LET
NOBODY
TURN US
AROUND

LET NOBODY TURN US AROUND

Voices of Resistance, Reform, and Renewal

AN AFRICAN AMERICAN ANTHOLOGY

Second Edition

editors
Manning Marable
Leith Mullings

ROWMAN & LITTLEFIELD PUBLISHERS, INC.
Lanham • Boulder • New York • Oxford

ROWMAN & LITTLEFIELD PUBLISHERS, INC.

Published in the United States of America
by Rowman & Littlefield Publishers, Inc.
A wholly owned subsidary of The Rowman & Littlefield Publishing Group, Inc.
4501 Forbes Boulevard, Suite 200, Lanham, Maryland 20706
www.rowmanlittlefield.com

Estover Road
Plymouth PL6 7PY
United Kingdom

British Library Cataloguing in Publication Information Available

Library of Congress Cataloging-in-Publication Data
Let nobody turn us around : an African American anthology : voices of resistance, reform, and renewal / Manning Marable and Leith Mullings, editors. — 2nd ed.
        p.   cm.
    Includes bibliographical references and index.
    ISBN 978-0-7425-6056-7 (cloth : alk. paper)
    ISBN 978-0-7425-6057-4 (pbk. : alk. paper
    ISBN 978-0-7425-6545-6 (electronic)
    1. African Americans—History—Sources. 2. African Americans—Civil rights—History—Sources. 3. African Americans—Social conditions—Sources. I. Marable, Manning, 1950– II. Mullings, Leith.
    E184.6.L48 2009
    973'.0496073—dc22
                                                                    2009005113

Printed in the United States of America

♾™ The paper used in this publication meets the minimum requirements of American National Standard for Information Sciences—Permanence of Paper for Printed Library Materials, ANSI Z39.48–1984.

CONTENTS

PREFACE TO THE FIRST EDITION

Nearly four years ago we jointly taught a graduate seminar offered at both City University Graduate School and Columbia University that was called, "Identity, Inequality, and Power." The basic idea behind the course was to identify significant and provocative ethnographic, historical, and theoretical articles and sources that explored the complex connections between the imagined communities such as those of race, gender, and nation, and the structures of social inequality, state power, and economic exploitation. We wanted to talk about the African-American experience in a manner that placed black people at the center of the forces of history. We believed that the greatest weight in the judgments made by social scientists in researching the black experience should be given to the voices of black people themselves. In countless ways—from speeches and religious sermons, personal letters to friends and family, political manifestos and editorials, through the development of common rituals and ceremonies that convey membership in kinship networks—African-American people made themselves. Their notions of identity, of who they were, were constructed over time through their collective struggles and experiences against inequality, as well as from memories and traditions they had brought from Africa.

We attempted to locate texts or anthologies that were appropriate for the seminar. We found, of course, a number of excellent social histories and ethnographic studies of different aspects of the experience of black people in the United States. Many of these works have interwoven the historical narrative with the voices and insights of black people themselves. That is to say, the authors of these works attempted to write history from the vantage point of being a participant observer of the culture. To theorize issues of identity, or questions about how any people understand the institutions of power that circumscribe their lives, scholars should first listen and learn from the people themselves. However, we were disappointed to find that in the past decade and more, very few anthologies designed for classroom usage incorporating this perspective into the collection and organization of sources have been published. What we wanted

was a collection of primary materials, rare published articles, speeches, and
other sources that told the story of how black people made themselves and interpreted the world in which they lived, in their own words and specifically from
their own point of view.

After teaching the seminar, we decided to collaborate in the writing of two
books on black American history and culture. The first is a long-term project, a
study of the black experience from within, over a series of seven generations.
We would like to develop a text that explores the ways in which African
Americans have perceived themselves as a people, how they understood the
structural barriers that denied them real opportunity, and how through their
culture they found their own imagination, voice, and agency. The book is a
work-in-progress, with the tentative title *The African Americans: A People's
History*. The second book was conceived as a comprehensive anthology of
African-American social thought, broadly defined as the bodies of knowledge
through which black people theorized from their experiences and social conditions, and proposed strategies and programs to enhance their power. Politics
begins at the moment when any group recognizes for itself its specific objective
interests and aspirations, and seeks agency to realize those interests. Black
social and political thought is the expression of how people of African descent
articulated and constructed the means to permit their communities to survive,
to resist, and to reform or transform the structures of white power all around
them. That story is what we hope *Let Nobody Turn Us Around* presents. More
than one hundred documents represent widely different ideological and political perspectives, reflecting an ongoing debate within the black community over
the appropriate strategies and tactics to achieve social change. It is by examining that diversity that we may discern the common ground that the vast majority of African Americans occupy.

There were a number of individuals who provided invaluable help in the
research and publication of this anthology. Columbia University doctoral candidates Johanna Fernandez and Devin Fergus assisted in the identification of
primary and secondary sources that were reviewed at the initial stage of preparing the text. Michele Hay, a graduate student at City University of New York,
helped to select important documents and did background research that was
important in the preparation of the biographical profiles and historical notes
that accompanied each text. We would especially like to express our gratitude
for the efforts of John McMillian, a doctoral candidate in history at Columbia
University. Over a period of more than one year, John reviewed and evaluated
the entire list of documents, tracked down hard-to-find biographical details on
a number of subjects, and wrote the first drafts of many biographical profiles.
John's careful attention to details and his enthusiasm and interest in the project
greatly enhanced the character of the book.

The book manuscript went through three major revisions and reorganizations during two years. We appreciate the efforts of the secretarial staff of the Institute for Research in African-American Studies at Columbia University—Diane Tinsley-Hatcher, Jennifer Jones, and Theresa Wilcox—who typed and revised the book throughout its many stages of development. Jennifer Jones, Sherell Daniels, and Andrea Queeley were also especially helpful in proofreading the final text and carefully checking for errors.

A major architect of this work is our editor Dean Birkenkamp at Rowman & Littlefield. When the concept of this book was initially discussed in 1996, Dean provided strong support for its development. Dean is an author's ideal editor—patient but persistent, and always helpful in thinking through problems connected with the technical aspects of putting a book together. Sallie Greenwood was extraordinarily diligent in identifying and securing permissions for all the sources—no small accomplishment given the large number of documents she was asked to review.

Finally and most importantly, we wish to dedicate this anthology to our five children, Alia, Malaika, Sojourner, Joshua, and Michael. We hope that our efforts to help rediscover and document the visions of black folk past and present may provide part of that knowledge necessary to assist the next generation of black children to win that freedom which their foremothers and forefathers struggled for so long to achieve.

MANNING MARABLE
LEITH MULLINGS
September 6, 1999

PREFACE TO THE SECOND EDITION

n the past two decades, the African-American community has experienced profound transformations. For many, the long freedom struggle has significantly recast how "race" is lived. There are African-American millionaires, politicians, and, most amazingly, Barack Obama, an African American, has been elected as the forty-fourth president of the United States. Clearly, the freedom struggle has also substantially modified the public discourse about race and the meaning of racial difference. Furthermore the immigration of millions of Latinos, Asians, and others since 1980, as well as a biracial president, has altered the racial and ethnic composition of the United States, undermining the older bipolar categories of white and black.

But simultaneously, African Americans have experience new forms of bound labor, massive incarceration, and deepening class stratification. Continuing racial and class inequality is largely masked by a new racial ideology—color-blind racism—the claims that the civil rights struggle has eliminated all forms of discrimination, and that the United States has successfully been transformed into a "color-blind society" in which each individual is free to determine her or his own destiny. In this sense, the U.S. racial system appears to be moving toward a model that characterized much of Latin America, where racial discrimination is maintained and reproduced, but is not sanctioned by law and often vigorously denied.

The contours of the freedom movement have consequently shifted. Electoral political struggles have intensified, but black candidates, especially in federal and statewide elections, are no longer answerable only to the black community. In the recent period, much of the freedom movement has not been waged in the large overarching organizations that characterized the civil rights struggle, but on the ground—in neighborhood networks and locally-based organizations concerned with a living wage, tenants' rights, prisoners' rights, environmental racism, education, and health. In many of these grassroots movements, women not only constitute the great majority of the cadre, but are also the leaders and theoreticians. As neoliberal capitalism is increasingly unable to meet the basic needs of most citizens and residents, calls for trans-formation from the most oppressed sectors of society have become louder and more determined.

Four centuries ago, people of African descent were among the first to expe-rience the destructive effects of globalization. The most recent phase of glob-alized capitalism has had a major and largely negative impact on African Americans. For many, it has contributed to increased poverty and marginaliza-tion. But globalization has also provided new opportunities: new global tech-nologies have facilitated innovative forms of communication, fostering new transnational networks and promoting mobilizing efforts. As the world has become smaller, the space for traditional race-based organizing based on older historical models has become increasingly constricted. Yet paradoxically, race-based movements, often inspired by the history of African-American struggle, have emerged in many parts of the globe in the past decade. Internationalism has always been a central feature of the U.S. black freedom struggle, but new transnational networks make it possible for activists to collectively challenge "global apartheid." The emergent discourse of "diaspora" encompasses a broad range of imagined communities and reframes the context for social change pro-jects led by black people in diverse national contexts.

As we observed at the beginning of the introduction of the first edition, African Americans are a people who have created themselves under the most difficult conditions. The sojourn of black people has been at times defined by a crucible of exploitation. Yet it has also been a triumph of the human spirit, a call for jus-tice in a wasteland of oppression. In this way, people who were not considered to be citizens with inalienable rights fought to redefine the character of the nation and how it was run. Through the 240 years of slavery, followed by nearly a century of Jim Crow segregation and only 45 years of desegregation, black people learned more than survival skills. They struggled to become trade union leaders and social workers, doctors and lawyers, engineers and architects.

Only six generations ago, it was forbidden by law to teach slaves to read and write. Today some of the greatest novelists, playwrights, and poets produced in the United States are African American. Less than seventy years ago black peo-ple were barred from professional athletics; today they dominate them. Black popular culture, relegated to obscurity as "race music" in the early twentieth century, now largely defines U.S. popular culture. As late as 1960, the majority of African Americans had never been permitted to vote in a presidential elec-tion, and were largely excluded from the electoral political system in the South. Today, the U.S. president is African American, there are over 10,000 black elected officials, and black voters comprise the essential core group for a liberal and progressive political coalition in national elections. African Americans have done more than make "contributions": they have instead largely reshaped and redefined what U.S. life and society are about. All these gains were the result of the struggles of ordinary people. Our struggle continues.

The acknowledgments of the second edition of *Let Nobody Turn Us Around* reflects these old and new contexts. The bibliographies have been updated throughout the volume. The final section, section V, has been significantly revised and expanded, with a new introduction and the addition of readings that bring the book up-to-date and address the new debates about culture, politics, and possible the directions of the black freedom struggle.

We would like to thank Karen Williams, a graduate student in anthropology at the Graduate Center of City University of New York, for her invaluable help with the new edition. She tracked down the new documents and wrote the first draft of several of the new profiles. We are also grateful to Courtney Teague and Sara Ingram for their assistance in preparing the manuscript.

MANNING MARABLE
LEITH MULLINGS
November 24, 2008
New York City

INTRODUCTION

Resistance, Reform, and Renewal
in the Black Experience

Throughout their entire history as a people, African Americans have created themselves. They did so in the context of the transatlantic slave trade and two-and-a-half centuries of chattel slavery—a structure of overwhelming inequality and brutality characterized by the sale of human beings and routine rapes and executions. They constructed their cultural identity and notions of humanity in a country that denied them citizenship and basic human dignity for hundreds of years. Beginning as enslaved Africans from various locations and ethnic and language groups across the continent of Africa, within several generations they found their voice, meaning, and consciousness as a special people.

Those captured from Africa were not people without history and culture. They were mothers and fathers, sons and daughters, and descendants of ancestors; they were religious specialists and supplicants, chiefs and commoners, cooks, musicians, metalworkers, scribes, farmers, and griots; they belonged to states, clans, lineages, age grades, men's and women's associations, artisan guilds, and secret societies. Their memories of how life should be lived, of womanhood and manhood, of beauty and aesthetics, of worship and spirituality, were not annihilated by the Middle Passage. But what they could do with these memories was very much constrained by the conditions in which they found themselves—the racial and class structure of enslavement. To paraphrase a well-known observation, African Americans created themselves, but not just as they pleased, not under circumstances chosen by themselves, but under circumstances directly encountered, given, and transmitted from the past. It was in the context of their African history and the prevailing social and economic relationships that African Americans created culture, religion, family, art forms, political institutions, and social and political theory.

Social and political theory—bodies of knowledge by which African Americans attempted to analyze and address the social, cultural, and political issues they confronted—emerged from everyday practices to reform and resist the structures of oppression, and to renew their community through imagining and enacting its continuity. Attempts to reform, utilizing group and individual resources to mitigate the worst aspects of the society and to enhance black interests within the state apparatus, ranged from petitions to the colonial legislatures and federal government for redress, lobbying for the abolition of slavery, and participation in various political parties to influence white liberal opinion on issues of race. Resistance was found in the various degrees of opposition to institutional racism: from day-to-day sabotage (disruption, noncompliance, refusals to work, running away) to overt rebellion (the murder of slaveholders, flight to the North, the underground railroad, joining forces with American Indian tribes to combat the U.S. army, the creation of maroon communities, and the slave uprisings of Nat Turner, Denmark Vesey, Gabriel Prosser, and Cinque). Throughout their history African Americans nurtured and renewed their emerging community—creating and maintaining cultural forms and building viable institutions to provide goods, services, and cultural and educational sustenance.

Yet social and political theory is not merely reactive. Though it was a collective effort to address existing social institutions and structures of power, it was also a search for meaning and voice. Social thought sought to understand who we are, envision new directions, and imagine a new society. The purpose was not only to advocate, but to realize our meaning and being.

The themes of reform, resistance, and renewal formed the cultural and social matrix of black consciousness, community, and public discourse. They were the foundations for the construction of a black American society that was self-conscious and motivated to define and achieve its specific interests. It was within this political culture and this web of increasingly elaborate social institutions—black religious denominations, Masonic lodges, free African societies, schools, newspapers—that competing strategic visions of how best to achieve group empowerment and self-organization began to crystallize.

The decisive historical period in the construction of black ideologies was between 1830 and 1865. The free black community in the North numbered more than one hundred thousand. The immediate question confronting African Americans was how to dismantle slavery—the oppression of four million people of African descent. But the larger issue was whether and how black people could find freedom, in the United States or elsewhere, while preserving what was valuable and central to their collective identity as a people. Are we Africans, or are we both Africans and Americans? Is our collective future inextricably linked to the U.S. state and American society? It was in the context of the national debate about slavery that two overlapping political ideologies emerged among black Americans, representing two different aspects of the same racial dilemma: the possibility of black Americans achieving equality within America's racialized social body.

What became known in the twentieth century as "integrationism" actually originated among the free black communities in the North prior to the Civil

War. A core of free black leaders—journalists, teachers, ministers, small entre-preneurs, abolitionists—concluded that the fight to abolish slavery could be won, but that it would represent only one part of a greater struggle: to expand the limited boundaries of American democracy to include people of African descent. The task ahead was to bring Negroes into every profession and to ensure their full participation in voting, serving on juries, and running for elec-tive office. Black people would have the unalienable right to own property, to have unfettered access to public accommodation and schools, and the freedom to hire themselves out for a fair wage. The only limitations on any individual's success would be determined by intellect and ambition, not by race.

The goal of integrationists was a society where color was insignificant and where individual achievement and hard work largely determined the life chances of most black people. Inherent in this ideological perspective was an inner paradox. Integrationist reformers often had no choice but to build black organizations behind the walls of segregation, to mobilize their supporters, and to appeal to sympathetic whites. At times, race consciousness among African Americans was used to challenge Jim Crow. A. Philip Randolph's Negro March on Washington, D.C., in 1941 and Martin Luther King, Jr.'s construction of the Southern Christian Leadership Conference in 1957 are two of many examples. Building on a racial base could be useful, but only for the long-term goal of eradicating all racial classifications and caste privileges that penalized Negroes simply because of the color of their skin. In other words, the struggle for inte-gration often had to be waged from within the boundaries of racial identity. This strategy also implied that what was "wrong" with the United States could be made right, if restrictions on the basis of race could be eliminated and if blacks and other disadvantaged groups could be more fully represented in the structures of civil and political authority.

In contrast, the black nationalist tradition was built on a no-nonsense set of assumptions about the relative permanence of white supremacy. Blacks would have to place their energies in building economic and social institutions that would provide goods and services to other black people. By hiring blacks, they could utilize racial segregation as a barrier to create a black consumer market. Some nationalists also saw these steps as stopgap measures. Only when a sig-nificant number of African Americans established their own separate geo-political space—perhaps a territory, a group or state, or resettlement to another country or continent—could ultimate security and the integrity of black people be achieved. The nationalists often saw themselves as accidental Americans, or Africans-in-exile. They frequently distrusted white liberals and reformers who expressed sympathy toward blacks even more than they distrusted white supremacist groups, because they felt the latter represented the true feelings of the white majority. Some felt that race war inside the United States, and indeed globally, was probably inevitable, and the best thing African Americans could do was to prepare for it. In 1852, Martin R. Delany called upon African

Americans to emigrate because "we love our country, dearly love her, but she doesn't love us—she despises us, and bids us begone, driving us from her embraces; but we shall not go where she desires us; but when we do go, whatever love we have for her, we shall love the country none the less that receives us as her adopted children" (section 1, document 17). Similarly, the first point in Marcus Garvey's 1920 "Declaration of Rights of the Negro Peoples of the World" reads: ". . . nowhere in the world, with few exceptions, are black men accorded equal treatment with white men, although in the same situation and circumstances, but, on the contrary, are discriminated against and denied the common rights due to human beings for no other reason than their race and color" (section 3, document 4). Almost fifty years later, Malcolm X observed, ". . . it is not necessary to change the white man's mind. We have to change our own mind. You can't change his mind about us" (section 4, document 13). These were the most extreme positions of the integrationist–nationalist ideological axis, but most African Americans during the century between the Civil War and the Civil Rights movement oscillated somewhere in between these two poles of racial opinion. In periods of political optimism, when the bar of institutional racism seemed to be in retreat, the integrationist perspective was usually dominant. But in times of white reaction and retrenchment from racial justice—such as the 1850s, 1920s, late 1960s, and early 1970s—black nationalism resurfaced.

A third strategic vision subsequently emerged, with the developing consciousness of the black working class and the growing intensity of labor struggles in the United States. This perspective neither accepted the structure of the contemporary society nor called for a separate black society, but rather advocated a radical transformation of the United States based on a fundamental redistribution of resources. This perspective did not merely push for the expansion of democracy but challenged the basic inequality of the economic structure. The objective here was to dismantle all forms of class hierarchy and social privilege. For T. Thomas Fortune, a printer who was born a slave, the working people's struggles of the 1880s underscored the importance of class in understanding and transforming society: "The iniquity of privileged class and concentrated wealth . . . does not admit of the argument that every man born into the world is justly entitled to so much of the produce of nature as will satisfy his physical necessities . . ." (section 2, document 4). In 1912 Hubert Henry Harrison declared that "socialism stands for the emancipation of the wage slaves" (section 2, document 16).

This perspective coalesces in the period from 1915 to 1954, with the consolidation of the black working class and its struggle for jobs and for access to employment at an equitable wage. It became a social force in the emergence of the African Blood Brotherhood in 1922 (section 3, document 3); the "Don't Buy Where You Can't Work" campaign in Harlem during the Great Depression (section 3, document 14); and the organization of the Sleeping Car Porters (section

3, document 17). The rise of working-class "organic intellectuals"—many of whom were associated with the Communist Party, such as southern organizers Angelo Herndon (section 3, document 11) and Hosea Hudson (section 3, document 12)—was particularly notable during this period. However, white racism, including that of white workers, continued to be a major obstacle.

These social visions—integration, nationalism, and transformation—are not mutually exclusive but are in fact broad, overlapping traditions. Throughout the twentieth century, these tendencies have been present, to varying degrees, in virtually every major mass movement in which black people have been engaged, from the desegregationist campaigns of the 1950s to the anti-apartheid mobilization of the 1980s. Though some organizations and individuals may have exemplified one tendency or the other, organizations and movements usually displayed a spectrum of views. Individuals often began their activist careers with one set of perspectives and moved to another as they perceive limitations of that paradigm. This was the case with Hubert Henry Harrison, W. E. B. Du Bois, Martin Luther King, and Malcolm X.

These three competing paradigms continue to underlie the Black Freedom movement. The broad range of forces in the desegregation struggle included the Urban League, which conceptualized civil rights as an expression of extending rights to black people, and the Southern Christian Leadership Conference, which had "the basic aim of achieving full citizenship rights, equality, and the integration of the Negro in all aspects of American life" (section 4, document 3). On the other hand, the left wing of the Civil Rights movement envisioned the necessity of a more far-reaching change. In 1963 John Lewis declared, "[t]he revolution is at hand, and we must free ourselves of the chains of political and economic slavery" (section 4, document 8).

Similarly the Black Power movement—a move toward nationalism that arose when the weaknesses of integrationism become evident—encompassed competing visions of the meaning of political power. Floyd McKissick, in his endorsement of Black Power, established the black capitalist venture of Soul City. On the other hand, the Black Panthers embraced a Marxist analysis of capitalism. Black Panther co-founder Huey P. Newton observed that "[t]he Black Panther Party bases its ideology and philosophy on a concrete analysis of concrete conditions, using dialectical materialism as our analytical method" (section 4, document 17). Fred Hampton called for class struggle, observing that "[w]e have to understand very clearly that there is a man in our community called a capitalist" (section 4, document 18). Angela Davis, a member of the Che-Lumumba Club of the Communist Party, explained why she is a Communist: "I am a Communist because I am convinced that the reason we have been forcefully compelled to eke out an existence at the lowest level of American society has to do with the nature of capitalism. . . . I am a Communist because I believe that black people, with whose labor and blood this country was built, have a right to a great deal of the wealth that has been hoarded in the hands of the Hughes, the Rockefellers, the

Kennedys, the DuPonts, all the super-powerful white capitalists of America" (section 4, document 19). During this period of Black Power, the militant tradition of black workers found expression in the creation of the Dodge Revolutionary Union Movement (DRUM) in Detroit, and in the more moderate Coalition of Black Trade Unionists.

Race, and to a lesser extent class, have been central to theorizing African-American liberation. But since its inception, African-American social theory has also included a lively discussion about gender, though this has received little attention until relatively recently. The unusual position of African-American women has made the issue of gender critical—both in practice and for the development of theory. The denial of "the protections of private patriarchy" throughout their history has made the situation of African-American women exceptional in American life. Often doing the same work as men during slavery, after Reconstruction they worked both outside and inside the home. Exploited as labor, but also oppressed on the basis of gender and race, their history has created an experience distinct from that of both black men and white women. Though triply oppressed, they also occupy a creative space from which to critique U.S. social structure from multiple sites. As Anna Julia Cooper noted in 1892, to be an African-American woman was "to have a heritage . . . unique in all the ages" (section 2, document 7).

Given the significance of black women in the slave community, in the struggle for abolition and emancipation, and as workers and activists, it may be that many African-American men were more open to issues of gender than white men—advocating access to education for women and other nontraditional gendered roles—though often in terms of the optimal requirements for motherhood. Martin Delany, who called for the emigration of black people from the United States in 1852, declared: "Let our young women have an education; let their minds be well informed; well stored with useful information and practical proficiency. . . . Our females must be qualified, because they are to be the mothers of our children" (section 1, document 17). Frederick Douglass and W. E. B. Du Bois were among the most consistent and vocal advocates for the rights of women.

But it is also true that, in subtle ways, the struggle for freedom was often framed in masculine terms. Abolitionist leader William Wells Brown lamented: "If I wish to stand up and say, 'I am a man,' I must leave the land that gave me birth" (section 1, document 14). Upon being expelled from the Georgia legislature in 1868, Henry McNeal Turner declared: "Am I a man? If I am such, I claim the rights of a man . . ." (section 2, document 2); and Frederick Douglass equates "what the black man wants" with the interests of the race as a whole (section 2, document 1). While clearly these formulations have to do with the semantic use of "man" for humankind, it is also true that they embodied often-unstated assumptions about the masculine privileges that nationhood entails. During Reconstruction, the demand for the hierarchical gender roles of the dominant society became integrally connected with the demand for freedom.

But black women have not had the luxury of defining freedom in patriarchal terms, and early on created an analysis of race, class, and gender that emerged from their experiences. While fully supporting the struggle for freedom, black women have addressed the issues of both gender and race. In 1851 Sojourner Truth declared "I am a woman's rights. I have as much muscle as any man, and can do as much work as any man" (section 1, document 15). Anticipating the feminist theorizing of the 1980s and 1990s, in 1892 Anna Julia Cooper wrote that the African-American woman is "confronted by both a woman question and a race problem, and is as yet an unknown or an unacknowledged factor in both" (section 2, document 7).

The consolidation of a black working-class perspective enhanced the development of a race- and class-based feminism. Domestic workers and women toiling in the cotton fields spoke out about their own conditions and created the context for a feminism grounded in the experiences of working women. A description of women workers in the cotton fields published in *Crisis* in 1938 laid the foundation for a sophisticated analysis of these issues, which were rediscovered by scholars in the 1980s, such as the double day and the unpaid labor of women. The following passage presents an analysis of the relationships between production and reproduction that is valid today (section 3, document 15):

> In the past, this woman was compelled to reproduce a large number of children because a large labor supply was in demand. Large families also mean a cheaper form of labor, for children, as well as women, generally represent labor that does not have to be paid. Consequently, the "overhead" falls upon the family instead of the landlord. The landlord himself has enforced this monopoly by letting his farm go to the tenant or cropper having the largest family. . . . Now the tenant-croppers are charged with "over-population" by the economists and agriculturalists who disregard the unwholesome economic factors that have caused an increase in farm tenancy. . . . As one solution to the "over-population," proponents of the sterilization racket are endeavoring to work up an agitation for sterilization of these cotton workers.

In 1949, Claudia Jones, a leader in the Communist Party, argued for a class- and race-based feminism. Her remarkable historical analysis, clearly articulating the triple oppression of race, class, and gender, anticipated the race, class, and gender theorists of the 1980s and 1990s. She analyzed the important role of negative representations of African-American women, presented an early formulation of "the personal is political," and called for the organization of domestic workers.

As women activists took militant and leading roles in the Civil Rights and Black Power movements—in SCLC, SNCC, and the Black Panther Party— they confronted real problems of how to deal in practice with the dilemmas of race, class, and gender. Activists such as Fannie Lou Hamer spoke eloquently of the solidarities of race and the contradictions of gender and class: ". . . we are here to work side by side with this black man in trying to bring liberation to all people" (section 4, document 10). In the 1980s there was a proliferation of work on gender that seriously attends to the centrality of race and racism in the lives of African-American women, and critiques the essentialist view put forward by Euro-American feminists. But divergent perspectives also emerged that reflect the differences in strategic social visions among the African-American people as a whole. While most feminist theorists now write of the integration of race, class, and gender, there are clear differences in how women of diverse class backgrounds and experiences understand these relationships, their visions of a new society, and their notions of how to get there.

This book is an attempt to compile a representative sample of a range of writings that reflect the political thought of black Americans in the United States from colonial times to the end of the twentieth century. We have attempted to include varied opinions from women and men, workers, and the intelligentsia.

As in any anthology, there are limitations. This is not a typical encyclopedia of African-American thought. We wanted the book to reflect the full range of African-American thought, but as extensive as the scope of this volume is, there are some obvious omissions. In several cases copyright problems limited our access to certain materials. In another instance, one prominent black conservative economist refused to permit his published work to appear in this volume. Because it is a collection of social *theory*, the focus on thought, to some extent, abstracts it from practice. The purpose of this book is not to assess social and political movements, but rather to present the theories that informed them. Furthermore, the emphasis on available written sources omits a body of popular reflections that might tell us much about "organic" social theory.

Section 1 begins with the period from 1768 to 1861. This was the era of slavery and the issue motivating African Americans was abolitionism and efforts at reform, resistance, and revolt against slavery. It was also the time of the birth of African-American culture and society. Section 2 covers 1861 to 1915. The Civil War, Reconstruction, and the establishment of Jim Crow segregation defined the politics of this period. African Americans were overwhelmingly rural and the majority continued to live in the South, as two generations of African Americans coped with the aftermath of slavery and the War.

Section 3 concerns the years 1915 to 1954, which marks the period of the "great migration," when African Americans in large numbers migrated from the rural South to the urban North. Two world wars, the "Red Summer" of 1919, the consolidation of the modern black working-class, the rise of black radicalism, and the emergence of the Civil Rights movement are also part of this era.

During the period covered by section 4—1954 to 1975—the Black Freedom movement flourishes through the Civil Rights struggle and the Black Power movement.

The years since 1975, treated in section 5, have been described as the second post-Reconstruction era. A time of rapidly developing class stratification both globally and within the United States, it has been characterized by new divisions and ideological debates among African Americans.

Whatever the site or political perspective from which African Americans theorize and struggle for freedom, resistance has had real consequences. In these pages you will read the words of people who, from different ideological vantage points, have fought for freedom. For those who have opposed the dominant society, taking a stand has often exacted a price: Marcus Garvey and Claudia Jones were exiled; W. E. B. Du Bois and Paul Robeson were severely harassed and denied passports; Henry Winston, Angela Davis, and Angelo Herndon spent years in jail; Fannie Lou Hamer and John Lewis were brutally beaten. From the mysterious death of David Walker to the executions and/or assassinations of Nat Turner, Malcolm X, Martin Luther King, Fred Hampton, the Attica Brothers, and countless known and unknown others, freedom for black people has always been won at a dear price. To these brave women and men we dedicate this book.

New York City
September 1999

FOUNDATIONS: SLAVERY AND ABOLITIONISM, 1768–1861

INTRODUCTION

African Americans created themselves through a series of vast historical events and social forces that greatly transformed the global political economy over half a millennium. Chief among these were the development of the transatlantic slave trade, beginning at the dawn of the sixteenth century, which transported at least fifteen million Africans against their will into the Americas and the Caribbean; the subsequent institutionalization and expansion of monocrop agricultural production relying on forced labor; and, with these, the establishment of the new world settler societies based on the extermination of indigenous populations. These broad historical forces were the context for the development of the British colonies in North America, which in 1787 would become the United States. Within these states about 650,000 Africans were resettled as slaves between 1619 and the eve of the Civil War.

The Africans were immediately confronted with the harsh realities of chattel enslavement, the brutal domination of their bodies and labor power for the benefit of others. Within this stratified social order, people of African descent were explicitly denied access to the courts, excluded from participation in public life, and legally categorized as private property. A process of racial stigmatization developed in which people of African descent were penalized for their physical appearance and phenotype, and Europeans began transforming themselves into the privileged racial category of whiteness. By the middle of the eighteenth century, the innate inferiority of black people was generally accepted by white Americans, including even most white critics of the slave trade, such as the Quakers. The relative permanence of physical markers combined with institutions of coercion helped to construct a social universe that in most respects confined African Americans to the most oppressive conditions within society.

Several of the documents in section 1 present in moving detail the inhumanity of life as a slave in the American South. Approximately three-fourths of all slaves worked in the fields, with the remainder assigned to household tasks, or laboring as mechanics and skilled workmen. Regardless of their tasks, all were expected to work without compensation. The slave was a commodity, and it was rare that a black person did not experience the loss of spouse, parents, children, or friends through sale. Document 10, "The Selling of Slaves," is drawn from an advertisement posted in New Orleans in 1835, presenting individuals from the same family for sale to the highest bidder. On the auction block were Chole, thirty-six years old, with her daughter Fanny, age sixteen, who was described as bilingual, "a good seamstress and ladies' maid . . . smart, intelligent and a first rate character." Dandridge, a twenty-six-year-old carpenter and servant, was offered for sale along with his wife, Nancy, twenty-four years of age, and their seven-year-old daughter Mary Ann, who was termed "smart, active and intelligent." The terms of this business transaction were straightforward: one-half cash, the rest paid within six months, "with special mortgage on the Slaves until final payment." As indicated in document 7, slaveholders recognized the potential dangers of teaching African Americans to read and write, which created "a tendency to excite dissatisfaction in their minds, and to produce insurrection and rebellion." In 1831 North Carolina law mandated that slaves who were caught instructing other slaves in reading and writing "receive thirty-nine lashes on his or her bare back." Whites who violated this prohibition against slave literacy were instead to be fined or imprisoned.

How did African Americans respond to this structure of oppression? Resistance always assumed many forms. As the narrative of Equiano (document 2) suggests, it began aboard the slave ships as enslaved Africans attempted to starve themselves or jump overboard. Perhaps the most common manifestation of protest is what many historians have called "day-to-day resistance." There is a large body of evidence from slaves' narratives and other literature suggesting that most black people fought in ways that would not openly communicate hostility or anger against their masters. Instead of violent confrontations, many used other tactics to harm and disrupt the normal business of daily life. Slaves engaged in deliberate work slowdowns; the destruction of farming implements, tools, and other property; the burning of crops or food supplies; and the refusal to carry out commands. Slaves routinely pretended to be ill or physically incapacitated. Enslaved women practiced contraception and sometimes infanticide in order to control their fertility. Some slaves ran off to wooded areas outside whites' settlements, in some instances creating maroon, or runaway slave, communities. Occasionally, black resistance took the form of outright revolt or rebellion. "The Statement of Nat Turner" (document 6) illustrates that slaves fully comprehended their exploitation and looked forward to the time "when the first should be last and the last should be first." When asked whether he regretted his bloody actions against whites, Turner bluntly replied, "Was not Christ crucified?"

Resistance to slavery among the free black community in the North took the form of vigilance committees—networks that provided safe shelter, food, and transportation to runaway slaves. Even free blacks were always in danger of being arrested, claimed as property by whites, and transported back to the South. The free black community in the North also organized a series of regional and national conferences bringing together the leading voices of African-American public opinion. The documents and speeches from these "Negro Conventions" provide excellent insights into the political and social thought of antebellum black America. The famous speech by Henry Highland Garnet (document 13) at the 1843 Negro convention for example, emphasizes the right of the oppressed to "use every means, both moral, intellectual and physical, that promises success." African Americans in the North and South alike were exhorted to use their power "to torment the God-cursed slaveholders, that they will be glad to let you go free. . . . Let your motto be resistance! resistance! RESISTANCE! No oppressed people have ever secured their liberty without resistance." Garnet's militant rhetoric in many ways prefigures the protest language of Malcolm X and Huey P. Newton a century later.

While resistance was essential, African Americans also understood that they would have to utilize any means at their disposal to modify the restrictions of white authority over the lives of black people. In other words, free blacks had to agitate for fundamentals that materially benefited African Americans within the existing political, economic, and social structure. The abolition of slavery could not be achieved by black people alone, and early on there was an awareness that a segment of the white population could be won to emancipation. The slave narratives, beginning with the classical 1789 account of Olaudah Equiano (document 2), were primarily designed to educate and inform European and white American audiences about the lives and perspectives of black people. African-American women were particularly effective in linking the struggles of black people with other reform movements, such as the pursuit of equality for women. Maria W. Stewart, a prominent public speaker in the 1830s, frequently linked the struggles of black people with other reform movements, such as temperance and women's rights. Similarly, Sojourner Truth, Frances Ellen Watkins Harper, and Mary Ann Shadd Cary spoke powerfully for the rights of African-American women.

The long-term goal of black reform was the redefinition of American democracy itself: the elimination of all restrictions to the full participation of African Americans in the larger society. David Walker's "Appeal" (document 5) carries this thesis to its logical conclusion: that blacks, because of their experiences of suffering and struggle in this country, were more American than whites: "Will any of us leave our homes and go to Africa? I hope not. . . . Let no man of us budge one step, and let slaveholders come to beat us from our country. America is more our country, than it is the whites—we have enriched it with our blood and tears." Making a similar point, Frederick Douglass's well-known 1852 address, "What to the Slave Is the

Fourth of July?," challenges white Americans to recognize their political hypocrisy by celebrating its democratic institution in a country filled with four million slaves (document 18). To the slave, Douglass declares, the national holiday "is a sham; your boasted liberty an unholy license; your national greatness, swelling vanity; your sounds of rejoicing are empty and heartless; your denunciation of tyrants, brass-fronted impudence; your shouts of liberty and equality, hollow mockery. . . ." The righteous anger in Douglass's words should not obscure his real objective: to convince his white audience that "the great principle of political freedom and of natural justice, embodied in that Declaration of Independence," should be extended to African Americans. To some extent, the struggle had to be waged within the paradigm and boundaries of debate set by the larger society. Slaveholders argued that enslaved people were an inferior species—African Americans asserted their humanity. Whites insisted that African Americans were not capable of voting—Frederick Douglass argued that they would develop the capabilities.

Black survival in an aggressively racist society also depended on the ability of African Americans to create, preserve, and renew their communities. Enslaved Africans who were forced into servitude in the western hemisphere were not blank slates, but brought with them memories and cultural values. As Equiano's account (document 2) demonstrates, his particularly detailed recollections ranged from family and religion to notions of beauty: "[I]deas of beauty are wholly relative. I remember while in Africa to have seen three Negro children who were tawny, and another quite white, who were universally regarded by myself and the natives in general, as far as related to their complexions, as deformed." But it is within the structural constraints of slavery and discrimination that they must create a culture—utilizing, transforming, and giving new meanings to cultural material from Africa and the Americas as they seek to imagine and invent the institutions that would ensure their survival. For example, though nowhere did the enslaved people have the right to marry, they continued to affirm their bonds of family, community, and humanity (document 9). During slavery, the church was the only legal institution through which enslaved people could congregate and exchange information as well as worship. Throughout African-American history, the church continued to be a major site of political organizing, and charismatic leadership was a hallmark of black politics.

In practical terms, this meant the constructing of socioeconomic institutions that provided goods, services, and resources to the black people. By the late eighteenth century, free blacks in several northern cities had established mutual-benefit associations—social organizations that helped black families in need. Free women of color were particularly active in organizing activities that would contribute to the abolition of slavery and black self-help. In April 1816, Richard Allen founded the African Methodist Episcopal Church (document 4), thereby laying the foundations of the black church, which to this day remains the largest and most influential force inside the black community. To a great extent it reshaped Christianity within the context of the needs of the African-American community. Prince Hall's Masonic lodge for African Americans (document 3) would also grow into a massive social network that was actively involved in all aspects of black civic and cultural life. From these early social institutions would ultimately derive the black press, schools and colleges, hospitals, insurance companies, banks, and commercial enterprises of all kinds.

What is particularly interesting is that the construction of this elaborate internal black world of which most whites were ignorant was achieved through conscious appeals to black solidarity and collective self-help. It was necessary for African Americans to become the keepers of their own history. In his call for resistance, Henry Highland Garnet (document 13) recounts the stories of the leaders of slave rebellions: Denmark Vessey, Nat Turner, Joseph Cinque, and Madison Washington. Similarly, as we shall see in the next section (section 2, document 8), Mary Church Terrell recounted the successes of black women.

There were boundaries of blackness: the expectations that African Americans should remain loyal to their race, that they should support the goals and values generally accepted as the cultural norm for their communities. One of the earliest expressions of the boundaries of blackness is by David Walker (document 5). He condemns some of his "brethren" who were "in league with tyrants, and who receive a great portion of their daily bread, of the moneys which they acquire from the blood and tears of their more miserable brethren, whom they scandalously delivered into the hands of our natural enemies!" An aspect of Walker's exhortation was a frank belief in the innate superiority of black people over whites: "[G]lory, honour and praise to Heaven's King . . . the sons and daughters of Africa, will, in spite of all the opposition of their enemies, stand forth in all the dignity and glory that is granted by the Lord to his creature man." In a society so grounded and permeated with white-supremacist ideology, African Americans such as Walker—and later figures such as Marcus Garvey, Elijah Muhammad, and Louis Farrakhan—emphasized the mental and physical superiority of black people in order to counter the allegations of inferiority.

The outbreak of the Civil War led to the destruction of one form of racial domination—slavery—but would ultimately be replaced by another: Jim Crow segregation. Over 180,000 African Americans fought in the Union army to liberate their people. This section presents some of the key ideas and leaders who contributed to the black struggle for freedom.

⚊ 1 ⚊

"On Being Brought from Africa to America," Phillis Wheatley, 1768

Phillis Wheatley (1753?–1784) was born in Gambia, West Africa, and is recognized as the first African American to publish a book. Transported to the

United States when she was about seven, Wheatley was an enslaved domestic servant in the household of John and Susanna Wheatley, who taught her to read and write and supported her interests in poetry. The public, however, could not believe that a domestic slave had the artistic and intellectual capabilities to create poetry. In 1772, Wheatley was brought before a courtroom in Boston to determine if she indeed could craft literature. The judges produced a written document that stated that "the poems specified . . . were . . . written by Phillis, a young Negro Girl." This statement was instrumental in Wheatley's ability to secure publication of her first book, *Poems on Various Subjects, Religious and Moral*. Controversy surrounding Wheatley's poetry continues to this day. Though it has been criticized for its weak stance on slavery, recent interpretations are more sympathetic, pointing out that Wheatley was a product of her times. Wheatley's second manuscript was lost, but in the past decade, remnants of this manuscript have surfaced. Despite her acclaim in both the United States and Britain, Wheatley died in abject poverty.

＝~

'TWAS mercy brought me from my Pagan land,
Taught my benighted soul to understand
That there's a God, that there's a Saviour too:
Once I redemption neither sought nor knew.
Some view our sable race with scornful eye,
"Their colour is a diabolic die."
Remember, Christians, Negros, black as Cain,
May be refin'd, and join th' angelic train

Source: Phillis Wheatley, *Complete Writings*, ed. by Vincent Carretta (New York: Penguin Books, 2001), pg. 13.

BIBLIOGRAPHIC RESOURCES:

Mukhtar Ali Isani, "'Gambia on My Soul': Africa and the African in the Writings of Phillis Wheatley," *MELUS* 6, no. 1 (Spring 1979), pp. 64–72.

Helen Burke, "Problematizing American Dissent: The Subject of Phillis Wheatley," in *Cohesion and Dissent in America*, ed. by Carol Colatrella and Joseph Alkana (Albany: State University of New York Press, 1994), pp. 193–209.

Helen M. Burke, "The Rhetoric and Politics of Marginality: The Subject of Phillis Wheatley," *Tulsa Studies in Women's Literature* 10, no. 1 (Spring 1991), pp. 31–45.

Henry Louis Gates, "Phillis Wheatley on Trial," *The New Yorker* (January 20, 2003).

———, *The Trials of Phillis Wheatley: America's First Black Poet and Her Encounters with the Founding Fathers* (New York: Basic Civitas Books, 2003).

John C. Shields, ed., *The Collected Works of Phillis Wheatley* (New York: Oxford University Press, 1989).

⤚ **2** ⤚

"The Interesting Narrative of the Life of Olaudah Equiano," Olaudah Equiano, 1789

There are questions about the birthplace and the life story of Olaudah Equiano (1745–1797). Recent scholarship suggests that Equiano was born not on the African continent but in South Carolina, and did not personally endure the Middle Passage. Nevertheless, he created a public persona rooted in an African past and slavery that was presented in his autobiography, *The Interesting Narrative of the Life of Olaudah Equiano, or Gustavus Vasa, the African, Written by Himself*, first published in 1789. Equiano claimed that he was born in the African village of Essaka (now part of eastern Nigeria), and was captured and sold into slavery at the age of eleven. He was first owned by a lieutenant in the English navy, who gave him the name Gustavus Vasa, and was later purchased by a Philadelphia merchant and Quaker. In 1766, he was finally able to buy his own freedom. Over the years Equiano traveled extensively and established several successful business ventures. Notwithstanding the debates about his origins and experience of the Middle Passage, his autobiography represented an influential text in the abolitionist movement, going through thirty-six editions between 1789 and 1857. Equiano died in London in 1797.

⤚

That part of Africa known by the name of Guinea to which the trade of slaves is carried on extends along the coast above 3,400 miles, from the Senegal to Angola, and includes a variety of kingdoms. Of these the most considerable is the kingdom of Benin, both as to extent and wealth, the richness and cultivation of the soil, the power of its king, and the number and warlike disposition of the inhabitants. It is situated nearly under the line and extends along the coast about 170 miles, but runs back into the interior part of Africa to a distance hitherto I believe unexplored by any traveller, and seems only terminated at length by the empire of Abyssinia, near 1,500 miles from its beginning. This kingdom is divided into many provinces or districts, in one of the most remote and fertile of which, called Eboe, I was born in the year 1745, situated in a charming fruitful vale, named Essaka. The distance of this province from the capital of Benin and the sea coast must be very considerable, for I had never heard of white men or Europeans, nor of the sea, and our subjection to the king of Benin was little more than nominal; for every transaction of the government, as far as my slender observation extended, was conducted by the chiefs or elders of the place. The manners and government of a people who have little commerce with other countries are generally very simple, and the history of what passes in one family or village may serve as a specimen of a nation. My father was one of those elders or chiefs I have spoken of and was styled Embrenché, a term as I remember importing the high-est distinction, and signifying in our language a *mark* of grandeur. This mark is conferred on the person entitled to it by cutting the skin across at the top of the forehead and drawing it down to the eyebrows, and while it is in this situation applying a warm hand and rubbing it until it shrinks up into a thick *weal* across the lower part of the forehead. Most of the judges and senators were thus marked; my father had long borne it. I had seen it conferred on one of my broth-ers, and I was also *destined* to receive it by my parents. . . .

We are almost a nation of dancers, musicians, and poets. Thus every great event such as a triumphant return from battle or other cause of public rejoicing is cel-ebrated in public dances, which are accompanied with songs and music suited to the occasion. The assembly is separated into four divisions, which dance either apart or in succession, and each with a character peculiar to itself. The first divi-sion contains the married men, who in their dances frequently exhibit feats of arms and the representation of a battle. To these succeed the married women, who dance in the second division. The young men occupy the third and the maid-ens the fourth. Each represents some interesting scene of real life, such as a great achievement, domestic employment, a pathetic story, or some rural sport, and as the subject is generally founded on some recent event it is therefore ever new. This gives our dances a spirit and variety which I have scarcely seen elsewhere. We have many musical instruments, particularly drums of different kinds, a piece of music which resembles a guitar, and another much like a stickado. These last are chiefly used by betrothed virgins who play on them on all grand festivals.

As our manners are simple, our luxuries are few. The dress of both sexes is nearly the same. It generally consists of a long piece of calico or muslin, wrapped loosely round the body somewhat in the form of a highland plaid. This is usually dyed blue, which is our favourite colour. It is extracted from a berry and is brighter and richer than any I have seen in Europe. Besides this our women of distinction wear golden ornaments, which they dispose with some profusion on their arms and legs. When our women are not employed with the men in tillage, their usual occupation is spinning and weaving cotton, which they afterwards dye and make into garments. They also manufacture earthen vessels, of which we have many kinds. Among the rest tobacco pipes, made after the same fashion and used in the same manner, as those in Turkey.

Our manner of living is entirely plain, for as yet the natives are unacquainted with those refinements in cookery which debauch the taste: bullocks, goats, and poultry, supply the greatest part of their food. These constitute likewise the prin-cipal wealth of the country and the chief articles of its commerce. The flesh is usually stewed in a pan; to make it savoury we sometimes use also pepper and other spices, and we have salt made of wood ashes. Our vegetables are mostly plantains, eadas, yams, beans, and Indian corn. The head of the family usually eats alone; his wives and slaves have also their separate tables. Before we taste food we always wash our hands: indeed our cleanliness on all occasions is extreme, but on this it is an indispensable ceremony. After washing, libation is made by pouring out a small portion of the drink on the floor, and tossing a small quantity of the food in a certain place for the spirits of departed relations, which the natives suppose to preside over their conduct and guard them from evil. They are totally unacquainted with strong or spirituous liquors, and their principal beverage is palm wine. This is got from a tree of that name by tapping it at the top and fastening a large gourd to it, and sometimes one tree will yield three or four gallons in a night. When just drawn it is of a most delicious sweetness, but in a few days it acquires a tartish and more spirituous flavour, though I never saw anyone intoxicated by it. The same tree also produces nuts and oil. Our principal luxury is in perfumes; one sort of these is an odoriferous wood of delicious fragrance, the other a kind of earth, a small portion of which thrown into the fire diffuses a more powerful odour. We beat this wood into powder and mix it with palm oil, with which both men and women perfume themselves.

In our buildings we study convenience rather than ornament. Each master of a family has a large square piece of ground, surrounded with a moat or fence or enclosed with a wall made of red earth tempered, which when dry is as hard as brick. Within this are his houses to accommodate his family and slaves which if numerous frequently present the appearance of a village. In the middle stands the principal building, appropriated to the sole use of the master and consisting of two apartments, in one of which he sits in the day with his family. The other is left apart for the reception of his friends. He has besides these a distinct apartment in which he sleeps, together with his male children. On each side are the apartments of his wives, who have also their separate day and night houses. The habitations of the slaves and their families are distributed throughout the rest of the enclosure. These houses never exceed one story in height: they are always built of wood or stakes driven into the ground, crossed with wattles, and neatly plastered within and without. The roof is thatched with reeds. Our day-houses are left open at the sides, but those in which we sleep are always covered, and plastered in the inside with a composition mixed with cow-dung to keep off the different insects which annoy us during the night. The walls and floors also of these are generally covered with mats. Our beds consist of a platform raised three or four feet from the ground, on which are laid skins and different parts of a spungy tree called plantain. Our covering is calico or muslin, the same as our dress. The usual seats are a few logs of wood, but we have benches, which are generally perfumed to accommodate strangers: these compose the greater part of our household furniture. Houses so constructed and furnished require but little skill to erect them. Every man is a sufficient architect for the purpose. The whole neighborhood afford their unanimous assistance in building them and in return receive and expect no other recompense than a feast.

As we live in a country where nature is prodigal of her favours, our wants are few and easily supplied; of course we have few manufactures. They consist for the most part of calicoes, earthenware, ornaments, and instruments of war and husbandry. But these make no part of our commerce, the principal articles of which, as I have observed, are provisions. In such a state money is of little use; however we have some small pieces of coin, if I may call them such. They are made something like an anchor, but I do not remember either their value or denomination.

We have also markets, at which I have been frequently with my mother. These are sometimes visited by stout mahogany-coloured men from the southwest of us: we call them *Oye-Eboe*, which term signifies red men living at a distance. They generally bring us firearms, gunpowder, hats, beads, and dried fish. The last we esteemed a great rarity as our waters were only brooks and springs. These articles they barter with us for odoriferous woods and earth, and our salt of wood ashes. They always carry slaves through our land, but the strictest account is exacted of their manner of procuring them before they are suffered to pass. Some times indeed we sold slaves to them, but they were only prisoners of war, or such among us as had been convicted of kidnapping, or adultery, and some other crimes which we esteemed heinous. This practice of kidnapping induces me to think that, notwithstanding all our strictness, their principal business among us was to trepan our people. I remember too they carried great sacks along with them, which not long after I had an opportunity of fatally seeing applied to that infamous purpose.

Our land is uncommonly rich and fruitful, and produces all kinds of vegetables in great abundance. We have plenty of Indian corn, and vast quantities of cotton and tobacco. Our pineapples grow without culture; they are about the size of the largest sugar-loaf and finely flavoured. We have also spices of different kinds, particularly pepper, and a variety of delicious fruits which I have never seen in Europe, together with gums of various kinds and honey in abundance. All our industry is exerted to improve those blessings of nature. Agriculture is our chief employment, and everyone, even the children and women, are engaged in it. Thus we are all habituated to labour from our earliest years. Everyone contributes something to the common stock, and as we are unacquainted with idleness we have no beggars. The benefits of such a mode of living are obvious. The West India planters prefer the slaves of Benin or Eboe to those of any other part of Guinea for their hardiness, intelligence, integrity, and zeal. Those benefits are felt by us in the general healthiness of the people, and in their vigour and activity; I might have added too in their comeliness. Deformity is indeed unknown amongst us, I mean that of shape. Numbers of the natives of Eboe now in London might be brought in support of this assertion, for in regard to complexion, ideas of beauty are wholly relative. I remember while in Africa to have seen three negro children who were tawny, and another quite white, who were universally regarded by myself and the natives in general, as far as related to their complexions, as deformed. Our women too were in my eyes at least uncommonly graceful, alert, and modest to a degree of bashfulness; nor do I remember to have ever heard of an instance of incontinence amongst them before marriage. They are also remarkably cheerful. Indeed cheerfulness and affability are two of the leading characteristics of our nation.

Our tillage is exercised in a large plain or common, some hours walk from our dwellings, and all the neighbours resort thither in a body. They use no beasts of husbandry, and their only instruments are hoes, axes, shovels, and beaks, or pointed iron to dig with. Sometimes we are visited by locusts, which come in large clouds so as to darken the air and destroy our harvest. This however happens rarely, but when it does a famine is produced by it. I remember an instance or two wherein this happened. This common is often the theatre of war, and therefore when our people go out to till their land they not only go in a body but generally take their arms with them for fear of a surprise, and when they apprehend an invasion they guard the avenues to their dwellings by driving sticks into the ground, which are so sharp at one end as to pierce the foot and are generally dipped in poison. From what I can recollect of these battles, they appear to have been irruptions of one little state or district on the other to obtain prisoners or booty. Perhaps they were incited to this by those traders who brought the European goods I mentioned amongst us. Such a mode of obtaining slaves in Africa is common, and I believe more are procured this way and by kidnapping than any other. When a trader wants slaves he applies to a chief for them and tempts him with his wares. It is not extraordinary if on this occasion he yields to the temptation with as little firmness, and accepts the price of his fellow creatures liberty with as little reluctance as the enlightened merchant. Accordingly he falls on his neighbours and a desperate battle ensues. If he prevails and takes prisoners, he gratifies his avarice by selling them; but if his party be vanquished and he falls into the hands of the enemy, he is put to death: for as he has been known to foment their quarrels it is thought dangerous to let him survive, and no ransom can save him, though all other prisoners may be redeemed. . . .

The first object which saluted my eyes when I arrived on the coast was the sea, and a slave ship, which was then riding at anchor, and waiting for its cargo. These filled me with astonishment, which was soon converted into terror, when I was carried on board I was immediately handled, and tossed up, to see if I were sound, by some of the crew; and I was now persuaded that I had got into a world of bad spirits, and that they were going to kill me. Their complexions too differing so much from ours, their long hair, and the language they spoke (which was very different from any I had ever heard) united to confirm me in this belief. Indeed such were the horrors of my views and fears at the moment, that, if ten thousand worlds had been my own, I would have freely parted with them all to have exchanged my condition with that of the meanest slave in my own country. When I looked round the ship too and saw a large furnace or copper boiling, and a multitude of black people of every description chained together, every one of their countenances expressing dejection and sorrow, I no longer doubted of my fate; and, quite overpowered with horror and anguish, I fell motionless on the deck and fainted. When I recovered a little I found some black people about me, who I believed were some of those who had brought me on board, and had been receiving their pay; they talked to me in order to cheer me, but all in vain. I asked them if we were not to be eaten by those white men with horrible looks, red faces, and long hair. They told me I was not; and one of the crew brought me a small portion of spirituous liquor in a wine-glass; but being afraid of him, I would not take it out of his hand. One of the blacks therefore took it from him and gave it to me, and I took a little down my palate, which, instead of reviving me, as they thought it would, threw me into the greatest consternation at the strange feeling it produced, having never tasted any such liquor before. Soon after this the blacks who brought me on board went off, and left me abandoned to despair. I now saw myself deprived of all chance of returning to my native country, or even the least glimpse of hope of gaining the shore, which I now considered as friendly; and I even wished for my former slavery in preference to my present situation, which was filled with horrors of every kind, still heightened by my ignorance of what I was to undergo. I was not long suffered to indulge my grief; I was soon put down under the decks, and there I received such a salutation in my nostrils as I had never experienced in my life: so that with the loathsomeness of the stench, and crying together, I became so sick and low that I was not able to eat, nor had I the least desire to taste any thing. I now wished for the last friend, death, to relieve me; but soon, to my grief, two of the white men offered me eatables; and, on my refusing to eat, one of them held me fast by the hands, and laid me across, I think the windlass, and tied my feet, while the other flogged me severely. I had never experienced any thing of this kind before: and, although not being used to the water, I naturally feared that element the first time I saw it, yet, nevertheless, could I have got over the nettings, I would have jumped over the side, but I could not; and, besides, the crew used to watch us very closely who were not chained down to the decks, lest we should leap into the water: and I have seen some of these poor African prisoners most severely cut for attempting to do so, and hourly whipped for not eating. This indeed was often the case with myself. In a little time after, amongst the poor chained men, I found some of my own nation, which in a small degree gave ease to my mind. I inquired of these what was to be done with us? they gave me to understand we were to be carried to these white people's country to work for them. I then was a little revived, and thought, if it were no worse than working, my situation was not so desperate: but still I feared I should be put to death, the white people looked and acted, as I thought, in so savage a manner; for I had never seen among any people such instances of brutal cruelty; and this not only shown towards us blacks, but also to some of the whites themselves. One white man in particular I saw, when we were permitted to be on deck, flogged so unmercifully with a large rope near the foremast, that he died in consequence of it; and they tossed him over the side as they would have done a brute. This made me fear these people the more; and I expected nothing less than to be treated in the same manner. I could not help expressing my fears and apprehensions to some of my countrymen: I asked them if these people had no country, but lived in this hollow place (the ship)? they told me they did not, but came from a distant one, "Then," said I, "how comes it in all our country we never heard of them!" They told me, because they lived so very far off. I then asked where were their women? had they any like themselves? I was told they had: "And why," said I, "do we not see them?" they answered, because they were left behind. I asked how the vessel could go? they told me they could not tell; but that there were cloth put upon the masts by the help of the ropes I saw, and then the vessel went on; and the white men had some spell or magic they put in the water when they liked in order to stop the vessel, I was exceedingly amazed at this account, and really thought they were spirits. I therefore wished much to be from amongst them, for I expected they would sacrifice me: but my wishes were vain; for we were so quartered that it was impossible for any of us to make our escape. While we stayed on the coast I was mostly on deck; and one day, to my great astonishment, I saw one of these vessels coming in with the sails up. As soon as the whites saw it, they gave a great shout, at which we were amazed: and the more so as the vessel appeared larger by approaching nearer. At last she came to an anchor in my sight, and when the anchor was let go I and my countrymen who saw it were lost in astonishment to observe the vessel stop; and were now convinced it was done by magic. Soon after this the other ship got her boats out, and they came on board of us, and the people of both ships seemed very glad to see each other. Several of the strangers also shook hands with us black people, and made motions with their hands, signifying I suppose, we were to go to their country; but we did not understand them. At last, when the ship we were in, had got in all her cargo, they made ready with many fearful noises, and we were all put under deck, so that we could not see how they managed the vessel. But this disappointment was the least of my sorrow. The stench of the hold while we were on the coast was so intolerably loathsome, that it was dangerous to remain there for any time, and some of us had been permitted to stay on the deck for the fresh air; but now that the whole ship's cargo were confined together, it became absolutely pestilential. The closeness of the place, and the heat of the climate, added to the number in the ship, which was so crowded that each had scarcely room to turn himself, almost suffocated us. This produced copious perspirations, so that the air soon became unfit for respiration, from a variety of loathsome smells, and brought on a sickness amongst the slaves, of which many died, thus falling victims to the improvident avarice, as I may call it, of their purchasers. This wretched situation was again aggravated by the galling of the chains, now become insupportable; and the filth of the necessary tubs, into which the children often fell, and were almost suffocated. The shrieks of the women, and the groans of the dying, rendered the whole a scene of horror almost inconceivable. Happily perhaps for myself I was soon reduced so low here that it was thought necessary to keep me almost always on deck; and from my extreme youth I was not put in fetters. In this situation I expected every hour to share the fate of my companions, some of whom were almost daily brought upon deck at the point of death, which I began to hope would soon put an end to my miseries. Often did I think many of the inhabitants of the deep much more happy than myself, I envied them the freedom they enjoyed, and as often wished I could change my condition for theirs. Every circumstance I met with served only to render my state more painful, and heightened my apprehensions and my opinion of the cruelty of the whites. One day they had taken a number of fishes; and when they had killed and satisfied themselves with as many as they thought fit, to our astonishment who were on the deck, rather than give any of them to us to eat, as we expected, they tossed the remaining fish into the sea again, although we begged and prayed for some as well as we could, but in vain; and some of my countrymen, being pressed by hunger, took an opportunity, when they thought no one saw them, of trying to get a little privately; but they were discovered, and the attempt procured them some very severe floggings. One day, when we had a smooth sea and moderate wind, two of my wearied countrymen who were chained together (I was near them at the time), preferring death to such a life of misery, somehow made through the nettings and jumped into the sea: immediately another quite dejected fellow, who on account of his illness, was suffered to be out of irons, also followed their example; and I believe many more would very soon have done the same if they had not been prevented by the ship's crew who were instantly alarmed. Those of us that were the most active were in a moment put down under the deck, and there was such a noise and confusion amongst the people of the ship as I never heard before, to stop her, and get the boat out to go after the slaves. However two of the wretches were drowned, but they got the other, and afterwards flogged him unmercifully for thus attempting to prefer death to slavery. In this manner we continued to undergo more hardships than I can now relate, hardships which are inseparable from this accursed trade. Many a time we were near suffocation from the want of fresh air, which we were often without for whole days together. This, and the stench of the necessary tubs, carried off many. During our passage I first saw flying fishes, which surprised me very much: they used frequently to fly across the ship, and many of them fell on the deck. I also now first saw the use of the quadrant; I had often with astonishment seen the mariners make observations with it, and I could not think what it meant. They at last took notice of my surprise: and one of them, willing to increase it, as well as to gratify my curiosity, made me one day look through it. The clouds appeared to me to be land, which disappeared as they passed along. This heightened my wonder; and I was now more persuaded than ever that I was in another world, and that every thing about me was magic. At last we came in sight of the island of Barbadoes, at which the whites on board gave a great shout, and made many signs of joy to us. We did not know what to think of this; but as the vessel drew nearer, we plainly saw the harbour, and other ships of different kinds and sizes; and we soon anchored amongst them off Bridge-Town. Many merchants and planters now came on board, though it was in the evening. They put us in separate parcels, and examined us attentively. They also made us jump, and pointed to the land, signifying we were to go there. We thought by this we should be eaten by these ugly men, as they appeared to us; and, when soon after we were all put down under the deck again, there was much dread and trembling among us, and nothing but bitter cries to be heard all the night from these apprehensions, insomuch that at last the white people got some old slaves from the land to pacify us. They told us we were not to be eaten, but to work, and were soon to go on land, where we should see many of our country people. This report eased us much; and sure enough, soon after we landed, there came to us Africans of all languages. We were conducted immediately to the merchant's yard, where we were all pent up together like so many sheep in a fold, without regard to sex or age. As every object was new to me, every thing I saw filled me with surprise. What struck me first was that the houses were built with bricks and stories, and in every other respect different from those I had seen in Africa: but I was still more astonished on seeing people on horseback. I did not know what this could mean; and indeed I thought these people were full of nothing but magical arts. While I was in this astonishment one of my fellow prisoners spoke to a countryman of his about the horses, who said they were the same kind they had in their country. I understood them, though they were from a distant part of Africa, and I thought it odd I had not seen any horses there; but afterwards when I came to converse with different Africans, I found they had many horses amongst them, and much larger than those I saw. We were not many days in the merchant's custody before we were sold after their usual manner, which is this:—On a signal given, (as the beat of a drum) the buyers rush at once into the yard where the slaves are confined, and make choice of that parcel they like best. The noise and clamour with which this is attended, and the eagerness visible in the countenances of the buyers, serve not a little to increase the apprehension of terrified Africans, who may well be supposed to consider them as the ministers of that destruction to which they think themselves devoted. In this manner, without scruple, are relations and friends separated, most of them never to see each other again. I remember in the vessel in which I was brought over, in the men's apartment, there were several brothers, who, in the sale were sold in different lots; and it was very moving on this occasion to see and hear their cries at parting. O, ye nominal Christians! might not an African ask you, learned you this from your God, who says unto you, Do unto all men as you would men should do unto you? Is it not enough that we are torn from our country and friends, to toil for your luxury and lust of gain? Must every tender feeling be likewise sacrificed to your avarice? Are the dearest friends and relations, now rendered more dear by their separation from their kindred, still to be parted from each other, and thus prevented from cheering the gloom of slavery with the small comfort of being together, and mingling their sufferings and sorrows? Why are parents to lose their children, brothers their sisters, or husbands their wives? Surely this is a new refinement in cruelty, which, while it has no advantage to atone for it, thus aggravates distress, and adds fresh horrors even to the wretchedness of slavery.

Source: Excerpt from Olaudah Equiano, *The Interesting Narrative of the Life of Olaudah Equiano, or Gustav Vasa, the African in 2 volumes* (New York, 1789 and 1791).

SELECT BIBLIOGRAPHY:

Houston Baker, *The Journey Back: Issues in Black Literature and Criticism* (Chicago: University of Chicago Press, 1980).

Stephen Butterfield, *Black Autobiography in America* (Amherst: University of Massachusetts Press, 1974).

Alexander X. Byrd, "Captives & Voyagers Black Migrants Across the Eighteenth-Century World of Olaudah Equiano" (Ph.D. diss., Duke University, 2001).

Vincent Carretta, *Equiano, The African: Biography of a Self-Made Man* (Athens: University of Georgia Press, 2005).

Angelo Constanzo, *Surprising Narrative: Olaudah Equiano and the Beginnings of Black Autobiography* (New York: Greenwood Press, 1987).

⇒ **3** ⇒

"Thus Doth Ethiopia Stretch Forth Her Hand from Slavery, to Freedom and Equality," Prince Hall, 1797

Questions remain about the birth, parentage, and early life of Prince Hall (1735?–1807). It is generally accepted by historians that Prince Hall was owned by a

Boston leather-dresser, William Hall, who freed him on April 9, 1770, as a reward for twenty-one years' service. In July 1775, Hall helped to initiate the first Masonic lodge for African Americans. Hall's efforts would ultimately establish Masonry as one of the major social institutions in black America. Less well known, but equally important, were Hall's contributions to the early abolitionist movement. Hall's 1788 petition to the Massachusetts legislature calling for an end to the slave trade was a contributing factor in its abolition. This sermon, originally delivered to a black fraternal order in Menotomy (later West Cambridge), Massachusetts, is notable as one of the earliest published speeches of an African American.

Beloved brethren of the African Lodge: It is now five years since I delivered a charge to you on some parts and points of Masonry. As one branch of super-structure of the foundation, I endeavored to show you the duty of a mason to a mason, and of charity and love to all mankind, as the work and image of the great God and the Father of the human race. I shall now attempt to show you that it is our duty to sympathize with our fellow men under their troubles, and with the families of our brethren who are gone, we hope, to the Grand Lodge above.

We are to have sympathy, but this, after all, is not to be confined to parties or colors, nor to towns or states, nor to a kingdom, but to the kingdoms of the whole earth, over whom Christ the King is head and Grand Master for all in distress.

Among these numerous sons and daughters of a distress, let us see our friends and brethren; and first let us see *them* dragged from their native country, by the iron hand of tyranny and oppression, from their dear friends and connections, with weeping eyes and aching hearts, to a strange land, and among a strange peo-ple, whose tender mercies are cruel, and there to bear the iron yoke of slavery and cruelty, till death, as a friend, shall relieve them. And must not the unhappy con-dition of these, our fellow men, draw forth our hearty prayers and wishes for their deliverance from those merchants and traders, whose characters you have described in Revelations 17:11–13? And who knows but these same sort of traders may, in a short time, in like manner bewail the loss of the African traffic to their shame and confusion? The day dawns now in some of the West Indies Islands. God can and will change their condition and their hearts, too, and let Boston and the world know that He hath no respect of persons, and that that bulwark of envy, pride, scorn and contempt, which is so visible in some, shall fall.

Jethro, an Ethiopian, gave instructions to his son-in-law, Moses, in establishing government. Exodus 18:22–24. Thus, Moses was not ashamed to be instructed by a black man. Phillip was not ashamed to take a seat beside the Ethiopian Eunuch and to instruct him in the gospel. The Grand Master Solomon was not ashamed to hold conference with the Queen of Sheba. Our Grand Master Solomon did not divide the living child, whatever he might do with the dead one; neither did he pretend to make a law to forbid the parties from having free intercourse with one another, without the fear of censure, or be turned out of the synagogue.

Now, my brethren, nothing is stable; all things are changeable. Let us seek those things which are sure and steadfast, and let us pray God that, while we remain here, he would give us the grace of patience and strength to bear up under all our troubles, which, at this day, God knows, we have our share of. Patience, I say; for were we not possessed of a great measure of it, we could not bear up under the daily insults we meet with in the streets of Boston, much more on public days of recreation. How, at such times, are we shamefully abused, and that to such a degree that we may truly be said to carry our lives in our hands, and the arrows of death are flying about our heads. Helpless women have their clothes torn from their backs. . . . And by whom are these disgraceful and abusive actions committed? Not by the men born and bred in Boston—they are better bred—but by a mob or horde of shameless, low-lived, envious, spiteful persons, some of them not long since servants in gentlemen's kitchens scouring knives, horse tenders, chaise drivers. I was told by a gentleman who saw the filthy behavior in the Common that, in all places he had been in, he never saw so cruel behavior in all his life; and that a slave in the West Indies on Sundays or holidays enjoys himself and friends without molestation. Not only this man, but many in town who have seen their behavior to us, and that without provocation twenty or thirty cowards have fallen upon one man. (Oh, the patience of the blacks!) 'Tis not for want of courage in you, for they know that they do not face you man for man; but in a mob, which we despise, and would rather suffer wrong than to do wrong, to the disturbance of the community, and the disgrace of our reputation; for every good citizen doth honor to the laws of the state where he resides.

My brethren, let us not be cast down under these and many other abuses we at present are laboring under, for the darkest hour is just before the break of day. My brethren, let us remember what a dark day it was with our African brethren, six years ago, in the French West Indies. Nothing but the snap of the whip was heard, from morning to evening. Hanging, breaking on the wheel, burning, and all manner of tortures were inflicted upon those unhappy people. But, blessed be God, the scene is changed. They now confess that God hath no respect of person and, therefore, receive them as their friends and treat them as brothers. Thus doth Ethiopia stretch forth her hand from slavery, to freedom and equality.

Source: Excerpt of speech delivered at black Masonic lodge, Menotomy, Massachusetts, June 24, 1797. Originally published in William C. Nell, *The Colored Patriots of the American Revolution* (Boston: R. F. Wallcut, 1855, pp. 61–64; also in Philip S. Foner, ed., *The Voice of Black America* (New York: Simon and Schuster, 1972), pp. 13–15.

SELECT BIBLIOGRAPHY:

Joanna Brooks, "Prince Hall, Freemasonry, and Genealogy," *African American Review* 34, no. 2 (2000), pp. 197–216.

George Williamson Crawford, *Prince Hall and His Followers: Being a Monograph on the Legitimacy of the Negro Masonry* (New York: AMS Press, 1914; reprint, 1971).

Harry E. Davis, *A History of Freemasonary among Negroes in America* (Published under auspices of the United Supreme Council, ancient and accepted Scottish rite of Freemasonry, Northern jurisdiction, U.S.A. [Prince Hall Affiliation] incorporated, 1946).

Sidney Kaplan, *The Black Presence in the Era of the American Revolution, 1770–1780*, rev. ed. (Amherst: University of Massachusetts Press, 1989).

Charles H. Wesley, *Prince Hall, Life and Legacy* (Washington, D.C.: United Supreme Council, Southern Jurisdiction, Prince Hall Affiliation, 1977).

⚊ 4 ⚊

The Founding of the African Methodist Episcopal Church, *Richard Allen, 1816*

Richard Allen (1760–1831) was born a slave in Philadelphia. At about the age of twenty, Allen joined the Methodist Church and quickly began to lead local meetings. Allen converted his master to Methodism, and eventually purchased his freedom. In 1787 Allen helped to establish the independent Free African Society, the first mutual and beneficial assistance association for African Americans. Allen's greatest accomplishment was his leadership in founding the African Methodist Episcopal (AME) Church in April 1816. Allen was active in antislavery efforts and helped sponsor the first national convention of black Americans in 1830. This document, taken from Allen's biography, describes the establishment of the AME Church.

⚊

December 1784, General Conference sat in Baltimore, the first General Conference ever held in America. The English preachers just arrived from Europe were, Rev. Dr. Coke, Richard Whatcoat and Thomas Vassey. This was the beginning of the Episcopal Church amongst the Methodists. Many of the ministers were set apart in holy orders at this conference, and were said to be entitled to the gown; and I have thought religion has been declining in the church ever since. There was a pamphlet published by some person, which stated, that when the Methodists were no people, then they were a people; and now they have become a people they were no people; which had often serious weight upon my mind.

In 1785 the Rev. Richard Whatcoat was appointed on Baltimore circuit. He was, I believe, a man of God. I found great strength in travelling with him—a father in Israel. In his advice he was fatherly and friendly. He was of a mild and serene disposition. My lot was cast in Baltimore, in a small meeting-house called Methodist Alley. I stopped at Richard Mould's, and was sent to my lodgings, and lodged at Mr. McCannon's. I had some happy meetings in Baltimore. I was introduced to Richard Russell, who was very kind and affectionate to me, and attended several meetings. Rev. Bishop Asbury sent for me to meet him at Henry Gaff's. I did so. He told me he wished me to travel with him. He told me that in the slave countries, Carolina and other places, I must not intermix with the slaves, and I would frequently have to sleep in his carriage, and he would allow me my victuals and clothes. I told him I would not travel with him on these conditions. He asked me my reason. I told him if I was taken sick, who was to support me? and that I thought people ought to lay up something while they were able, to support themselves in time of sickness or old age. He said that was as much as he got, his victuals and clothes. I told him he would be taken care of, let his afflictions be as they were, or let him be taken sick where he would, he would be taken care of; but I doubted whether it would be the case with myself. He smiled, and told me he would give me from then until he returned from the eastward to make up my mind, which would be about three months. But I made up my mind that I would not accept of his proposals. Shortly after I left Hartford Circuit, and came to Pennsylvania, on Lancaster circuit. I travelled several months on Lancaster circuit with the Rev. Peter Morratte and Irie Ellis. They were very kind and affectionate to me in building me up; for I had many trials to pass through, and I received nothing from the Methodist connection. My usual method was, when I would get bare of clothes, to stop travelling and go to work, so that no man could say I was chargeable to the connection. My hands administered to my necessities. The autumn of 1785 I returned again to Radnor. I stopped at George Giger's, a man of God, and went to work. His family were all kind and affectionate to me. I killed seven beeves, and supplied the neighbors with meat; got myself pretty well clad through my own industry—thank God—and preached occasionally. The elder in charge in Philadelphia frequently sent for me to come to the city. February, 1786, I came to Philadelphia. Preaching was given out for me at five o'clock in the morning at St. George church. I strove to preach as well as I could, but it was a great cross to me; but the Lord was with me. We had a good time, and several souls were awakened, and were earnestly seeking redemption in the blood of Christ. I thought I would stop in Philadelphia a week or two. I preached at different places in the city. My labor was much blessed. I soon saw a large field open in seeking and instructing my African brethren, who had been a long forgotten people and few of them attended public worship. I preached in the commons, in Southwark, Northern Liberties, and wherever I could find an opening. I frequently preached twice a day, at 5 o'clock in the morning and in the evening, and it was not uncommon for me to preach from four to five times a day. I established prayer meetings; I raised a society in 1786 for forty-two members. I saw the necessity of erecting a place of worship for the colored people. I proposed it to the most respectable people of color in this city; but here I met with opposition. I had but three colored brethren that united with me in erecting a place of worship—the Rev. Absalom Jones, William White and Dorus Ginnings. These united with me as soon as it became public and known by the elder who was stationed in the city. The Rev. C— B— opposed the plan, and would not submit to any argument we could raise; but he was shortly removed from the charge. The Rev. Mr. W— took the charge, and the Rev. L— G—, Mr. W— was much opposed to an African church, and used very degrading and insulting language to us, to try and prevent us from going on. We all belonged to St. George's church—Rev. Absalom Jones, William White and Dorus Ginnings. We felt ourselves much cramped; but my dear Lord was with us, and we believed, if it was his will, the work would go on, and that we would be able to succeed in building the house of the Lord. We established prayer meetings and meetings of exhortation, and the Lord blessed our endeavors, and many souls were awakened; but the elder soon forbid us holding any such meetings; but we viewed the forlorn state of our colored brethren, and that they were destitute of a place of worship. They were considered as a nuisance.

A number of us usually attended St. George's church in Fourth street; and when the colored people began to get numerous in attending the church, they moved us from the seats we usually sat on, and placed us around the wall, and on

Sabbath morning we went to church and the sexton stood at the door, and told us to go in the gallery. He told us to go, and we would see where to sit. We expected to take the seats over the ones we formerly occupied below, not knowing any better. We took those seats. Meeting had begun, and they were nearly done singing, and just as we got to the seats, the elder said, "Let us pray." We had not been long upon our knees before I heard considerable scuffling and low talking. I raised my head up and saw one of the trustees, H— M—, having hold of the Rev. Absalom Jones, pulling him up off of his knees, and saying, "You must get up—you must not kneel here." Mr. Jones replied, "Wait until prayer is over." Mr. H— M— said, "No, you must get up now, or I will call for aid and force you away." Mr. Jones said, "Wait until prayer is over, and I will get up and trouble you no more." With that he beckoned to one of the other trustees, Mr. L— S— to come to his assistance. He came, and went to William White to pull him up. By this time prayer was over, and we all went out of the church in a body, and they were no more plagued with us in the church. This raised a great excitement and inquiry among the citizens, in so much that I believe they were ashamed of their conduct. But my dear Lord was with us, and we were filled with fresh vigor to get a house erected to worship God in. Seeing our forlorn and distressed situation, many of the hearts of our citizens were moved to urge us forward; notwithstanding we had subscribed largely towards finishing St. George's church, in building the gallery and laying new floors, and just as the house was made comfortable, we were turned out from enjoying the comforts of worshipping therein. We then hired a store-room, and held worship by ourselves. Here we were pursued with threats of being disowned, and read publicly out of meeting if we did continue worship in the place we had hired; but we believed the Lord would be our friend. We got subscription papers out to raise money to build the house of the Lord. By this time we had waited on Dr. Rush and Mr. Robert Ralston, and told them of our distressing situation. We considered it a blessing that the Lord had put it into our hearts to wait upon those gentlemen. They pitied our situation, and subscribed largely towards the church, and were very friendly towards us, and advised us how to go on. We appointed Mr. Ralston our treasurer. Dr. Rush did much for us in public by his influence. I hope the name of Dr. Benjamin Rush and Robert Ralston will never be forgotten among us. They were the first two gentlemen who espoused the cause of the oppressed, and aided us in building the house of the Lord for the poor Africans to worship in. Here was the beginning and rise of the first African church in America. But the elder of the Methodist Church still pursued us. Mr. J— M— called upon us and told us if we did not erase our names from the subscription paper, and give up the paper, we would be publicly turned out of meeting. We asked him if we had violated any rules of discipline by so doing. He replied, "I have the charge given to me by the Conference, and unless you submit I will read you publicly out of meeting." We told him we were willing to abide by the discipline of the Methodist Church, "And if you will show us where we have violated any law of discipline of the Methodist Church, we will submit; and if there is no rule violated in the discipline we will proceed on." He replied, "We will read you all out." We told him if he turned us out contrary to rule of discipline, we should seek further redress. We told him we were dragged off of our knees in St. George's church, and treated worse than heathens; and we were determined to seek out for ourselves, the Lord being our helper. He told us we were not Methodists, and left us. Finding we would go on in raising money to build the church, he called upon us again, and wished to see us all together. We met him. He told us that he wished us well, that he was a friend to us, and used many arguments to convince us that we were wrong in building a church. We told him we had no place of worship; and we did not mean to go to St. George's church any more, as we were so scandalously treated in the presence of all the congregation present; "and if you deny us your name, you cannot seal up the scriptures from us, and deny us a name in heaven. We believe heaven is free for all who worship in spirit and truth." And he said, "So you are determined to go on." We told him "Yes, God being our helper." He then replied, "We will disown you all from the Methodist connection." We believed if we put our trust in the Lord, he would stand by us. This was a trial that I never had to pass through before. I was confident that the great head of the church would support us. My dear Lord was with us. . . . Robert R. Roberts, the resident elder, came to Bethel, insisted on preaching to us and taking the spiritual charge of the congregation, for we were Methodists he was told he should come on some terms with the trustees; his answer was, that "He did not come to consult with Richard Allen or other trustees, but to inform the congregation, that on next Sunday afternoon, he would come and take the spiritual charge." We told him he could not preach for us under existing circumstances. However, at the appointed time he came, but having taken previous advice we had our preacher in the pulpit when he came, and the house was so fixed that he could not get but more than half way to the pulpit. Finding himself disappointed he appealed to those who came with him as witnesses, that "That man (meaning the preacher), had taken his appointment." Several respectable white citizens who knew the colored people had been ill-used, were present, and told us not to fear, for they would see us righted, and not suffer Roberts to preach in a forcible manner, after which Roberts went away.

The next elder stationed in Philadelphia was Robert Birch, who, following the example of his predecessor, came and published a meeting for himself. But the method just mentioned was adopted and he had to go away disappointed. In consequence of this, he applied to the Supreme Court for a writ of mandamus, to know why the pulpit was denied him. Being elder, this brought on a lawsuit, which ended in our favor. Thus by the Providence of God we were delivered from a long, distressing and expensive suit, which could not be resumed, being determined by the Supreme Court. For this mercy we desire to be unfeignedly thankful.

About this time, our colored friends in Baltimore were treated in a similar manner by the white preachers and trustees, and many of them driven away who were disposed to seek a place of worship, rather than go to law.

Many of the colored people in other places were in a situation nearly like those of Philadelphia and Baltimore, which induced us, in April 1816, to call a general meeting, by way of Conference. Delegates from Baltimore and other places which met those of Philadelphia, and taking into consideration their grievances, and in order to secure the privileges, promote union and harmony among themselves, it was resolved: "That the people of Philadelphia, Baltimore, etc., etc., should become one body, under the name of the African Methodist Episcopal Church." We deemed it expedient to have a form of discipline, whereby we may guide our people in the fear of God, in the unity of the Spirit, and in the bonds of peace, and preserve us from that spiritual despotism which we have so recently experienced—remembering that we are not to lord it over God's heritage, as greedy dogs that can never have enough. But with long suffering and bowels of compassion, to bear each other's burdens, and so fulfill the Law of Christ, praying that our mutual striving together for the promulgation of the Gospel may be crowned with abundant success. . . .

Source: Excerpt from Richard Allen, *The Life, Experience and Gospel Labors of the Rt. Rev. Richard Allen* (Philadelphia: Lee & Yocum, 1888), pp. 11–17, 23–24.

SELECT BIBLIOGRAPHY:
Carol V. R. George, *Segregated Sabbaths: Richard Allen and the Emergence of Independent Black Churches, 1760–1840* (New York: Oxford University Press, 1973).
Harry Reed, *Platforms for Change: The Foundations of the Northern Free Black Community* (East Lansing: Michigan State University Press, 1994).
Charles H. Wesley, *Richard Allen: Apostle of Freedom* (Washington, D.C.: Associated Publishers, 1935).

⟿ 5 ⟿

David Walker's "Appeal," *1829–1830*

David Walker (1785–1830) was born in Wilmington, Ohio, and moved to Boston in 1827, where he became a well-known spokesperson against slavery, and contributed to the first African-American newspaper, *Freedom's Journal*. Walker was uncompromising in denouncing what he saw as the "evils" of slavery, and urged enslaved African Americans to employ any tactics, including violence, to achieve liberation. Walker's militancy is clearly presented in his famous *Appeal in Four Articles*, which was reprinted several times in 1829 and 1830. Walker died mysteriously in 1830, possibly due to poisoning.

⟿

APPEAL, &c.

PREAMBLE

My dearly beloved Brethren and Fellow Citizens.

Having travelled over a considerable portion of these United States, and having, in the course of my travels, taken the most accurate observations of things as they exist—the result of my observations has warranted the full and unshaken conviction, that we, (coloured people of these United States,) are the most degraded, wretched, and abject set of beings that ever lived since the world began; and I pray God that none like us ever may live again until time shall be no more. They tell us of the Israelites in Egypt, the Helots in Sparta, and of the Roman Slaves, which last were made up from almost every nation under heaven, whose sufferings under those ancient and heathen nations, were, in comparison with ours, under this enlightened and Christian nation, no more than a cypher—or, in other words, those heathen nations of antiquity, had but little more among them than the name and form of slavery; while wretchedness and endless miseries were reserved, apparently in a phial, to be poured out upon our fathers, ourselves and our children, by *Christian* Americans!

These positions I shall endeavour, by the help of the Lord, to demonstrate in the course of this *Appeal*, to the satisfaction of the most incredulous mind—and may God Almighty, who is the Father of our Lord Jesus Christ, open your hearts to understand and believe the truth.

The *causes*, my brethren, which produce our wretchedness and miseries, are so very numerous and aggravating, that I believe the pen only of a Josephus or a Plutarch, can well enumerate and explain them. Upon subjects, then, of such incomprehensible magnitude, so impenetrable, and so notorious, I shall be obliged to omit a large class of, and content myself with giving you an exposition of a few of those, which do indeed rage to such an alarming pitch, that they cannot but be a perpetual source of terror and dismay to every reflecting mind.

I am fully aware, in making this appeal to my much afflicted and suffering brethren, that I shall not only be assailed by those whose greatest earthly desires are, to keep us in abject ignorance and wretchedness, and who are of the firm conviction that Heaven has designed us and our children to be slaves and *beasts of burden* to them and their children. I say, I do not only expect to be held up to the public as an ignorant, impudent and restless disturber of the public peace, by such avaricious creatures, as well as a mover of insubordination—and perhaps put in prison or to death, for giving a superficial exposition of our miseries, and exposing tyrants. But I am persuaded, that many of my brethren, particularly those who are ignorantly in league with slave-holders or tyrants, who acquire their daily bread by the blood and sweat of their more ignorant brethren—and not a few of those too, who are too ignorant to see an inch beyond their noses, will rise up and call me cursed—Yea, the jealous ones among us will perhaps use more abject subtlety, by affirming that this work is not worth perusing, that we are well situated, and there is no use in trying to better our condition, for we cannot. I will ask one question here.—Can our condition be any worse?—Can it be more mean and abject? If there are any changes, will they not be for the better, though they may appear for the worst at first? Can they get us any lower? Where can they get us? They are afraid to treat us worse, for they know well, the day they do it they are gone. But against all accusations which may or can be preferred against me, I appeal to Heaven for my motive in writing—who knows that my object is, if possible, to awaken in the breasts of my afflicted, degraded and slumbering brethren, a spirit of inquiry and investigation respecting our miseries and wretchedness in this *Republican Land of Liberty!!!!!!*

The sources from which our miseries are derived, and on which I shall comment, I shall not combine in one, but shall put them under distinct heads and expose them in their turn; in doing which, keeping truth on my side, and not departing from the strictest rules of morality, I shall endeavour to penetrate, search out, and lay them open for your inspection. If you cannot or will not profit by them, I shall have done *my* duty to you, my country and my God.

And as the inhuman system of *slavery*, is the *source* from which most of our miseries proceed, I shall begin with that *curse to nations*, which has spread terror and devastation through so many nations of antiquity, and which is raging to such a pitch at the present day in Spain and in Portugal. It had one tug in England, in France, and in the United States of America; yet the inhabitants thereof, do not learn wisdom, and erase it entirely from their dwellings and from all with whom they have to do. The fact is, the labour of slaves comes so cheap to the avaricious usurpers, and is (as they think) of such great utility to the country where it exists, that those who are actuated by sordid avarice only, overlook the evils, which will as sure as the Lord lives, follow after the good. In fact, they are so happy to keep in ignorance and degradation, and to receive the homage and the labour of the slaves, they forget that God rules in the armies of heaven and among the inhabitants of the earth, having his ears continually open to the cries, tears and groans of his oppressed people; and being a just and holy Being will at one day appear fully in behalf of the oppressed, and arrest the progress of the avaricious oppressors; for although the destruction of the oppressors God may not effect by the oppressed, yet the Lord our God will bring other destructions upon them—for not unfrequently will he cause them to rise up one against another, to be split and divided, and to oppress each other, and sometimes to open hostilities with sword in hand. Some may ask, what is the matter with this united and happy people?— Some say it is the cause of political usurpers; tyrants, oppressors, &c. But has not the Lord an oppressed and suffering people among them? Does the Lord condescend to hear their cries and see their tears in consequence of oppression? Will he let the oppressors rest comfortably and happy always? Will he not cause the very children of the oppressors to rise up against them, and oftimes put them to death? "God works in many ways his wonders to perform."

All persons who are acquainted with history, and particularly the Bible, who are not blinded by the God of this world, and are not actuated solely by avarice—who are able to lay aside prejudice long enough to view candidly and impartially, things as they were, are, and probably will be—who are willing to admit that God made man to serve Him *alone*, and that man should have no other Lord or Lords but Himself—that God Almighty is the *sole proprietor* or *master* of the WHOLE human family, and will not on any consideration admit of a colleague, being unwilling to divide his glory with another—and who can dispense with prejudice long enough to admit that we are *men*, notwithstanding our *improminent noses* and *woolly heads*, and believe that we feel for our fathers, mothers, wives and children, as well as the whites do for theirs.—I say, all who are permitted to see and believe these things, can easily recognize the judgments of God among the Spaniards. Though others may lay the cause of the fierceness with which they cut each other's throats, to some other circumstance, yet they who believe that God is a God of justice, will believe that SLAVERY *is the principal cause*.

While the Spaniards are running about upon the field of battle cutting each other's throats, has not the Lord an afflicted and suffering people in the midst of them, whose cries and groans in consequence of oppression are continually pouring into the ears of the God of justice? Would they not cease to cut each other's throats, if they could? But how can they? The very support which they draw from government to aid them in perpetrating such enormities, does it not arise in a great degree from the wretched victims of oppression among them? And yet they are calling for *Peace!—Peace!!* Will any peace be given unto them? Their destruction may indeed be procrastinated awhile, but can it continue long, while they are oppressing the Lord's people? Has He not the hearts of all men in His hand? Will he suffer one part of his creatures to go on oppressing another like brutes always, with impunity? And yet, those avaricious wretches are calling for *Peace!!!!* I declare, it does appear to me, as though some nations think God is asleep, or that he made the Africans for nothing else but to dig their mines and work their farms, or they cannot believe history, sacred or profane. I ask every man who has a heart, and is blessed with the privilege of believing—Is not God a God of justice to *all* his creatures? Do you say he is? Then if he gives peace and tranquillity to tyrants, and permits them to keep our fathers, our mothers, ourselves and our children in eternal ignorance and wretchedness, to support them and their families, would he be to us a God of *justice?* I ask, O ye *Christians!!!* who hold us and our children in the most abject ignorance and degradation, that ever a people were afflicted with since the world began—I say, if God gives you peace and tranquillity, and suffers you thus to go on afflicting us, and our children, who have never given you the least provocation—would he be to us *a God of justice?* If you will allow that we are MEN, who feel for each other, does not the blood of our fathers and of us their children, cry aloud to the Lord of Sabaoth against you, for the cruelties and murders with which you have, and do continue to afflict us. But it is time for me to close my remarks on the suburbs, just to enter more fully into the interior of this system of cruelty and oppression. . . .

 . . . I saw a paragraph, a few years since, in a South Carolina paper, which, speaking of the barbarity of the Turks, it said: "The Turks are the most barbarous people in the world—they treat the Greeks more like *brutes* than human beings." And in the same paper was an advertisement, which said: "Eight well built Virginia and Maryland *Negro fellows* and four *wenches* will positively be *sold* this day, *to the highest bidder!*" And what astonished me still more was, to see in this same *humane* paper!! the cuts of three men, with clubs and budgets on their backs, and an advertisement offering a considerable sum of money for their apprehension and delivery. I declare, it is really so amusing to hear the Southerners and Westerners of this country talk about *barbarity*, that it is positively, enough to make a man *smile*.

The sufferings of the Helots among the Spartans, were somewhat severe, it is true, but to say that theirs, were as severe as ours among the Americans, I do most strenuously deny—for instance, can any man show me an article on a page of ancient history which specifies, that, the Spartans chained, and hand-cuffed the Helots, and dragged them from their wives and children, children from their parents, mothers from their suckling babes, wives from their husbands, driving them from one end of the country to the other? Notice the Spartans were heathens, who lived long before our Divine Master made his appearance in the flesh. Can Christian Americans deny these barbarous cruelties? Have you not, Americans, having subjected us under you, added to these miseries, by insulting us in telling us to our face, because we are helpless, that we are not of the human family? I ask you, O! Americans, I ask you in the name of the Lord, can you deny these charges? Some perhaps may deny, by saying, that they never thought or said that we were not men. But do not actions speak louder than words?—have they not made provisions for the Greeks, and Irish? Nations who have never done the least thing for them, while *we*, who have enriched their country with our blood and tears—have dug up gold and silver for them and their children, from generation to generation, and are in more miseries than any other people under heaven, are not seen, but by comparatively, a handful of the American people? There are indeed, more ways to kill a dog, besides choking it to death with butter. Further— The Spartans or Lacedemonians, had some frivolous pretext, for enslaving the Helots, for they (Helots) while being free inhabitants of Sparta, stirred up an intestine commotion, and were, by the Spartans subdued, and made prisoners of war. Consequently they and their children were condemned to perpetual slavery.[1]

I have been for years troubling the pages of historians, to find out what our fathers have done to the *white Christians of America*, to merit such condign punishment as they have inflicted on them, and do continue to inflict on us their children. But I must aver, that my researches have hitherto been to no effect. I have therefore, come to the immoveable conclusion, that they (Americans) have, and do continue to punish us for nothing else, but for enriching them and their country. For I cannot conceive of any thing else. Nor will I ever believe otherwise, until the Lord shall convince me. . . .

⟜⟝

Article II: Our Wretchedness in Consequence of Ignorance
Ignorance, my brethren, is a mist, low down into the very dark and almost impenetrable abyss in which, our fathers for many centuries have been plunged. The Christians, and enlightened of Europe, and some of Asia, seeing the ignorance and consequent degradation of our fathers, instead of trying to enlighten them, by teaching them that religion and light with which God had blessed them, they have plunged them into wretchedness ten thousand times more intolerable, than if they had left them entirely to the Lord, and to add to their miseries, deep down into which they have plunged them tell them, that they are an *inferior* and *distinct race* of beings, which they will be glad enough to recall and swallow by and

by. Fortune and misfortune, two inseparable companions, lay rolled up in the wheel of events, which have from the creation of the world, and will continue to take place among men until God shall dash worlds together.

When we take a retrospective view of the arts and sciences—the wise legislators—the Pyramids, and other magnificent buildings—the turning of the channel of the river Nile, by the sons of Africa or of Ham, among whom learning originated, and was carried thence into Greece, where it was improved upon and refined. Thence among the Romans, and all over the then enlightened parts of the world, and it has been enlightening the dark and benighted minds of men from then, down to this day. I say, when I view retrospectively, the renown of that once mighty people, the children of our great progenitor I am indeed cheered. Yea further, when I view that mighty son of Africa, HANNIBAL, one of the greatest generals of antiquity, who defeated and cut off so many thousands of the white Romans or murderers, and who carried his victorious arms, to the very gate of Rome, and I give it as my candid opinion, that had Carthage been well united and had given him good support, he would have carried that cruel and barbarous city by storm. But they were dis-united, as the coloured people are now, in the United States of America, the reason our natural enemies are enabled to keep their feet on our throats.

Beloved brethren—here let me tell you, and believe it, that the Lord our God, as true as he sits on his throne in heaven, and as true as our Saviour died to redeem the world, will give you a Hannibal, and when the Lord shall have raised him up, and given him to you for your possession, O my suffering brethren! remember the divisions and consequent sufferings of *Carthage* and of *Hayti*. Read the history particularly of Hayti, and see how they were butchered by the whites, and do you take warning. The person whom God shall give you, give him your support and let him go his length, and behold in him the salvation of your God. God will indeed, deliver you through him from your deplorable and wretched condition under the Christians of America. I charge you this day before my God to lay no obstacle in his way, but let him go.

The whites want slaves, and want us for their slaves, but some of them will curse the day they ever saw us. As true as the sun ever shone in its meridian splendor, my colour will root some of them out of the very face of the earth. They shall have enough of making slaves of, and butchering, and murdering us in the manner which they have. No doubt some may say that I write with a bad spirit, and that I being a black, wish these things to occur. Whether I write with a bad or a good spirit, I say if these things do not occur in their proper time, it is because the world in which we live does not exist, and we are deceived with regard to its existence.—It is immaterial however to me, who believe, or who refuse—though I should like to see the whites repent peradventure God may have mercy on them, some however, have gone so far that their cup must be filled. . . .

Ignorance and treachery one against the other—a grovelling servile and abject submission to the lash of tyrants, we see plainly, my brethren, are not the natural elements of the blacks, as the Americans try to make us believe; but these are misfortunes which God has suffered our fathers to be enveloped in for many ages, no doubt in consequence of their disobedience to their Maker, and which do, indeed, reign at this time among us, almost to the destruction of all other principles: for I must truly say, that ignorance, the mother of treachery and deceit, gnaws into our very vitals. Ignorance, as it now exits among us, produces a state of things, Oh my Lord! too horrible to present to the world. Any man who is curious to see the full force of ignorance developed among the coloured people of the United States of America, has only to go into the southern and western states of this confederacy, where, if he is not a tyrant, but has the feelings of a human being, who can feel for a fellow creature, he may see enough to make his very heart bleed! He may see there, a son take his mother, who bore almost the pains of death to give him birth, and by the command of a tyrant, strip her as naked as she came into the world, and apply the cow-hide to her, until she falls a victim to death in the road! He may see a husband take his dear wife, not unfrequently in a pregnant state, and perhaps far advanced, and beat her for an unmerciful wretch, until his infant falls a lifeless lump at her feet! Can the Americans escape God Almighty? If they do, can he be to us a God of Justice? God is just, and I know it—for he has convinced me to my satisfaction—I cannot doubt him. My observer may see fathers beating their sons, mothers their daughters, and children their parents, all to pacify the passions of unrelenting tyrants. He may also see them telling news and lies, making mischief one upon another. These are some of the productions of ignorance, which he will see practised among my dear brethren, who are held in unjust slavery and wretchedness, by avaricious and unmerciful tyrants, to whom, and their hellish deeds, I would suffer my life to be taken before I would submit. And when my curious observer comes to take notice of those who are said to be free, (which assertion I deny) and who are making some frivolous pretentions to common sense, he will see that branch of ignorance among the slaves assuming a more cunning and deceitful course of procedure.— He may see some of my brethren in league with tyrants, selling their own brethren into *hell upon earth*, not dissimilar to the exhibitions in Africa, but in a more secret, servile and abject manner. Oh Heaven! I am full!!! I can hardly move my pen!!! and as I expect some will try to put me to death, to strike terror into others, and to obliterate from their minds the notion of freedom, so as to keep my brethren the more secure in wretchedness, where they will be permitted to stay but a short time (whether tyrants believe it or not)—I shall give the world a development of facts, which are already witnessed in the courts of heaven. My observer may see some of those ignorant and treacherous creatures (coloured people) sneaking about in the large cities, endeavouring to find out all strange coloured people, where they work and where they reside, asking them questions, and trying to ascertain whether they are runaways or not, telling them, at the same time, that they always have been, are, and always will be, friends to their brethren; and, perhaps, that they themselves are absconders, and a thousand such treacherous lies to get the better information of the more ignorant!!! There have been and are at this day in Boston, New-York, Philadelphia, and Baltimore, coloured men; who are in league with tyrants, and who receive a great portion of their daily bread, of the moneys which they acquire from the blood and tears of their more miserable brethren, whom they scandalously delivered into the hands of our *natural enemies!!!!!!* . . .

. . . I say, from the beginning, I do not think that we were natural enemies to each other. But the whites having made us so wretched, by subjecting us to slavery, and having murdered so many millions of us, in order to make us work for them, and out of devilishness—and they taking our wives, whom we love as we do ourselves—our mothers, who bore the pains of death to give us birth—our fathers and dear little children, and ourselves, and strip and beat us one before the other—chain, hand-cuff, and drag us about like rattle-snakes—shoot us down like wild bears, before each other's faces, to make us submissive to, and work to support them and their families. They (the whites) know well, if we are *men*—and there is a secret monitor in their hearts which tells them we are—they know, I say, if we *are* men, and see them treating us in the manner they do, that there can be nothing in our hearts but death alone, for them, notwithstanding we may appear cheerful, when we see them murdering our dear mothers and wives, because we cannot help ourselves. Man, in all ages and all nations of the earth, is the same. Man is a peculiar creature—he is the image of his God, though he may be subjected to the most wretched condition upon earth, yet the spirit and feeling which constitute the creature, man, can never be entirely erased from his breast, because the God who made him after his own image, planted it in his heart; he cannot get rid of it. The whites knowing this, they do not know what to do; they know that they have done us so much injury, they are afraid that we, being men, and not brutes, will retaliate, and woe will be to them; therefore, that dreadful fear, together with an avaricious spirit, and the natural love in them, to be called masters, (which term will yet honour them with to their sorrow) bring them to the resolve that they will keep us in ignorance and wretchedness, as long as they possibly can,[2] and make the best of their time, while it lasts. Consequently they, themselves, (and not us) render themselves our natural enemies, by treating us so cruel. They keep us miserable now, and call us their property, but some of them will have enough of us by and by—their stomachs shall run over with us; they want us for their slaves, and shall have us to their fill. (We are all in the world together!!—I said above, because we cannot help ourselves, (viz. we cannot help the whites murdering our mothers and our wives) but this statement is incorrect—for we can help ourselves; for, if we lay aside abject servility, and be determined to act like men, and not brutes—the murders among the whites would be afraid to show their cruel heads. But O, my God!—in sorrow I must say it, that my colour, all over the world, have a mean, servile spirit. They yield in a moment to the whites, let them be right or wrong—the reason they are able to keep their feet on our throats. Oh! my coloured brethren, all over the world, when shall we arise from this death-like apathy?—And be men!! You will notice, if ever we become men, I mean *respectable* men, such as other people are,) we must exert ourselves to the full. For remember, that it is the greatest desire and object of the greater part of the whites, to keep us ignorant, and make us work to support them and their families. . . . Will any of us leave our homes and go to Africa? I hope not.[3] Let them commence their attack upon us as they did on our brethren in Ohio, driving and beating us from our country, and my soul for theirs, they will have enough of it. Let no man of us budge one step, and let slave-holders come to beat us from our country. America is more our country, than it is the whites—we have enriched it with our *blood and tears*. The greatest riches in all America have arisen from our blood and tears:—and will they drive us from our property and homes, which we have earned with our *blood?* They must look sharp or this very thing will bring swift destruction upon them. The Americans have got so fat on our blood and groans, that they have almost forgotten the God of armies. But let them go on.

ADDITION.—I will give here a very imperfect list of the cruelties inflicted on us by the enlightened Christians of America.—First, no trifling portion of them will beat us nearly to death, if they find us on our knees praying to God,—They hinder us from going to hear the word of God—they keep us sunk in ignorance, and will not let us learn to read the word of God, nor write—If they find us with a book of any description in our hand, they will beat us nearly to death—they are so afraid we will learn to read, and enlighten our dark and benighted minds—They will not suffer us to meet together to worship the God who made us—they brand us with hot iron—they cram bolts of fire down our throats—they cut us as they do horses, bulls, or hogs—they crop our ears and sometimes cut off bits of our tongues—they chain and hand-cuff us, and while in that miserable and wretched condition, beat us with cow-hides and clubs—they keep us half naked and starve us sometimes nearly to death under their infernal whips or lashes (which some of them shall have enough of yet)—They put on us fifty-sixes and chains, and make us work in that cruel situation, and in sickness, under lashes to support them and their families.—They keep us three or four hundred feet under ground working in their mines, night and day to dig up gold and silver to enrich them and their children.—They keep us in the most death-like ignorance by keeping us from all source of information, and call us, who are free men and next to the Angels of God, their property!!!!!! They make us fight and murder each other, many of us being ignorant, not knowing any better,—They take us, (being ignorant,) and put us as drivers one over the other, and make us afflict each other as bad as they themselves afflict us—and to crown the whole of this catalogue of cruelties, they tell us that we the (blacks) are an inferior race of beings! incapable of self government!!—We would be injurious to society and ourselves, if tyrants should loose their unjust hold on us!!! That if we were free we would not work, but would live on plunder or theft!!!! that we are the meanest and laziest set of beings in the world!!!!! That they are obliged to keep us in bondage to do us good!!!!!!—That we are satisfied to rest in slavery to them and their children!!!!!!—That we ought not to be set free in America, but ought to be sent away to Africa!!!!!!!—That if we were set free in America, we would involve the country in a civil war, which assertion is altogether at variance with our feeling or design, for we ask them for nothing but the rights of man, viz. for them to set us free, and treat us like men, and there will be no danger, for we will love and respect them, and protect our country—but cannot conscientiously do these things until they treat us like men.

How cunning slave-holders think they are!!!—How much like the king of Egypt who, after he saw plainly that God was determined to bring out his people, in spite of him and his, as powerful as they were. He was willing that Moses, Aaron and the Elders of Israel, but not all the people should go and serve the Lord. But God deceived him as he will Christian Americans, unless they are very cautious how they move. What would have become of the United States of America, was it not for those among the whites, who not in words barely, but in truth and in deed, love and fear the Lord?—Our Lord and Master said:—[4] "Who so shall offend one of these little ones which believe in me, it were better for him that a millstone were hanged about his neck, and that he were drowned in the depth of the sea." But the Americans with this very threatening of the Lord's, not only beat his little ones among the Africans, but many of them they put to death or murder. Now the avaricious Americans, think that the Lord Jesus Christ will let them off, because his words are no more than the words of a man!!! In fact, many of them are so avaricious and ignorant, that they do not believe in our Lord and Saviour Jesus Christ. Tyrants may think they are so skillful in State affairs is the reason that the government is preserved. But I tell you, that this country would have been given up long ago, was it not for the lovers of the Lord. They are indeed, the salt of the earth. Remove the people of God among the whites, from this land of blood, and it will stand until they cleverly get out of the way. . . .

Notes: 1. See Dr. Goldsmith's *History of Greece*, page 9. See also, Plutarch's *Lives*. The Helots subdued by Agis, king of Sparta. 2. And still hold us up with indignity as being incapable of acquiring knowledge!!! See the inconsistency of the assertions of those wretches— they beat us inhumanely, sometimes almost to death, for attempting to inform ourselves, by reading the *Word* of our Maker, and at the same time tell us, that we are beings *void of intellect!!!!* How admirably their practices agree with their professions in this case. Let me cry shame upon you Americans, for such outrages upon human nature!!! If it were possible for the whites always to keep us ignorant and miserable, and make us work to enrich them and their children, and insult our feelings by representing us as *talking Apes*, what would they do? But glory, honour and praise to Heaven's King, that the sons and daughters of Africa, will, in spite of all the opposition of their enemies, stand forth in all the dignity and glory that is granted by the Lord to his creature man. 3. Those who are ignorant enough to go to Africa, the coloured people ought to be glad to have them go, for if they are ignorant enough to let the whites *fool* them off to Africa, they would be no small injury to us if they reside in this country. 4. See St. Matthew's Gospel, chap. xviii. 6.

Source: Excerpt from David Walker, *David Walker's Appeal in Four Articles; Together with a Preamble, to the Coloured Citizens of the World, but in Particular and Very Expressly, to those of the United States of America* (Boston: Revised and published by David Walker, 3rd ed., 1830).

SELECT BIBLIOGRAPHY:

Houston A. Baker, Jr., *Long Black Song* (Charlottesville: University Press of Virginia, 1972).
Lerone Bennett, *Pioneers in Protest* (Chicago: Johnson Publishing Co., 1968).
Hasan Crockett, "The Incendiary Pamphlet: David Walker's Appeal in Georgia," *Journal of Negro History* 86, no. 3 (2001), pp. 305–318.
Peter P. Hinks, *To Awaken My Affiliated Brethren: David Walker and the Problems of Antebellum Slave Resistance* (University Park: Pennsylvania State University Press, 1997).
Vernon Loggins, *The Negro Author* (New York: Columbia University, 1931).

⌐ **6** ⌐

The Statement of Nat Turner, *1831*

Probably the most famous slave revolt in American history was led by Nat Turner (1800–1831). Turner was born in Southampton County, Virginia, the child of slave parents. On August 22, 1831, Turner and a group of sixty to eighty slaves initiated an insurrection, killing about sixty whites in the span of forty hours. The revolt was viciously suppressed by local and state authorities. Over two hundred slaves, most of whom had little knowledge of the uprising and had not participated in it, were killed in retaliation. Turner himself was captured on October 30, 1831, and summarily tried and executed on November 11, 1831. Before his trial, Turner was interviewed by a court-appointed attorney, Thomas Gray. The document produced by Gray, which was published as *Turner's Confessions*, became the basis for a controversial novel by author William Styron depicting the revolt. Turner's actions symbolized to successive generations of African Americans a fierce determination to achieve freedom. It is important to keep in mind that Gray's account was surely influenced by his racism, and that there is no independent source that can verify the statements attributed to Turner.

⌐

. . . I was thirty-one years of age the second of October last, and born the property of Benjamin Turner, of this county. In my childhood a circumstance occurred which made an indelible impression on my mind, and laid the groundwork of that enthusiasm which has terminated so fatally to many, both white and black, and for which I am about to atone at the gallows. It is here necessary to relate this circumstance. Trifling as it may seem, it was the commencement of that belief which has grown with time; and even now, sir, in his dungeon, helpless and forsaken as I am, I cannot divest myself of. Being at play with other children, when three or four years old, I was telling them something, which my mother, overhearing, said it had happened before I was born. I stuck to my story, however, and related some things which went, in her opinion, to confirm it. Others being called on, were greatly astonished, knowing that these things had happened, and caused them to say, in my hearing, I surely would be a prophet, as the Lord had shown me things that had happened before my birth. And my mother and grandmother strengthened me in this my first impression, saying, in my presence, I was intended for some great purpose, which they had always thought from certain marks on my head and breast. . . .

My grandmother, who was very religious, and to whom I was much attached—my master, who belonged to the church, and other religious persons who visited the house, and whom I often saw at prayers, noticing the singularity of my manners, I suppose, and my uncommon intelligence for a child, remarked I had too much sense to be raised, and, if I was, I would never be of any service to any one as a slave. To a mind like mine, restless, inquisitive, and observant of everything that was passing, it is easy to suppose that religion was the subject to which it would be directed; and, although this subject principally occupied my thoughts, there was nothing that I saw or heard of to which my attention was not directed. The manner in which I learned to read and write, not only had great influence on my own mind, as I acquired it with the most perfect ease,—so much so, that I have no recollection whatever of learning the alphabet; but, to the astonishment of the family, one day, when a book was shown me, to keep me from crying, I began spelling the names of different objects. This was a source of wonder to all in the neighborhood, particularly the blacks—and this learning was constantly improved at all opportunities. When I got large enough to go to work, while employed I was reflecting on many things that would present themselves to my imagination; and whenever an opportunity occurred of looking at a book, when the school-children were getting their lessons, I would find many things that the fertility of my own imagination had depicted to me before. All my time, not devoted to my master's service, was spent either in prayer, or in making experiments in casting different things in moulds made of earth, in attempting to make paper, gunpowder, and many other experiments, that, although I could not perfect, yet convinced me of its practicability if I had the means.[1]

I was not addicted to stealing in my youth, nor have ever been; yet such was the confidence of the Negroes in the neighborhood, even at this early period of my life, in my superior judgment, that they would often carry me with them when they were going on any roguery, to plan for them. Growing up among them with this confidence in my superior judgment, and when this, in their opinions, was perfected by Divine inspiration, from the circumstances already alluded to in my infancy, and which belief was ever afterwards zealously inculcated by the austerity of my life and manners, which became the subject of remark by white and black; having soon discovered to be great, I must appear so, and therefore studiously avoided mixing in society, and wrapped myself in mystery, devoting my time to fasting and prayer.

By this time, having arrived to man's estate, and hearing the Scriptures commented on at meetings, I was struck with that particular passage which says, "Seek ye the kingdom of heaven, and all things shall be added unto you." I reflected much on this passage, and prayed daily for light on this subject. As I was praying one day at my plough, the Spirit spoke to me, saying, "Seek ye the kingdom of heaven, and all things shall be added unto you." *Question.* "What do you mean by the Spirit?" *Answer.* "The Spirit that spoke to the prophets in former days,"—and I was greatly astonished, and for two years prayed continually, whenever my duty would permit; and then again I had the same revelation, which fully confirmed me in the impression that I was ordained for some great purpose in the hands of the Almighty. Several years rolled round, in which many events occurred to strengthen me in this my belief. At this time I reverted in my mind to the remarks made of me in my childhood, and the things that had been shown me; and as it had been said of me in my childhood, by those by whom I had been taught to pray, both white and black, and in whom I had the greatest confidence, that I had too much sense to be raised, and if I was I would never be of any use to any one as a slave; now, finding I had arrived to man's estate, and was a slave, and these revelations being made known to me, I began to direct my attention to this great object, to fulfill the purpose for which, by this time, I felt assured I was intended. Knowing the influence I had obtained over the minds of my fellow-servants—(not by the means of conjuring and such-like tricks—for to them I always spoke of such things with contempt), but by the communion of the Spirit, whose revelations I often communicated to them, and they believed and said my wisdom came from God,—I now began to prepare them for my purpose, by telling them something was about to happen that would terminate in fulfilling the great promise that had been made to me.

About this time I was placed under an overseer, from whom I ran away, and after remaining in the woods thirty days, I returned, to the astonishment of the Negroes on the plantation, who thought I had made my escape to some other part of the country, as my father had done before. But the reason of my return was, that the Spirit appeared to me and said I had my wishes directed to the things of this world, and not to the kingdom of heaven, and that I should return to the service of my earthly master—"For he who knoweth his Master's will, and doeth it not, shall be beaten with many stripes, and thus have I chastened you." And the Negroes found fault, and murmured against me, saying that if they had my sense they would not serve any master in the world. And about this time I had a vision—and I saw white spirits and black spirits engaged in battle, and the sun was darkened—the thunder rolled in the heavens, and blood flowed in streams—and I heard a voice saying, "Such is your luck, such you are called to see; and let it come rough or smooth, you must surely bear it."

I now withdrew myself as much as my situation would permit from the intercourse of my fellow-servants, for the avowed purpose of serving the Spirit more fully; and it appeared to me, and reminded me of the things it had already shown me, and that it would then reveal to me the knowledge of the elements, the revolution of the planets, the operation of tides, and changes of the seasons. After this revelation in the year 1825, and the knowledge of the elements being made known to me, I sought more than ever to obtain true holiness before the great day of judgment should appear, and then I began to receive the true knowledge of faith. And from the first steps of righteousness until the last, was I made perfect; and the Holy Ghost was with me, and said, "Behold me as I stand in the heavens." And I looked and saw the forms of men in different attitudes; and there were lights in the sky, to which the children of darkness gave other names than what they really were; for they were the lights of the Saviour's hands, stretched forth from east to west, even as they were extended on the cross on Calvary for the redemption of sinners. And I wondered greatly at these miracles, and prayed to be informed of a certainty of the meaning thereof; and shortly afterwards, while laboring in the field, I discovered drops of blood on the corn, as though it were dew from heaven; and I communicated it to many, both white and black, in the neighborhood—and I then found on the leaves in the woods hieroglyphic characters and numbers, with the forms of men in different attitudes, portrayed in blood, and representing the figures I had seen before in the heavens. And now the Holy Ghost had revealed itself to me, and made plain the miracles it had shown me; for as the blood of Christ had been shed on this earth, and had ascended to heaven for the salvation of sinners, and was now returning to earth again in the form of dew,— and as the leaves on the trees bore the impression of the figures I had seen in the heavens,—it was plain to me that the Saviour was about to lay down the yoke he had borne for the sins of men, and the great day of judgment was at hand.

About this time I told these things to a white man (Etheldred T. Brantley), on whom it had a wonderful effect; and he ceased from his wickedness, and was attacked immediately with a cutaneous eruption, and blood oozed from the pores of his skin, and after praying and fasting nine days he was healed. And the Spirit appeared to me again, and said, as the Saviour had been baptized, so should we be also; and when the white people would not let us be baptized by the church, we went down into the water together, in the sight of many who reviled us, and were baptized by the Spirit. After this I rejoiced greatly, and gave thanks to God. And on the 12th of May, 1828, I heard a loud noise in the heavens, and the Spirit instantly appeared to me and said the Serpent was loosened, and Christ had laid down the yoke he had borne for the sins of men, and that I should take it on and fight against the Serpent, for the time was fast approaching when the first should be last and the last should be first. *Ques.* "Do you not find yourself mistaken now?"—*Ans.* "Was not Christ crucified?" And by signs in the heavens that it would make known to me when I should commence the great work, and until the first sign appeared I should conceal it from the knowledge of men; and on the appearance of the sign (the eclipse of the sun, last February[2]), I should arise and prepare myself, and slay my enemies with their own weapons. And immediately on the sign appearing in the heavens, the seal was removed from my lips, and I communicated the great work laid out for me to do, to four in whom I had the greatest confidence (Henry, Hark, Nelson, and Sam). It was intended by us to have begun the work of death on the 4th of July last. Many were the plans formed and rejected by us, and it affected my mind to such a degree that I fell sick, and the time passed without our coming to any determination how to commence— still forming new schemes and rejecting them, when the sign appeared again, which determined me not to wait longer.

Since the commencement of 1830 I had been living with Mr. Joseph Travis, who was to me a kind master, and placed the greatest confidence in me; in fact, I had no cause to complain of his treatment to me. On Saturday evening, the 20th of August, it was agreed between Henry, Hark, and myself, to prepare a dinner the next day for the men we expected, and then to concert a plan, as we had not yet determined on any. Hark, on the following morning, brought a pig, and Henry brandy; and being joined by Sam, Nelson, Will, and Jack, they prepared in the woods a dinner, where, about three o'clock, I joined them.

Q. Why were you so backward in joining them?

A. The same reason that had caused me not to mix with them years before,

I saluted them on coming up, and asked Will how came he there. He answered, his life was worth no more than others, and his liberty as dear to him. I asked him if he thought to obtain it. He said he would, or lose his life. This was enough to put him in full confidence. Jack, I knew, was only a tool in the hands of Hark. It was quickly agreed we should commence at home (Mr. J. Travis') on that night; and until we had armed and equipped ourselves, and gathered sufficient force, neither age nor sex was to be spared—which was invariably adhered to. We remained at the feast until about two hours in the night, when we went to the house and found Austin. . . .

I took my station in the rear, and, as it was my object to carry terror and devastation wherever we went, I placed fifteen or twenty of the best armed and most to be relied on in front, who generally approached the houses as fast as their horses could run. This was for two purposes—to prevent their escape, and strike terror to the inhabitants; on this account I never got to the houses, after leaving Mrs. Whitehead's, until the murders were committed, except in one case. I sometimes got in sight in time to see the work of death completed; viewed the mangled bodies as they lay, in silent satisfaction, and immediately started in quest of other victims. Having murdered Mrs. Waller and ten children, we started for Mr. Wm. Williams',—having killed him and two little boys that were there; while engaged in this, Mrs. Williams fled and got some distance from the house, but she was pursued, overtaken, and compelled to get up behind one of the company, who brought her back, and, after showing her the mangled body of her lifeless husband, she was told to get down and lay by his side, where she was shot dead.

The white men pursued and fired on us several times. Hark had his horse shot under him, and I caught another for him as it was running by me; five or six of my men were wounded, but none left on the field. Finding myself defeated here, I instantly determined to go through a private way, and cross the Nottoway River at the Cypress Bridge, three miles below Jerusalem, and attack that place in the rear, as I expected they would look for me on the other road, and I had a great desire to get there to procure arms and ammunition. After going a short distance in this private way, accompanied by about twenty men, I overtook two or three, who told me the others were dispersed in every direction.

On this, I gave up all hope for the present; and on Thursday night, after having supplied myself with provisions from Mr. Travis', I scratched a hole under a pile of fence-rails in a field, where I concealed myself for six weeks, never leaving my hiding-place but for a few minutes in the dead of the night to get water, which was very near. Thinking by this time I could venture out, I began to go about in the night, and eavesdrop the houses in the neighborhood; pursuing this course for about a fortnight, and gathering little or no intelligence, afraid of speaking to any human being, and returning every morning to my cave before the dawn of day. I know not how long I might have led this life, if accident had not betrayed me. A dog in the neighborhood passing by my hiding-place one night while I was out, was attracted by some meat I had in my cave, and crawled in and stole it, and was coming out just as I returned. A few nights after, two Negroes having started to go hunting with the same dog, and passed that way, the dog came again to the place, and having just gone out to walk about, discovered me and barked; on which, thinking myself discovered, I spoke to them to beg concealment. On making myself known, they fled from me. Knowing then they would betray me, I immediately left my hiding-place, and was pursued almost incessantly, until I was taken, a fortnight afterwards, by Mr. Benjamin Phipps, in a little hole I had dug out with my sword, for the purpose of concealment, under the top of a fallen tree.

During the time I was pursued, I had many hair-breadth escapes, which your time will not permit you to relate. I am here loaded with chains, and willing to suffer the fate that awaits me.

Notes: 1. When questioned as to the manner of manufacturing those different articles, he was found well informed. [Footnote in original.] 2. An event which caused much alarm throughout the nation.

Source: "Autobiographical Statement of Nat Turner," published in Thomas R. Gray, ed., *The Confessions of Nat Turner, the leader of the late insurrection in Southampton, Va.* (Baltimore: 1831).

SELECT BIBLIOGRAPHY:
Makungu M. Akinyela, "Battling the Serpent: Nat Turner, Africanized Christianity, and a Black Ethos," *Journal of Black Studies* 33, no. 3 (January 2003), pp. 255–80.

Herbert Aptheker, *Nat Turner's Slave Rebellion: Together with the text of the So-Called Confessions of Nat Turner Made in Prison in 1831* (New York: Humanities Press, 1966).

John Henrik Clarke, ed., *William Styron's The Confessions of Nat Turner: Ten Black Writers Respond* (Boston: Beacon Press, 1968).

John B. Duff and Peter M. Mitchell, eds., *The Nat Turner Rebellion: The Historical Event and the Modern Controversy* (New York: Harper & Row, 1971).

Kenneth S. Greenberg, ed., *Nat Turner a Slave Rebellion in History and Memory* (Oxford: Oxford University Press, 2004).

Stephen B. Oates, *The Fires of Jubilee: Nat Turner's Fierce Rebellion* (New York: Harper & Row, 1975).

William Styron, *The Confessions of Nat Turner* (New York: Random House, 1967).

⌒ 7 ⌒

Slaves Are Prohibited to Read and Write by Law

Slavemasters understood that their social control of the slaves could not be based solely on physical coercion. Knowledge was power, and virtually all slave codes established in the United States set restrictions making it illegal to teach slaves to read or write. The statute below, passed by the state of North Carolina in 1830–1831, was fairly typical.

AN ACT TO PREVENT ALL PERSONS FROM TEACHING SLAVES
TO READ OR WRITE, THE USE OF FIGURES EXCEPTED.

Whereas the teaching of slaves to read and write, has a tendency to excite dissatisfaction in their minds, and to produce insurrection and rebellion, to the manifest injury of the citizens of this State:
Therefore,
Be it enacted by the General Assembly of the State of North Carolina, and it is hereby enacted by the authority of the same, That any free person, who shall hereafter teach, or attempt to teach, any slave within the State to read or write, the use of figures excepted, or shall give or sell to such slave or slaves any books or pamphlets, shall be liable to indictment in any court of record in this State having jurisdiction thereof, and upon conviction, shall, at the discretion of the court, if a white man or woman, be fined not less than one hundred dollars, nor more than two hundred dollars, or imprisoned; and if a free person of color, shall be fined, imprisoned, or whipped, at the discretion of the court, not exceeding thirty nine lashes, nor less than twenty lashes.

II. *Be it further enacted*, That if any slave shall hereafter teach, or attempt to teach, any other slave to read or write, the use of figures excepted, he or she may be carried before any justice of the peace, and on conviction thereof, shall be sentenced to receive thirty nine lashes on his or her bare back.

III. *Be it further enacted*, That the judges of the Superior Courts and the justices of the County Courts shall give this act in charge to the grand juries of their respective counties.

Source: "Act Passed by the General Assembly of the State of North Carolina at the Session of 1830–1831" (Raleigh: 1831).

SELECT BIBLIOGRAPHY:

Ira Berlin, ed., *Free at Last: A Documentary History of Slavery, Freedom, and the Civil War* (New York: New Press, 1992).

Robert Starobin, ed., *Blacks in Bondage: Letters of American Slaves* (New York: New View Points, 1974).

⌐ 8 ⌐

"What If I Am a Woman?" *Maria W. Stewart, 1833*

Maria W. Stewart (1803–1879) was born in Hartford, Connecticut, and was orphaned at age five. Though she lacked any formal education, she played a brief but important political role as a public advocate of African Americans and of women—an achievement that is all the more notable given the social mores of her period, which generally limited the scope and content of women's activism to temperance societies and literary clubs. In 1831 she published a small pamphlet, *Religion and the Pure Principles of Mortality, the Sure Foundation on Which We Must Build,* and in 1832–1833 traveled on the public lecture circuit. Later in life, Stewart was a public school teacher in New York City, Washington, D.C., and Baltimore.

~

African rights and liberty is a subject that ought to fire the breast of every free man of color in these United States, and excite in his bosom a lively, deep, decided and heart-felt interest. When I cast my eyes on the long list of illustrious names that are enrolled on the bright annals of fame amongst the whites, I turn my eyes within, and ask my thoughts, "Where are the names of our illustrious ones?" It must certainly have been for the want of energy on the part of the free people of color that they have been long willing to bear the yoke of oppression. It must have been the want of ambition and force that has given the whites occasion to say that our natural abilities are not as good, and our capacities by nature inferior to theirs. They boldly assert that, did we possess a natural independence of soul, and feel a love for liberty within our breasts, some one of our sable race, long before this, would have testified it, notwithstanding the disadvantages under which we labor. We have made ourselves appear altogether unqualified to speak in our own defence, and are therefore looked upon as objects of pity and commiseration. We have been imposed upon, insulted and derided on every side; and now, if we complain, it is considered as the height of impertinence. We have suffered ourselves to be considered as dastards, cowards, mean, faint-hearted wretches; and on this account, (not because of our complexion,) many despise us and would gladly spurn us from their presence.

These things have fired my soul with a holy indignation, and compelled me thus to come forward, and endeavor to turn their attention to knowledge and improvement; for knowledge is power. I would ask, is it blindness of mind, or stupidity of soul, or the want of education, that has caused our men who are 60 or 70 years of age, never to let their voices be heard nor their hands be raised in behalf of their color? Or has it been for the fear of offending the whites? If it has, O ye fearful ones, throw off your fearfulness, and come forth in the name of the Lord, and in the strength of the God of Justice, and make yourselves useful and active members in society; for they admire a noble and patriotic spirit in others—and should they not admire it in us? If you are men, convince them that you possess the spirit of men; and as your day, so shall your strength be. Have the sons of Africa no souls? feel they no ambitious desires? shall the chains of ignorance forever confine them? shall the insipid appellation of "clever negroes," or "good creatures," any longer content them? Where can we find amongst ourselves the man of science, or a philosopher, or an able statesman, or a counsellor at law? Show me our fearless and brave, our noble and gallant ones. Where are our lecturers on natural history, and our critics in useful knowledge? There may be a few such men amongst us, but they are rare. It is true, our fathers bled and died in the revolutionary war, and others fought bravely under the command of Jackson, in defence of liberty. But where is the man that has distinguished himself in these modern days by acting wholly in the defence of African rights and liberty? There was one—although he sleeps, his memory lives.

I am sensible that there are many highly intelligent gentlemen of color in these United States, in the force of whose arguments, doubtless, I should discover my inferiority; but if they are blest with wit and talent, friends and fortune, why have they not made themselves men of eminence, by striving to take all the reproach that is cast upon the people of color, and in endeavoring to alleviate the woes of their brethren in bondage? Talk, without effort, is nothing; you are abundantly capable, gentlemen, of making yourselves men of distinction; and this gross neglect, on your part, causes my blood to boil within me. Here is the grand cause which hinders the rise and progress of the people of color. It is their want of laudable ambition and requisite courage.

Individuals have been distinguished according to their genius and talents, ever since the first formation of man, and will continue to be whilst the world stands. The different grades rise to honor and respectability as their merits may deserve. History informs us that we sprung from one of the most learned nations of the whole earth—from the seat, if not the parent of science; yes, poor, despised Africa was once the resort of sages and legislators of other nations, was esteemed the school for learning, and the most illustrious men in Greece flocked thither for instruction. But it was our gross sins and abominations that provoked the Almighty to frown thus heavily upon us, and give our glory unto others. Sin and prodigality have caused the downfall of nations, kings and emperors; and were it not that God in wrath remembers mercy, we might indeed despair; but a promise is left us; "Ethiopia shall again stretch forth her hands unto God."

But it is of no use for us to boast that we sprung from this learned and enlightened nation, for this day a thick mist of moral gloom hangs over millions of our race. Our condition as a people has been low for hundreds of years, and it will continue to be so, unless, by the true piety and virtue, we strive to regain that which we have lost. White Americans, by their prudence, economy and exertions, have sprung up and become one of the most flourishing nations in the world, distinguished for their knowledge of the arts and sciences, for their polite literature. Whilst our minds are vacant and starving for want of knowledge, theirs are filled to overflowing. Most of our color have been taught to stand in fear of the white man from their earliest infancy, to work as soon as they could walk, and call "master" before they scarce could lisp the name of mother. Continual fear and laborious servitude have in some degree lessened in us that natural force and energy which belong to man; or else, in defiance of opposition, our men before this would have nobly and boldly contended for their rights. But give the man of color an equal opportunity with the white, from the cradle to manhood, and from manhood to the grave, and you would discover the dignified statesman, the man of science, and the philosopher. But there is no such opportunity for the sons of Africa, and I fear that our powerful ones are fully determined that there never shall be. Forbid, ye Powers on High, that it should any longer be said that our men possess no force. O ye sons of Africa, when will your voices be heard in our legislative halls, in defiance of your enemies, contending for equal rights and liberty?

How can you, when you reflect from what you have fallen, refrain from crying mightily unto God, to turn away from us the fierceness of his anger, and remember our transgressions against us no more forever. But a God of infinite purity will not regard the prayers of those who hold religion in one hand, and prejudice, sin and pollution in the other; he will not regard the prayers of self-righteousness and hypocrisy. Is it possible, I exclaim, that for the want of knowledge, we have labored for thousands of years to support others, and been content to receive what they chose to give us in return? Cast your eyes about—look as far as you can see—all, all is owned by the lordly white, except here and there a lowly dwelling which the man of color, midst deprivations, fraud and opposition, has been scarce able to procure. Like King Solomon, who put neither nail nor hammer to the temple, yet received the praise; so also have the white Americans gained themselves a name, like the names of the great men who are in the earth, whilst in reality we have been their principal foundation and support. We have pursued the shadow, they have obtained the substance; we have performed the labor, they have received the profits; we have planted the vines, they have eaten the fruits of them.

I would implore our men, and especially our rising youth, to flee from the gambling board and the dance hall; for we are poor, and have no money to throw away. I do not consider dancing as criminal in itself, but it is astonishing to me that our young men are so blind to their own interest and the future welfare of their children, as to spend their hard earnings for this frivolous amusement; for it has been carried on among us to such an unbecoming extent that it has become absolutely disgusting. "Faithful are the wounds of a friend, but the kisses of an enemy are deceitful." Had those men amongst us, who have had an opportunity, turned their attention as assiduously to mental and moral improvement as they have to gambling and dancing, I might have remained quietly at home, and they stood contending in my place. These polite accomplishments will never enroll your names on the bright annals of fame, who admire the belle void of intellectual knowledge, or applaud the dandy that talks largely on politics, without striving to assist his fellow in the revolution, when the nerves and muscles of every other man forced him into the field of action. You have a right to rejoice, and to let your hearts cheer you in the days of your youth; yet remember that for all these things God will bring you into judgment. Then, O ye sons of Africa, turn your mind from these perishable objects, and contend for the cause of God and the rights of man. Form yourselves into temperance societies. There are temperate men amongst you; then why will you any longer neglect to strive, by your example, to suppress vice in all its abhorrent forms? You have been told repeatedly of the glorious results arising from temperance, and can you bear to see the whites arising in honor and respectability, without endeavoring to grasp after that honor and respectability also?

But I forbear. Let our money, instead of being thrown away as heretofore, be appropriated for schools and seminaries of learning for our children and youth. We ought to follow the example of the whites in this respect. Nothing would raise our respectability, add to our peace and happiness and reflect so much honor upon us, as to be ourselves the promoters of temperance, and the supporters, as far as we are able, of useful and scientific knowledge. The rays of light and knowledge have been hid from our view; we have been taught to consider ourselves as scarce superior to the brute creation; and have performed the most laborious part of American drudgery. Had we as people received one half the early advantages the whites have received, I would defy the government of these United States to deprive us any longer of our rights.

I am informed that the agent of the Colonization Society has recently formed an association of young men, for the purpose of influencing those of us to go to Liberia who may feel disposed. The colonizationists are blind to their own interest, for should the nations of the earth make war with America, they would find their forces much weakened by our absence; or should we remain here, can our "brave soldiers" and "fellow citizens," as they were termed in time of calamity, condescend to defend the rights of the whites, and be again deprived of their own, or sent to Liberia in return? O, if the colonizationists are real friends to Africa, let them expend the money which they collect in erecting a college to educate her injured sons in this land of gospel light and liberty; for it would be most thankfully received on our part, and convince us of the truth of their professions, and save time, expense and anxiety. Let them place before us noble objects, worthy of pursuit, and see if we prove ourselves to be those unambitious Negroes they term us. But ah! methinks their hearts are so frozen towards us, they had rather their money should be sunk in the ocean than to administer it to our relief; and I fear, if they dared, like Pharaoh king of Egypt, they would order every male child amongst us to be drowned. But the most high God is still as able to subdue the lofty pride of these white Americans, as He was the heart of that ancient rebel. They say though we are looked upon as things, yet we sprang from a scientific people. Had our men the requisite force and energy, they would soon convince them, by their efforts both in public and private, that they were men, or things in the shape of men. Well may the colonizationists laugh us to scorn for our negligence; well may they cry, "Shame to the sons of Africa." As the burden of the Israelites was too great for Moses to bear, so also is our burden too great for our noble advocate to bear. You must feel interested, my brethren, in what he undertakes, and hold up his hands by your good words, or in spite of himself his soul will become discouraged, and his heart will die within him; for he has, as it were, the strong bulls of Bashan to contend with.

It is of no use for us to wait any longer for a generation of well-educated men to arise. We have slumbered and slept too long already; the day is far spent; the night of death approaches; and you have sound sense and good judgment sufficient to begin with, if you feel disposed to make a right use of it. Let every man of color throughout the United States, who possesses the spirit and principles of a man, sign a petition to Congress to abolish slavery in the District of Columbia, and grant you the rights and privileges of common free citizens; for if you had had faith as a grain of mustard seed, long before this the mountains of prejudice might have been removed. We are all sensible that the Anti-Slavery Society has taken hold of the arm of our whole population, in order to raise them out of the mire. Now all we have to do is, by a spirit of virtuous ambition to strive to raise ourselves; and I am happy to have it in my power thus publicly to say that the colored inhabitants of this city, in some respects, are beginning to improve. Had the free people of color in these United States nobly and boldly contended for their rights, and showed a natural genius and talent, although not so brilliant as some; had they held up, encouraged and patronized each other; nothing could have hindered us from being a thriving and flourishing people. There has been a fault amongst us. The reason why our distinguished men have not made themselves more influential is, because they fear the strong current of opposition through which they must pass, would cause their downfall and prove their overthrow. And what gives rise to this opposition? Envy. And what has it amounted to? Nothing. And who are the cause of it? Our whited sepulchres who want to be great, and don't know how; who love to be called of men "Rabbi, Rabbi," who put on false sanctity, and humble themselves to their brethren, for the sake of acquiring the highest place in the synagogue, and the uppermost seats at the feast. You, dearly beloved, who are the genuine followers of our Lord Jesus Christ, the salt of the earth and the light of the world, are not so culpable. As I told you, in the very first of my writing, I tell you again, I am but as one drop in the bucket—as one particle of the small dust of the earth. God will surely raise up those amongst us who will plead the cause of virtue, and the pure principles of morality, more eloquently than I am able to do.

It appears to me that America has become like the great city of Babylon, for she has boasted in her heart,—"I sit a queen, and am no widow, and shall see no sorrow." She is indeed a seller of slaves and the souls of men; she has made the Africans drunk with the wine of her fornication; she has put them completely beneath her feet, and she means to keep them there; her right hand supports the reins of government, and her left hand the wheel of power, and she is determined not to let go her grasp. But many powerful sons and daughters of Africa will shortly arise, who will put down vice and immorality amongst us, and declare by Him that sitteth upon the throne, that they will have their rights; and if refused, I am afraid they will spread horror and devastation around. I believe that the oppression of injured Africa has come up before the majesty of Heaven; and when our cries shall have reached the ears of the Most High, it will be a tremendous day for the people of this land; for strong is the arm of the Lord God Almighty.

Life has almost lost its charms for me; death has lost its sting and the grave its terrors; and at times I have a strong desire to depart and dwell with Christ, which is far better. Let me entreat my white brethren to awake and save our sons from dissipation, and our daughters from ruin. Lend the hand of assistance to feeble merit, and plead the cause of virtue amongst our sable race; so shall our curses upon you be turned into blessings; and though you shall endeavor to drive us from these shores, still we will cling to you the more firmly; nor will we attempt to rise above you; we will presume to be called equals only.

The unfriendly whites first drove the native American from his much-loved home. Then they stole our fathers from their peaceful and quiet dwellings, and brought them hither and made bond men and bond women of them and their little ones; they have obliged our brethren to labor, kept them in utter ignorance, nourished them in vice and raised them in degradation; and now that we have enriched their soil, and filled their coffers, they say that we are not capable of becoming like white men, and that we never can rise to respectability in this country. They would drive us to a strange land. But before I go, the bayonet shall pierce me through. African rights and liberty is a subject that ought to fire the breast of every free man of color in these United States, and excite in his bosom a lively, deep, decided and heartfelt interest.

Source: "Mrs. Stewart's Farewell Address to Her Friends in the City of Boston, Delivered September 21, 1833," published as *Productions of Mrs. Maria W. Stewart* (Boston: William Lloyd Garrison and Knapp, 1832).

SELECT BIBLIOGRAPHY:
Marilyn Richardson, ed., *Maria W. Stewart: America's First Black Woman Political Writer: Essays and Speeches* (Bloomington: Indiana University Press, 1987).
Lora Romero, *Home Fronts: Domesticity and Its Critics in the Antebellum United States* (Durham: Duke University Press, 1997).
Rodger Streitmatter, "Maria W. Stewart: The First Female African-American Journalist," *Historical Journal of Massachusetts* 21, no. 2 (1993), pp. 44–59.

⌐ 9 ⌐

A Slave Denied the Rights to Marry, *1834*

Although many African-American slaves married and had children, such marriages were never formally recognized by law and were always tenuous. Slaves were essentially private property, and most owners had little interest or concern about the family life of their chattel. In many instances, slaveowners simply refused to give their permission to allow their slaves to marry, especially if their intended partner was someone else's property. Slaves always feared that their spouse or children could be sold. Many historians do not adequately present the terrible human dimensions that this form of coercion must have had upon the slave community. This letter illustrates one example of the larger tragedy of human bondage.

⌐

MILO THOMPSON (SLAVE) TO LOUISA BETHLEY

Oct. 15th 1834

Miss Louisa Bethley

I have got greatly disappointed in my expectations on next Saturday. I will be compelled to disappoint you at that time but I regret it very much. Master says I must put it off a little longer, until he can see farther into the matter. he says probably Mr. Birney may break up house keeping or something of the kind and he dont know what may become of you, for that reason we must defer it a little longer. I will come up and see you shortly and then we will make some arrangements about it. it is with great reluctance that I put it off any longer, but I am compelled to do it owing to the circumstances I have related. I shall remain your affectionate lover until death.

Milo Thompson

Source: Letter from Milo Thompson (slave) to Louisa Bethley, October 15, 1834, in Dwight L. Diamond, ed., *Letters of James G. Birney, 1831–1857*, Vol. I (New York: Appleton-Century, 1938), p. 144.

SELECT BIBLIOGRAPHY:

Ira Berlin and Leslie S. Rowland, eds., *Families and Freedom: A Documentary History of African-American Kinship in the Civil War Era* (New York: New Press, 1977).

B.A. Botkin, ed., *Lay My Burden Down: Folk History of Slavery* (Athens: University of Georgia Press, 1989).

Herbert George Gutman, *The Black Family in Slavery and Freedom, 1750–1925* (New York: Vintage Books, 1977).

Julius Lester, ed., *To Be a Slave* (New York: Dial Press, 1968).

Dylan Penningroth, "Claiming Kin and Property: African American Life Before and After Emancipation" (Ph.D. diss., University of Michigan, 2000).

ᕲ 10 ᕲ

The Selling of Slaves, *1835*

Although the transatlantic slave trade was technically outlawed in the early nineteenth century, the barter, sale, and transportation of slaves—the domestic slave trade—continued until the Civil War. Because slaves were legally defined as property, they could be exchanged for land, goods, or services. Slave auctions were advertised in local newspapers to attract potential buyers.

BY HEWLETT & BRIGHT

SALE OF VALUABLE SLAVES (On account of departure)

The Owner of the following named and valuable Slaves, being on the eve of departure for Europe, will cause the same to be offered for sale, at the NEW EXCHANGE, corner of St. Louis and Chartres streets, on *Saturday*, May 16, at Twelve o'Clock, *viz*.

1. SARAH, a mulatress, aged 45 years, a good cook and accustomed to house work in general, is an excellent and faithful nurse for sick persons, and in every respect a first rate character.

2. DENNIS, her son, a mulatto, aged 24 years, a first rate cook and steward for a vessel, having been in that capacity for many years on board one of the Mobile packets; is strictly honest, temperate, and a first rate subject.

3. CHOLE, a mulatress, aged 36 years, she is, without exception, one of the most competent servants in the country, a first rate washer and ironer, does up lace, a good cook, and for a bachelor who wishes a house-keeper she would be invaluable; she is also a good ladies' maid, having travelled to the North in that capacity.

4. FANNY, her daughter, a mulatress, aged 16 years, speaks French and English, is a superior hair-dresser, (pupil of Guilliae,) a good seamstress and ladies' maid, is smart, intelligent, and a first rate character.

5. DANDRIDGE, a mulatoo, aged 26 years, a first rate dining-room servant, a good painter and rough carpenter, and has but few equals for honesty and sobriety.

6. NANCY, his wife, aged about 24 years, a confidential house servant, good seamstress, mantuamaker and tailoress, a good cook, washer and ironer, etc.

7. MARY ANN, her child, a creole, aged 7 years, speaks French and English, is smart, active and intelligent.

8. FANNY or FRANCES, a mulatress, aged 22 years, is a first rate washer and ironer, good cook and house servant, and has an excellent character.

9. EMMA, an orphan, aged 10 or 11 years, speaks French and English, has been in the country 7 years, has been accustomed to waiting on table, sewing etc., is intelligent and active.

10. FRANK, a mulatto, aged about 32 years speaks French and English, is a first rate hostler and coachman, understands perfectly well the management of horses, and is, in every respect, a first rate character, with the exception that he will occasionally drink, though not an habitual drunkard.

All the above named Slaves are acclimated and excellent subjects: they were purchased by their present vendor many years ago, and will, therefore, be severally warranted against all vices and maladies prescribed by law, save and except FRANK, who is fully guaranteed in every other respect but the one above mentioned.

TERMS:—One-half Cash, and the other half in notes at Six months, drawn and endorsed to the satisfaction of the Vendor, with special mortgage on the Slaves until final payment. The Acts of Sale to be passed before WILLIAM BOSWELL, *Notary Public*, at the expense of the Purchaser.

New-Orleans, May 13, 1835

Source: Advertisement, "Hewlett and Bright Sale of Valuable Slaves," New Orleans, May 13, 1835. Copy at the New-York Historical Society.

SELECT BIBLIOGRAPHY:

Ira Berlin and Leslie S. Rowland, eds., *Families and Freedom: A Documentary History of African-American Kinship in the Civil War Era* (New York: New Press, 1997).

B.A. Botkin, ed., *Lay My Burden Down: Folk History of Slavery* (Athens: University of Georgia Press, 1989).

Vincent Harding, *There Is a River: The Black Struggle for Freedom in America* (New York: Vintage Books, 1983).

George Rawick, gen. ed.; Jan Milleagas, Ken Lawrence, eds., *The American Slave: A Comprise Autobiography* (Westport, Conn.: Greenwood Publishing, 1978).

～ 11 ～

Solomon Northrup Describes a New Orleans Slave Auction, *1841*

Solomon Northrup (1808–1862?) was born free in Sandy Hill (now Hudson Falls), New York. He led a quiet and undistinguished life as a manual laborer, learned to read and write, was married in 1829, and started a family. In 1841 he was suddenly kidnapped into slavery from Washington, D.C. Northrup was made to labor as human chattel for twelve years before he made a dramatic escape from a Louisiana plantation. As a result, Northrup's 1853 narrative, *Twelve Years a Slave*, was a best-seller of its genre. Frederick Douglass at the time stated, "its truth is stranger than fiction."

～

In the first place we were required to wash thoroughly, and those with beards to shave. We were then furnished with a new suit each, cheap, but clean. The men had hat, coat, shirt, pants and shoes; the women frocks of calico, and handkerchief to bind about their heads. We were now conducted into a large room in the front part of the building to which the yard was attached, in order to be properly trained, before the admission of customers. The men were arranged on one side of the room, the women at the other. The tallest was placed at the head of the row, then the next tallest, and so on in the order of their respective heights. Emily was at the foot of the line of women. Freeman [Theophilus Freeman, owner of the slave-pen.] charged us to remember our places; exhorted us to appear smart and lively,—sometimes threatening, and again, holding out various inducements. During the day he exercised us in the art of "looking smart," and of moving to our places with exact precision.

After being fed, in the afternoon, we were again paraded and made to dance. Bob, a colored boy, who had some time belonged to Freeman, played on the violin. Standing near him, I made bold to inquire if he could play the "Virginia Reel." He answered he could not, and asked me if I could play. Replying in the affirmative, he handed me the violin. I struck up a tune, and finished it. Freeman ordered me to continue playing, and seemed well pleased, telling Bob that I far excelled him—a remark that seemed to grieve my musical companion very much.

Next day many customers called to examine Freeman's "new lot." The latter gentleman was very loquacious, dwelling at much length upon our several good points and qualities. He would make us hold up our heads, walk briskly back and forth, while customers would feel of our hands and arms and bodies, turn us about, ask us what we could do, make us open our mouths and show our teeth, precisely as a jockey examines a horse which he is about to barter for or purchase. Sometimes a man or woman was taken back to the small house in the yard, stripped, and inspected more minutely. Scars upon a slave's back were considered evidence of a rebellious or unruly spirit, and hurt his sale.

An old gentleman, who said he wanted a coachman, appeared to take a fancy to me. From his conversation with Burch [Freeman's business associate], I learned he was a resident in the city. I very much desired that he would buy me, because I conceived it would not be difficult to make my escape from New Orleans on some northern vessel. Freeman asked him fifteen hundred dollars for me. The old gentleman insisted it was too much as times were very hard. Freeman, however, declared that I was sound of health, of a good constitution, and intelligent. He made it a point to enlarge upon my musical attainments. The old gentleman argued quite adroitly that there was nothing extraordinary about the Negro, and finally, to my regret, went out, saying he would call again. During the day, however, a number of sales were made. David and Caroline were purchased together by a Natchez planter. They left us, grinning broadly, and in a most happy state of mind, caused by the fact of their not being separated. Sethe was sold to a planter of Baton Rouge, her eyes flashing with anger as she was led away.

The same man also purchased Randall. The little fellow was made to jump, and run across the floor, and perform many other feats, exhibiting his activity and condition. All the time the trade was going on, Eliza was crying aloud, and wringing her hands. She besought the man not to buy him, unless he also bought herself and Emily. She promised, in that case, to be the most faithful slave that ever lived. The man answered that he could not afford it, and then Eliza burst into a paroxysm of grief, weeping plaintively. Freeman turned round to her, savagely, with his whip in his uplifted hand, ordering her to stop her noise, or he would flog her. He would not have such work—such snivelling; and unless she ceased that minute, he would take her to the yard and give her a hundred lashes. Yes, he would take the nonsense out of her pretty quick—if he didn't, might he be d—d. Eliza shrunk before him, and tried to wipe away her tears, but it was all in vain. She wanted to be with her children, she said, the little time she had to live. All the frowns and threats of Freeman, could not wholly silence the afflicted mother. She kept on begging and beseeching them, most piteously, not to separate the three. Over and over again she told them how she loved her boy. A great many times she repeated her former promises—how very faithful and obedient she would be; how hard she would labor day and night, to the last moment of her life, if he would only buy them all together. But it was of no avail; the man could not afford it. The bargain was agreed upon, and Randall must go alone. Then Eliza ran to him; embraced him passionately; kissed him again and again; told him to remember her—all the while her tears falling in the boy's face like rain.

Freeman damned her, calling her a blubbering, bawling wench, and ordered her to go to her place, and behave herself, and be somebody. He swore he wouldn't stand such stuff but a little longer. He would soon give her something to cry about, if she was not mighty careful, and *that* she might depend upon.

The planter from Baton Rouge, with his new purchase, was ready to depart.

"Don't cry, mama. I will be a good boy. Don't cry," said Randall, looking back, as they passed out of the door.

What has become of the lad, God knows. It was a mournful scene indeed. I would have cried myself if I had dared.

Source: Solomon Northrup, *Twelve Years a Slave* (Auburn, N.Y.: 1853), p. 78.

SELECT BIBLIOGRAPHY:

Solomon Northrup, *Twelve Years a Slave*, ed. Sue Eakins and Joseph Logsdon (Baton Rouge: Louisiana State University Press, 1968).

Carver Wendell Waters, "Voice into Slave Narratives of Olaudah Equiano, Frederick Douglass, and Solomon Northrup" (Ph.D. diss., University of Southwestern Louisiana, 1988).

~ 12 ~

Cinque and the *Amistad* Revolt, *1841*

In 1839, a group of Africans who had been captured by slave traders and were being transported to a Cuban port seized control of the ship. The Spanish schooner *Amistad* eventually landed in the United States. President Martin Van Buren urged that the Africans be turned over to the Spanish authorities. However, former president John Quincy Adams represented the Africans before the U.S. Supreme Court. In 1841 after reviewing the evidence, the court decided to free the Africans. Associate Justice Joseph Story held that when the revolt on the *Amistad* occurred, the "free native Africans" had been in effect kidnapped, and therefore they had the right to be free. Several artists, including filmmaker Steven Spielberg in 1997, have produced artistic depictions of the revolt. The *Amistad* incident symbolizes the coerced migrations of roughly 15 million African people to the western hemisphere, and illustrates that, despite the odds against them, many captives resisted.

MR. JUSTICE STORY, delivered the opinion of the court.

This is the case of an appeal from the decree of the circuit court of the district of Connecticut, sitting in admiralty. The leading facts, as they appear upon the transcript of the proceedings, are as follows: On the 27th of June 1839, the schooner "L'Amistad," being the property of Spanish subjects, cleared out from the port of Havana, in the island of Cuba, for Puerto Principe, in the same island.

On board of the schooner were the master, Ramon Ferrer, and Jose Ruiz and Pedro Montez, all Spanish subjects. The former had with him a negro boy, named Antonio, claimed to be his slave. Jose Ruiz had with him forty-nine negroes, claimed by him as his slaves, and stated to be his property, in a certain pass or document, signed by the governor-general of Cuba. Pedro Montez had with him four other negroes, also claimed by him as his slaves, and stated to be his property, in a similar pass or document, also signed by the governor-general of Cuba.

On the voyage, and before the arrival of the vessel at her port of destination, the negroes rose, killed the master, and took possession of her. On the 26th of August, the vessel was discovered by Lieutenant Gedney, of the United States brig "Washington," at anchor on the high seas, at the distance of half a mile from the shore of Long Island. A part of the negroes were then on shore, at Culloden Point, Long Island, who were seized by Lieutenant Gedney, and brought on board. The vessel, with the negroes and other persons on board, was brought by Lieutenant Gedney into the district of Connecticut, and there libelled for salvage in the district court of the United States. A libel for salvage was also filed by Henry Green and Pelatiah Fordham, of Sag Harbor, Long Island. On the 18th of September, Ruiz and Montez filed claims and libels, in which they asserted their ownership of the negroes as their slaves, and of certain parts of the cargo, and prayed that the same might be "delivered to them, or to the representatives of her Catholic Majesty, as might be most proper." On the 19th of September, the attorney of the United States for the district of Connecticut filed an information or libel, setting forth, that the Spanish minister had officially presented to the proper department of the government of the United States, a claim for the restoration of the vessel, cargo, and slaves, as the property of Spanish subjects, which had arrived within the jurisdictional limits of the United States, and were taken possession of by the said public armed brig of the United States, under such circumstances as made it the duty of the United States to cause the same to be restored to the true proprietors, pursuant to the treaty between the United States and Spain; and praying the court, on its being made legally to appear that the claim of the Spanish minister was well founded, to make such order for the disposal of the vessel, cargo and slaves, as would best enable the United States to comply with their treaty stipulations. But if it should appear, that the negroes were persons transported from Africa, in violation of the laws of the United States, and brought within the United States, contrary to the same laws; he then prayed the court to make such order for their removal to the coast of Africa, pursuant to the laws of the United States, as it should deem fit. . . .

On the 7th of January 1840, the negroes, Cinque and others, with the exception of Antonio, by their counsel, filed an answer, denying that they were slaves, or the property of Ruiz and Montez, or that the court could, under the constitution or laws of the United States, or under any treaty, exercise any jurisdiction over their persons, by reason of the premises; and praying that they might be dismissed. They specially set forth and insisted in this answer, that they were native-born Africans; born free, and still, of right, ought to be free and not slaves; that they were, on or about the 15th of April 1839, unlawfully kidnapped, and forcibly and wrongfully carried on board a certain vessel, on the coast of Africa, which was unlawfully engaged in the slave-trade, and were unlawfully transported in the same vessel to the island of Cuba, for the purpose of being there unlawfully sold as slaves; that Ruiz and Montez, well knowing the premises, made a pretended purchase of them; that afterwards, on or about the 28th of June 1839, Ruiz and Montez, confederating with Ferrer (master of the Amistad), caused them, without law or right, to be placed on board of the Amistad, to be transported to some place unknown to them, and there to be enslaved for life; that, on the voyage, they rose on the master, and took possession of the vessel, intending to return therewith to their native country, or to seek an asylum in some free state; and the vessel arrived, about the 26th of August 1839, off Montauk Point, near Long Island; a part of them were sent on shore, and were seized by Lieutenant Gedney, and carried on board; and all of them were afterwards brought by him into the district of Connecticut. . . .

No question has been here made, as to the proprietary interests in the vessel and cargo. It is admitted, that they belong to Spanish subjects, and that they ought to be restored. The only point on this head is, whether the restitution ought to be upon the payment of salvage, or not? The main controversy is, whether these negroes are the property of Ruiz and Montez, and ought to be delivered up; and to this, accordingly, we shall first direct our attention.

It has been argued on behalf of the United States, that the court are bound to deliver them up, according to the treaty of 1795, with Spain, which has in this particular been continued in full force, by the treaty of 1819, ratified in 1821. The sixth article of that treaty seems to have had, principally in view, cases where the property of the subjects of either state had been taken possession of within the territorial jurisdiction of the other, during war. The eighth article provides for cases where the shipping of the inhabitants of either state are forced, through stress of weather, pursuit of pirates or enemies, or any other urgent necessity, to seek shelter in the ports of the other. There may well be some doubt entertained, whether the present case, in its actual circumstances, falls within the purview of this article. But it does not seem necessary, for reasons hereafter stated, absolutely to decide it. The ninth article provides, "that all ships and merchandize, of what nature soever, which shall be rescued out of the hands of any pirates or robbers, on the high seas, shall be brought into some port of either state, and shall be delivered to the custody of the officers of that port, in order to be taken care of and restored, entire, to the true proprietor, as soon as due and sufficient proof shall be made concerning the property thereof." This is the article on which the main reliance is placed on behalf of the United States, for the restitution of these negroes. To bring the case within the article, it is essential to establish: 1st, That these negroes, under all the circumstances, fall within the description of merchandize, in the sense of the treaty. 2d, That there has been a rescue of them on the high seas, out of the hands of the pirates and robbers; which, in the present case, can only be, by showing that they themselves are pirates and robbers; and 3d, That Ruiz and Montez, the asserted proprietors, are the true proprietors, and have established their title by competent proof.

If these negroes were, at the time, lawfully held as slaves, under the laws of Spain, and recognised by those laws as property, capable of being lawfully bought and sold; we see no reason why they may not justly be deemed, within the intent of the treaty, to be included under the denomination of merchandize, and as such ought to be restored to the claimants; for upon that point the laws of Spain would seem to furnish the proper rule of interpretation. But admitting this, it is clear, in our opinion, that neither of the other essential facts and requisites has been established in proof; and the *onus probandi* of both lies upon the claimants to give rise to the *casus foederis*. It is plain, beyond controversy, if we examine the evidence, that these negroes never were the lawful slaves of Ruiz or Montez, or of any other Spanish subjects. They are natives of Africa, and were kidnapped there, and were unlawfully transported to Cuba, in violation of the laws and treaties of Spain, and the most solemn edicts and declarations of that government. By those laws and treaties, and edicts, the African slave-trade is utterly abolished; the dealing in that trade is deemed a heinous crime; and the negroes thereby introduced into the dominions of Spain, are declared to be free. Ruiz and Montez are proved to have made the pretended purchase of these negroes, with a full knowledge of all the circumstances. And so cogent and irresistible is the evidence in this respect, that the district-attorney has admitted in open court, upon the record, that these negroes were native Africans, and recently imported into Cuba, as alleged in their answers to the libels in the case. The supposed proprietary interest of Ruiz and Montez is completely displaced, if we are at liberty to look at the evidence, or the admissions of the district-attorney.

If then, these negroes are not slaves, but are kidnapped Africans, who, by the laws of Spain itself, are entitled to their freedom, and were kidnapped and illegally carried to Cuba, and illegally detained and restrained on board the Amistad; there is no pretence to say, that they are pirates or robbers. We may lament the dreadful acts by which they asserted their liberty, and took possession of the Amistad, and endeavored to regain their native country; but they cannot be deemed pirates or robbers, in the sense of the law of nations, or the treaty with Spain, or the laws of Spain itself; at least, so far as those laws have been brought to our knowledge. Nor do the libels of Ruiz or Montez assert them to be such.

This posture of the facts would seem, of itself, to put an end to the whole inquiry upon the merits. But it is argued, on behalf of the United States, that the ship and cargo, and negroes, were duly documented as belonging to Spanish subjects, and this court have no right to look behind these documents; that full faith and credit is to be given to them; and that they are to be held conclusive evidence in this cause, even although it should be established by the most satisfactory proofs, that they have been obtained by the grossest frauds and impositions upon the constituted authorities of Spain. To this argument, we can, in no wise, assent. There is nothing in the treaty which justifies or sustains the argument. We do not here meddle with the point, whether there has been any connivance in this illegal traffic, on the part of any of the colonial authorities or subordinate officers of Cuba; because, in our view, such an examination is unnecessary, and ought not to be pursued, unless it were indispensable to public justice, although it has been strongly pressed at the bar. What we proceed upon is this, that although public documents of the government, accompanying property found on board of the private ships of a foreign nation, certainly are to be deemed *prima facie* evidence of the facts which they purport to state, yet they are always open to be impugned for fraud; and whether that fraud be in the original obtaining of these documents, or in the subsequent fraudulent and illegal use of them, when once it is satisfactorily established, it overthrows all their sanctity, and destroys them as proof. Fraud will vitiate any, even the most solemn, transactions; and an asserted title to property, founded upon it, is utterly void. The very language of the ninth article of the treaty of 1795, requires the proprietor to make due and sufficient proof of his property. And how can that proof be deemed either due or sufficient, which is but a connected and stained tissue of fraud? This is not a mere rule of municipal jurisprudence. Nothing is more clear in the law of nations, as an established rule to regulate their rights and duties, and intercourse, than the doctrine, that the ship's papers are but *prima facie* evidence, and that, if they are shown to be fraudulent, they are not to be held proof of any valid title. This rule is familiarly applied, and, indeed, is of every-day's occurrence in cases of prize, in the contests between belligerents and neutrals, as is apparent from numerous cases to be found in the reports of this court; and it is just as applicable to the transactions of civil intercourse between nations, in times of peace. If a private ship, clothed with Spanish papers, should enter the ports of the United States, claiming the privileges and immunities, and rights, belonging to *bona fide* subjects of Spain, under our treaties or laws, and she should, in reality, belong to the subjects of another nation, which was not entitled to any such privileges, immunities or rights, and the proprietors were seeking, by fraud, to cover their own illegal acts, under the flag of Spain; there can be no doubt, that it would be the duty of our courts to strip off the disguise, and to look at the case, according to its naked realities. In the solemn treaties between nations, it can never be presumed, that either state intends to provide the means of perpetrating or protecting frauds; but all the provisions are to be construed as intended to be applied to *bona fide* transactions. The 17th article of the treaty with Spain, which provides for certain passports and certificates, as evidence of property on board of the ships of both states, is, in its terms, applicable only to cases where either of the parties is engaged in a war. This article required a certain form of passport to be agreed upon by the parties, and annexed to the treaty; it never was annexed; and therefore, in the case of *The Amiable Isabella*, 6 Wheat. 1, it was held inoperative.

It is also a most important consideration, in the present case, which ought not to be lost sight of, that, supposing these African negroes not to be slaves, but kidnapped, and free negroes, the treaty with Spain cannot be obligatory upon them; and the United States are bound to respect their rights as much as those of Spanish subjects. The conflict of rights between the parties, under such circumstances, becomes positive and inevitable, and must be decided upon the eternal principles of justice and international law. If the contest were about any goods on board of this ship, to which American citizens asserted a title, which was denied by the Spanish claimants, there could be no doubt of the right of such American citizens to litigate their claims before any competent American tribunal, notwithstanding the treaty with Spain. *A fortiori*, the doctrine must apply, where human life and human liberty are in issue, and constitute the very essence of the controversy. The treaty with Spain never could have intended to take away the equal rights of all foreigners, who should contest their claims before any of our courts, to equal justice; or to deprive such foreigners of the protection given them by other treaties, or by the general law of nations. Upon the merits of the case, then, there does not seem to us to be any ground for doubt, that these negroes ought to be deemed free; and that the Spanish treaty interposes no obstacle to the just assertion of their rights. . . .

Source: Excerpts from the *United States Appellants v. the Libellants and Claimants of the Schooner Amistad,* Supreme Court of the United States, 15 Pet. (40 U.S.) 581, 587 (1841).

SELECT BIBLIOGRAPHY:
Arthur Abraham, *The Amistad Revolt: An Historical Legacy of Sierra Leone and the United States* (Freetown, Sierra Leone: U.S. Information Service, 1985).

Matthew James Christensen, "Of Rebellions and Revolutions: Masculinity, Race, and Transnational Modernity in Late Twentieth-Century U.S. and Sierra Leonean Representations of the *Amistad* Slave Revolt" (Ph.D. diss., University of California, Los Angeles, 2002).

Helen Kromer, *Amistad: The Slave Uprising Aboard the Spanish Schooner* (Cleveland: Pilgrim Press, 1987).

Christopher Martin, *The Amistad Affair* (London and New York: Abelard-Schuman, 1970).

H. D. Motyl, *The Voyage of La Amistad a Quest for Freedom* [United States]: MPI Home Video, 2005. DVD Video.

Iyunolu Folayan Osagie, *The Amistad Revolt: Memory, Slavery, and the Politics of Identity in the United States and Sierra Leone* (Athens: University of Georgia Press, 2000).

William A. Owens, *Black Mutiny: The Revolt on the Schooner Amistad*, with Introductions by Derrick Bell and Michael Eric Dyson (Baltimore: Black Classics Press, 1997).

Steven Spielberg, *Amistad*, Universal City: DreamWorks, 1998. DVD Video.

⁓ 13 ⁓

"Let Your Motto Be Resistance!" *Henry Highland Garnet, 1843*

Henry Highland Garnet (1815–1882) was born in Maryland, where he and his family lived until they escaped to New York in 1825. Educated as a minister, Garnet became actively involved in antislavery organizing efforts. At the 1843 National Negro Convention, Garnet delivered a controversial speech, "Address to the Slaves of the United States of America." In tones that a century later would be echoed by Malcolm X, Garnet called for the use of violence to overthrow the system of slavery. Garnet's speech was published in 1848, along with the text of

Davis Walker's *Appeal*. After the Compromise of 1850, Garnet became more pessimistic about the possibility of racial justice inside the United States, and actively explored the alternative of African-American colonization. During the Civil War, Garnet was an adviser to President Abraham Lincoln. Garnet helped to establish the Cuban Anti-Slavery Society in New York City in 1872. He was appointed United States Minister to Liberia and died there in 1882.

Brethren and Fellow-Citizens:—Your brethren of the North, East, and West have been accustomed to meet together in National Conventions, to sympathize with each other, and to weep over your unhappy condition. In these meetings we have addressed all classes of the free, but we have never, until this time, sent a word of consolation and advice to you. We have been contented in sitting still and mourning over your sorrows, earnestly hoping that before this day your sacred liberties would have been restored. But, we have hoped in vain. Years have rolled on, and tens of thousands have been borne on streams of blood and tears, to the shores of eternity. While you have been oppressed, we have also been partakers with you; nor can we be free while you are enslaved. We, therefore, write to you as being bound with you.

Many of you are bound to us, not only by the ties of a common humanity, but we are connected by the more tender relations of parents, wives, husbands, children, brothers, and sisters, and friends. As such we most affectionately address you.

Slavery has fixed a deep gulf between you and us, and while it shuts out from you the relief and consolation which your friends would willingly render, it afflicts and persecutes you with a fierceness which we might not expect to see in the fiends of hell. But still the Almighty Father of mercies has left to us a glimmering ray of hope, which shines out like a lone star in a cloudy sky. Mankind are becoming wiser, and better—the oppressor's power is fading, and you, every day, are becoming better informed, and more numerous. Your grievances, brethren, are many. We shall not attempt, in this short address, to present to the world all the dark catalogue of this nation's sins, which have been committed upon an innocent people. Nor is it indeed necessary, for you feel them from day to day, and all the civilized world look upon them with amazement.

Two hundred and twenty-seven years ago, the first of our injured race were brought to the shores of America. They came not with glad spirits to select their homes in the New World. They came not with their own consent, to find an unmolested enjoyment of the blessings of this fruitful soil. The first dealings they had with men calling themselves Christians, exhibited to them the worst features of corrupt and sordid hearts: and convinced them that no cruelty is too great, no villainy and no robbery too abhorrent for even enlightened men to perform, when influenced by avarice and lust. Neither did they come flying upon the wings of Liberty, to a land of freedom. But they came with broken hearts, from their beloved native land, and were doomed to unrequited toil and deep degradation.

Nor did the evil of their bondage end at their emancipation by death. Succeeding generations inherited their chains, and millions have come from eternity into time, and have returned again to the world of spirits, cursed and ruined by American slavery.

The propagators of the system, or their immediate ancestors, very soon discovered its growing evil, and its tremendous wickedness, and secret promises were made to destroy it. The gross inconsistency of a people holding slaves, who had themselves "ferried o'er the wave" for freedom's sake, was too apparent to be entirely overlooked. The voice of Freedom cried, "Emancipate your slaves." Humanity supplicated with tears for the deliverance of the children of Africa. Wisdom urged her solemn plea. The bleeding captive plead his innocence, and pointed to Christianity who stood weeping at the cross. Jehovah frowned upon the nefarious institution, and thunderbolts, red with vengeance, struggled to leap forth to blast the guilty wretches who maintained it. But all was vain. Slavery had stretched its dark wings of death over the land, the Church stood silently by—the priests prophesied falsely, and the people loved to have it so. Its throne is established, and now it reigns triumphant.

Nearly three millions of your fellow-citizens are prohibited by law and public opinion, (which in this country is stronger than law,) from reading the Book of Life. Your intellect has been destroyed as much as possible, and every ray of light they have attempted to shut out from your minds. The oppressors themselves have become involved in the ruin. They have become weak, sensual, and rapacious—they have cursed you—they have cursed themselves—they have cursed the earth which they have trod.

The colonists threw the blame upon England. They said that the mother country entailed the evil upon them, and that they would rid themselves of it if they could. The world thought they were sincere, and the philanthropic pitied them. But time soon tested their sincerity. In a few years the colonists grew strong, and severed themselves from the British Government. Their independence was declared, and they took their station among the sovereign powers of the earth. The declaration was a glorious document. Sages admired it, and the patriotic of every nation reverenced the God-like sentiments which it contained. When the power of Government returned to their hands, did they emancipate the slaves? No; they rather added new links to our chains. Were they ignorant of the principles of Liberty? Certainly they were not. The sentiments of their revolutionary orators fell in burning eloquence upon their hearts, and with one voice they cried, LIBERTY OR DEATH. Oh what a sentence was that! It ran from soul to soul like electric fire, and nerved the arm of thousands to fight in the holy cause of Freedom. Among the diversity of opinions that are entertained in regard to physical resistance, there are but a few found to gainsay that stern declaration. We are among those who do not.

SLAVERY! How much misery is comprehended in that single word. What mind is there that does not shrink from its direful effects? Unless the image of God be obliterated from the soul, all men cherish the love of Liberty. The nice discerning political economist does not regard the sacred right more than the untutored

African who roams in the wilds of Congo. Nor has the one more right to the full enjoyment of his freedom than the other. In every man's mind the good seeds of liberty are planted, and he who brings his fellow down so low, as to make him contented with a condition of slavery, commits the highest crime against God and man. Brethren, your oppressors aim to do this. They endeavor to make you as much like brutes as possible. When they have blinded the eyes of your mind— when they have embittered the sweet waters of life—when they have shut out the light which shines from the word of God—then, and not till then, has American slavery done its perfect work.

TO SUCH DEGRADATION IT IS SINFUL IN THE EXTREME FOR YOU TO MAKE VOLUNTARY SUBMISSION. The divine commandments you are in duty bound to reverence and obey. If you do not obey them, you will surely meet with the displeasure of the Almighty. He requires you to love him supremely, and your neighbor as yourself—to keep the Sabbath day holy—to search the Scriptures—and bring up your children with respect for his laws, and to worship no other God but him. But slavery sets all these at nought, and hurls defiance in the face of Jehovah. The forlorn condition in which you are placed, does not destroy your moral obligation to God. You are not certain of heaven, because you suffer yourselves to remain in a state of slavery, where you cannot obey the commandments of the Sovereign of the universe. If the ignorance of slavery is a passport to heaven, then it is a blessing, and no curse, and you should rather desire its perpetuity than its abolition. God will not receive slavery, nor ignorance, nor any other state of mind, for love and obedience to him. Your condition does not absolve you from your moral obligation. The diabolical injustice by which your liberties are cloven down, NEITHER GOD, NOR ANGELS, OR JUST MEN, COMMAND YOU TO SUFFER FOR A SINGLE MOMENT. THEREFORE IT IS YOUR SOLEMN AND IMPERATIVE DUTY TO USE EVERY MEANS, BOTH MORAL, INTELLECTUAL, AND PHYSICAL, THAT PROMISES SUCCESS. If a band of heathen men should attempt to enslave a race of Christians, and to place their children under the influence of some false religion, surely, Heaven would frown upon the men who would not resist such aggression, even to death. If, on the other hand, a band of Christians should attempt to enslave a race of heathen men, and to entail slavery upon them, and to keep them in heathenism in the midst of Christianity, the God of heaven would smile upon every effort which the injured might make to disenthral themselves.

Brethren, it is as wrong for your lordly oppressors to keep you in slavery, as it was for the man thief to steal our ancestors from the coast of Africa. You should therefore now use the same manner of resistance, as would have been just in our ancestors, when the bloody foot-prints of the first remorseless soul-thief was placed upon the shores of our fatherland. The humblest peasant is as free in the sight of God as the proudest monarch that ever swayed a sceptre. Liberty is a spirit sent out from God, and like its great Author, is no respecter of persons.

Brethren, the time has come when you must act for yourselves. It is an old and true saying that, "if hereditary bondmen would be free, they must themselves strike the blow." You can plead your own cause, and do the work of emancipation better than any others. The nations of the old world are moving in the great cause of universal freedom, and some of them at least will, ere long, do you justice. The combined powers of Europe have placed their broad seal of disapprobation upon the African slave trade. But in the slaveholding parts of the United States, the trade is as brisk as ever. They buy and sell you as though you were brute beasts. The North has done much—her opinion of slavery in the abstract is known. But in regard to the South, we adopt the opinion of the *New York Evangelist*—"We have advanced so far, that the cause apparently waits for a more effectual door to be thrown open than has been yet." We are about to point you to that more effectual door. Look around you, and behold the bosoms of your loving wives heaving with untold agonies! Hear the cries of your poor children! Remember the stripes your fathers bore. Think of the torture and disgrace of your noble mothers. Think of your wretched sisters, loving virtue and purity, as they are driven into concubinage and are exposed to the unbridled lusts of incarnate devils. Think of the undying glory that hangs around the ancient name of Africa:—and forget not that you are native-born American citizens, and as such, you are justly entitled to all the rights that are granted to the freest. Think how many tears you have poured out upon the soil which you have cultivated with unrequited toil and enriched with your blood; and then go to your lordly enslavers and tell them plainly, that you *are determined to be free*. Appeal to their sense of justice, and tell them that they have no more right to oppress you, than you have to enslave them. Entreat them to remove the grievous burdens which they have imposed upon you, and to remunerate you for your labor. Promise them renewed diligence in the cultivation of the soil, if they will render to you an equivalent for your services. Point them to the increase of happiness and prosperity in the British West-Indies since the Act of Emancipation. Tell them in language which they cannot misunderstand, of the exceeding sinfulness of slavery, and of a future judgment, and of the righteous retributions of an indignant God. Inform them that all you desire is FREEDOM, and that nothing else will suffice. Do this, and for ever after cease to toil for the heartless tyrants, who give you no other reward but stripes and abuse. If they then commence the work of death, they, and not you, will be responsible for the consequences. You had far better all die—*die immediately*, than live slaves, and entail your wretchedness upon your posterity. If you would be free in this generation, here is your only hope. However much you and all of us may desire it, there is not much hope of redemption without the shedding of blood. If you must bleed, let it all come at once—rather *die freemen, than live to be the slaves*. It is impossible, like the children of Israel, to make a grand exodus from the land of bondage. The Pharaohs are on both sides of the blood-red waters! You cannot move *en masse*, to the dominions of the British Queen—nor can you pass through Florida and overrun Texas, and at last find peace in Mexico. The propagators of American slavery are spending their blood and treasure, that they may plant the black flag in the heart of Mexico and riot in the halls of Montezumas. In the language of the Rev. Robert Hall, when addressing the volunteers of Bristol, who were rushing forth to repel the invasion of Napoleon, who threatened to lay waste the fair homes of England, "Religion is too much interested in your behalf, not to shed over you her most gracious influences."

You will not be compelled to spend much time in order to become inured to hardships. From the first moment that you breathed the air of heaven, you have been accustomed to nothing else but hardships. The heroes of the American Revolution were never put upon harder fare than a peck of corn and a few herrings per week. You have not become enervated by the luxuries of life. Your sternest energies have been beaten out upon the anvil of severe trial. Slavery has done this, to make you subservient to its own purposes; but it has done more than this, it has prepared you for any emergency. If you receive good treatment, it is what you could hardly expect; if you meet with pain, sorrow, and even death, these are the common lot of the slaves.

Fellow-men! patient sufferers! behold your dearest rights crushed to the earth! See your sons murdered, and your wives, mothers and sisters doomed to prostitution. In the name of the merciful God, and by all that life is worth, let it no longer be a debatable question, whether it is better to choose *Liberty* or *death*.

In 1822, Denmark Veazie, of South Carolina, formed a plan for the liberation of his fellow-men. In the whole history of human efforts to overthrow slavery, a more complicated and tremendous plan was never formed. He was betrayed by the treachery of his own people, and died a martyr to freedom. Many a brave hero fell, but history, faithful to her high trust, will transcribe his name on the same monument with Moses, Hampden, Tell, Bruce and Wallace, Toussaint L'Ouverture, Lafayette and Washington. That tremendous movement shook the whole empire of slavery. The guilty soul-thieves were overwhelmed with fear. It is a matter of fact, that at that time, and in consequence of the threatened revolution, the slave States talked strongly of emancipation. But they blew but one blast of the trumpet of freedom, and then laid it aside. As these men became quiet, the slaveholders ceased to talk about emancipation: and now behold your condition to-day! Angels sigh over it, and humanity has long since exhausted her tears in weeping on your account!

The patriotic Nathaniel Turner followed Denmark Veazie. He was goaded to desperation by wrong and injustice. By despotism, his name has been recorded on the list of infamy, and future generations will remember him among the noble and brave.

Next arose the immortal Joseph Cinque, the hero of the *Amistad*. He was a native African, and by the help of God he emancipated a whole ship-load of his fellow men on the high seas. And he now sings of liberty on the sunny hills of Africa and beneath his native palm-trees, where he hears the lion roar and feels himself as free as that king of the forest.

Next arose Madison Washington, that bright star of freedom, and took his station in the constellation of true heroism. He was a slave on board the brig Creole, of Richmond, bound to New Orleans, that great slave mart, with a hundred and four others. Nineteen struck for liberty or death. But one life was taken, and the whole were emancipated, and the vessel was carried into Nassau, New Providence.

Noble men! Those who have fallen in freedom's conflict, their memories will be cherished by the true-hearted and the God-fearing in all future generations; those who are living, their names are surrounded by a halo of glory.

Brethren, arise, arise! Strike for your lives and liberties. Now is the day and the hour. Let every slave throughout the land do this, and the days of slavery are numbered. You cannot be more oppressed than you have been—you cannot suffer greater cruelties than you have already. *Rather die freemen than live to be slaves.* Remember that you are FOUR MILLIONS!

It is in your power so to torment the God-cursed slaveholders, that they will be glad to let you go free. If the scale was turned, and black men were the masters and white men the slaves, every destructive agent and element would be employed to lay the oppressor low. Danger and death would hang over their heads day and night. Yes, the tyrants would meet with plagues more terrible than those of Pharaoh. But you are a patient people. You act as though you were made for the special use of these devils. You act as though your daughters were born to pamper the lusts of your masters and overseers. And worse than all, you tamely submit while your lords tear your wives from your embraces and defile them before your eyes. In the name of God, we ask, are you men? Where is the blood of your fathers? Has it all run out of your veins? Awake, awake; millions of voices are calling you! Your dead fathers speak to you from their graves. Heaven, as with a voice of thunder, calls on you to arise from the dust.

Let your motto be resistance! *resistance!* RESISTANCE! No oppressed people have ever secured their liberty without resistance. What kind of resistance you had better make, you must decide by the circumstances that surround you, and according to the suggestion of expediency. Brethren, adieu! Trust in the living God. Labor for the peace of the human race, and remember that you are FOUR MILLIONS.

Source: "An Address to the Slaves of the United States of America," 1843, reprinted in Garnet, *A Memorial Discourse by Rev. Henry Highland Garnet* (Philadelphia: Joseph M. Wilson, 1865), pp. 44–51.

SELECT BIBLIOGRAPHY:

Henry Highland Garnet, *The Condition, Elevation, Emigration, and Destiny of the Colored People of the United States, Politically Considered* (Philadelphia: Privately Printed, 1852).

James Arthur Holmes, "Black Nationalism and Theodicy: A Comparison of the Thought of Henry Highland Garnet, Alexander Crummell, and Henry McNeal Turner" (Th.D. diss., Boston University School of Theology, 1997).

Earl Ofari, *Let Your Motto Be Resistance: The Life and Thought of Henry Highland Garnet* (Boston: Beacon Press, 1972).

Martin B. Pasternak, *Rise Now and Fly to Arms: The Life of Henry Highland Garnet* (New York: Garland Publishing, 1995).

Joel Schor, *Henry Highland Garnet: A Voice of Black Radicalism in the Nineteenth Century* (Westport, Conn.: Greenwood Press, 1977).

Sterling Stuckey, "A Last Stern Struggle: Henry Highland Garnet and Liberation Theory," in *Black Leaders of the Nineteenth Century*, ed. Leon Litwack and August Meier (Urbana: University of Illinois Press, 1988), pp. 129–48.

~ 14 ~

"Slavery as It Is," *William Wells Brown, 1847*

William Wells Brown (1814?–1884) was born a slave near Lexington, Kentucky. After one unsuccessful escape attempt, Brown managed to free himself by escaping to Cleveland. Brown first came to prominence as an effective lecturer for the New York Anti-Slavery Society. Brown's widely read 1848 autobiography, *Narrative of William Wells Brown, A Fugitive Slave*, and his novel *Clotel: or, The President's Daughter*, published in 1853, were important contributions to early African-American literature. Brown became a major leader in a variety of social reform movements, speaking on behalf of temperance and women's suffrage. Brown's most important, though neglected, work, *Rising Son: or, The Antecedents and Advancement of the Colored Race*, published after the Civil War, was one of the earliest texts presenting the history of black people from their own perspective.

~

. . . It is deplorable to look at the character of the American people, the character that has been given to them by the institution of slavery. The profession of the American people is far above the profession of the people of any other country. Here the people profess to carry out the principles of Christianity. The American people are a sympathizing people. They not only profess, but appear to be a sympathizing people to the inhabitants of the whole world. They sympathize with everything else but the American slave. When the Greeks were struggling for liberty, meetings were held to express sympathy. Now they are sympathizing with the poor downtrodden serfs of Ireland, and are sending their sympathy across the ocean to them.

But what will the people of the Old World think? Will they not look upon the American people as hypocrites? Do they not look upon your professed sympathy as nothing more than hypocrisy? You may hold your meetings and send your words across the ocean; you may ask Nicholas of Russia to take the chains from his poor downtrodden serfs, but they look upon it all as nothing but hypocrisy. Look at our twenty thousand fugitive slaves, running from under the stars and stripes, and taking refuge in the Canadas; *twenty thousand*, some leaving their wives, some their husbands, some leaving their children, some their brothers, and some their sisters—fleeing to take refuge in the Canadas. Wherever the stars and stripes are seen flying in the United States of America, they point him out as a slave.

If I wish to stand up and say, "I am a man," I must leave the land that gave me birth. If I wish to ask protection as a man, I must leave the American stars and stripes. Wherever the stars and stripes are seen flying upon American soil, I can receive no protection; I am a slave, a chattel, a thing. I see your liberty poles around in your cities. If tomorrow morning you are hoisting the stars and stripes upon one of your liberty poles, and I should see the man following me who claims my body and soul as his property, I might climb to the very top of your liberty pole, I might cut the cord that held your stars and stripes and bind myself with it as closely as I could to your liberty pole, I might talk of law and the Constitution, but nothing could save me unless there be public sentiment enough in Salem. I could not appeal to law or the Constitution; I could only appeal to public sentiment; and if public sentiment would not protect me, I must be carried back to the plantations of the South, there to be lacerated, there to drag the chains that I left upon the Southern soil a few years since.

This is deplorable. And yet the American slave can find a spot where he may be a man—but it is not under the American flag. Fellow citizens, I am the last to eulogize any country where they oppress the poor. I have nothing to say in behalf of England or any other country, any further than as they extend protection to mankind. I say that I honor England for protecting the black man. I honor every country that shall receive the American slave, that shall protect him, and that shall recognize him as a man.

I know that the United States will not do it; but I ask you to look at the efforts of other countries. Even the Bey of Tunis, a few years since, has decreed that there shall not be a slave in his dominions; and we see that the subject of liberty is being discussed throughout the world. People are looking at it; they are examining it; and it seems as though every country and every people and every government were doing something, excepting the United States. But Christian, democratic, republican America is doing nothing at all. It seems as though she would be the last. It seems as though she was determined to be the last to knock the chain from the limbs of the slave. Shall the American people be behind the people of the Old World? Shall they be behind those who are represented as almost living in the dark ages?

> Shall every flap of England's flag
> Proclaim that all around are free,
> From farthest Ind to each blue crag
> That beetles o'er the western sea?
> And shall we scoff at Europe's kings,
> When Freedom's fire is dimmed with us;
> And round our country's alter clings
> The damning shade of Slavery's curse?

Shall we, I ask, shall the American people be the last? I am here, not for the purpose of condemning the character of the American people, but for the purpose of trying to protect or vindicate their character. I would to God that there were some feature that I could vindicate. There is no liberty here for me; there is no liberty for those with whom I am associated; there is no liberty for the American slave; and yet we hear a great deal about liberty! How do the people of the Old World regard the American people? Only a short time since, an American gentleman, in traveling through Germany, passed the window of a bookstore where he saw a number of pictures. One of them was a cut representing an American slave on his knees, with chains upon his limbs. Over him stood a white man, with a long whip; and underneath was written, "the latest specimen of American democracy." I ask my audience, Who placed that in the hands of those that drew it? It was the people of the United States. Slavery, as it is to be found in this country, has given the serfs of the Old World an opportunity of branding the American people as the most tyrannical people upon God's footstool.

Only a short time since, an American man-of-war was anchored in the bay opposite Liverpool. The English came down by the hundreds and thousands. The stars and stripes were flying; and there stood those poor persons that had never seen an American man-of-war, but had heard a great deal of American democracy. Some were eulogizing the American people; some were calling it the "land of the free and the home of the brave." And while they stood there, one of their number rose up, and pointing his fingers to the American flag, said:

> United States, your banner wears
> Two emblems,—one of fame;
> Alas, the other that it bears,
> Reminds us of your shame.
> The white man's liberty entyped,
> Stands blazoned by your stars;
> But what's the meaning of your stripes?
> They mean your Negro scars.

What put that in the mouth of that individual? It was the system of American slavery; it was the action of the American people; the inconsistency of the American people; their profession of liberty, and their practice in opposition to their profession. . . .

Source: "A Lecture Delivered before the Female Anti-Slavery Society of Salem at Lyceum Hall, November 4, 1847, by William Wells Brown, A Fugitive Slave," reported by Henry M. Parkhurst, Boston, 1847.

SELECT BIBLIOGRAPHY:

Bernard W. Bell, *The Afro-American Novel and Its Tradition* (Amherst: University of Massachusetts Press, 1987).

William Wells Brown, *Narrative of William Wells Brown, A Fugitive Slave* (Boston: Anti-Slavery Office, 1848).

———, *Clotel; or, The President's Daughter* (1853; reprint, New York: Arno Press, 1969).

———, *Rising Son; or, The Antecedents and Advancement of the Colored Race* (Boston: A.G. Brown, 1876).

William Edward Farrison, *William Wells Brown: Author and Reformer* (Chicago: University of Chicago Press, 1969).

Paul Jefferson, ed., *The Travels of William Wells Brown* (New York: Markus Weiner Publishing, 1991).

L. H. Whelchel, *My Chains Fell Off: William Wells Brown, Fugitive Abolitionist* (Lanham, Md.: University Press of America).

⚬ **15** ⚬

"A'n't I a Woman?" *Sojourner Truth, 1851*

Sojourner Truth (c. 1799–1883) was a legendary figure in the struggle to abolish human bondage in the United States. Born in slavery as Isabella Bomefree, she was liberated by the New York State Emancipation Act of 1827. In 1843 she assumed the name Sojourner Truth, and began to travel across the country as an abolitionist itinerant preacher. Truth worked closely with leading abolitionists such as Frederick Douglass, and became involved in the early women's rights movement. In the 1970s and 1980s, black feminist scholars such as bell hooks cited the example of Truth as a model of black feminism's activism and courage within the male-dominated abolitionist movement. The memorable phrase "A'n't I a Woman?" was underscored in a famous speech attributed to Truth at a women's rights conventions held in Akron, Ohio, in May 1851. There are two different accounts of Truth's address, the first published in *The Anti-Slavery Bugle* in June 1851, and the second, better-known version by feminist abolitionist France Dana Gage, published twelve years later. According to historian Nell Irvin Painter, the latter was a largely fictive narrative. We have provided both texts.

⚬

One of the most unique and interesting speeches of the Convention was made by Sojourner Truth, an emancipated slave. It is impossible to transfer it to paper, or convey any adequate idea of the effect it produced upon the audience. Those only can appreciate it who saw her powerful form, her whole-souled, earnest gesture, and listened to her strong and truthful tones. She came forward to the platform and addressing the President said with great simplicity: "May I say a few words?" Receiving an affirmative answer, she proceeded:

I want to say a few words about this matter. I am a woman's rights. I have as much muscle as any man, and can do as much work as any man. I have plowed and reaped and husked and chopped and mowed, and can any man do more than that? I have heard much about the sexes being equal. I can carry as much as any man, and can eat as much too, if I can get it. I am as strong as any man that is now. As for intellect, all I can say is, if woman have a pint, and man a quart—why can't she have her little pint full? You need not be afraid to give us our rights for fear we will take too much,—for we can't take more than our pint'll hold. The poor men seem to be all in confusion, and don't know what to do. Why children, if you have woman's rights, give it to her and you will feel better. You will have your own rights, and they won't be so much trouble. I can't read, but I can hear. I have heard the bible and have learned that Eve caused man to sin. Well, if woman upset the world, do give her a chance to set it right side up again. The Lady has spoken about Jesus, how he never spurned woman from him, and she was right. When Lazarus died, Mary and Martha came to him with faith and love and besought him to raise their brother. And Jesus wept and Lazarus came forth. And how came Jesus into the world? Through God who created him and a woman who bore him. Man, where is your part? But the women are coming up blessed be God and a few of the men are coming up with them. But man is in a tight place, the poor slave is on him, woman is coming on him, he is surely between a hawk and a buzzard.

Wall, chilern, whar dar is so much racket dar must be somethin' out of kilter. I tink dat 'twixt de niggers of de Souf and de womin at de Norf, all talkin' 'bout rights, de white men will be in a fix pretty soon. But what's all dis here talkin' 'bout?

Dat man ober dar say dat womin needs to be helped into carriages and lifted ober ditches, and to hab de best place everywhar. Nobody eber helps me into carriages, or ober mud puddles, or gibs me any best place! And a'n't I a woman? Look at my arm! I have ploughed, and planted, and gathered into barns, and no man could head me! And a'n't I a woman? I could work as much and eat as much as a man—when I could get it—and bear de lash as well! And a'n't I a woman? I have borne thirteen chilren, and seen 'em mos' all sold off to slavery, and when I cried out with my mother's grief, none but Jesus heard me! And a'n't I a woman?

Den dey talks 'bout dis ting in de head: what dis dey call it? ("Intellect," whispered some one near.) Dat's it, honey. What dat got to do wid womin's rights or nigger's rights? If my cup won't hold but a pint, and yourn holds a quart, wouldn't ye be mean not to let me have my little half-measure full?

Den dat little man in black dar, he say women can't have as much rights as men, 'cause Christ wan't a woman! Whar did your Christ come from? Whar did your Christ come from? From God and a woman! Man had nothin' to do wid Him!

If de fust woman God ever made was strong enough to turn de world upside down all alone, dese women togedder (and she glanced her eye over the platform) ought to be able to turn it back, and get it right side up again! And now dey is asking to do it, de men better let 'em.

Sources: (1) Excerpt from *The Anti-Slavery Bugle*, June 21, 1851; and (2) Reported in Elizabeth Cady Stanton, Susan B. Anthony, and M. J. Gage, *History of Women Suffrage*, Vol. I (Rochester, N.Y.: 1887).

SELECT BIBLIOGRAPHY:

Jacqueline Bernard, *Journey Toward Freedom: The Story of Sojourner Truth* (New York: Feminist Press of the City University of New York, 1990).

Nell Irvin Painter, "Representing Truth: Sojourner Truth's Knowing and Becoming Known," *Journal of American History* 81, no. 2 (September 1994), pp. 461–492.

———, *Sojourner Truth: A Life, a Symbol* (New York: W. W. Norton, 1998).

Dorothy Sterling, *We Are Your Sisters: Black Women in the Nineteenth Century* (New York: W. W. Norton, 1984).

Erlene Stetson and Linda David, *Glorying in Tribulation: The Lifework of Sojourner Truth* (East Lansing: Michigan State University Press, 1994).

Sojourner Truth, with Francis W. Titus, ed., *Narrative of Sojourner Truth; a Bondswoman of Olden Time, with a History of Her Labors and Correspondence Drawn from her "Book of Life"* (Battle Creek, Mich.: Privately Published, 1875, 1878; republished, Jeffery Stewart, ed., 1991).

⚞ 16 ⚟

"A Plea for Emigration, or, Notes of Canada West," *Mary Ann Shadd Cary, 1852*

Mary Ann Shadd Cary (1823–1893) was born in Wilmington, Delaware, the eldest of thirteen children. Although Delaware was a slave state, the Shadd family was part of an elite free black community. Mary Ann Shadd's parents were active supporters of the antislavery movement and their next home in West Chester, Pennsylvania, served as a way station on the Underground Railroad. Shadd was educated in a Quaker School, and in 1839 she began a career teaching African Americans. Shadd's first essay, "Hints to the Colored People of the North" (1849) called for antislavery reform, and in particular, advised middle-class blacks to become "producers instead of mere consumers." After the passing of the Fugitive Slave Act of 1850, Mary Ann Shadd fled to Canada, where she established a school educating former slaves and free blacks. In the pamphlet, "A Plea for Emigration or, Notes on Canada West," published in 1852, Shadd presented a powerful plea to African Americans to move north. In 1854, she assumed management of *The Provincial Freeman* to become the first African-American woman editor and publisher in North America. With the outbreak of the American Civil War, Shadd Cary returned to the United States. She later became the first African-American woman to enroll in Howard University Law School, graduating in 1883.

INTRODUCTORY REMARKS

The increasing desire on the part of the coloured people to become thoroughly informed respecting the Canadas, and particularly that part of the Province called Canada West—to learn of the climate, soil and productions, and of the inducements offered generally to emigrants, and to them particularly, since that the passage of the odious Fugitive Slave Law has made a residence in the United States to many of them dangerous in the extreme—this consideration, and the absence of condensed information accessible to all, is my excuse for offering this tract to the notice of the public.

The people are in a strait. On the one hand, a pro-slavery administration, with its entire controllable force, is bearing upon them with fatal effect. On the other, the Colonization Society, in the garb of *Christianity* and *Philanthropy*, is seconding the efforts of the first named power, by bringing into the lists a vast social and immoral influence, thus making more effective the agencies employed. Information is needed. Tropical Africa, the land of promise of the colonizationists, teeming as she is with the breath of pestilence, a burning sun and fearful maladies, bids them welcome; she feelingly invites to moral and physical death, under a voluntary escort of their most bitter enemies at home. Again, many look with dreadful forebodings to the probability of worse than inquisitorial inhumanity in the Southern States from the operation of the Fugitive Law. Certain that neither a home in Africa, nor in the Southern States, is desirable under present circumstances, inquiry is made respecting Canada.

I have endeavored to furnish information to a certain extent, to that end, and believing that more reliance would be placed upon a statement of facts obtained in the country, from reliable sources and from observation, than upon a repetition of current statement, made elsewhere, however honestly made, I determined to visit Canada, and to there collect such information as most persons desire. These pages contain the result of much inquiry: matter obtained both from individuals and from documents and papers of unquestionable character in the Province.

THE FRENCH AND FOREIGN POPULATIONS

. . . Persons emigrating to Canada need not hope to find the general state of society as it is in the States. There is, as in the old country, a strong class feeling—lines are as completely drawn between the different classes, and aristocracy in the Canadas is the same in its manifestations as aristocracy in England, Scotland and elsewhere. There is no approach to Southern chivalry, nor the sensitive democracy prevalent at the North; but there is an aristocracy of birth, not of skin, as with Americans. In the ordinary arrangements of society, from wealthy and titled immigrants and visitors from the mother country, down through the intermediate circles to Yankees and Indians, it appears to have been settled by common consent, that one class should not "see any trouble over another"; but the common ground on which all honest and respectable men meet is that of innate hatred of American Slavery.

RECAPITULATION

The conclusion arrived at in respect to Canada by an impartial person is that no settled country in America offers stronger inducements to coloured people. The climate is healthy, and they enjoy as good health as other settlers, or as the natives; the soil is of the first quality; the laws of the country give to them, at first, the same protection and privileges as to other persons not born subjects; and after compliance with Acts of Parliament affecting them, as taking oath, they may enjoy full "privileges of British birth in the Province." The general tone of society is healthy; vice is discountenanced, and infractions of the law promptly punished; and, added to this, there is an increasing anti-slavery sentiment, and a progressive system of religion.

Source: Excerpts from Mary Ann Shadd Cary, *A Plea for Emigration, or, Notes of Canada West*, ed. by Richard Almonte (Toronto: Mercury Press, 1998), pp. 43–44 and 88–89.

SELECT BIBLIOGRAPHY:

Richard Almonte, ed., *A Plea for Emigration, or, Notes of Canada West* (Toronto: Mercury Press, 1998).

Jim Bearden, and Linda Jean Butler, *Shadd: The Life and Times of Mary Shadd Cary* (Toronto: NC Press, 1977).

Jane Rhodes, *Mary Ann Shadd Cary: The Black Press and Protest in the Nineteenth Century* (Bloomington: Indiana University Press, 1999).

Shirley J. Yee, "Finding a Place: Mary Ann Shadd Cary and the Dilemmas of Black Migration to Canada, 1850–1870," *Frontiers: A Journal of Women Studies* 18, no. 3 (1997), pp. 1–16.

~ 17 ~

A Black Nationalist Manifesto, *Martin R. Delany, 1852*

Martin R. Delany (1812–1885) was a major theoretical and political architect of what today we call "black nationalism." Born in Virginia, of Gullah and Mandingo descent, Delany assumed many different vocations throughout his long career, among them educator, physician, African explorer, unsuccessful political candidate, author, and journalist. In 1843 Delany produced one of the earliest African-American newspapers, *The Mystery*. Although he worked briefly with Frederick Douglass to produce *The North Star* newspaper, the two black leaders differed sharply over the strategies and philosophies for the African-American community. Delany's *The Condition, Elevation, Emigration, and Destiny of the Colored People of the United States, Politically Considered* presented a program of racial separatism and advocated colonization as the only long-term hope to achieve black freedom. In the Civil War, Delany became a major in the 104th U.S. colored troops. During Reconstruction he ran unsuccessfully for lieutenant governor of South Carolina.

~

THE CONDITION, ELEVATION, EMIGRATION, AND DESTINY OF THE COLORED PEOPLE OF THE UNITED STATES, POLITICALLY CONSIDERED

V. MEANS OF ELEVATION

Moral theories have long been resorted to by us, as a means of effecting the redemption of our brethren in bonds, and the elevation of the free colored people in this country. Experience has taught us, that speculations are not enough; that the *practical* application of principles adduced, the thing carried out, is the only true and proper course to pursue.

We have speculated and moralised much about equality—claiming to be as good as our neighbors, and everybody else—all of which, may do very well in ethics—but not in politics. We live in society among men, conducted by men, governed by rules and regulations. However arbitrary, there are certain policies that regulate all well-organized institutions and corporate bodies. We do not intend here to speak of the legal political relations of society, for those are treated on elsewhere. The business and social, or voluntary and mutual policies, are those that now claim our attention. Society regulates itself—being governed by mind, which like water, finds its own level. "Like seeks like," is a principle in the laws of matter, as well as of mind. There is such a thing as inferiority of things, and positions; at least society has made them so; and while we continue to live among men, we must agree to all *just* measures—all those we mean, that do not necessarily infringe on the rights of others. By the regulations of society, there is no equality of persons, where there is not an equality of attainments. By this, we do not wish to be understood as advocating the actual equal attainments of every individual; but we mean to say, that if these attainments be necessary for the elevation of the white man, they are necessary for the elevation of the colored man. That some colored men and women, in a like proportion to the whites, should be qualified in all the attainments possessed by them. It is one of the regulations of society the world over, and we shall have to conform to it, or be discarded as unworthy of the associations of our fellows.

Cast our eyes about us and reflect for a moment, and what do we behold! every thing that presents to view gives evidence of the skill of the white man. Should we purchase a pound of groceries, a yard of linen, a vessel of crockeryware, a piece of furniture, the very provisions that we eat,—all, all are the products of the white man, purchased by us from the white man, consequently, our earnings and means, are all given to the white man.

Pass along the avenues of any city or town, in which you live—behold the trading shops—the manufactories—see the operations of the various machinery—see the stage-coaches coming in, bringing the mails of intelligence—look at the railroads interlining every section, bearing upon them their mighty trains, flying with the velocity of the swallow, ushering in the hundreds of industrious, enterprising travelers. Cast again your eyes widespread over the ocean—see the vessels in every direction with their white sheets spread to the winds of heaven, freighted with the commerce, merchandise and wealth of many nations. Look as you pass along through the cities, at the great and massive buildings—the beautiful and extensive structures of architecture—behold the ten thousand cupolas, with their spires all reared up towards heaven, intersecting the territory of the clouds—all standing as mighty living monuments, of the industry, enterprise, and intelligence of the white man. And yet, with all these living truths, rebuking us with scorn, we strut about, place our hands akimbo, straighten up ourselves to our greatest height, and talk loudly about being "as good as any body." How do we compare with them? Our fathers are their coachmen, our brothers their cookmen, and ourselves their waiting-men. Our mothers their nurse-women, our sisters their scrub-women, our daughters their maid-women, and our wives their washer-women. Until colored men, attain to a position above permitting their mothers, sisters, wives, and daughters, to do the drudgery and menial offices of other men's wives and daughters; it is useless, it is nonsense, it is pitiable mockery, to talk about equality and elevation in society. The world is looking upon us, with feelings of commiseration, sorrow, and contempt. We scarcely deserve sympathy, if we peremptorily refuse advice, bearing upon our elevation. . . .

White men are producers—we are consumers. They build houses, and we rent them. They raise produce, and we consume it. They manufacture clothes and wares, and we garnish ourselves with them. They build coaches, vessels, cars, hotels, saloons, and other vehicles and places of accommodation, and we deliberately wait until they have got them in readiness, then walk in, and contend with as much assurance for a "right," as though the whole thing was bought by, paid for, and belonged to us. By their literary attainments, they are the contributors to, authors and teachers of, literature, science, religion, law, medicine, and all other useful attainments that the world now makes use of. We have no reference to ancient times—we speak of modern things.

These are the means by which God intended man to succeed: and this discloses the secret of the white man's success with all of his wickedness, over the head of the colored man, with all of his religion. We have been pointed and plain, on this part of the subject, because we desire our readers to see persons and things in their true position. Until we are determined to change the condition of things, and raise ourselves above the position in which we are now prostrated, we must hang our heads in sorrow, and hide our faces in shame. It is enough to know that these things are so; the causes we care little about. Those we have been examining, complaining about, and moralising over, all our life time. This we are weary of. What we desire to learn now is, how to effect a *remedy*; this we have endeavored to point out. Our elevation must be the result of *self-efforts*, and work of our *own hands*. No other human power can accomplish it. If we but determine it shall be so, it will be so. Let each one make the case his own, and endeavor to rival his neighbor, in honorable competition.

These are the proper and only means of elevating ourselves and attaining equality in this country or any other, and it is useless, utterly futile, to think about going any where, except we are determined to use these as the necessary means of developing our manhood. The means are at hand, within our reach. Are we willing to try them? Are we willing to raise ourselves superior to the condition of slaves, or continue the meanest underlings, subject to the beck and call of every creature bearing a pale complexion? If we are, we had as well remained in the South, as to have come to the North in search of more freedom. What was the object of our parents in leaving the South, if it were not for the purpose of attaining equality in common with others of their fellow citizens, by giving their children access to all the advantages enjoyed by others? Surely this was their object. They heard of liberty and equality here, and they hastened on to enjoy it, and no people are more astonished and disappointed than they, who for the first time, on beholding the position we occupy here in the free North—what is called, and what they expect to find, the free States. They at once tell us, that they have as much liberty in the South as we have in the North—that there as free people, they are protected in their rights—that we have nothing more—that in other respects they have the same opportunity, indeed the preferred opportunity, of being their maids, servants, cooks, waiters, and menials in general, there, as we have here—that had they known for a moment, before leaving, that such was to be the only position they occupied here, they would have remained where they were, and never left. Indeed, such is the disappointment in many cases, that they immediately return back again, completely insulted at the idea, of having us here at the north, assume ourselves to be their superiors. Indeed, if our superior advantages of the free States, do not induce and stimulate us to the higher attainments in life, what in the name of degraded humanity will do it?

VI. THE UNITED STATES OUR COUNTRY

Our common country is the United States. Here were we born, here raised and educated; here are the scenes of childhood; the pleasant associations of our school going days; the loved enjoyments of our domestic and fireside relations, and the sacred graves of our departed fathers and mothers, and from here will we not be driven by any policy that may be schemed against us.

We are Americans, having a birthright citizenship—natural claims upon the country—claims common to all others of our fellow citizens—natural rights, which may, by virtue of unjust laws, be obstructed, but never can be annulled. Upon these do we place ourselves, as immovably fixed as the decrees of the living God. But according to the economy that regulates the policy of nations, upon which rests the basis of justifiable claims to all freemen's rights, it may be necessary to take another view of, and enquire into the political claims of colored men. . . .

XXI. CENTRAL AND SOUTH AMERICA AND THE WEST INDIES

Central and South America, are evidently the ultimate destination and future home of the colored race on this continent; the advantages of which in preference to all others, will be apparent when once pointed out.[1]

The advantages to the colored people of the United States, to be derived from emigration to Central, South America, and the West Indies, are incomparably greater than that of any other parts of the world at present.

In the first place, there never have existed in the policy of any of the nations of Central or South America, an inequality on account of race or color, and any prohibition of rights, has generally been to the white, and not to the colored races.[2] To the whites, not because they were white, not on account of their color, but because of the policy pursued by them towards the people of other races than themselves. The population of Central and South America, consist of fifteen millions two hundred and forty thousand, adding the ten millions of Mexico; twenty-five millions two hundred and forty thousand, of which vast population, but *one-seventh* are whites, or the pure European race. Allowing a deduction of one- seventh of this population for the European race that may chance to be in those countries, and we have in South and Central America alone, the vast colored population of *thirteen millions one hundred and seventy-seven thousand*; and including Mexico, a *colored* population on this glorious continent of *twenty-one millions, six hundred and forty thousand.*

This vast number of people, our brethren—because they are precisely the same people as ourselves and share the same fate with us, as the case of numbers of them have proven, who have been adventitiously thrown among us—stand ready and willing to take us by the hand—nay, are anxiously waiting, and earnestly importuning us to come, that they may make common cause with us, and we all share the same fate. There is nothing under heaven in our way—the people stand with open arms ready to receive us. The climate, soil, and productions—the vast rivers and beautiful sea-coast—the scenery of the landscape, and beauty of the starry heavens above—the song of the birds—the voice of the people say come— and God our Father bids us go.—Will we go? Go we must, and go we will, as there is no alternative. To remain here in North America, and be crushed to the earth in vassalage and degradation, we never will.

Talk not about religious biases—we have but one reply to make. We had rather be a Heathen *freeman*, than a Christian *slave*.

There need be no fear of annexation in these countries—the prejudices of the people are all against it, and with our influences infused among them, the aversion would be ten-fold greater. Neither need there be any fears of an attempt on the part of the United States, at a subjugation of these countries. Policy is against it, because the United States has too many colored slaves in their midst, to desire to bring under their government, twenty-one millions of disfranchised people, whom it would cost them more to keep under subjection, than ten-fold the worth of the countries they gained. Besides, let us go to whatever parts of Central and South America we may, we shall make common cause with the people, and shall hope, by one judicious and signal effort, to assemble one day—and a glorious day it will be—in a great representative convention, and form a glorious union of South American States, "inseparably connected one and forever."

This can be done, easily done, if the proper course be pursued, and necessity will hold them together as it holds together the United States of North America— self-preservation. As the British nation serves to keep in check the Americans; so would the United States serve to keep in Union the South American States.

We should also enter into solemn treaties with Great Britain, and like other free and independent nations, take our chance, and risk consequences. Talk not of consequences; we are now in chains; shall we shake them off and go to a land of liberty? shall our wives and children be protected, secure, and affectionately cherished, or shall they be debased and degraded as our mothers and fathers were? By the light of heaven, no! By the instincts of nature, no!

Talk not about consequences. White men seek responsibilities; shall we shun them? They brave dangers and risk consequences; shall we shrink from them? What are consequences, compared in the scale of value, with liberty and freedom; the rights and privileges of our wives and children? In defence of our liberty—the rights of my wife and children; had we the power, we would command the vault of a volcano, charged with the wrath of heaven, and blast out of existence, every thing that dared obstruct our way.

The time has now fully arrived, when the colored race is called upon by all the ties of common humanity, and all the claims of consummate justice, to go forward and take their position, and do battle in the struggle now being made for the redemption of the world. Our cause is a just one; the greatest at present that elicits the attention of the world. For if there is a remedy; that remedy is now at hand. God himself as assuredly as he rules the destinies of nations, and entereth measures into the "hearts of men," has presented these measures to us. Our race is to be redeemed; it is a great and glorious work, and we are the instrumentalities by which it is to be done. But we must go from among our oppressors; it never can be done by staying among them. God has, as certain as he has ever designed any thing, has designed this great portion of the New World, for us, the colored races; and as certain as we stubborn our hearts, and stiffen our necks against it, his protecting arm and fostering care will be withdrawn from us.

Shall we be told that we can live nowhere, but under the will of our North American oppressors; that this (the United States,) is the country most favorable to our improvement and progress? Are we incapable of self-government, and making such improvements for ourselves as we delight to enjoy after American white men have made them for themselves? No, it is not true. Neither is it true that the United States is the best country for our improvement. That country is the best, in which our manhood can be best developed; and that is Central and South America, and the West Indies—all belonging to this glorious Continent. . . .

—

XXII. NICARAGUA AND NEW GRENADA

As it is not reasonable to suppose, that all who read this volume—especially those whom it is intended most to benefit—understand geography; it is deemed advisable, to name some particular places, as locality of destination.

We consequently, to begin with, select NICARAGUA, in Central America, North, and NEW GRENADA, the Northern part of South America, South of Nicaragua, as the most favorable points at present, in every particular, for us to emigrate to.

In the first place, they are the nearest points to be reached, and countries at which the California adventurers are now touching, on their route to that distant land, and not half the distance of California.

In the second place, the advantages for all kinds of enterprise, are equal if not superior, to almost any other points—the climate being healthy and highly favorable.

In the third place, and by no means the least point of importance, the British nation is bound by solemn treaty, to protect both of those nations from foreign imposition, until they are able to stand alone.

Then there is nothing in the way, but everything in favor, and opportunities for us to rise to the full stature of manhood. Remember this fact, that in these countries, colored men now fill the highest places in the country: and colored people have the same chances there, that white people have in the United States. All that is necessary to do, is to go, and the moment your foot touches the soil, you have all the opportunities for elevating yourselves as the highest, according to your industry and merits.

Nicaragua and New Grenada, are both Republics, having a President, Senate, and Representatives of the people. The municipal affairs are well conducted; and remember, however much the customs of the country may differ, and appear strange to those you have left behind—remember that you are free; and that many who, at first sight, might think that they could not become reconciled to the new order of things, should recollect, that they were once in a situation in the United States, (in *slavery*,) where they were compelled to be content with customs infinitely more averse to their feelings and desires. And that customs become modified, just in proportion as people of different customs from different parts, settle in the same communities together. All we ask is Liberty—the rest follows as a matter of course.

$$\sim$$

XXIII. THINGS AS THEY ARE

"And if thou boast TRUTH to utter,
SPEAK, and leave the rest to God."

In presenting this work, we have but a single object in view, and that is, to inform the minds of the colored people at large, upon many things pertaining to their elevation, that but few among us are acquainted with. Unfortunately for us, as a body, we have been taught to believe, that we must have some person to think for us, instead of thinking for ourselves. So accustomed are we to submission and this kind of training, that it is with difficulty, even among the most intelligent of the colored people, an audience may be elicited for any purpose whatever, if the expounder is to be a colored person; and the introduction of any subject is treated with indifference, if not contempt, when the originator is a colored person. Indeed, the most ordinary white person, is almost revered, while the most qualified colored person is totally neglected. Nothing from them is appreciated.

We have been standing comparatively still for years, following in the footsteps of our friends, believing that what they promise us can be accomplished, just because they say so, although our own knowledge should long since, have satisfied us to the contrary. Because even were it possible, with the present hate and jealousy that the whites have towards us in this country, for us to gain equality of rights with them; we never could have an equality of the exercise and enjoyment of those rights—because, the great odds of numbers are against us. We might indeed, as some at present, have the right of the elective franchise—nay, it is not the elective franchise, because the *elective franchise* makes the enfranchised, *eligible* to any position attainable; but we may exercise the right of *voting* only, which to us, is but poor satisfaction; and we by no means care to cherish the privilege of voting somebody into office, to help to make laws to degrade us.

In religion—because they are both *translators* and *commentators*, we must believe nothing, however absurd, but what our oppressors tell us. In Politics, nothing but such as they promulge; in Anti-Slavery, nothing but what our white brethren and friends say we must; in the mode and manner of our elevation, we must do nothing, but that which may be laid down to be done by our white brethren from some quarter or other; and now, even in the subject of emigration, there are some colored people to be found, so lost to their own interest and self-respect, as to be gulled by slave owners and colonizationists, who are led to believe there is no other place in which they can become elevated, but Liberia, a government of American slaveholders, as we have shown—simply, because white men have told them so.

Upon the possibility, means, mode and manner, of our Elevation in the United States—Our Original Rights and Claims as Citizens—Our Determination not to be Driven from our Native Country—the Difficulties in the Way of our Elevation—Our Position in Relation to our Anti-Slavery Brethren—the Wicked Design and Injurious Tendency of the American Colonization Society—Objections to Liberia—Objections to Canada—Preferences to South America, &c., &c., all of which we have treated without reserve; expressing our mind freely, and with candor, as we are determined that as far as we can at present do so, the minds of our readers shall be enlightened. The custom of concealing information upon vital and important subjects, in which the interest of the people is involved, we do not agree with, nor favor in the least; we have therefore, laid this cursory treatise before our readers, with the hope that it may prove instrumental in directing the attention of our people in the right way, that leads to their Elevation. Go or stay—of course each is free to do as he pleases—one thing is certain; our Elevation is the work of our own hands. And Mexico, Central America, the West Indies, and South America, all present now, opportunities for the individual enterprise of our young men, who prefer to remain in the United States, in preference to going where they can enjoy real freedom, and equality of rights. Freedom of Religion, as well as of politics, being tolerated in all of these places.

Let our young men and women, prepare themselves for usefulness and business; that the men may enter into merchandise, trading, and other things of importance; the young women may become teachers of various kinds, and otherwise fill places of usefulness. Parents must turn their attention more to the education of their children. We mean, to educate them for useful practical business purposes. Educate them for the Store and the Counting House—to do every-day practical business. Consult the children's propensities, and direct their education according to their inclinations. It may be, that there is too great a desire on the part of parents, to give their children a professional education, before the body of the people, are ready for it. A people must be a business people, and have more to depend upon than mere help in people's houses and Hotels, before they are either able to support, or capable of properly appreciating the services of professional men among them. This has been one of our great mistakes—we have gone in advance of ourselves. We have commenced at the superstructure of the building, instead of the foundation—at the top instead of the bottom. We should first be mechanics and common tradesmen, and professions as a matter of course would grow out of the wealth made thereby. Young men and women, must now prepare for usefulness—the day of our Elevation is at hand—all the world now gazes at us—and Central and South America, and the West Indies, bid us come and be men and women, protected, secure, beloved and Free.

The branches of Education most desirable for the preparation of youth, for practical useful every-day life, are Arithmetic and good Penmanship, in order to be Accountants; and a good rudimental knowledge of Geography—which has ever been neglected, and underestimated—and of Political Economy; which without the knowledge of the first, no people can ever become adventurous—nor of the second, never will be an enterprising people. Geography, teaches a knowledge of the world, and Political Economy, a knowledge of the wealth of nations; or how to make money. These are not abstruse sciences, or learning not easily acquired or understood; but simply, common School Primer learning, that every body may get. And, although it is the very Key to prosperity and success in common life, but few know anything about it. Unfortunately for our people, so soon as their children learn to read a Chapter in the New Testament, and scribble a miserable hand, they are pronounced to have "Learning enough"; and taken away from School, no use to themselves, nor community. This is apparent in our Public Meetings, and Official Church Meetings; of the great number of men present, there are but few capable of filling a Secretaryship. Some of the large cities may be an exception to this. Of the multitudes of Merchants, and Business men throughout this country, Europe, and the world, few are qualified, beyond the branches here laid down by us as necessary for business. What did John Jacob Astor, Stephen Girard, or do the millionaires and the greater part of the merchant princes, and mariners, know about Latin and Greek, and the Classics? Precious few of them know any thing. In proof of this, in 1841, during the Administration of President Tyler, when the mutiny was detected on board of the American Man of War Brig Somers, the names of the Mutineers, were recorded by young S—a Midshipman in Greek. Captain Alexander Slidell McKenzie, Commanding, was unable to read them; and in his despatches to the Government, in justification of his policy in executing the criminals, said that he "discovered some curious characters which he was unable to read," &c.; showing thereby, that that high functionary, did not understand even the Greek Alphabet, which was only necessary, to have been able to read proper names written in Greek.

What we most need then, is a good business practical Education; because, the Classical and Professional education of so many of our young men, before their parents are able to support them, and community ready to patronize them, only serves to lull their energy, and cripple the otherwise, praiseworthy efforts they would make in life. A Classical education, is only suited to the wealthy, or those who have a prospect of gaining a livelihood by it. The writer does not wish to be understood, as underrating a Classical and Professional education; this is not his intention; he fully appreciates them, having had some such advantages himself; but he desires to give a proper guide, and put a check to the extravagant idea that is fast obtaining, among our people especially, that a Classical, or as it is named, a "finished education," is necessary to prepare one for usefulness in life. Let us have an education, that shall practically develop our thinking faculties and manhood; and then, and not until then, shall we be able to vie with our oppressors, go where we may. We as heretofore, have been on the extreme; either no qualification at all, or a Collegiate education. We jumped too far; taking a leap from the deepest abyss to the highest summit; rising from the ridiculous to the sublime; without medium or intermission.

Let our young women have an education; let their minds be well informed; well stored with useful information and practical proficiency, rather than the light superficial acquirements, popularly and fashionably called accomplishments. We desire accomplishments, but they must be useful.

Our females must be qualified, because they are to be the mothers of our children. As mothers are the first nurses and instructors of children; from them children consequently, get their first impressions, which being always the most lasting, should be the most correct. Raise the mothers above the level of degradation, and the offspring is elevated with them. In a word, instead of our young men, transcribing in their blank books, recipes for *Cooking*; we desire to see them making the transfer of *Invoices of Merchandise*. Come to our aid then; the *morning* of our *Redemption* from degradation, adorns the horizon.

In our selection of individuals, it will be observed, that we have confined ourself entirely to those who occupy or have occupied positions among the whites, consequently having a more general bearing as useful contributors to society at large. While we do not pretend to give all such worthy cases, we gave such as we possessed information of, and desire it to be understood, that a large number of our most intelligent and worthy men and women, have not been named, because from their more private position in community, it was foreign to the object and design of this work. If we have said aught to offend, "take the will for the deed," and be assured, that it was given with the purest of motives, and best intention, from a true-hearted man and brother; deeply lamenting the sad fate of his race in this country, and sincerely desiring the elevation of man, and submitted to the serious consideration of all, who favor the promotion of the cause of God and humanity.

⸺

XXIV. A GLANCE AT OURSELVES—CONCLUSION

> With broken hopes—sad devastation;
> A race *resigned* to DEGRADATION!

. . . If we did not love our race superior to others, we would not concern ourself about their degradation; for the greatest desire of our heart is, to see them stand on a level with the most elevated of mankind. No people are ever elevated above the condition of their *females*; hence, the condition of the mother determines the condition of the child. To know the position of a people, it is only necessary to know the *condition* of their females; and despite themselves, they cannot rise above their level. Then what is our condition? Our *best ladies* being washerwomen, chambermaids, children's traveling nurses, and common house servants, and menials, we are all a degraded, miserable people, inferior to any other people as a whole, on the face of the globe.

These great truths, however unpleasant, must be brought before the minds of our people in its true and proper light, as we have been too delicate about them, and too long concealed them for fear of giving offence. It would have been infinitely better for our race, if these facts had been presented before us half a century ago—we would have been now proportionably benefitted by it.

As an evidence of the degradation to which we have been reduced, we dare premise, that this chapter will give offence to many, very many, and why? Because they may say, "He dared to say that the occupation of a *servant* is a degradation." It is not necessarily degrading; it would not be, to one or a few people of a kind; but a *whole race of servants* are a degradation to that people.

Efforts made by men of qualifications for the toiling and degraded millions among the whites, neither gives offence to that class, nor is it taken unkindly by them; but received with manifestations of gratitude; to know that they are thought to be, equally worthy of, and entitled to stand on a level with the elevated classes; and they have only got to be informed of the way to raise themselves, to make the effort and do so as far as they can. But how different with us. Speak of our position in society, and it at once gives insult. Though we are servants; among ourselves we claim to be *ladies* and *gentlemen*, equal in standing, and as the popular expression goes, "Just as good as any body"—and so believing, we make no efforts to raise above the common level of menials; because the *best* being in that capacity, all are content with the position. We cannot at the same time, be domestic and lady; servant and gentleman. We must be the one or the other. Sad, sad indeed, is the thought, that hangs drooping in our mind, when contemplating the picture drawn before us. Young men and women, "we write these things unto you, because ye are strong," because the writer, a few years ago, gave unpardonable offence to many of the young people of Philadelphia and other places, because he dared tell them, that he thought too much of them, to be content with seeing them the servants of other people. Surely, she that could be the mistress, would not be the maid; neither would he that could be the master, be content with being the servant; then why be offended, when we point out to you, the way that leads from the menial to the mistress or the master. All this we seem to reject with fixed determination, repelling with anger, every effort on the part of our intelligent men and women to elevate us, with true Israelitish degradation, in reply to any suggestion or proposition that may be offered, "Who made thee a ruler and judge?"

The writer is no "Public Man," in the sense in which this is understood among our people, but simply an humble individual, endeavoring to seek a livelihood by a profession obtained entirely by his own efforts, without relatives and friends able to assist him; except such friends as he gained by the merit of his course and conduct, which he here gratefully acknowledges; and whatever he has accomplished, other young men may, by making corresponding efforts, also accomplish.

In our own country, the United States, there are *three million five hundred thousand slaves*; and we, the nominally free colored people, are *six hundred thousand* in number; estimating one-sixth to be men, we have *one hundred thousand* able bodied freemen, which will make a powerful auxiliary in any country to which we may become adopted—an ally not to be despised by any power on earth. We love our country, dearly love her, but she doesn't love us—she despises us, and bids us begone, driving us from her embraces; but we shall not go where she desires us; but when we do go, whatever love we have for her, we shall love the country none the less that receives us as her adopted children.

For the want of business habits and training, our energies have become paralyzed; our young men never think of business, any more than if they were so many bondmen, without the right to pursue any calling they may think most advisable. With our people in this country, dress and good appearances have been made the only test of gentleman and ladyship, and that vocation which offers the best opportunity to dress and appear well, has generally been preferred, however menial and degrading, by our young people, without even, in the majority of cases, an effort to do better; indeed, in many instances, refusing situations equally lucrative, and superior in position; but which would not allow as much display of dress and personal appearance. This, if we ever expect to rise, must be discarded from among us, and a high and respectable position assumed.

One of our great temporal curses is our consummate poverty. We are the poorest people, as a class, in the world of civilized mankind—abjectly, miserably poor, no one scarcely being able to assist the other. To this, of course, there are noble exceptions; but that which is common to, and the very process by which white men exist, and succeed in life, is unknown to colored men in general. In any and every considerable community may be found, some one of our white fellow-citizens, who is worth more than all the colored people in that community put together. We consequently have little or no efficiency. We must have means to be practically efficient in all the undertakings of life; and to obtain them, it is necessary that we should be engaged in lucrative pursuits, trades, and general business transactions. In order to be thus engaged, it is necessary that we should occupy positions that afford the facilities for such pursuits. To compete now with the mighty odds of wealth, social and religious preferences, and political influences of this country, at this advanced stage of its national existence, we never may expect. A new country, and new beginning, is the only true, rational, politic remedy for our disadvantageous position; and that country we have already pointed out, with triple golden advantages, all things considered, to that of any country to which it has been the province of man to embark.

Every other than we, have at various periods of necessity, been a migratory people; and all when oppressed, shown a greater abhorrence of oppression, if not a greater love of liberty, than we. We cling to our oppressors as the objects of our love. It is true that our enslaved brethren are here, and we have been led to believe that it is necessary for us to remain, on that account. Is it true, that all should remain in degradation, because a part are degraded? We believe no such thing. We believe it to be the duty of the Free, to elevate themselves in the most speedy and effective manner possible; as the redemption of the bondman depends entirely upon the elevation of the freeman; therefore, to elevate the free colored people of America, anywhere upon this continent; forebodes the speedy redemption of the slaves. We shall hope to hear no more of so fallacious a doctrine—the necessity of the free remaining in degradation, for the sake of the oppressed. Let us apply, first, the lever to ourselves; and the force that elevates us to the position of manhood's considerations and honors, will cleft the manacle of every slave in the land.

When such great worth and talents—for want of a better sphere—of men like Rev. Jonathan Robinson, Robert Douglass, Frederick A. Hinton, and a hundred others that might be named, were permitted to expire in a barber-shop; and such living men as may be found in Boston, New York, Philadelphia, Baltimore, Richmond, Washington City, Charleston (S.C.), New Orleans, Cincinnati, Louisville, St. Louis, Pittsburg, Buffalo, Rochester, Albany, Utica, Cleveland, Detroit, Milwaukee, Chicago, Columbus, Zanesville, Wheeling, and a hundred other places, confining themselves to barber-shops and waiterships in Hotels; certainly the necessity of such a course as we have pointed out, must be cordially acknowledged; appreciated by every brother and sister of oppression; and not rejected as heretofore, as though they preferred inferiority to equality. These minds must become "unfettered," and have "space to rise." This cannot be in their present positions. A continuance in any position, becomes what is termed "Second Nature"; it begets an *adaptation*, and *reconciliation* of *mind* to such condition. It changes the whole physiological condition of the system, and adapts man and woman to a higher or lower sphere in the pursuits of life. The offsprings of slaves and peasantry, have the general characteristics of their parents; and nothing but a different course of training and education, will change the character.

The slave may become a lover of his master, and learn to forgive him for continual deeds of maltreatment and abuse; just as the Spaniel would couch and fondle at the feet that kick him; because he has been taught to reverence them, and consequently, becomes adapted in body and mind to his condition. Even the shrubbery-loving Canary, and lofty-soaring Eagle, may be tamed to the cage, and learn to love it from habit of confinement. It has been so with us in our position among our oppressors; we have been so prone to such positions, that we have learned to love them. When reflecting upon this all important, and to us, all absorbing subject; we feel in the agony and anxiety of the moment, as though we could cry out in the langauge of a Prophet of old: "Oh that my head were waters, and mine eyes a fountain of tears, that I might weep day and night for the" degradation "of my people! Oh that I had in the wilderness a lodging place of wayfaring men; that I might leave my people, and go from them!"

The Irishman and German in the United States, are very different persons to what they were when in Ireland and Germany, the countries of their nativity. There their spirits were depressed and downcast; but the instant they set their foot upon unrestricted soil; free to act and untrammelled to move; their physical condition undergoes a change, which in time becomes physiological, which is transmitted to the offspring, who when born under such circumstances, is a decidedly different being to what it would have been, had it been born under different circumstances.

A child born under oppression, has all the elements of servility in its constitution; who when born under favorable circumstances, has to the contrary, all the elements of freedom and independence of feeling. Our children then, may not be expected, to maintain that position and manly bearing; born under the unfavorable circumstances with which we are surrounded in this country; that we so much desire. To use the language of the talented Mr. Whipper, "they cannot be raised in this country, without being stoop shouldered." Heaven's pathway stands unobstructed, which will lead us into a Paradise of bliss. Let us go on and possess the land, and the God of Israel will be our God.

The lessons of every school book, the pages of every history, and columns of every newspaper, are so replete with stimuli to nerve us on to manly aspirations, that those of our young people, who will now refuse to enter upon this great theatre of Polynesian adventure, and take their position on the stage of Central and South America, where a brilliant engagement, of certain and most triumphant success, in the drama of human equality awaits them; then, with the blood of *slaves*, write upon the lintel of every door in sterling Capitals, to be gazed and hissed at by every passer by—

> Doomed by the Creator
> To servility and degradation;
> The SERVANT of the *white man*,
> And despised of every nation!

Notes: 1. The native language of these countries, as well as the greater part of South America, is *Spanish*, which is the easiest of all foreign languages to learn. It is very remarkable and worthy of note, that with a view of going to Mexico or South America, the writer several years ago paid some attention to the Spanish language; and now, a most singular coincidence, without preunderstanding, in almost every town, where there is any intelligence among them, there are some *colored persons* of both sexes, who are studying the Spanish language. Even the Methodist and other clergymen, among them. And we earnestly entreat all colored persons who can, to study, and have their children taught Spanish. No foreign language will be of such *import* to colored people, in a very short time, as the Spanish. Mexico, Central and South America, importune us to speak their language; and if nothing else, the silent indications of Cuba, urge us to learn the Spanish tongue. 2. The Brazilians have formed a Colonization Society, for the purpose of colonizing free blacks to Africa. The Brazilians are Portuguese, the only nation that can be termed white, and the only one that is a real slave holding nation in South America. Even the black and colored men have equal privileges with whites; and the action of this society will probably extend only to the sending back of such captives as may be taken from piratical slaves. Colonization in Brazil, has doubtless been got up under the influence of United States slaveholders and their abettors, such as the consuls and envoys, who are sent out to South America, by the government. Chevalier Niteroi, *charge de affaires* from Brazil near the government of Liberia, received by the President on the 28th of last January, is also charged with the mission of establishing a colony of free blacks in Liberia. The Chevalier was once a Captain in the Brazilian navy on the coast of Africa; and no doubt is conversant with the sentiments of Roberts, who was charged with the slave trade at one time. The scheme of United States slaveholders and President J.J. Roberts, their agent of Liberia, will not succeed, in establishing prejudice against the black race; not even in slaveholding Brazil. We have no confidence in President Roberts of Liberia, believing him to be wholly without principle—seeking only self-aggrandizement; even should it be done, over the ruined prospects of his staggering infant country. The people of Liberia, should beware of this man. His *privy councillors* are to be found among *slaveholders* in the United States.

Source: Excerpt from *The Condition, Elevation, Emigration, and Destiny of the Colored People of the United States, Politically Considered* (Philadelphia: Privately Printed, 1852).

SELECT BIBLIOGRAPHY:

Tunde Adeleke, "Martin R. Delany's Philosophy of Education: A Neglected Aspect of African American Liberation Thought," *Journal of Negro Education* 63, no. 2 (Spring 1994), pp. 221–36.

Benjamin G. Brawley, *Early Negro American Writers* (Chapel Hill: University of North Carolina Press, 1935).

Cyril E. Griffith, *The African Dream: Martin R. Delany and the Emergence of Pan-African Thought* (University Park: Pennsylvania State University Press, 1975).

Robert S. Levine Martin, ed., *Martin R. Delany: A Documentary Reader* (Chapel Hill: University of North Carolina Press, 2003).

Tolagbe Ogunleye, "Dr. Martin Robison Delany, 19th-Century Africana Womanists: Reflections on His Avant-Garde Politics Concerning Gender, Colorism, and Nation Building," *Journal of Black Studies* 28, no. 5 (May 1998), pp. 628–49.

Tommie Shelby, "Two Conceptions of Black Nationalism: Martin Delany on the Meaning of Black Political Solidarity," *Political Theory* 31, no. 5 (October 2003), pp. 664–92.

Dorothy Sterling, *The Making of an Afro-American: Martin Robinson Delany, 1812–1885* (New York: Da Capo Press, 1996).

Victor Ullman, *Martin R. Delany: The Beginnings of Black Nationalism* (Boston: Beacon Press, 1971).

⌐ 18 ⌐

"What to the Slave Is the Fourth of July?" *Frederick Douglass, 1852*

Frederick Douglass (1818–1895) was the most influential African-American leader of the nineteenth century. After escaping from slavery in 1838, Douglass worked as an agent for the Massachusetts Anti-Slavery Society. Douglass was so eloquent as a public speaker that many whites doubted that he had ever been a slave. Partially to silence his critics, Douglass authored *Narrative of the Life of Frederick Douglass* in 1845. After the publication of the autobiography, Douglass was forced to leave the United States, living for two years in Great Britain. In 1847, returning to the United States, Douglass established *The North Star* newspaper, which was later renamed *Frederick Douglass' Paper*. Douglass was a prominent abolitionist, but was also extensively involved in many other reform movements, especially women's suffrage. After the Civil War, Douglass became a central figure in the national Republican Party.

Fellow Citizens: Pardon me, and allow me to ask, why am I called upon to speak here today? What have I or those I represent to do with your national independence? Are the great principles of political freedom and of natural justice, embodied in that Declaration of Independence, extended to us? And am I, therefore, called upon to bring our humble offering to the national altar, and to confess the benefits, and express devout gratitude for the blessings resulting from your independence to us?

Would to God, both for your sakes and ours, that an affirmative answer could be truthfully returned to these questions. Then would my task be light, and my burden easy and delightful. For who is there so cold that a nation's sympathy could not warm him? Who so obdurate and dead to the claims of gratitude, that would not thankfully acknowledge such priceless benefits? Who so stolid and selfish that would not give his voice to swell the halleluiahs of a nation's jubilee, when the chains of servitude had been torn from his limbs? I am not that man. In a case like that, the dumb might eloquently speak, and the "lame man leap like a hare."

But such is not the state of the case. I say it with a sad sense of disparity between us. I am not included within the pale of this glorious anniversary! Your high independence only reveals the immeasurable distance between us. The blessings in which you this day rejoice are not enjoyed in common. The rich inheritance of justice, liberty, prosperity, and independence bequeathed by your fathers is shared by you, not by me. The sunlight that brought life and healing to you has brought stripes and death to me. This Fourth of July is *yours*, not *mine*. *You* may rejoice, I must mourn. To drag a man in fetters into the grand illuminated temple of liberty, and call upon him to join you in joyous anthems, were inhuman mockery and sacrilegious irony. Do you mean, citizens, to mock me, by asking me to speak today? If so, there is a parallel to your conduct. And let me warn you, that it is dangerous to copy the example of a nation whose crimes, towering up to heaven, were thrown down by the breath of the Almighty, burying that nation in irrecoverable ruin. I can today take up the lament of a peeled and woe-smitten people.

"By the rivers of Babylon, there we sat down. Yes! We wept when we remembered Zion. We hanged our harps upon the willows in the midst thereof. For there they that carried us away captive, required of us a song; and they who wasted us, required of us mirth, saying, Sing us one of the songs of Zion. How can we sing the Lord's song in a strange land? If I forget thee, O Jerusalem, let my right hand forget her cunning. If I do not remember thee, let my tongue cleave to the roof of my mouth."

Fellow citizens, above your national, tumultuous joy, I hear the mournful wail of millions, whose chains, heavy and grievous yesterday, are today rendered more intolerable by the jubilant shouts that reach them. If I do forget, if I do not remember those bleeding children of sorrow this day, "may my right hand forget her cunning, and may my tongue cleave to the roof of my mouth!" To forget them, to pass lightly over their wrongs, and to chime in with the popular theme, would be treason most scandalous and shocking, and would make me a reproach before God and the world. My subject, then, fellow citizens, is "American Slavery." I shall see this day and its popular characteristics from the slave's point of view. Standing here, identified with the American bondman, making his wrongs mine, I do not hesitate to declare, with all my soul, that the character and conduct of this nation never looked blacker to me than on this Fourth of July. Whether we turn to the declarations of the past, or to the professions of the present, the conduct of the nation seems equally hideous and revolting. America is false to the past, false to the present, and solemnly binds herself to be false to the future. Standing with God and the crushed and bleeding slave on this occasion, I will, in the name of humanity, which is outraged, in the name of liberty, which is fettered, in the name of the Constitution and the Bible, which are disregarded and trampled upon, dare to call in question and to denounce, with all the emphasis I can command, everything that serves to perpetuate slavery—the great sin and shame of America! "I will not equivocate; I will not excuse"; I will use the severest language I can command, and yet not one word shall escape me that any man, whose judgment is not blinded by prejudice, or who is not at heart a slave-holder, shall not confess to be right and just.

But I fancy I hear some of my audience say it is just in this circumstance that you and your brother Abolitionists fail to make a favorable impression on the public mind. Would you argue more and denounce less, would you persuade more and rebuke less, your cause would be much more likely to succeed. But, I submit, where all is plain there is nothing to be argued. What point in the antislavery creed would you have me argue? On what branch of the subject do the people of this country need light? Must I undertake to prove that the slave is a man? That point is conceded already. Nobody doubts it. The slaveholders themselves acknowledge it in the enactment of laws for their government. They acknowledge it when they punish disobedience on the part of the slave. There are seventy-two crimes in the State of Virginia, which, if committed by a black man (no matter how ignorant he be), subject him to the punishment of death; while only two of these same crimes will subject a white man to like punishment. What is this but the acknowledgment that the slave is a moral, intellectual, and responsible being? The manhood of the slave is conceded. It is admitted in the fact that Southern statute-books are covered with enactments, forbidding, under severe fines and penalties, the teaching of the slave to read and write. When you can point to any such laws in reference to the beasts of the field, then I may consent to argue the manhood of the slave. When the dogs in your streets, when the fowls of the air, when the cattle on your hills, when the fish of the sea, and the reptiles that crawl, shall be unable to distinguish the slave from a brute, then I will argue with you that the slave is a man!

For the present it is enough to affirm the equal manhood of the Negro race. Is it not astonishing that, while we are plowing, planting, and reaping, using all kinds of mechanical tools, erecting houses, constructing bridges, building ships, working in metals of brass, iron, copper, silver, and gold; that while we are reading, writing, and cyphering, acting as clerks, merchants, and secretaries, having among us lawyers, doctors, ministers, poets, authors, editors, orators, and teachers; that while we are engaged in all the enterprises common to other men—digging gold in California, capturing the whale in the Pacific, feeding sheep and cattle on the hillside, living, moving, acting, thinking, planning, living in families as husbands, wives, and children, and above all, confessing and worshipping the Christian God, and looking hopefully for life and immortality beyond the grave—we are called upon to prove that we are men?

Would you have me argue that man is entitled to liberty? That he is the rightful owner of his own body? You have already declared it. Must I argue the wrongfulness of slavery? Is that a question for republicans? Is it to be settled by the rules of logic and argumentation, as a matter beset with great difficulty, involving a doubtful application of the principle of justice, hard to understand? How should I look today in the presence of Americans, dividing and subdividing a discourse, to show that men have a natural right to freedom, speaking of it relatively and positively, negatively and affirmatively? To do so would be to make myself ridiculous, and to offer an insult to your understanding. There is not a man beneath the canopy of heaven who does not know that slavery is wrong *for him.*

What! Am I to argue that it is wrong to make men brutes, to rob them of their liberty, to work them without wages, to keep them ignorant of their relations to their fellow men, to beat them with sticks, to flay their flesh with the last, to load their limbs with irons, to hunt them with dogs, to sell them at auction, to sunder their families, to knock out their teeth, to burn their flesh, to starve them into obedience and submission to their masters? Must I argue that a system thus marked with blood and stained with pollution is wrong? No; I will not. I have better employment for my time and strength than such arguments would imply.

What, then, remains to be argued? Is it that slavery is not divine; that God did not establish it; that our doctors of divinity are mistaken? There is blasphemy in the thought. That which is inhuman cannot be divine. Who can reason on such a proposition? They that can, may; I cannot. The time for such argument is past.

At a time like this, scorching irony, not convincing argument, is needed. Oh! had I the ability, and could I reach the nation's ear, I would today pour out a fiery stream of biting ridicule, blasting reproach, withering sarcasm, and stern rebuke. For it is not light that is needed, but fire; it is not the gentle shower, but thunder. We need the storm, the whirlwind, and the earthquake. The feeling of the nation must be quickened; the conscience of the nation must be roused; the propriety of the nation must be startled; the hypocrisy of the nation must be exposed; and its crimes against God and man must be denounced.

What to the American slave is your Fourth of July? I answer, a day that reveals to him more than all other days of the year, the gross injustice and cruelty to which he is the constant victim. To him your celebration is a sham; your boasted liberty an unholy license; your national greatness, swelling vanity; your sounds of rejoicing are empty and heartless; your denunciation of tyrants, brass-fronted impudence; your shouts of liberty and equality, hollow mockery; your prayers and hymns, your sermons and thanksgivings, with all your religious parade and solemnity, are to him mere bombast, fraud, deception, impiety, and hypocrisy— a thin veil to cover up crimes which would disgrace a nation of savages. There is not a nation of the earth guilty of practices more shocking and bloody than are the people of these United States at this very hour.

Go where you may, search where you will, roam through all the monarchies and despotisms of the Old World, travel through South America, search out every abuse and when you have found the last, lay your facts by the side of the every-day practices of this nation, and you will say with me that, for revolting barbarity and shameless hypocrisy, America reigns without a rival.

Source: Alice Moore Dunbar, ed., *Masterpieces of Negro Eloquence* (New York: Bookery Publishing, 1914), pp. 42–47.

SELECT BIBLIOGRAPHY:

William L. Andrews, *Critical Essays on Frederick Douglass* (Boston: G.K. Hall, 1991).

John Blassingame, ed., *The Frederick Douglass Papers*, 2 Vols. (New Haven, Conn.: Yale University Press, 1979).

James A. Colaiaco, *Frederick Douglass and the Fourth of July* (New York: Palgrave Macmillan, 2006).

Frederick Douglass, *My Bondage, My Freedom* (New York: Miller, Orton and Mulligan, 1885).

———, *Life and Times of Frederick Douglass. Written by Himself. His Early Life as a Slave, His Escape from Bondage, and His Complete History to the Present Time, including His Connection with the Anti-Slavery Movement* (new revised edition, Boston: Dewolfe Fishe, 1892).

Philip S. Foner, *Frederick Douglass, a Biography* (New York: Citadel Press, 1964).

Nathan I. Huggins, *Slave and Citizen: The Life of Frederick Douglass* (New York: Harper Collins, 1980).

Christoph K. Lohmann, ed., *Radical Passion: Ottilie Assing's Reports from America and Letters to Frederick Douglass*, trans. Christoph K. Lohmann (New York: P. Lang, 1999).

Waldo Martin, *The Mind of Frederick Douglass* (Chapel Hill: University of North Carolina Press, 1984).

James Oakes, *The Radical and the Republican: Frederick Douglass, Abraham Lincoln, and the Triumph of Antislavery Politics* (New York: W. W. Norton & Co., 2007).

～ 19 ～

"No Rights That a White Man Is Bound to Respect": The Dred Scott Case and Its Aftermath

Dred Scott (1795–1858) was born a slave in Southampton, Virginia, and later became a litigator in one of the most famous cases of the nineteenth century. Scott sued for his freedom, and in a second trial, won on the grounds that his slave status was nullified when his master took him to Illinois (a free state) and Wisconsin (a free territory). In 1857, however, the U.S. Supreme Court ruled against Scott. Because slaves were not legal citizens, they were deemed to have no standing in the courts. Chief Justice Roger B. Taney's decision went well beyond the actual details of the case, by voiding the Missouri Compromise of 1820, and permitting the expansion of slavery into states that had been defined as free. The decision greatly accelerated political conflict over the issue of slavery, leading to the Civil War. Frederick Douglass and other abolitionists immediately denounced this decision. Immediately after the Supreme Court's negative decision, Scott's owner, Irene Emerson, freed him.

Dred Scott vs. Alex. Sandford, Saml. Russell, and Irene Emerson
To the Honorable, the Circuit Court within and for the County of St. Louis.

Your petitioner, Dred Scott, a man of color, respectfully represents that sometime in the year 1835 your petitioner was purchased as a slave by one John Emerson, since deceased, who afterwards, to-wit; about the year 1836 or 1837, conveyed your petitioner from the State of Missouri to Fort Snelling, a fort then occupied by the troops of the United States and under the jurisdiction of the United States, situated in the territory ceded by France to the United States under the name of Louisiana, lying north of 36 degrees and 30′ North latitude, now included in the State of Missouri, and resided and continued to reside at Fort Snelling upwards of one year, and held your petitioner in slavery at such Fort during all that time in violation of the Act of Congress of 1806 and 1820, entitled An Act to Authorize the People of Missouri Territory to form a Constitution and State Government, and for the admission of such State into the Union on an equal footing with the original states, and to Prohibit Slavery in Certain Territories.

Your petitioner avers that said Emerson has since departed this life, leaving his widow Irene Emerson and an infant child whose name is unknown to your petitioner; and that one Alexander Sandford administered upon the estate of said Emerson and that your petitioner is now unlawfully held in slavery by said Sandford and by said administrator and said Irene Emerson claims your petitioner as part of the estate of said Emerson and by one Samuel Russell.

Your petitioner therefore prays your Honorable Court to grant him leave to sue as a poor person, in order to establish his right to freedom, and that the necessary orders may be made in the premises.

Dred Scott

State of Missouri
County of St. Louis

This day personally came before me, the undersigned, a Justice of the Peace, Dred Scott, the person whose name is affixed to the foregoing petition, and made oath that the facts set forth in the above petition are true to the best of his knowledge and belief, that he is entitled to his freedom. Witness my hand this 1st day of July, 1847.

his
Dred **X** Scott
mark

Sworn to and subscribed before me this 1st day of July, 1847.

Peter W. Johnstone
Justice of the Peace

ROGER B. TANEY, OPINION ON *DRED SCOTT V. SANDFORD*

The question is simply this: Can a Negro, whose ancestors were imported into this country, and sold as slaves, become a member of the political community formed and brought into existence by the Constitution of the United States, and as such become entitled to all the rights, and privileges, and immunities, guaranteed by that instrument to the citizen? One of which rights is the privilege of suing in a court of the United States in the cases specified in the Constitution.

It will be observed, that the plea applies to that class of persons only whose ancestors were Negroes of the African race, and imported into this country, and sold and held as slaves. The only matter in issue before the court, therefore, is whether the descendants of such slaves, when they shall be emancipated, or who are born of parents who had become free before their birth, are citizens of a State, in the sense in which the word citizen is used in the Constitution of the United States. . . .

The words "people of the United States" and "citizens" are synonymous terms, and mean the same thing. They both describe the political body who, according to our republican institutions, from the sovereignty, and who hold the power and conduct the government through their representatives. They are what we familiarly call the "sovereign people," and every citizen is one of this people, and a constituent member of this sovereignty. The question before us is, whether the class of persons described in the plea in abatement compose a portion of this people, and are constituent members of this sovereignty? We think they are not, and that they are not included, and were not intended to be included, under the word "citizens" in the Constitution, and can, therefore, claim none of the rights and privileges which that instrument provides for and secures to citizens of the United States. On the contrary, they were at that time considered as a subordinate and inferior class of beings, who had been subjugated by the dominant race, and whether emancipated or not, yet remained subject to their authority, and had no rights or privileges but such as those who held the power and the government might choose to grant them. . . .

It is very clear, therefore, that no State can, by any Act or law of its own, passed since the adoption of the Constitution, introduce a new member into the political community created by the Constitution of the United States. It cannot make him a member of this community by making him a member of its own. And for the same reason it cannot introduce any person, or description of persons, who were not intended to be embraced in this new political family, which the Constitution brought into existence, but were intended to be excluded from it. . . .

In the opinion of the court, the legislation and histories of the times, and the language used in the Declaration of Independence, show, that neither the class of persons who had been imported as slaves, nor their descendants, whether they had become free or not, were then acknowledged as a part of the people, nor intended to be included in the general words used in that memorable instrument.

It is difficult at this day to realize the state of public opinion in relation to that unfortunate race, which prevailed in the civilized and enlightened portions of the world at the time of the Declaration of Independence, and when the Constitution of the United States was framed and adopted. . . .

They had for more than a century before been regarded as beings of an inferior order and altogether unfit to associate with the white race, either in social or political relations; and so far inferior that they had no rights which the white man was bound to respect; and that the Negro might justly and lawfully be reduced to slavery for his benefit. He was bought and sold and treated as an ordinary article of merchandise and traffic whenever a profit could be made by it. This opinion was at that time fixed and universal in the civilized portion of the white race. It was regarded as an axiom in morals as well. . . .

. . . A Negro of the African race was regarded . . . as an article of property and held and bought and sold as such in every one of the thirteen Colonies which united in the Declaration of Independence and afterward formed the Constitution of the United States. The slaves were more or less numerous in the different Colonies, as slave labor was found more or less profitable. But no one seems to have doubted the correctness of the prevailing opinion of the time. . . .

The language of the Declaration of Independence is equally conclusive:

It begins by declaring that "When, in the course of human events, it becomes necessary for one people to dissolve the political bands which have connected them with another, and to assume, among the powers of the earth the separate and equal station to which the laws of nature and nature's God entitle them, a decent respect for the opinions of mankind requires that they should declare the causes which impel them to the separation."

It then proceeds to say: "We hold these truths to be self-evident: that all men are created equal; that they are endowed by their Creator with certain inalienable rights; that among these are life, liberty, and the pursuit of happiness; that to secure these rights, governments are instituted, deriving their just powers from the consent of the governed."

The general words above quoted would seem to embrace the whole human family, and if they were used in a similar instrument at this day would be so understood. But it is too clear for dispute that the enslaved African race were not intended to be included and formed no part of the people who framed and adopted this declaration; for if the language, as understood in that day, would embrace them, the conduct of the distinguished men who framed the Declaration of Independence would have been utterly and flagrantly inconsistent with the principles they asserted; and instead of the sympathy of mankind, to which they so confidently appealed, they would have deserved and received universal rebuke and reprobation.

Yet the men who framed this declaration were great men—high in literary acquirements—high in their sense of honor, and incapable of asserting principles inconsistent with those on which they were acting. They perfectly understood the meaning of the language they used and how it would be understood by others; and they knew that it would not in any part of the civilized world be supposed to embrace the Negro race, which, by common consent, had been excluded from civilized governments and the family of nations and doomed to slavery. They spoke and acted according to the then established doctrine and principles and in the ordinary language of the day, and no one misunderstood them. The unhappy black race were separated from the white by indelible marks, and laws long before established, and were never thought of or spoken of except as property and when the claims of the owner or the profit of the trader were supposed to need protection.

This state of public opinion had undergone no change when the Constitution was adopted, as is equally evident from its provisions and language.

The brief preamble sets forth by whom it was formed, for what purposes, and for whose benefit and protection. It declares that it is formed by the *people* of the United States; that is to say, by those who were members of the different political communities in the several states; and its great object is declared to be to secure the blessing of liberty to themselves and their posterity. It speaks in general terms of the *people* of the United States, and of *citizens* of the several states, when it is providing for the exercise of the powers granted or the privileges secured to the citizen. It does not define what description of persons are intended to be included under these terms, or who shall be regarded as a citizen and one of the people. It uses them as terms so well understood that no further description or definition was necessary. . . .

But there are two clauses in the Constitution which point directly and specifically to the Negro race as a separate class of persons, and show clearly that they were not regarded as a portion of the people or citizens of the Government then formed.

One of these clauses reserves to each of the thirteen States the right to import slaves until the year 1808, if it thinks it proper. And the importation which it thus sanctions was unquestionably of persons of the race of which we are speaking, as the traffic in slaves in the United States had always been confined to them. And by the other provision the States pledge themselves to each other to maintain the right of property of the master, by delivering up to him any slave who may have escaped from his service, and be found within their respective territories. . . . And these two provisions show, conclusively, that neither the description of persons therein referred to, nor their descendants, were embraced in any of the other provisions of the Constitution; for certainly these two clauses were not intended to confer on them or their posterity the blessings of liberty, or any of the personal rights so carefully provided for the citizen. . . .

Indeed, when we look to the condition of this race in the several States at the time, it is impossible to believe that these rights and privileges were intended to be extended to them. . . .

The legislation of the States therefore shows, in a manner not to be mistaken, the inferior and subject condition of that race at the time the Constitution was adopted, and long afterwards, throughout the thirteen States by which that instrument was framed; and it is hardly consistent with the respect due to these States, to suppose that they regarded at that time, as fellow-citizens and members of the sovereignty, a class of beings whom they had thus stigmatized.

FREDERICK DOUGLASS'S SPEECH DENOUNCING THE DECISION

While four millions of our fellow countrymen are in chains—while men, women, and children are bought and sold on the auction-block with horses, sheep, and swine—while the remorseless slave-whip draws the warm blood of our common humanity—it is meet that we assemble as we have done today, and lift up our hearts and voices in earnest denunciation of the vile and shocking abomination. It is not for us to be governed by our hopes or our fears in this great work; yet it is natural on occasions like this, to survey the position of the great struggle which is going on between slavery and freedom, and to dwell upon such signs of encouragement as may have been lately developed, and the state of feeling these signs or events have occasioned in us and among the people generally. It is a fitting time to take an observation to ascertain where we are, and what our prospects are.

To many, the prospects of the struggle against slavery seem far from cheering. Eminent men, North and South, in Church and State, tell us that the omens are all against us. Emancipation, they tell us, is a wild, delusive idea; the price of human flesh was never higher than now; slavery was never more closely entwined about the hearts and affections of the southern people than now; that whatever of conscientious scruple, religious conviction, or public policy, which opposed the system of slavery forty or fifty years ago, has subsided; and that slavery never reposed upon a firmer basis than now. Completing this picture of the happy and prosperous condition of this system of wickedness, they tell us that this state of things is to be set to our account. Abolition agitation has done it all. How deep is the misfortune of my poor, bleeding people, if this be so! How lost their condition, if even the efforts of their friends but sink them deeper in ruin!

Without assenting to this strong representation of the increasing strength and stability of slavery, without denouncing what of untruth pervades it, I own myself not insensible to the many difficulties and discouragements that beset us on every hand. They fling their broad and gloomy shadows across the pathway of every thoughtful colored man in this country. For one, I see them clearly, and feel them sadly. With an earnest, aching heart, I have long looked for the realization of the hope of my people. Standing, as it were, barefoot, and treading upon the sharp and flinty rocks of the present, and looking out upon the boundless sea of the future, I have sought, in my humble way, to penetrate the intervening mists and clouds, and, perchance, to descry, in the dim and shadowy distance, the white flag of freedom, the precise speck of time at which the cruel bondage of my people should end, and the long entombed millions rise from the foul grave of slavery and death. But of that time I can know nothing, and you can know nothing. All is uncertain at that point. One thing, however, is certain; slaveholders are in earnest, and mean to cling to their slaves as long as they can, and to the bitter end. They show no sign of a wish to quit their iron grasp upon the sable throats of their victims. Their motto is, "a firmer hold and a tighter grip" for every new effort that is made to break their cruel power. The case is one of life or death with them, and they will give up only when they must do that or do worse.

In one view the slaveholders have a decided advantage over all opposition. It is well to notice this advantage—the advantage of complete organization. They are organized; and yet were not at the pains of creating their organizations. The State governments, where the system of slavery exists, are complete slavery organizations. The church organizations in those States are equally at the service of slavery; while the Federal Government, with its army and navy, from the chief magistracy in Washington, to the Supreme Court, and thence to the chief marshalship at New York, is pledged to support, defend, and propagate the crying curse of human bondage. The pen, the purse, and the sword, are united against the simple truth, preached by humble men in obscure places.

This is one view. It is, thank God, only one view; there is another, and a brighter view. David, you know, looked small and insignificant when going to meet Goliath, but looked larger when he had slain his foe. The Malakoff was, to the eye of the world, impregnable, till the hour it fell before the shot and shell of the allied army. Thus hath it ever been. Oppression, organized as ours is, will appear invincible up to the very hour of its fall. Sir, let us look at the other side, and see if there are not some things to cheer our heart and nerve us up anew in the good work of emancipation.

Take this fact—for it is a fact—the anti-slavery movement has, from first to last, suffered no abatement. It has gone forth in all directions, and is now felt in the remotest extremities of the Republic.

It started small, and was without capital either in men or money. The odds were all against it. It literally had nothing to lose, and everything to gain. There was ignorance to be enlightened, error to be combatted, conscience to be awakened, prejudice to be overcome, apathy to be aroused, the right of speech to be secured, mob violence to be subdued, and a deep, radical change to be inwrought in the mind and heart of the whole nation. This great work, under God, has gone on, and gone on gloriously.

Amid all changes, fluctuations, assaults, and adverses of every kind, it has remained firm in its purpose, steady in its aim, onward and upward, defying all opposition, and never losing a single battle. Our strength is in the growth of anti-slavery conviction, and this has never halted.

There is a significant vitality about this abolition movement. It has taken a deeper, broader, and more lasting hold upon the national heart than ordinary reform movements. Other subjects of much interest come and go, expand and contract, blaze and vanish, but the huge question of American Slavery, comprehending, as it does, not merely the weal or the woe of four millions, and their countless posterity, but the weal or the woe of this entire nation, must increase in magnitude and in majesty with every hour of its history. From a cloud not bigger than a man's hand, it has overspread the heavens. It has risen from a grain not bigger than a mustard seed. Yet see the fowls of the air, how they crowd its branches.

Politicians who cursed it, now defend it; ministers, once dumb, now speak in its praise; and presses, which once flamed with hot denunciations against it, now surround the sacred cause as by a wall of living fire. Politicians go with it as a pillar of cloud by day, and the press as a pillar of fire by night. With these ancient tokens of success, I, for one, will not despair of our cause.

Those who have undertaken to suppress and crush out this agitation for Liberty and humanity, have been most woefully disappointed. Many who have engaged to put it down, have found themselves put down. The agitation has pursued them in all their meanderings, broken in upon their seclusion, and, at the very moment of fancied security, it has settled down upon them like a mantle of unquenchable fire. Clay, Calhoun, and Webster each tried his hand at suppressing the agitation; and they went to their graves disappointed and defeated.

Loud and exultingly have we been told that the slavery question is settled, and settled forever. You remember it was settled thirty-seven years ago, when Missouri was admitted into the Union with a slaveholding constitution, and slavery prohibited in all territory north of thirty-six degrees of north latitude. Just fifteen years afterwards, it was settled again by voting down the right of petition, and gagging down free discussion in Congress. Ten years after this it was settled again by the annexation of Texas, and with it the war with Mexico. In 1850 it was again settled. This was called a final settlement. By it slavery was virtually declared to be the equal of Liberty, and should come into the Union on the same terms. By it the right and the power to hunt down men, women, and children, in every part of this country, was conceded to our southern brethren, in order to keep them in the Union. Four years after this settlement, the whole question was once more settled, and settled by a settlement which unsettled all the former settlements.

The fact is, the more the question has been settled, the more it has needed settling. The space between the different settlements has been strikingly on the decrease. The first stood longer than any of its successors.

This last settlement must be called the Taney settlement. We are now—the second, ten years—the third, five years—the fourth stood four years—and the fifth has stood the brief space of two years.

This last settlement must be called the Taney settlement. We are now told, in tones of lofty exultation, that the day is lost—all lost—and that we might as well give up the struggle. The highest authority has spoken. The voice of the Supreme Court has gone out over the troubled waves of the National Conscience, saying peace, be still.

This infamous decision of the Slaveholding wing of the Supreme Court maintains that slaves are within the contemplation of the Constitution of the United States, property; that slaves are property in the same sense that horses, sheep, and swine are property; that the old doctrine that slavery is a creature of local law is false; that the right of the slaveholder to his slave does not depend upon the local law, but is secured wherever the Constitution of the United States extends; that Congress has no right to prohibit slavery anywhere; that slavery may go in safety anywhere under the star-spangled banner; that colored persons of African descent have no rights that white men are bound to respect; that colored men of African descent are not and cannot be citizens of the United States.

You will readily ask me how I am affected by this devilish decision—this judicial incarnation of wolfishness? My answer is, and no thanks to the slaveholding wing of the Supreme Court, my hopes were never brighter than now.

I have no fear that the National Conscience will be put to sleep by such an open, glaring, and scandalous tissue of lies as that decision is, and has been, over and over, shown to be.

The Supreme Court of the United States is not the only power in this world. It is very great, but the Supreme Court of the Almighty is greater. Judge Taney can do many things, but he cannot perform impossibilities. He cannot bale out the ocean, annihilate the firm old earth, or pluck the silvery star of liberty from our Northern sky. He may decide, and decide again; but he cannot reverse the decision of the Most High. He cannot change the essential nature of things— making evil good, and good evil.

Happily for the whole human family, their rights have been defined, declared, and decided in a court higher than the Supreme Court. "There is a law," says Brougham, "above all the enactments of human codes, and by that law, unchangeable and eternal, man cannot hold property in man."

Your fathers have said that man's right to liberty is self-evident. There is no need of argument to make it clear. The voices of nature, of conscience, of reason, and of revelation, proclaim it as the right of all rights, the foundation of all trust, and of all responsibility. Man was born with it. It was his before he comprehended it. The *deed* conveying it to him is written in the center of his soul, and is recorded in Heaven. The sun in the sky is not more palpable to the sight than man's right to liberty is to the moral vision. To decide against this right in the person of Dred Scott, or the humblest and most whip-scarred bondman in the land, is to decide against God. It is an open rebellion against God's government. It is an attempt to undo what God has done, to blot out the broad distinction instituted by the *Allwise* between men and things, and to change the image and superscription of the everliving God into a speechless piece of merchandise.

Such a decision cannot stand. God will be true though every man be a liar. We can appeal from this hell-black judgment of the Supreme Court, to the court of common sense and common humanity. We can appeal from man to God. If there is no justice on earth, there is yet justice in heaven. You may close your Supreme Court against the black man's cry for justice, but you cannot, thank God, close against him the ear of a sympathising world, nor shut up the Court of Heaven. All that is merciful and just, on earth and in Heaven, will execrate and despise this edict of Taney.

If it were at all likely that the people of these free States would tamely submit to this demoniacal judgment, I might feel gloomy and sad over it, and possibly it might be necessary for my people to look for a home in some other country. But as the case stands, we have nothing to fear.

In one point of view, we, the abolitionists and colored people, should meet this decision, unlooked for and monstrous as it appears, in a cheerful spirit. This very attempt to blot out forever the hopes of an enslaved people may be one necessary link in the chain of events preparatory to the downfall and complete overthrow of the whole slave system.

The whole history of the anti-slavery movement is studded with proof that all measures devised and executed with a view to ally and diminish the anti-slavery agitation, have only served to increase, intensify, and embolden that agitation. This wisdom of the crafty has been confounded, and the counsels of the ungodly brought to nought. It was so with the Fugitive Slave Bill. It was so with the Kansas-Nebraska Bill; and it will be so with this last and most shocking of all pro-slavery devices, this Taney decision.

When great transactions are involved, where the fate of millions is concerned, where a long enslaved and suffering people are to be delivered, I am superstitious enough to believe that the finger of the Almighty may be seen bringing good out of evil, and making the wrath of man redound to his honor, hastening the triumph of righteousness.

The American people have been called upon, in a most striking manner, to abolish and put away forever the system of slavery. The subject has been pressed upon their attention in all earnestness and sincerity. The cries of the slave have gone forth to the world, and up to the throne of God. This decision, in my view, is a means of keeping the nation awake on the subject. It is another proof that God does not mean that we shall go to sleep, and forget that we are a slaveholding nation.

Step by step we have seen the slave power advancing; poisoning, corrupting, and perverting the institutions of the country; growing more and more haughty, imperious, and exacting. The white man's liberty has been marked out for the same grave with the black man's.

The ballot box is desecrated, God's law set at nought, armed legislators stalk the halls of Congress, freedom of speech is beaten down in the Senate. The rivers and highways are infested by border ruffians, and white men are made to feel the iron heel of slavery. This ought to arouse us to kill off the hateful thing. They are solemn warnings to which the white people, as well as the black people, should take heed.

If these shall fail, judgment, more fierce or terrible, may come. The lightning, whirlwind, and earthquake may come. Jefferson said that he trembled for his country when he reflected that God is just, and his justice cannot sleep forever. The time may come when even the crushed worm may turn under the tyrant's feet. Goaded by cruelty, stung by a burning sense of wrong, in an awful moment of depression and desperation, the bondman and bondwoman at the south may rush to one wild and deadly struggle for freedom. Already slaveholders go to bed with bowie knives, and apprehend death at their dinners. Those who enslave, rob, and torment their cooks, may well expect to find death in their dinner-pots.

The world is full of violence and fraud, and it would be strange if the slave, the constant victim of both fraud and violence, should escape the contagion. He, too, may learn to fight the devil with fire, and for one, I am in no frame of mind to pray that this may be long deferred.

Two remarkable occurrences have followed the presidential election; one was the unaccountable sickness traced to the National Hotel at Washington, and the other was the discovery of a plan among the slaves, in different localities, to slay their oppressors. Twenty or thirty of the suspected were put to death. Some were shot, some hanged, some burned, and some died under the lash. One brave man owned himself well acquainted with the conspiracy, but said he would rather die than disclose the facts. He received seven hundred and fifty lashes, and his noble spirit went away to the God who gave it. The name of this hero has been by the meanness of tyrants suppressed. Such a man redeems his race. He is worthy to be mentioned with the Hoffers and Tells, the noblest heroes of history. These insurrectionary movements have been put down, but they may break out at any time, under the guidance of higher intelligence, and with a more invincible spirit.

> The fire thus kindled, may be revived again;
> The flames are extinguished, but the embers remain;
> One terrible blast may produce an ignition,
> Which shall wrap the whole South in wild conflagration.
>
> The pathway of tyrants lies over volcanoes
> The very air they breathe is heavy with sorrows;
> Agonizing heart-throbs convulse them while sleeping,
> And the wind whispers Death as over them sweeping.

By all the laws of nature, civilization, and of progress, slavery is a doomed system. Not all the skill of politicians, North and South, not all the sophistries of Judges, not all the fulminations of a corrupt press, not all the hypocritical prayers, or the hypocritical refusals to pray of a hollow-hearted priesthood, not all the devices of sin and Satan, can save the vile thing from extermination.

Already a gleam of hope breaks upon us from the southwest. One Southern city has grieved and astonished the whole South by a preference for freedom. The wedge has entered. Dred Scott, of Missouri, goes into slavery, but St. Louis declares for freedom. The judgment of Taney is not the judgment of St. Louis.

It may be said that this demonstration in St. Louis is not to be taken as an evidence of sympathy with the slave; that it is purely a white man's victory. I admit it. Yet I am glad that white men, bad as they generally are, should gain a victory over slavery. I am willing to accept a judgment against slavery, whether supported by white or black reasons—though I would much rather have it supported by both. He that is not against us, is on our part.

Come what will, I hold it to be morally certain that, sooner or later, by fair means or foul means, in quiet or in tumult, in peace or in blood, in judgment or in mercy, slavery is doomed to cease out of this otherwise goodly land, and liberty is destined to become the settled law of this Republic.

I base my sense of the certain overthrow of slavery, in part, upon the nature of the American Government, the Constitution, the tendencies of the age, and the character of the American people; and this, notwithstanding the important decision of Judge Taney.

I know of no soil better adapted to the growth of reform than American soil. I know of no country where the conditions for affecting great changes in the settled order of things, for the development of right ideas of liberty and humanity, are more favorable than here in these United States.

The very groundwork of this government is a good repository of Christian civilization. The Constitution, as well as the Declaration of Independence, and the sentiments of the founders of the Republic, give us a platform broad enough, and strong enough, to support the most comprehensive plans for the freedom and elevation of all the people of this country, without regard to color, class, or clime.

There is nothing in the present aspect of the anti-slavery question which should drive us into the extravagance and nonsense of advocating a dissolution of the American Union as a means of overthrowing slavery, or freeing the North from the malign influence of slavery upon the morals of the Northern people. While the press is at liberty, and speech is free, and the ballot-box is open to the people of the sixteen free States; while the slaveholders are but four hundred thousand in number, and we are fourteen millions; while the mental and moral power of the nation is with us; while we are really the strong and they are the weak, it would look worse than cowardly to retreat from the Union.

If the people of the North have not the power to cope with these four hundred thousand slaveholders inside the Union, I see not how they could get out of the Union. The strength necessary to move the Union must ever be less than is required to break it up. If we have got to conquer the slave power to get out of the Union, I for one would much rather conquer, and stay in the Union. The latter, it strikes me, is the far more rational mode of action.

I make these remarks in no servile spirit, nor in any superstitious reverence for a mere human arrangement. If I felt the Union to be a curse, I should not be far behind the very chiefest of the disunion Abolitionists in denouncing it. But the evil to be met and abolished is not in the Union. The power arrayed against us is not a parchment.

It is not in changing the dead form of the Union, that slavery is to be abolished in this country. We have to do not with the dead, but the living; not with the past, but the living present.

Those who seek slavery in the Union, and who are everlastingly dealing blows upon the Union, in the belief that they are killing slavery, are most woefully mistaken. They are fighting a dead form instead of a living and powerful reality. It is clearly not because of the peculiar character of our Constitution that we have slavery, but the wicked pride, love of power, and selfish perverseness of the American people. Slavery lives in this country not because of any paper Constitution, but in the moral blindness of the American people, who persuade themselves that they are safe, though the rights of others may be struck down.

Besides, I think it would be difficult to hit upon any plan less likely to abolish slavery than the dissolution of the Union. The most devoted advocates of slavery, those who make the interests of slavery their constant study, seek a dissolution of the Union as their final plan for preserving slavery from Abolition, and their ground is well taken. Slavery lives and flourishes best in the absence of civilization;

a dissolution of the Union would shut up the system in its own congenial barbarism.

The dissolution of the Union would not give the North one single additional advantage over slavery to the people of the North, but would manifestly take from them many which they now certainly possess.

Within the Union we have a firm basis of anti-slavery operation. National welfare, national prosperity, national reputation and honor, and national scrutiny; common rights, common duties, and common country, are so many bridges over which we can march to the destruction of slavery. To fling away these advantages because James Buchanan is President or Judge Taney gives a lying decision in favor of slavery, does not enter into my notion of common sense.

Mr. Garrison and his friends have been telling us that, while in the Union, we are responsible for slavery; and in so telling us, he and they have told us the truth. But in telling us that we shall cease to be responsible for slavery by dissolving the Union, he and they have not told us the truth.

There now, clearly, is no freedom from responsibility for slavery, but in the Abolition of slavery. We have gone too far in this business now to sum up our whole duty in the cant phrase of "no Union with slaveholders."

To desert the family hearth may place the recreant husband out of the sight of his hungry children, but it cannot free him from responsibility. Though he should roll the waters of three oceans between him and them, he could not roll from his soul the burden of his responsibility to them; and, as with the private family, so in this instance with the national family. To leave the slave in his chains, in the hands of cruel masters who are too strong for him, is not to free ourselves from responsibility. Again: If I were on board of a pirate ship, with a company of men and women whose lives and liberties I had put in jeopardy, I would not clear my soul of their blood by jumping in the long boat, and singing out no union with pirates. My business would be to remain on board, and while I never would perform a single act of piracy again, I should exhaust every means given me by my position, to save the lives and liberties of those against whom I had committed piracy. In like manner, I hold it is our duty to remain inside this Union, and use all the power to restore to enslaved millions their precious and God-given rights. The more we have done by our voice and our votes, in times past, to rivet their galling fetters, the more clearly and solemnly comes the sense of duty to remain, to undo what we have done. Where, I ask, could the slave look for release from slavery if the Union were dissolved? I have an abiding conviction founded upon long and careful study of the certain effects of slavery upon the moral sense of slaveholding communities, that if the slaves are ever delivered from bondage, the power will emanate from the free States. All hope that the slaveholders will be self-moved to this great act of justice, is groundless and delusive. Now, as of old, the Redeemer must come from above, not from beneath. To dissolve the Union would be to withdraw the emancipating power from the field.

But I am told this is the argument of expediency. I admit it, and am prepared to show that what is expedient in this instance is right. "Do justice, though the heavens fall." Yes, that is a good motto, but I deny that it would be doing justice to the slave to dissolve the Union and leave the slave in his chains to get out by the clemency of his master, or the strength of his arms. Justice to the slave is to break his chains, and going out of the union is to leave him in his chains, and without any probable chance of getting out of them.

But I come now to the great question as to the constitutionality of slavery. The recent slaveholding decision, as well as the teachings of anti-slavery men, make this a fit time to discuss the constitutional pretensions of slavery.

The people of the North are a law-abiding people. They love order and respect the means to that end. This sentiment has sometimes led them to the folly and wickedness of trampling upon the very life of law, to uphold its dead form. This was so in the execution of that thrice accursed Fugitive Slave Bill. Burns and Simms were sent back to the hell of slavery after they had looked upon Bunker Hill, and heard liberty thunder in Faneuil Hall. The people permitted this outrage in obedience to the popular sentiment of reverence for law. While men thus respect law, it becomes a serious matter so to interpret the law as to make it operate against liberty. I have a quarrel with those who fling the Supreme Law of this land between the slave and freedom. It is a serious matter to fling the weight of the Constitution against the cause of human liberty, and those who do it, take upon them a heavy responsibility. Nothing but absolute necessity, shall, or ought to drive me to such a concession to slavery.

When I admit that slavery is constitutional, I must see slavery recognized in the Constitution. I must see that it is there plainly stated that one man of a certain description has a right of property in the body and soul of another man of a certain description. There must be no room for a doubt. In a matter so important as the loss of liberty, everything must be proved beyond all reasonable doubt.

The well-known rules of legal interpretation bear me out in this stubborn refusal to see slavery where slavery is not, and only to see slavery where it is.

The Supreme Court has, in its day, done something better than make slaveholding decisions. It has laid down rules of interpretation which are in harmony with the true idea and object of law and liberty.

It has told us that the intention of legal instruments must prevail; and that this must be collected from its words. It told us that language must be construed strictly in favor of liberty and justice.

It has told us where rights are infringed, where fundamental principles are overthrown, where the general system of the law is departed from, the Legislative intention must be expressed with irresistible clearness, to induce a court of justice to suppose a design to effect such objects.

These rules are as old as law. They rise out of the very elements of law. It is to protect human rights, and promote human welfare. Law is in its nature opposed to wrong, and must everywhere be presumed to be in favor of the right. The pound of flesh, but not one drop of blood, is a sound rule of legal interpretation.

Besides there is another rule of law as well of common sense, which requires us to look to the ends for which a law is made, and to construe its details in harmony with the ends sought.

Now let us approach the Constitution from the standpoint thus indicated, and instead of finding in it a warrant for the stupendous system of robbery, comprehended in the term slavery, we shall find it strongly against that system.

"We, the people of the United States, in order to form a more perfect Union, establish justice, insure domestic tranquility, provide for the common defence, promote the general welfare, and secure the blessings of liberty to ourselves and our posterity, do ordain and establish this constitution for the United States of America."

Such are the objects announced by the instrument itself, and they are in harmony with the Declaration of Independence, and the principles of human well-being.

Six objects are here declared, "Union," "defence," "welfare," "tranquility," and "justice," and "liberty."

Neither in the preamble nor in the body of the Constitution is there a single mention of the term *slave* or *slave holder*, *slave master* or *slave state*, neither is there any reference to the color, or the physical peculiarities of any part of the people of the United States. Neither is there anything in the Constitution standing alone, which would imply the existence of slavery in this country.

"We, the people"—not we, the white people—not we, the citizens, or the legal voters—not we, the privileged class, and excluding all other classes but we, the people; not we, the horses and cattle, but we the people—the men and women, the human inhabitants of the United States, do ordain and establish this Constitution, &c.

I ask, then, any man to read the Constitution, and tell me where, if he can, in what particular that instrument affords the slightest sanction of slavery?

Where will he find a guarantee for slavery? Will he find it in the declaration that no person shall be deprived of life, liberty, or property, without due process of law? Will he find it in the declaration that the Constitution was established to secure the blessing of liberty? Will he find it in the right of the people to be secure in their persons and papers, and houses, and effects? Will he find it in the clause prohibiting the enactment by any State of a bill of attainder?

These all strike at the root of slavery, and any one of them, but faithfully carried out, would put an end to slavery in every State in the American Union.

Take, for example, the prohibition of a bill of attainder. That is a law entailing on the child the misfortunes of the parent. This principle would destroy slavery in every State of the Union.

The law of slavery is a law of attainder. The child is property because its parent was property, and suffers as a slave because its parent suffered as a slave.

Thus the very essence of the whole slave code is in open violation of a fundamental provision of the Constitution, and is in open and flagrant violation of all the objects set forth in the Constitution.

While this and much more can be said, and has been said, and much better said, by Lysander Spooner, William Goodell, Beriah Green, and Gerrit Smith, in favor of the entire unconstitutionality of slavery, what have we on the other side?

How is the constitutionality of slavery made out, or attempted to be made out?

First, by discrediting and casting away as worthless the most beneficent rules of legal interpretation; by disregarding the plain and common-sense reading of the instrument itself; by showing that the Constitution does not mean what it says, and says what it does not mean, by assuming that the written Constitution is to be interpreted in the light of a secret and unwritten understanding of its framers, which understanding is declared to be in favor of slavery. It is in this mean, contemptible, underhand method that the Constitution is pressed into the service of slavery.

They do not point us to the Constitution itself, for the reason that there is nothing sufficiently explicit for their purpose; but they delight in supposed intentions—intentions nowhere expressed in the Constitution, and everywhere contradicted in the Constitution.

Judge Taney lays down this system of interpreting in this wise:

"The general words above quoted would seem to embrace the whole human family, and, if they were used in a similar instrument at this day, would be so understood. But it is too clear for dispute that the enslaved African race were not intended to be included, and formed no part of the people who framed and adopted this declaration; for if the language, as understood in that day, would embrace them, the conduct of the distinguished men who framed the Declaration of Independence would have been utterly and flagrantly inconsistent with the principles they asserted; and instead of the sympathy of mankind, to which they appealed, they would have deserved and received universal rebuke and reprobation.

"It is difficult, at this day, to realize the state of public opinion respecting that unfortunate class with the civilized and enlightened portion of the world at the time of the Declaration of Independence and the adoption of the Constitution; but history shows they had, for more than a century, been regarded as beings of an inferior order, and unfit associates for the white race, either socially or politically, and had no rights which white men are bound to respect; and the black man might be reduced to slavery, bought and sold, and treated as an ordinary article of merchandise. This opinion, at that time, was fixed and universal with the civilized portion of the white race. It was regarded as an axiom of morals, which no one thought of disputing, and everyone habitually acted upon it, without doubting, for a moment, the correctness of the opinion. And in no nation was this opinion more fixed, and generally acted upon, than in England; the subjects of which government not only seized them on the coast of Africa, but took them, as ordinary merchandise, to where they could make a profit on them. The opinion, thus entertained, was universally maintained on the colonies this side of the Atlantic; accordingly, Negroes of the African race were regarded by them as property, and held and bought and sold as such in every one of the thirteen colonies, which united in the Declaration of Independence, and afterwards formed the Constitution."

The argument here is, that the Constitution comes down to us from a slaveholding period and a slaveholding people; and that, therefore, we are bound to suppose that the Constitution recognizes colored persons of African descent, the victims of slavery at that time, as debarred forever from all participation in the benefit of the Constitution and the Declaration of Independence, although the plain reading of both includes them in their beneficent range.

As a man, an American, a citizen, a colored man of both Anglo-Saxon and African descent, I denounce this representation as a most scandalous and devilish perversion of the Constitution, and a brazen misstatement of the facts of history.

But I will not content myself with mere denunciation; I invite attention to the facts.

It is a fact, a great historic fact, that at the time of the adoption of the Constitution, the leading religious denominations in this land were anti-slavery, and were laboring for the emancipation of the colored people of African descent.

The church of a country is often a better index of the state of opinion and feeling than is even the government itself.

The Methodists, Baptists, Presbyterians, and the denomination of Friends, were actively opposing slavery, denouncing the system of bondage, with language as burning and sweeping as we employ at this day.

Take the Methodists. In 1780, that denomination said: "The Conference acknowledges that slavery is contrary to the laws of God, man, and nature, and hurtful to society—contrary to the dictates of conscience and true religion, and doing to others that we would not do unto us." In 1784, the same church declared, "that those who buy, sell, or give slaves away, except for the purpose to free them, shall be expelled immediately." In 1785, it spoke even more stringently on the subject. It then said: "We hold in the deepest abhorrence the practice of slavery, and shall not cease to seek its destruction by all wise and proper means."

So much for the position of the Methodist Church in the early history of the Republic, in those days of darkness to which Judge Taney refers.

Let us now see how slavery was regarded by the Presbyterian Church at that early date.

In 1794, the General Assembly of that body pronounced the following judgment in respect to slavery, slaveholders, and slaveholding.

"1st Timothy, 1st chapter, 10th verse: 'The law was made for manstealers.' 'This crime among the Jews exposed the perpetrators of it to capital punishment.' Exodus, xxi, 15.—And the apostle here classes them with sinners of the first rank. The word he uses in its original import, comprehends all who are concerned in bringing any of the human race into slavery, or in retaining them in it. Stealers of men are all those who bring off slaves or freemen, and keep, sell, or buy them. 'To steal a freeman,' says Grotius, 'is the highest kind of theft.' In other instances, we only steal human property, but when we steal or retain men in slavery, we seize those who, in common with ourselves, are constituted, by the original grant, lords of the earth."

I might quote, at length, from the sayings of the Baptist Church and the sayings of eminent divines at this early period, showing that Judge Taney has grossly falsified history, but will not detain you with these quotations.

The testimony of the church, and the testimony of the founders of this Republic, from the declaration downward, prove Judge Taney false; as false to history as he is to law.

Washington and Jefferson, and Adams, and Jay, and Franklin, and Rush, and Hamilton, and a host of others, held no such degrading views on the subject of slavery as are imputed by Judge Taney to the Fathers of the Republic.

All, at that time, looked for the gradual but certain abolition of slavery, and shaped the constitution with a view to this grand result.

George Washington can never be claimed as a fanatic, or as the representative of fanatics. The slaveholders impudently use his name for the base purpose of giving respectability to slavery. Yet, in a letter to Robert Morris, Washington uses this language—language which, at this day, would make him a terror of the slaveholders, and the natural representative of the Republican party.

"There is not a man living, who wishes more sincerely than I do, to see some plan adopted for the abolition of slavery; but there is only one proper and effectual mode by which it can be accomplished, and that is by Legislative authority; and this, as far as my suffrage will go, shall not be wanting."

Washington only spoke the sentiment of his times. There were, at that time, Abolition societies in the slave States—Abolition societies in Virginia, in North Carolina, in Maryland, in Pennsylvania, and in Georgia—all slaveholding States. Slavery was so weak, and liberty so strong, that free speech could attack the monster to its teeth. Men were not mobbed and driven out of the presence of slavery, merely because they condemned the slave system. The system was then on its knees imploring to be spared, until it could get itself decently out of the world.

In the light of these facts, the Constitution was framed, and framed in conformity to it.

It may, however, be asked, if the Constitution were so framed that the rights of all the people were naturally protected by it, how happens it that a large part of the people have been held in slavery ever since its adoption? Have the people mistaken the requirements of their own Constitution?

The answer is ready. The Constitution is one thing, its administration is another, and, in this instance, a very different and opposite thing. I am here to vindicate the law, not the administration of the law. It is the written Constitution, not the unwritten Constitution, that is now before us. If, in the whole range of the Constitution, you can find no warrant for slavery, then we may properly claim it for liberty.

Good and wholesome laws are often found dead on the statute book. We may condemn the practice under them and against them, but never the law itself. To condemn the good law with the wicked practice, is to weaken, not to strengthen our testimony.

It is no evidence that the Bible is a bad book, because those who profess to believe the Bible are bad. The slaveholders of the South, and many of their wicked allies at the North, claim the Bible for slavery; shall we, therefore, fling the Bible away as a pro-slavery book? It would be as reasonable to do so as it would be to fling away the Constitution.

We are not the only people who have illustrated the truth, that a people may have excellent law, and detestable practices. Our Savior denounces the Jews, because they made void the law by their traditions. We have been guilty of the same sin.

The American people have made void our Constitution by just such traditions as Judge Taney and Mr. Garrison have been giving to the world of late, as the true light in which to view the Constitution of the United States. I shall follow neither. It is not what Moses allowed for the hardness of heart, but what God requires, ought to be the rule.

It may be said that it is quite true that the Constitution was designed to secure the blessings of liberty and justice to the people who made it, and to the posterity of the people who made it, but was never designed to do any such thing for the colored people of African descent.

This is Judge Taney's argument, and it is Mr. Garrison's argument, but it is not the argument of the Constitution. The Constitution imposes no such mean and satanic limitations upon its own beneficent operation. And, if the Constitution makes none, I beg to know what right has anybody, outside of the Constitution, for the special accommodation of slaveholding villainy, to impose such a construction upon the Constitution?

The Constitution knows all the human inhabitants of this country as "the people." It makes, as I have said before, no discrimination in favor of, or against, any class of the people, but is fitted to protect and preserve the rights of all, without reference to color, size, or any physical peculiarities. Besides, it has been shown by William Goodell and others, that in eleven out of the old thirteen States, colored men were legal voters at the time of the adoption of the Constitution.

In conclusion, let me say, all I ask of the American people is, that they live up to the Constitution, adopt its principles, imbibe its spirit, and enforce its provisions.

When this is done, the wounds of my bleeding people will be healed, the chain will no longer rust on their ankles, their backs will no longer be torn by the bloody lash, and liberty, the glorious birthright of our common humanity, will become the inheritance of all the inhabitants of this highly favored country—May 1857.

Sources: (1) Dred Scott petitions for his freedom, July 1847, Missouri Court Records, St. Louis; (2) Roger B. Taney, excerpt from "*Obiter Dictum* on Dred Scott v. Sandford," 1857; and (3) excerpt from Frederick Douglass, "A Most Scandalous and Devilish Perversion of the Constitution," speech denouncing the Dred Scott decision, May,1857.

SELECT BIBLIOGRAPHY:

Austin Allen, *Origins of the Dred Scott Case: Jacksonian Jurisprudence and the Supreme Court, 1837–1857* (Athens: University of Georgia Press, 2006).

Walter Ehrlich, *They Have No Rights: Dred Scott's Struggle for Freedom* (Westport, Conn.: Greenwood Press, 1979).

Don E. Fehrenbacher, *The Dred Scott Case: Its Significance in American Law and Politics* (New York: Oxford University Press, 1978).

Paul Finkelman, *Dred Scott v. Sandford: A Brief History with Documents* (Boston: Bedford Books, 1997).

Stanley Kutler, ed., *The Dred Scott Decision: Law or Politics?* (Boston: Houghton Mifflin, 1997).

Earl M. Maltz, *Dred Scott and the Politics of Slavery* (Lawrence: University Press of Kansas, 2007).

~ 20 ~

"Whenever the Colored Man Is Elevated, It Will Be by His Own Exertions," John S. Rock, 1858

John S. Rock (1825–1866) was an abolitionist, teacher, dentist, physician, and lawyer. In 1865 he became the first African American to be accorded the privilege of pleading before the Supreme Court. In the speech that follows, which was originally presented to an audience in Boston's Faneuil Hall in March 1858, Rock proved prescient both in his analysis of racism and in his anticipation of much of the discourse on "black pride" that became a central part of the Black Power movement a century later.

~

Ladies and Gentlemen:

YOU WILL not expect a lengthened speech from me to-night. My health is too poor to allow me to indulge much in speech-making. But I have not been able to resist the temptation to unite with you in this demonstration of respect for some of my noble but misguided ancestors.

White Americans have taken great pains to try to prove that we are cowards. We are often insulted with the assertion, that if we had had the courage of the Indians or the white man, we would never have submitted to be slaves. I ask if Indians and white men have never been slaves? The white man tested the Indian's courage here when he had his organized armies, his battle-grounds, his places of retreat, with everything to hope for and everything to lose. The position of the African slave has been very different. Seized a prisoner of war, unarmed, bound hand and foot, and conveyed to a distant country among what to him were worse than cannibals; brutally beaten, half-starved, closely watched by armed men, with no means of knowing their own strength or the strength of their enemies, with no weapons, and without a probability of success. But if the white man will take the trouble to fight the black man in Africa or in Hayti, and fight him as fair as the black man will fight him there—if the black man does not come off victor, I am deceived in his prowess. But, take a man, armed or unarmed, from his home, his country, or his friends, and place him among savages, and who is he that would not make good his retreat? 'Discretion is the better part of valor,' but for a man to resist where he knows it will destroy him, shows more fool-hardiness than courage. There have been many Anglo-Saxons and Anglo-Americans enslaved in Africa, but I have never heard that they successfully resisted any government. They always resort to running indispensables.

The courage of the Anglo-Saxon is best illustrated in his treatment of the negro. A score or two of them can pounce upon a poor negro, tie and beat him, and then call him a coward because he submits. Many of their most brilliant victories have been achieved in the same manner. But the greatest battles which they have fought have been upon paper. We can easily account for this; their trumpeter is dead. He died when they used to be exposed for sale in the Roman market, about the time that Cicero cautioned his friend Atticus not to buy them, on account of their stupidity. A little more than half a century ago, this race, in connection with their Celtic neighbors, who have long been considered (by themselves, of course,) the bravest soldiers in the world, so far forgot themselves, as to attack a few cowardly, stupid negro slaves, who, according to their accounts, had not sense enough to go to bed. And what was the result? Why, sir, the negroes drove them out from the island like so many sheep, and they have never dared to show their faces, except with hat in hand.

Our true and tried friend, Rev. Theodore Parker, said, in his speech at the State House, a few weeks since, that 'the stroke of the axe would have settled the question long ago, but the black man would not strike.' Mr. Parker makes a very low estimate of the courage of his race, if he means that one, two or three millions of these ignorant and cowardly black slaves could, without means, have brought to their knees five, ten, or twenty millions of intelligent, brave white men, backed up by a rich oligarchy. But I know of no one who is more familiar with the true character of the Anglo-Saxon race than Mr. Parker. I will not dispute this point with him, but I will thank him or any one else to tell us how it could have been done. His remark calls to my mind the day which is to come, when one shall chase a thousand, and two put ten thousand to flight. But when he says that 'the black man *would not* strike,' I am prepared to say that he does us great injustice. The black man is not a coward. The history of the bloody struggles for freedom in Hayti, in which the blacks whipped the French and the English, and gained their independence, in spite of the perfidy of that villainous First Consul, will be a lasting refutation of the malicious aspersions of our enemies. The history of the struggles for the liberty of the U.S. ought to silence every American calumniator. I have learned that even so late as the Texan war, a number of black men were silly enough to offer themselves as living sacrifices for our country's shame. A gentleman who delivered a lecture before the New York Legislature, a few years since, whose name I do not now remember, but whose language I give with some precision, said, 'In the Revolution, colored soldiers fought side by side with you in your struggles for liberty, and there is not a battle-field from Maine to Georgia that has not been crimsoned with their blood, and whitened with their bones.' In 1814, a bill passed the Legislature of New York, accepting the services of 2000 colored volunteers. Many black men served under Com. McDonough when he conquered on lake Champlain. Many were in the battles of Plattsburgh and Sackett's Harbor, and General Jackson called out colored troops from Louisiana and Alabama, and in a solemn proclamation attested to their fidelity and courage.

The white man contradicts himself who says, that if he were in our situation, he would throw off the yoke. Thirty millions of white men of this proud Caucasian race are at this moment held as slaves, and bought and sold with horses and cattle. The iron heel of oppression grinds the masses of all European races to the dust. They suffer every kind of oppression, and no one dares to open his mouth to protest against it. Even in the Southern portion of this boasted land of liberty, no white man dares advocate so much of the Declaration of Independence as declares that 'all men are created free and equal, and have an inalienable right to life, liberty,' &c.

White men have no room to taunt us with tamely submitting. If they were black men, they would work wonders; but, as white men, they can do nothing. 'O, Consistency, thou art a jewel!'

Now, it would not be surprising if the brutal treatment which we have received for the past two centuries should have crushed our spirits. But this is not the case. Nothing but a superior force keeps us down. And when I see the slaves rising up by hundreds annually, in the majesty of human nature, bidding defiance to every slave code and its penalties, making the issue Canada or death, and that too while they are closely watched by paid men armed with pistols, clubs and bowie-knives, with the army and navy of this great Model Republic arrayed against them, I am disposed to ask if the charge of cowardice does not come with ill-grace.

But some men are so steeped in folly and imbecility; so lost to all feelings of their own littleness; so destitute of principle, and so regardless of humanity, that they dare attempt to destroy everything which exists in opposition to their interests or opinions which their narrow comprehensions cannot grasp.

We ought not to come here simply to honor those brave men who shed their blood for freedom, or to protest against the Dred Scott decision, but to take counsel of each other, and to enter into new vows of duty. Our fathers fought nobly for freedom, but they were not victorious. They fought for liberty, but they got slavery. The white man was benefitted, but the black man was injured. I do not envy the white American the little liberty which he enjoys. It is his right, and he ought to have it. I wish him success, though I do not think he deserves it. But I would have all men free. We have had much sad experience in this country, and it would be strange indeed if we do not profit by some of the lessons which we have so dearly paid for. Sooner or later, the clashing of arms will be heard in this country, and the black man's services will be needed: 150,000 freemen capable of bearing arms, and not all cowards and fools, and three quarters of a million slaves, wild with the enthusiasm caused by the dawn of the glorious opportunity of being able to strike a genuine blow for freedom, will be a power which white men will be "bound to respect." Will the blacks fight? Of course they will. The black man will never be neutral. He could not if he would, and he would not if he could. Will he fight for this country, right or wrong? This the common sense of every one answers; and when the time comes, and come it will, the black man will give an intelligent answer. Judge Taney may outlaw us; Caleb Cushing may show the depravity of his heart by abusing us; and this wicked government may oppress us; but the black man will live when Judge Taney, Caleb Cushing and this wicked government are no more. White man may despise, ridicule, slander and abuse us; they may seek as they always have done to divide us, and make us feel degraded; but no man shall cause me to turn my back upon my race. With it I will sink or swim.

The prejudice which some white men have, or affected to have, against my color gives me no pain. If any man does not fancy my color, that is his business, and I shall not meddle with it. I shall give myself no trouble because he lacks good taste. If he judges my intellectual capacity by my color, he certainly cannot expect much profundity, for it is only skin deep, and is really of no very great importance to any one but myself. I will not deny that I admire the talents and noble characters of many white men. But I cannot say that I am particularly pleased with their physical appearance. If old mother nature had held out as well as she commenced, we should, probably, have had fewer varieties in the races. When I contrast the fine tough muscular system, the beautiful, rich color, the full broad features, and the gracefully frizzled hair of the Negro, with the delicate physical organization, wan color, sharp features and lank hair of the Caucasian, I am inclined to believe that when the white man was created, nature was pretty well exhausted—but determined to keep up appearances, she pinched up his features, and did the best she could under the circumstances. (Great laughter.)

I would have you understand, that I not only love my race, but am pleased with my color; and while many colored persons may feel degraded by being called negroes, and wish to be classed among other races more favored, I shall feel it my duty, my pleasure and my pride, to concentrate my feeble efforts in elevating to a fair position a race to which I am especially identified by feelings and by blood.

My friends, we can never become elevated until we are true to ourselves. We can come here and make brilliant speeches, but our field of duty is elsewhere. Let us go to work—each man in his place, determined to do what he can for himself and his race. Let us try to carry out some of the resolutions which we have made, and are so fond of making. If we do this, friends will spring up in every quarter, and where we least expect them. But we must not rely on them. They cannot elevate us. Whenever the colored man is elevated, it will be by his own exertions. Our friends can do what many of them are nobly doing, assist us to remove the obstacles which prevent our elevation, and stimulate the worthy to persevere. The colored man who, by dint of perseverance and industry, educates and elevates himself, prepares the way for others, gives character to the race, and hastens the day of general emancipation. While the negro who hangs around the corners of the streets, or lives in the grog-shops or by gambling, or who has no higher ambition than to serve, is by his vocation forging fetters for the slave, and is 'to all intents and purposes' a curse to his race. It is true, considering the circumstances under which we have been placed by our white neighbors, we have a right to ask them not only to cease to oppress us, but to give us that encouragement which our talents and industry may merit. When this is done, they will see our minds expand, and our pockets filled with rocks. How very few colored men are encouraged in their trades or business! Our young men see this, and become disheartened. In this country, where money is the great sympathetic nerve which ramifies society, and has a ganglia in every man's pocket, a man is respected in proportion to his success in business. When the avenues to wealth are opened to us, we will then become educated and wealthy, and then the roughest looking colored man that you ever saw, or ever will see, will be pleasanter than the harmonies of Orpheus, and black will be a very pretty color. It will make our jargon, wit—our words, oracles; flattery will then take the place of slander, and you will find no prejudice in the Yankee whatever. We do not expect to occupy a much better position than we now do, until we shall have our educated and wealthy men, who can wield a power that cannot be misunderstood. Then, and not till then, will the tongue of slander be silenced, and the lip of prejudice sealed. Then, and not till then, will we be able to enjoy true equality, which can exist only among peers.

Source: Speech from *The Liberator*, March 12, 1858.

SELECT BIBLIOGRAPHY:

J. Harlan Buzby, *John Stewart Rock: Teacher, Healer, Counselor* (Salem: Salem County Historical Society, 2002).

George S. Levesque, "Boston's Black Brahmin: Dr. John S. Rock," *Civil War History* 26, no. 4 (1980), pp. 326–46.

Benjamin Quarles, *The Black Abolitionists* (New York: Oxford University Press, 1969).

Paul E. Teed, "Racial Nationalism and Its Challengers: Theodore Parker, John Rock, and the Antislavery Movement," *Civil War History* 41, no. 2 (1995), pp. 142–60.

Louise Tompkins Wright, "The Civil Rights Activities of Three Great Negro Physicians (1840–1940)," *Journal of Negro History* 52, no. 3 (1967), pp. 169–84.

〜 21 〜

The Spirituals: "Go Down, Moses" and "Didn't My Lord Deliver Daniel"

Throughout the African-American experience, spirituality has been a source for human renewal, survival, and resistance. The meaning of faith in the black mind in slavery was a rock upon which the oppressed could find human dignity and hope for the future. The slaves logically interpreted the stories of the Old Testament in the context of their own collective suffering. They came to believe that their faith in God and themselves would create a path leading eventually toward freedom. Many historians have observed that the same spirituals contained hidden meanings or messages that could serve as a coded language, communicating information among slaves without the knowledge of overseers and masters. The themes of suffering and struggle, faith and transcendence, are all pivotal in the development of the African-American spirituals.

〜

"Go Down, Moses"

> Go down, Moses,
> 'Way down in Egypt land,
> Tell ole Pharaoh,
> To let my people go.
> Go down, Moses,

'Way down in Egypt land,
Tell ole Pharaoh,
To let my people go.

When Israel was in Egypt land,
Let my people go,
Oppressed so hard they could not stand,
Let my people go,

Thus spoke the Lord, bold Moses said,
Let my people go,
If not I'll smite your first-born dead,
Let my people go.

Go down, Moses,
'Way down in Egypt land,
Tell ole Pharaoh,
To let my people go.

"Didn't My Lord Deliver Daniel"

Didn't my Lord deliver Daniel,
deliver Daniel, deliver Daniel,
Didn't my Lord deliver Daniel,
An' why not every man.

He delivered Daniel from the lion's den,
Jonah from the belly of the whale,
An' the Hebrew chillun from the fiery furnace,
An' why not every man.

Didn't my Lord deliver Daniel,
deliver Daniel, deliver Daniel,
Didn't my Lord deliver Daniel,
An' why not every man.

The moon run down in a purple stream,
The sun forbear to shine,
An' every star disappear,
King Jesus shall-a be mine.

The win' blows eas' an' the win' blows wes',
It blows like the judg-a-ment day,
An' ev'ry po' soul that never did pray'll
Be glad to pray that day.

Didn't my Lord deliver Daniel,
deliver Daniel, deliver Daniel,

Didn't my Lord deliver Daniel,
An' why not every man.

Source: Traditional spirituals.

SELECT BIBLIOGRAPHY:

William Francis Allen, *Slave Songs of the United States* (New York: Dover, 1995).

Richard Newman, *Go Down Moses: A Celebration of the African-Spiritual* (New York: Clarkson Potter, 1998).

Erskine Peters, ed., *Lyrics of the Afro-American Spiritual* (Westport, Conn.: Greenwood Press, 1993).

Albert J. Raboteau, *Slave Religion: The "Invisible Institution" in the Antebellum South* (New York: Oxford University Press, 1978).

ADDITIONAL RESOURCES:

Ed Bell and Thomas Lennon, *Unchained Memories: Readings from the Slave Narratives*: HBO Documentary Films, 2003. DVD Video.

Ira Berlin, *Generations of Captivity: A History of African-American Slaves* (Cambridge, Mass.; London: Belknap, 2004).

———, *Slaves without Masters: The Free Negro in the Antebellum South* (New York: New Press, 2007).

Sylvia R. Frey, *Water from the Rock: Black Resistance in a Revolutionary Age* (Princeton: Princeton University Press, 1991).

Library of Congress, "Voices from the Days of Slavery," http://memory.loc.gov/ammem /collections/voices/.

Jennifer L. Morgan, *Laboring Women: Reproduction and Gender in New World Slavery* (Philadelphia: University of Pennsylvania Press, 2004).

James Oliver Horton and Lois E. Horton, *In Hope of Liberty: Culture, Community and Protest among Northern Free Blacks, 1700–1860* (New York: Oxford University Press, 1998).

PBS, "The Africans in America Web Site," www.pbs.org/wgbh/aia/home.html.

———, "Slavery and the Making of America" http://www.pbs.org/wnet/slavery/index.html.

"Race and Slavery Petition Project," library.uncg.edu/slavery_petitions/index.asp.

"Recovered Histories: Reawakening the Narratives of Enslavement, Resistance and the Fight for Freedom," www.recoveredhistories.org/index.php.

"Suolair—Africa South of the Sahara," www-sul.stanford.edu/depts/ssrg/africa/history/ hislavery.html.

Deborah G. White, *Ar'n't I a Woman?: Female Slaves in the Plantation South*, rev. ed. (New York: W. W. Norton, 1999).

RECONSTRUCTION AND REACTION: THE AFTERMATH OF SLAVERY AND THE DAWN OF SEGREGATION, 1861–1915

INTRODUCTION

The human toll exacted by the Civil War was, by any standard, enormous. Over 600,000 Americans were killed in combat; and there was the destruction of property that would today be equivalent to billions of dollars. Most white Northerners fought the war, as Lincoln insisted, "to preserve the Union," rather than to extend full equality to the Negro. But once slavery had been destroyed, black people had no intention of being confined to a social and political status of permanent servitude. Even before the military conflict ended, black leaders were pressuring the government to go well beyond the Emancipation Proclamation, to full voting rights and political representation for black men. As Douglass warned in 1865 (document 1), "if abolitionists fail to press it [black male suffrage] now, we may not see, for centuries to come, the same disposition that exists at this moment." Once the right to vote was guaranteed, Douglass believed that black men could be expected to compete fairly within society. "What I ask for the Negro is not benevolence, not pity, not sympathy, but simply justice," Douglass emphasized. "If you will only untie his hands, and give him a chance . . . he will work as readily for himself as the white man."

The essence of Reconstruction was a concerted effort by African Americans and their white allies to extend the principles of democratic government to black people, and to give them, at the minimum, the basic educational skills and economic resources necessary for their future development. For more than two decades, African Americans fought vigorously in southern state legislatures and in the U.S. Congress for the legal protections they needed to preserve their newly won freedom. Yet in pursuing these objectives, the majority of black leaders did not seek to achieve an economic revolution. They respected the rights of private property, and sought opportunity rather than redistribution. One typical example of this moderate perspective is the 1868 speech of Henry McNeal Turner, given just before he and other black elected officials were expelled from the Georgia state legislature by racist whites: "We have built up your country; we have worked in your fields, and garnered your harvests, for two hundred and fifty years!" Turner declared. "And what do we ask of you in return? Do we ask you for compensation for the sweat our fathers bore for you—for the tears you have caused, and the hearts you have broken, and the lives you have curtailed, and the blood you have spilled? We ask it not. We are willing to let the dead past bury its dead, but we ask you now for our RIGHTS" (document 2).

Despite the efforts of black reformers, the Compromise of 1877 and the withdrawal of federal troops from the South effectively ended the gains of Reconstruction. For the next quarter-century, African Americans experienced the steady erosion of their political and civil rights, gradually usurped by state legislatures, courts, and law enforcement agencies. Mississippi led the way in 1890 with the adoption of its white-supremacist state constitution, largely excluding black males from voting. By 1904, all other southern states had also held new racist constitutional conventions or had adopted restrictive legislation, such as "Grandfather clauses" or all-white primary elections. Blacks were soon eliminated from state legislatures, and were ejected from the U.S. Congress by 1901. Economically, millions of poor southern blacks were trapped in sharecropping, a system structured to ensure that they provided cheap agricultural labor for the benefit of white landlords. The sharecropping system often degenerated into debt peonage, in which black families would be permanently indentured to their landlords through financial obligation, creating conditions barely different from enslavement. Throughout the South, blacks began to be excluded from all public accommodations, denied access to schools and other essential services, and restricted from living in certain residential areas. Thousands of skilled black workers—plumbers, carpenters, brick masons, mechanics—lost their jobs when these vocations were redefined as "white men's work." Essential to the racist assault against black people's rights was lynching. Thousands of African Americans were executed without trials, convictions, or, sometimes, even accusations of having committed crimes; many were mutilated and sometimes even burned at the stake. It was as if white America had turned viciously against black interests in every quarter.

During this reactionary period, black leaders were forced to rethink their political and social agendas. If racial integration was out of the question, how could the black community empower itself or even survive in a hostile white environment? One widespread response was the rebirth of black nationalism: the ideas of racial uplift, self-help, and black cultural pride that were embedded in the ideology of earlier nationalists such as Delany. Many African-American leaders could see progress only in the repatriation of blacks to the African continent. Two such leaders were Edward Wilmot Blyden and Alexander Crummell. Blyden was in many respects the first authentic "Pan-Africanist," espousing the goals of West African political unity and the migration of blacks from the Caribbean and the Americas to Africa (document 5). Crummell was a noted Episcopalian minister who had lived and worked in Liberia for twenty years, and whose appeals to the cultivation of "the Negro intellect" prefigured W. E. B. Du Bois's theory of the "Talented Tenth" (document 6).

The central African-American leader during this period was Booker T. Washington. A profoundly pragmatic man, Washington cautioned blacks against protesting segregation and disenfranchisement. In exchange for accepting white supremacy, Washington sought the public space to develop black-owned businesses, banks, and other enterprises. He astutely realized that racial segregation would, in this context, be beneficial, as it would create a black consumer market for black businesses. Washington's conservative ideas gained widespread acceptance through his control of several major black newspapers, his influence in black churches, and his founding of the Tuskegee Institute in 1881—an institution dedicated to industrial and agricultural training for African Americans. As Washington declared in his Atlanta Exposition address in 1895: "In all things that are purely social we can be as separate as the fingers, yet one as the hand in all things essential to mutual progress. . . . The wisest among my race understand that the agitation of questions of social equality is the extremist folly, and that progress in the enjoyment of all privileges that will come to us must be the result of severe and constant struggle rather than artificial forcing" (document 10).

Washington's policies of racial self-help and political accommodation were criticized by a number of black intellectuals, journalists, and political leaders. The crusading journalist and newspaper editor Ida B. Wells-Barnett wrote exposés documenting the crime of lynching across the South. In her essay included here (document 13), Wells-Barnett calls for federal anti-lynching legislation. William Monroe Trotter, editor of the *Boston Guardian*, repeatedly denounced Washington as "this Benedict Arnold of the Negro race" (document 11). Du Bois was slowly drawn into the public struggle against Washington's influence, but never attacked him with the angry rhetoric of Trotter. Indeed, it was Du Bois's more nuanced and measured criticism of the Tuskegee philosophy of accommodation that won him significant support. Du Bois's central argument against Washington was threefold: first, economic power did not translate directly or even necessarily into political power, and black-owned businesses and farms, while necessary, would always be vulnerable to white authority in a rigidly segregated society; second, that a political movement had to be constructed to challenge the legitimacy and legality of Jim Crow; and third, that a liberal-arts–educated black middle class, the "Talented Tenth," should be the vanguard in the struggle to achieve a genuinely multiracial democracy (document 14).

Many critics of Washington, including Du Bois, came together in 1905 to initiate the Niagara Movement, a group of several hundred intellectuals, clergymen, journalists, and lawyers who opposed accommodation and Jim Crow segregation. The Declaration of Principles of the Niagara Movement presented a striking alternative to the Tuskegee philosophy: "We believe in manhood suffrage; we believe that no man is so good, intelligent, or wealthy as to be entrusted wholly with the welfare of his neighbor. . . . All American citizens have the right to equal treatment in places of public entertainment. . . . We demand upright judges in courts, juries selected without discrimination on account of color, and the same measure of punishment and the same efforts of reformation for black as for white offenders. . . . Any discrimination based simply on race or color is barbarous, we care not how hallowed it be by custom, expediency, or prejudice" (document 15). The Niagara Movement never succeeded in offering more than token opposition to Washington's political organization, the "Tuskegee Machine." Yet within five years the Niagara Movement would help set into motion another reform organization coalesced around a similarly liberal racial program—the National Association for the Advancement of Colored People (NAACP).

Although the period between the demise of Reconstruction and World War I has often been characterized in African-American historiography by the conflict between Washington and Du Bois, there were many significant social movements and cultural currents that existed outside this debate. Both Washington and Du Bois were in certain respects trapped in a racial discourse, and conceived of their politics in racial categories. Washington had reluctantly accepted the reality of racial segregation and worked to maneuver around it. Du Bois rejected Jim Crow, but sought to supersede race by dismantling its legal and social structures of inequality. Like Douglass before them, both men were largely engaged in a political discourse with sections of the white establishment: Washington appealed to the Republican Party, philanthropists, and industrialists, while Du Bois sought the support of white reformers, liberals, and the intelligentsia. Well before 1900, however, the objective conditions existed for a different kind of black politics that was grounded not solely in racial terminologies and categories, but in the language of gender and class.

African-American middle-class women had been active for decades in both the antislavery movement and the struggle for women's equality. In the years immediately after Reconstruction, black women leaders began to establish local associations promoting racial uplift and women's rights as well as addressing the negative representations of black women that rationalized their exploitation. In 1894, Josephine St. Pierre Ruffin organized the Women's Era Club, bringing together sixty prominent blacks in the Boston area. Mary Church Terrell helped form the Colored Women's League in Washington, D.C., and was the central leader in bringing together black women's groups from all over the country to establish the National Association of Colored Women in 1896. Margaret Murray Washington (the wife of Booker T. Washington) and Terrell served, respectively, as president and second vice president of the International Council of Women of the Darker Races in the 1920s. In her 1904 speech cited here (document 8), Terrell eloquently makes the case for a politics based on gender emancipation as well as race: "Not only are colored women with ambition and aspiration handicapped on account of their sex, but they are almost everywhere baffled and mocked because of their race. Not only because they are women, but because they are colored women are discouragement and disappointment meeting them at every turn. . . . [Yet] with tireless energy and eager zeal, colored women have worked in every conceivable way to elevate their race." Black women were in the forefront of struggles to halt the convict-leasing system and the petitioning of southern legislatures to repeal "the obnoxious Jim-Crow-car laws." Through these and other organized efforts, "colored women who are working for the emancipation and elevation of their race know where their duty lies."

One of the most significant black intellectuals of this period was Anna Julia Cooper. Her 1892 book, *A Voice from the South*, could be described as the first text of African-American feminist thought. Cooper writes (document 7):

The colored woman of today occupies, one may say, a unique position in the country. In a period of itself transitional and unsettled, her status seems one of the least ascertainable and definitive of all forces which make for our civilization. She is confronted by both a woman question and a race problem, and is as yet an unknown or an unacknowledged factor in both. . . . But no woman can possibly put herself or her sex outside any of the interests that affect humanity. All departments in the new era are to be hers, in the sense that her interests are in all and through all; and it is incumbent on her to keep intelligently and sympathetically en rapport with all the great movements of her time, that she may know on which side to throw the weight of her influence. . . . To be a woman in such an age carries with it a privilege and an opportunity never implied before. But to be a woman of the Negro race in America, and to be able to grasp the deep significance of the possibilities of the crisis, is to have a heritage . . . unique in the ages.

In her extraordinary public career, Cooper was the only woman to be selected for membership in the American Negro Academy, the first black intellectual society, established in 1897 by Crummell. She was only one of two black women to speak at the first Pan-African Conference held in London in 1900, giving a presentation on "The Negro Problem in America." In 1925, Cooper became the fourth African-American woman to receive a doctorate degree.

During this period, African-American workers began to create their own organizations to fight for increased wages and improved working conditions. They were confronted with blatant racial discrimination in hiring policies and in union membership. Nevertheless, a growing number of black working women and men began defining their political interests in terms of class as much as in terms of race. In 1869, the Colored National Labor Union, a precursor to other black labor formations, was formed in Washington, D.C. In this section, we have included "The Race Question a Class Question," first published in the journal *The Worker* in October 1904 (document 12), which makes a frank appeal to African Americans to join workers' movements: "It is part of the instinctive policy of the capital class to perpetuate itself by creating and playing upon race hatred in order to keep working men of all races and nationalities from uniting to overthrow the infamous industrial system by which the capitalists profit." The document issued in 1912 by the Brotherhood of Timber Workers in Alexandria, Louisiana, exhorts black laborers to join with white workers to help "blaze freedom's pathway through the jungles of the South." White Supremacy was an empty slogan to impoverished white workers, meaning "starvation wages and child slavery . . . the supremacy of misery and the equality of rags." Black and white unity was thought to be essential for the empowerment of the entire working class: "Workers of the world, unite! You have nothing but your chains to lose! You have a world to gain!"

The socialist-inspired appeals of white workers' movements frequently underestimated the significance of racism as a barrier to constructing multiracial trade unions. Although some black workers, intellectuals, and journalists such as T. Thomas Fortune (document 4) were attracted to socialism, many were wary of the racism of white workers and the racially exclusionary policies of the trade unions. In 1904, Du Bois declared himself a "socialist-of-the-path" and in 1911 joined the Socialist Party, but left it a year later. One of the first African-American radicals who tried to bridge the political divide between race-conscious protest and the class struggle of the workers' movements was Hubert Henry Harrison. Harrison recognized that "the great labor problem with which all working people are faced is made harder for black working people by the addition of a race problem." But in reality, one problem "grows out of the other. . . . It pays the capitalist to keep the workers divided. So he creates and keeps alive these prejudices. He gets them to believe that their interests are different" (document 16). But eventually, Harrison concluded that racism was so strong within the white left and labor movement that it was necessary for the African Americans to develop their own race-based protest organizations. This led Harrison to support the black nationalist movement of Marcus Garvey, and he served for a time as editor of Garvey's publication, *The Negro World*.

The boundaries of blackness still largely set the parameters for social and political thought within the African-American community. The omnipresence of segregation and the racialization of nearly every aspect of public life forced the vast majority of black people to frame their political ideas and practices in reference to the racial state, either by accommodating to it, as counseled by Washington, or demanding reforms within it, as pursued by Du Bois. But a new politics, based on gender and class, also found a small yet growing constituency in black America. But as long as Jim Crow was hegemonic within U.S. society, the political discourse of black America would continue to be articulated through the context of race.

⇌ 1 ⇌

"What the Black Man Wants," *Frederick Douglass, 1865*

By the end of the Civil War, Douglass had become the most influential spokesperson for African Americans' rights. In this address, Douglass attempts to identify some of the major issues and objectives for the black community in the aftermath of slavery's demise. He puts forward a radical democratic program of black empowerment that unfortunately was never achieved during the Reconstruction period.

⇌

I came here, as I come always to the meetings in New England, as a listener, and not as a speaker; and one of the reasons why I have not been more frequently to the meetings of this society, has been because of the disposition on the part of some of my friends to call me out upon the platform, even when they knew that there was some difference of opinion and of feeling between those who rightfully belong to this platform and myself; and for fear of being misconstrued, as desiring to interrupt or disturb the proceedings of these meetings, I have usually kept away, and have thus been deprived of that educating influence, which I am always free to confess is of the highest order, descending from this platform. I have felt, since I have lived out West, that in going there I parted from a great deal that was valuable; and I feel, every time I come to these meetings, that I have lost a great deal by making my home west of Boston, west of Massachusetts; for, if anywhere in the country there is to be found the highest sense of justice, or the truest demands for my race, I look for it in the East, I look for it here. The ablest discussions of the whole question of our rights occur here, and to be deprived of the privilege of listening to those discussions is a great deprivation.

I do not know, from what has been said, that there is any difference of opinion as to the duty of abolitionists, at the present moment. How can we get up any difference at this point, or any point, where we are so united, so agreed? I went especially, however, with that word of Mr. Phillips, which is the criticism of Gen. Banks and Gen. Banks' policy. I hold that that policy is our chief danger at the present moment; that it practically enslaves the Negro, and makes the Proclamation of 1863 a mockery and delusion. What is freedom? It is the right to choose one's own employment. Certainly it means that, if it means anything; and when any individual or combination of individuals undertakes to decide for any man when he shall work, where he shall work, at what he shall work, and for what he shall work, he or they practically reduce him to slavery. He is a slave. That I understand Gen. Banks to do—to determine for the so-called freedman, when, and where, and at what, and for how much he shall work, when he shall be punished, and by whom punished. It is absolute slavery. It defeats the beneficent intention of the Government, if it has beneficent intentions, in regards to the freedom of our people.

I have had but one idea for the last three years to present to the American people, and the phraseology in which I clothe it is the old abolition phraseology. I am for the "immediate, unconditional, and universal" enfranchisement of the black man, in every State in the Union. Without this, his liberty is a mockery; without this, you might as well almost retain the old name of slavery for his condition; for in fact, if he is not the slave of the individual master, he is the slave of society, and holds his liberty as a privilege, not as a right. He is at the mercy of the mob, and has no means of protecting himself.

It may be objected, however, that this pressing of the Negro's right to suffrage is premature. Let us have slavery abolished, it may be said, let us have labor organized, and then, in the natural course of events, the right of suffrage will be extended to the Negro. I do not agree with this. The constitution of the human mind is such, that if it once disregards the conviction forced upon it by a revelation of truth, it requires the exercise of a higher power to produce the same conviction afterwards. The American people are now in tears. The Shenandoah has run blood—the best blood of the North. All around Richmond, the blood of New England and of the North has been shed—of your sons, your brothers and your fathers. We all feel, in the existence of this Rebellion, that judgments terrible, wide-spread, far-reaching, overwhelming, are abroad in the land; and we feel, in view of these judgments, just now, a disposition to learn righteousness. This is the hour. Our streets are in mourning, tears are falling at every fireside, and under the chastisement of this Rebellion we have almost come up to the point of conceding this great, this all-important right of suffrage. I fear that if we fail to do it now, if abolitionists fail to press it now, we may not see, for centuries to come, the same disposition that exists at this moment. Hence, I say, now is the time to press this right.

It may be asked, "Why do you want it? Some men have got along very well without it. Women have not this right." Shall we justify one wrong by another? This is a sufficient answer. Shall we at this moment justify the deprivation of the Negro of the right to vote, because some one else is deprived of that privilege? I hold that women, as well as men, have the right to vote, and my heart and my voice go with the movement to extend suffrage to woman; but that question rests upon another basis than that on which our right rests. We may be asked, I say, why we want it. I will tell you why we want it. We want it because it is our *right*, first of all. No class of men can, without insulting their own nature, be content with any deprivation of their rights. We want it again, as a means for educating our race. Men are so constituted that they derive their conviction of their own possibilities largely from the estimate formed of them by others. If nothing is expected of a people, that people will find it difficult to contradict that expectation. By depriving us of suffrage, you affirm our incapacity to form an intelligent judgment respecting public men and public measures; you declare before the world that we are unfit to exercise the elective franchise, and by this means lead us to undervalue ourselves, to put a low estimate upon ourselves, and to feel that we have no possibilities like other men. Again, I want the elective franchise, for one, as a colored man, because ours is a peculiar government, based upon a peculiar idea, and that idea is universal suffrage. If I were in a monarchial government, or an autocratic or aristocratic government, where the few bore rule and the many were subject, there would be no special stigma resting upon me, because I did not exercise the elective franchise. It would do me no great violence. Mingling with the mass I should partake of the strength of the mass; I should be supported by the mass, and I should have the same incentives to endeavor with the mass of my fellow-men; it would be no particular burden, no particular deprivation; but here where universal suffrage is the rule, where that is the fundamental idea of the Government, to rule us out is to make us an exception, to brand us with the stigma of inferiority, and to invite to our heads the missiles of those about us; therefore, I want the franchise for the black man.

There are, however, other reasons, not derived from any consideration merely of our rights, but arising out of the conditions of the South, and of the country—considerations which have already been referred to by Mr. Phillips—considerations which must arrest the attention of statesmen. I believe that when the tall heads of this Rebellion shall have been swept down, as they will be swept down, when the Davises and Toombses and Stephenses, and others who are leading this Rebellion shall have been blotted out, there will be this rank undergrowth of treason, to which reference has been made, growing up there, and interfering with, and thwarting the quiet operation of the Federal Government in those States. You will see those traitors, handing down, from sire to son, the same malignant spirit which they have manifested, and which they are now exhibiting, with malicious hearts, broad blades, and bloody hands in the field, against our sons and brothers. That spirit will still remain; and whoever sees the Federal Government extended over those Southern States will see that Government in a strange land, and not only in a strange land, but in an enemy's land. A post-master of the United States in the South will find himself surrounded by a hostile spirit; a collector in a Southern port will find himself surrounded by a hostile spirit; a United States marshal or United States judge will be surrounded there by a hostile element. That enmity will not die out in a year, will not die out in an age. The Federal Government will be looked upon in those States precisely as the Governments of Austria and France are looked upon in Italy at the present moment. They will endeavor to circumvent, they will endeavor to destroy, the peaceful operation of this Government. Now, where will you find the strength to counterbalance this spirit, if you do not find it in the Negroes of the South? They are your friends, and have always been your friends. They were your friends even when the Government did not regard them as such. They comprehended the genius of this war before you did. It is a significant fact, it is a marvellous fact, it seems almost to imply a direct interposition of Providence, that this war, which began in the interest of slavery on both sides, bids fair to end in the interest of liberty on both sides. It was begun, I say, in the interest of slavery on both sides. The South was fighting to take slavery out of the Union, and the North fighting to keep it in the Union; the South fighting to get it beyond the limits of the United States Constitution, and the North fighting to retain it within those limits; the South fighting for new guarantees, and the North fighting for the old guarantees;—both despising the Negro, both insulting the Negro. Yet, the Negro, apparently endowed with wisdom from on high, saw more clearly the end from the beginning than we did. When Seward said the status of no man in the country would be changed by the war, the Negro did not believe him. When our generals sent their underlings in shoulder-straps to hunt the flying Negro back from our lines into the jaws of slavery, from which he had escaped, the Negroes thought that a mistake had been made, and that the intentions of the Government had not been rightly understood by our officers in shoulder-straps, and they continued to come into our lines, threading their way through bogs and fens, over briers and thorns, fording streams, swimming rivers, bringing us tidings as to the safe path to march, and pointing out the dangers that threatened us. They are our only friends in the South, and we should be true to them in this their trial hour, and see to it that they have the elective franchise.

I know that we are inferior to you in some things—virtually inferior. We walk about among you like dwarfs among giants. Our heads are scarcely seen above the great sea of humanity. The Germans are superior to us; the Irish are superior to us; the Yankees are superior to us; they can do what we cannot, that is, what we have not hitherto been allowed to do. But while I make this admission, I utterly deny, that we are originally, or naturally, or practically, or in any way, or in any important sense, inferior to anybody on this globe. This charge of inferiority is an old dodge. It has been made available for oppression on many occasions. It is only about six centuries since the blue-eyed and fair-haired Anglo-Saxons were considered inferior by the haughty Normans, who once trampled upon them. If you read the history of the Norman Conquest, you will find that this proud Anglo-Saxon was once looked upon as of coarser clay than his Norman master, and might be found in the highways and byways of old England laboring with a brass collar on his neck, and the name of his master marked upon it. *You* were down then! You are up now. I am glad you are up, and I want you to be glad to help us up also.

The story of our inferiority is an old dodge, as I have said; for wherever men oppress their fellows, wherever they enslave them, they will endeavor to find the needed apology for such enslavement and oppression in the character of the people oppressed and enslaved. When we wanted, a few years ago, a slice of Mexico, it was hinted that the Mexicans were an inferior race, that the old Castilian blood had become so weak that it would scarcely run down hill, and that Mexico needed the long, strong and beneficent arm of the Anglo-Saxon care extended over it. We said that it was necessary to its salvation, and a part of the "manifest destiny" of this Republic, to extend our arm over that dilapidated government. So, too, when Russia wanted to take possession of a part of the Ottoman Empire, the Turks were "an inferior race." So, too, when England wants to set the heel of her power more firmly in the quivering heart of old Ireland, the Celts are an "inferior race." So, too, the Negro, when he is to be robbed of any right which is justly his, is an "inferior man." It is said that we are ignorant; I admit it. But if we know enough to be hung, we know enough to vote. If the Negro knows enough to pay taxes to support the government, he knows enough to vote; taxation and representation should go together. If he knows enough to shoulder a musket and fight for the flag, fight for the government, he knows enough to vote. If he knows as much when he is sober as an Irishman knows when drunk, he knows enough to vote, on good American principles.

But I was saying that you needed a counterpoise in the persons of the slaves to the enmity that would exist at the South after the Rebellion is put down. I hold that the American people are bound, not only in self-defence, to extend this right to the freedmen of the South, but they are bound by their love of country, and by all their regard for the future safety of those Southern States, to do this—to do it as a measure essential to the preservation of peace there. But I will not dwell upon this. I put it to the American sense of honor. The honor of a nation is an important thing. It is said in the Scriptures, "What doth it profit a man if he gain the whole world, and lose his own soul?" It may be said, also, What doth it profit a nation if it gain the whole world, but lose its honor? I hold that the American government has taken upon itself a solemn obligation of honor, to see that this war—let it be long or let it be short, let it cost much or let it cost little—that this war shall not cease until every freedman at the South has the right to vote. It has bound itself to it. What have you asked the black men of the South, the black men of the whole country, to do? Why, you have asked them to incur the deadly enmity of their masters, in order to befriend you and to befriend this Government. You have asked us to call down, not only upon ourselves, but upon our children's children, the deadly hate of the entire Southern people. You have called upon us to turn our backs upon our masters, to abandon their cause and espouse yours; to turn against the South and in favor of the North; to shoot down the Confederacy and uphold the flag—the American flag. You have called upon us to expose ourselves to all the subtle machinations of their malignity for all time. And now, what do you propose to do when you come to make peace? To reward your enemies, and trample in the dust your friends? Do you intend to sacrifice the very men who have come to the rescue of your banner in the South, and incurred the lasting displeasure of their masters thereby? Do you intend to sacrifice them and reward your enemies? Do you mean to give your enemies the right to vote, and take it away from your friends? Is that wise policy? Is that honorable? Could American honor withstand such a blow? I do not believe you will do it. I think you will see to it that we have the right to vote. There is something too mean in looking upon the Negro, when you are in trouble, as a citizen, and when you are free from trouble, as an alien. When this nation was in trouble, in its early struggles, it looked upon the Negro as a citizen. In 1776 he was a citizen. At the time of the formation of the Constitution the Negro had the right to vote in eleven States out of the old thirteen. In your trouble you have made us citizens. In 1812 Gen. Jackson addressed us as citizens—"fellow-citizens." He wanted us to fight. We were citizens then! And now, when you come to frame a conscription bill, the Negro is a citizen again. He has been a citizen just three times in the history of this government, and it has always been in time of trouble. In time of trouble we are citizens. Shall we be citizens in war, and aliens in peace? Would that be just?

I ask my friends who are apologizing for not insisting upon this right, where can the black man look, in this country, for the assertion of his right, if he may not look to the Massachusetts Anti-Slavery Society? Where under the whole heavens can he look for sympathy, in asserting this right, if he may not look to this platform? Have you lifted us up to a certain height to see that we are men, and then are any disposed to leave us there, without seeing that we are put in possession of all our rights? We look naturally to this platform for the assertion of all our rights, and for this one especially. I understand the anti-slavery societies of this country to be based on two principles,—first, the freedom of the blacks of this country; and, second, the elevation of them. Let me not be misunderstood here. I am not asking for sympathy at the hands of abolitionists, sympathy at the hands of any. I think the American people are disposed often to be generous rather than just. I look over this country at the present time, and I see Educational Societies, Sanitary Commissions, Freedmen's Associations, and the like,—all very good: but in regard to the colored people there is always more that is benevolent, I perceive, than just, manifested towards us. What I ask for the Negro is not benevolence, not pity, not sympathy, but simply *justice*. The American people have always been anxious to know what they shall do with us. Gen. Banks was distressed with solicitude as to what he should do with the Negro. Everybody has asked the question, and they learned to ask it early of the abolitionists, "What shall we do with the Negro?" I have had but one answer from the beginning. Do nothing with us! Your doing with us has already played the mischief with us. Do nothing with us! If the apples will not remain on the tree of their own strength, if they are wormeaten at the core, if they are early ripe and disposed to fall, let them fall! I am not for tying or fastening them on the tree in any way, except by nature's plan, and if they will not stay there, let them fall. And if the Negro cannot stand on his own legs, let him fall also. All I ask is, give him a chance to stand on his own legs! Let him alone! If you see him on his way to school, let him alone, don't disturb him! If you see him going to the dinner-table at a hotel, let him go! If you see him going to the ballot-box, let him alone, don't disturb him! If you see him going into a work-shop, just let him alone,—your interference is doing him a positive injury. Gen. Banks' "preparation" is of a piece with this attempt to prop up the Negro. Let him fall if he cannot stand alone! If the Negro cannot live by the line of eternal justice, so beautifully pictured to you in the illustration used by Mr. Phillips, the fault will not be yours, it will be his who made the Negro, and established that line for his government. Let him live or die by that. If you will only untie his hands, and give him a chance, I think he will live. He will work as readily for himself as the white man. A great many delusions have been swept away by this war. One was, that the Negro would not work; he has proved his ability to work. Another was, that the Negro would not fight; that he possessed only the most sheepish attributes of humanity; was a perfect lamb, or an "Uncle Tom"; disposed to take off his coat whenever required, fold his hands, and be whipped by anybody who wanted to whip him. But the war has proved that there is a great deal of human nature in the Negro, and that "he will fight," as Mr. Quincy, our President, said, in earlier days than these, "when there is a reasonable probability of his whipping anybody."

Source: Excerpt from "What the Black Man Wants," speech delivered in 1865.

SELECT BIBLIOGRAPHY:
William Andrews, ed., *Critical Essays on Frederick Douglass* (Boston: G.K. Hall, 1991).
David W. Blight, *Frederick Douglass' Civil War: Keeping Faith in Jubilee* (Baton Rouge: Louisiana State University Press, 1989).
Eric J. Sundquist, ed., *Frederick Douglass: New Literary and Historical Essays* (Cambridge: Cambridge University Press, 1990).

～ 2 ～

Henry McNeal Turner, Black Christian Nationalist

Henry McNeal Turner (1834–1915) was born near Abbeville, South Carolina, the son of free black parents. His father died when he was young, and he was forced to work picking cotton with slaves. After running away from home as a teenager, Turner first found employment as an office boy in a law firm. In 1851 he became an itinerant minister in the Methodist Episcopal Church, and seven years later joined the African Methodist Episcopal (AME) Church. Turner's rise in the church was rapid. In 1862, he became pastor of the Union Bethel AME Church, the capital's largest African-American congregation. President Abraham Lincoln appointed Turner the first black U.S. army chaplain. Turner accompanied black troops into battle, and briefly served in the Freedman's Bureau. During Reconstruction, Turner was assigned to build the AME Church in Georgia. Elected to the Georgia constitutional convention in 1867, Turner quickly became a central figure in black politics in the state. After being elected to the Georgia state legislature in 1868, Turner and twenty-six other African Americans were expelled from office by racist white legislators. Moments before Turner led the black delegation from the capitol building in protest, he made the following address. In later life, Turner become an AME bishop in 1880, and the founder and first president of Morris Brown College in Atlanta in 1890. Traveling to Africa four times between 1891 and 1898, Turner became a noted proponent of black emigration to Africa. In 1906, Turner, W. E. B. Du Bois, and other black leaders established the Georgia Equal Rights Association.

Mr. Speaker:

Before proceeding to argue this question upon its intrinsic merits, I wish the members of this House to understand the position that I take. I hold that I am a member of this body. Therefore, sir, I shall neither fawn or cringe before any party, nor stoop to beg them for my rights. Some of my colored fellow members, in the course of their remarks, took occasion to appeal to the sympathies of Members on the opposite side, and to eulogize their character for magnanimity. It reminds me very much, sir, of slaves begging under the lash. I am here to demand my rights, and to hurl thunderbolts at the men who would dare to cross the threshold of my manhood. There is an old aphorism which says, "Fight the Devil with fire," and if I should observe the rule in this instance, I wish gentlemen to understand that it is but fighting them with their own weapon.

The scene presented in this House, to-day, is one unparalleled in the history of the world. From this day, back to the day when God breathed the breath of life into Adam, no analogy for it can be found. Never, in the history of the world, has a man been arraigned before a body clothed with legislative, judicial or executive functions, charged with the offence of being of a darker hue than his fellowmen. I know that questions have been before the Courts of this country, and of other countries, involving topics not altogether dissimilar to that which is being discussed here to-day. But, sir, never in all the history of the great nations of this world—never before—has a man been arraigned, charged with an offence committed by the God of Heaven Himself. Cases may be found where men have been deprived of their rights for crimes and misdemeanors; but it has remained for the

State of Georgia, in the very heart of the nineteenth century, to call a man before the bar, and there charge him with an act for which he is no more responsible than for the head which he carries upon his shoulders. The Anglo-Saxon race, sir, is a most surprising one. No man has ever been more deceived in that race than I have been for the last three weeks. I was not aware that there was in the character of that race so much cowardice, or so much pusillanimity. The treachery which has been exhibited in it by gentlemen belonging to that race has shaken my confidence in it more than anything that has come under my observation from the day of my birth.

What is the question at issue? Why, sir, this Assembly, to-day, is discussing and deliberating on a judgment; there is not a Cherubim that sits around God's eternal Throne, to-day, that would not tremble—even were an order issued by the Supreme God Himself—to come down here and sit in judgment on my manhood. Gentlemen may look at this question in whatever light they choose, and with just as much indifference as they may think proper to assume, but I tell you, sir, that this is a question which will not die to-day. This event shall be remembered by posterity for ages yet to come, and while the sun shall continue to climb the hills of heaven.

Whose Legislature is this? Is it a white man's Legislature, or is it a black man's Legislature? Who voted for a Constitutional Convention, in obedience to the mandate of the Congress of the United States? Who first rallied around the standard of Reconstruction? Who set the ball of loyalty rolling in the State of Georgia? And whose voice was heard on the hills and in the valleys of this State? It was the voice of the brawny-armed Negro, with the few humanitarian-hearted white men who came to our assistance. I claim the honor, sir, of having been the instrument of convincing hundreds—yea, thousands—of white men, that to reconstruct under the measures of the United States Congress was the safest and the best course for the interest of the State.

Let us look at some facts in connection with this matter. Did half the white men of Georgia vote for this Legislature? Did not the great bulk of them fight, with all their strength, the Constitution under which we are acting? And did they not fight against the organization of this Legislature? And further, sir, did they not vote against it? Yes, sir! And there are persons in this Legislature to-day, who are ready to spit their poison in my face, while they themselves opposed, with all their power, the ratification of this Constitution. They question my right to a seat in this body, to represent the people whose legal votes elected me. This objection, sir, is an unheard of monopoly of power. No analogy can be found for it, except it be the case of a man who should go into my house, take possession of my wife and children, and then tell me to walk out. I stand very much in the position of a criminal before your bar, because I dare to be the exponent of the views of those who sent me here. Or, in other words, we are told that if black men want to speak, they must speak through white trumpets; if black men want their sentiments expressed, they must be adulterated and sent through white messengers, who will quibble, and equivocate, and evade, as rapidly as the pendulum of a clock. If this be not done, then the black men have committed an outrage, and their

Representatives must be denied the right to represent their constituents.

The great question, sir, is this: Am I a man? If I am such, I claim the rights of a man. Am I not a man because I happen to be of a darker hue than honorable gentlemen around me? . . .

But Mr. Speaker, I do not regard this movement as a thrust at me, it is a thrust at the Bible—a thrust at the God of the Universe, for making a man and not finishing him; it is simply calling the Great Jehovah a fool. Why, sir, though we are not white, we have accomplished much. We have pioneered civilization here; we have built up your country; we have worked in your fields, and garnered your harvests, for two hundred and fifty years! And what do we ask of you in return? Do we ask you for compensation for the sweat our fathers bore for you—for the tears you have caused, and the hearts you have broken, and the lives you have curtailed, and the blood you have spilled? Do we ask retaliation? We ask it not. We are willing to let the dead past bury its dead; but we ask you now for our RIGHTS. You have all the elements of superiority upon your side; you have our money and your own; you have our education and your own; and you have your land and our own, too. We, who number hundreds of thousands in Georgia, including our wives and families, with not a foot of land to call our own— strangers in the land of our birth; without money, without education, without aid, without a roof to cover us while we live, nor sufficient clay to cover us when we die! It is extraordinary that a race such as yours, professing gallantry, and chivalry, and education, and superiority, living in a land where ringing chimes call child and sire to the Church of God—a land where Bibles are read and Gospels truths are spoken, and where courts of justice are presumed to exist; it is extraordinary to say, that, with all these advantages on your side, you can make war upon the poor defenseless black man. . . .

You may expel us, gentlemen, but I firmly believe that you will someday repent it. The black man cannot protect a country, if the country doesn't protect him; and if, tomorrow, a war should arise, I would not raise a musket to defend a country where my manhood is denied. The fashionable way in Georgia when hard work is to be done, is, for the white man to sit at his ease, while the black man does the work; but, sir, I will say this much to the colored men of Georgia, as if I should be killed in this campaign, I may have no opportunity of telling them at any other time: Never lift a finger nor raise a hand in defense of Georgia, unless Georgia acknowledges that you are men, and invests you with the rights pertaining to manhood. Pay your taxes, however, obey all orders from your employers, take good counsel from friends, work faithfully, earn an honest living, and show, by your conduct, that you can be good citizens. . . .

You may expel us, gentlemen, by your votes, today; but while you do it, remember that there is a just God in Heaven, whose All-Seeing Eye beholds alike the acts of the oppressor and the oppressed, and who, despite the machinations of the wicked, never fails to vindicate the cause of Justice, and the sanctity of His own handiwork.

Source: Speech delivered on September 3, 1868, before the Georgia State Legislature.

SELECT BIBLIOGRAPHY:

Stephen Ward Angell, *Bishop Henry McNeal Turner and African American Religion in the South* (Knoxville: University of Tennessee Press, 1992).

Gregory Mixon, "Henry McNeal Turner Versus the Tuskegee Machine: Black Leadership in the Nineteenth Century," *Journal of Negro History* 79, no. 4 (Autumn 1994), pp. 363–80.

Mongo Melanchthron Ponton, *Life and Times of Henry M. Turner* (Atlanta: A.B. Caldwell Publishing, 1917).

Edwin S. Redkey, *Black Exodus: Black Nationalist and Back-to-Africa Movements* (New Haven, Conn.: Yale University Press, 1969).

———, ed., *Respect Black: The Writings and Speeches of Henry McNeal Turner* (New York: Arno Press, 1971).

Henry McNeal Turner, *Methodist Polity, or the Genius and Theory of Methodism* (Philadelphia: A.M.E. Book Concern, 1885).

Robert R. Wright, Jr., *The Bishops of the African Methodist Episcopal Church* (Nashville, Tenn.: A.M.E. Sunday School Union, 1963).

~ **3** ~

Black Urban Workers during Reconstruction

In the aftermath of the Civil War, large numbers of African Americans migrated to northern cities. In most cases, these black workers were trying to escape the oppressive labor conditions of the South. Yet increased competition from foreign-born whites, who largely outnumbered African Americans in the North, meant that labor conditions were difficult there as well. In December 1869, African Americans gathered in Washington, D.C., to organize the National Colored Labor Union, which lasted until 1872. Subsequently, for many decades the majority of black urban workers was marginalized in segregated unions, or shut out of unions altogether.

~

ANONYMOUS DOCUMENT ON THE NATIONAL COLORED
LABOR CONVENTION, 1869

The Convention of colored men at Washington last week was in some respects the most remarkable one we ever attended. We had always had full faith in the capacity of the negro for self-improvement, but were not prepared to see, fresh from slavery, a body of two hundred men, so thoroughly conversant with public affairs, so independent in spirit, and so anxious apparently to improve their social condition, as the men who represented the South, in that convention. . . . The convention was called to order by Mr. Myers, of Baltimore, and Geo. T. Downing, of Rhode Island, was chosen temporary chairman. . . .

. . . rare tact [was] shown by their permanent president, the Hon. John B. Harris of North Carolina. . . .

. . . they formed a National Labor Union . . . and may be said to be fairly in the field as an organized body of laborers.

Isaac Myers, a member of the present Labor Union, was chosen their permanent President for the ensuing year, with a good list of other officers. . . .

Washington, D.C. (1869)

NEW YORK TRIBUNE ARTICLE ON AFRICAN-AMERICAN WORKERS, 1870

. . . Baltimore contains a larger proportion of skilled colored labor than any portion of the country, New Orleans not excepted. . . . One of the best evidences of thrift and enterprise I have noticed . . . are the building and other self-help associations which exist here. The first-named societies were inspired by the successful economy and activity of the Germans. There are at least 25 colored societies in the city. There are several known as "The National Relief Association No. 1," etc. The admission fee is $2.50 and ten cents a week is required thereafter. . . .

Among the noteworthy efforts is an operative brickyard, owned in five-dollar shares, and run by the share-holders themselves. It is doing very well. . . .

. . . The most interesting movement I have found is that known as the Chesapeake Marine Railway and Dry Dock Company, which, as it illustrates the tyranny of caste and the manner by which it can be defeated, when even energy, industry, skill, and determination [are] combined, deserves some extended notice. The company, or rather its leading corporators, have already attained more than a local fame, from the fact that from among them came the movement which resulted in the recognition last year at the Philadelphia Labor Congress of colored labor delegates, and subsequently of the organization at Washington, in December following, of the National Colored Labor union. Now for the origin of this enterprise. Baltimore had always been famous as a ship-building and repairing entrepot. In slave times a large portion of the ship caulkers especially were colored men, as were also many ship-carpenters. In all other trade connected with this interest, a considerable share of the skilled, and nearly all of the unskilled labor, was colored. As a rule they were and are excellent mechanics. Frederick Douglass once worked in the very yard now owned by colored men. When last in Baltimore, he visited the yard, and took the caulker's tool in hand once again. The slave power was strong enough to protect these colored mechanics, many of them being slaves. When the war terminated, however, the bitter hostility, hitherto suppressed, against colored labor, manifested itself in violent combinations. As Mr. Gaines, the present manager of the company, informed me, extermination of colored mechanics was openly declared to be the aim of their white rivals. The combination was against all labor, but manifested mostly in the shipbuilding trades. The white mechanics all struck, even refusing to work, where colored cartmen and stevedores were employed. There was no antagonism or complaint on account of wages, as the colored men were as strenuous as the whites in demanding full pay. The Trades Unions, to which, of course, colored men were not admitted, organized the movement. In the yards on one side of the Patapaco River the colored caulkers were driven off in 1865. In 1866 the general strike was organized. The bosses did not sympathize with the white mechanics, and to the credit of many . . . they stood out as long as possible. Very soon the strike threatened to become general against all colored labor, mechanical or otherwise; the violence threatened to be extended even to hotel waiters of the proscribed race. This atrocious movement was industriously fomented by the active men in Andrew Jackson's reaction.

At last the leading colored caulkers, carpenters, and mechanics, seeing what the crusade meant, determined on a vigorous protective effort. Their conclusion was reached in the organization of the Maryland Mutual Joint Stock Railway Company, whose capital was to consist of 10,000 shares at $50. About 2000 shares were taken within a few days, and $10,000 subscribed, 100 shares being the largest amount taken by any one person. Most of the shares were taken in ones, twos, and threes, by mechanics, caulkers, laborers, even the barbers and washerwomen being represented. The shipyard and marine railway they now own belonged to Jas. L. Mullen and Son, earnest Union men and warm defenders of equal rights to their workmen. They offered to sell and asked no more than the place was worth—$40,000. The bargain was closed; another honorable gentleman, Capt. Sipplegarth, ship-owner, builder and navigator, came forward and loaned them the remaining $30,000, on six years' time, at moderate interest, with the privilege of paying at any time within the six years, taking a mortgage on the property itself.

. . . The Company was organized and got to work by Feb. 2, 1866, employing at first 62 hands, nearly all skilled men, and some of them white. Business was depressed, the outrageous strike having driven it away from the port, and the work did not average for some months more than four days per week, at the average wages of $3 per day. At the present time the Company are able to employ, fulltime, 75 hands. From Feb. 2, 1866, to Jan. 1, 1867, its business amounted to about $60,000, on which the profits were nearly or quite 25 percent or $15,000. The next year was better for them, though business was generally very dull. In carrying on their work and paying their men, they had to resort to borrowing as a rule. They never had a note protested. Within four years from organization they completed the payment for their yard and railway, lifting the mortgage in June last. In 1868 they were incorporated by the title I have given, having done business previously under the firm name of John H. Smith and Co. Most of their trade is with Eastern ship-owners and masters. At the present time they do, and have done for three years past, more repairing than any other company on the Patapaco River. This success has not been achieved without serious trouble. Intimidation has been practiced on their patrons. In two instances, where profitable jobs were pending they have been driven off by white mobs; in one case a white man who took charge of their working force was shot dead. What added point to the act was the fact that he was ordinarily one of their bitterest antagonists. On another occasion, having hired the Canton Marine Railway to take up a large ship which they were caulking and repairing, the whites threatened to strike, and so the Railway Company refused to allow its use. Still they have persevered, and today are masters of the situation. They have had some good contracts, in one case repairing Government dredges and tugs.

The managers think the feeling against them decidedly subsiding. They accredited this fact mainly to their ability to employ labor and pay for it promptly. They think that men have been forced to a sense of shame by finding no resentments cherished on the part of the corporators of the Chesapeake Company. To some extent, more recently, they believe that the dread of Chinese labor induces the ultra-trades unionists to desire their (the colored mechanics') favor. It is worth noting that they are not, and never have been, members of the trades unions. Their business rules, as stated to me by the manager, are simple. Asking why they did more ship repair work than other firms or companies possessing equal facilities, the reply was: 1st, because our labor is of the best; the men we employ are thoroughly skilled, and 2nd, we seek to retain custom as well as make money. We have never lost a patron except by outside intimidation. We try to accommodate, work hard and overtime to finish jobs, and always use the best materials. These are good rules, and this is a good record. . . .

Sources: (1) Excerpt, "The National Colored Labor Convention, 1869," *American Workman*, Boston (December 25, 1869), p. 2; and (2) excerpt, article on African-American workers in Baltimore, *New York Tribune* (September 1, 1870).

SELECT BIBLIOGRAPHY:

John H. Bracey, ed., *Black Workers and Organized Labor* (Belmont, Ca.: Wadsworth Publishing, 1971).

Philip S. Foner, ed., *Organized Labor and the Black Worker, 1619–1973* (New York: International Publishers, 1976).

Philip S. Foner and Ronald L. Lewis, eds., *Black Workers: A Documentary History from Colonial Times to the Present* (Philadelphia: Temple University Press, 1989).

Michael K. Honey, *Black Workers Remember: An Oral History of Segregation, Unionism, and the Freedom Struggle* (Berkeley: University of California Press, 1999).

Bruce Nelson, *Divided We Stand: American Workers and the Struggle for Black Equality, Politics and Society in Twentieth-Century America* (Princeton: Princeton University Press, 2001).

Elizabeth H. Pleck, *Black Migration and Poverty: Boston, 1865–1900* (New York: Academic Press, 1979).

~ 4 ~

"Labor and Capital Are in Deadly Conflict," *T. Thomas Fortune, 1886*

T. Thomas Fortune (1856–1928) was considered the leading African-American journalist of his day. Born a slave in Marianna, Florida, he began his career as a compositor on the *New York Witness* without any formal education but with a practical knowledge of the printer's trade. In 1879 he became the founding editor of the *New York Globe* (later renamed the *New York Age*). Karl Marx was an important influence on Fortune's thought, and in 1884 he authored the important book, *Black and White: Land, Labor, and Politics in the South*. As Jim Crow segregation became consolidated in the South, the political environment for Fortune's radical politics virtually disappeared. Personal and economic problems may have contributed to Fortune's growing dependency on the support of conservative educator Booker T. Washington. By the early 1900s Fortune edited many of Washington's addressees and was a ghostwriter for some of his major articles.

I do not exaggerate the gravity of the subject when I say that it is now the very first in importance not only in the United States but in every country in Europe. Indeed the wall of industrial discontent encircles the civilized globe.

The iniquity of privileged class and concentrated wealth has become so glaring and grievous to be borne that a thorough agitation and an early readjustment of the relation which they sustain to labor can no longer be delayed with safety to society.

It does not admit of argument that every man born into the world is justly entitled to so much of the produce of nature as will satisfy his physical necessities; it does not admit of argument that every man, by reason of his being, is justly entitled to the air he must breathe, the water he must drink, the food he must eat and the covering he must have to shield him from the inclemency of the weather. These are self-evident propositions, not disputed by the most orthodox advocate of excessive wealth on the one hand and excessive poverty on the other. That nature intended these as the necessary correlations of physical being is abundantly proved in the primitive history of mankind and in the freedom and commonality of possession which now obtain everywhere among savage people. The moment you deny to a man the unrestricted enjoyment of all the elements upon which the breath he draws is dependent, that moment you deny to him the inheritance to which he was born.

I maintain that organized society, as it obtains today, based as it is upon feudal conditions, is an outrageous engine of torture and an odious tyranny; that it places in the hands of a few the prime elements of human existence, regardless of the great mass of mankind; that the whole aim and necessity of the extensive and costly machinery of the law we are compelled to maintain grows out of the fact that this fortunate or favored minority would otherwise be powerless to practice upon the masses of society the gross injustice which everywhere prevails.

For centuries the aim and scope of all law have been to more securely hedge about the capitalist and the landowner and to repress labor within a condition wherein bare subsistence was the point aimed at.

From the institution of feudalism to the present time the inspiration of all conflict has been that of capitalist, landowner and hereditary aristocracy against the larger masses of society—the untitled, the disinherited proletariat of the world.

This species of oppression received its most memorable check in the great French Revolution, wherein a new doctrine became firmly rooted in the philosophy of civil government—that is, that the toiling masses of society possessed certain inherent rights which kingcraft, hereditary aristocracy, landlordism and usury mongers must respect. As a result of the doctrine studiously inculcated by the philosophers of the French Revolution, we had the revolt of the blacks of Haiti, under the heroic Touissaint L'Ouverture, the bloody Dessalines and the suave, diplomatic and courtly Christophe, by which the blacks secured forever their freedom as free men and their independence as a people; and our own great Revolution, wherein the leading complaint was taxation by the British government of the American colonies without conceding them proportionate representation. At bottom in each case, bread and butter was the main issue. So it has always been. So it will continue to be, until the scales of justice are made to strike a true balance between labor on the one hand and the interest on capital invested and the wages of superintendence on the other. Heretofore the interest on capital and the wages of superintendence have absorbed so much of the wealth produced as to leave barely nothing to the share of labor.

It should be borne in mind that of this trinity labor is the supreme potentiality. Capital, in the first instance, is the product of labor. If there had never been any labor there would not now be any capital to invest. Again, if a bonfire were made of all the so-called wealth of the world it would only require a few years for labor to reproduce it; but destroy the brawn and muscle of the world and it could not be reproduced by all the gold ever delved from the mines of California and Australia and the fabulous gems from the diamond fields of Africa. In short, labor has been and is the producing agency, while capital has been and is the absorbing or parasitical agency.

Should we, therefore, be surprised that with the constantly growing intelligence and democratization of mankind labor should have grown discontented at the systematic robbery practiced upon it for centuries, and should now clamor for a more equitable basis of adjustment of the wealth it produces?

I could name you a dozen men who have in the last forty or fifty years amassed among them a billion dollars, so that a millionaire has become as common a thing almost as a pauper. How came they by their millions? Is it possible for a man in his lifetime, under the most favorable circumstances, to amass a million dollars? Not at all! The constitution of our laws must be such that they favor one as against the other to permit of such a glaring disparity.

I have outlined for you the past and present relations of capital and labor. The widespread discontent of the labor classes in our own country and in Europe gives emphasis to the position here taken.

I abhor injustice and oppression wherever they are to be found, and my best sympathies go out freely to the struggling poor and the tyranny-ridden of all races and lands. I believe in the divine right of man, not of caste or class, and I believe that any law made to perpetuate or to give immunity to these as against the masses of mankind is an infamous and not-to-be-borne infringement of the just laws of the Creator, who sends each of us into the world as naked as a newly fledged jay bird and crumbles us back into the elements of Mother Earth by the same processes of mutation and final dissolution.

The social and material differences which obtain in the relations of mankind are the creations of man, not of God. God never made such a spook as a king or a duke; he never made such an economic monstrosity as a millionaire; he never gave John Jones the right to own a thousand or a hundred thousand acres of land, with their complement of air and water. These are the conditions of man, who has sold his birthright to the Shylocks of the world and received not even a mess of pottage for his inheritance. The thing would really be laughable, if countless millions from the rice swamps of the Carolinas to the delvers in the mines of Russian Siberia, were not ground to powder to make a holiday for some selfish idler.

Everywhere labor and capital are in deadly conflict. The battle has been raging for centuries, but the opposing forces are just now in a position for that death struggle which it was inevitable must come before the end was. Nor is it within the scope of finite intelligence to forecast the lines upon which the settlement will be made. Capital is entrenched behind ten centuries of law and conservatism, and controlled withal by the wisest and coolest heads in the world. The inequality of the forces joined will appear very obvious. Yet the potentiality of labor will be able to force concessions from time to time, even as the commoners of England have through centuries been able to force from royalty relinquishment of prerogative after prerogative, until, from having been among the most despotic of governments under Elizabeth, the England of today under Queen Victoria is but a royal shadow. So the time may come when the forces of labor will stand upon absolute equality with those of capital, and that harmony between them obtain which has been sought for by wise men and fools for a thousand years.

Source: Speech delivered on April 20, 1886, Brooklyn Literary Union, printed in the *New York Freeman*, May 1, 1886.

SELECT BIBLIOGRAPHY:

T. Thomas Fortune, *Black and White: Land, Labor, and Politics in the South* (New York: Fords, Howard & Hubert, 1884; reprinted, New York: Arno, 1968).

August Meier, *Negro Thought in America, 1880–1915* (Ann Arbor: University of Michigan Press, 1966).

Emma Lou Thornbrough, *T. Thomas Fortune: Militant Abolitionist* (Chicago: University of Chicago Press, 1972).

⤙ 5 ⤚

Edward Wilmot Blyden and the African Diaspora

Edward Wilmot Blyden (1832–1912) was in many respects the first important theorist of Pan-Africanism—the concept that people of African descent have a com-

mon cultural, social, and political destiny, and that struggles for black empowerment and nationalism must transcend geographical boundaries. Born in Charlotte
Amalie, St. Thomas, Danish Virgin Islands, of free parents, Blyden moved to
Liberia in 1851. He rose rapidly as an educator, minister, and journalist. In 1855
he edited the *Liberia Herald*, and in 1864 was named Liberia's Secretary of State.
As a professor of classics, Greek, and Latin at Liberia College from 1861 to 1871,
he actively encouraged blacks in the United States to emigrate to Liberia. In his
later career, Blyden served as Liberia's Ambassador to Great Britain and as President of the American Colonization Society. Blyden's most famous work, *Christianity, Islam and the Negro Race*, published in 1887, promoted Islam as a religion
that could unify and advance the black world. *Negro*, a periodical published by
Blyden, was the first journal that openly advocated the ideas of Pan-Africanism.

〜

THE AFRICAN PROBLEM AND THE METHOD OF ITS SOLUTION

I am seriously impressed with a sense of the responsibility of my position to-night.
I stand in the presence of the representatives of that great organization which
seems first of all the associations in this country to have distinctly recognized the
hand of God in the history of the Negro race in America—to have caught something of the meaning of the Divine purpose in permitting their exile to and
bondage in this land. I stand also in the presence of what, for the time being at
least, must be considered the foremost congregation of the land—the religious
home of the President of the United States. There are present, also, I learn, on
this occasion, some of the statesmen and lawmakers of the land.

My position, then, is one of honor as well as of responsibility, and the message
I have to deliver, I venture to think, concerns directly or indirectly the whole
human race. I come from that ancient country, the home of one of the great original races, occupied by the descendants of one of the three sons to whom, according to Biblical history, the whole world was assigned—a country which is now
engaging the active attention of all Europe. I come, also, from the ancestral home
of at least five millions in this land. Two hundred millions of people have sent me
on an errand of invitation to their blood relations here. Their cry is, "Come over
and help us." And I find among hundreds of thousands of the invited an eager and
enthusiastic response. . . .

. . . It would appear that the world outside of Africa has not yet stopped to consider the peculiar conditions which lift that continent out of the range of the ordinary agencies by which Europe has been able to occupy other countries and sub-
jugate or exterminate their inhabitants.

They have not stopped to ponder the providential lessons on this subject scattered through the pages of history, both past and contemporary.

First. Let us take the most obvious lesson as indicated in the climatic conditions. Perhaps in no country in the world is it so necessary (as in Africa) that the
stranger or new comer should possess the *mens sana in corpore sano*—the sound
mind in sound body; for the climate is most searching, bringing to the surface any
and every latent physical or mental defect. If a man has any chronic or hereditary

disease it is sure to be developed, and if wrong medical treatment is applied it is very apt to be exaggerated and often to prove fatal to the patient. And as with the body so with the mind. Persons of weak minds, either inherited or brought on by excessive mental application or troubles of any kind, are almost sure to develop an impatience or irritability, to the surprise and annoyance of their friends who knew them at home. The Negro immigrant from a temperate region sometimes suffers from these climatic inconveniences, only in his case, after a brief process of acclimatization, he becomes himself again, while the white man never regains his soundness in that climate, and can retain his mental equilibrium only by periodical visits to his native climate. The regulation of the British Government for West Africa is that their officials are allowed six months' leave of absence to return to Europe after fifteen month's residence at Sierra Leone and twelve months on the Gold Coast or Lagos; and for every three days during which they are kept on the coast after the time for their leave arrives, they are allowed one day in Europe. The neglect of this regulation is often attended with most serious consequences.

Second. When we come into the moral and intellectual world it would seem as if the Almighty several times attempted to introduce the foreigner and a foreign civilization into Africa and then changed his purpose. The Scriptures seem to warrant the idea that in some way inexplicable to us, and incompatible with our conception of the character of the Sovereign of the Universe, the unchangeable Being sometimes reverses His apparent plans. We read that, "it repented God," &c. For thousands of years the northeastern portion of Africa witnessed a wonderful development of civilization. The arts and sciences flourished in Egypt for generations, and that country was the centre of almost universal influence; but there was no effect produced upon the interior of Africa. So North Africa became the seat of a great military and commercial power which flourished for 700 years. After this the Roman Catholic Church constructed a mighty influence in the same region, but the interior of the continent received no impression from it.

In the fifteenth century the Congo country, of which we now hear so much, was the scene of extensive operations of the Roman Catholic Church. Just a little before the discovery of America thousands of the natives of the Congo, including the most influential families, were baptized by Catholic missionaries; and the Portuguese, for a hundred years, devoted themselves to the work of African evangelization and exploration. It would appear that they knew just as much of interior Africa as is known now after the great exploits of Speke and Grant and Livingstone, Baker and Cameron and Stanley. It is said that there is a map in the Vatican, three hundred years old, which gives all the general physical relief and the river and lake systems of Africa with more or less accuracy; but the Arab geographers of a century before had described the mountain system, the great lakes, and the course of the Nile.

Just about the time that Portugal was on the way to establish a great empire on that continent, based upon the religious system of Rome, America was discovered, and, instead of the Congo, the Amazon became the seat of Portuguese power. Neither Egyptian, Carthaginian, Persian, or Roman influence was allowed to establish itself on that continent. It would seem that in the providential purpose no solution of the African problem was to come from alien sources. Africans were not doomed to share the fate of some other dark races who have come in contact with the aggressive European. Europe was diverted to the Western Hemisphere. The energies of that conquering race, it was decreed, should be spent in building up a home for themselves on this side. Africa followed in chains.

The Negro race was to be preserved for a special and important work in the future. Of the precise nature of that work no one can form any definite conception. It is probable that if foreign races had been allowed to enter their country they would have been destroyed. So they were brought over to be helpers in this country and at the same time to be preserved. It was not the first time in the history of the world that a people have been preserved by subjection to another people. We know that God promised Abraham that his seed should inherit the land of Canaan; but when He saw that in their numerically weak condition they would have been destroyed in conflicts with the indigenous inhabitants, he took them down to Egypt and kept them there in bondage four hundred years that they might be fitted, both by discipline and numerical increase, for the work that would devolve upon them. Slavery would seem to be a strange school in which to preserve a people; but God has a way of salting as well as purifying by fire.

The Europeans, who were fleeing from their own country in search of wider areas of freedom and larger scope for development, found here an aboriginal race unable to co-operate with them in the labors required for the construction of the material framework of the new civilization. The Indians would not work, and they have suffered the consequences of that indisposition. They have passed away. To take their place as accessories in the work to be done God suffered the African to be brought hither, who could work and would work, and could endure the climatic conditions of a new southern country, which Europeans could not. Two currents set across the Atlantic towards the west for nigh three hundred years—the one from Europe, the other from Africa. The one from Africa had a crimson color. From that stream of human beings millions fell victims to the cruelties of the middle passage, and otherwise suffered from the brutal instincts of their kidnappers and enslavers. I do not know whether Africa has been invited to the celebration of the fourth centenary of the discovery of America; but she has quite as much reason, if not as much right, to participate in the demonstration of that occasion as the European nations. Englishman, Hollander, and Huguenot, Nigritian and Congo came together. If Europe brought the head, Africa furnished the hands for a great portion of the work which has been achieved here, though it was the opinion of an African chief that the man who discovered America ought to have been imprisoned for having uncovered one people for destruction and opened a field for the oppression and suffering of another.

But when the new continent was opened Africa was closed. The veil, which was being drawn aside, was replaced, and darkness once more enveloped the land, for then not the *country* but the *people* were needed. They were to do a work elsewhere, and meanwhile their country was to be shut out from the view of the outside world.

The first Africans landed in this country in the State of Virginia in the year 1619. Then began the first phase of what is called the Negro problem. These people did not come hither of their own accord. Theirs was not a voluntary but a compulsory expatriation. The problem, then, on their arrival in this country, which confronted the white people was how to reduce to effective and profitable servitude an alien race which it was neither possible nor desirable to assimilate. This gave birth to that peculiar institution, established in a country whose *raison d'etre* was that all men might enjoy the "right to life, liberty, and the pursuit of happiness." Laws had to be enacted by Puritans, Cavaliers, and Roundheads for slaves, and every contrivance had to be devised for the safety of the institution. It was a difficult problem, in the effort to solve which both master and slave suffered.

It would seem, however, that in the first years of African slavery in this country, the masters upon many of whom the relationship was forced, understood its providential origin and purpose, until after a while, avarice and greed darkened their perceptions, and they began to invent reasons, drawn even from the Word of God, to justify their holding these people in perpetual bondage for the advantage of themselves and their children forever. But even after a blinding cupidity had captured the generality by its bewitching spell, there were those (far-sighted men, especially after the yoke of Great Britain had been thrown off) who saw that the abnormal relation could not be permanent under the democratic conditions established by the fundamental law of the land. It was Thomas Jefferson, the writer of the Declaration of Independence, who made the celebrated utterance: "Nothing is more clearly written in the Book of Destiny than the emancipation of the blacks; and it is equally certain that the two races will never live in a state of equal freedom under the same Government, so insurmountable are the barriers which nature, habit, and opinion have established between them."

For many years, especially in the long and weary period of the antislavery conflict, the latter part of this dictum of Jefferson was denounced by many good and earnest men. The most intelligent of the colored people resented it as a prejudiced and anti-Christian conception. But as the years go by and the Negroes rise in education and culture, and therefore in love and pride of race, and in proper conception of race gifts, race work and race destiny, the latter clause of that famous sentence is not only being shorn of its obscurity and repulsiveness, but is being welcomed as embodying a truth indispensable to the preservation and prosperity of both races, and as pointing to the regeneration of the African Fatherland. There are some others of the race who, recognizing Jefferson's principle, would make the races one by amalgamation.

It was under the conviction of the truth expressed by that statesman that certain gentlemen of all political shades and differing religious views, met together in this city in the winter of 1816–'17, and organized the American Colonization Society. Though friendly to the antislavery idea, and anxious for the extinction of the abnormal institution, these men did not make their views on that subject prominent in their published utterances. They were not Abolitionists in the political or technical sense of that phrase. But their labors furnished an outlet and encouragement for persons desiring to free their slaves, giving them the assurance that their freedmen would be returned to their Fatherland, carrying thither what light of Christianity and civilization they had received. It seems a pity that this humane, philanthropic, and far-seeing work should have met with organized opposition from another band of philanthropists, who, anxious for a speedy deliverance of the captives, thought they saw in the Colonization Society an agency for riveting instead of breaking the fetters of the slave, and they denounced it with all the earnestness and eloquence they could command, and they commanded, both among whites and blacks, some of the finest orators the country has ever produced. And they did a grand work, both directly and indirectly, for the Negro and for Africa. They did their work and dissolved their organization. But when their work was done the work of the Colonization Society really began.

In the development of the Negro question in this country the colonizationists might be called the prophets and philosophers; the abolitionists, the warriors and politicians. Colonizationists saw what was coming and patiently prepared for its advent. Abolitionists attacked the first phase of the Negro problem and labored for its immediate solution; colonizationists looked to the last phase of the problem and labored to get both the whites and blacks ready for it. They labored on two continents, in America and in Africa. Had they not begun as early as they did to take up lands in Africa for the exiles, had they waited for the abolition of slavery, it would now have been impossible to obtain a foothold in their fatherland for the returning hosts. The colonizationist, as prophet, looked at the State as it would be; the abolitionist, as politician, looked at the State as it was. The politician sees the present and is possessed by it. The prophet sees the future and gathers inspiration from it. The politician may influence legislation; the prophet, although exercising great moral influence, seldom has any legislative power. The agitation of the politician may soon culminate in legal enactments; the teachings of the prophet may require generations before they find embodiment in action. The politician has today; the prophet, to-morrow. The politician deals with facts, the prophet with ideas, and ideas take root very slowly. Though nearly three generations have passed away since Jefferson made his utterance, and more than two since the organization of the Colonization Society, yet the conceptions they put forward can scarcely be said to have gained maturity, much less currency, in the public mind. But the recent discussions in the halls of Congress show that the teachings of the prophet are now beginning to take hold of the politician. It may take many years yet before the people come up to these views, and, therefore, before legislation upon them may be possible, but there is evidently movement in that direction.

The first phase of the Negro problem was solved at Appomattox, after the battle of the warrior, with confused noise and garments rolled in blood. The institution of slavery, for which so many sacrifices had been made, so many of the principles of humanity had been violated, so many of the finer sentiments of the heart had been stifled, was at last destroyed by violence.

Now the nation confronts the second phase, the educational, and millions are being poured out by State governments and by individual philanthropy for the education of the freedmen, preparing them for the third and last phase of the problem, viz: EMIGRATION.

In this second phase, we have that organization, which might be called the successor of the old Anti-Slavery Society, taking a most active and effective part. I mean the American Missionary Association. I have watched with constant gratitude and admiration the course and operations of that Society, especially when I remember that, organized in the dark days of slavery, twenty years before emancipation, it held aloft courageously the banner on which was inscribed freedom for the Negro and no fellowship with his oppressors. And they, among the first, went South to lift the freedmen from the mental thraldom and moral degradation in which slavery had left him. They triumphed largely over the spirit of their opponents. They braved the dislike, the contempt, the apprehension with which their work was at first regarded, until they succeeded by demonstrating the advantages of knowledge over ignorance, to bring about that state of things to which Mr. Henry Grady, in his last utterances, was able to refer with such satisfaction, viz., that since the war the South has spent $122,000,000 in the cause of public education, and this year it is pledged to spend $37,000,000, in the benefits of which the Negro is a large participant.

It is not surprising that some of those who, after having been engaged in the noble labors of solving the first phase of the problem—in the great anti-slavery war—and are now confronting the second phase, should be unable to receive with patience the suggestion of the third, which is the emigration phase, when the Negro, freed in body and in mind, shall bid farewell to these scenes of his bondage and discipline and betake himself to the land of his fathers, the scene of larger opportunities and loftier achievements. I say it is not surprising that the veterans of the past and the present should be unable to give much enthusiasm to the work of the future. It is not often given to man to labor successfully in the land of Egypt, in the wilderness and across the Jordan. Some of the most effective workers, must often, with eyes undimmed and natural force unabated, lie down and die on the borders of full freedom, and if they live, life to them is like a dream. The young must take up the work. To old men the indications of the future are like a dream. Old men are like them that dream. Young men see visions. They catch the spirit of the future and are able to place themselves in accord with it.

But things are not yet ready for the solution of the third and last phase of the problem. Things are not ready in this country among whites or blacks. The industrial condition of the South is not prepared for it. Things are not yet ready in Africa for a complete exodus. Europe is not yet ready; she still thinks that she can take and utilize Africa for her own purposes. She does not yet understand that Africa is to be for the African or for nobody. Therefore she is taking up with renewed vigor, and confronting again, with determination, the African problem. Englishmen, Germans, Italians, Belgians, are taking up territory and trying to wring from the grey-haired mother of civilization the secret of the ages. Nothing has come down from Egypt so grand and impressive as the Sphinxes that look at you with calm and emotionless faces, guarding their secret to-day as they formerly guarded the holy temples. They are a symbol of Africa. She will not be forced. She only can reveal her secret. Her children trained in the house of bondage will show it to the world. Some have already returned and have constructed an independent nation as a beginning of this work on her western borders.

It is a significant fact that Africa was completely shut up until the time arrived for the emancipation of her children in the Western World. When Jefferson and Washington and Hamilton and Patrick Henry were predicting and urging the freedom of the slave, Mungo Park was beginning that series of explorations by English enterprise which has just ended in the expedition of Stanley. Just about the time that England proclaimed freedom throughout her colonies, the brothers Lander made the great discovery of the mouth of the Niger; and when Lincoln issued the immortal proclamation, Livingstone was unfolding to the world that wonderful region which Stanley has more fully revealed and which is becoming now the scene of the secular and religious activities of Christendom. The King of the Belgians has expended fortunes recently in opening the Congo and in introducing the appliances of civilization, and by a singular coincidence a bill has been brought forward in the U.S. Senate to assist the emigration of Negroes to the Fatherland just at the time when that philanthropic monarch has despatched an agent to this country to invite the co-operation in his great work of qualified freedmen. This is significant.

What the King of the Belgians has just done is an indication of what other European Powers will do when they have exhausted themselves in costly experiments to utilize white men as colonists in Africa. They will then understand the purpose of the Almighty in having permitted the exile and bondage of the Africans, and they will see that for Africa's redemption the Negro is the chosen instrument. They will encourage the establishment and building up of such States as Liberia. They will recognize the scheme of the Colonization Society as the providential one.

The little nation which has grown up on that coast as a result of the efforts of this Society, is now taking hold upon that continent in a manner which, owing to inexperience, it could not do in the past. The Liberians have introduced a new article into the commerce of the world—the Liberian coffee. They are pushing to the interior, clearing up the forests, extending the culture of coffee, sugar, cocoa, and other tropical articles, and are training the aborigines in the arts of civilization and in the principles of Christianity. The Republic occupies five hundred miles of coast with an elastic interior. It has a growing commerce with various countries of Europe and America. No one who has visited that country and has seen the farms on the banks of the rivers and in the interior, the workshops, the schools, the churches, and other elements and instruments of progress will say that the United States, through Liberia, is not making a wholesome impression upon Africa—an impression which, if the members of the American Congress understood, they would not begrudge the money required to assist a few hundred thousand to carry on in that country the work so well begun. They would gladly spare them from the laboring element of this great nation to push forward the enterprises of civilization in their Fatherland, and to build themselves up on the basis of their race manhood.

If there is an intelligent Negro here to-night I will say to him, let me take you with me in imagination to witness the new creation or development on that distant shore; I will not paint you an imaginary picture, but will describe an historical fact; I will tell you of reality. Going from the coast, through those depressing alluvial plains which fringe the eastern and western borders of the continent, you reach, after a few miles' travel, the first high or undulating country, which, rising abruptly from the swamps, enchants you with its solidity, its fertility, its verdure, its refreshing and healthful breezes. You go further, and you stand upon a higher elevation where the wind sings more freshly in your ears, and your heart beats fast as you survey the continuous and unbroken forests that stretch away from your feet to the distant horizon. The melancholy cooing of the pigeons in some unseen retreat or the more entrancing music of livelier and picturesque songsters alone disturb the solemn and almost oppressive solitude. You hear no human sound and see the traces of no human presence. You decline to pursue your adventurous journey. You refuse to penetrate the lonely forest that confronts you. You return to the coast, thinking of the long ages which have elapsed, the seasons which, in their onward course, have come and gone, leaving those solitudes undisturbed. You wonder when and how are those vast wildernesses to be made the scene of human activity and to contribute to human wants and happiness. Finding no answer to your perplexing question you drop the subject from your thoughts. After a few years—a very few it may be—you return to those scenes. To your surprise and gratification your progress is no longer interrupted by the inconvenience of bridle-paths and tangled vines. The roads are open and clear. You miss the troublesome creeks and drains which, on your previous journey, harassed and fatigued you. Bridges have been constructed, and without any of the former weariness you find yourself again on the summit, where in loneliness you had stood sometime before. What do you now see? The gigantic trees have disappeared, houses have sprung up on every side. As far as the eye can see the roofs of comfortable and homelike cottages peep through the wood. The waving corn and rice and sugar-cane, the graceful and fragrant coffee tree, the unbrageous cocoa, orange, and mango plum have taken the place of the former sturdy denizens of the forest. What has brought about the change? The Negro emigrant has arrived from America, and, slender though his facilities have been, has produced these wonderful revolutions. You look beyond and take in the forests that now appear on the distant horizon. You catch glimpses of native villages embowered in plantain trees, and you say these also shall be brought under civilized influences, and you feel yourself lifted into manhood, the spirit of the teacher and guide and missionary comes upon you, and you say, "There, below me and beyond lies the world into which I must go. There must I cast my lot. I feel I have a message to it, or a work in it"; and the sense that there are thousands dwelling there, some of whom you may touch, some of whom you may influence, some of whom may love you or be loved by you, thrills you with a strange joy and expectation, and it is a thrill which you can never forget; for ever and anon it comes upon you with increased intensity. In that hour you are born again. You hear forevermore the call ringing in your ears, "Come over and help us."

These are the visions that rise before the Liberian settler who has turned away from the coast. This is the view that exercises such an influence upon his imagination, and gives such tone to his character, making him an independent and productive man on the continent of his fathers.

As I have said, this is no imaginary picture, but the embodiment of sober history. Liberia, then, is a fact, an aggressive and progressive fact, with a great deal in its past and everything in its future that is inspiring and uplifting.

It occupies one of the most charming countries in the western portion of that continent. It has been called by qualified judges the garden spot of West Africa. I love to dwell upon the memories of scenes which I have passed through in the interior of that land. I have read of countries which I have not visited—the grandeur of the Rocky Mountains and the charms of the Yosemite Valley, and my imagination adds to the written description and becomes a gallery of delightful pictures. But of African scenes my memory is a treasure house in which I delight to revel. I have distinctly before me the days and dates when I came into contact with their inexhaustible beauties. Leaving the coast line, the seat of malaria, and where are often seen the remains of the slaver's barracoons, which always give an impression of the deepest melancholy, I come to the high tablelands with their mountain scenery and lovely valleys, their meadow streams and mountain rivulets, and there amid the glories of a changeless and unchanging nature, I have taken off my shoes and on that consecrated ground adored the God and Father of the Africans.

This is the country and this is the work to which the American Negro is invited. This is the opening for him which, through the labors of the American Colonization Society, has been effected. This organization is more than a *colonization* society, more than an emigration society. It might with equal propriety and perhaps with greater accuracy be called the African *Repatriation* Society; or since the idea of planting towns and introducing extensive cultivation of the soil is included in its work, it might be called the African Repatriation and Colonization Society, for then you bring in a somewhat higher idea than mere colonization—the mere settling of a new country by strangers—you bring in the idea of restoration, of compensation to a race and country much and long wronged.

Colonizationists, notwithstanding all that has been said against them, have always recognized the manhood of the Negro and been willing to trust him to take care of himself. They have always recognized the inscrutable providence by which the African was brought to these shores. They have always taught that he was brought hither to be trained out of his sense of irresponsibility to a knowledge of his place as a factor in the great work of humanity; and that after having been thus trained he could find his proper sphere of action only in the land of his origin to make a way for himself. They have believed that it has not been given to the white man to fix the intellectual or spiritual status of this race. They have recognized that the universe is wide enough and God's gifts are varied enough to allow the man of Africa to find out a path of his own within the circle of genuine human interests, and to contribute from the field of his particular enterprise to the resources—material, intellectual, and moral—of the great human family.

But will the Negro go to do this work?

Is he willing to separate himself from a settled civilization which he has helped to build up to betake himself to the wilderness of his ancestral home and begin anew a career on his own responsibility?

I believe that he is. And if suitable provision were made for their departure to-morrow hundreds of thousands would avail themselves of it. The African question, or the Negro problem, is upon the country, and it can no more be ignored than any other vital interest. The chief reason, it appears to me, why it is not more seriously dealt with is because the pressure of commercial and political exigencies does not allow time and leisure to the stronger and richer elements of the nation to study it. It is not a question of color simply—that is a superficial accident. It lies deeper than color. It is a question of race, which is the outcome not only of climate, but of generations subjected to environments which have formed the mental and moral constitution.

It is a question in which two distinct races are concerned. This is not a question then purely of reason. It is a question also of instinct. Races feel; observers theorize.

The work to be done beyond the seas is not to be a reproduction of what we see in this country. It requires, therefore, distinct race perception and entire race devotion. It is not to be the healing up of an old sore, but the unfolding of a new bud, an evolution; the development of a new side of God's character and a new phase of humanity. God said to Moses, "I am that I am"; or, more exactly, "I shall be that I shall be." Each race sees from its own standpoint a different side of the Almighty. The Hebrews could not see or serve God in the land of the Egyptians; no more can the Negro under the Anglo-Saxon. He can serve *man* here. He can furnish the labor of the country, but to the inspiration of the country he must ever be an alien.

In that wonderful sermon of St. Paul on Mars Hill in which he declared that God hath made of one blood all nations of men to dwell on all the face of the earth and hath determined the bounds of their habitation, he also said, "In Him we live and move and have our being." Now it cannot be supposed that in the types and races which have already displayed themselves God has exhausted himself. It is by God in us, where we have freedom to act out ourselves, that we do each our several work and live out into action, through our work, whatever we have within us of noble and wise and true. What we do is, if we are able to be true to our nature, the representation of some phase of the Infinite Being. If we live and move and have our being in Him, God also lives, and moves and has His being in us. This is why slavery of any kind is an outrage. It spoils the image of God as it strives to express itself through the individual or the race. As in the Kingdom of Nature, we see in her great organic types of being, in the movement, changes, and order of the elements, those vast thoughts of God, so in the great types of man, in the various races of the world, as distinct in character as in work, in the great divisions of character, we see the will and character and consciousness of God disclosed to us. According to this truth a distinct phase of God's character is set forth to be wrought out into perfection in every separate character. As in every form of the inorganic universe we see some noble variation of God's thought and beauty, so in each separate man, in each separate race, something of the absolute is incarnated. The whole of mankind is a vast representation of the Deity. Therefore we cannot extinguish any race either by conflict or amalgamation without serious responsibility.

You can easily see then why one race overshadowed by another should long to express itself—should yearn for the opportunity to let out the divinity that stirs within it. This is why the Hebrews cried to God from the depths of their affliction in Egypt, and this is why thousands and thousands of Negroes in the South are longing to go to the land of their fathers. They are not content to remain where everything has been done on the line of another race. They long for the scenes where everything is to be done under the influence of a new racial spirit, under the impulse of new skies and the inspiration of a fresh development. Only those are fit for this new work who believe in the race—have faith in its future—a prophetic insight into its destiny from a consciousness of its possibilities. The inspiration of the race is in the race.

Only one race has furnished the prophets for humanity—the Hebrew race; and before they were qualified to do this they had to go down to the depths of servile degradation. Only to them were revealed those broad and pregnant principles upon which every race can stand and work and grow; but for the special work of each race the prophets arise among the people themselves.

What is pathetic about the situation is, that numbers among whites and blacks are disposed to ignore the seriousness and importance of the question. They seem to think it a question for political manipulation and to be dealt with by partisan statesmanship, not recognizing the fact that the whole country is concerned. I freely admit the fact, to which attention has been recently called, that there are many Afro-Americans who have no more to do with Africa than with Iceland, but this does not destroy the truth that there are millions whose life is bound up with that continent. It is to them that the message comes from their brethren across the deep, "Come over and help us."

Source: Lecture delivered at the American Colonization Society, Washington, D.C., January 19, 1890.

SELECT BIBLIOGRAPHY:
Edward Wilmot Blyden, *Black Spokesman: Select Published Writings of Edward Wilmot Blyden*, ed. Hollis R. Lynch (New York: Humanities Press, 1971).

Howard Brotz, ed., *Negro Social and Political Thought: 1850–1920* (New York: Basic Books, 1966).

James Conyers, "An Afrocentric Study of the Philosophy of Edward Wilmot Blyden" (Ph.D. diss., Temple University, 1998).

Hollis R. Lynch, *Edward Wilmot Blyden: Pan-Negro Patriot, 1832–1912* (New York: Oxford University Press, 1967).

Richard Brent Turner, "Edward Wilmot Blyden and Pan-Africanism: The Ideological Roots of Islam and Black Nationalism in the United States," *Muslim World: A Quarterly Review of History, Culture, Religions & the Christian Mission in Islamdom* 87 (April 1997), pp. 169–82.

～ 6 ～

"The Democratic Idea Is Humanity," *Alexander Crummell, 1888*

Alexander Crummell (1819–1898) was born in New York City, and as a young man was trained to become an Episcopal priest. Refused admission to the Diocese of Pennsylvania because of his race, he traveled to England in 1848. He enrolled in Cambridge University, graduating in 1853. For nearly two decades, Crummell lived in Liberia. Appointed as a professor at Liberia College in 1861, he authored several books on African-American and African issues. Returning to the United States in 1872, he founded and pastored St. Luke's Episcopal Church. Crummell taught at Howard University from 1895 to 1897. One of his major achievements was the establishment of the American Negro Academy in 1897, which was the first society of black scholars in the United States. Crummell deeply influenced the thinking of the young W. E. B. Du Bois, who dedicated a chapter to his mentor in *The Souls of Black Folk.*

～

THE RACE PROBLEM IN AMERICA

The residence of various races of men in the same national community, is a fact which has occurred in every period of time and in every quarter of the globe. So well known is this fact of history that the mention of a few special instances will be sufficient for this occasion.

It took place in earliest times on the plains of Babylon. It was seen on the banks of the Nile, in the land of the Pharaohs. The same fact occurred again when the barbarian hosts of the North fell upon effete Roman society, and changed the fate of Europe. Once more we witness the like fact when the Moors swept along the banks of the Mediterranean, and seated themselves in might and majesty on the hills of Granada and along the fertile slopes of Arragon and Castile. And now, in the 19th century, we have the largest illustration of the same fact in our own Republic, where are gathered together, in one national community, sixty millions of people of every race and kindred under the sun. It might be supposed that an historical fact so large and multiform would furnish a solution of the great race-problem, which now invites attention in American society. We read the future by the past. And without doubt there are certain principles of population which are invariable in their working and universal in their results. Such principles are inductions from definite conditions, and may be called the laws of population. They are, too, both historical and predictive. One cannot only ascertain through them the past condition of States and peoples, but they give a light which opens up with clearness the future of great commonwealths.

But, singular as it may seem, there is no fixed law of history by which to determine the probabilities of the race-problem in the United States. We can find nowhere such invariability of result as to set a principle or determine what may be called an historical axiom.

Observe just here the inevitable confusion which is sure to follow the aim after historical precedent in this problem.

The descendants of Nimrod and Assur, people of two different stocks, settled in Babylon; and the result was amalgamation.[1]

The Jews and the Egyptians under the Pharaohs inhabited the same country 400 years; but antagonism was the result, and expulsion the final issue.

The Tartars overran China in the tenth century, and the result has been amalgamation.

The Goths and Vandals poured into Italy like a flood, and the result has been absorption.

The Celts and Scandinavians clustered like bees from the fourth to the sixth centuries in the British Isles, and the result has been absorption.

The Northmen and Gauls have lived side by side in Normandy since the tenth century, and the result has been absorption.

The Moors and Spaniards came into the closest contact in the sixth century, and it resulted in constant antagonism and in final expulsion.

The Caucasian and the Indian have lived in close neighborhood on this continent since 1492, and the result has been the extinction of the Indian.

The Papuan and the Malay have lived side by side for ages in the tropical regions of the Pacific, and have maintained every possible divergence of tribal life, of blood, government, and religion, down to the present, and yet have remained perpetually and yet peacefully separate and distinct.[2]

These facts, circling deep historic ages, show that we can find no definite historical precedent or principle applicable to the race-problem in America.

Nevertheless we are not entirely at sea with regard to this problem. There are certain tendencies, seen for over 200 years in our population, which indicate settled, determinate proclivities, and which show, if I mistake not, the destiny of races.

What, then, are the probabilities of the future? Do the indications point to amalgamation or to absorption as the outcome of race-life in America? Are we to have the intermingling of our peoples into one common blood or the perpetuity of our diverse stocks, with the abiding integrity of race, blood, and character?

I might meet the theory which anticipates amalgamation by the great principle manifested in every sphere, viz: "That nature is constantly departing from the simple to the complex; starting off in new lines from the homogeneous to the heterogeneous"; striking out in divers ways into variety; and hence we are hedged in, in the aim after blood-unity, by a law of nature which is universal, and which excludes the notion of amalgamation.

But I turn from the abstract to history. It is now about 268 years since the tides of immigration began to beat upon our shores. This may be called a brief period, but 268 years is long enough to fix a new type of man. Has such a new type sprung up here to life? Has a new commingled race, the result of our diverse elements, come forth from the crucible of our heterogeneous nationality?

We will indulge in no speculation upon this subject. We will exclude even the faintest tinge of the imagination. The facts alone shall speak for themselves.

First of all is the history of the Anglo-Saxon race in America. In many respects it has been the foremost element in the American population; in largeness of numbers, in civil polity and power, in educational impress, and in religious influence. What has become of this element of our population? Has it been lost in the current of the divergent streams of life which have been spreading abroad throughout the land?

Why, every one knows that in New England, in Virginia, in the Far West, along the Atlantic Seaboard, that fully three-fifths of the whole American population are the offspring of this same hardy, plodding, common-sense people that they were centuries ago, when their fathers pressed through the forests of Jamestown or planted their feet upon the sterile soil of Plymouth.

Some of you may remember the remark of Mr. Lowell, on his return in 1885 from his mission to England. He said that when English people spoke to him of Americans as a people different from themselves, he always told them that in blood he was just as much an Englishman as they were; and Mr. Lowell in this remark was the spokesman of not less than thirty-six millions of men of as direct Anglo-Saxon descent as the men of Kent or the people of Yorkshire.

The Celtic element came to America in two separate columns. The French entered Canada in 1607. They came with all that glow, fervor, gallantry, social aptitudes, and religious loyalty which, for centuries, have characterized the Gallic blood, and which are still conspicuous features on both sides of the Atlantic.

The other section of the Celtic family began their immigration about 1640; and they have almost depopulated Ireland to populate America; and their numbers now are millions.

One or two facts are observable concerning the French and Irish, viz: (1) That, although kindred in blood, temperament, and religion, they have avoided both neighborhood of locality and marital alliance; and (2) so great has been the increase of the Hibernian family that in Church life and political importance they form a vast solidarity in the nation.

The German, like the Celtic family, came over in two sections. The Batavian stock came first from Holland in 1608, and made New York, New Jersey, and Pennsylvania their habitat. The Germans proper, or High Germans, have been streaming into the Republic since 1680, bringing with them that steadiness and sturdiness, that thrift and acquisitiveness, that art and learning, that genius and acumen, which have given an elastic spring to American culture, depth to philosophy, and inspiration to music and to art.

And here they are in great colonies in the Middle and Western States, and in vast sections of our great cities. And yet where can one discover any decline in the purity of German blood, or the likelihood of its ultimate loss in the veins of alien people?

The Negro contingent was one of the earliest contributions to the American population. The black man came quickly on the heel of the Cavalier at Jamestown, and before the arrival of the Puritan in the east. "That fatal, that perfidious bark" of Sir John Hawkins, that "ferried the slave captive o'er the sea" from

Africa, preceded the Mayflower one year and five months.

From that small cargo and its after arrivals have arisen the large black population, variously estimated from 8 to 10,000,000. It is mostly, especially in the wide rural areas of the South, a purely Negro population. In the large cities there is a wide intermixture of blood. This, by some writers, is taken as the indication of ultimate and entire amalgamation. But the past in this incident is no sign of the future. The gross and violent intermingling of the blood of the southern white man cannot be taken as an index of the future of the black race.

Amalgamation in its exact sense means the approach of affinities. The word applied to human beings implies will, and the consent of two parties. In *this* sense there has been no amalgamation of the two races; for the Negro in this land has ever been the truest of men, in marital allegiance, to his own race.

Intermixture of blood there has been—not by the amalgamation, which implies consent, but through the victimizing of the helpless black woman. But even this has been limited in extent. Out of 4,500,000 of this race in the census of 1861, 400,000 were set down as of mixed blood. Thousands of these were the legitimate offspring of colored parents; and the probability is that not more than 150,000 had white fathers. Since emancipation the black woman has gained possession of her own person, and it is the testimony of Dr. Haygood and other eminent Southerners that the base process of intermixture has had a wide and sudden decline, and that the likelihood of the so-called amalgamation of the future is fast dying out.

And now, after this survey of race tides and race life during 268 years, I repeat the question: "Has a *new* race, the product of our diverse elements, sprung up here in America? Or, is there any such a probability for the future?"

Let me answer this question by a recent and striking reference.

Dr. Strong, in his able, startling, striking Tractate, entitled *"Our Country,"* speaks, in ch. 4, p. 44, of the Helvetian settlement in southern Wisconsin. He deprecates the preservation of its race, its language, its worship, and its customs in their integrity. In this, you see, he forgets the old Roman adage that "though men cross the seas they do not change their nature." He then protests (and rightly, too) against the perpetuation of race antipathies, and closes his criticism with the suggestion, similar to that of Canon Rawlinson, of Oxford, viz., that the American people should seek the solution of the race-problem by universal assimilation of blood.

Dr. Strong evidently forgets that the principle of race is one of the most persistent of all things in the constitution of man. It is one of those structural facts in our nature which abide with a fixed, vital, and reproductive power.

Races, like families, are the organisms and the ordinance of God; and race feeling, like the family feeling, is of divine origin. The extinction of race feeling is just as possible as the extinction of family feeling. Indeed, a race *is* a family. The principle of continuity is as masterful in races as it is in families—as it is in nations.

History is filled with the attempts of kings and mighty generals and great statesmen to extinguish this instinct. But their failures are as numerous as their futile attempts; for this sentiment, alike subtle and spontaneous, has both pervaded and stimulated society in every quarter. Indeed, as Lord Beaconsfield says, "race is the key to history." When once the race-type gets fixed as a new variety, then it acts precisely as the family life; for, 1ST, it propagates itself by that divine instinct of reproduction, vital in all living creatures, and next, 2ND, it has a growth as a "seed after its own kind and in itself," whereby the race-type becomes a perpetuity, with its own distinctive form, constitution, features, and structure. Heredity is just as true a fact in races as in families, as it is in individuals.

Nay, we see, not seldom, a special persistency in the race life. We see families and tribes and clans swept out of existence, while race "goes on forever." Yea, even nations suffer the same fate. Take, for instance, the unification of States now constantly occurring. One small nation after another is swallowed up by another to magnify its strength and importance, and thus the great empires of the world become colossal powers. But it is observable that the process of unification leaves untouched the vitality and the persistency of race. You have only to turn to Great Britain and to Austria to verify this statement. In both nations we see the intensity of race cohesion, and at the same time the process of unification. Indeed, on all sides, in Europe, we see the consolidation of States; and at the same time the integration of race: Nature and Providence thus developing that principle of unity which binds the universe, and yet at the same time manifesting that conserving power which tends everywhere to fixity of type. And this reminds us of the lines of Tennyson:

> That nature lends such evil dreams?
> Are God and nature, then, at strife,
> So careful of the type she seems,
> So careless of the single life.

Hence, when a race once seats itself permanently in a land it is almost as impossible to get rid of it as it is to extirpate a plant that is indigenous to its soil. You can drive out a family from a community. You can rid yourself of a clan or a single tribe by expulsion. You can swallow up by amalgamation a simple emigrant people.

But when a RACE, *i.e.*, a compact, homogeneous population of one blood, ancestry, and lineage—numbering, perchance, some eight or ten millions—once enters a land and settles therein as its home and heritage, then occurs an event as fixed and abiding as the rooting of the Pyrenees in Spain or the Alps in Italy.

The race-problem, it will thus be seen, cannot be settled by extinction of race. No amalgamating process can eliminate it. It is not a carnal question—a problem of breeds, or blood, or lineage.

And even if it were, amalgamation would be an impossibility. How can any one persuade seven or eight millions of people to forget the ties of race? No one could *force* them into the arms of another race. And even then it would take generations upon generations to make the American people homogeneous in blood and essential qualities. Thus take one single case: There are thirty millions of Negroes on the American *continent* (eight or more millions in the United States of

America), and constantly increasing at an immense ratio. Nothing but the sheerest, haziest imagination can anticipate the future dissolution of this race and its final loss; and so, too, of the other races of men in America.

Indeed, the race-problem is a moral one. It is a question entirely of ideas. Its solution will come especially from the domain of principles. Like all the other great battles of humanity, it is to be fought out with the weapons of truth. The race-problem is a question of organic life, and it must be dealt with as an ethical matter by the laws of the Christian system. "As diseases of the mind are invisible, so must their remedies be."

And this brings me to the one vast question that still lingers, *i.e.*, the question of AMITY. Race-life is a permanent element in our system. Can it be maintained in peace? Can these races give the world the show of brotherhood and fraternity? Is there a moral remedy in this problem?

Such a state of concord is, we must admit, a rare sight, even in christendom. There is great friction between Celt and Saxon in Britain. We see the violence of both Russ and German against the Jew. The bitterness is a mutual one between Russia on the one hand and Bulgaria and the neighboring dependent principalities on the other, and France and Germany stand facing one another like great fighting cocks.

All this is by no means assuring, and hence we cannot dismiss this question in an off-hand and careless manner.

The current, however, does not set all one way. There is another aspect to this question.

Thus, the Norman and the Frank have lived together harmoniously for centuries; the Welsh, English, and Scotch in England; the Indian, the Spaniard, and Negro in Brazil, and people of very divergent lineage in Spain.

And now the question arises: What are the probabilities of amity in a land where exists such wide divergence of race as the Saxon on the one hand and the Negro on the other?

First of all, let me say that the social idea is to be entirely excluded from consideration. It is absolutely a personal matter, regulated by taste, condition, or either by racial or family affinities; and there it must remain undisturbed forever. The Jews in this land are sufficient for themselves. So are the Germans, the Italians, the Irish, and so are the Negroes. Civil and political freedom trench in no way upon the domestic state or social relations.

Besides, there is something ignoble in any man, any class, any race of men whining and crying because they cannot move in spheres where they are not wanted.

But, beyond the social range there should be no compromise; and this country should be agitated and even convulsed till the battle of liberty is won, and every man in the land is guaranteed fully every civil and political right and prerogative.

The question of equality pertains entirely to the two domains of civil and political life and prerogative.

Now, I wish to show that the probabilities tend toward the complete and entire civil and political equality of all the peoples of this land.

1st. Observe that this is the age of civil freedom. It has not as yet gained its fullest triumphs; neither yet has Christianity.

But it is to be observed in the history of man that, in due time, certain principles get their set in human society, and there is no such thing as successfully resisting them. Their rise is not a matter of chance or haphazard. It is God's hand in history. It is the providence of the Almighty, and no earthly power can stay it.

Such, pre-eminently, was the entrance of Christianity in the centre of the world's civilization, and the planting of the idea of human brotherhood amid the ideas in the laws and legislation of great nations. *That* was the seed from which have sprung all the great revolutions in thought and governmental policies during the Christian era. Its work has been slow, but it has been certain and unfailing. I cannot pause to narrate all its early victories. We will take a limited period. We will begin at the dawn of modern civilization, and note the grand achievements of the idea of Christian brotherhood.

It struck at the doctrine of the Divine Right of Kings, and mortally wounded it. It demanded the extinction of Feudalism, and it got it. It demanded the abolition of the Slave Trade, and it got it. It demanded the abolition of Russian Serfage, and it got it. It demanded the education of the masses, and it got it.

In the early part of the eighteenth century this principle of brotherhood sprouted forth into a grander and more consummate growth, and generated the spirit of democracy.

When I speak of the spirit of democracy I have no reference to that spurious, blustering, self-sufficient spirit which derides God and authority on the one hand, and crushes the weak and helpless on the other. The democratic spirit I am speaking of is that which upholds the doctrine of human rights; which demands honor to all men; which recognizes manhood in all conditions; which uses the State as the means and agency for the unlimited progress of humanity. This principle has its root in the Scriptures of God, and it has come forth in political society to stay! In the hands of man it has indeed suffered harm. It has been both distorted and exaggerated, and without doubt it needs to be chastised, regulated, and sanctified. But the democratic principle in its essence is of God, and in its normal state it is the consummate flower of Christianity, and is irresistible because it is the mighty breath of God.

It is democracy which has demanded the people's participation in government and the extension of suffrage, and it got it. It has demanded a higher wage for labor, and it has got it, and will get more. It has demanded the abolition of Negro slavery, and it has got it. Its present demand is the equality of man in the State, irrespective of race, condition, or lineage. The answer to this demand is the solution of the race-problem.

In this land the crucial test in the race-problem is the civil and political rights of the black man. The only question now remaining among us for the full triumph of Christian democracy is the equality of the Negro.

Nay, I take back my own words. It is NOT the case of the Negro in this land. It is the nation which is on trial. The Negro is only the touch-stone. By this black man she stands or falls.

If the black man cannot be free in this land, if he cannot tread with firmness every pathway to preferment and superiority, neither can the white man. "A bridge is never stronger than its weakest point."

> In nature's chain, whatever link you strike,
> Tenth or ten-thousandth, breaks the chain alike.

So compact a thing is humanity that the despoiling of an individual is an injury to society.

This nation has staked her existence on this principle of democracy in her every fundamental political dogma, and in every organic State document. The democratic idea is neither Anglo-Saxonism, nor Germanism, nor Hibernianism, but HUMANITY, and humanity can live when Anglo-Saxonism or any class of the race of man has perished. Humanity anticipated all human varieties by thousands of years, and rides above them all, and outlives them all, and swallows up them all!

If this nation is not truly democratic then she must die! Nothing is more destructive to a nation than an organic falsehood! This nation cannot live—this nation does not deserve to live—on the basis of a lie!

Her fundamental idea is democracy; and if this nation will not submit herself to the domination of this idea—if she refuses to live in the spirit of this creed— then she is already doomed, and she will certainly be damned.

But neither calamity, I ween, is her destiny.

The democratic spirit is of itself a prophecy of its own fulfillment. Its disasters are trivialities; its repulses only temporary. In this nation the Negro has been the test for over 200 years. But see how far the Negro has traveled this time.

In less than the lifetime of such a man as the great George Bancroft, observe the transformation in the status of the Negro in this land. When *he* was a child the Negro was a marketable commodity, a beast of the field, a chattel in the shambles, outside of the pale of the law, and ignorant as a pagan.

Nay, when I was a boy of 13, I heard the utterance fresh from the lips of the great J. C. Calhoun, to wit, that if he could find a Negro who knew the Greek syntax he would then believe that the Negro was a human being and should be treated as a man.

If he were living to-day he would come across scores of Negroes, not only versed in the Greek syntax, but doctors, lawyers, college students, clergymen, some learned professors, and *one* the author of a new Greek Grammar.

But just here the caste spirit interferes in this race-problem and declares: "You Negroes may get learning; you may get property; you may have churches and religion; but this is your limit! This is a white man's Government! No matter how many millions you may number, we Anglo-Saxons are to rule!" This is the edict constantly hissed in the Negro's ear, in one vast section of the land.

Let me tell you of a similar edict in another land:

Some sixty years ago there was a young nobleman, an undergraduate at Oxford University, a youth of much talent, learning, and political ambition; but, at the same time, he was *then* a foolish youth! His patrician spirit rose in bitter protest against the Reform Bill of that day, which lessened the power of the British aristocracy and increased the suffrages of the Commons. He was a clever young fellow, and he wrote a brilliant poem in defense of his order, notable, as you will see, for its rhythm, melody, and withal for its—silliness! Here are two lines from it:

> Let Laws and Letters, Arts and Learning die;
> But give us still our old Nobility.

Yes, let everything go to smash! Let civilization itself go to the dogs, if only an oligarchy may rule, flourish, and dominate!

We have a blatant provincialism in our own country, whose only solution of the race-problem is the eternal subjection of the Negro, and the endless domination of a lawless and self-created aristocracy.

Such men forget that the democratic spirit rejects the factious barriers of caste, and stimulates the lowest of the kind to the very noblest ambitions of life. They forget that nations are no longer governed by races, but by ideas. They forget that the triumphant spirit of democracy has bred an individualism which brooks not the restraints of classes and aristocracies. They forget that, regardless of "Pope, Consul, King," or oligarchy, this same spirit of democracy lifts up to place and power her own agents for the rule of the world; and brings to the front, now a Dane as King of Greece, and now a Frenchman as King of Sweden; now a Jewish D'Israeli as Prime Minister of England, and now a Gallatin and a Schurz as cabinet ministers in America. They forget that a Wamba and a Gurth in one generation, whispering angry discontent in secret places, become, by the inspiration of democracy, the outspoken Hampdens and Sydneys of another. They forget that, as letters ripen and education spreads, the "Sambos" and "Pompeys" of to-day will surely develop into the Touissants and the Christophes, the Wards and the Garnets of the morrow, champions of their race and vindicators of their rights. They forget that democracy, to use the words of De Tocqueville, "has severed every link of the chain" by which aristocracy had fixed every member of the community, "from the peasant to the king."[3]

They forget that the Church of God is in the world; that her mission is, by the Holy Ghost, "to take the weak things of the world to confound the mighty," "to put down the mighty from their seats, and to exalt them of low degree"; that now, as in all the ages, she will, by the Gospel, break up tyrannies and useless dynasties, and lift up the masses to nobleness of life, and exalt the humblest of men to excellence and superiority.

Above all things, they forget that "the King invisible, immortal, eternal" is upon the throne of the universe; that thither caste, and bigotry, and race-hate can never reach; that He is everlastingly committed to the interests of the oppressed; that He is constantly sending forth succors and assistances for the rescue of the wronged and injured; that He brings all the forces of the universe to grind to powder all the enormities of earth, and to rectify all the ills of humanity, and so hasten on the day of universal brotherhood.

By the presence and the power of that Divine Being all the alienations and disseverances of men shall be healed; all the race-problems of this land easily be solved; and love and peace prevail among men.

Notes: 1. "Duties of Higher toward Lower Races." Canon Rawlinson, *Princeton Review*. Nov., 1878. 2. See "Physics and Politics," by Bagehot, pp. 84, 85. 3. *Democracy in America*, B. 2, Ch. 2.

Source: Excerpt from 1888 speech, "The Race Problem in America," in *Africa and America: Addresses and Discourses* (Springfield, Mass.: Wiley, 1891), pp. 39–57.

SELECT BIBLIOGRAPHY:

Alexander Crummell, *Africa and America* (Springfield, Mass.: Wiley, 1891).

———, *The Relations and Duties of Free Colored Men in America to Africa* (Hartford, Conn.: Lockwood, 1861).

Rayford W. Logan and Michael R. Winston, eds., *Dictionary of American Negro Biography* (New York: W.W. Norton, 1982).

William Jeremiah Moses, *Alexander Crummell: A Study of Civilization and Discontent* (New York: Oxford University Press, 1989).

———, ed., *Destiny and Race: Selected Writings, 1840–1898* (Amherst: University of Massachusetts Press, 1992).

J. R. Oldfield, *Alexander Crummell (1819–1898) and the Creation of an African-American Church in Liberia* (Lewiston: E. Mellen Press, 1990).

———, ed., *Civilization and Black Progress: Selected Writings of Alexander Crummell on the South* (Charlottesville: University Press of Virginia, 1995).

Gregory U. Rigsby, *Alexander Crummell: A Pioneer in Nineteenth-Century Pan-African Thought* (New York: Greenwood Press, 1987).

~ 7 ~

"A Voice from the South," *Anna Julia Cooper, 1892*

Anna Julia Cooper (1858–1964) was born in Raleigh, North Carolina, the daughter of a free black woman and a slave father. She was educated at St. Augustine's Normal and Collegiate Institute in Raleigh. In 1877 she married an Episcopal clergyman, George Christopher Cooper, who died two years later. Cooper enrolled in Oberlin College in 1881, received her B.A. degree in 1884 and master's degree in 1887. Cooper's outstanding career as an educator, scholar, and public lecturer was unequaled for her time. For 39 years she taught mathematics and later Latin at the M Street High School in Washington, D.C. Cooper participated in the Pan-African Conference held in London in 1900. She undertook graduate studies at Columbia University from 1913 to 1916, and received her doctorate from the University of Paris in 1925. In the 1930s she served as president of Frelinghuysen University. Her 1892 book, *A Voice from the South*, is one of the pivotal early texts in the development of black feminist thought.

To-day America counts her millionaires by the thousand; questions of tariff and questions of currency are the most vital ones agitating the public mind. In this period, when material prosperity and well earned ease and luxury are assured facts from a national standpoint, woman's work and woman's influence are needed as never before; needed to bring a heart power into this money getting, dollar-worshipping civilization; needed to bring a moral force into the utilitarian motives and interests of the time; needed to stand for God and Home and Native Land *versus gain and greed and grasping selfishness.*

There can be no doubt that this fourth centenary of America's discovery which we celebrate at Chicago, strikes the keynote of another important transition in the history of this nation; and the prominence of woman in the management of its celebration is a fitting tribute to the part she is is destined to play among the forces of the future. This is the first congressional recognition of woman in this country, and this Board of Lady Managers constitute the first women legally appointed by any government to act in a national capacity. This of itself marks the dawn of a new day.

Now the periods of discovery, of settlement, of developing resources and accumulating wealth have passed in rapid succession. Wealth in the nation as in the individual brings leisure, repose, reflection. The struggle with nature is over, the struggle with ideas begins. We stand then, it seems to me, in this last decade of the nineteenth century, just in the portals of a new and untried movement on a higher plain and in a grander strain than any the past has called forth. It does not require a prophet's eye to divine its trend and image its possibilities from the forces we see already at work around us; nor is it hard to guess what must be the status of woman's work under the new regime.

In the pioneer days her role was that of a camp-follower, an additional something to fight for and be burdened with, only repaying the anxiety and labor she called forth by her own incomparable gifts of sympathy and appreciative love; unable herself ordinarily to contend with the bear and the Indian, or to take active part in clearing the wilderness and constructing the home.

In the second or wealth producing period her work is abreast of man's, complementing and supplementing, counteracting excessive tendencies, and mollifying over rigorous proclivities.

In the era now about to dawn, her sentiments must strike the keynote and give the dominant tone. And this because of the nature of her contribution to the world.

Her kingdom is not over physical forces. Not by might, nor by power can she prevail. Her position must ever be inferior where strength of muscle creates leadership. If she follows the instincts of her nature, however, she must always stand for the conservation of those deeper moral forces which make for the happiness of homes and the righteousness of the country. In a reign of moral ideas she is easily queen.

There is to my mind no grander and surer prophecy of the new era and of woman's place in it, than the work already begun in the waning years of the nineteenth century by the W.C.T.U.[1] in America, an organization which has even now reached not only national but international importance, and seems destined to permeate and purify the whole civilized world. It is the living embodiment of woman's activities and woman's ideas, and its extent and strength rightly prefigure her increasing power as a moral factor.

The colored woman of to-day occupies, one may say, a unique position in this country. In a period of itself transitional and unsettled, her status seems one of the least ascertainable and definitive of all the forces which make for our civilization. She is confronted by both a woman question and a race problem, and is as yet an unknown or an unacknowledged factor in both. While the women of the white race can with calm assurance enter upon the work they feel by nature appointed to do, while their men give loyal support and appreciative countenance to their efforts, recognizing in most avenues of usefulness the propriety and the need of woman's distinctive co-operation, the colored woman too often finds herself hampered and shamed by a less liberal sentiment and a more conservative attitude on the part of those for whose opinion she cares most. That this is not universally true I am glad to admit. There are to be found both intensely conservative white men and exceedingly liberal colored men. But as far as my experience goes the average man of our race is less frequently ready to admit the actual need among the sturdier forces of the world for woman's help or influence. That great social and economic questions await her interference, that she could throw any light on problems of national import, that her intermeddling could improve the management of school systems, or elevate the tone of public institutions, or humanize and sanctify the far reaching influence of prisons and reformatories and improve the treatment of lunatics and imbeciles,—that she has a word worth hearing on mooted questions in political economy, that she could contribute a suggestion on the relations of labor and capital, or offer a thought on honest money and honorable trade, I fear the majority of "Americans of the colored variety" are not yet prepared to concede. It may be that they do not yet see these questions in their right perspective, being absorbed in the immediate needs of their own political complications. A good deal depends on where we put the emphasis in this world; and our men are not perhaps to blame if they see everything colored by the light of those agitations in the midst of which they live and move and have their being. The part they have had to play in American history during the last twenty-five or thirty years has tended rather to exaggerate the importance of mere political advantage, as well as to set a fictitious valuation on those able to secure such advantage. It is the astute politician, the manager who can gain preferment for himself and his favorites, the demagogue known to stand in with the powers at the White House and consulted on the bestowal of government plums, whom we set in high places and denominate great. It is they who receive the hosannas of the multitude and are regarded as leaders of the people. The thinker and the doer, the man who solves the problem by enriching his country with an invention worth thousands or by a thought inestimable and precious is given neither bread nor a stone. He is too often left to die in obscurity and neglect even if spared in his life the bitterness of fanatical jealousies and detraction.

And yet politics, and surely American politics, is hardly a school for great minds. Sharpening rather than deepening, it develops the faculty of taking advantage of present emergencies rather than the insight to distinguish between the true and the false, the lasting and the ephemeral advantage. Highly cultivated selfishness rather than consecrated benevolence is its passport to success. Its votaries are never seers. At best they are but manipulators—often only jugglers. It is conducive neither to profound statesmanship nor to the higher type of manhood. Altruism is its *mauvais succès* and naturally enough it is indifferent to any factor which cannot be worked into its own immediate aims and purposes. As woman's influence as a political element is as yet nil in most of the commonwealth of our republic, it is not surprising that with those who place the emphasis on mere political capital she may yet seem almost a nonentity so far as it concerns the solution of great national or even racial perplexities.

There are those, however, who value the calm elevation of the thoughtful spectator who stands aloof from the heated scramble; and, above the turmoil and din of corruption and selfishness, can listen to the teachings of eternal truth and righteousness. There are even those who feel that the black man's unjust and unlawful exclusion temporarily from participation in the elective franchise in certain states is after all but a lesson "in the desert" fitted to develop in him insight and discrimination against the day of his own appointed time. One needs occasionally to stand aside from the hum and rush of human interests and passions to hear the voices of God. And it not unfrequently happens that the All-loving gives a great push to certain souls to thrust them out, as it were, from the distracting current for awhile to promote their discipline and growth, or to enrich them by communion and reflection. And similarly it may be woman's privilege from her peculiar coigne of vantage as a quiet observer, to whisper just the needed suggestion or the almost forgotten truth. The colored woman, then, should not be ignored because her bark is resting in the silent waters of the sheltered cove. She is watching the movements of the contestants none the less and is all the better qualified, perhaps, to weigh and judge and advise because not herself in the excitement of the race. Her voice, too, has always been heard in clear, unfaltering tones, ringing the changes on those deeper interests which make for permanent good. She is always sound and orthodox on questions affecting the well-being of her race. You do not find the colored woman selling her birthright for a mess of pottage. Nay, even after reason has retired from the contest, she has been known to cling blindly with the instinct of a turtle dove to those principles and policies which to her mind promise hope and safety for children yet unborn. It is notorious that ignorant black women in the South have actually left their husbands' homes and repudiated their support for what was understood by the wife to be race disloyalty, or "voting away," as she expresses it, the privileges of herself and little ones.

It is largely our women in the South to-day who keep the black men solid in the Republican party. The latter as they increase in intelligence and power of discrimination would be more apt to divide on local issues at any rate. They begin to see that the Grand Old Party regards the Negro's cause as an outgrown issue, and on Southern soil at least finds a too intimate acquaintanceship with him a somewhat unsavory recommendation. Then, too, their political wits have been sharpened to appreciate the fact that it is good policy to cultivate one's neighbors and not depend too much on a distant friend to fight one's home battles. But the black woman can never forget—however lukewarm the party may to-day appear—that it was a Republican president who struck the manacles from her own wrists and gave the possibilities of manhood to her helpless little ones; and to her mind a Democratic Negro is a traitor and a time-server. Talk as much as you like of venality and manipulation in the South, there are not many men, I can tell you, who would dare face a wife quivering in every fiber with the consciousness that her husband is a coward who could be paid to desert her deepest and dearest interests.

Not unfelt, then, if unproclaimed has been the work and influence of the colored women of America.[2] Our list of chieftains in the service, though not long, is not inferior in strength and excellence, I dare believe, to any similar list which this country can produce.

Among the pioneers, Frances Watkins Harper could sing with prophetic exaltation in the darkest days, when as yet there was not a rift in the clouds overhanging her people:

> Yes, Ethiopia shall stretch
> Her bleeding hands abroad;
> Her cry of agony shall reach the burning throne of God.
> Redeemed from dust and freed from chains
> Her sons shall lift their eyes,
> From cloud-capt hills and verdant plains
> Shall shouts of triumph rise.

Among preachers of righteousness, an unanswerable silencer of cavilers and objectors, was Sojourner Truth, that unique and rugged genius who seemed carved out without hand or chisel from the solid mountain mass; and in pleasing contrast, Amanda Smith, sweetest of natural singers and pleaders in dulcet tones for the things of God and of His Christ.

Sarah Woodson Early and Martha Briggs, planting and watering in the school room, and giving off from their matchless and irresistible personality an impetus and inspiration which can never die so long as there lives and breathes a remote descendant of their disciples and friends.

Charlotte Forten Grimké, the gentle spirit whose verses and life link her so beautifully with America's great Quaker poet and loving reformer.

Hallie Quinn Brown, charming reader, earnest, effective lecturer and devoted worker of unflagging zeal and unquestioned power.

Fanny Jackson Coppin, the teacher and organizer, pre-eminent among women of whatever country or race in constructive and executive force.

These women represent all shades of belief and as many departments of activity; but they have one thing in common—their sympathy with the oppressed race in America and the consecration of their several talents in whatever line to the work of its deliverance and development.

Fifty years ago woman's activity according to orthodox definitions was on a pretty clearly cut "sphere," including primarily the kitchen and the nursery, and rescued from the barrenness of prison bars by the womanly mania for adorning every discoverable bit of china or canvass with forlorn looking cranes balanced idiotically on one foot. The woman of today finds herself in the presence of responsibilities which ramify through the profoundest and most varied interests of her country and race. Not one of the issues of this plodding, toiling, sinning, repenting, falling, aspiring humanity can afford to shut her out, or can deny the reality of her influence. No plan for renovating society, no scheme for purifying politics, no reform in church or in state, no moral, social, or economic question, no movement upward or downward in the human plane is lost on her. A man once said when told his house was afire: "Go tell my wife; I never meddle with household affairs." But no woman can possibly put herself or her sex outside any of the interests that affect humanity. All departments in the new era are to be hers, in the sense that her interests are in all and through all; and it is incumbent on her to keep intelligently and sympathetically *en rapport* with all the great movements of her time, that she may know on which side to throw the weight of her influence. She stands now at the gateway of this new era of American civilization. In her hands must be moulded the strength, the wit, the statesmanship, the morality, all the psychic force, the social and economic intercourse of that era. To be alive at such an epoch is a privilege, to be a woman then is sublime.

In this last decade of our century, changes of such moment are in progress, such new and alluring vistas are opening out before us, such original and radical suggestions for the adjustment of labor and capital, of government and the governed, of the family, the church and the state, that to be a possible factor though an infinitesimal in such a movement is pregnant with hope and weighty with responsibility. To be a woman in such an age carries with it a privilege and an opportunity never implied before. But to be a woman of the Negro race in America, and to be able to grasp the deep significance of the possibilities of the crisis, is to have a heritage, it seems to me, unique in the ages. In the first place, the race is young and full of the elasticity and hopefulness of youth. All its achievements are before it. It does not look on the masterly triumphs of nineteenth-century civilization with that *blasé* world-weary look which characterized the old washed out and worn out races which have already, so to speak, seen their best days. . . .

Notes: 1. W.C.T.U.: Woman's Christian Temperance Union, an organization of women that crusaded against saloons and the drinking of alcohol. 2. In the paragraphs following, Cooper discusses the nineteenth century's most influential "colored women of America": Frances Watkins Harper (1825–1911), writer, lecturer, and poet, author of the quoted "Yes, Ethiopia . . ."; Sojourner Truth (1797–1883), evangelist, abolitionist, and feminist; Amanda Smith (1837–1915), evangelist and reformer; Sarah Woodson Early (1825–1907), pioneer black feminist-nationalist; Martha Briggs (1838–1889), faculty member and public school administrator; Charlotte Forten Grimké (1837–1914), antislavery poet, educator, and minister's wife; Hallie Quinn Brown (1845–1949), educator and social reformer, a founder of the National Association of Colored Women; and Fanny Jackson Coppin (1837–1913), educator and missionary.

Source: Excerpt from *A Voice from the South, By a Black Woman from the South* (Xenia, Ohio: Aldine Printing House, 1892).

SELECT BIBLIOGRAPHY:

Cathryn Bailey, "Anna Julia Cooper: 'Dedicated in the Name of My Slave Mother to the Education of Colored Working People,'" *Hypatia* 19, no. 2 (Spring 2004), pp. 56–73.

Karen Baker-Fletcher, *A Singing Something: Womanist Reflections on Anna Julia Cooper* (New York: Crossroad, 1994).

Ruth Bogin and Bert Lowenburg, *Black Women in Nineteenth-Century American Life: Their Words, Their Thoughts, Their Feelings* (University Park: Pennsylvania State University Press, 1985).

Kevin Gaines, *Uplifting the Race: Black Leadership, Politics and Culture in the Twentieth Century* (Chapel Hill: University of North Carolina Press, 1996).

Kathy L. Glass, "Tending to the Roots: Anna Julia Cooper's Sociopolitical Thought and Activism," *Meridians: Feminism, Race, Transnationalism* 6, no. 1 (October 2005), pp. 23–55.

LaRese Charmell Hubbard, "An Afrocentric Study of the Intellectual Thought of Anna Julia Cooper" (Ph.D. diss., Temple University, 2005).

Charles C. Lemert, and Esme Bhan, eds., *The Voice of Anna Julia Cooper: Including a Voice from the South and Other Important Essays, Papers, and Letters* (Lanham, Md.: Rowman & Littlefield, 1998).

Vivian M. May, *Anna Julia Cooper, Visionary Black Feminist: A Critical Introduction* (London: Routledge, 2007).

———, "Thinking from the Margins, Acting at the Intersections: Anna Julia Cooper's a Voice from the South," *Hypatia* 19, no. 2 (Spring 2004), pp. 74–91.

Christiane Warren-Christian, "Anna Julia Cooper: Feminist and Scholar" (Ph.D. diss., Drew University, 2003).

⫷ 8 ⫸

The National Association of Colored Women: Mary Church Terrell and Josephine St. Pierre Ruffin

Mary Church Terrell (1863–1954) was born in Memphis, Tennessee, into an affluent black family. Educated at Oberlin College, she received her bachelor's degree in 1884 and her master's degree four years later. In 1892 she was the first woman president of the Bethel Literary and Historical Association. In 1895 Terrell was appointed to the Board of Education in Washington, D.C., probably the first black women to be named to a school board in the United States. Terrell was a cofounder and the first president of the National Association of Colored Women (NACW) in 1896. She was active in civil rights and women's rights causes. While her husband, Robert Terrell, was a judge and a political ally of Booker T. Washington, she fearlessly attacked racial segregation. Terrell was for many years the vice president of the NAACP. At the age of ninety she led and participated in desegregation demonstrations and picket lines.

Josephine St. Pierre Ruffin (1842–1924) was born and educated in Boston, worked locally as an advocate of civil rights and women's suffrage, and maintained friendships with Frederick Douglass and William Lloyd Garrison. She gained further prominence through her interest in the Women's Club Movement, and she served as president of the National Federation of Afro-American Women. In 1896, her organization merged into Terrell's NACW, where she became vice-president. Ruffin died in Boston in 1924.

~~~

"The Progress of Colored Women," Mary Church Terrell

When one considers the obstacles encountered by colored women in their effort to educate and cultivate themselves, since they became free, the work they have accomplished and the progress they have made will bear favorable comparison, at least with that of their more fortunate sisters, from whom the opportunity of acquiring knowledge and the means of self-culture have never been entirely withheld. Not only are colored women with ambition and aspiration handicapped on account of their sex, but they are almost everywhere baffled and mocked because of their race. Not only because they are women, but because they are colored women are discouragement and disappointment meeting them at every turn. But in spite of the obstacles encountered, the progress made by colored women along many lines appears like a veritable miracle of modern times. Forty years ago for the great masses of colored women there was no such thing as home. Today in each and every section of the country there are hundreds of homes among colored people, the mental and moral tone of which is as high and as pure as can be found among the best people of any land.

To the women of the race may be attributed in large measure the refinement and purity of the colored home. The immorality of colored women is a theme upon which those who know little about them or those who maliciously misrepresent them love to descant. Foul aspersions upon the character of colored women are assiduously circulated by the press of certain sections and especially by the direct descendants of those who in years past were responsible for the moral degradation of their female slaves. And yet, in spite of the fateful heritage of slavery, even though the safeguards usually thrown around maidenly youth and innocence are in some sections entirely withheld from colored girls, statistics compiled by men not inclined to falsify in favor of my race show that immorality among the colored women of the United States is not so great as among women with similar environment and temptations in Italy, Germany, Sweden and France.

Scandals in the best colored society are exceedingly rare, while the progressive game of divorce and remarriage is practically unknown.

The intellectual progress of colored women has been marvelous. So great has been their thirst for knowledge and so Herculean their efforts to acquire it that there are few colleges, universities, high and normal schools in the North, East and West from which colored girls have not graduated with honor. In Wellesley, Vassar, Ann Arbor, Cornell and in Oberlin, my dear alma mater, whose name will always be loved and whose praise will always be sung as the first college in the country broad, just and generous enough to extend a cordial welcome to the Negro and to open its doors to women on an equal footing with the men, colored girls by their splendid records have forever settled the question of their capacity and worth. The instructors in these and other institutions cheerfully bear testimony to their intelligence, their diligence and their success.

As the brains of colored women expanded, their hearts began to grow. No sooner had the heads of a favored few been filled with knowledge than their hearts yearned to dispense blessings to the less fortunate of their race. With tireless energy and eager zeal, colored women have worked in every conceivable way to elevate their race. Of the colored teachers engaged in instructing our youth it is probably no exaggeration to say that fully 80 percent are women. In the backwoods, remote from the civilization and comforts of the city and town colored women may be found courageously battling with those evils which such conditions always entail. Many a heroine of whom the world will never hear has thus sacrificed her life to her race amid surroundings and in the face of privations which only martyrs can bear.

Through the medium of their societies in the church, beneficial organizations out of it and clubs of various kinds, colored women are doing a vast amount of good. It is almost impossible to ascertain exactly what the Negro is doing in any field, for the records are so poorly kept. This is particularly true in the case of the women of the race. During the past forty years there is no doubt that colored women in their poverty have contributed large sums of money to charitable and educational institutions as well as to the foreign and home missionary work. Within the twenty-five years in which the educational work of the African Methodist Episcopal Church has been systematized, the women of that organization have contributed at least five hundred thousand dollars to the cause of education. Dotted all over the country are charitable institutions for the aged, orphaned and poor which have been established by colored women. Just how many it is difficult to state, owing to the lack of statistics bearing on the progress, possessions and prowess of colored women.

Among the charitable institutions either founded, conducted or supported by colored women, may be mentioned the Hale Infirmary of Montgomery, Alabama, the Carrie Steel Orphanage of Atlanta, the Reed Orphan Home of Covington, and the Hains Industrial School of Augusta, all three in the state of Georgia; a home for the aged of both races in New Bedford, and St. Monica's Home of Boston, in Massachusetts, Old Folks Home of Memphis, Tennessee, and the Colored Orphan's Home of Lexington, Kentucky, together with others which lack of space forbids me to mention. Mt. Meigs Institute is an excellent example of a work originated and carried into successful execution by a colored woman. The school was established for the benefit of colored people on the plantations in the black belt of Alabama. In the township of Mt. Meigs the population is practically all colored. Instruction given in this school is of the kind best suited to the needs of the people for whom it was established. Along with some scholastic training, girls are taught everything pertaining to the management of the home, while boys are taught practical farming, wheelwrighting, blacksmithing, and have some military training. Having started with almost nothing, at the end of eight years the trustees of the school owned nine acres of land

and five buildings in which several thousand pupils had received instructions, all through the energy, the courage and the sacrifice of one little woman.

Up to date, politics have been religiously eschewed by colored women, although questions affecting our legal status as a race is sometimes agitated by the most progressive class. In Louisiana and Tennessee colored women have several times petitioned the legislatures of their respective states to repel the obnoxious Jim-Crow-car laws. Against the convict-lease system, whose atrocities have been so frequently exposed of late, colored women here and there in the South are waging a ceaseless war. So long as hundreds of their brothers and sisters, many of whom have committed no crime or misdemeanor whatever, are thrown into cells whose cubic contents are less than those of a good-size grave, to be overworked, underfed and only partially covered with vermin-infested rags, and so long as children are born to the women in those camps who breathe the polluted atmosphere of these dens of horror and vice from the time they utter their first cry in the world till they are released from their suffering by death, colored women who are working for the emancipation and elevation of their race know where their duty lies. By constant agitation of this painful and hideous subject they hope to touch the conscience of the country, so that this stain upon its escutcheon shall be forever wiped away.

Alarmed at the rapidity with which the Negro is losing ground in the world of trade, some of the farsighted women are trying to solve the labor question, so far as it concerns the women at least, by urging the establishment of schools of domestic science wherever means therefor can be secured. Those who are interested in this particular work hope and believe that if colored women and girls are thoroughly trained in domestic service, the boycott which has undoubtedly been placed upon them in many sections of the country will be removed. With so few vocations open to the Negro and with the labor organizations increasingly hostile to him, the future of the boys and girls of the race appears to some of our women very foreboding and dark.

The cause of temperance has been eloquently espoused by two women, each of whom has been appointed national superintendent of work among colored people by the Woman's Christian Temperance Union. In business, colored women have had signal success. There is in Alabama a large milling and cotton business belonging to and controlled by a colored woman, who has sometimes as many as seventy-five men in her employ. Until a few years ago the principal ice plant of Nova Scotia was owned and managed by a colored woman, who sold it for a large amount. In the professions there are dentists and doctors whose practice is lucrative and large. Ever since a book was published in 1773 entitled "Poems on Various Subjects. Religious and Moral by Phillis Wheatley, Negro Servant of Mr. John Wheatley," of Boston, colored women have given abundant evidence of literary ability. In sculpture we are represented by a woman upon whose chisel Italy has set her seal of approval; in painting by one of Bouguereau's pupils and in music by young women holding diplomas from the best conservatories in the land.

In short, to use a thought of the illustrious Frederick Douglass, if judged by the depths from which they have come, rather than by the heights to which those blessed with centuries of opportunities have attained, colored women need not hang their heads in shame. They are slowly but surely making their way up to the heights, wherever they can be scaled. In spite of handicaps and discouragements they are not losing heart. In a variety of ways they are rendering valiant service to their race. Lifting as they climb, onward and upward they go struggling and striving and hoping that the buds and blossoms of their desires may burst into glorious fruition ere long. Seeking no favors because of their color nor charity because of their needs they knock at the door of Justice and ask for an equal chance.

~

LETTER TO THE LADIES OF THE GEORGIA EDUCATIONAL LEAGUE, JOSEPHINE ST. PIERRE RUFFIN

Ladies of the Georgia Educational League:

The telegram which you sent to Governor Northern to read to his audience, informing the people of the North of your willingness to undertake the moral training of the colored children of Georgia, merits more than a passing notice. It is the first time, we believe, in the history of the South where a body of representative Southern white women have shown such interest in the moral welfare of the children of their former slaves as to be willing to undertake to make them more worthy the duties and responsibilities of citizenship. True, there have been individual cases where courageous women have felt their moral responsibility, and have nobly met it, but one of the saddest things about the sad condition of affairs in the South has been the utter indifference which Southern women, who were guarded with unheard of fidelity during the war, have manifested to the mental and moral welfare of the children of their faithful slaves, who, in the language of Henry Grady, placed a black mass of loyalty between them and dishonor. This was a rare opportunity for you to have shown your gratitude to your slaves and your interest in their future welfare.

The children would have grown up in utter ignorance had not the North sent thousands of her noblest daughters to the South on this mission of heroic love and mercy; and it is worthy of remark of those fair daughters of the North, that, often eating with Negroes, and in the earlier days sleeping in their humble cabins, and always surrounded by thousands of them, there is not one recorded instance where one has been the victim of violence or insult. If because of the bitterness of your feelings, of your deep poverty at the close of the war, conditions were such that you could not do this work yourselves, you might have give a Christian's welcome to the women who came a thousand miles to do the work, that, in all gratitude and obligation belonged to you,—but instead, these women were often persecuted, always they have been ruthlessly ostracised, even until this day; often they were lonely, often longed for a word of sympathy, often craved association with their own race, but for thirty years they have been treated by the Christian white women of the South,—simply because they were doing your work,—the work committed to you by your Saviour, when he said, "Inasmuch as you did it to one of the least of these my brethren, you did it unto me,"—with a contempt that would serve to justify a suspicion that instead of being the most cultured women, the purest, bravest missionaries in America, they were outcasts and lepers.

But at last a change has come. And so you have "decided to take up the work of moral and industrial training of the Negroes," as you "have been doing this work among the whites with splendid results." This is one of the most hopeful stars that have shot through the darkness of the Southern sky. What untold blessings might not the educated Christian women of the South prove to the Negro groping blindly in the darkness of the swamps and bogs of prejudice for a highway out of servitude, oppression, ignorance, and immorality!

The leading women of Georgia should not ask Northern charity to do what they certainly must have the means for making a beginning of themselves. If your heart is really in this work—and we do not question it—the very best way for you to atone for your negligence in the past is to make a start yourselves. Surely if the conditions are as serious as you represent them to be, your husbands, who are men of large means, who are able to run great expositions and big peace celebrations, will be willing to provide you with the means to protect your virtue and that of your daughters by the moral training you propose to give in the kindergartens.

There is much you might do without the contribution of a dollar from any pocket, Northern or Southern. On every plantation there are scores, if not hundreds, of little colored children who could be gathered about you on a Sabbath afternoon and given many helpful inspiring lessons in morals and good conduct.

It is a good augury of better days, let us hope, when the intelligent, broad-minded women of Georgia, spurning the incendiary advice of that human firebrand who would lynch a thousand Negroes a month, are willing to join in this great altruistic movement of the age and endeavor to lift up the degraded and ignorant, rather than to exterminate them. Your proposition implies that they may be uplifted and further, imports a tacit confession that if you had done your duty to them at the close of the war, which both gratitude and prudence should have prompted you to do, you would not now be confronted with a condition which you feel it necessary to check, in obedience to the great first law of nature—self-protection. If you enter upon this work you will doubtless be criticised by a class of your own people who think you are lowering your own dignity, but the South has suffered too much already from that kind of false pride to let it longer keep her recreant to the spirit of the age.

If, when you have entered upon it, you need the cooperation, either by advice or other assistance, of the colored women of the North, we beg to assure you that they will not be lacking,—until then, the earnest hope goes out that you will bravely face and sternly conquer your former prejudices and quickly undertake this missionary work which belongs to you.

Sources: (1) Mary Church Terrell, "The Progress of Colored Women," excerpt from a speech originally published in *The Voice of the Negro* (July 1904), pp. 292–94; and (2) Josephine St.

Pierre Ruffin, excerpt from "Letter to the Ladies of the Georgia Educational League," June 1889, published in Alice Moore Dunbar, ed., *Masterpieces of Negro Eloquence* (New York: Bookery Publishing, 1914), pp. 173–76.

SELECT BIBLIOGRAPHY:

Sharon Harley, "Mary Church Terrell: Genteel Militant," in *Black Leaders of the Nineteenth Century*, ed. Leon Litwack and August Meier (Urbana: University of Illinois Press, 1988), pp. 291–307.

Beverly Washington Jones, *Quest for Equality: The Life and Writings of Mary Eliza Church Terrell, 1863–1954* (Brooklyn, N.Y.: Carlson Publishing, 1990).

Gladys B. Shepperd, *Mary Church Terrell: Respectable Person* (Baltimore: Human Relations Press, 1959).

Dorothy Sterling, *Black Foremothers: Three Lives* (Old Westbury, N.Y.: Feminist Press, 1979).

Mary Church Terrell, *A Colored Woman in a White World* (Washington, D.C.: Ransdell, 1940).

Teresa Blue Holden, "'Earnest Women Can Do Anything': The Public Career of Josephine St. Pierre Ruffin, 1842–1904" (Ph.D. diss., St. Louis University, 2006).

≈ 9 ≈

"I Know Why the Caged Bird Sings," *Paul Laurence Dunbar*

Born in Dayton, Ohio, Paul Laurence Dunbar (1872–1906) would become the most popular African-American poet in the early twentieth century. In 1893 his poetry began to receive favorable attention in the press. But it was Dunbar's *Majors and Minors* (1895) that catapulted him to prominence as one of America's most prominent poets. Dunbar was best known for his "dialect poetry," which was based on the language and idioms of rural black culture. At least half of Dunbar's prose and poetry was not written in the dialect style, and some of his work, such as his famous poem "We Wear the Mask," hints at a political and social critique of white racism. Unfairly criticized by some for representing African Americans solely as racial stereotypes, Dunbar's best work still retains its creativity and originality.

≈

"Ode to Ethiopia"

> O Mother Race! to thee I bring
> This pledge of faith unwavering,
> This tribute to thy glory.
> I know the pangs which thou didst feel,
> When Slavery crushed thee with its heel,
> With thy dear blood all gory.
>
> Sad days were those—ah, sad indeed!
> But through the land the fruitful seed

Of better times was growing.
The plant of freedom upward sprung,
And spread its leaves so fresh and young—
Its blossoms now are blowing.

On every hand in this fair land,
Proud Ethiope's swarthy children stand
Beside their fairer neighbour;
The forests flee before their stroke,
Their hammers ring, their forges smoke,—
they stir in honest labour.

They tread the fields where honour calls;
Their voices sound through senate halls
In majesty and power.
To right they cling; the hymns they sing
Up to the skies in beauty ring,
And bolder grow each hour.

Be proud, my Race, in mind and soul;
Thy name is writ on Glory's scroll
In characters of fire.
High 'mid the clouds of Fame's bright sky
Thy banner's blazoned folds now fly,
And truth shall lift them higher.

Thou hast the right to noble pride.
Whose spotless robes were purified
By blood's severe baptism.
Upon thy brow the cross was laid,
And labour's painful sweat-beads made
A consecrating chrism.

No other race, or white or black,
When bound as thou wert, to the rack,
So seldom stooped to grieving;
No other race, when free again,
Forgot the past and proved them men
So noble in forgiving.

Go on and up! Our souls and eyes
Shall follow thy continuous rise;
Our ears shall list thy story
From bards who from thy root shall spring,
And proudly tune their lyres to sing
Of Ethiopia's glory.

"We Wear the Mask"

> We wear the mask that grins and lies,
> It hides our cheeks and shades our eyes,—
> this Debt we pay to human guile;
> With torn and bleeding hearts we smile,
> And mouth with myriad subtleties.
>
> Why should the world be overwise,
> In counting all our tears and sighs?
> Nay, let them only see us, while
>   We wear the mask.
>
> We smile, but, O great Christ, our cries
> To thee from tortured souls arise.
> We sing, but oh the clay is vile
> Beneath our feet, and long the mile;
> But let the world dream otherwise,
>   We wear the mask!

"Sympathy"

> I know what the caged bird feels, alas!
>   When the sun is bright on the upland slopes;
> When the wind stirs soft through the springing grass,
> And the river flows like a stream of glass;
>   When the first bird sings and the first bud opes,
> And the faint perfume from its chalice steals:
> I know what the caged bird feels!
>
> I know why the caged bird beats his wing
>   Till its blood is red on the cruel bars;
> For he must fly back to his perch and cling
> When he fain would be on the bough a-swing;
>   And a pain still throbs in the old, old scars
> And they pulse again with a keener sting:
> I know why he beats his wing!
>
> I know why the caged bird sings, ah me,
>   When his wing is bruised and his bosom sore:
> When he beats his bars and he would be free;
> It is not a carol of joy or glee,
>   But a prayer that he sends from his heart's deep core,
> But a plea, that upward to Heaven he flings:
> I know why the caged bird sings!

Source: "Ode to Ethiopia" (1893), "We Wear the Mask" (1895), and "Sympathy" (1899) from Joanne M. Braxton, ed., *Collected Poetry of Paul Laurence Dunbar* (Charlottesville: University Press of Virginia, 1993). Reprinted by permission of the University Press of Virginia.

SELECT BIBLIOGRAPHY:

Virginia Cunningham, *Paul Laurence Dunbar and His Song* (New York: Dodd, Mead, 1974).

Kevin Gaines, *Uplifting the Race: Black Leadership, Politics, and Culture in the 20th Century* (Chapel Hill: University of North Carolina Press, 1996).

Jay Martin, ed., *Singer in the Dawn: A Reinterpretation of Paul Laurence Dunbar* (New York: Dodd, Mead, 1975).

Jay Martin and Gossie H. Hudson, eds., *The Paul Laurence Dunbar Reader* (New York: Dodd, Mead, 1975).

E. W. Metcalf, *Paul Laurence Dunbar: A Bibliography* (Metuchen, N.J.: Scarecrow Press, 1975).

Peter Revell, *Paul Laurence Dunbar* (Boston: Twayne Publishers, 1979).

Herbert Woodward Martin and Ronald Primeau, eds., *In His Own Voice: The Dramatic and Other Uncollected Works of Paul Laurence Dunbar* (Athens: Ohio University Press, 2002).

⁓ 10 ⁓

Booker T. Washington and the Politics of Accommodation

Booker T. Washington (1856–1915) was the most powerful and influential African-American politician from the end of Reconstruction until the emergence of the Civil Rights movement. Born in slavery, Washington's remarkable climb to personal prominence was in many ways a Horatio Alger story. Working his way through Hampton Institute, at the age of twenty-six Washington founded Tuskegee Institute in the heart of Alabama's Black Belt. With few resources, within twenty years he had built the largest black vocational and agricultural school in the United States. Washington first became famous among whites for his "Atlanta Compromise" address of 1895, where he appeared to renounce civil rights and racial equality in favor of segregated economic development. Washington's ideology of hard work, self-help, and black capitalism appealed to white business, philanthropic, and political leaders, who lavished resources on Tuskegee. Washington founded the National Negro Business League in 1900. His network of supporters formed the powerful "Tuskegee Machine," which had a vast influence among African-American institutions in the early 1900s. Although Washington privately lobbied against the political disfranchisement of blacks, he was accused of directly contributing to lynchings and racial segregation by critics such as William Monroe Trotter. Washington's real influence rested with his strong support from Republican presidents such as Theodore Roosevelt, and philanthropists like Andrew Carnegie. But with the presidential election of Woodrow Wilson in 1912, much of Washington's patronage diminished. Washington's last major essay, "My View of

Segregation Laws," which is excerpted here, represented a modest move away from his accommodationist stance on Jim Crow.

~~

ATLANTA EXPOSITION ADDRESS

One-third of the population of the South is of the Negro race. No enterprise seeking the material, civil, or moral welfare of this section can disregard this element of our population and reach the highest success. I but convey to you, Mr. President and Directors, the sentiment of the masses of my race when I say that in no way have the value and manhood of the American Negro been more fittingly and generously recognized than by the managers of this magnificent exposition at every stage of its progress. It is a recognition that will do more to cement the friendship of the two races than any occurrence since the dawn of our freedom.

Not only this, but the opportunity here afforded will awaken among us a new era of industrial progress. Ignorant and inexperienced, it is not strange that in the first years of our new life we began at the top instead of at the bottom; that a seat in Congress or the State Legislature was more sought than real estate or industrial skill; that the political convention or stump-speaking had more attraction than starting a dairy farm or truck garden.

A ship lost at sea for many days suddenly sighted a friendly vessel. From the mast of the unfortunate vessel was seen a signal: "Water, water; we die of thirst!" The answer from the friendly vessel at once came back: "Cast down your bucket where you are." A second time the signal, "Water, water; send us water!" ran up from the distressed vessel, and was answered: "Cast down your bucket where you are." And a third and fourth signal for water was answered, "Cast down your bucket where you are." The captain of the distressed vessel, at last heeding the injunction, cast down his bucket, and it came up full of fresh, sparkling water from the mouth of the Amazon River. To those of my race who depend upon bettering their condition in a foreign land, or who underestimate the importance of cultivating friendly relations with the Southern white man who is their next-door neighbor, I would say: "Cast down your bucket where you are"—cast it down in making friends, in every manly way, of the people of all races by whom we are surrounded.

Cast it down in agriculture, mechanics, in commerce, in domestic service, and in the professions. And in this connection it is well to bear in mind that whatever other sins the South may be called to bear, when it comes to business, pure and simple, it is in the South that the Negro is given a man's chance in the commercial world, and in nothing is this Exposition more eloquent than in emphasizing this chance. Our greatest danger is that in the great leap from slavery to freedom we may overlook the fact that the masses of us are to live by the productions of our hands, and fail to keep in mind that we shall prosper in proportion as we learn to dignify and glorify common labor, and put brains and skill into the common occupations of life; shall prosper in proportion as we learn to draw the line between the superficial and the substantial, the ornamental gewgaws of life and the useful. No race can prosper till it learns that there is as much dignity in tilling a field as in writing a poem. It is at the bottom of life we must begin, and not at the top. Nor should we permit our grievances to overshadow our opportunities.

To those of the white race who look to the incoming of those of foreign birth and strange tongue and habits for the prosperity of the South, were I permitted, I would repeat what I say to my own race, "Cast down your bucket where you are." Cast it down among the eight million Negroes whose habits you know, whose fidelity and love you have tested in days when to have proved treacherous meant the ruin of your firesides. Cast down your bucket among these people who have without strikes and labor wars tilled your fields, cleared your forests, builded your railroads and cities, brought forth treasures from the bowels of the earth, and helped make possible this magnificent representation of the progress of the South. Casting down your bucket among my people, helping and encouraging them as you are doing on these grounds, and, with education of head, hand, and heart, you will find that they will buy your surplus land, make blossom the waste places in your fields, and run your factories. While doing this, you can be sure in the future, as in the past, that you and your families will be surrounded by the most patient, faithful, law-abiding, and unresentful people that the world has seen. As we have proved our loyalty to you in the past, in nursing your children, watching by the sick bed of your mothers and fathers, and often following them with tear-dimmed eyes to their graves, so in the future, in our humble way, we shall stand by you with a devotion that no foreigner can approach, ready to lay down our lives, if need be, in defense of yours, interlacing our industrial, commercial, civil, and religious life with yours in a way that shall make the interests of both races one. In all things that are purely social we can be as separate as the fingers, yet one as the hand in all things essential to mutual progress.

There is no defense or security for any of us except in the highest intelligence and development of all. If anywhere there are efforts tending to curtail the fullest growth of the Negro, let these efforts be turned into stimulating, encouraging, and making him the most useful and intelligent citizen. Effort or means so invested will pay a thousand per cent interest. These efforts will be twice blessed —"Blessing him that gives and him that takes."

There is no escape through law of man or God from the inevitable:

> The laws of changeless justice bind
>   Oppressor with oppressed;
> And close as sin and suffering joined
>   We march to fare abreast.

Nearly sixteen millions of hands will aid you in pulling the load upward, or they will pull, against you, the load downward. We shall constitute one-third and more of the ignorance and crime of the South, or one-third its intelligence and progress; we shall contribute one-third to the business and industrial prosperity of the South, or we shall prove a veritable body of death, stagnating, depressing, retarding every effort to advance the body politic.

Gentlemen of the Exposition, as we present to you our humble effort at an exhibition of our progress, you must not expect overmuch. Starting thirty years ago with ownership here and there in a few quilts and pumpkins and chickens (gathered from miscellaneous sources), remember, the path that has led from these to the inventions and production of agricultural implements, buggies, steam engines, newspapers, books, statuary carving, paintings, the management of drug-stores and banks, has not been trodden without contact with thorns and thistles. While we take pride in what we exhibit as a result of our independent efforts, we do not for a moment forget that our part in this exhibition would fall far short of your expectations but for the constant help that has come to our educational life, not only from the Southern states, but especially from Northern philanthropists, who have made their gifts a constant stream of blessing and encouragement.

The wisest among my race understand that the agitation of questions of social equality is the extremest folly, and that progress in the enjoyment of all the priv-ileges that will come to us must be the result of severe and constant struggle rather than of artificial forcing. No race that has anything to contribute to the markets of the world is long, in any degree, ostracized. It is important and right that all privileges of the law be ours, but it is vastly more important that we be prepared for the exercise of those privileges. The opportunity to earn a dollar in a factory just now is worth infinitely more than the opportunity to spend a dollar in an opera house.

In conclusion, may I repeat that nothing in thirty years has given us more hope and encouragement, and drawn us so near to you of the white race, as this oppor-tunity offered by the Exposition; and here bending, as it were, over the altar that represents the results of the struggles of your race and mine, both starting practi-cally empty-handed three decades ago, I pledge that, in your effort to work out the great and intricate problem which God has laid at the doors of the South, you shall have at all times the patient, sympathetic help of my race; only let this be con-stantly in mind, that while, from representations in these buildings of the product of field, of forest, of mine, of factory, letters, and art, much good will come, yet far above and beyond material benefits will be that higher good, that, let us pray God, will come in a blotting out of sectional differences and racial animosities and sus-picions, in a determination to administer absolute justice, in a willing obedience among all classes to the mandates of law. This, coupled with our material pros-perity, will bring into our beloved South a new heaven and a new earth.

My View of Segregation Laws

In all of my experience I have never yet found a case where the masses of the people of any given city were interested in the matter of the segregation of white and colored people; that is, there has been no spontaneous demand for segrega-tion ordinances. In certain cities politicians have taken the leadership in intro-ducing such segregation ordinances into city councils, and after making an appeal to racial prejudices have succeeded in securing a backing for ordinances which would segregate the Negro people from their white fellow citizens. After such ordinances have been introduced it is always difficult, in the present state of public opinion in the South, to have any considerable body of white people oppose them, because their attitude is likely to be misrepresented as favoring Negroes against white people. They are, in the main, afraid of the stigma, "Negro-lover."

It is probably useless to discuss the legality of segregation; that is a matter which the courts will finally pass upon. It is reasonably certain, however, that the courts in no section of the country would uphold a case where Negroes sought to segregate white citizens. This is the most convincing argument that segregation is regarded as illegal, when viewed on its merits by the whole body of our white citizens.

Personally I have little faith in the doctrine that it is necessary to segregate the whites from the blacks to prevent race mixture. The whites are the dominant race in the South, they control the courts, the industries and the government in all of the cities, counties and states except in those few communities where the Negroes, seeking some form of self-government, have established a number of experimental towns or communities.

I have never viewed except with amusement the sentiment that white people who live next to Negro populations suffer physically, mentally and morally because of their proximity to colored people. Southern white people who have been brought up in this proximity are not inferior to other white people. The President of the United States was born and reared in the South in close contact with black people. Five members of the present Cabinet were born in the South; and many of them, I am sure, had black "mammies." The Speaker of the House of Representatives is a Southern man, the chairman of leading committees in both the United States Senate and the Lower House of Congress are Southern men. Throughout the country to-day, people occupying the highest positions not only in the government but in education, industry and science, are persons born in the South in close contact with the Negro.

Attempts at legal segregation are unnecessary for the reason that the matter of residence is one which naturally settles itself. Both colored and whites are likely to select a section of the city where they will be surrounded by congenial neighbors. It is unusual to hear of a colored man attempting to live where he is surrounded by white people or where he is not welcome. Where attempts are being made to segregate the races legally, it should be noted that in the matter of business no attempt is made to keep the white man from placing his grocery store, his dry goods store, or other enterprise right in the heart of a Negro district. This is another searching test which challenges the good faith of segregationists.

It is true that the Negro opposes these attempts to restrain him from residing in certain sections of a city or community. He does this not because he wants to mix with the white man socially, but because he feels that such laws are unnecessary. The Negro objects to being segregated because it usually means that he will receive inferior accommodations in return for the taxes he pays. If the Negro is segregated, it will probably mean that the sewerage in his part of the city will be inferior; that the streets and sidewalks will be neglected, that the street lighting will be poor; that his section of the city will not be kept in order by the police and other authorities, and that the "undesirables" of other races will be placed near him, thereby making it difficult for him to rear his family in decency. It should always be kept in mind that while the Negro may not be directly a large taxpayer, he does pay large taxes indirectly. In the last analysis, all will agree that the man who pays house rent pays large taxes, for the price paid for the rent includes payment of the taxes on the property.

Right here in Alabama nobody is thinking or talking about land and home segregation. It is rather remarkable that in the very heart of the Black Belt where the black man is most ignorant the white people should not find him so repulsive as to set him away off to himself. If living side by side is such a menace as some people think, it does seem as if the people who have had the bulk of the race question to handle during the past fifty years would have discovered the danger and adjusted it long ago.

A segregated Negro community is a terrible temptation to many white people. Such a community invariably provides certain types of white men with hiding-places—hiding-places from the law, from decent people of their own race, from their churches and their wives and daughters. In a Negro district in a certain city in the South a house of ill-repute for white men was next door to a Negro denominational school. In another town a similar kind of house is just across the street from the Negro grammar school. In New Orleans the legalized vice section is set in the midst of the Negro section, and near the spot where stood a Negro school and a Negro church, and near the place where the Negro orphanage now operates. Now when a Negro seeks to buy a house in a reputable street he does it not only to get police protection, lights and accommodations, but to remove his children to a locality in which vice is not paraded.

In New Orleans, Atlanta, Birmingham, Memphis—indeed in nearly every large city in the South—I have been in the homes of Negroes who live in white neighborhoods, and I have yet to find any race friction; the Negro goes about his business, the white man about his. Neither the wives nor the children have the slightest trouble.

White people who argue for the segregation of the masses of black people forget the tremendous power of objective teaching. To hedge any set of people off in a corner and sally among them now and then with a lecture or a sermon is merely to add misery to degradation. But put the black man where day by day he sees how the white man keeps his lawns, his windows; how he treats his wife and children, and you will do more real helpful teaching than a whole library of lectures and sermons. Moreover, this will help the white man. If he knows that his life is to be taken as a model, that his hours, dress, manners, are all to be patterns for someone less fortunate, he will deport himself better than he would otherwise. Practically all the real moral uplift the black people have got from the whites—and this has been great indeed—has come from this observation of the white man's conduct. The South to-day is still full of the type of Negro with gentle manners. Where did he get them? From some master or mistress of the same type.

Summarizing the matter in the large, segregation is ill-advised because

1. It is unjust.
2. It invites other unjust measures.
3. It will not be productive of good, because practically every thoughtful Negro resents its injustice and doubts its sincerity. Any race adjustment based on injustice finally defeats itself. The Civil War is the best illustration of what results where it is attempted to make wrong right or seem to be right.
4. It is unnecessary.
5. It is inconsistent. The Negro is segregated from his white neighbor, but white business men are not prevented from doing business in Negro neighborhoods.
6. There has been no case of segregation of Negroes in the United States that has not widened the breach between the two races. Wherever a form of segregation exists it will be found that it has been administered in such a way as to embitter the Negro and harm more or less the moral fibre of the white man. That the Negro does not express this constant sense of wrong is no proof that he does not feel it.

It seems to me that the reasons given above, if carefully considered, should serve to prevent further passage of such segregation ordinances as have been adopted in Norfolk, Richmond, Louisville, Baltimore, and one or two cities in South Carolina.

Finally, as I have said in another place, as white and black learn daily to adjust, in a spirit of justice and fair play, those interests which are individual and racial, and to see and feel the importance of those fundamental interests which are common, so will both races grow and prosper. In the long run no individual and no race can succeed which sets itself at war against the common good; for "in the gain or loss of one race, all the rest have equal claim."

Sources: (1) Excerpt from "Atlanta Exposition Address," delivered in Atlanta, Georgia, September 18, 1895, reprinted in Washington, *Up from Slavery: An Autobiography* (New York: Doubleday, Page, 1900); and (2) "My View of Segregation Laws," *New Republic* 5, no. 57 (December 4, 1915), pp. 113–14.

SELECT BIBLIOGRAPHY:
Kevin Gaines, *Uplifting the Race: Black Leadership, Politics, and Culture in the 20th Century* (Chapel Hill: University of North Carolina Press, 1996).
Louis R. Harlan, *Booker T. Washington: The Making of a Black Leader, 1865–1901* (New York: Oxford University Press, 1972).
———, *Booker T. Washington: The Wizard of Tuskegee, 1901–1915* (New York: Oxford University Press, 1983).
———, ed., *Booker T. Washington Papers*, 14 Vols. (Urbana: University of Illinois Press, 1972–1989).
August Meier, *Negro Thought in America, 1980–1915* (Ann Arbor: University of Michigan Press, 1963).
Booker T. Washington, *Up from Slavery: An Autobiography* (New York: Doubleday, Page, 1900).

Houston A. Baker, *Turning South Again: Re-Thinking Modernism/Re-Reading Booker T.* (Durham: Duke University Press, 2001).

W. Fitzhugh Brundage, ed., *Booker T. Washington and Black Progress: Up from Slavery 100 Years Later* (Gainesville: University Press of Florida, 2003).

Rebecca Carroll, ed., *Uncle Tom or New Negro? African Americans Reflect on Booker T. Washington and Up from Slavery One Hundred Years Later* (New York: Broadway Books/Harlem Moon, 2006).

Michael Rudolph West, *The Education of Booker T. Washington: American Democracy and the Idea of Race Relations* (New York: Columbia University Press, 2006).

⚊ 11 ⚊

William Monroe Trotter and the *Boston Guardian*

The most bitter critic of Booker T. Washington was William Monroe Trotter (1872–1934). Born in Springfield Township, Ohio, Trotter received his B.A. degree from Harvard, graduating magna cum laude in 1895, and earned his M.A. from Harvard the following year. Trotter hated all forms of racial segregation and believed that Washington was nothing less than a traitor to his people. Trotter's publication, the *Boston Guardian*, became a leading voice for black radicalism. With W. E. B. Du Bois he initiated the Niagara Movement in 1905. Trotter was active in the Negro American Political League from 1908 to 1913. Trotter's confrontational style created as many enemies as friends, yet his ideas were instrumental in the development of the modern black freedom movement.

⚊

Under the caption, "Principal Washington Defines His Position," the *Tuskegee Student*, the official organ of Tuskegee, prints the institute letter in which Mr. Washington said: "We cannot elevate and make useful a race of people unless there is held out to them the hope of reward for right living. Every revised constitution throughout the southern states has put a premium upon intelligence, ownership of property, thrift and character." This little sheet begins by saying that the letter "appeared in all of the important papers of the country on Nov. 28. It has been unstintingly praised from one section of the country to the other for its clarity and forcefulness of statement, and for its ringing note of sincerity." Although such words are to be expected from the employees of the school they are for the most part only too true. It is true that, although the letter was sent to the *Age Herald* of Birmingham, Alabama, it appeared simultaneously "in all the important papers of the country." Then its effect must be admitted to have been greater than if any other Negro had written it, for admittedly no other Negro's letter could have obtained such wide publicity. If it had in it aught that was injurious to the Negro's welfare or to his manhood rights, therefore, such worked far more damage than if any other Negro or any other man, save the president himself, had written the words.

What man is there among us, whether friend or foe of the author of the letter, who was not astounded at the reference to the disfranchising constitutions quoted above. "Every revised constitution throughout the southern states has put a premium upon intelligence, ownership of property, thrift and character," and all the more so because Mr. Washington had not been accused by even the southerners of opposing these disfranchising constitutions. . . . If the statement is false, if it is misleading, if it is injurious to the Negro, all the more blamable and guilty is the author because the statement was gratuitous on his part.

Is it the truth? Do these constitutions encourage Negroes to be thrifty, to be better and more intelligent? For this sort of argument is the most effective in favor of them. . . . Where is the Negro who says the law was or is ever intended to be fairly applied? . . . If so, then every reputable Negro orator and writer, from Hon. A. H. Grimke on, have been mistaken. If so, every Negro clergyman of standing, who has spoken on the subject . . . have been misinformed. We happen to know of an undertaker who has an enormous establishment in Virginia, who now can't vote. Is that encouraging thrift? Two letter carriers, who have passed the civil service examinations, are now sueing because disfranchised. Is that encouraging intelligence? . . . Even a Republican candidate for governor in Virginia recently said Negro domination was to be feared if 10 Negroes could vote because they could have the balance of power. Mr. Washington's statement is shamefully false and deliberately so.

But even were it true, what man is a worse enemy to a race than a leader who looks with equanimity on the disfranchisement of his race in a country where other races have universal suffrage by constitutions that make one rule for his race and another for the dominant race, by constitutions made by conventions to which his race is not allowed to send its representatives, by constitutions that his race although endowed with the franchise by law are not allowed to vote upon, and are, therefore, doubly illegal, by constitutions in violation to the national constitution, because, forsooth, he thinks such disfranchising laws will benefit the moral character of his people. Let our spiritual advisers condemn this idea of reducing a people to serfdom to make them good.

But what was the effect of Mr. Washington's letter on the northern white people? . . .

No thinking Negro can fail to see that, with the influence Mr. Washington yields [wields] in the North and the confidence reposed in him by the white people on account of his school, a fatal blow has been given to the Negro's political rights and liberty by his statement. The benevolence idea makes it all the more deadly in its effect. It comes very opportunely for the Negro, too, just when Roosevelt declares the Negro shall hold office, . . . when Congress is being asked to enforce the Negro's constitutional rights, when these laws are being carried to the Supreme Court. And here Mr. Washington, having gained sufficient influence through his doctrines, his school and his elevation by the President, makes all these efforts sure of failure by killing public sentiment against the disfranchising constitutions.

And Mr. Washington's word is the more effective for, discreditable as it may seem, not five Negro papers even mention a statement that belies all their editorials and that would have set aflame the entire Negro press of the country, if a less wealthy and less powerful Negro had made it. Nor will Negro orators nor Negro preachers dare now to pick up the gauntlet thrown down by the great "educator." Instead of being universally repudiated by the Negro race his statement will be practically universally endorsed by its silence because Washington said it, though it sounds the death-knell of our liberty. The lips of our leading politicians are sealed, because, before he said it, Mr. Washington, through the President, put them under obligation to himself. Nor is there that heroic quality now in our race that would lead men to throw off the shackles of fear, of obligation, of policy and denounce a traitor though he be a friend, or even a brother. It occurs to none that silence is tantamount to being virtually an accomplice in the treasonable act of this Benedict Arnold of the Negro race.

O, for a black Patrick Henry to save his people from this stigma of cowardice; to rouse them from their lethargy to a sense of danger; to score the tyrant and to inspire his people with the spirit of those immortal words: "Give Me Liberty or Give Me Death."

Source: Excerpt from editorial, *Boston Guardian*, December 20, 1902.

SELECT BIBLIOGRAPHY:
Stephen R. Fox, *Guardian of Boston: William Monroe Trotter* (New York: Atheneum, 1970).
August Meier, *Negro Thought in America, 1880 1915* (Ann Arbor: University of Michigan Press, 1963).
William Jeremiah Moses, *The Golden Age of Black Nationalism, 1850–1925* (New York: Archon Books, 1978).

☞ 12 ☞

Race and the Southern Worker

The demise of Reconstruction and the consolidation of Jim Crow segregation did not destroy efforts to build coalitions between black and white working-class and poor people in the South. The rapid expansion of industries in southern states created the basis for the growth of biracial unions. The documents reprinted here illustrate that a significant number of African-American and white workers recognized their common class interests.

☞

A Negro Woman Speaks
I am a colored woman, wife and mother. I have lived all my life in the South, and have often thought what a peculiar fact it is that the more ignorant the Southern

whites are of us the more vehement they are in their denunciation of us. They boast that they have little intercourse with us, never see us in our homes, churches or places of amusement, but still they know us thoroughly.

They also admit that they know us in no capacity except as servants, yet they say that we are at our best in that single capacity. What philosophers they are! The Southerners saw we Negroes are a happy, laughing set of people, with no thought of tomorrow. How mistaken they are! The educated, thinking Negro is just the opposite. There is a feeling of unrest, insecurity, almost panic among the best class of Negroes in the South. In our homes, in our churches, wherever two or three are gathered together, there is a discussion of what is best to do. Must we remain in the South or go elsewhere? Where can we go to feel that security which other people feel? Is it best to go in great numbers or only in several families? These and many other things are discussed over and over.

People who have security in their homes, whose children can go on the street unmolested, whose wives and daughters are treated as women, cannot, perhaps, sympathize with the Southern Negro's anxieties and complaints. I ask forbearance of such people. . . .

I know of houses occupied by poor Negroes in which a respectable farmer would not keep his cattle. It is impossible for them to rent elsewhere. All Southern real estate agents have "white property" and "colored property." In one of the largest Southern cities there is a colored minister, a graduate of Harvard, whose wife is an educated, Christian woman, who lived for weeks in a tumble-down rookery because he could neither rent nor buy in a respectable locality.

Many colored women who wash, iron, scrub, cook or sew all the week to help pay the rent for these miserable hovels and help fill the many small mouths, would deny themselves some of the necessaries of life if they could take their little children and teething babies on the cars to the parks of a Sunday afternoon and sit under the trees, enjoy the cool breezes and breathe God's pure air for only two or three hours; but this is denied them. Some of the parks have signs, "No Negroes allowed on these grounds except as servants." Pitiful, pitiful customs and laws that make war on women and babes! There is no wonder that we die; the wonder is that we persist in living.

Fourteen years ago I had just married. My husband had saved sufficient money to buy a small home. On account of our limited means we went to the suburbs, on unpaved streets, to look for a home, only asking for a high, healthy locality. Some real estate agents were "sorry, but had nothing to suit," some had "just the thing," but we discovered on investigation that they had "just the thing" for an unhealthy pigsty. Others had no "colored property." One agent said that he had what we wanted, but we should have to go to see the lot after dark, or walk by and give the place a casual look; for, he said, "all the white people in the neighborhood would be down on me." Finally we bought this lot. When the house was being built we went to see it. Consternation reigned. We had ruined this neighborhood of poor people; poor as we, poorer in manners at least. The people who lived next door received the sympathy of their friends. When we walked on the street (there were no sidewalks) we were embarrassed by the stare of many unfriendly eyes.

Two years passed before a single woman spoke to me, and only then because I helped one of them when a little sudden trouble came to her. Such was the reception, I a happy young woman, just married, received from people among whom I wanted to make a home. Fourteen years have now passed, four children have been born to us, and one has died in this same home, among these same neighbors. Although the neighbors speak to us, and occasionally one will send a child to borrow the morning's paper or ask the loan of a pattern, not one woman has ever been inside of my house, not even at the times when a woman would doubly appreciate the slightest attention of a neighbor.

The Southerner boasts that he is our friend; he educates our children, he pays us for work and is most noble and generous to us. Did not the Negro by his labor for over three hundred years help to educate the white man's children? Is thirty equal to three hundred? Does a white man deserve praise for paying a black man for his work?

The Southerner also claims that the Negro get justice. Not long ago a Negro man was cursed and struck in the face by an electric-car conductor. The Negro knocked the conductor down and although it was clearly proven in a court of "jus tice" that the conductor was in the wrong the Negro had to pay a fine of $10. The judge told him "I fine you that much to teach you that you must respect white folks." The conductor was acquitted. "Most noble judge! A second Daniel!" This is the South's idea of justice.

A noble man, who has established rescue homes for fallen women all over the country, visited a Southern city. The women of the city were invited to meet him in one of the churches. The fallen women were especially invited and both good and bad went. They sat wherever they could find a seat, so long as their faces were white; but I, a respectable married woman, was asked to sit apart. A colored woman, however respectable, is lower than the white prostitute. The Southern white woman will declare that no Negro women are virtuous, yet she places her innocent children in their care. . . .

The Southerner says "the Negro must keep in his place." That means the particular place the white man says is his. . . . A self-respecting colored man who does not cringe but walks erect, supports his family, educates his children, and by example and precept teaches them that God made all men equal, is called a "dangerous Negro"; "he is too smart"; "he wants to be white and act like white people." Now we are told that the Negro has the worst traits of the whole human family and the Southern white man the best; but we must not profit by his example or we are regarded as "dangerous Negroes."

White agents and other chance visitors who come into our homes ask questions that we must not dare ask their wives. They express surprise that our children have clean faces and that their hair is combed. You cannot insult a colored woman, you know. . . .

There are aristocrats in crime, in poverty and in misfortune in the South. The white criminal cannot think of eating or sleeping in the same part of the penitentiary with the Negro criminal. The white pauper is just as exclusive; and although the blind cannot see color, nor the insane care about it, they must be kept separate, at great extra expense. Lastly, the dead white man's bones must not be contaminated with the dead black man's. . . .

Whenever a crime is committed, in the South the policemen look for the Negro in the case. A white man with face and hands blackened can commit any crime in the calendar. The first friendly stream soon washes away his guilt and he is ready to join in the hunt to lynch the "big, black burly brute." When a white man in the South does commit a crime, that is simply one white man gone wrong. If his crime is especially brutal he is a freak or temporarily insane. If one low, ignorant black wretch commits a crime, that is different. All of us must bear his guilt. A young white boy's badness is simply the overflowing of young animal spirits; the black boy's badness is badness, pure and simple. . . .

When we were shouting for Dewey, Sampson, Schley and Hobson, and were on tiptoe to touch the hem of their garments, we were delighted to know that some of our Spanish-American heroes were coming where we could get a glimpse of them. Had not black men helped in a small way to give them their honors? In the cities of the South, where these heroes went, the white school children were assembled, flags were waved, flowers strewn, speeches made, and "My Country, 'tis of Thee, Sweet Land of Liberty," was sung. Our children who need to be taught so much, were not assembled, their hands waved no flags, they threw no flowers, heard no thrilling speech, sang no song of their country. And this is the South's idea of justice. Is it surprising that feeling grows more bitter, when the white mother teaches her boy to hate my boy, not because he is mean, but because his skin is dark? I have seen very small white children hang their black dolls. It is not the child's fault, he is simply an apt pupil.

Someone will at last arise who will champion our cause and compel the world to see that we deserve justice; as other heroes compelled it to see that we deserved freedom.

꜒

THE RACE QUESTION A CLASS QUESTION

"There is no clash between the white man of the South and the negro of MY CLASS!" said John Mitchell, Jr., President of the Mechanics' Savings Bank of Richmond, Va., at the convention of the Bankers' Association in New York City. Mr. Mitchell declared that no color line was drawn between the "better class" of whites and the "better class" of blacks, and that the negro was learning that as a business man the negro would be respected and not discriminated against. "He was received with enthusiasm and his brief remarks proved to be one of the memorable features of the convention. Among the Southern delegates a feeling of genuine satisfaction was expressed and they united in praising Mr. Mitchell's speech," says the New York *Evening Post.* And when the colored banker had finished and was being cheered and congratulated on all sides, the bankers were roused to new enthusiasm by a response from one of the South's best-known financiers, Col. Robert J. Lowry of Atlanta, who said: "I am delighted to hear from my Southern brother. There is no fight, no hostility, between his class and my race in Georgia— or anywhere else. I am glad to hear this gentleman from Virginia. The gentleman is right in what he says."

This touching scene in which the Southern white capitalist greeted the black capitalist as a gentleman and a brother in a striking proof of the fact that the race question is at bottom, like all other questions, a class question.

It is undoubtedly true that the negro has suffered much discrimination and outrage merely because of race feeling, and on the surface it may seem that the hatred of blacks is wholly caused, by repugnance to those of another race. But the real source of this race feeling is to be found in the fact that the negroes AS A RACE were once, as slaves, almost the sole working class in the North together with the fact that most of them are now working people—wage slaves instead of chattel slaves.

The nonproductive ruling class, whether it be a slave-holding class or capitalist class, always looks down upon and despises the other class which toils and sweats for it and feeds it and produces all the wealth upon which it lives in luxury. The capitalist's contempt of the white workingman is restrained only by the consideration that it is necessary to get his vote, by the fact that it is necessary to maintain the illusion of social and political equality in order to keep the white workingman contented with his lot. The white workingman is used to believing himself "as good as any man" and it is therefore necessary for the capitalists to keep up this flattering illusion in order to persuade him to continue to submit to the present industrial system of legalized robbery. But because the negro working class is not long used to political freedom, and because the master class of the South once owned him bodily as a chattel slave, the contempt of the Southern ruling class for the negro workingman is entirely unrestrained, and the negro's age-long habit of submission is taken advantage of to throw out his vote or disfranchise him.

That the Southerner's contempt for the negro is not really based on any physical repugnance to him as a person is proven by the fact that the rich whites of the South think nothing of tolerating the presence of the black man as a personal servant waiting upon them, shaving them, attending them in baths and performing all sorts of services which bring the colored man into the closest personal contact with his master. And the thousands of mulattoes in the South are living proofs that many of the white men who express their horror at the thought of "social equality" freely enter into the most intimate of all personal relations with the women of the black race, as did many of the old slaveholders who considered their female slaves as sexual property as well as sources of material profit.

As a matter of fact there is no "social equality" between the workingmen and the rich men of any race. The white capitalist moves in the "cultured and respectable society" of his own class and would regard as preposterous and abhorrent the idea of receiving the "coarse and vulgar workingman" on a basis of equality; the workingman is admitted to his circles only in a despised menial capacity in some places special street cars for workingmen have been proposed (just as the South has its "Jim Crow" cars for negroes) in order that the fine ladies and gentlemen of the capitalist class may not have to soil themselves by riding in the same cars with "the dirty, ignorant workingmen."

That the Southern capitalist has no more regard for the workingman of his own race than he has for the negro is shown by the fact that wherever white working-men go on strike, the capitalists never hesitate to replace them with negro scabs, and the black man who will do any equal amount of work for less wages can always get the job of the white. When a question of capitalist profit is involved race lines disappear and class division, regardless of race, stands out clearly for all to see. And that the negro is despised by the Southern upper class really for the reason that he is a workingman, and consequently poor, is proven by the fact that both the negroes and the prosperous whites consider the "poor white trash" of the South still lower than the black race itself.

The speech of the colored capitalist at the convention of the Bankers' Association, and the way to which it was received by the Southern gentry present, prove that the Southern capitalist does not say: "All 'coons' look alike to me." To the Southern capitalist the black banker is evidently a "gentleman" and a brother in the fraternity of capitalist parasites, but the black workingman is despised as a "loafer" and an inferior being, as is the white workingman. And the black banker has a delightfully simple solution of the race problem: Just let all negroes become bankers or business men and then they will be respected and race hatred will dis-appear. White workingmen are familiar with the same advice: Just let them save enough capital out of their wages, by the practise of industry, thrift, frugality and other capitalist virtues, to compete with multi-million-dollar trusts and then they will be eminently respectable citizens.

It is part of the instinctive policy of the capitalist class to perpetuate itself by creating and playing upon race hatred in order to keep workingmen of all races and nationalities from uniting to overthrow the infamous industrial system by which the capitalists profit. And it is also part of capitalist policy to use a weaker race to undermine the efforts of the more intelligent workingmen to better their conditions and emancipate their class. So it happens that Booker T. Washington and other prominent colored men are coddled by the ruling capitalist class and need to teach the colored men to be hardworking, submissive and contented under the tyranny of capitalism. . . .

Booker T. Washington, the best type of the negro leader who is entirely satis-factory to the capitalist, has recently been put to a crucial test on the question of working class vs. capitalist class. During the recent great meat strike, in which so many of his race were used as strike breakers, he was asked by the union of the workers in the stockyards to address a meeting, which both union and non-union workingmen were invited to attend, on the question: "Should negroes act as strike breakers?" In this position, so awkward for a man who has dined with the capi-talist President who stands for the "open shop," Booker escaped by pleading the convenient excuse of "a previous engagement" which would prevent his being present.

Some negro papers openly advise the colored man to show his "faithfulness" and his industrial power by taking a job wherever he can get it, even if he is thus helping to break a strike, and promise that this will result in capitalist favor and respect; notwithstanding the fact that the strike breaker is always despised even by the capitalist himself and kicked out when he can no longer be used.

The Socialist movement, on the other hand, appeals to all workingmen, without regard to race, color, or previous condition of servitude (but with very lively regard to present condition of servitude), to realize that their interests are in common and against the interests of all capitalists and to unite to overthrow capitalist rule.

Many of the Southern trade unions are realizing this, in some measure, by admitting the negroes to membership equally with the white, just as the bankers recognize their common class interest by welcoming the negro banker.

To the negro Socialism says: As a workingman you are oppressed by your capitalist boss as you were as a slave by your master, you are enslaved and robbed of the product of your labor under wage-slavery as you were under chattel slavery; you must unite with all other workingmen in the Socialist movement to free yourselves.

To the white workingman Socialism says: "If you do not realize your common interests with your black fellow-workman he will be used against you by the capitalist, who is the enemy of both of you. You must recognize that his interests as a workingman are the same as yours and must enroll him as a comrade in the fight against capitalism.

And to the white Southerner who fears the bugaboo of "social equality" with the negro, and objects to Socialism on that ground, it may be said. No one who objects to "social equality" with the negro, or with anyone else, can be forced to associate with those who are uncongenial to them under Socialism or under any other system. No one need invite to his home or seek the company of those who are displeasing to him. Socialism stands for political and economic equality, and in all public relations men of all races must have the same rights as human beings; but private association is a matter for each individual to decide for himself. And finally it should be remembered that as repugnance to the colored man has its chief source in his subservient position as a worker, together with all the lack of advantages which that position implies, therefore under Socialism, when opportunity for education and culture will be open to all, the negro and all others who are now crushed and degraded by capitalism will develop to a point where they will no longer be "inferior," and consequently no longer repellent or uncongenial.

NEGRO WORKERS!
Don't Allow Yourselves to be Divided from Your Fellow Workers by the Vicious Lumber Trust.

To all Negro Workers, and especially to the Negro Forest and Lumber Workers of the South, we send this message and appeal:

Fellow Worker:

When the forest slaves of Louisiana and Texas revolted against peonage and began, about two years ago, the organization of the Brotherhood of Timber Workers, an industrial union taking in all the workers in the sawmills and camps, the lumber kings at once recognized the power inherent in such a movement and immediately began a campaign of lying and violence against the Union and all persons connected with it or suspected of sympathizing with us.

First among the cries they raised against us was, of course, the bunco cries of "white supremacy" and "social equality" coupled with that other cry: "They are organizing negroes against whites!" which the capitalists and landlords of the South and their political buzzard and social carrion crows always raise in order to justify the slugging and assassination of white and colored working men who seek to organize and better the condition of their class. From the day you, the negro workers were "freed," down to the present hour these cries have been used to cloak the vilest crimes against workers, white and colored, and to hide the whole-sale rape of the commonwealth of the South by as soulless and cold blooded a set of industrial scalawags and carpetbaggers as ever drew the breath of life.

For a generation, under the influence of these specious cries, they have kept us fighting each other—we to secure the "white supremacy" of a tramp and YOU the "social equality" of a vagrant. Our fathers "feel for it," but we, their children, have come to the conclusion that porterhouse steaks and champagne will look as well on your tables as on those of the industrial scalawags and carpetbaggers; that the "white supremacy" that means starvation wages and child slavery for us and the "social equality" that means the same for you, though they may mean the "high life" and "Christian civilization" to the lumber kings and landlords, will have to go. As far as we, the workers of the South, are concerned, the only "supremacy" and "equality" they have ever granted us is the supremacy of misery and the equality of rags. This supremacy and this equality we, the Brotherhood of Timber Workers, mean to stand no longer than we have an organization big and strong enough to enforce our demands, chief among which is "A man's life for all the workers in the mills and forests of the South." Because the negro workers comprise one-half or more of the labor employed in the Southern lumber industry, this battle cry of ours, "A man's life for all the workers," has been considered a menace and therefore a crime in the eyes of the Southern oligarchy, for they, as well as we, are fully alive to the fact that we can never raise our standard of living and better our conditions so long as they can keep us split, whether on race, craft, religions or national lines, and they have tried and are trying all these methods of division in addition to their campaign of terror, wherein deeds have been and are being committed that would make Diaz blush with shame, they are so atrocious in their white-livered cruelty. For this reason, that they sought to organize all the workers, A. L. Emerson, president of the Brotherhood, and 63 other Union men, are now in prison at Lake Charles, La. under indictment, as a result of the Massacre of Grabow where three Union men and one Association gunman were killed, charged with murder in the first degree, indicted for killing their own brothers, and they will be sent to the gallows, or, worse, to the frightful penal farms and levees of Louisiana, unless a united working class comes to their rescue with the funds necessary to defend them and the action that will bring them all free of the grave and levees.

Further words are idle. It is a useless waste of paper to tell you, the negro workers, of the merciless injustice of the Southern Lumber Operators' Association, for YOUR RACE has learned through tears and blood the hyenaism we are fighting. Enough. Emerson and his associates are in prison because they fought for the unity of all the workers.

Will you remain silent, turn no hand to help them in this, their hour of great danger?

Our fight is your fight, and we appeal to you to do your duty by these men, the bravest of the brave! Help us free them all. Join the Brotherhood and help us blaze freedom's pathway through the jungles of the South.

"Workers of the world, unite! You have nothing but your chains to lose! You have a world to gain!"

> COMMITTEE OF DEFENSE,
> BROTHERHOOD OF TIMBER WORKERS,
> Box 78, Alexandria, La.

Solidarity, September 28, 1912

Sources: (1) "A Negro Woman Speaks," *The Independent* 54 (September 18, 1902), pp. 2221–24; (2) "The Race Question a Class Question," *The Worker* (October 2, 1904); and (3) "Negro Workers!" appeal drafted by the Committee of Defense, Brotherhood of Timber Workers, Alexandria, Louisiana, published in *Solidarity* (September 28, 1912).

SELECT BIBLIOGRAPHY:

John Bracey, August Meier, and Elliot Rudwick, *Black Workers and Organized Labor* (Belmont, Ca.: Wadsworth Publishing, 1971).

Lawrence Goodwyn, *The Populist Moment: A Short History of the Agrarian Revolt in America* (New York: Oxford University Press, 1978).

Jacqueline Jones, *The Dispossessed: America's Underclass from the Civil War to the Present* (New York: Basic Books, 1992).

———, *A Social History of the Laboring Classes: From Colonial Times to the Present, Problems in American History* (Malden: Blackwell Publishers, 1999).

Sterling D. Spero and Abram L. Harris, *The Black Worker: The Negro and the Labor Movement* (New York: Columbia University Press, 1931).

⁓ 13 ⁓

Ida B. Wells-Barnett, Crusader for Justice

Ida B. Wells-Barnett (1862–1931) was, in our opinion, the greatest African-American political journalist in history. Wells was born in Holly Springs, Mississippi, during the Civil War. Her parents died when she was a teenager. Wells worked as a teacher and journalist. In 1891 she moved to Memphis, where she became co-owner of the *Memphis Free Speech and Headlight* newspaper. Wells's fiery editorials and investigative reporting outraged the local white establishment. In 1892, after white racists destroyed her printing press, Wells moved to the North and continued her campaign against lynching. Wells was an associate of Susan B. Anthony, an outspoken supporter of women's rights. She was an active member of the Niagara Movement, and a cofounder of the National Association for the Advancement of Colored People (NAACP). Her popular political essays and journalistic commentaries inspired several generations of black activists.

The lynching record for a quarter of a century merits the thoughtful study of the American people. It presents three salient facts:

First: Lynching is color-line murder.

Second: Crimes against women is the excuse, not the cause.

Third: It is a national crime and requires a national remedy.

Proof that lynching follows the color line is to be found in the statistics which have been kept for the past twenty-five years. During the few years preceding this period and while frontier lynch law existed, the executions showed a majority of white victims. Later, however, as law courts and authorized judiciary extended into the far West, lynch law rapidly abated, and its white victims became few and far between.

Just as the lynch-law regime came to a close in the West, a new mob movement started in the South. This was wholly political, its purpose being to suppress the colored vote by intimidation and murder. Thousands of assassins banded together under the name of Ku Klux Klans, "Midnight Raiders," "Knights of the Golden Circle," et cetera, et cetera, spread a reign of terror, by beating, shooting and killing colored people by the thousands. In a few years, the purpose was accomplished, and the black vote was suppressed. But mob murder continued.

From 1882, in which year fifty-two were lynched, down to the present, lynching has been along the color line. Mob murder increased yearly until in 1892 more than two hundred victims were lynched and statistics show that 3,284 men, women and children have been put to death in this quarter of a century. During the last ten years from 1899 to 1908 inclusive the number lynched was 959. Of this number 102 were white, while the colored victims numbered 857. No other nation, civilized or savage, burns its criminals: only under the Stars and Stripes is the human holocaust possible. Twenty-eight human beings burned at the stake, one of them a woman and two of them children, is the awful indictment against American civilization—the gruesome tribute which the nation pays to the color line.

Why is mob murder permitted by a Christian nation? What is the cause of this awful slaughter? This question is answered almost daily—always the same shameless falsehood that "Negroes are lynched to protect womanhood." Standing before a Chautauqua assemblage, John Temple Graves, at once champion of lynching and apologist for lynchers, said: "The mob stands today as the most potential bulwark between the women of the South and such a carnival of crime as would infuriate the world and precipitate the annihilation of the Negro race. This is the never-varying answer of lynchers and their apologists. All know that it is untrue. The cowardly lyncher revels in murder, then seeks to shield himself from public execration by claiming devotion to woman. But truth is mighty and the lynching record discloses the hypocrisy of the lyncher as well as his crime.

The Springfield, Illinois, mob rioted for two days, the militia of the entire state was called out, two men were lynched, hundreds of people driven from their homes, all because a white woman said a Negro assaulted her. A mad mob went to the jail, tried to lynch the victim of her charge and, not being able to find him, proceeded to pillage and burn the town and to lynch two innocent men. Later, after the police had found that the woman's charge was false, she published a retraction, the indictment was dismissed and the intended victim discharged. But the lynched victims were dead. Hundreds were homeless and Illinois was disgraced.

As a final and complete refutation of the charge that lynching is occasioned by crimes against women, a partial record of lynchings is cited; 285 persons were lynched for causes as follows:

Unknown cause, 92; no cause, 10; race prejudice, 49, miscegenation, 7; informing, 12; making threats, 11; keeping saloon, 3; practicing fraud, 5; practicing voodooism, 2; bad reputation, 8; unpopularity, 3; mistaken identity, 5; using improper language, 3; violation of contract, 1; writing insulting letter, 2; eloping, 2; poisoning horse, 1; poisoning well, 2; by white caps, 9; vigilantes, 14; Indians, 1; moonshining, 1; refusing evidence, 2; political causes, 5; disputing, 1; disobeying quarantine regulations, 2; slapping a child, 1; turning state's evidence, 3; protecting a Negro, 1; to prevent giving evidence, 1; knowledge of larceny, 1; writing letter to white woman, 1; asking white woman to marry, 1; jilting girl, 1; having smallpox, 1; concealing criminal, 2; threatening political exposure, 1; self-defense, 6; cruelty, 1; insulting language to woman, 5; quarreling with white man, 2; colonizing Negroes, 1; throwing stones, 1; quarreling, 1; gambling, 1.

Is there a remedy, or will the nation confess that it cannot protect its protectors at home as well as abroad? Various remedies have been suggested to abolish the lynching infamy, but year after year, the butchery of men, women and children continues in spite of plea and protest. Education is suggested as a preventive, but it is as grave a crime to murder an ignorant man as it is a scholar. True, few educated men have been lynched, but the hue and cry once started stops at no bounds, as was clearly shown by the lynchings in Atlanta, and in Springfield, Illinois.

Agitation, though helpful, will not alone stop the crime. Year after year statistics are published, meetings are held, resolutions are adopted and yet lynchings go on. Public sentiment does measurably decrease the sway of mob law, but the irresponsible bloodthirsty criminals who swept through the streets of Springfield, beating an inoffensive law-abiding citizen to death in one part of the town, and in another torturing and shooting to death a man who for threescore years had made a reputation for honesty, integrity and sobriety, had raised a family and had accumulated property, were not deterred from their heinous crimes by either education or agitation.

The only certain remedy is an appeal to law. Lawbreakers must be made to know that human life is sacred and that every citizen of this country is first a citizen of the United States and secondly a citizen of the state in which he belongs. This nation must assert itself and defend its federal citizenship at home as well as abroad. The strong arm of the government must reach across state lines whenever unbridled lawlessness defies state laws and must give to the individual citizen under the Stars and Stripes the same measure of protection which it gives to him when he travels in foreign lands.

Federal protection of American citizenship is the remedy for lynching. Foreigners are rarely lynched in America. If, by mistake, one is lynched, the national government quickly pays the damages. The recent agitation in California against the Japanese compelled this nation to recognize that federal power must yet assert itself to protect the nation from the treason of sovereign states. Thousands of American citizens have been put to death and no President has yet raised his hand in effective protest, but a simple insult to a native of Japan was quite sufficient to stir the government at Washington to prevent the threatened wrong. If the government has power to protect a foreigner from insult, certainly it has power to save a citizen's life.

The practical remedy has been more than once suggested in Congress. Senator Gallinger, of New Hampshire, in a resolution introduced in Congress called for an investigation "with the view of ascertaining whether there is a remedy for lynching which Congress may apply." The Senate Committee has under consideration a bill drawn by A. E. Pillsbury, formerly Attorney General of Massachusetts, providing for federal prosecution of lynchers in cases where the state fails to protect citizens or foreigners. Both of these resolutions indicate that the attention of the nation has been called to this phase of the lynching question.

As a final word, it would be a beginning in the right direction if this conference can see its way clear to establish a bureau for the investigation and publication of the details of every lynching, so that the public could know that an influential body of citizens has made it a duty to give the widest publicity to the facts in each case; that it will make an effort to secure expressions of opinion all over the country against lynching for the sake of the country's fair name; and lastly, but by no means least, to try to influence the daily papers of the country to refuse to become accessory to mobs either before or after the fact. Several of the greatest riots and most brutal burnt offerings of the mobs have been suggested and incited by the daily papers of the offending community. If the newspaper which suggests lynching in its accounts of an alleged crime, could be held legally as well as morally responsible for reporting that "threats of lynching were heard"; or, "it is feared that if the guilty one is caught, he will be lynched"; or, "there were cries of 'lynch him,' and the only reason the threat was not carried out was because no leader appeared," a long step toward a remedy will have been taken.

In a multitude of counsel there is wisdom. Upon the grave question presented by the slaughter of innocent men, women and children there should be an honest, courageous conference of patriotic, law-abiding citizens anxious to punish crime promptly, impartially and by due process of law, also to make life, liberty and property secure against mob rule.

Time was when lynching appeared to be sectional, but now it is national—a blight upon our nation, mocking our laws and disgracing our Christianity. "With malice toward none but with charity for all" let us undertake the work of making the "law of the land" effective and supreme upon every foot of American soil—a shield to the innocent; and to the guilty, punishment swift and sure.

Source: Excerpt from a speech delivered at the National Negro Conference, 1909 (*Proceedings: National Negro Conference*, 1909, pp. 174–79).

SELECT BIBLIOGRAPHY:

Carolyn Karcher, "Ida B. Wells and Her Allies against Lynching," *Comparative American Studies* 3, no. 2 (June 2005), pp. 131–151.

Patricia Ann Schechter, *Ida B. Wells-Barnett and American Reform, 1880–1930* (Chapel Hill: University of North Carolina Press, 2001).

Dorothy Sterling, *Black Foremothers: Three Lives* (Old Westbury, N.Y.: Feminist Press, 1979).

Mildred I. Thompson, *Ida B. Wells-Barnett: An Exploratory Study of an American Black Woman* (Brooklyn, N.Y.: Carlson Publishing, 1990).

Emilie M. Townes, *Womanist Justice, Womanist Hope* (Atlanta: Scholars Press, 1993).

James West Davidson, *'They Say': Ida B. Wells and the Reconstruction of Race* (Oxford: Oxford University Press, 2007).

⚊ **14** ⚊

William Edward Burghardt Du Bois

The most influential black intellectual of the twentieth century was unquestionably W. E. B. Du Bois (1868–1963). Born in Great Barrington, Massachusetts, Du Bois received bachelor's degrees from Fisk University in 1888 and from Harvard College two years later. He completed graduate studies at the University of Berlin and received his Ph.D. in history from Harvard University in 1895. Du Bois taught for two years at Wilberforce University, and after holding a research position at the University of Pennsylvania, accepted a professorship at Atlanta University in 1897. Du Bois's sociological research, notably his study of the black urban community of Philadelphia, and his annual research conferences and edited volumes produced at Atlanta University, established the field of African-American sociology. Du Bois helped to initiate the Pan-Africanist movement in 1900. He was founder of the Niagara Movement in 1905 and was the most prominent black leader in the establishment of the NAACP in 1910. Reluctantly, Du Bois left his academic research at Atlanta University to assume the editorship of the NAACP's journal, *Crisis*, from 1910 until 1934. Du Bois is perhaps best known for his collection of essays, *The Souls of Black Folk*, which was written between 1897 and 1903. The documents cited here illustrate the evolution of Du Bois's ideas about race and the obligations of the African-American middle class and intelligentsia, that he would soon term the "Talented Tenth," to uplift the masses of black people.

⌒

EXCERPTS FROM "THE CONSERVATION OF RACES"

The American Negro has always felt an intense personal interest in discussions as to the origins and destinies of races: primarily because back of most discussions of race with which he is familiar, have lurked certain assumptions as to his natural abilities, as to his political, intellectual and moral status, which he felt were wrong. He has, consequently, been led to deprecate and minimize race distinctions, to believe intensely that out of one blood God created all nations, and to speak of human brotherhood as though it were the possibility of an already dawning to-morrow.

Nevertheless, in our calmer moments we must acknowledge that human beings are divided into races; that in this country the two most extreme types of the world's races have met, and the resulting problem as to the future relations of these types is not only of intense and living interest to us, but forms an epoch in the history of mankind.

It is necessary, therefore, in planning our movements, in guiding our future development, that at times we rise above the pressing, but smaller questions of separate schools and cars, wage-discrimination and lynch law, to survey the whole question of race in human philosophy and to lay, on a basis of broad knowledge and careful insight, those large lines of policy and higher ideals which may form our guiding lines and boundaries in the practical difficulties of every day. For it is certain that all human striving must recognize the hard limits of natural law, and that any striving, no matter how intense and earnest, which is against the constitution of the world, is vain. The question, then, which we must seriously consider is this: What is the real meaning of Race; what has, in the past, been the law of race development, and what lessons has the past history of race development to teach the rising Negro people?

When we thus come to inquire into the essential difference of races we find it hard to come at once to any definite conclusion. Many criteria of race differences have in the past been proposed, as color, hair, cranial measurements and language. And manifestly, in each of these respects, human beings differ widely. They vary in color, for instance, from the marble-like pallor of the Scandinavian to the rich, dark brown of the Zulu, passing by the creamy Slav, the yellow Chinese, the light brown Sicilian and the brown Egyptian. Men vary, too, in the texture of hair from the obstinately straight hair of the Chinese to the obstinately tufted and frizzled hair of the Bushman. In measurement of heads, again, men vary; from the broad-headed Tartar to the medium-headed European and the narrow-headed Hottentot; or, again in language, from the highly-inflected Roman tongue to the monosyllabic Chinese. All these physical characteristics are patent enough, and if they agreed with each other it would be very easy to classify mankind. Unfortunately for scientists, however, these criteria of race are most exasperatingly intermingled. Color does not agree with texture of hair, for many of the dark races have straight hair; nor does color agree with the breadth of the head, for the yellow Tartar has a broader head than the German; nor, again, has the science of language as yet succeeded in clearing up the relative authority of these various and contradictory criteria. The final word of science, so far, is that we have at least two, perhaps three, great families of human beings—the whites and Negroes, possibly the yellow race. That other races have arisen from the intermingling of the blood of these two. This broad division of the world's races which men like Huxley and Raetzel have introduced as more nearly true than the old five-race scheme of Blumenbach, is nothing more than an acknowledgment that, so far as purely physical characteristics are concerned, the differences between men do not explain all the differences of their history. It declares, as Darwin himself said, that great as is the physical unlikeness of the various races of men their likenesses are greater, and upon this rests the whole scientific doctrine of Human Brotherhood.

Although the wonderful developments of human history teach that the grosser physical differences of color, hair and bone go but a short way toward explaining the different roles which groups of men have played in Human Progress, yet there are differences—subtle, delicate and elusive, though they may be—which have silently but definitely separated men into groups. While these subtle forces have generally followed the natural cleavage of common blood, descent and physical peculiarities, they have at other times swept across and ignored these. At all times, however, they have divided human beings into races, which, while they perhaps transcend scientific definition, nevertheless, are clearly defined to the eye of the Historian and Sociologist.

If this be true, then the history of the world is the history, not of individuals, but of groups, not of nations, but of races, and he who ignores or seeks to override the race idea in human history ignores and overrides the central thought of all history. What, then, is a race? It is a vast family of human beings, generally of common blood and language, always of common history, traditions and impulses, who are both voluntarily and involuntarily striving together for the accomplishment of certain more or less vividly conceived ideals of life.

Turning to real history, there can be no doubt, first, as to the widespread, nay, universal, prevalence of the race idea, the race spirit, the race ideal, and as to its efficiency as the vastest and most ingenious invention for human progress. We, who have been reared and trained under the individualistic philosophy of the Declaration of Independence and the laisser-faire philosophy of Adam Smith, are loath to see and loath to acknowledge this patent fact of human history. We see the Pharaohs, Caesars, Toussaints and Napoleons of history and forget the vast races of which they were but epitomized expressions. We are apt to think in our

American impatience, that while it may have been true in the past that closed race groups made history, that here in conglomerate America *nous avons changer tout cela*—we have changed all that, and have no need of this ancient instrument of progress. This assumption of which the Negro people are especially fond, can not be established by a careful consideration of history.

We find upon the world's stage today eight distinctly differentiated races, in the sense in which History tells us the word must be used. They are, the Slavs of eastern Europe, the Teutons of middle Europe, the English of Great Britain and America, the Romance nations of Southern and Western Europe, the Negroes of Africa and America, the Semitic people of Western Asia and Northern Africa, the Hindoos of Central Asia and the Mongolians of Eastern Asia. There are, of course, other minor race groups, as the American Indians, the Esquimaux and the South Sea Islanders; these larger races, too, are far from homogeneous; the Slav includes the Czech, the Magyar, the Pole and the Russian; the Teuton includes the German, the Scandinavian and the Dutch; the English include the Scotch, the Irish and the conglomerate American. Under Romance nations the widely differing Frenchman, Italian, Sicilian and Spaniard are comprehended. The term Negro is, perhaps, the most indefinite of all, combining the Mulattoes and Zamboes of America and the Egyptians, Bantus and Bushmen of Africa. Among the Hindoos are traces of widely differing nations, while the great Chinese, Tartar, Corean and Japanese families fall under the one designation—Mongolian.

The question now is: What is the real distinction between these nations? Is it the physical differences of blood, color and cranial measurements? Certainly we must all acknowledge that physical differences play a great part, and that, with wide exceptions and qualifications, these eight great races of to-day follow the cleavage of physical race distinctions; the English and Teuton represent the white variety of mankind; the Mongolian, the yellow; the Negroes, the black. Between these are many crosses and mixtures, where Mongolian and Teuton have blended into the Slav, and other mixtures have produced the Romance nations and the Semites. But while race differences have followed mainly physical race lines, yet no mere physical distinctions would really define or explain the deeper differences—the cohesiveness and continuity of these groups. The deeper differences are spiritual, psychical, differences—undoubtedly based on the physical, but infinitely transcending them. The forces that bind together the Teuton nations are, then, first, their race identity and common blood; secondly, and more important, a common history, common laws and religion, similar habits of thought and a conscious striving together for certain ideals of life. The whole process which has brought about these race differentiations has been a growth, and the great characteristic of this growth has been the differentiation of spiritual and mental differences between great races of mankind and the integration of physical differences.

The age of nomadic tribes of closely related individuals represents the maximum of physical differences. They were practically vast families, and there were as many groups as families. As the families came together to form cities the physical differences lessened, purity of blood was replaced by the requirement of domicile, and all who lived within the city bounds became gradually to be regarded as members of the group; *i.e.*, there was a slight and slow breaking down of physical barriers. This, however, was accompanied by an increase of the spiritual and social differences between cities. This city became husbandmen, this, merchants, another warriors, and so on. The *ideals of life* for which the different cities struggled were different. When at last cities began to coalesce into nations there was another breaking down of barriers which separated groups of men. The larger and broader differences of color, hair and physical proportions were not by any means ignored, but myriads of minor differences disappeared, and the sociological and historical races of men began to approximate the present division of races as indicated by physical researches. At the same time the spiritual and physical differences of race groups which constituted the nations became deep and decisive. The English nation stood for constitutional liberty and commercial freedom; the German nation for science and philosophy; the Romance nations stood for literature and art, and the other race groups are striving, each in its own way, to develop for civilization its particular message, its particular ideal, which shall help to guide the world nearer and nearer that perfection of human life for which we all long, that "one far off Divine event."

This has been the function of race differences up to the present time. What shall be its function in the future? Manifestly some of the great races of today—particularly the Negro race—have not as yet given to civilization the full spiritual message which they are capable of giving. I will not say that the Negro race has as yet given no message to the world, for it is still a mooted question among scientists as to just how far Egyptian civilization was Negro in its origin; if it was not wholly Negro, it was certainly very closely allied. Be that as it may, however the fact still remains that the full, complete Negro message of the whole Negro race has not as yet been given to the world: that the messages and ideal of the yellow race have not been completed, and that the striving of the mighty Slavs has but begun. The question is, then: How shall this message be delivered; how shall these various ideals be realized? The answer is plain: By the development of these race groups, not as individuals, but as races. For the development of Japanese genius, Japanese literature and art, Japanese spirit, only Japanese, bound and welded together, Japanese inspired by one vast ideal, can work out in its fullness the wonderful message which Japan has for the nations of the earth. For the development of Negro genius, of Negro literature and art, of Negro spirit, only Negroes bound and welded together, Negroes inspired by one vast ideal, can work out in its fullness the great message we have for humanity. We cannot reverse history; we are subject to the same natural laws as other races, and if the Negro is ever to be a factor in the world's history—if among the gaily-colored banners that deck the broad ramparts of civilization is to hang one uncompromising black, then it must be placed there by black hands, fashioned by black heads and hallowed by the travail of 200,000,000 black hearts beating in one glad song of jubilee.

For this reason, the advance guard of the Negro people—the 8,000,000 people of Negro blood in the United States of America—must soon come to realize that if they are to take their just place in the van of Pan-Negroism, then their destiny is *not* absorption by the white Americans. That if in America it is to be proven for the first time in the modern world that not only Negroes are capable of evolving individual men like Toussaint, the Saviour, but are a nation stored with wonderful possibilities of culture, then their destiny is not a servile imitation of Anglo-Saxon culture, but a stalwart originality which shall unswervingly follow Negro ideals.

It may, however, be objected here that the situation of our race in America renders this attitude impossible; that our sole hope of salvation lies in our being able to lose our race identity in the commingled blood of the nation; and that any other course would merely increase the friction of races which we call race prejudice, and against which we have so long and so earnestly fought.

Here, then, is the dilemma, and it is a puzzling one, I admit. No Negro who has given earnest thought to the situation of his people in America has failed, at some time in life, to find himself at these cross-roads; has failed to ask himself at some time: What, after all, am I? Am I an American or am I a Negro? Can I be both? Or is it my duty to cease to be a Negro as soon as possible and be an American? If I strive as a Negro, am I not perpetuating the very cleft that threatens and separates Black and White America? Is not my only possible practical aim the subduction of all that is Negro in me to the American? Does my black blood place upon me any more obligation to assert my nationality than German, or Irish or Italian blood would?

It is such incessant self-questioning and the hesitation that arises from it, that is making the present period a time of vacillation and contradiction for the American Negro; combined race action is stifled, race responsibility is shirked, race enterprises languish, and the best blood, the best talent, the best energy of the Negro people cannot be marshalled to do the bidding of the race. They stand back to make room for every rascal and demagogue who chooses to cloak his selfish deviltry under the veil of race pride.

Is this right? Is it rational? Is it good policy? Have we in America a distinct mission as a race—a distinct sphere of action and an opportunity for race development, or is self-obliteration the highest end to which Negro blood dare aspire?

If we carefully consider what race prejudice really is, we find it, historically, to be nothing but the friction between different groups of people; as is the difference in aim, in feeling, in ideals of two different races; if, now, this difference exists touching territory, laws, language, or even religion, it is manifest that these people cannot live in the same territory without fatal collision; but if, on the other hand, there is substantial agreement in laws, language and religion; if there is a satisfactory adjustment of economic life, then there is no reason why, in the same country and on the same street, two or three great national ideals might not thrive and develop, that man of different races might not strive together for their race ideals as well, perhaps even better, than in isolation. Here, it seems to me, is the reading of the riddle that puzzles so many of us. We are Americans, not only by birth and by citizenship, but by our political ideals, our language, our religion. Farther than that, our Americanism does not go. At that point, we are Negroes, members of a vast historic race that from the very dawn of creation has slept, but half awakening in the dark forests of its African fatherland. We are the first fruits of this new nation, the harbinger of that black to-morrow which is yet destined to soften the whiteness of the Teutonic to-day. We are that people whose subtle sense of song has given America its only American music, its only American fairy tales, its only touch of pathos and humor amid its mad money-getting plutocracy. As such, it is our duty to conserve our physical powers, our intellectual endowments, our spiritual ideals; as a race we must strive by race organization, by race solidarity, by race unity to the realization of that broader humanity which freely recognizes differences in men, but sternly deprecates inequality in their opportunities of development.

For the accomplishment of these ends we need race organizations: Negro colleges, Negro newspapers, Negro business organizations, a Negro school of literature and art, and an intellectual clearing house, for all these products of the Negro mind, which we may call a Negro Academy. Not only is all this necessary for positive advance, it is absolutely imperative for negative defense. Let us not deceive ourselves at our situation in this country. Weighted with a heritage of moral iniquity from our past history, hard pressed in the economic world by foreign immigrants and native prejudice, hated here, despised there and pitied everywhere; our one haven of refuge is ourselves, and but one means of advance, our own belief in our great destiny, our own implicit trust in our ability and worth. There is no power under God's high heaven that can stop the advance of eight thousand thousand honest, earnest, inspired and united people. But—and here is the rub they *must* be honest, fearlessly criticising their own faults, zealously correcting them; they must be *earnest*. No people that laughs at itself, and ridicules itself, and wishes to God it was anything but itself ever wrote its name in history; it *must* be inspired with the Divine faith of our black mothers, that out of the blood and dust of battle will march a victorious host, a mighty nation, a peculiar people, to speak to the nations of earth a Divine truth that shall make them free. And such a people must be united; not merely united for the organized theft of political spoils, not united to disgrace religion with whoremongers and wardheelers; not united merely to protest and pass resolutions, but united to stop the ravages of consumption among the Negro people, united to keep black boys from loafing, gambling and crime; united to guard the purity of black women and to reduce that vast army of black prostitutes that is today marching to hell; and united in serious organizations, to determine by careful conference and thoughtful interchange of opinion the broad lines of policy and action for the American Negro.

This is the reason for being which the American Negro Academy has. It aims at once to be the epitome and expression of the intellect of the black-blooded people of America, the exponent of the race ideals of one of the world's great races. As such, the Academy must, if successful, be

(a). Representative in character.
(b). Impartial in conduct.
(c). Firm in leadership.

It must be representative in character; not in that it represents all interests or all factions, but in that it seeks to comprise something of the *best* thought, the most unselfish striving and the highest ideals. There are scattered in forgotten nooks and corners throughout the land, Negroes of some considerable training, of high minds, and high motives, who are unknown to their fellows, who exert far too little influence. These the Negro Academy should strive to bring into touch with each other and to give them a common mouthpiece.

The Academy should be impartial in conduct; while it aims to exalt the people it should aim to do so by truth—not by lies, by honesty—not by flattery. It should continually impress the fact upon the Negro people that they must not expect to have things done for them—they MUST DO FOR THEMSELVES; that they have on their hands a vast work of self-reformation to do, and that a little less complaint and whining, and a little more dogged work and manly striving would do us more credit and benefit than a thousand Force or Civil Rights bills.

Finally, the American Negro Academy must point out a practical path of advance to the Negro people; there lie before every Negro today hundreds of questions of policy and right which must be settled and which each one settles now, not in accordance with any rule, but by impulse or individual preference; for instance: What should be the attitude of Negroes toward the educational qualification for voters? What should be our attitude toward separate schools? How should we meet discriminations on railways and in hotels? Such questions need not so much specific answers for each part as a general expression of policy, and nobody should be better fitted to announce such a policy than a representative honest Negro Academy.

All this, however, must come in time after careful organization and long conference. The immediate work before us should be practical and have direct bearing upon the situation of the Negro. The historical work of collecting the laws of the United States and of the various States of the Union with regard to the Negro is a work of such magnitude and importance that no body but one like this could think of undertaking it. If we could accomplish that one task we would justify our existence.

In the field of Sociology an appalling work lies before us. First, we must unflinchingly and bravely face the truth, not with apologies, but with solemn earnestness. The Negro Academy ought to sound a note of warning that would echo in every black cabin in the land: *Unless we conquer our present vices they will conquer us*; we are diseased, we are developing criminal tendencies, and an alarmingly large percentage of our men and women are sexually impure. The Negro Academy should stand and proclaim this over the housetops, crying with Garrison: *I will not equivocate, I will not retreat a single inch, and I will be heard.* The Academy should seek to gather about it the talented, unselfish men, the pure and noble-minded women, to fight an army of devils that disgraces our manhood and our womanhood. There does not stand today upon God's earth a race more capable in muscle, in intellect, in morals, than the American Negro, if he will bend his energies in the right direction; if he will

Burst his birth's invidious bar
And grasp the skirts of happy chance,
And breast the blows of circumstance,
And grapple with his evil star.

In science and morals, I have indicated two fields of work for the Academy. Finally, in practical policy, I wish to suggest the following *Academy Creed*:

1. We believe that the Negro people, as a race, have a contribution to make to civilization and humanity, which no other race can make.

2. We believe it the duty of the Americans of Negro descent, as a body, to maintain their race identity until this mission of the Negro people is accomplished, and the ideal of human brotherhood has become a practical possibility.

3. We believe that, unless modern civilization is a failure, it is entirely feasible and practicable for two races in such essential political, economic, and religious harmony as the white and colored people of America, to develop side by side in peace and mutual happiness, the peculiar contribution which each has to make to the culture of their common country.

4. As a means to this end we advocate, not such social equality between these races as would disregard human likes and dislikes, but such a social equilibrium as would, throughout all the complicated relations of life, give due and just consideration to culture, ability, and moral worth, whether they be found under white or black skins.

5. We believe that the first and greatest step toward the settlement of the present friction between the races—commonly called the Negro Problem—lies in the correction of the immorality, crime, and laziness among the Negroes themselves, which still remains as a heritage from slavery. We believe that only earnest and long-continued efforts on our own part can cure these social ills.

6. We believe that the second great step toward a better adjustment of the relations between the races should be a more impartial selection of ability in the economic and intellectual world, and a greater respect for personal liberty and worth, regardless of race. We believe that only earnest efforts on the part of the white people of this country will bring much-needed reform in these matters.

7. On the basis of the foregoing declaration, and firmly believing in our high destiny, we, as American Negroes, are resolved to strive in every honorable way for the realization of the best and highest aims, for the development of strong manhood and pure womanhood, and for the rearing of a race ideal in America and Africa, to the glory of God and the uplifting of the Negro people.

—

EXCERPTS FROM *THE SOULS OF BLACK FOLK*

O water, voice of my heart, crying in the sand,
    All night long crying with a mournful cry,
As I lie and listen, and cannot understand
    The voice of my heart in my side or the voice of the sea,

O water, crying for rest, is it I, is it I?
  All night long the water is crying to me.

Unresting water, there shall never be rest
  Till the last moon droop and the last tide fail,
And the fire of the end begin to burn in the west;
  And the heart shall be weary and wonder and cry like the sea,
All life long crying without avail,
  As the water all night long is crying to me.

ARTHUR SIMONS

Between me and the other world there is ever an unasked question: unasked by some through feelings of delicacy; by others through the difficulty of rightly framing it. All, nevertheless, flutter round it. They approach me in a half-hesitant sort of way, eye me curiously or compassionately, and then, instead of saying directly, How does it feel to be a problem? they say, I know an excellent colored man in my town; or, I fought at Mechanicsville; or, Do not these Southern outrages make your blood boil? At these I smile, or am interested, or reduce the boiling to a simmer, as the occasion may require. To the real question, How does it feel to be a problem? I answer seldom a word.

And yet, being a problem is a strange experience,—peculiar even for one who has never been anything else, save perhaps in babyhood and in Europe. It is in the early days of rollicking boyhood that the revelation first bursts upon one, all in a day, as it were. I remember well when the shadow swept across me. I was a little thing, away up in the hills of New England, where the dark Housatonic winds between Hoosac and Taghkanic to the sea. In a wee wooden schoolhouse, something put it into the boys' and girls' heads to buy gorgeous visiting-cards—ten cents a package—and exchange. The exchange was merry, till one girl, a tall newcomer, refused my card,—refused it peremptorily, with a glance. Then it dawned upon me with a certain suddenness that I was different from the others; or like, mayhap, in heart and life and longing, but shut out from their world by a vast veil. I had thereafter no desire to tear down that veil, to creep through; I held all beyond it in common contempt, and lived above it in a region of blue sky and great wandering shadows. That sky was bluest when I could beat my mates at examination-time, or beat them at a foot-race, or even beat their stringy heads. Alas, with the years all this fine contempt began to fade; for the worlds I longed for, and all their dazzling opportunities, were theirs, not mine. But they should not keep these prizes, I said; some, all, I would wrest from them. Just how I would do it I could never decide: by reading law, by healing the sick, by telling the wonderful tales that swam in my head,—some way. With other black boys the strife was not so fiercely sunny: their youth shrunk into tasteless sycophancy, or into silent hatred of the pale world about them and mocking distrust of everything white; or wasted itself in a bitter cry, Why did God make me an outcast and a stranger in mine own house? The shades of the prison-house closed round about us all: walls strait and stubborn to the whitest, but relentlessly narrow, tall, and unscalable to sons of night who must plod darkly on in resignation, or beat unavailing palms against the stone, or steadily, half hopelessly, watch the streak of blue above.

After the Egyptian and Indian, the Greek and Roman, the Teuton and Mongolian, the Negro is a sort of seventh son, born with a veil, and gifted with second-sight in this American world,—a world which yields him no true self-consciousness, but only lets him see himself through the revelation of the other world. It is a peculiar sensation, this double-consciousness, this sense of always looking at one's self through the eyes of others, of measuring one's soul by the tape of a world that looks on in amused contempt and pity. One ever feels his two-ness,—an American, a Negro; two souls, two thoughts, two unreconciled strivings; two warring ideals in one dark body, whose dogged strength alone keeps it from being torn asunder.

The history of the American Negro is the history of this strife,—this longing to attain self-conscious manhood, to merge his double self into a better and truer self. In this merging he wishes neither of the older selves to be lost. He would not Africanize America, for America has too much to teach the world and Africa. He would not bleach his Negro soul in a flood of white Americanism, for he knows that Negro blood has a message for the world. He simply wishes to make it possible for a man to be both a Negro and an American, without being cursed and spit upon by his fellows, without having the doors of Opportunity closed roughly in his face.

This, then, is the end of his striving: to be a co-worker in the kingdom of culture, to escape both death and isolation, to husband and use his best powers and his latent genius. These powers of body and mind have in the past been strangely wasted, dispersed, or forgotten. The shadow of a mighty Negro past flits through the tale of Ethiopia the Shadowy and of Egypt the Sphinx. Throughout history, the powers of single black men flash here and there like falling stars, and die sometimes before the world has rightly gauged their brightness. Here in America, in the few days since Emancipation, the black man's turning hither and thither in hesitant and doubtful striving has often made his very strength to lose effectiveness, to seem like absence of power, like weakness. And yet it is not weakness,—it is the contradiction of double aims. The double-aimed struggle of the black artisan—on the one hand to escape white contempt for a nation of mere hewers of wood and drawers of water, and on the other hand to plough and nail and dig for a poverty-stricken horde—could only result in making him a poor craftsman, for he had but half a heart in either cause. By the poverty and ignorance of his people, the Negro minister or doctor was tempted toward quackery and demagogy; and by the criticism of the other world, toward ideals that made him ashamed of his lowly tasks. The would-be black *savant* was confronted by the paradox that the knowledge his people needed was a twice-told tale to his white neighbors, while the knowledge which would teach the white world was Greek to his own flesh and blood. The innate love of harmony and beauty that set the ruder souls of his people a-dancing and a-singing raised but confusion and doubt in the soul of the black artist; for the beauty revealed to him was the soul-beauty of a race which his larger audience despised, and he could not articulate the message of another people. This waste of double aims, this seeking to satisfy two unreconciled ideals, has wrought sad havoc with the courage and faith and deeds of ten thousand thousand people,—has sent them often wooing false gods and invoking false means of salvation, and at times has even seemed about to make them ashamed of themselves.

Away back in the days of bondage they thought to see in one divine event the end of all doubt and disappointment; few men ever worshipped Freedom with half such unquestioning faith as did the American Negro for two centuries. To him, so far as he thought and dreamed, slavery was indeed the sum of all villainies, the cause of all sorrow, the root of all prejudice; Emancipation was the key to a promised land of sweeter beauty than ever stretched before the eyes of wearied Israelites. In song and exhortation swelled one refrain—Liberty; in his tears and curses the God he implored had Freedom in his right hand. At last it came,— suddenly, fearfully, like a dream. With one wild carnival of blood and passion came the message in his own plaintive cadences:—

> "Shout, O children!
> Shout, you're free!
> For God has bought your liberty!"

Years have passed away since then,—ten, twenty, forty; forty years of national life, forty years of renewal and development, and yet the swarthy spectre sits in its accustomed seat at the Nation's feast. In vain do we cry to this our vastest social problem:—

> "Take any shape but that, and my firm nerves
> Shall never tremble!"

The Nation has not yet found peace from its sins; the freedman has not yet found in freedom his promised land. Whatever of good may have come in these years of change, the shadow of a deep disappointment rests upon the Negro people,—a disappointment all the more bitter because the unattained ideal was unbounded save by the simple ignorance of a lowly people.

The first decade was merely a prolongation of the vain search for freedom, the boon that seemed ever barely to elude their grasp,—like a tantalizing will-o'-the-wisp, maddening and misleading the headless host. The holocaust of war, the terrors of the Ku-Klux Klan, the lies of carpet-baggers, the disorganization of industry, and the contradictory advice of friends and foes, left the bewildered serf with no new watchword beyond the old cry for freedom. As the time flew, however, he began to grasp a new idea. The ideal of liberty demanded for its attainment powerful means, and these the Fifteenth Amendment gave him. The ballot, which before he had looked upon as a visible sign of freedom, he now regarded as the chief means of gaining and perfecting the liberty with which war had partially endowed him. And why not? Had not votes made war and emancipated millions? Had not votes enfranchised the freedmen? Was anything impossible to a power that had done all this? A million black men started with renewed zeal to vote themselves into the kingdom. So the decade flew away, the revolution of 1876 came, and left the half-free serf weary, wondering, but still inspired. Slowly but steadily, in the following years, a new vision began gradually to replace the dream of political power,—a powerful movement, the rise of another ideal to guide the unguided, another pillar of fire by night after a clouded day. It was the ideal of "book-learning"; the curiosity, born of compulsory ignorance, to know and test the power of the cabalistic letters of the white man, the longing to know. Here at last seemed to have been discovered the mountain path to Canaan; longer than the highway of Emancipation and law, steep and rugged, but straight, leading to heights high enough to overlook life.

Up the new path the advance guard toiled, slowly, heavily, doggedly; only those who have watched and guided the faltering feet, the misty minds, the dull understandings, of the dark pupils of these schools know how faithfully, how piteously, this people strove to learn. It was weary work. The cold statistician wrote down the inches of progress here and there, noted also where here and there a foot had slipped or some one had fallen. To the tired climbers, the horizon was ever dark, the mists were often cold, the Canaan was always dim and far away. If, however, the vistas disclosed as yet no goal, no resting-place, little but flattery and criticism, the journey at least gave leisure for reflection and self-examination; it changed the child of Emancipation to the youth with dawning self-consciousness, self-realization, self-respect. In those sombre forests of his striving his own soul rose before him, and he saw himself,—darkly as through a veil; and yet he saw in himself some faint revelation of his power, of his mission. He began to have a dim feeling that, to attain his place in the world, he must be himself, and not another. For the first time he sought to analyze the burden he bore upon his back, that dead-weight of social degradation partially masked behind a half-named Negro problem. He felt his poverty; without a cent, without a home, without land, tools, or savings, he had entered into competition with rich, landed, skilled neighbors. To be a poor man is hard, but to be a poor race in a land of dollars is the very bottom of hardships. He felt the weight of his ignorance,—not simply of letters, but of life, of business of the humanities; the accumulated sloth and shirking and awkwardness of decades and centuries shackled his hands and feet. Nor was his burden all poverty and ignorance. The red stain of bastardy, which two centuries of systematic legal defilement of Negro women had stamped upon his race, meant not only the loss of ancient African chastity, but also the hereditary weight of a mass of corruption from white adulterers, threatening almost the obliteration of the Negro home.

A people thus handicapped ought not to be asked to race with the world, but rather allowed to give all its time and thought to its own social problems. But alas! while sociologists gleefully count his bastards and his prostitutes, the very soul of the toiling, sweating black man is darkened by the shadow of a vast despair. Men call the shadow prejudice, and learnedly explain it as the natural defence of culture against barbarism, learning against ignorance, purity against crime, the "higher" against the "lower" races. To which the Negro cries Amen! and swears that to so much of this strange prejudice as is founded on just homage to civilization, culture, righteousness, and progress, he humbly bows and meekly does obeisance. But before that nameless prejudice that leaps beyond all this he stands helpless, dismayed, and well-nigh speechless; before that personal disrespect and mockery, the ridicule and systematic humiliation, the distortion of fact and wan-

ton license of fancy, the cynical ignoring of the better and the boisterous welcoming of the worse, the all-pervading desire to inculcate disdain for everything
black, from Toussaint to the devil,—before this there rises a sickening despair
that would disarm and discourage any nation save that black host to whom "discouragement" is an unwritten word.

But the facing of so vast a prejudice could not but bring the inevitable self-
questioning, self-disparagement, and lowering of ideals which ever accompany
repression and breed in an atmosphere of contempt and hate. Whisperings and
portents came borne upon the four winds: Lo! we are diseased and dying, cried
the dark hosts; we cannot write, our voting is vain; what need of education, since
we must always cook and serve? And the Nation echoed and enforced this self-
criticism, saying: Be content to be servants, and nothing more; what need of
higher culture for half-men? Away with the black man's ballot, by force or
fraud,—and behold the suicide of a race! Nevertheless, out of the evil came
something of good,—the more careful adjustment of education to real life, the
clearer perception of the Negroes' social responsibilities, and the sobering realization of the meaning of progress.

So dawned the time of *Sturm und Drang:* storm and stress to-day rocks our little boat on the mad waters of the world-sea; there is within and without the sound
of conflict, the burning of body and rending of soul; inspiration strives with doubt,
and faith with vain questionings. The bright ideals of the past,—physical freedom,
political power, the training of brains and the training of hands,—all these in turn
have waxed and waned, until even the last grows dim and overcast. Are they all
wrong,—all false? No, not that, but each alone was over-simple and incom-
plete,—the dreams of a credulous race-childhood, or the fond imaginings of the
other world which does not know and does not want to know our power. To be
really true, all these ideals must be melted and welded into one. The training of
the schools we need to-day more than ever,—the training of deft hands, quick
eyes and ears, and above all the broader, deeper, higher culture of gifted minds
and pure hearts. The power of the ballot we need in sheer self-defence,—else
what shall save us from a second slavery? Freedom, too, the long-sought, we still
seek,—the freedom of life and limb, the freedom to work and think, the freedom
to love and aspire. Work, culture, liberty,—all these we need, not singly but
together, not successively but together, each growing and aiding each, and all
striving toward that vaster ideal that swims before the Negro people, the ideal of
human brotherhood, gained through the unifying ideal of Race; the ideal of fostering and developing the traits and talents of the Negro, not in opposition to or
contempt for other races, but rather in large conformity to the greater ideals of
the American Republic, in order that some day on American soil two world-races
may give each to each those characteristics both so sadly lack. We the darker ones
come even now not altogether empty-handed: there are to-day no truer expo-
nents of the pure human spirit of the Declaration of Independence than the
American Negroes; there is no true American music but the wild sweet melodies
of the Negro slave; the American fairy tales and folk-lore are Indian and African;
and, all in all, we black men seem the sole oasis of simple faith and reverence in

a dusty desert of dollars and smartness. Will America be poorer if she replace her brutal dyspeptic blundering with light-hearted but determined Negro humility? or her coarse and cruel wit with loving jovial good-humor? or her vulgar music with the soul of the Sorrow Songs?

Merely a concrete test of the underlying principles of the great republic is the Negro Problem, and the spiritual striving of the freedmen's sons is the travail of souls whose burden is almost beyond the measure of their strength, but who bear it in the name of an historic race, in the name of this the land of their fathers' fathers, and in the name of human opportunity.

And now what I have briefly sketched in large outline let me on coming pages tell again in many ways, with loving emphasis and deeper detail, that men may listen to the striving in the souls of black folk.

Sources: Excerpts from "The Conservation of Races," paper presented to the American Negro Academy, Occasional Papers, No. 2 (Washington, D.C., 1897); and (2) excerpts from chapter I, "Of Our Spiritual Strivings," and chapter II, "Of the Dawn of Freedom," from *The Souls of Black Folk* (Chicago: A.C. McClurg, 1903).

SELECT BIBLIOGRAPHY:

W. E. B. Du Bois, *The Suppression of the African Slave-Trade to the United States of America, 1638–1870* (New York: Longmans, Green, 1896).

———, *The Philadelphia Negro: A Social Study* (Boston: Ginn and Company, 1899).

———, *The Souls of Black Folk: Essays and Sketches* (Chicago: A.C. McClurg, 1903).

———, *Darkwater: Voices from the Veil* (New York: Harcourt, Brace and Stratford, 1920).

David Levering Lewis, ed., *W. E. B. Du Bois: A Reader* (New York: Holt, 1995).

Manning Marable, *W.E.B. Du Bois: Black Radical Democrat* (Boulder: Paradigm Publishers, 2005).

Adolph Reed, *W. E. Du Bois and American Political Thought: Fabianism and the Color Line* (New York: Oxford University Press, 1997).

Eric J. Sundquist, ed., *The Oxford W. E. B. Du Bois Reader* (New York: Oxford University Press, 1996).

Raymond Wolters, *Du Bois and His Rivals* (Columbia: University of Missouri Press, 2002).

⌐ 15 ⌐

The Niagara Movement, *1905*

At the invitation of W. E. B. Du Bois, a group of socially conscious black intellectuals and leaders gathered together at Niagara Falls in 1905. This meeting initiated the Niagara Movement. Many participants were motivated by their opposition to the conservative leadership of Booker T. Washington, who was widely criticized in some circles not simply for his policy of racial accommodationism but also for his heavy-handed political tactics against those who dared to challenge him. Though the Niagara Movement represented the growing voice of dissent within black America and forcefully challenged the racial oppression of Jim Crow, the success of the project was limited. Washington used his influence with major African-American newspapers, churches, and colleges to undermine and discredit his opponents. Tensions between Du Bois and Trotter also contributed to the demise of this group.

PROGRESS: The members of the conference, known as the Niagara Movement, assembled in annual meeting at Buffalo, July 11th, 12th and 13th, 1905, congratulate the Negro-Americans on certain undoubted evidences of progress in the last decade, particularly the increase of intelligence, the buying of property, the checking of crime, the uplift in home life, the advance in literature and art, and the demonstration of constructive and executive ability in the conduct of great religious, economic and educational institutions.

Suffrage: At the same time, we believe that this class of American citizens should protest emphatically and continually against the curtailment of their political rights. We believe in manhood suffrage; we believe that no man is so good, intelligent or wealthy as to be entrusted wholly with the welfare of his neighbor.

Civil Liberty: We believe also in protest against the curtailment of our civil rights. All American citizens have the right to equal treatment in places of public entertainment according to their behavior and deserts.

Economic Opportunity: We especially complain against the denial of equal opportunities to us in economic life; in the rural districts of the South this amounts to peonage and virtual slavery; all over the South it tends to crush labor and small business enterprises; and everywhere American prejudice, helped often by iniquitous laws, is making it more difficult for Negro-Americans to earn a decent living.

Education: Common school education should be free to all American children and compulsory. High school training should be adequately provided for all, and college training should be the monopoly of no class or race in any section of our common country. We believe that, in defense of our own institutions, the United States should aid common school education, particularly in the South, and we especially recommend concerted agitation to this end. We urge an increase in public high school facilities in the South, where the Negro-Americans are almost wholly without such provisions. We favor well-equipped trade and technical schools for the training of artisans, and the need of adequate and liberal endowment for a few institutions of higher education must be patent to sincere well-wishers of the race.

Courts: We demand upright judges in courts, juries selected without discrimination on account of color and the same measure of punishment and the same efforts at reformation for blacks as for white offenders. We need orphanages and farm schools for dependent children, juvenile reformatories for delinquents, and the abolition of the dehumanizing convict-lease system.

Public Opinion: We note with alarm the evident retrogression in this land of sound public opinion on the subject of manhood rights, republican government and human brotherhood, and we pray God that this nation will not degenerate into a mob of boasters and oppressors, but rather will return to the faith of the fathers, that all men were created free and equal, with certain unalienable rights.

Health: We plead for health—for an opportunity to live in decent houses and localities, for a chance to rear our children in physical and moral cleanliness.

Employers and Labor Unions: We hold up for public execration the conduct of two opposite classes of men: The practice among employers of importing ignorant Negro-American laborers in emergencies, and then affording them neither protection nor permanent employment; and the practice of labor unions in proscribing and boycotting and oppressing thousands of their fellow-toilers, simply because they are black. These methods have accentuated and will accentuate the war of labor and capital, and they are disgraceful to both sides.

Protest: We refuse to allow the impression to remain that the Negro-American assents to inferiority, is submissive under oppression and apologetic before insults. Through helplessness we may submit, but the voice of protest of ten million Americans must never cease to assail the ears of their fellows, so long as America is unjust.

Color-Line: Any discrimination based simply on race or color is barbarous, we care not how hallowed it be by custom, expediency or prejudice. Differences made on account of ignorance, immorality, or disease are legitimate methods of fighting evil, and against them we have no word of protest; but discriminations based simply and solely on physical peculiarities, place of birth, color of skin, are relics of that unreasoning human savagery of which the world is and ought to be thoroughly ashamed.

"Jim Crow" Cars: We protest against the "Jim Crow" car, since its effect is and must be to make us pay first-class fare for third-class accommodations, render us open to insults and discomfort and to crucify wantonly our manhood, womanhood and self-respect.

Soldiers: We regret that this nation has never seen fit adequately to reward the black soldiers who, in its five wars, have defended their country with their blood, and yet have been systematically denied the promotions which their abilities deserve. And we regard as unjust, the exclusion of black boys from the military and naval training schools.

War Amendments: We urge upon Congress the enactment of appropriate legislation for securing the proper enforcement of those articles of freedom, the thirteenth, fourteenth and fifteenth amendments of the Constitution of the United States.

Oppression: We repudiate the monstrous doctrine that the oppressor should be the sole authority as to the rights of the oppressed. The Negro race in America stolen, ravished and degraded, struggling up through difficulties and oppression, needs sympathy and receives criticism; needs help and is given hindrance, needs protection and is given mob-violence, needs justice and is given charity, needs leadership and is given cowardice and apology, needs bread and is given a stone. This nation will never stand justified before God until these things are changed.

The Church: Especially are we surprised and astonished at the recent attitude of the church of Christ—of an increase of a desire to bow to racial prejudice, to narrow the bounds of human brotherhood, and to segregate black men to some outer sanctuary. This is wrong, unchristian and disgraceful to the twentieth century civilization.

Agitation: Of the above grievances we do not hesitate to complain, and to complain loudly and insistently. To ignore, overlook, or apologize for these wrongs is to prove ourselves unworthy of freedom. Persistent manly agitation is the way to liberty, and toward this goal the Niagara Movement has started and asks the cooperation of all men of all races.

Help: At the same time we want to acknowledge with deep thankfulness the help of our fellowmen from the abolitionist down to those who today still stand for equal opportunity and who have given and still give of their wealth and of their poverty for our advancement.

Duties: And while we are demanding, and ought to demand, and will continue to demand the rights enumerated above, God forbid that we should ever forget to urge corresponding duties upon our people:

The duty to vote.
The duty to respect the rights of others.
The duty to work.
The duty to obey the laws.
The duty to be clean and orderly.
The duty to send our children to school.
The duty to respect ourselves, even as we respect others.

This statement, complaint and prayer we submit to the American people, and Almighty God.

Source: "The Niagara Movement Declaration of Principles," 1905. Originally published in the *Cleveland Gazette,* July 22, 1905.

SELECT BIBLIOGRAPHY:

W. E. B. Du Bois, *The Oxford W. E. B. Du Bois Reader,* ed. Eric J. Sundquist (New York: Oxford University Press, 1996).

David Levering Lewis, *W. E. B. Du Bois: Biography of a Race, 1868–1919* (New York: Holt, 1993).

Manning Marable, *W. E. B. Du Bois: Black Radical Democrat* (Boulder: Parodiem Publishers, 2005).

August Meier, *Negro Thought in America, 1880–1915: Racial Ideologies in the Age of Booker T. Washington* (Ann Arbor: University of Michigan Press, 1963).

Elliot M. Rudwick, "The Niagara Movement," *Journal of Negro History* 42, no. 3 (1957), pp. 177–200.

————, *W. E. B. Du Bois: A Study in Minority Group Leadership* (Philadelphia: University of Pennsylvania Press, 1960).

⌁ 16 ⌁

Hubert Henry Harrison, Black Revolutionary Nationalist

Hubert Henry Harrison (1883–1927) was born in St. Croix, Danish West Indies, and moved to New York as a teenager. Harrison read widely in history, literature, and the social sciences, and became a socialist after arriving at the conclusion that racism was largely driven by class exploitation. Harrison acquired a popular following as a charismatic street speaker both on Harlem's Lenox Avenue and at Madison Square in Manhattan. The racial prejudice Harrison encountered among white socialists pushed him in the direction of black nationalism. Harrison served for a time as editor of Marcus Garvey's newspaper, *The Negro World*. His most ambitious book, *When Africa Awakes*, presents a powerful perspective of what would later be defined as "revolutionary nationalism."

⌁

. . . Today, fellow sufferers, they tell us that we are free. But are we? If you will think for a moment you will see that we are not free at all. We have simply changed one form of slavery for another. Then it was chattel slavery, now it is wage slavery. For that which was the essence of chattel slavery is the essence of wage slavery. It is only a difference in form. The chattel slave was compelled to work by physical force; the wage slave is compelled to work by starvation. The product of the chattel slave's labor was taken by his master; the product of the wage slave's labor is taken by the employer.

The United States government has made a study of the wealth-producing power of the wage slaves and has shown that the average worker *produces* $2,451 a year. The government has also made a study of wages in the United States, and that study shows that the average worker gets $437 a year. This means that the average employer takes away from the average wage slave $2,014 a year. In the good old days the master took away the wealth produced by the slave in the simplest form; today he takes it away in the form of profits. But in one respect the wage slave is worse off than the chattel slave. Under chattel slavery the master owned the man and the land; he had to feed and clothe the man. Under wage slavery the man feeds and clothes himself. Under chattel slavery it was to the interest of the owner to give the slave work and to keep him from starving to death. Under wage slavery, if the man is out of work the employer doesn't care; that is no loss to him; and if the man dies, there are millions of others eager to take his place, because, as I said before, they must either work for him or starve.

There is one very striking parallel between the two cases. Today there are many people who say that this system is divinely appointed—is a law of nature—just as they said the same thing of chattel slavery. Well, there are millions of workers who say it is wrong. Under chattel slavery black workers were robbed; under wage slavery all the workers are robbed. The Socialist party says that this robbing shall cease; that no worker black or white shall be exploited for profit. And it says, further, that there is one sure and certain way of putting an end to the system, and that is by working for the success of Socialism. . . .

Under the old system, the capitalist owned the man; today he owns the tools with which the man must work. These tools are the factories, the mines, and the machines. The system that owns them owns you and me and all the rest of us, black, white, brown, red and yellow. We can't live unless we have access to these tools, and our masters the capitalists see to it that we are separated from what we make by using these things, except so much as is necessary to keep us alive that we may be able to make more—for them. This little bit is called wages. They wouldn't give us even that if they thought that we could live without it. In the good old days the chattel slave would be fastened with a chain if they thought that he might escape. Today no chain is necessary to bind us to the tools. We are as free as air. Of course. We are free to starve. And that chain of the fear of starvation binds us to the tools owned by the capitalist as firmly as any iron chain ever did. And this system doesn't care whether the slaves who are bound in this new way are white or black. To the capitalist system all workers are equal—in so far as they have a stomach.

Now the one great fact for the Negro in America today is *race prejudice*. The great labor problem with which all working people are faced is made harder for black working people by the addition of a race problem. I want to show you how one grows out of the other and how, at bottom, they are both the same thing. In other words, I want you to see the economic reason for race prejudice.

In the first place, do you know that the most rabid, Negro-hating, Southern aristocrat has not the slightest objection to sleeping in the same house with a Negro—if that Negro sleeps there as his servant? He doesn't care if his food is prepared by a Negro cook and handled by a Negro waiter before it gets to him; he will eat it. But if a Negro comes into the same public restaurant to buy and eat food, then—oh my!—he gets all hot up about it. But why? What's the difference? I will tell you. The aristocrat wants the black man to feel that he is on a lower level. When he is "in his place," he is liked. But he must not be allowed to do anything to make him forget that he is on this lower level; he must be kept "in his place," which means the place which the aristocrat wants him to keep. You see, the black man carries the memory of slavery with him. Everybody knows that the slaves were the exploited working class of the South. That put them in a class by themselves, down at the bottom, downtrodden, despised, "inferior."

Do you begin to see now that race prejudice is only another name for *caste prejudice*? If our people had never been slaves; had never been exploited workers, and so, at the bottom of the ladder, there would be no prejudice against them now. In every case where there has been a downtrodden class of workers at the bottom, that class has been despised by the class that lived by their labor. Do you doubt it? Then look at the facts. If you had picked up a daily paper in New York in 1848 you would have found at the end of many an advertisement for butler, coachman, lady's maid, clerk or bookkeeper these words: "No Irish need apply." There was a race prejudice against the Irish then, because most of the manual unskilled laborers were Irish. They were at the bottom, exploited and despised. But they have changed things since then. Beginning in the seventies, when Jewish laborers began to come here from Russia, Austria and Germany, and lasting even to our own day, there has been race prejudice against the Jews. And today, when the Italian has taken the place which the Irish laborer vacated—at the bottom— he too comes in for his share of prejudice. In every one of these cases it was the condition of the people at the bottom—as despised, exploited, wage slaves—that was responsible for the race prejudice. And it is just so in the black man's case— with this difference: his color marks what he once was, and even though he should wear a dress suit every evening and own an automobile or a farm, he can always be picked out and reminded.

Now, under the present system, exploiting the wage slave is respectable. I have already shown you that wherever the worker is exploited he is despised. So you will see that despising the wage slave is quite fashionable. . . . As long as the present system continues, the workers will be despised; as long as the workers are despised, the black man will be despised, robbed and murdered, because they are least able to defend themselves. Now ask yourself whether you haven't a very special interest in changing the present system.

Of course, you will ask: "But haven't white working people race prejudice too?" Sure, they have. Do you know why? It pays the capitalist to keep the workers divided. So he creates and keeps alive these prejudices. He gets them to believe that their interests are different. Then he uses one half of them to club the other half with. In Russia when the working men demand reform, the capitalists sick them on the Jews. In America they sick them on the Negroes. That makes them forget their own condition; as long as they can be made to look down upon another class. "But then," you will say, "the average wage slave must be a chump." Sure, he is. That's what the capitalist counts on. And Socialism is working to educate the workers to see this and to unite them in doing away with the present system.

Socialism stands for the emancipation of the wage slaves. Are you a wage slave? Do you want to be emancipated? Then join hands with the Socialists. Hear what they have to say. Read some of their literature. Get a Socialist leaflet, a pamphlet, or, better still, a book. You will be convinced of two things: that Socialism is right, and that it is inevitable. It is right because any order of things in which those who work have least while those who work them have most, is wrong. It is inevitable because a system under which the wealth produced by the labor of human hands amounts to more than two hundred and twenty billions a year while many millions live on the verge of starvation, is bound to break down. Therefore, if you wish to join with the other class-conscious, intelligent wage earners—in putting an end to such a system; if you want to better living conditions for black men as well as for white men; to make this woeful world of ours a little better for you children and your children's children, study Socialism—and think and work your way out. . . .

Source: Excerpt from speech originally delivered in about 1912, first published in Harrison, *The Negro and the Nation* (New York: 1917[?]), pp. 48–58.

SELECT BIBLIOGRAPHY:

John G. Jackson, *Hubert Henry Harrison: The Black Socrates* (Austin, Tex.: American Athiest Press, 1987).

Jeffrey Babcock Perry, "Hubert Henry Harrison, The Father of Harlem Radicalism: The Early Years, 1883 through the Founding of the Liberty League and the Voice in 1917" (Ph.D. diss., Columbia University, 1986).

ADDITIONAL RESOURCES:

"The Avalon Project at Yale Law School: African-Americans—Biography, Autobiography and History," www.yale.edu/lawweb/avalon/treatise/african_americans.htm.

"Race and Place—An African-American Community in Jim Crow: Charlottesville, VA," www.vcdh.virginia.edu/afam/raceandplace/index.html.

Edward L. Ayers, *The Promise of the New South: Life after Reconstruction* (Oxford: Oxford University Press, 2007).

Jane Elizabeth Dailey, Glenda Elizabeth Gilmore, and Bryant Simon, eds., *Jumpin' Jim Crow: Southern Politics from Civil War to Civil Rights* (Princeton: Princeton University Press, 2000).

Eric Foner, *Reconstruction: America's Unfinished Revolution, 1863–1877.* (New York: History Book Club, 2005).

Eric Foner and illustrations edited and with commentary by Joshua Brown, *Forever Free: The Story of Emancipation and Reconstruction*, 1st ed. (New York: Knopf, 2005).

Evelyn Nakano Glenn, *Unequal Freedom: How Race and Gender Shaped American Citizenship and Labor* (Cambridge: Harvard University Press, 2004).

Darlene Clark Hine, *Black Women in the Nursing Profession: A Documentary History, The History of American Nursing* (New York: Garland, 1985).

———, *Black Women in White: Racial Conflict and Cooperation in the Nursing Profession, 1890–1950, Blacks in the Diaspora* (Bloomington: Indiana University Press, 1989).

Gilbert Jonas and with a forward by Julian Bond, *Freedom's Sword: The NAACP and the Struggle against Racism in America, 1909–1969* (London: Routledge, 2007).

William Miles, *Men of Bronze: The Black American Heroes of World War I*, Santa Monica: Direct Cinema Ltd., 1995. DVD Video.

Roger L. Ransom and Richard Sutch, *One Kind of Freedom: The Economic Consequences of Emancipation*, 2nd ed. (Cambridge: Cambridge University Press, 2001).

FROM PLANTATION TO GHETTO: THE GREAT MIGRATION, HARLEM RENAISSANCE, AND WORLD WAR, 1915–1954

INTRODUCTION

The four decades considered in section 3 were a period of both continuity and tremendous change for the national African-American community. The central political reality for black Americans was, of course, Jim Crow segregation. By the 1920s, the United States had become a thoroughly segregated society, in which constitutional safeguards and civil liberties rarely applied to black people. Like the South African system known years later as *apartheid*, the United States was in effect a "racist state," in which access to voting rights, political representation, and economic and social development was rigidly determined for racialized minorities through governmental authorities and, more informally, through deliberate acts of extralegal terror. Black Americans were increasingly subjected to de facto segregation in many northern cities, and white-owned banks frequently denied credit and capital to African Americans starting businesses or buying homes in predominantly white areas. The actual political accomplishments of Reconstruction were distorted in standard scholarship, or viciously parodied in racist films such as *The Birth of a Nation* (1915). The high tide of white supremacy occurred in the years immediately following World War I. In what would later be called the "Red Summer of 1919," hundreds of African Americans were murdered and thousands were left homeless by the attacks of racist mobs. The Ku Klux Klan, originally established as a white southern vigilante group during Reconstruction, was revived and achieved tremendous support. By the early 1920s, several million whites, most of whom lived outside the South, actively participated in the Ku Klux Klan and supported its candidates for public office. Both major national political parties, the Republicans and Democrats, repudiated support for the rights of Negroes. This environment of white supremacy and unqualified racial repression led to new developments in the political character and protest organizations of African-American people.

A second factor in the transformation of black political and social life was the Great Migration—the vast relocation of millions of African Americans from the rural, agricultural South to the urban, industrial North. Sociologists and historians have long debated the fundamental factors that accounted for the decision of so many African Americans to leave the South. The mechanization of southern agriculture and the decline of cotton farming pushed thousands of sharecroppers off the land. Many black workers were attracted to better-paying jobs in the manufacturing and industrial factories of the Midwest and Northeast. Others simply wanted to escape the political persecution, lynching, and racial oppression. As millions of black people resettled in the North, they quickly created new urban communities with elaborate social infrastructures: black newspapers, churches, schools, funeral establishments, beauty and barber shops, fraternal organizations, Masonic lodges, theater groups, and similar institutions. By 1930, Harlem had become the largest black urban center in North America, and was virtually the mecca of black culture and the arts. Boston's Roxbury, Chicago's South Side, and Cleveland's Hough district also became identifiably black metropolises. Soon after World War II, south-central Los Angeles and East Oakland in California would join this growing list of African-American urban communities. By the end of the war, about forty percent of all black Americans lived outside the South, and more than half lived in cities.

The flowering of the Harlem Renaissance in the 1920s was the literary and cultural expression of the social forces that produced the Great Migration and the modern ghetto. In the writings of Jean Toomer, Claude McKay, Nella Larsen, Zora Neale Hurston, and Countee Cullen, a new generation of artists and intellectuals, born in the age of jazz, found their own unique voice. As Langston Hughes suggested in his 1926 essay, "The Negro Artist and the Racial Mountain," the power and creativity of black art would be found within a celebration and understanding of the culture of "black common people. . . . They furnish a wealth of colorful, distinctive material for any artist because they still hold their own individuality in the face of American standardizations. And perhaps these common people will give to the world its truly great Negro artist, the one who is not afraid to be himself" (document 6).

The Harlem Renaissance also involved a social critique. The phrase "the New Negro" was used to characterize the new levels of militancy, racial consciousness, and cultural energy that were most visibly represented in Harlem. For poets and politicians alike, the black metropolis was the new frontier for black life and social development. "To my mind," NAACP national secretary James Weldon Johnson wrote in 1925, "Harlem is more than a Negro community; it is a large-scale laboratory experiment in the race problem. . . . I believe that the Negro's advantages and opportunities are greater in Harlem than in any other place in the country, and that Harlem will become the intellectual, the cultural, and the financial center for Negroes of the United States, and will exert a vital influence upon all Negro peoples" (document 8).

These complex factors—the Great Migration to the North, the explosive growth of black urban communities, the development of a black working class, all within the constraints of racial segregation—created the space for new protest ideologies and formations. Booker T. Washington's death in 1915 and the negotiated peace between the Tuskegee Machine and the liberal integrationists led by Du Bois at the Amenia conference the following year, destroyed accommodation as a viable political strategy. By 1919, *The Crisis* claimed over one hundred thousand readers, and the NAACP had clearly won the ideological battle to become the voice and political agent of the black middle class. But in the wake of the Red Summer of 1919, Du Bois's leadership was severely challenged from several quarters. The principal spokesperson for black nationalism and racial separatism was Jamaican-born Marcus Garvey, founder of the Universal Negro Improvement Association (UNIA) in 1914. Arriving in the United States in 1916, Garvey used his charismatic oratory and organizing skills to quickly establish a mass following among hundreds of thousands of black poor and working-class people. Unlike the NAACP and Frederick Douglass before him, Garvey did not desire a pluralistic, integrated American society in which Negroes freely participated. The UNIA's "Declaration of Rights of the Negro Peoples of the World," ratified in Harlem in August 1920, presents an alternative vision of black self-determination and racial separatism that drew from the earlier ideas of Delany and Blyden: "We declare that Negroes, wheresoever they form a community among themselves, should be given the right to elect their own representatives to represent them in legislatures, courts of law, or such institutions as may exercise control over that particular community. . . . We believe in the freedom of Africa for the Negro people of the world, and by the principle of Europe for the Europeans and Asia for the Asiatics; we also demand Africa for the Africans at home and abroad." Garvey was convinced that the NAACP was nothing less "than a scheme to destroy the Negro Race" and that "Du Bois represents a group that hates the Negro blood in its veins . . ." (document 4).

The liberal integrationists also came under intense attack from the left. Influenced by the Bolshevik Revolution of 1917, black socialists interpreted the oppression of African Americans as part of the larger exploitation of the proletariat. What the black masses needed was not Garvey's racial chauvinism, the black radicals believed, but world revolution. Cyril V. Briggs's African Blood Brotherhood (ABB) combined the race militancy reflected in the UNIA with a Marxist analysis of class struggle. The ABB's program explicitly condemned "those Negroes who would distract the attention of the Negro workers from the fight for better conditions in the United States to an illusory empire or republic on the continent of Africa. . . . The ABB believes in interracial cooperation—not the sham cooperation of the oppressed Negro workers and their oppressors, but the honest cooperation of colored and white workers based upon mutual appreciation of the fact of the identity of their interests as members of the working class" (document 3).

Throughout the 1920s, the Marxist left did not play a dominant role in African-American politics and society. The existence of Jim Crow served to anchor nearly all black political discourse to the "race question"; whether one supported racial integration or Garvey's "back to Africa" program, racial categories and assumptions set the parameters of politics. All of this changed, however, with the onset of the Great Depression. By 1932, nearly half of all African-American workers were unemployed. Millions were homeless and hungry. The NAACP had no effective program to attack black unemployment, and Du Bois himself was pressured to resign from the organization in 1934 over his support for a strategy of economic "self-segregation." Garvey had been harassed by the federal government, imprisoned in 1925, and permanently expelled from the United States in 1927. The UNIA, which was for a brief time the largest mass-membership organization in black history, virtually disappeared. Into this vacuum entered a series of radical workers, intellectuals, leaders, organizers, and organizations that favored neither liberal integration nor racial separatism, but rather what can be termed "transformation": the complete dismantling of institutional racism, the democratization of the U.S. state and the fundamental redistribution of economic wealth and resources throughout society, and the elimination of all social manifestations of human inequality and gender discrimination.

In this section, economist Abram L. Harris outlines the theoretical justification for a radical movement within the black community: "Progressives must realize that Negro economic and political leadership is opportunistic and petty bourgeois," Harris observes. "Thus progressives [must] carry to the Negro masses some realization of the causes of unemployment, low wages, and the need for labor unionism and cooperation . . ." (document 9). It was through the activism of blacks in the Communist Party that Harris's academic Marxist critique became a social force. The struggles to save the lives of the Scottsboro boys in Alabama, and to free political prisoner Angelo Herndon in Georgia in the 1930s, attracted thousands of African Americans to the Communist Party (documents 10, 11). The left helped to organize a series of protest associations involving African Americans, including tenants' rights groups, sharecroppers' unions, and the Southern Negro Youth Conference (document 16). From the point of view of many black workers, the Communist Party provided the rare opportunity to discuss important political issues affecting their communities with whites on the basis of full equality. Hosea Hudson's personal account of his experiences inside the Communist Party provides some insights for the movement's popularity at this time: "I found this Party, a party of the working class, gave me rights equal with all others regardless of color, sex, or age or educational standards. I with my uneducation could express myself, without being made fun of by others who could read well and fast, using big words. I was treated with high respect. I had a right to help make the policy" (document 12). At a time when southern black people were routinely denied the right to vote, to serve on juries, or to freely express their opinions in public, the experience of the Communist Party's democratic procedures was a striking contrast.

The growing influence of the left served to revitalize liberal reformist organizations, and led to the formation of new protest movements. In Harlem, Reverend Adam Clayton Powell, Jr., minister of the Abyssinian Baptist Church, became the leader of a mass campaign to boycott and picket businesses that refused to employ black workers (document 14). A. Philip Randolph, leader of the Brotherhood of Sleeping Car Porters, inspired the Negro March on Washington Movement in 1941, successfully pressuring the Roosevelt administration to grant Executive Order 8802, which outlawed racial discriminatory hiring policies in defense plants (document 17). The identification of areas of unity in the class and race questions that occurred during this era transformed the political landscape for both labor and African-American struggles. Under the visionary guidance of attorney Charles Hamilton Houston, the NAACP pursued gradual but steady judicial assault against the legal justifications for the racist "separate but equal" policy.

Throughout these years, black women played central roles in the shaping of all three major political currents within black America: liberal integrationism, black nationalism, and transformationism. In the 1920s and 1930s, the foremost voice for women's rights among the Negro middle class was educator Mary McLeod Bethune, president of what would later become Bethune-Cookman College. In her 1935 speech reprinted here (document 13), she encourages the NAACP to "continue to struggle toward the goal of social justice. . . . Let us cease now to render our allegiance to the creed of belief in the inherent superiority of white and the inherent inferiority of black." Amy Euphemia Jacques Garvey, a black nationalist leader and women's rights advocate, challenged African-American males to overcome their patriarchal attitudes about politics (document 5):

> We are tired of hearing Negro men say, "There is a better day coming," while they do nothing to usher in the day. We are becoming so impatient that we are getting in the front ranks, and serve notice on the world that we will brush aside the halting, cowardly Negro men, and with prayer on our lips and arms prepared for any fray, we will press on and on until victory is over. Africa must be for Africans, and Negroes everywhere must be independent. . . . Mr. Black man, watch your step! Ethiopia's queens will reign again, and her Amazons protect her shores and people. Strengthen your shaking knees, and move forward, or we will displace you and lead on to victory and to glory

From the vantage point of the left, perhaps the most important radical feminist voice was that of Claudia Jones. Crafting a Marxian analysis of race, gender, and class, she points out in her 1949 essay (document 19) that "Negro women—as workers, as Negroes, and as women—are the most oppressed stratum of the whole population. . . . The super-exploitation of the Negro woman worker is thus revealed not only in that she receives, as woman, less than equal pay for equal work with men, but in that the majority of Negro women get less than half the pay of white women." Consequently, she observes, there is "little wonder" that black maternity and infant mortality rates are so high. Because of their triple burden of gender, race, and class exploitation, African-American women could potentially become the most revolutionary social group in the country. Jones's theoretical formulation of how these three social categories are related anticipates by thirty years the analysis of black Marxist feminists such as Angela Y. Davis and other race, class, and gender feminists:

> A developing consciousness on the woman question today, therefore, must not fail to recognize that the Negro question in the United States is *prior* to, and not equal to, the woman question; that only to the extent that we fight all chauvinist expressions and actions as regards the Negro people and fight for the full equality of the Negro people, can women as a whole advance their struggle for equal rights. For the progressive women's movement, the Negro woman, who combines in her status the worker, the Negro, and the woman, is the vital link to this heightened political consciousness.

The hopes for domestic social reform on issues of both race and class were extinguished for nearly a decade, as World War II gave way to the Cold War. The armed global confrontation between the Soviet Union and the United States rationalized a government-sponsored purge of millions of American radicals and even liberals from public and private institutions. Approximately one million workers in Communist-led unions were expelled from the AFL-CIO. States passed laws defining membership in the Communist Party as a crime. Leaders and organizers of the Communist Party were jailed. Claudia Jones was imprisoned and expelled from the United States. The State Department seized the passports of Du Bois and black actor and activist Paul Robeson for eight years, illegally denying them the right to travel. Robeson's annual income fell from over $100,000 to virtually nothing, since he was denied access to speak and perform. Moderate integrationists such as NAACP leader Walter White were silent, and at times, even encouraged the persecution of black radicals.

By the mid-1950s, the transformationist, radical current of black political thought and activism had been seriously weakened by McCarthyism. But as events in Montgomery, Alabama, in 1955 would show, the black freedom movement would soon experience another renaissance.

⚊ 1 ⚊

Black Conflict over World War I

When the United States declared war on Germany and entered what was then called the Great War, African Americans were bitterly divided over the conflict. Socialists such as A. Philip Randolph and Hubert H. Harrison attacked the war effort as imperialist. More moderate black leaders such as Du Bois saw the war as an opportunity for Negroes to gain political advantages. Woodrow Wilson's pledge to make the world "safe for democracy," if extended to African Americans, should mean the elimination of Jim Crow segregation and European colonialism. Unfortunately, blacks who joined the war effort discovered that American democracy was still reserved for "whites only."

⚊

CLOSE RANKS, W. E. B. DU BOIS
This is the crisis of the world. For all the long years to come men will point to the year 1918 as the great Day of Decision, the day when the world decided whether it would submit to military despotism and an endless armed peace—if peace it could be called—or whether they would put down the menace of German militarism and inaugurate the United States of the World.

We of the colored race have no ordinary interest in the outcome. That which the German power represents today spells death to the aspirations of Negroes and all darker races for equality, freedom and democracy. Let us not hesitate. Let us, while this war lasts, forget our special grievances and close our ranks shoulder to shoulder with our own white fellow citizens and the allied nations that are fighting for democracy. We make no ordinary sacrifice, but we make it gladly and willingly with our eyes lifted to the hills.

⌒⌒

THE DESCENT OF DU BOIS, HUBERT H. HARRISON

In a recent bulletin of the War Department it was declared that "justifiable grievances" were producing and had produced "not disloyalty, but an amount of unrest and bitterness which even the best efforts of their leaders may not be able always to guide." This is the simple truth. The essence of the present situation lies in the fact that the people whom our white masters have "recognized" as our leaders (without taking the trouble to consult us) and those who, by our own selection, had actually attained to leadership among us are being revaluated and, in most cases, rejected.

The most striking instance from the latter class is Dr. W. E. Du Bois, the editor of *The Crisis*. Du Bois's case is the more significant because his former services to his race have been undoubtedly of a high and courageous sort. Moreover, the act by which he has brought upon himself the stormy outburst of disapproval from his race is one which of itself, would seem to merit no such stern condemnation. To properly gauge the value and merit of this disapproval one must view it in the light of its attendant circumstances and of the situation in which it arose.

Dr. Du Bois first palpably sinned in his editorial "Close Ranks" in the July number of *The Crisis*. But this offense (apart from the trend and general tenor of the brief editorial) lies in a single sentence: "Let us, while this war lasts, *forget our special grievances* and close our ranks, shoulder to shoulder with our white fellow citizens and the allied nations that are fighting for democracy." From the latter part of the sentence there is no dissent, so far as we know. The offense lies in that part of the sentence which ends with the italicized words. It is felt by all his critics, that Du Bois, of all Negroes, knows best that our "special grievances" which the War Department Bulletin describes as "justifiable" consist of lynching, segregation and disfranchisement, and that the Negroes of America can not preserve either their lives, their manhood or their vote (which is their political life and liberties) with these things in existence. The doctor's critics feel that America can not use the Negro people to any good effect unless they have life, liberty and manhood assured and guaranteed to them. Therefore, instead of the war for democracy making these things less necessary, it makes them more so.

"But," it may be asked, "why should not these few words be taken merely as a slip of the pen or a venal error in logic? Why all this hubbub?" Is it because the so-called leaders of the first-mentioned class have already established an unsavory reputation by advocating this same surrender of life, liberty and manhood, masking their cowardice behind the pillars of war-time sacrifice? Du Bois's statement, then, is believed to mark his entrance into that class, and is accepted as a "surrender" of the principles which brought him into prominence—and which alone kept him there.

Later, when it was learned that Du Bois was being preened for a berth in the War Department as a captain-assistant (adjutant) to Major Spingarn, the words used by him in the editorial acquired a darker and more sinister significance. The two things fitted too well together as motive and self-interest.

For these reasons Du Bois is regarded much in the same way as a knight in the middle ages who had had his armor stripped from him, his arms reversed and his spurs hacked off. This ruins him as an influential person among Negroes at this time, alike whether he becomes a captain or remains an editor.

RETURNING SOLDIERS, W. E. B. DU BOIS

We are returning from war! The Crisis and tens of thousands of black men were drafted into a great struggle. For bleeding France and what she means and has meant and will mean to us and humanity and against the threat of German race arrogance, we fought gladly and to the last drop of blood; for America and her highest ideals, we fought in far-off hope; for the dominant southern oligarchy entrenched in Washington, we fought in bitter resignation. For the America that represents and gloats in lynching, disfranchisement, caste, brutality and devilish insult—for this, in the hateful upturning and mixing of things, we were forced by vindictive fate to fight also.

But today we return! We return from the slavery of uniform which the world's madness demanded us to don to the freedom of civil garb. We stand again to look America squarely in the face and call a spade a spade. We sing: This country of ours, despite all its better souls have done and dreamed, is yet a shameful land.

It *lynches*.

And lynching is barbarism of a degree of contemptible nastiness unparalleled in human history. Yet for fifty years we have lynched two Negroes a week, and we have kept this up right through the war.

It *disfranchises* its own citizens.

Disfranchisement is the deliberate theft and robbery of the only protection of poor against rich and black against white. The land that disfranchises its citizens and calls itself a democracy lies and knows it lies.

It encourages *ignorance*.

It has never really tried to educate the Negro. A dominant minority does not want Negroes educated. It wants servants, dogs, whores and monkeys. And when this land allows a reactionary group by its stolen political power to force as many black folk into these categories as it possibly can, it cries in contemptible hypocrisy: "They threaten us with degeneracy; they cannot be educated."

It *steals* from us.

It organizes industry to cheat us. It cheats us out of our land; it cheats us out of our labor. It confiscates our savings. It reduces our wages. It raises our rent. It steals our profit. It taxes us without representation. It keeps us consistently and universally poor, and then feeds us on charity and derides our poverty.

It *insults* us.

It has organized a nation-wide and latterly a world-wide propaganda of deliberate and continuous insult and defamation of black blood wherever found. It decrees that it shall not be possible in travel nor residence, work nor play, education nor instruction for a black man to exist without tacit or open acknowledgment of his inferiority to the dirtiest white dog. And it looks upon any attempt to question or even discuss this dogma as arrogance, unwarranted assumption and treason.

This is the country to which we Soldiers of Democracy return. This is the fatherland for which we fought! But it is *our* fatherland. It was right for us to fight. The faults of *our* country are *our* faults. Under similar circumstances, we would fight again. But by the God of Heaven, we are cowards and jackasses if now that that war is over, we do not marshal every ounce of our brain and brawn to fight a sterner, longer, more unbending battle against the forces of hell in our own land.

We *return*.

We *return from fighting*.

We *return fighting*.

Make way for Democracy! We saved it in France, and by the Great Jehovah, we will save it in the United States of America, or know the reason why.

Sources: (1) W. E. B. Du Bois, "Close Ranks," *Crisis* 16 (July 1918), reprinted by permission of *The Crisis*; (2) excerpt from Hubert H. Harrison, "The Descent of Du Bois," in *When Africa Awakens* (New York: Porro Press, 1920); and (3) Du Bois, "Returning Soldiers," *Crisis* 18 (May 1919), pp. 13–14, reprinted by permission of *The Crisis*. The editors wish to thank the Crisis Publishing Co., Inc., the publisher of the magazine of the National Association for the Advancement of Colored People, for the use of the material from *The Crisis*.

SELECT BIBLIOGRAPHY:

Mark Ellis, *Race, War, and Surveillance: African Americans and the United States Government During World War I* (Bloomington: Indiana University Press, 2001).

William Irwin MacIntyre, *Colored Soldiers* (Macon, Ga.: J.W. Burke, 1923).

Maj. Warner A. Ross, *My Colored Batallion* (Chicago: W.A. Ross, 1920).

Allison William Sweeney, *History of the American Negro in the Great War: His Splendid Record in the Battle Zones of Europe* (New York: Johnson reprint, 1970).

〜 2 〜

"If We Must Die," *Claude McKay, 1919*

In the years following the end of World War I, a rising tide of white racism swept across the United States. Several million whites joined the Ku Klux Klan. White mobs began to attack black communities, destroying homes, schools, and churches. Scores of African Americans were lynched, some of them while still wearing their U.S. army uniforms. Jamaican-born radical Claude McKay (1889– 1948) was outraged by these racial atrocities, and expressed his militancy in poetry and essays.

"If We Must Die"

> If we must die—let it not be like hogs
> Hunted and penned in an inglorious spot,
> While round us bark the mad and hungry dogs,
> Making their mock at our accursed lot.
> If we must die—oh, let us nobly die,
> So that our precious blood may not be shed
> In vain; then even the monsters we defy
> Shall be constrained to honor us though dead!
> Oh, Kinsmen! We must meet the common foe;
> Though far outnumbered, let us show us brave,
> And for their thousand blows deal one deathblow!
> What though before us lies the open grave?
> Like men we'll face the murderous, cowardly pack,
> Pressed to the wall, dying, but fighting back!

Source: "If We Must Die," *Liberator* 2 (July 1919), p. 21. Reprinted from *Selected Poems of Claude McKay* (New York: Bookman Associates, 1953), p. 36.

SELECT BIBLIOGRAPHY:

Wayne F. Cooper, *Claude McKay: Rebel Sojourner in the Harlem Renaissance: A Biography* (Baton Rouge: Louisiana State University Press, 1987).

Addison Gayle, *Claude McKay: The Black Poet at War* (Detroit: Broadside Press, 1972).

Josh Gosciak, *The Shadowed Country: Claude McKay and the Romance of the Victorians* (New Brunswick: Rutgers University Press, 2006).

Winston James, *A Fierce Hatred of Injustice: Claude McKay's Jamaica and His Poetry of Rebellion* (London: Verso, 2001).

Claude McKay, *Complete Poems*, ed. by William J. Maxwell (Urbana: University of Illinois Press, 2004).

Kotti Sree Ramesh and K. Nirupa Rani, *Claude McKay: The Literary Identity from Jamaica to Harlem and Beyond* (Jefferson: McFarland, 2006).

Tyrone Tillery, *Claude McKay: A Black Poet's Struggle for Identity* (Amherst: University of Massachusetts Press, 1992).

⟿ 3 ⟿

Black Bolsheviks: Cyril V. Briggs and Claude McKay

Cyril V. Briggs (1887–1966) was born in the British Leeward Islands, and emigrated to New York on July 4, 1905. Shortly upon arriving, Briggs began writing for the *Amsterdam News*. Later, he became the primary organizer, executive head, and "Primary Chief" of the African Blood Brotherhood (ABB), a radical black organization that emerged in 1921. The ABB declared its primary goal as the advancement of black rights and the "immediate protection and ultimate liberation of Negroes everywhere." Building on the revolutionary nationalism of Hubert H. Harrison, Briggs integrated the ideology of Bolshevism. The Brotherhood was frankly critical of the NAACP and the "Talented Tenth," and placed its faith in the collective consciousness and militancy of the black working class. At first somewhat sympathetic to Garveyism, it quickly turned bitterly against the movement. At its height, the ABB had seven thousand members. Briggs and other ABB leaders joined the Communist Party, and formed the major black constituency of the radical left throughout the 1920s.

⟿

"WHAT THE AFRICAN BLOOD BROTHERHOOD STANDS FOR," CYRIL V. BRIGGS TALKING POINTS on the Great Negro Exodus from the South; the reasons for the Exodus; Its Effect on Northern Labor; the Relationship between Colored and White Workers, Etc.

With an Appeal to the Self-Interest of All Workers
Labor Unions and the Negro
(A Statement by a White Labor Leader)

"Among the many short-sighted policies of conservative union leaders few are more harmful than the unfair attitude adopted in many cases toward the admission of colored workers into labor organizations. The Negroes are becoming an ever greater factor in industry. In order that this progress should be accomplished in an orderly fashion, and so that the colored workers should not be used against the white workers, the intelligent thing to do is for the organized white workers to go to great lengths to teach them the necessity for united action of both races as against the exploitation set up by the employers. Unfortunately, however, too often this has not been done. The result is that in many cases the Negro workers, feeling themselves discriminated against, have allowed themselves to be used by the employers to break down union conditions. Many a strike has thus been lost, and many more will be lost if the situation is not remedied. An intelligent policy toward the colored workers is one of the prime needs of the present-day labor movement. Unless it is worked out, organized white labor will pay bitterly enough for its folly by having the employers use the Negroes in industry as an army of strike-breakers. Labor already has more enemies than it can handle. To force the colored workers on to the employers' side, through a stupid union policy, is to invite disaster. The doors of the trade union movement must be thrown wide open to the Negro workers."—Wm. Z. Foster in "The World To-morrow," May, 1923.

And in the Meantime—

the Great Migration of Negro workers from the South continues. Negro workers are pouring North to escape the hellish conditions described in another part of this folder and in search of higher wages and better living conditions. Shall they be tools for the employers' Open Shop plot against Labor or will Organized Labor move to win these workers to its ranks by (1) opening the doors of the labor unions to them on terms of full equality with white workers, not in theory only but in practice; (2) eliminating all discriminatory practices, non-promotable and "dead-line" clauses, unfair legislative enactments, etc., and (3) acquainting the Negro workers with the benefits of unionism and actively bidding for their membership.

A Workers' Organization
What the A.B.B. Is
What It Stands For
What It Is Doing

The African Blood Brotherhood is an organization of Negro workers pledged by its Constitution and Program:

To gain for Negro labor a higher rate of compensation and to prevent capitalist exploitation and oppression of the workers of the Race—Sec. 7, Art. 2, of its Constitution.

To establish a true rapprochement and fellowship within the darker races and with the truly class-conscious white workers—Sec. 9, Art. 3, of its Constitution.

Under the caption of "Higher Wages for Negro Labor, Shorter Hours and Better Living Conditions," the program of the A.B.B. declares:

To gain for Negro Labor a higher rate of compensation and to prevent exploitation because of lack of protective organization we must encourage industrial unionism among our people and at the same time fight to break down the prejudice in the unions which is stimulated and encouraged by the employers. This prejudice is already meeting the attack of the radical and progressive element among white labor union men and must eventually give way before the united onslaught of Colored and White Workers. Wherever it is found impossible to enter the existing labor unions, independent unions should be formed, that Negro Labor be enabled to protect its interests.

The A.B.B. Seeks

To bring about co-operation between colored and white workers on the basis of their identity of interest as workers;

To educate the Negro in the benefits of unionism and to gain admission for him on terms of full equality to the unions;

To bring home to the Negro worker his class interests as a worker and to show him the real source of his exploitation and oppression;

To organize the Negro's labor power into labor and farm organizations;

To foster the principles of consumers' co-operatives as an aid against the high cost of living;

To oppose with counter propaganda the vicious capitalist propaganda against the Negro as a race, which is aimed to keep the workers of both races apart and thus facilitate their exploitation;

To realize a United front of Negro workers and organizations as the first step in an effective fight against oppression and exploitation;

To acquaint the civilized world with the facts about lynchings, peonage, jim-crow-ism, disfranchisement and other manifestations of race prejudice and mob rule.

Towards These Ends the A.B.B.

Supports a press service—the Crusader Service—for the dissemination to the Negro Press of the facts about conditions and events in the sphere of organized labor; reports of labor's changing and increasingly enlightened attitude towards the colored workers; and sends out news of general race interest, interpreted from the working class point of view. The Service is mailed twice each week and is used regularly by over a hundred Negro papers.

Sends organizers and lecturers into industrial sections to propagate the doctrines of unionism and enlist Negro workers into the ranks of the most militant organization of Negro workers in the country.

Operates forums and classes with the aim of arousing (1) the race consciousness of the Negro workers and (2) their class consciousness. (This is the natural process.)

Guards against the use of the Negro migrants as tools for the Open Shop advocates and other unscrupulous employers who seek to break the power of Organized Labor and to destroy all those gains won for the working class during the last twenty years by those workers who had the good sense to organize for their protection.

Exposes the existence of mob-law, peonage, and other barbarisms in the South and wages relentless war against these evil conditions which force the Southern Negro to flee the South and seek employment in the industrial sections.

The Message to You—

Class-conscious white worker or race-conscious Negro (and the A.B.B. has only one message for both!)—shocked by the conditions under which the Negro is forced to live in the South; the conditions which are driving him northward to create new alignments and strange problems in the industrial sections of the North—you cannot fail to realize the potentialities evoked by this steady stream of unorganized workers from the South. If you are a thinking, rational being you cannot fail to recognize THAT THIS IS YOUR FIGHT and you must help us wage it! The A.B.B. is a workers' organization. It has no source of income other than its membership and the masses. It is upon the workers it must depend. *You* must help us in the work of reaching the Negro masses with the message of unionism, the message of organized power, the message of united action by the workers of both races against the capitalist combinations; against the Wall Streets, the Chambers of Commerce, the Rotarian gang, the Ku Klux Klan, (the American Fascisti) and against all the tools of the interests who would keep the workers apart in order the more effectively to exploit them.

This Is Your Fight! So Help Wage It!

Race-conscious Negro, show that you recognize the source of your oppression!

Class-conscious White Worker, show that you realize the fact of the identity of the interests of the workers of all races!

Reasons for the Negro Exodus from the South

A glimpse of hell was given newspaper readers a few weeks ago in connection with the conditions of peonage in the State of Florida under which young Martin Talbert, a white lad of North Dakota, was wantonly murdered under the lash of a boss-driver's whip. Here's some more of hell!

Mob Law

"In some counties the Negro is being driven out as though he were a wild beast. In others he is being held as a slave. In others, no Negroes remain.

". . . If the condition indicated by these charges should continue, both God and man would justly condemn Georgia more severely than man and God have condemned Belgium and Leopold for the Congo atrocities.

"In only two of the 135 cases cited is the 'usual crime' against white women involved."—Extracts from Governor Dorsey's Statements As to the Negro in Georgia.

Peonage

Case No. 135—"March 30, a Negro, said to have been held in peonage, appealed to a justice of the peace. In the presence of the justice, a Marshal is reported to have beaten the Negro with an axe handle. Nothing has been done to the Marshal."

Case No. 134.—"December, 1920, a white man is reported to have killed a Negro for trying to leave his place. The white man has not been arrested."—Extracts from Governor Dorsey's Statements As to the Negro in Georgia.

The Negro and the Courts

Southern courts are justly notorious for the brand of justice they hand out to the Negro worker. This brand ranges from a fine of $25 for "keeping late hours," with a convict farm and a boss-driver in the offing if the "offender" cannot raise the money, to sentences to death and long term imprisonments for Negroes accused of resisting exploitation. For example, when in Phillips County, Ark., colored farm hands got together to protest and secure legal action against vicious exploitation and downright robbery under the share-cropping system of the South, those colored farm hands were attacked and shot down by their employers and their gangsters. Those who escaped the massacre were locked up charged with inciting to an insurrection against the white people of the county. In an atmosphere charged with race prejudice and the most virulent hatred, twelve of these men were sentenced to death and sixty-seven to long prison terms.

And this horrible frame-up, with its death sentences for 12 and long prison terms for 67, is only one of many such incidents that occur throughout the Southland and, with night-riding, whipping and lynching, contribute to keep the Negro population in a constant state of terrorism and have led to the present Great Migration, coupled with long hours of toil, low wages, unhealthy living conditions, and other forms of savage exploitation.

A Free Africa:—The A.B.B. stands for the waging of a determined and unceasing fight for the liberation of Africa without, however, making any surrenders or compromises on other fronts. We have no patience, therefore, with those Negroes who would distract the attention of the Negro workers from the fight for better conditions in the United States to an illusory empire or republic on the continent of Africa. We believe that the Negro workers of America can best help their blood-brothers in Africa by first making of their own group a power in America. The position of 12,000,000 Negroes at the heart of an imperialist power could not long be ignored were those Negroes intelligently organized, courageously led, and co-operating with the organized white workers on the basis of identity of interests of the entire working-class of the world.

"To Be a Negro in a Day Like This"

THE NEGRO IS

reduced to peonage in the Southern States;
shut out from labor unions in the North;
forced to an inferior status before the courts of the land;
made a subject of public contempt everywhere;
lynched and mobbed with impunity;
deprived of the ballot in the South;
segregated in vile, unsanitary districts in cities, both North and South;
degraded economically, politically and socially;
often persecuted by reason of his very thrift and ambition;
denied (and in this he is not unlike most workers) the security of life guaranteed by the Constitution.

The A.B.B. believes in inter-racial co-operation—not the sham co-operation of the oppressed Negro workers and their oppressors, but the honest co-operation of colored and white workers based upon mutual appreciation of the fact of the identity of their interests as members of the working class. This is the only inter-racial co-operation the A.B.B. believes in!

The Negro's Rock of Gibraltar!

That to a large extent is what the A.B.B. is today. That is what it must be to a much greater degree tomorrow. And that is the task before every member of the A.B.B. And the way to successfully achieve our task is to organize every Negro into the A.B.B. that we possibly can. Get the intelligent and aggressive. Get the race-conscious. Get those who know the source of their oppression and are accordingly class-conscious as well as race-conscious. Get them all! Organize every Negro into the Brotherhood. Once in, it will be our duty to educate them to become effective units for the waging of the Negro Liberation Struggle. Our educational machinery is functioning perfectly. It has yet to be taxed to capacity. Get them in!

SOVIET RUSSIA AND THE NEGRO, CLAUDE MCKAY

The label of propaganda will be affixed to what I say here. I shall not mind; propaganda has now come into its respectable rights and I am proud of being a propagandist. The difference between propaganda and art was impressed on my boyhood mind by a literary mentor, Milton's poetry and his political prose set side by side as the supreme examples. So too, my teacher,—splendid and broadminded though he was, yet unconsciously biased against what he felt was propaganda—thought that that gilt-washed artificiality, *The Picture of Dorian Gray*, would outlive *Arms and the Man* and *John Bull's Other Island*. But inevitably as I grew older I had perforce to revise and change my mind about propaganda. I lighted on one of Milton's greatest sonnets that was pure propaganda and a widening horizon revealed that some of the finest spirits of modern literature—Voltaire, Hugo, Heine, Swift, Shelley, Byron, Tolstoy, Ibsen—had carried the taint of propaganda. The broader view did not merely include propaganda literature in my literary outlook; it also swung me away from the childish age of the enjoyment of creative work for pleasurable curiosity to another extreme where I have always sought for the motivating force or propaganda intent that underlies all literature of interest. My birthright, and the historical background of the race that gave it to me, made me very respectful and receptive of propaganda and world events since the year 1914 have proved that it is no mean science of convincing information.

American Negroes are not as yet deeply permeated with the mass movement spirit and so fail to realize the importance of organized propaganda. It was Marcus Garvey's greatest contribution to the Negro movement; his pioneer work in that field is a feat that the men of broader understanding and sounder ideas who will follow him must continue. It was not until I first came to Europe in 1919 that I came to a full realization and understanding of the effectiveness of the insidious propaganda in general that is maintained against the Negro race. And it was not by the occasional affront of the minority of civilized fiends—mainly those Europeans who had been abroad, engaged in the business of robbing colored peoples in their native land—that I gained my knowledge, but rather through the questions about the Negro that were put to me by genuinely sympathetic and cultured persons.

The average Europeans who read the newspapers, the popular books and journals, and go to see the average play and a Mary Pickford movie, are very dense about the problem of the Negro; and they are the most important section of the general public that the Negro propagandists would reach. For them the tragedy of the American Negro ended with *Uncle Tom's Cabin* and Emancipation. And since then they have been aware only of the comedy—the Negro minstrel and vaudevillian, the boxer, the black mammy and butler of the cinematograph, the caricatures of the romances and the lynched savage who has violated a beautiful white girl.

A very few ask if Booker T. Washington is doing well or if the "Black Star Line" is running; perhaps some one less discreet than sagacious will wonder how colored men can hanker so much after white women in face of the lynching penalty. Misinformation, indifference and levity sum up the attitude of western Europe towards the Negro. There is the superior but very fractional intellectual minority that knows better, but whose influence on public opinion is infinitesimal, and so it may be comparatively easy for white American propagandists—whose interests behoove them to misrepresent the Negro—to turn the general indifference into hostile antagonism if American Negroes who have the intellectual guardianship of racial interests do not organize effectively, and on a world scale, to combat their white exploiters and traducers.

The world war has fundamentally altered the status of Negroes in Europe. It brought thousands of them from America and the British and French colonies to participate in the struggle against the Central Powers. Since then serious clashes have come about in England between the blacks that later settled down in the seaport towns and the natives. France has brought in her black troops to do police duty in the occupied districts of Germany. The color of these troops, and their customs too, are different and strange and the nature of their work would naturally make their presence irritating and unbearable to the inhabitants whose previous knowledge of Negroes has been based, perhaps, on their prowess as cannibals. And besides, the presence of these troops provides rare food for the chauvinists of a once proud and overbearing race, now beaten down and drinking the dirtiest dregs of humiliation under the bayonets of the victor. . . .

The world upheaval having brought the three greatest European nations— England, France and Germany—into closer relationship with Negroes, colored Americans should seize the opportunity to promote finer inter-racial understanding. As white Americans in Europe are taking advantage of the situation to intensify their propaganda against the blacks, so must Negroes meet that with a strong counter-movement. Negroes should realize that the supremacy of American capital today proportionately increases American influence in the politics and social life of the world. Every American official abroad, every smug tourist, is a protagonist of dollar culture and a propagandist against the Negro. Besides brandishing the Rooseveltian stick in the face of the lesser new world natives, America holds an economic club over the heads of all the great European nations, excepting Russia, and so those bold individuals in Western Europe who formerly sneered at dollar culture may yet find it necessary and worth while to be discreetly silent. As American influence increases in the world, and especially in Europe, through the extension of American capital, the more necessary it becomes for all struggling minorities of the United States to organize extensively for the world wide propagation of their grievances. Such propaganda efforts, besides strengthening the cause at home, will certainly enlist the sympathy and help of those foreign groups that are carrying on a life and death struggle to escape the octuple arms of American business interests. And the Negro, as the most suppressed and persecuted minority, should use this period of ferment in international affairs to lift his cause out of his national obscurity and force it forward as a prime international issue.

Though Western Europe can be reported as being quite ignorant and apathetic of the Negro in world affairs, there is one great nation with an arm in Europe that is thinking intelligently on the Negro as it does about all international problems. When the Russian workers overturned their infamous government in 1917, one of the first acts of the new Premier, Lenin, was a proclamation greeting all the oppressed peoples throughout the world, exhorting them to organize and unite against the common international oppressor—Private Capitalism. Later on in Moscow, Lenin himself grappled with the question of the American Negroes and spoke on the subject before the Second Congress of the Third International. He consulted with John Reed, the American journalist, and dwelt on the urgent necessity of propaganda and organizational work among the Negroes of the South. The subject was not allowed to drop. When Sen Katayama of Japan, the veteran revolutionist, went from the United States to Russia in 1921 he placed the American Negro problem first upon his full agenda. And ever since he has been working unceasingly and unselfishly to promote the cause of the exploited American Negro among the Soviet councils of Russia.

With the mammoth country securely under their control, and despite the great energy and thought that are being poured into the revival of the national industry, the vanguard of the Russian workers and the national minorities, now set free from imperial oppression are thinking seriously about the fate of the oppressed classes, the suppressed national and racial minorities in the rest of Europe, Asia, Africa and America. They feel themselves kin in spirit to these people. They want to help make them free. And not the least of the oppressed that fill the thoughts of the new Russia are the Negroes of America and Africa. If we look back two decades to recall how the Czarist persecution of the Russian Jews agitated Democratic America, we will get some idea of the mind of Liberated Russia towards the Negroes of America. The Russian people are reading the terrible history of their own recent past in the tragic position of the American Negro to-day. Indeed, the Southern States can well serve the purpose of showing what has happened in Russia. For if the exploited poor whites of the South could ever transform themselves into making common cause with the persecuted and plundered Negroes, overcome the oppressive oligarchy—the political crackers and robber landlords—and deprive it of all political privileges, the situation would be very similar to that of Soviet Russia to-day. . . .

I met with this spirit of sympathetic appreciation and response prevailing in all circles in Moscow and Petrograd. I never guessed what was awaiting me in Russia. I had left America in September of 1922 determined to get there, to see into the new revolutionary life of the people and report on it. I was not a little dismayed when, congenitally averse to notoriety as I am, I found that on stepping upon Russian soil I forthwith became a notorious character. And strangely enough there was nothing unpleasant about my being swept into the surge of revolutionary Russia. For better or for worse every person in Russia is vitally affected by the revolution. No one but a soulless body can live there without being stirred to the depths by it.

I reached Russia in November—the month of the Fourth Congress of the Communist International and the Fifth Anniversary of the Russian Revolution. The whole revolutionary nation was mobilized to honor the occasion, Petrograd was magnificent in red flags and streamers. Red flags fluttered against the snow from all the great granite buildings. Railroad trains, street cars, factories, stores, hotels, schools—all wore decorations. It was a festive month of celebration in which I, as a member of the Negro race, was a very active participant. I was received as though the people had been apprised of, and were prepared for, my coming. When Max Eastman and I tried to bore our way through the dense crowds, that jammed the Tverskaya Street in Moscow on the 7th of November, I was caught, tossed up into the air, and passed along by dozens of stalwart youths.

"How warmly excited they get over a strange face!" said Eastman. A young Russian Communist remarked: "But where is the difference? Some of the Indians are as dark as you." To which another replied: "The lines of the face are different, the Indians have been with us long. The people instinctively see the difference." And so always the conversation revolved around me until my face flamed. The Moscow press printed long articles about the Negroes in America, a poet was inspired to rhyme about the Africans looking to Soviet Russia and soon I was in demand everywhere—at the lectures of poets and journalists, the meetings of soldiers and factory workers. Slowly I began losing self-consciousness with the realization that I was welcomed thus as a symbol as a member of the great American Negro group—kin to the unhappy black slaves of European Imperialism in Africa—that the workers of Soviet Russia, rejoicing in their freedom, were greeting through me.

Russia, in broad terms, is a country where all the races of Europe and of Asia meet and mix. The fact is that under the repressive power of the Czarist bureaucracy the different races preserved a degree of kindly tolerance towards each other. The fierce racial hatreds that flame in the Balkans never existed in Russia. Where in the South no Negro might approach a *"cracker"* as a man for friendly offices, a Jewish pilgrim in old Russia could find rest and sustenance in the home of an orthodox peasant. It is a problem to define the Russian type by features. The Hindu, the Mongolian, the Persian, the Arab, the West European—all these types may be traced woven into the distinctive polyglot population of Moscow. And so, to the Russian, I was merely another type, but stranger, with which they were not yet familiar. They were curious with me, all and sundry, young and old, in a friendly, refreshing manner. Their curiosity had none of the intolerable impertinence and often downright affront that any very dark colored man, be he Negro, Indian or Arab, would experience in Germany and England. . . .

The evenings of the proletarian poets held in the Arbot were much more serious affairs. The leadership was communist, the audience working class and attentive like diligent, elementary school children. To these meetings also came some of the keener intellects from the Domino Café. One of these young women told me that she wanted to keep in touch with all the phases of the new culture. In Petrograd the meetings of the intelligentsia seemed more formal and inclusive. There were such notable men there as Chukovsky the critic, Eugene Zamiatan the celebrated novelist and Marshack the poet and translator of Kipling. The artist and theatre world were also represented. There was no communist spirit in

evidence at these intelligentsia gatherings. Frankly there was an undercurrent of
hostility to the bolshevists. But I was invited to speak and read my poems whenever I appeared at any of them and treated with every courtesy and consideration
as a writer. Among those sophisticated and cultured Russians, many of them
speaking from two to four languages, there was no overdoing of the correct thing,
no vulgar wonderment and bounderish superiority over a Negro's being a poet. I
was a poet, that was all, and their keen questions showed that they were much
more interested in the technique of my poetry, my views on and my position
regarding the modern literary movements than in the difference of my color.
Although I will not presume that there was no attraction at all in that little difference! . . .

During the first days of my visit I felt that the great demonstration of friendliness was somehow expressive of the enthusiastic spirit of the glad anniversary days,
that after the month was ended I could calmly settle down to finish the book about
the American Negro that the State Publishing Department of Moscow had com-
missioned me to write, and in the meantime quietly go about making interesting
contacts. But my days in Russia were a progression of affectionate enthusiasm of
the people towards me. Among the factory workers, the red-starred and chevroned
soldiers and sailors, the proletarian students and children, I could not get off as
lightly as I did with the intelligentsia. At every meeting I was received with boisterous acclaim, mobbed with friendly demonstration. The women workers of the
great bank in Moscow insisted on hearing about the working conditions of the colored women of America and after a brief outline I was asked the most exacting
questions concerning the positions that were most available to colored women,
their wages and general relationship with the white women workers. The details I
could not give; but when I got through, the Russian women passed a resolution
sending greetings to the colored women workers of America, exhorting them to
organize their forces and send a woman representative to Russia. I received a similar message from the Propaganda Department of the Petrograd Soviet which is
managed by Nicoleva, a very energetic woman. There I was shown the new status
of the Russian women gained through the revolution of 1917. Capable women can
fit themselves for any position; equal pay with men for equal work; full pay during
the period of pregnancy and no work for the mother two months before and two
months after the confinement. Getting a divorce is comparatively easy and not
influenced by money power, detective chicanery and wire pulling. A special
department looks into the problems of joint personal property and the guardianship and support of the children. There is no penalty for legal abortion and no legal
stigma of illegitimacy attaching to children born out of wedlock.

There were no problems of the submerged lower classes and the suppressed
national minorities of the old Russia that could not bear comparison with the
grievous position of the millions of Negroes in the United States to-day. Just as
Negroes are barred from the American Navy and the higher ranks of the Army,
so were the Jews and the sons of the peasantry and proletariat discriminated
against in the Russian Empire. It is needless repetition of the obvious to say that

Soviet Russia does not tolerate such discriminations, for the actual government of the country is now in the hands of the combined national minorities, the peasantry and the proletariat. By the permission of Leon Trotsky, Commissar-in-chief of the military and naval forces of Soviet Russia, I visited the highest military schools in the Kremlin and environs of Moscow. And there I saw the new material, the sons of the working people in training as cadets by the old officers of the upper classes. For two weeks I was a guest of the Red navy in Petrograd with the same eager proletarian youth of new Russia, who conducted me through the intricate machinery of submarines, took me over aeroplanes captured from the British during the counter-revolutionary war around Petrograd and showed me the making of a warship ready for action. And even of greater interest was the life of the men and the officers, the simplified discipline that was strictly enforced, the food that was served for each and all alike, the extra political educational classes and the extreme tactfulness and elasticity of the political commissars, all communists, who act as advisers and arbitrators between the men and students and the officers. Twice or thrice I was given some of the *kasha* which is sometimes served with the meals. In Moscow I grew to like this food very much, but it was always difficult to get. I had always imagined that it was quite unwholesome and unpalatable and eaten by the Russian peasant only on account of extreme poverty. But on the contrary I found it very rare and sustaining when cooked right with a bit of meat and served with butter—a grain food very much like the common but very delicious West Indian rice-and-peas.

The red cadets are seen in the best light at their gymnasium exercises and at the political assemblies when discipline is set aside. Especially at the latter where a visitor feels that he is in the midst of the early revolutionary days, so hortatory are the speeches, so intense the enthusiasm of the men. At all these meetings I had to speak and the students asked me general questions about the Negro in the American Army and Navy, and when I gave them the common information, known to all American Negroes, students, officers and commissars were unanimous in wishing that a group of young American Negroes would take up training to become officers in the Army and Navy of Soviet Russia.

The proletarian students of Moscow were eager to learn of the life and work of Negro students. They sent messages of encouragement and good will to the Negro students of America and, with a fine gesture of fellowship, elected the Negro delegate of the American Communist Party and myself to honorary membership in the Moscow Soviet.

Those Russian days remain the most memorable of my life. The intellectual Communists and the intelligentsia were interested to know that America had produced a formidable body of Negro intelligentsia and professionals, possessing a distinctive literature and cultural and business interests alien to the white man's. And they think naturally, that the militant leaders of the intelligentsia must feel and express the spirit of revolt that is slumbering in the inarticulate Negro masses, precisely as the emancipation movement of the Russian masses had passed through similar phases.

Russia is prepared and waiting to receive couriers and heralds of good will and interracial understanding from the Negro race. Her demonstration of friendliness and equality for Negroes may not conduce to promote healthy relations between Soviet Russia and democratic America, the anthropologists of 100 per cent pure white Americanism may soon invoke Science to prove that the Russians are not at all God's white people. I even caught a little of American anti-Negro propaganda in Russia. A friend of mine, a member of the Moscow intelligentsia repeated to me the remarks of the lady correspondent of a Danish newspaper: that I should not be taken as a representative Negro for she had lived in America and found all Negroes lazy, bad and vicious, a terror to white women. In Petrograd I got a like story from Chukovsky, the critic, who was on intimate terms with a high worker of the American Relief Administration and his southern wife. Chukovsky is himself an intellectual "westerner," the term applied to those Russians who put Western-European civilization before Russian culture and believe that Russia's salvation lies in becoming completely westernized. He had spent an impressionable part of his youth in London and adores all things English, and during the world war was very pro-English. For the American democracy, also, he expresses unfeigned admiration. He has more Anglo-American books than Russian in his fine library and considers the literary section of *The New York Times* a journal of a very high standard. He is really a maniac of Anglo-Saxon American culture. Chukovsky was quite incredulous when I gave him the facts of the Negro's status in American civilization.

"The Americans are a people of such great energy and ability," he said, "how could they act so petty towards a racial minority?" And then he related an experience of his in London that bore a strong smell of *cracker* breath. However, I record it here in the belief that it is authentic for Chukovsky is a man of integrity: About the beginning of the century, he was sent to England as correspondent of a newspaper in Odessa, but in London he was more given to poetic dreaming and studying English literature in the British Museum and rarely sent any news home. So he lost his job and had to find cheap, furnished rooms. A few weeks later, after he had taken up his residence in new quarters, a black guest arrived, an American gentleman of the cloth. The preacher procured a room on the top floor and used the dining and sitting room with the other guests, among whom was a white American family. The latter protested the presence of the Negro in the house and especially in the guest room. The landlady was in a dilemma, she could not lose her American boarders and the cleryman's money was not to be despised. At last she compromised by getting the white Americans to agree to the Negro's staying without being allowed the privilege of the guest room, and Chukovsky was asked to tell the Negro the truth. Chukovsky strode upstairs to give the unpleasant facts to the preacher and to offer a little consolation, but the black man was not unduly offended:

"The white guests have the right to object to me," he explained, anticipating Garvey, "they belong to a superior race."

"But," said Chukovsky, "*I* do not object to you, *I* don't feel any difference; we don't understand color prejudice in Russia."

"Well," philosophized the preacher, "you are very kind, but taking the scriptures as authority, I don't consider the Russians to be white people."

Sources: (1) "What the African Blood Brotherhood Stands For," originally published in the *Communist Review* [London] 2 (April 1922), pp. 448–54; and (2) Claude McKay, excerpt from "Soviet Russia and the Negro," originally published in *The Crisis* 27 (December 1923), pp. 61–65, and (January 1924), pp. 114–18, reprinted by permission of *The Crisis*. The editors wish to thank the Crisis Publishing Co., Inc., the publisher of the magazine of the National Association for the Advancement of Colored People, for the use of the material from *The Crisis*.

SELECT BIBLIOGRAPHY:

Clifton C. Hawkins, "'Race First Versus Class First': An Intellectual History of Afro-American Radicalism, 1911–1928" (Ph.D. diss., University of California, Davis, 2000).

Winston James, *Holding Aloft the Banner of Ethiopia: Caribbean Radicalism in Early Twentieth-Century American* (London: Verso, 1998).

R. A. Kuykendall, "African Blood Brotherhood, Independent Marxist During the Harlem Renaissance," *Western Journal of Black Studies* 26, no 1 (Spring 2002), pp. 16–21.

Minkah Makalani, "For the Liberation of Black People Everywhere: The African Blood Brotherhood, Black Radicalism, and Pan-African Liberation in the New Negro Movement" (Ph.D. diss., University of Illinois at Urbana-Champaign, 2004).

Mark Solomon, *The Cry Was Unity: Communists and African-Americans, 1917–1936* (Jackson: University Press of Mississippi, 1998).

≃ 4 ≃

Marcus Garvey and the Universal Negro Improvement Association

Marcus Garvey (1887–1940) was the charismatic leader and organizer of the largest black nationalist movement in history, the Universal Negro Improvement Association (UNIA). Born in Jamaica, Garvey worked as a journalist and printer in the Caribbean, Central America, and Britain. Inspired by the ideas of Booker T. Washington, Garvey launched the UNIA as a self-help organization for people of African descent. Entering the United States in 1916, Garvey promptly built a mass-based organization of largely working-class and poor black people. His dynamic speaking ability and his flair for public demonstrations captured the popular imagination of the black masses. The UNIA established more than seven hundred branch organizations throughout the United States, and several hundred more across the Caribbean and Africa. British and U.S. authorities continually harassed and undermined Garvey's organizations, and Garvey himself was imprisoned in Atlanta in 1925. Deported from the United States two years later, the UNIA gradually declined as an organized movement. Garvey died in London in 1940, but his life and legacy continue to influence black nationalist and Pan-Africanist politics throughout the black diaspora.

DECLARATION OF RIGHTS OF THE NEGRO PEOPLES OF
THE WORLD PREAMBLE

"Be it Resolved, That the Negro people of the world, through their chosen representatives in convention assembled in Liberty Hall, in the City of New York and United States of America, from August 1 to August 31, in the year of our Lord, one thousand nine hundred and twenty, protest against the wrongs and injustices they are suffering at the hands of their white brethren, and state what they deem their fair and just rights, as well as the treatment they propose to demand of all men in the future."

We complain:

I. "That nowhere in the world, with few exceptions, are black men accorded equal treatment with white men, although in the same situation and circumstances, but, on the contrary, are discriminated against and denied the common rights due to human beings for no other reason than their race and color."

"We are not willingly accepted as guests in the public hotels and inns of the world for no other reason than our race and color."

II. "In certain parts of the United States of America our race is denied the right of public trial accorded to other races when accused of crime, but are lynched and burned by mobs, and such brutal and inhuman treatment is even practised upon our women."

III. "That European nations have parceled out among themselves and taken possession of nearly all of the continent of Africa, and the natives are compelled to surrender their lands to aliens and are treated in most instances like slaves."

IV. "In the southern portion of the United States of America, although citizens under the Federal Constitution, and in some states almost equal to the whites in population and are qualified land owners and taxpayers, we are, nevertheless, denied all voice in the making and administration of the laws and are taxed without representation by the state governments, and at the same time compelled to do military service in defense of the country."

V. "On the public conveyances and common carriers in the Southern portion of the United States we are jim-crowed and compelled to accept separate and inferior accommodations and made to pay the same fare charged for first-class accommodations, and our families are often humiliated and insulted by drunken white men who habitually pass through the jim-crow cars going to the smoking car."

VI. "The physicians of our race are denied the right to attend their patients while in the public hospitals of the cities and states where they reside in certain parts of the United States."

"Our children are forced to attend inferior separate schools for shorter terms than white children, and the public school funds are unequally divided between the white and colored schools."

VII. "We are discriminated against and denied an equal chance to earn wages for the support of our families, and in many instances are refused admission into labor unions, and nearly everywhere are paid smaller wages than white men."

VIII. "In Civil Service and departmental offices we are everywhere discriminated against and made to feel that to be a black man in Europe, America and the West Indies is equivalent to being an outcast and a leper among the races of men, no matter what the character and attainments of the black man may be."

IX. "In the British and other West Indian Islands and colonies, Negroes are secretly and cunningly discriminated against, and denied those fuller rights in government to which white citizens are appointed, nominated and elected."

X. "That our people in those parts are forced to work for lower wages than the average standard of white men and are kept in conditions repugnant to good civilized tastes and customs."

XI. "That the many acts of injustice against members of our race before the courts of law in the respective islands and colonies are of such nature as to create disgust and disrespect for the white man's sense of justice."

XII. "Against all such inhuman, unchristian and uncivilized treatment we here and now emphatically protest, and invoke the condemnation of all mankind."

"In order to encourage our race all over the world and to stimulate it to a higher and grander destiny, we demand and insist on the following Declaration of Rights:

1. "Be it known to all men that whereas, all men are created equal and entitled to the rights of life, liberty and the pursuit of happiness, and because of this we, the duly elected representatives of the Negro peoples of the world, invoking the aid of the just and Almighty God do declare all men, women and children of our blood throughout the world free citizens, and do claim them as free citizens of Africa, the Motherland of all Negroes."

2. "That we believe in the supreme authority of our race in all things racial; that all things are created and given to man as a common possession; that there should be an equitable distribution and apportionment of all such things, and in consideration of the fact that as a race we are now deprived of those things that are morally and legally ours, we believe it right that all such things should be acquired and held by whatsoever means possible."

3. "That we believe the Negro, like any other race, should be governed by the ethics of civilization, and, therefore, should not be deprived of any of those rights or privileges common to other human beings."

4. "We declare that Negroes, wheresoever they form a community among themselves, should be given the right to elect their own representatives to represent them in legislatures, courts of law, or such institutions as may exercise control over that particular community."

5. "We assert that the Negro is entitled to even-handed justice before all courts of law and equity in whatever country he may be found, and when this is denied him on account of his race or color such denial is an insult to the race as a whole and should be resented by the entire body of Negroes."

6. "We declare it unfair and prejudicial to the rights of Negroes in communi-

ties where they exist in considerable numbers to be tried by a judge and jury composed entirely of an alien race, but in all such cases members of our race are entitled to representation on the jury."

7. "We believe that any law or practice that tends to deprive any African of his land or the privileges of free citizenship within his country is unjust and immoral, and no native should respect any such law or practice."

8. "We declare taxation without representation unjust and tyrannous, and there should be no obligation on the part of the Negro to obey the levy of a tax by any law-making body from which he is excluded and denied representation on account of his race and color."

9. "We believe that any law especially directed against the Negro to his detriment and singling him out because of his race or color is unfair and immoral, and should not be respected."

10. "We believe all men entitled to common human respect, and that our race should in no way tolerate any insults that may be interpreted to mean disrespect to our color."

11. "We deprecate the use of the term 'nigger' as applied to Negroes, and demand that the word 'Negro' be written with a capital 'N.'"

12. "We believe that the Negro should adopt every means to protect himself against barbarous practices inflicted upon him because of color."

13. "We believe in the freedom of Africa for the Negro people of the world, and by the principle of Europe for the Europeans and Asia for the Asiatics; we also demand Africa for the Africans at home and abroad."

14. "We believe in the inherent right of the Negro to possess himself of Africa, and that his possession of same shall not be regarded as an infringement on any claim or purchase made by any race or nation."

15. "We strongly condemn the cupidity of those nations of the world who, by open aggression or secret schemes, have seized the territories and inexhaustible natural wealth of Africa, and we place on record our most solemn determination to reclaim the treasures and possession of the vast continent of our forefathers."

16. "We believe all men should live in peace one with the other, but when races and nations provoke the ire of other races and nations by attempting to infringe upon their rights, war becomes inevitable, and the attempt in any way to free one's self or protect one's rights or heritage becomes justifiable."

17. "Whereas, the lynching, by burning, hanging or any other means, of human beings is a barbarous practice, and a shame and disgrace to civilization, we therefore declare any country guilty of such atrocities outside the pale of civilization."

18. "We protest against the atrocious crime of whipping, flogging and overworking of the native tribes of Africa and Negroes everywhere. These are methods that should be abolished, and all means should be taken to prevent a continuance of such brutal practices."

19. "We protest against the atrocious practice of shaving the heads of Africans, especially of African women or individuals of Negro blood, when placed in prison as a punishment for crime by an alien race."

20. "We protest against segregated districts, separate public conveyances, industrial discrimination, lynchings and limitations of political privileges of any Negro citizen in any part of the world on account of race, color or creed, and will exert our full influence and power against all such."

21. "We protest against any punishment inflicted upon a Negro with severity, as against lighter punishment inflicted upon another of an alien race for like offense, as an act of prejudice and injustice, and should be resented by the entire race."

22. "We protest against the system of education in any country where Negroes are denied the same privileges and advantages as other races."

23. "We declare it inhuman and unfair to boycott Negroes from industries and labor in any part of the world."

24. "We believe in the doctrine of the freedom of the press, and we therefore emphatically protest against the suppression of Negro newspapers and periodicals in various parts of the world, and call upon Negroes everywhere to employ all available means to prevent such suppression."

25. "We further demand free speech universally for all men."

26. "We hereby protest against the publication of scandalous and inflammatory articles by an alien press tending to create racial strife and the exhibition of picture films showing the Negro as a cannibal."

27. "We believe in the self-determination of all peoples."

28. "We declare for the freedom of religious worship."

29. "With the help of Almighty God, we declare ourselves the sworn protectors of the honor and virtue of our women and children, and pledge our lives for their protection and defense everywhere, and under all circumstances from wrongs and outrages."

30. "We demand the right of unlimited and unprejudiced education for ourselves and our posterity forever."

31. "We declare that the teaching in any school by alien teachers to our boys and girls, that the alien race is superior to the Negro race, is an insult to the Negro people of the world."

32. "Where Negroes form a part of the citizenry of any country, and pass the civil service examination of such country, we declare them entitled to the same consideration as other citizens as to appointments in such civil service."

33. "We vigorously protest against the increasingly unfair and unjust treatment accorded Negro travelers on land and sea by the agents and employees of railroad and steamship companies and insist that for equal fare we receive equal privileges with travelers of other races."

34. "We declare it unjust for any country, State or nation to enact laws tending to hinder and obstruct the free immigration of Negroes on account of their race and color."

35. "That the right of the Negro to travel unmolested throughout the world be not abridged by any person or persons, and all Negroes are called upon to give aid to a fellow Negro when thus molested."

36. "We declare that all Negroes are entitled to the same right to travel over the world as other men."

37. "We hereby demand that the governments of the world recognize our leader and his representatives chosen by the race to look after the welfare of our people under such governments."

38. "We demand complete control of our social institutions without interference by any alien race or races."

39. "That the colors, Red, Black and Green, be the colors of the Negro race."

40. "Resolved, That the anthem 'Ethiopia, Thou Land of Our Fathers,' etc., shall be the anthem of the Negro race.". . .

41. "We believe that any limited liberty which deprives one of the complete rights and prerogatives of full citizenship is but a modified form of slavery."

42. "We declare it an injustice to our people and a serious impediment to the health of the race to deny to competent licensed Negro physicians the right to practice in the public hospitals of the communities in which they reside, for no other reason than their race and color."

43. "We call upon the various governments of the world to accept and acknowledge Negro representatives who shall be sent to the said governments to represent the general welfare of the Negro peoples of the world."

44. "We deplore and protest against the practice of confining juvenile prisoners in prisons with adults, and we recommend that such youthful prisoners be taught gainful trades under humane supervision."

45. "Be it further resolved, that we as a race of people declare the League of Nations null and void as far as the Negro is concerned, in that it seeks to deprive Negroes of their liberty."

46. "We demand of all men to do unto us as we would do unto them, in the name of justice; and we cheerfully accord to all men all the rights we claim herein for ourselves."

47. "We declare that no Negro shall engage himself in battle for an alien race without first obtaining the consent of the leader of the Negro people of the world, except in a matter of national self-defense."

48. "We protest against the practice of drafting Negroes and sending them to war with alien forces without proper training, and demand in all cases that Negro soldiers be given the same training as the aliens."

49. "We demand that instructions given Negro children in schools include the subject of 'Negro History,' to their benefit."

50. "We demand a free and unfettered commercial intercourse with all the Negro people of the world."

51. "We declare for the absolute freedom of the seas for all peoples."

52. "We demand that our duly accredited representatives be given proper recognition in all leagues, conferences, conventions or courts of international arbitration wherever human rights are discussed."

53. "We proclaim the 31st day of August of each year to be an international holiday to be observed by all Negroes."

54. "We want all men to know we shall maintain and contend for the freedom and equality of every man, woman and child of our race, with our lives, our fortunes and our sacred honor."

These rights we believe to be justly ours and proper for the protection of the Negro race at large, and because of this belief we, on behalf of the four hundred million Negroes of the world, do pledge herein the sacred blood of the race in defense, and we hereby subscribe our names as a guarantee of the truthfulness and faithfulness hereof in the presence of Almighty God, on the 13th day of August, in the year of our Lord one thousand nine hundred and twenty.

AN APPEAL TO THE CONSCIENCE OF THE BLACK RACE TO SEE ITSELF

It is said to be a hard and difficult task to organize and keep together large numbers of the Negro race for the common good. Many have tried to congregate us, but have failed, the reason being that our characteristics are such as to keep us more apart than together.

The evil of internal division is wrecking our existence as a people, and if we do not seriously and quickly move in the direction of a readjustment it simply means that our doom becomes imminently conclusive.

For years the Universal Negro Improvement Association has been working for the unification of our race, not on domestic-national lines only, but universally. The success which we have met in the course of our effort is rather encouraging, considering the time consumed and the environment surrounding the object of our concern.

It seems that the whole world of sentiment is against the Negro, and the difficulty of our generation is to extricate ourselves from the prejudice that hides itself beneath, as well as above, the action of an international environment.

Prejudice is conditional on many reasons, and it is apparent that the Negro supplies, consciously or unconsciously, all the reasons by which the world seems to ignore and avoid him. No one cares for a leper, for lepers are infectious persons, and all are afraid of the disease, so because the Negro keeps himself poor, helpless and undemonstrative, it is natural also that no one wants to be of him or with him.

Progress and Humanity

Progress is the attraction that moves humanity, and to whatever people or race this "modern virtue" attaches itself, there will you find the splendor of pride and self-esteem that never fail to win the respect and admiration of all.

It is the progress of the Anglo-Saxons that single them out for the respect of all the world. When their race had no progress or achievement to its credit, then, like all other inferior peoples, they paid the price in slavery, bondage, as well as through prejudice. We cannot forget the time when even the ancient Briton was regarded as being too dull to make a good Roman slave, yet today the influence of that race rules the world.

It is the industrial and commercial progress of America that causes Europe and the rest of the world to think appreciatively of the Anglo-American race. It is not because one hundred and ten million people live in the United States that the world is attracted to the republic with so much reverence and respect—a reverence and respect not shown to India with its three hundred millions, or to China with its four hundred millions. Progress of and among any people will advance them in the respect and appreciation of the rest of their fellows. It is such a progress that the Negro must attach to himself if he is to rise above the prejudice of the world.

The reliance of our race upon the progress and achievements of others for a consideration in sympathy, justice and rights is like a dependence upon a broken stick, resting upon which will eventually consign you to the ground.

Self-Reliance and Respect

The Universal Negro Improvement Association teaches our race self-help and self-reliance, not only in one essential, but in all those things that contribute to human happiness and well-being. The disposition of the many to depend upon the other races for a kindly and sympathetic consideration of their needs, without making the effort to do for themselves, has been the race's standing disgrace by which we have been judged and through which we have created the strongest prejudice against ourselves.

There is no force like success, and that is why the individual makes all efforts to surround himself throughout life with the evidence of it. As of the individual, so should it be of the race and nation. The glittering success of Rockefeller makes him a power in the American nation; the success of Henry Ford suggests him as an object of universal respect, but no one knows and cares about the bum or hobo who is Rockefeller's or Ford's neighbor. So, also, is the world attracted by the glittering success of races and nations, and pays absolutely no attention to the bum or hobo race that lingers by the wayside.

The Negro must be up and doing if he will break down the prejudice of the rest of the world. Prayer alone is not going to improve our condition, nor the policy of watchful waiting. We must strike out for ourselves in the course of material achievement, and by our own effort and energy present to the world those forces by which the progress of man is judged.

A Nation and Country

The Negro needs a nation and a country of his own, where he can best show evidence of his own ability in the art of human progress. Scattered as an unmixed and unrecognized part of alien nations and civilizations is but to demonstrate his imbecility, and point him out as an unworthy derelict, fit neither for the society of Greek, Jew nor Gentile.

It is unfortunate that we should so drift apart, as a race, as not to see that we are but perpetuating our own sorrow and disgrace in failing to appreciate the first great requisite of all peoples—organization.

Organization is a great power in directing the affairs of a race or nation toward a given goal. To properly develop the desires that are uppermost, we must first concentrate through some system or method, and there is none better than organization. Hence, the Universal Negro Improvement Association appeals to each and every Negro to throw in his lot with those of us who, through organization, are working for the universal emancipation of our race and the redemption of our common country, Africa.

No Negro, let him be American, European, West Indian or African, shall be truly respected until the race as a whole has emancipated itself through self-achievement and progress, from universal prejudice. The Negro will have to build his own government, industry, art, science, literature and culture, before the world will stop to consider him. Until then, we are but wards of a superior race and civilization, and the outcasts of a standard social system.

The race needs workers at this time, not plagiarists, copyists and mere imitators; but men and women who are able to create, to originate and improve, and thus make an independent racial contribution to the world and civilization.

Monkey Apings of "Leaders"

The unfortunate thing about us is that we take the monkey apings of our "so-called leading men" for progress. There is no progress in aping white people and telling us that they represent the best in the race, for in that respect any dressed monkey would represent the best of its species, irrespective of the creative matter of the monkey instinct. The best in a race is not reflected through or by the action of its apes, but by its ability to create of and by itself. It is such a creation that the Universal Negro Improvement Association seeks

Let us not try to be the best or worst of others, but let us make the effort to be the best of ourselves. Our own racial critics criticise us as dreamers and "fanatics," and call us "benighted" and "ignorant," because they lack racial backbone. They are unable to see themselves creators of their own needs. The slave instinct has not yet departed from them. They still believe that they can only live or exist through the good graces of their "masters." The good slaves have not yet thrown off their shackles; thus, to them, the Universal Negro Improvement Association is an "impossibility."

It is the slave spirit of dependence that causes our "so-called leading men" (apes) to seek the shelter, leadership, protection and patronage of the "master" in their organization and so-called advancement work. It is the spirit of feeling secured as good servants of the master, rather than as independents, why our modern Uncle Toms take pride in laboring under alien leadership and becoming surprised at the audacity of the Universal Negro Improvement Association in proclaiming for racial liberty and independence.

But the world of white and other men, deep down in their hearts, have much more respect for those of us who work for our racial salvation under the banner of the Universal Negro Improvement Association, than they could ever have in all eternity for a group of helpless apes and beggars who make a monopoly of undermining their own race and belittling themselves in the eyes of self-respecting people, by being "good boys" rather than able men.

Surely there can be no good will between apes, seasoned beggars and independent minded Negroes who will at least make an effort to do for themselves. Surely, the "dependents" and "wards" (and may I not say racial imbeciles?) will rave against and plan the destruction of movements like the Universal Negro Improvement Association that expose them to the liberal white minds of the world as not being representative of the best in the Negro, but, to the contrary, the worst. The best of a race does not live on the patronage and philanthropy of others, but makes an effort to do for itself. The best of the great white race doesn't fawn before and beg black, brown or yellow men; they go out, create for self and thus demonstrate the fitness of the race to survive; and so the white race of America and the world will be informed that the best in the Negro race is not the class of beggars who send out to other races piteous appeals annually for donations to maintain their coterie, but the groups within us that are honestly striving to do for themselves with the voluntary help and appreciation of that class of other races that is reasonable, just and liberal enough to give to each and every one a fair chance in the promotion of those ideals that tend to greater human progress and human love.

The work of the Universal Negro Improvement Association is clear and clean-cut. It is that of inspiring an unfortunate race with pride in self and with the determination of going ahead in the creation of those ideals that will lift them to the unprejudiced company of races and nations. There is no desire for hate or malice, but every wish to see all mankind linked into a common fraternity of progress and achievement that will wipe away the odor of prejudice, and elevate the human race to the height of real godly love and satisfaction.

Sources: (1) Excerpt from "Declaration of Rights of the Negro Peoples of the World," August 1920, originally published in Amy Jacques Garvey, ed., *Philosophy and Opinions of Marcus Garvey*, Vol. 2 (New York: Universal Publishing House, 1925), pp. 135–42; and (2) "An Appeal to the Conscience of the Black Race to See Itself," in *Philosophy and Opinions of Marcus Garvey*.

SELECT BIBLIOGRAPHY:

Randall K. Burkett, *Garveyism as a Religious Movement: The Institutionalization of a Black Civil Religion* (Metuchen, N.J.: Scarecrow Press, 1978).

Amy Jacques Garvey, *Garvey and Garveyism* (Kingston, Jamaica: A. Jacques Garvey, 1963).

Claudrena N. Harold, *The Rise and Fall of the Garvey Movement in the Urban South, 1918–1942* (London: Routledge, 2007).

Robert A. Hill and Association Universal Negro Improvement, eds., *The Marcus Garvey and Universal Negro Improvement Association Papers*, 10 vols. (Berkeley: University of California Press, 1983).

Rupert Lewis, *Marcus Garvey: Anti-Colonial Champion* (Trenton, N.J.: Africa World Press, 1988).

Mary G. Rolinson, Grassroots Garveyism: *The Universal Negro Improvement Association in the Rural South, 1920–1927* (Chapel Hill: University of North Carolina Press, 2007).

Jeannette Smith-Irvin, *Footsliders of the Universal Negro Improvement Association: Their Own Words* (Trenton, N.J.: Africa World Press, 1989).

Emory J. Tolbert, *The UNIA and Black Los Angeles: Ideology and Community in the American Garvey Movement* (Los Angeles: Center for Afro-American Studies, University of California Press, 1980).

Theodore G. Vincent, *Black Power and the Garvey Movement* (Berkeley, Ca.: Ramparts Press, 1971).

↝ 5 ↝

"Women as Leaders," *Amy Euphemia Jacques Garvey, 1925*

Amy Euphemia Jacques Garvey (1896–1973) was one of the key political leaders, archivists, and interpreters of the Garvey movement. As Garvey's second wife, she frequently represented her husband at public meetings and events. She was a regular columnist in the UNIA's newspaper, *The Negro World*. Garvey was a forceful advocate of women's rights and participated in the famous Fifth Pan-African Congress held in Manchester, England, in 1945. Her 1963 book *Garvey and Garveyism* was partially responsible for reviving interest in the UNIA and the Garvey movement.

↝

The exigencies of this present age require that women take their places beside their men. White women are rallying all their forces and uniting regardless of national boundaries to save their race from destruction, and preserve its ideals for posterity. . . . White men have begun to realize that as women are the backbone of the home, so can they, by their economic experience and their aptitude for details, participate effectively in guiding the destiny of nation and race.

No line of endeavor remains closed for long to the modern woman. She agitates for equal opportunities and gets them; she makes good on the job and gains the respect of men who heretofore opposed her. She prefers to be a breadwinner than a half-starved wife at home. She is not afraid of hard work, and by being independent she gets more out of the present-day husband than her grandmother did in the good old days.

The women of the East, both yellow and black, are slowly but surely imitating the women of the Western world, and as the white women are bolstering up a decaying white civilization, even so women of the darker races are sallying forth to help their men establish a civilization according to their own standards, and to strive for world leadership.

Women of all climes and races have as great a part to play in the development of their particular group as the men. Some readers may not agree with us on this issue, but do they not mould the minds of their children the future men and women? Even before birth a mother can so direct her thoughts and conduct as to bring into the world either a genius or an idiot. Imagine the early years of contact between mother and child, when she directs his form of speech, and is responsible for his conduct and deportment. Many a man has risen from the depths of poverty and obscurity and made his mark in life because of the advices and councils of a good mother whose influence guided his footsteps throughout his life.

Women therefore are extending this holy influence outside the realms of the home, softening the ills of the world by their gracious and kindly contact.

Some men may argue that the home will be broken up and women will become coarse and lose their gentle appeal. We do not think so, because everything can be done with moderation. . . . The doll-baby type of woman is a thing of the past, and the wide-awake woman is forging ahead prepared for all emergencies, and ready to answer any call, even if it be to face the cannons on the battlefield.

New York has a woman Secretary of State. Two States have women Governors, and we would not be surprised if within the next ten years a woman graces the White House in Washington, D.C. Women are also filling diplomatic positions, and from time immemorial women have been used as spies to get information for their country.

White women have greater opportunities to display their ability because of the standing of both races, and due to the fact that black men are less appreciative of their women than white men. The former will more readily sing the praises of white women than their own; yet who is more deserving of admiration than the black woman, she who has borne the rigors of slavery, the deprivations consequent on a pauperized race, and the indignities heaped upon a weak and defenseless people? Yet she has suffered all with fortitude, and stands ever ready to help in the onward march to freedom and power.

Be not discouraged black women of the world, but push forward, regardless of the lack of appreciation shown you. A race must be saved, a country must be redeemed, and unless you strengthen the leadership of vacillating Negro men, we will remain marking time until the Yellow race gains leadership of the world, and we be forced to subserviency under them, or extermination.

We are tired of hearing Negro men say, "There is a better day coming," while they do nothing to usher in the day. We are becoming so impatient that we are getting in the front ranks, and serve notice on the world that we will brush aside the halting, cowardly Negro men, and with prayer on our lips and arms prepared for any fray, we will press on and on until victory is over.

Africa must be for Africans, and Negroes everywhere must be independent, God being our guide. Mr. Black man, watch your step! Ethiopia's queens will reign again, and her Amazons protect her shores and people. Strengthen your shaking knees, and move forward, or we will displace you and lead on to victory and to glory.

Source: "Women as Leaders," from *The Negro World* (October 25, 1925).

SELECT BIBLIOGRAPHY:

Karen Adler, "'Always Leading Our Men in Service and Sacrifice': Amy Jacques Garvey, Feminist Black Nationalist," *Gender & Society* 6, no. 3 (September 1992), pp. 346–75.
Amy Jacques Garvey, *Garvey and Garveyism* (Kingston, Jamaica: A. Jacques Garvey, 1963).
Mark D. Matthews, "Our Women and What They Think, Amy Jacques Garvey and the Negro World," *Black Scholar* 10, nos. 8–9 (1979), pp. 2–18.
Ula Yvette Taylor, "The Veiled Garvey: The Life and Times of Amy Jacques Garvey" (Ph.D. diss., University of California, Santa Barbara, 1992).

~ 6 ~

Langston Hughes and the Harlem Renaissance

The rise of Harlem as a cultural and social center for black America created the context for a new black intelligentsia. Writers, musicians, and artists came to Harlem, attempting to redefine the parameters of Negro aesthetics and creativity. These "New Negroes" saw themselves as products of a modern age, breaking with established traditions and celebrating black life and culture. The Harlem Renaissance represents the artistic and cultural production of this generation, defined roughly from the Red Summer of 1919 through the early years of the Great Depression.

Along with Countee Cullen, Claude McKay, Nella Larsen, and Zora Neale Hurston, Langston Hughes (1902–1967) was a leading light of the Harlem Renaissance. Sometimes called "The Shakespeare of Harlem," Hughes studied at Columbia University and rose to prominence with his first collection of poetry, *Weary Blues* (1926). In addition to poetry, Hughes published plays, novels, stories, essays, and an autobiography. At the start of his career, Hughes's work often centered upon the daily lives of African Americans, and he employed black working-class vernacular drawn from African-American musical traditions (mainly blues). With the advent of the Great Depression, however, his work became more overtly political, reflecting his interest in Marxism. By World War II, Hughes's reputation as black America's most popular poet was firmly established.

~

THE NEGRO ARTIST AND THE RACIAL MOUNTAIN

One of the most promising of the young Negro poets said to me once, "I want to be a poet—not a Negro poet," meaning, I believe, "I want to write like a white poet"; meaning subconsciously, "I would like to be a white poet"; meaning behind that, "I would like to be white." And I was sorry the young man said that, for no great poet has ever been afraid of being himself. And I doubted then that, with his desire to run away spiritually from his race, this boy would ever be a great poet. But this is the mountain standing in the way of any true Negro art in America this urge within the race toward whiteness, the desire to pour racial individuality into the mold of American standardization, and to be as little Negro and as much American as possible.

But let us look at the immediate background of this young poet. His family is of what I suppose one would call the Negro middle class: people who are by no means rich yet never uncomfortable nor hungry—smug, contented, respectable folk, members of the Baptist church. The father goes to work every morning. He is a chief steward at a large white club. The mother sometimes does fancy sewing or supervises parties for the rich families of the town. The children go to a mixed school. In the home they read white papers and magazines. And the mother often says "Don't be like niggers" when the children are bad. A frequent phrase from the father is, "Look how well a white man does things." And so the word white comes to be unconsciously a symbol of all the virtues. It holds for the children beauty, morality, and money. The whisper of "I want to be white" runs silently through their minds. This young poet's home is, I believe, a fairly typical home of the colored middle class. One sees immediately how difficult it would be for an artist born in such a home to interest himself in interpreting the beauty of his own people. He is never taught to see that beauty. He is taught rather not to see it, or if he does, to be ashamed of it when it is not according to Caucasian patterns.

For racial culture the home of a self-styled "high-class" Negro has nothing better to offer. Instead there will perhaps be more aping of things white than in a less cultured or less wealthy home. The father is perhaps a doctor, lawyer, landowner, or politician. The mother may be a social worker, or a teacher, or she may do nothing and have a maid. Father is often dark but he has usually married the lightest woman he could find. The family attend a fashionable church where few really colored faces are to be found. And they themselves draw a color line. In the North they go to white theaters and white movies. And in the South they have at least two cars and a house "like white folks." Nordic manners, Nordic faces, Nordic hair, Nordic art (if any), and an Episcopal heaven. A very high mountain indeed for the would-be racial artist to climb in order to discover himself and his people.

But then there are the low-down folks, the so-called common element, and they are the majority—may the Lord be praised! The people who have their nip of gin on Saturday nights and are not too important to themselves or the community, or too well fed, or too learned to watch the lazy world go round. They live on Seventh Street in Washington or State Street in Chicago and they do not particularly care whether they are like white folks or anybody else. Their joy runs, bang! into ecstasy. Their religion soars to a shout. Work maybe a little today, rest a little tomorrow. Play awhile. Sing awhile. O, let's dance! These common people are not afraid of spirituals, as for a long time their more intellectual brethren were, and jazz is their child. They furnish a wealth of colorful, distinctive material for any artist because they still hold their own individuality in the face of American standardizations. And perhaps these common people will give to the world its truly great Negro artist, the one who is not afraid to be himself. Whereas the better-class Negro would tell the artist what to do, the people at least let him alone when he does appear. And they are not ashamed of him—if they know he exists at all. And they accept what beauty is their own without question.

Certainly there is, for the American Negro artist who can escape the restrictions the more advanced among his own group would put upon him, a great field of unused material ready for his art. Without going outside his race, and even among the better classes with their "white" culture and conscious American manners, but still Negro enough to be different, there is sufficient matter to furnish a black artist with a lifetime of creative work. And when he chooses to touch on the relations between Negroes and whites in this country with their innumerable overtones and undertones, surely, and especially for literature and the drama, there is an inexhaustible supply of themes at hand. To these the Negro artist can give his racial individuality, his heritage of rhythm and warmth, and his incongruous humor that so often, as in the Blues, becomes ironic laughter mixed with tears. But let us look again at the mountain.

A prominent Negro clubwoman in Philadelphia paid eleven dollars to hear Raquel Meller sing Andalusian popular songs. But she told me a few weeks before she would not think of going to hear "that woman," Clara Smith, a great black artist, sing Negro folksongs. And many an upper-class Negro church, even now, would not dream of employing a spiritual in its services. The drab melodies in white folks' hymnbooks are much to be preferred. "We want to worship the Lord correctly and quietly. We don't believe in 'shouting.' Let's be dull like the Nordics," they say, in effect.

The road for the serious black artist, then, who would produce a racial art is most certainly rocky and the mountain is high. Until recently he received almost no encouragement for his work from either white or colored people. The fine novels of Chesnutt go out of print with neither race noticing their passing. The quaint charm and humor of Dunbar's dialect verse brought to him, in his day, largely the same kind of encouragement one would give a side-show freak (A colored man writing poetry! How odd!) or a clown (How amusing!).

The present vogue in things Negro, although it may do as much harm as good for the budding colored artist, has at least done this: it has brought him forcibly to the attention of his own people among whom for so long, unless the other race had noticed him beforehand, he was a prophet with little honor. I understand that Charles Gilpin acted for years in Negro theaters without any special acclaim from his own, but when Broadway gave him eight curtain calls, Negroes, too, began to beat a tin pan in his honor. I know a young colored writer, a manual worker by day, who had been writing well for the colored magazines for some years, but it was not until he recently broke into the white publications and his first book was accepted by a prominent New York publisher that the "best" Negroes in his city took the trouble to discover that he lived there. Then almost immediately they decided to give a grand dinner for him. But the society ladies were careful to whisper to his mother that perhaps she'd better not come. They were not sure she would have an evening gown.

The Negro artist works against an undertow of sharp criticism and misunderstanding from his own group and unintentional bribes from the whites. "O, be respectable, write about nice people, show how good we are," say the Negroes. "Be stereotyped, don't go too far, don't shatter our illusions about you, don't amuse us too seriously. We will pay you," say the whites. Both would have told Jean Toomer not to write "Cane." The colored people did not praise it. The white people did not buy it. Most of the colored people who did read "Cane" hate it. They are afraid of it. Although the critics gave it good reviews the public remained indifferent. Yet (excepting the work of Du Bois) "Cane" contains the finest prose written by a Negro in America. And like the singing of Robeson, it is truly racial.

But in spite of the Nordicized Negro intelligentsia and the desires of some white editors we have an honest American Negro literature already with us. Now I await the rise of the Negro theater. Our folk music, having achieved world-wide fame, offers itself to the genius of the great individual American Negro composer who is to come. And within the next decade I expect to see the work of a growing school of colored artists who paint and model the beauty of dark faces and create with new technique the expressions of their own soul-world. And the Negro dancers who will dance like flame and the singers who will continue to carry our songs to all who listen—they will be with us in even greater numbers tomorrow.

Most of my own poems are racial in theme and treatment, derived from the life I know. In many of them I try to grasp and hold some of the meanings and rhythms of jazz. I am sincere as I know how to be in these poems and yet after every reading I answer questions like these from my own people: Do you think Negroes should always write about Negroes? I wish you wouldn't read some of your poems to white folks. How do you find anything interesting in a place like a cabaret? Why do you write about black people? You aren't black. What makes you do so many jazz poems?

But jazz to me is one of the inherent expressions of Negro life in America: the eternal tom-tom beating in the Negro soul—the tom-tom of revolt against weariness in a white world, a world of subway trains, and work, work, work; the tom-tom of joy and laughter, and pain swallowed in a smile. Yet the Philadelphia clubwoman is ashamed to say that her race created it and she does not like me to write about it. The old subconscious "white is best" runs through her mind. Years of study under white teachers, a life-time of white books, pictures, and papers, and white manners, morals, and Puritan standards made her dislike the spirituals. And now she turns up her nose at jazz and all its manifestations—likewise almost everything else distinctly racial. She doesn't care for the Winold Reiss portraits of Negroes because they are "too Negro." She does not want a true picture of herself from anybody. She wants the artist to flatter her, to make the white world believe that all Negroes are as smug and as near white in soul as she wants to be. But, to my mind, it is the duty of the younger Negro artist, if he accepts any duties at all from outsiders, to change through the force of his art that old whispering "I want to be white," hidden in the aspirations of his people, to "Why should I want to be white? I am a Negro—and beautiful!"

So I am ashamed for the black poet who says, "I want to be a poet, not a Negro poet," as though his own racial world were not as interesting as any other world. I am ashamed, too, for the colored artist who runs from the painting of Negro faces to the painting of sunsets after the manner of the academicians because he fears the strange un-whiteness of his own features. An artist must be free to choose what he does, certainly, but he must also never be afraid to do what he might choose.

Let the blare of Negro jazz bands and the bellowing voice of Bessie Smith singing Blues penetrate the closed ears of the colored near-intellectuals until they listen and perhaps understand. Let Paul Robeson singing Water Boy, and Rudolph Fisher writing about the streets of Harlem, and Jean Toomer holding the heart of Georgia in his hands, and Aaron Douglas drawing strange black fantasies cause the smug Negro middle class to turn from their white, respectable, ordinary books and papers to catch a glimmer of their own beauty. We younger Negro artists who create now intend to express our individual dark-skinned selves without fear or shame. If white people are pleased we are glad. If they are not, it doesn't matter. We know we are beautiful. And ugly too. The tom-tom cries and the tom-tom laughs. If colored people are pleased we are glad. If they are not, their displeasure doesn't matter either. We build our temples for tomorrow, strong as we know how, and we stand on top of the mountain, free within ourselves.

My America

This is my land, America. Naturally, I love it—it is home—and I am vitally concerned about its *mores*, its democracy, and its well-being. I try now to look at it with clear, unprejudiced eyes. My ancestry goes back at least four generations on American soil and, through Indian blood, many centuries more. My background and training is purely American—the schools of Kansas, Ohio, and the East. I am old stock as opposed to recent immigrant blood.

Yet many Americans who cannot speak English—so recent is their arrival on our shores—may travel about our country at will securing food, hotel, and rail accommodations wherever they wish to purchase them. *I may not.* These Americans, once naturalized, may vote in Mississippi or Texas, if they live there. *I may not.* They may work at whatever job their skills command. *But I may not.* They may purchase tickets for concerts, theatres, lectures wherever they are sold throughout the United States. *Often I may not.* They may repeat the Oath of Allegiance with its ringing phrase of "Liberty and justice for all," with a deep faith in its truth—as compared with the limitations and oppressions they have experienced in the Old World. I repeat the oath, too, but I know that the phrase about "liberty and justice" does not fully apply to me. I am an American—*but I am a colored American.*

I know that all these things I mention are not *all* true for *all* localities *all* over America. Jim Crowism varies in degree from North to South, from the mixed schools and free franchise of Michigan to the tumbledown colored schools and open terror at the polls of Georgia and Mississippi. All over America, however, against the Negro there has been an economic color line of such severity that since the Civil War we have been kept most effectively, as a racial group, in the lowest economic brackets. Statistics are not needed to prove this. Simply look around you on the Main Street of any American town or city. There are no colored clerks in any of the stores—although colored people spend their money there. There are practically never any colored street-car conductors or bus drivers—although these public carriers run over streets for which we pay taxes. There are no colored girls at the switchboards of the telephone company—but millions of Negroes have phones and pay their bills. Even in Harlem, nine times out of ten, the man who comes to collect your rent is white. Not even that job is given to a colored man by the great corporations owning New York real estate. From Boston to San Diego, the Negro suffers from job discrimination.

Yet America is a land where, in spite of its defects, I can write this article. Here the voice of democracy is still heard—Wallace, Willkie, Agar, Pearl Buck, Paul Robeson, Lillian Smith. America is a land where the poll tax still holds in the South—but opposition to the poll tax grows daily. America is a land where lynchers are not yet caught—but Bundists are put in jail, and majority opinion condemns the Klan. America is a land where the best of all democracies has been achieved for some people—but in Georgia, Roland Hayes, world-famous singer, is beaten for being colored and nobody is jailed—nor can Mr. Hayes vote in the State where he was born. Yet America is a country where Roland Hayes *can* come from a log cabin to wealth and fame—in spite of the segment that still wishes to maltreat him physically and spiritually, famous though he is.

This segment, the South, is not all of America. Unfortunately, however, the war with its increased flow of white Southern workers to Northern cities, has caused the Jim Crow patterns of the South to spread *all* over America, aided and abetted by the United States Army. The Army, with its policy of segregated troops, has brought Jim Crow into communities where it was but little, if at all, in existence before Pearl Harbor. From Camp Custer in Michigan to Guadalcanal in the South Seas, the Army has put its stamp upon official Jim Crow, in imitation of the Southern states where laws separating Negroes and whites are as much a part of government as are Hitler's laws segregating Jews in Germany. Therefore, any consideration of the current problems of the Negro people in America must concern itself seriously with the question of what to do about the South.

The South opposes the Negro's right to vote, and this right is denied us in most Southern states. Without the vote a citizen has no means of protecting his constitutional rights. For Democracy to approach its full meaning, the Negro *all over* America must have the vote. The South opposes the Negro's right to work in industry. Witness the Mobile shipyard riots, the Detroit strikes fomented by Southern whites against the employment of colored people, the Baltimore strikes of white workers who objected to Negroes attending a welding school which would give them the skill to rate upgrading. For Democracy to achieve its meaning, the Negro like other citizens must have the right to work, to learn skilled trades, and to be upgraded.

The South opposes the civil rights of Negroes and their protection by law. Witness lynchings where no one is punished, witness the Jim Crow laws that deny the letter and spirit of the Constitution. For Democracy to have real meaning, the Negro must have the same civil rights as any other American citizen. These three simple principles of Democracy—the vote, the right to work, and the right to protection by law—the South opposes when it comes to me. Such procedure is dangerous for *all* America. That is why, in order to strengthen Democracy, further the war effort, and achieve the confidence of our colored allies, we must institute a greater measure of Democracy for the eight million colored people of the South. And we must educate the white Southerners to an understanding of such democracy, so they may comprehend that decency toward colored peoples will lose them nothing, but rather will increase their own respect and safety in the modern world.

I live on Manhattan Island. For a New Yorker of color, truthfully speaking, the South begins at Newark. A half hour by tube from the Hudson Terminal, one comes across street-corner hamburger stands that will not serve a hamburger to a Negro customer wishing to sit on a stool. For the same dime a white pays, a Negro must take his hamburger elsewhere in a paper bag and eat it, minus a plate, a napkin, and a glass of water. Sponsors of the theory of segregation claim that it can be made to mean equality. Practically, it never works out that way. Jim Crow always means less for the one Jim Crowed and an unequal value for his money—no stool, no shelter, merely the hamburger, in Newark.

As the colored traveller goes further South by train, Jim Crow increases. Philadelphia is ninety minutes from Manhattan. There the all-colored grammar school begins its separate education of the races that Talmadge of Georgia so highly approves. An hour or so further down the line is Baltimore where segregation laws are written in the state and city codes. Another hour by train, Washington. There the conductor tells the Negro traveller, be he soldier or civilian, to go into the Jim Crow coach behind the engine, usually half a baggage car, next to trunks and dogs.

That this change to complete Jim Crow happens at Washington is highly significant of the state of American democracy in relation to colored peoples today. Washington is the capital of our nation and one of the great centers of the Allied war effort toward the achievement of the Four Freedoms. To a southbound Negro citizen told at Washington to change into a segregated coach the Four Freedoms have a hollow sound, like distant lies not meant to be the truth.

The train crosses the Potomac into Virginia, and from there on throughout the South life for the Negro, by state law and custom, is a hamburger in a sack without a plate, water, napkin, or stool—but at the same price as the whites pay—to be eaten apart from the others without shelter. The Negro can do little about this because the law is against him, he has no vote, the police are brutal, and the citizens think such caste-democracy is as it should be.

For his seat in the half-coach of the crowded Jim Crow car, a colored man must pay the same fare as those who ride in the nice air-cooled coaches further back in the train, privileged to use the diner when they wish. For his hamburger in a sack served without courtesy the Southern Negro must pay taxes but refrain from going to the polls, and must patriotically accept conscription to work, fight, and perhaps die to regain or maintain freedom for people in Europe or Australia when he himself hasn't got it at home. Therefore, to his ears most of the war speeches about freedom on the radio sound perfectly foolish, unreal, high-flown, and false. To many Southern whites, too, this grand talk so nobly delivered, so poorly executed, must seem like play-acting.

Liberals and persons of good will, North and South, including, no doubt, our President himself, are puzzled as to what on earth to do about the South—the poll-tax South, the Jim Crow South—that so shamelessly gives the lie to Democracy. With the brazen frankness of Hitler's *Mein Kampf*, Dixie speaks through Talmadge, Rankin, Dixon, Arnall, and Mark Ethridge.

In a public speech in Birmingham, Mr. Ethridge says: "All the armies of the world, both of the United States and the Axis, could not force upon the South an abandonment of racial segregation." Governor Dixon of Alabama refused a government war contract offered Alabama State Prison because it contained an anti-discrimination clause which in his eyes was an "attempt to abolish segregation of races in the South." He said: "We will not place ourselves in a position to be attacked by those who seek to foster their own pet social reforms." In other words, Alabama will not reform. It is as bull-headed as England in India, and its governor is not ashamed to say so.

As proof of Southern intolerance, almost daily the press reports some new occurrence of physical brutality against Negroes. Former Governor Talmadge was "too busy" to investigate when Roland Hayes and his wife were thrown into jail, and the great tenor beaten, on complaint of a shoe salesman over a dispute as to what seat in his shop a Negro should occupy when buying shoes. Nor did the governor of Mississippi bother when Hugh Gloster, professor of English at Morehouse College, riding as an inter-state passenger, was illegally ejected from a train in his state, beaten, arrested, and fined because, being in an overcrowded Jim Crow coach, he asked for a seat in an adjacent car which contained only two white passengers.

Legally, the Jim Crow laws do not apply to inter-state travellers, but the FBI has not yet gotten around to enforcing that Supreme Court ruling. En route from San Francisco to Oklahoma City, Fred Wright, a county probation officer of color, was beaten and forced into the Texas Jim Crow coach on a transcontinental train by order of the conductor in defiance of federal law. A seventy-six-year-old clergyman, Dr. Jackson of Hartford, Connecticut, going South to attend the National Baptist Convention, was set upon by white passengers for merely passing through a white coach on the way to his own seat. There have been many similar attacks upon colored soldiers in uniform on public carriers. One such attack resulted in death for the soldier, dragged from a bus and killed by civilian police. Every day now, Negro soldiers from the North, returning home on furlough from Southern camps, report incident after incident of humiliating travel treatment below the Mason-Dixon line.

It seems obvious that the South does not yet know what this war is all about. As answer Number One to the question, "What shall we do about the South?" I would suggest an immediate and intensive government-directed program of pro-democratic education, to be put into the schools of the South from the first grades of the grammar schools to the universities. As part of the war effort, this is urgently needed. The Spanish Loyalist Government had trench schools for its soldiers and night schools for civilians even in Madrid under siege. America is not under siege yet. We still have time (but not too much) to teach our people what we are fighting for, and to begin to apply those teachings to race relations at home. You see, it would be too bad for an emissary of color from one of the Latin American countries, say Cuba or Brazil, to arrive at Miami Airport and board a train for Washington, only to get beaten up and thrown off by white Southerners who do not realize how many colored allies we have—nor how badly we need them—and that it is inconsiderate and rude to beat colored people, anyway.

Because transportation in the South is so symbolic of America's whole racial problem, the Number Two thing for us to do is study a way out of the Jim Crow car dilemma at once. Would a system of first, second, and third class coaches help? In Europe, formerly, if one did not wish to ride with peasants and tradespeople, one could always pay a little more and solve that problem by having a first class compartment almost entirely to oneself. Most Negroes can hardly afford parlor car seats. Why not abolish Jim Crow entirely and let the whites who wish to do so, ride in coaches where few Negroes have the funds to be? In any case, our Chinese, Latin American, and Russian allies are not going to think much of our democratic pronunciamentos as long as we keep compulsory Jim Crow cars on Southern rails.

Since most people learn a little through education, albeit slowly, as Number Three, I would suggest that the government draft all the leading Negro intellectuals, sociologists, writers, and concert singers from Alain Locke of Oxford and W. E. B. Du Bois of Harvard to Dorothy Maynor and Paul Robeson of Carnegie Hall and send them into the South to appear before white audiences, carrying messages of culture and democracy, thus off-setting the old stereotypes of the Southern mind and the Hollywood movie, and explaining to the people without dialect what the war aims are about. With each, send on tour a liberal white Southerner like Paul Green, Erskine Caldwell, Pearl Buck, Lillian Smith, or William Seabrook. And, of course, include soldiers to protect them from the fascist-minded among us.

Number Four, as to the Army—draftees are in sore need of education on how to behave toward darker peoples. Just as a set of government suggestions has been issued to our soldiers on how to act in England, so a similar set should be given them on how to act in Alabama, Georgia, Texas, Asia, Mexico, and Brazil—wherever there are colored peoples. Not only printed words should be given them, but intensive training in the reasons for being decent to everybody. Classes in democracy and the war aims should be set up in every training camp in America and every unit of our military forces abroad. These forces should be armed with understanding as well as armament, prepared for friendship as well as killing.

I go on the premise that most Southerners are potentially reasonable people, but that they simply do not know nowadays what they are doing to America, or how badly their racial attitudes look toward the rest of the civilized world. I know their politicians, their schools, and the Hollywood movies have done their best to uphold prevailing reactionary viewpoints. Heretofore, nobody in America except a few radicals, liberals, and a handful of true religionists have cared much about either the Negroes or the South. Their sincere efforts to effect a change have been but a drop in a muddy bucket. Basically, the South needs universal suffrage, economic stabilization, a balanced diet, and vitamins for children. But until those things are achieved, on a lesser front to ameliorate—not solve—the Negro problem (and to keep Southern prejudice from contaminating all of America) a few mild but helpful steps might be taken.

It might be pointed out to the South that the old bugaboo of sex and social equality doesn't mean a thing. Nobody as a rule sleeps with or eats with or dances with or marries anybody else except by mutual consent. Millions of people of various races in New York, Chicago, and Seattle go to the same polls and vote without ever co-habiting together. Why does the South think it would be otherwise with Negroes were they permitted to vote there? Or to have a decent education? Or to sit on a stool in a public place and eat a hamburger? Why they think simple civil rights would force a Southerner's daughter to marry a Negro in spite of herself, I have never been able to understand. It must be due to some lack of instruction somewhere in their schooling.

A government-sponsored educational program of racial decency could, furthermore, point out to its students that cooperation in labor would be to the advantage of all—rather than to the disadvantage of anyone, white or black. It could show quite clearly that a million unused colored hands barred out of war industries might mean a million weapons lacking in the hands of our soldiers on some foreign front—therefore a million extra deaths—including Southern white boys needlessly dying under Axis fire—because Governor Dixon of Alabama and others of like mentality need a little education. It might also be pointed out that when peace comes and the Southerners go to the peace table, if they take there with them the traditional Dixie racial attitudes, there is no possible way for them to aid in forming any peace that will last. China, India, Brazil, Free French Africa, Soviet Asia and the whole Middle East will not believe a word they say.

Peace only to breed other wars is a sorry peace indeed, and one that we must plan now to avoid. Not only in order to win the war then, but to create peace along decent lines, we had best start *now* to educate the South—and all America—in racial decency. That education cannot be left to well-meaning but numerically weak civilian organizations. The government itself should take over—and vigorously. After all, Washington is the place where the conductor comes through every southbound train and tells colored people to change to the Jim Crow car ahead.

That car, in these days and times, has no business being "ahead" any longer. War's freedom train can hardly trail along with glory behind a Jim Crow coach. No matter how streamlined the other cars may be, that coach endangers all humanity's hopes for a peaceful tomorrow. The wheels of the Jim Crow car are about to come off and the walls are going to burst wide open. The wreckage of

Democracy is likely to pile up behind that Jim Crow car, unless America learns that it is to its own self-interest to stop dealing with colored peoples in so anti-quated a fashion. I do not like to see my land, America, remain provincial and unrealistic in its attitudes toward color. I hope the men and women of good will here of both races will find ways of changing conditions for the better.

Certainly it is not the Negro who is going to wreck our Democracy. (What we want is more of it, not less.) But Democracy is going to wreck itself if it continues to approach closer and closer to fascist methods in its dealings with Negro citi-zens—for such methods of oppression spread, affecting other whites, Jews, the foreign born, labor, Mexicans, Catholics, citizens of Oriental ancestry—and, in due time, they boomerang right back at the oppressor. Furthermore, American Negroes are now Democracy's current test for its dealings with the colored peo-ples of the whole world of whom there are many, many millions—*too many* to be kept indefinitely in the position of passengers in Jim Crow cars.

POEMS

"I, Too"

> I, too, sing America.
>
> I am the darker brother.
> They send me to eat in the kitchen
> When company comes,
> But I laugh,
> And eat well,
> And grow strong.
>
> Tomorrow, I'll be at the table
> When company comes.
> Nobody'll dare
> Say to me,
> "Eat in the kitchen,"
> Then.
>
> Besides,
> They'll see how beautiful I am
> And be ashamed—
>
> I, too, am America.

> 1925, 1959

"Harlem"

> What happens to a dream deferred?
> Does it dry up

like a raisin in the sun?
Or fester like a sore—
And then run?
Does it stink like rotten meat?
Or crust and sugar over—
like a syrupy sweet?

Maybe it just sags
like a heavy load.

Or does it explode?

1951, 1959

Sources: (1) "The Negro Artist and the Racial Mountain," *Nation* 122 (June 23, 1926), reprinted with permission; (2) "My America," from *What the Negro Wants* by Rayford W. Logan (Chapel Hill: University of North Carolina Press, 1944), pp. 299–307. Copyright 1944 by the University of North Carolina Press, renewed 1974 by Rayford W. Logan. Used by permission of the publisher; and (3) "I, Too" and "Harlem," from *Collected Poems by Langston Hughes* (New York: Alfred A. Knopf, 1994). Copyright 1994 by the Estate of Langston Hughes. Reprinted by permission of Alfred A. Knopf, Inc. For subscription information to the *Nation*, call 1-800-333-8536. Portions of each week's *Nation* magazine can be accessed at www.thenation.com.

SELECT BIBLIOGRAPHY:

Donald C. Dickinson, *A Bio-Bibliography of Langston Hughes, 1902–1967* (Hamden, Conn.: Archon Books, 1967).

Henry Louis Gate, Jr. and K. A. Appiah, eds., *Langston Hughes: Critical Perspectives Past and Present* (New York: Amistad [distributed by Penguin, USA], 1998).

Nathan I. Huggins, *Harlem Renaissance* (New York: Oxford University Press, 1971).

David L. Lewis, *When Harlem Was in Vogue* (New York: Knopf, 1981).

Arnold Rampersad, *The Life of Langston Hughes*, Vol. 1, *1902–1941* (New York: Oxford University Press, 1986).

Arnold Rampersad, *The Life of Langston Hughes*, 2 vols. (Oxford: Oxford University Press, 2002).

Jonathan Scott, *Socialist Joy in the Writing of Langston Hughes* (Columbia: University of Missouri Press, 2006).

~ 7 ~

"The Negro Woman and the Ballot," *Alice Moore Dunbar-Nelson, 1927*

Alice Dunbar-Nelson (1875–1935) was born Alice Ruth Moore in New Orleans, Louisiana, and attended both the University of Pennsylvania and Cornell University before becoming a well-known writer. At age twenty she published her first book of poetry, *Violet and Other Tales* (1895). She moved to Brooklyn, where she taught school and gave classes at Victoria Earle Matthews's White Rose Mission.

For several years she was married to poet Paul Laurence Dunbar. After Dunbar's death in 1906, she married a journalist, Robert John Nelson. Dunbar-Nelson and her husband published the *Wilmington Advocate* newspaper in the 1920s, and were active in black Republican Party politics. During the Harlem Renaissance, her work received renewed critical attention by a younger generation of African-American writers and poets. Dunbar-Nelson was an insightful political analyst, and was for decades widely read in black publications. With the publication of Dunbar-Nelson's diary in 1984, the existence of an active African-American lesbian network in the 1920s and her relationships with other women became known to scholars.

It has been six years since the franchise as a national measure has been granted women. The Negro woman has had the ballot in conjunction with her white sister, and friend and foe alike are asking the question, What has she done with it?

Six years is a very short time in which to ask for results from any measure or condition, no matter how simple. In six years a human being is barely able to make itself intelligible to listeners; is a feeble, puny thing at best, with undeveloped understanding, no power of reasoning, with a slight contributory value to the human race, except in a sentimental fashion. Nations in six years are but the beginnings of an idea. It is barely possible to erect a structure of any permanent value in six years, and only the most ephemeral trees have reached any size in six years.

So perhaps it is hardly fair to ask with a cynic's sneer, What has the Negro woman done with the ballot since she has had it? But, since the question continues to be hurled at the woman, she must needs be nettled into reply.

To those colored women who worked, fought, spoke, sacrificed, traveled, pleaded, wept, cajoled, all but died for the right of suffrage for themselves and their peers, it seemed as if the ballot would be the great objective of life. That with its granting, all the economic, political, and social problems to which the race had been subject would be solved. They did not hesitate to say—those militantly gentle workers for the vote—that with the granting of the ballot the women would step into the dominant place, politically, of the race. That all the mistakes which the men had made would be rectified. The men have sold their birthright for a mess of pottage, said the women. Cheap political office and little political preferment had dazzled their eyes so that they could not see the great issues affecting the race. They had been fooled by specious lies, fair promises and large-sounding works. Pre-election promises had inflated their chests, so that they could not see the post-election failures at their feet.

And thus on and on during all the bitter campaign of votes for women.

One of the strange phases of the situation was the rather violent objection of the Negro man to the Negro woman's having the vote. Just what his objection racially was, he did not say, preferring to hide behind the grandiloquent platitude of his white political boss. He had probably not thought the matter through; if he had, remembering how precious the ballot was to the race, he would have hesitated at withholding its privilege from another one of his own people.

But all that is neither here nor there. The Negro woman got the vote along with some tens of million other women in the country. And has it made any appreciable difference in the status of the race? . . . The Negro woman was going to be independent, she had averred. She came into the political game with a clean slate. No Civil War memories for her, and no deadening sense of gratitude to influence her vote. She would vote men and measures, not parties. She could scan each candidate's record and give him her support according to how he had stood in the past on the question of race. She owed no party allegiance. The name of Abraham Lincoln was not synonymous with her for blind G.O.P. allegiance. She would show the Negro man how to make his vote a power, and not a joke. She would break up the tradition that one could tell a black man's politics by the color of his skin.

And when she got the ballot she slipped quietly, safely, easily, and conservatively into the political party of her male relatives.

Which is to say, that with the exception of New York City, and a sporadic break here and there, she became a Republican. Not a conservative one, however. She was virulent and zealous. Prone to stop speaking to her friends who might disagree with her findings on the political issue, and vituperative in campaigns.

In other words the Negro woman has by and large been a disappointment in her handling of the ballot. She has added to the overhead charges of the political machinery, without solving racial problems.

One of two bright lights in the story hearten the reader. In the congressional campaign of 1922 the Negro woman cut adrift from party allegiance and took up the cudgel (if one may mix metaphors) for the cause of the Dyer Bill. The Anti-Lynching Crusaders, led by Mrs. Mary B. Talbot, found in several states—New Jersey, Delaware, and Michigan particularly—that its cause was involved in the congressional election. Sundry gentlemen had voted against the Dyer Bill in the House and had come up for re-election. They were properly castigated by being kept at home. The women's votes unquestionably had the deciding influence in the three states mentioned, and the campaign conducted by them was of a most commendable kind.

School bond issues here and there have been decided by the colored woman's votes—but so slight is the ripple on the smooth surface of conservatism that it has attracted no attention from the deadly monotony of the blind faith in the "Party of Massa Linkun."

As the younger generation becomes of age it is apt to be independent in thought and in act. But it is soon whipped into line by the elders, and by the promise of plums of preferment or of an amicable position in the community or of easy social relations—for we still persecute socially those who disagree with us politically. What is true of the men is true of the women. The very young is apt to let father, sweetheart, brother, or uncle decide her vote. . . .

Whether women have been influenced and corrupted by their male relatives and friends is a moot question. Were I to judge by my personal experience I would say unquestionably so. I mean a personal experience with some hundreds of women in the North Atlantic, Middle Atlantic, and Middle Western States.

High ideals are laughed at, and women confess with drooping wings how they have been scoffed at for working for nothing, for voting for nothing, for supporting a candidate before having first been "seen." In the face of this sinister influence it is difficult to see how the Negro woman could have been anything else but "just another vote."

All this is rather a gloomy presentment of a well-known situation. But it is not altogether hopeless. The fact that the Negro woman CAN be roused when something near and dear to her is touched and threatened is cheering. Then she throws off the influence of her male companion and strikes out for herself. Whatever the Negro may hope to gain for himself must be won at the ballot box, and quiet "going along" will never gain his end. When the Negro woman finds that the future of her children lies in her own hands—if she can be made to see this—she will strike off the political shackles she has allowed to be hung upon her, and win the economic freedom of her race.

Perhaps some Joan of Arc will lead the way.

Source: "The Negro Woman and the Ballot," *Messenger* 9 (April 1927), p. 111.

SELECT BIBLIOGRAPHY:

Eleanor Alexander, *Lyrics of Sunshine and Shadow: The Tragic Courtship and Marriage of Paul Laurence Dunbar and Alice Ruth Moore: A History of Love and Violence among the African American Elite* (New York: New York University Press, 2001).

Bruce D. Dickson, Jr., *Black American Writing from the Nadir: The Evolution of a Literary Tradition* (Baton Rouge: Louisiana State University Press, 1989).

Alice Dunbar-Nelson, *An Alice Dunbar-Nelson Reader*, ed. R. Ora Williams (Washington, D.C.: University Press of America, 1979).

———, *The Works of Alice Dunbar-Nelson*, Vols. 1–3, ed. Gloria T. Hull (New York: Oxford University Press, 1988).

Addison Gayle, Jr., *Oak and Ivy* (New York: Doubleday, 1971).

Gloria T. Hull, ed., *Give Us Each Day: The Diary of Alice Dunbar-Nelson* (New York: Norton, 1984).

8

James Weldon Johnson and Harlem in the 1920s

Born in Jacksonville, Florida, James Weldon Johnson (1871–1938) had a multifaceted career as a poet, novelist, lyricist, civil rights leader, diplomat, lawyer, and teacher. Among his considerable accomplishments, he is remembered as the lyricist of "Lift Every Voice and Sing" (the "Negro National Anthem"), and as the author of the enormously influential novel, *The Autobiography of an Ex-Coloured Man*, first published anonymously in 1912. Early in his public career Johnson was closely associated with Booker T. Washington's Tuskegee Machine. After Washington's death, Johnson and other black moderates gravitated toward the reformist politics of Du Bois and the NAACP. Johnson served as the first black national secretary of the NAACP, from 1920 to 1930. He was tragically killed in an automobile accident in 1938.

~~~

HARLEM: THE CULTURE CAPITAL

In the history of New York, the significance of the name Harlem has changed from Dutch to Irish to Jewish to Negro. Of these changes, the last has come most swiftly. Throughout colored America, from Massachusetts to Mississippi, and across the continent to Los Angeles and Seattle, its name, which as late as fifteen years ago had scarcely been heard, now stands for the Negro metropolis. Harlem is indeed the great Mecca for the sight-seer, the pleasure-seeker, the curious, the adventurous, the enterprising, the ambitious and the talented of the whole Negro world; for the lure of it has reached down to every island of the Carib Sea and has penetrated even into Africa.

In the make-up of New York, Harlem is not merely a Negro colony or community, it is a city within a city, the greatest Negro city in the world. It is not a slum or a fringe, it is located in the heart of Manhattan and occupies one of the most beautiful and healthful sections of the city. It is not a "quarter" of dilapidated tenements, but is made up of new-law apartments and handsome dwellings, with well-paved and well-lighted streets. It has its own churches, social and civic centers, shops, theaters and other places of amusement. And it contains more Negroes to the square mile than any other spot on earth. A stranger who rides up magnificent Seventh Avenue on a bus or in an automobile must be struck with surprise at the transformation which takes place after he crosses One Hundred and Twenty-fifth Street. Beginning there, the population suddenly darkens and he rides through twenty-five solid blocks where the passers-by, the shoppers, those sitting in restaurants, coming out of theaters, standing in doorways and looking out of windows are practically all Negroes; and then he emerges where the population as suddenly becomes white again. There is nothing just like it in any other city in the country, for there is no preparation for it; no change in the character of the houses and streets; no change, indeed, in the appearance of the people, except their color.

Negro Harlem is practically a development of the past decade, but the story behind it goes back a long way. There have always been colored people in New York. In the middle of the last century they lived in the vicinity of Lispenard, Broome and Spring Streets. When Washington Square and lower Fifth Avenue was the center of aristocratic life, the colored people, whose chief occupation was domestic service in the homes of the rich, lived in a fringe and were scattered in nests to the south, east and west of the square. As late as the 80s the major part of the colored population lived in Sullivan, Thompson, Bleecker, Grove, Minetta Lane and adjacent streets. It is curious to note that some of these nests still persist. In a number of the blocks of Greenwich Village and Little Italy may be found small groups of Negroes who have never lived in any other section of the city. By about 1890 the center of colored population had shifted to the upper Twenties and lower Thirties west of Sixth Avenue. Ten years later another considerable shift northward had been made to West Fifty-third Street.

The West Fifty-third Street settlement deserves some special mention because it ushered in a new phase of life among colored New Yorkers. . . .

The move to Fifty-third Street was the result of the opportunity to get into newer and better houses. About 1900 the move to Harlem began, and for the same reason. Harlem had been overbuilt with large, new-law apartment houses, but rapid transportation to that section was very inadequate—the Lenox Avenue Subway had not yet been built—and landlords were finding difficulty in keeping houses on the east side of the section filled. Residents along and near Seventh Avenue were fairly well served by the Eighth Avenue Elevated. A colored man, in the real estate business at this time, Philip A. Payton, approached several of these landlords with the proposition that he would fill their empty or partially empty houses with steady colored tenants. The suggestion was accepted, and one or two houses on One Hundred and Thirty-fourth Street east of Lenox Avenue were taken over. Gradually other houses were filled. The whites paid little attention to the movement until it began to spread west of Lenox Avenue; they then took steps to check it. They proposed through a financial organization, the Hudson Realty Company, to buy in all properties occupied by colored people and evict the tenants. The Negroes countered by similar methods. Payton formed the Afro-American Realty Company, a Negro corporation organized for the purpose of buying and leasing houses for occupancy by colored people. Under this counter stroke the opposition subsided for several years.

But the continually increasing pressure of colored people to the west over the Lenox Avenue dead line caused the opposition to break out again, but in a new and more menacing form. Several white men undertook to organize all the white people of the community for the purpose of inducing financial institutions not to lend money or renew mortgages on properties occupied by colored people. In this effort they had considerable success, and created a situation which has not yet been completely overcome, a situation which is one of the hardest and most unjustifiable the Negro property owner in Harlem has to contend with. The Afro-American Realty Company was now defunct, but two or three colored men of means stepped into the breach. Philip A. Payton and J. C. Thomas bought two five-story apartments, dispossessed the white tenants and put in colored. J. B. Nail bought a row of five apartments and did the same thing. St. Philip's Church bought a row of thirteen apartment houses on One Hundred and Thirty-fifth Street, running from Seventh Avenue almost to Lenox.

The situation now resolved itself into an actual contest. Negroes not only continued to occupy available apartment houses, but began to purchase private dwellings between Lenox and Seventh Avenues. Then the whole movement, in the eyes of the whites, took on the aspect of an "invasion"; they became panic-stricken and began fleeing as from a plague. The presence of one colored family in a block, no matter how well bred and orderly, was sufficient to precipitate a flight. House after house and block after block was actually deserted. It was a great demonstration of human beings running amuck. None of them stopped to reason why they were doing it or what would happen if they didn't. The banks and lending companies holding mortgages on these deserted houses were compelled to take them over. For some time they held these houses vacant, preferring to do that and carry the charges than to rent or sell them to colored people. But values dropped and continued to drop until at the outbreak of the war in Europe property in the northern part of Harlem had reached the *nadir*.

In the meantime the Negro colony was becoming more stable; the churches were being moved from the lower part of the city; social and civic centers were being formed; and gradually a community was being evolved. Following the outbreak of the war in Europe Negro Harlem received a new and tremendous impetus. Because of the war thousands of aliens in the United States rushed back to their native lands to join the colors and immigration practically ceased. The result was a critical shortage in labor.This shortage was rapidly increased as the United States went more and more largely into the business of furnishing munitions and supplies to the warring countries. To help meet this shortage of common labor Negroes were brought up from the South. The government itself took the first steps, following the practice in vogue in Germany of shifting labor according to the supply and demand in various parts of the country. The example of the government was promptly taken up by the big industrial concerns, which sent hundreds, perhaps thousands, of labor agents into the South who recruited Negroes by wholesale. I was in Jacksonville, Fla., for a while at that time, and I sat one day and watched the stream of migrants passing to take the train. For hours they passed steadily, carrying flimsy suit cases, new and shiny, rusty old ones, bursting at the seams, boxes and bundles and impedimenta of all sorts, including banjos, guitars, birds in cages and what not. Similar scenes were being enacted in cities and towns all over that region. The first wave of the great exodus of Negroes from the South was on. Great numbers of these migrants headed for New York or eventually got there, and naturally the majority went up into Harlem. But the Negro population of Harlem was not swollen by migrants from the South alone; the opportunity for Negro labor exerted its pull upon the Negroes of the West Indies, and those islanders in the course of time poured into Harlem to the number of twenty-five thousand or more. . . .

The question naturally arises, "Are the Negroes going to be able to hold Harlem?" If they have been steadily driven northward for the past hundred years and out of less desirable sections, can they hold this choice bit of Manhattan Island? It is hardly probable that Negroes will hold Harlem indefinitely, but when they are forced out it will not be for the same reasons that forced them out of former quarters in New York City. The situation is entirely different and without precedent. When colored people do leave Harlem, their homes, their churches, their investments and their businesses, it will be because the land has become so valuable they can no longer afford to live on it. But the date of another move northward is very far in the future. What will Harlem be and become in the meantime? Is there danger that the Negro may lose his economic status in New York and be unable to hold his property? Will Harlem become merely a famous ghetto, or will it be a center of intellectual, cultural and economic forces exerting an influence throughout the world, especially upon Negro peoples? Will it become a point of friction between the races in New York?

I think there is less danger to the Negroes of New York of losing out economically and industrially than to the Negroes of any large city in the North. In most of the big industrial centers Negroes are engaged in gang labor. They are employed by thousands in the stockyards in Chicago, by thousands in the automobile plants in Detroit; and in those cities they are likely to be the first to be let go, and in thousands, with every business depression. In New York there is hardly such a thing as gang labor among Negroes, except among the longshoremen, and it is in the longshoremen's unions, above all others, that Negroes stand on an equal footing. Employment among Negroes in New York is highly diversified; in the main they are employed more as individuals than as non-integral parts of a gang. Furthermore, Harlem is gradually becoming more and more a self-supporting community. Negroes there are steadily branching out into new businesses and enterprises in which Negroes are employed. So the danger of great numbers of Negroes being thrown out of work at once, with a resulting economic crisis among them, is less in New York than in most of the large cities of the North to which Southern migrants have come.

These facts have an effect which goes beyond the economic and industrial situation. They have a direct bearing on the future character of Harlem and on the question as to whether Harlem will be a point of friction between the races in New York. It is true that Harlem is a Negro community, well defined and stable; anchored to its fixed homes, churches, institutions, business and amusement places; having its own working, business and professional classes. It is experiencing a constant growth of group consciousness and community feeling. Harlem is, therefore, in many respects, typically Negro. It has many unique characteristics. It has movement, color, gayety, singing, dancing, boisterous laughter and loud talk. One of its outstanding features is brass band parades. Hardly a Sunday passes but that there are several of these parades of which many are gorgeous with regalia and insignia. Almost any excuse will do—the death of an humble member of the Elks, the laying of a cornerstone, the "turning out" of the order of this or that. In many of these characteristics it is similar to the Italian colony. But withal, Harlem grows more metropolitan and more a part of New York all the while. Why is it then that its tendency is not to become a mere "quarter"?

I shall give three reasons that seem to me to be important in their order. First, the language of Harlem is not alien; it is not Italian or Yiddish; it is English. Harlem talks American, reads American, thinks American. Second, Harlem is not physically a "quarter." It is not a section cut off. It is merely a zone through which four main arteries of the city run. Third, the fact that there is little or no gang labor gives Harlem Negroes the opportunity for individual expansion and individual contacts with the life and spirit of New York. A thousand Negroes from Mississippi put to work as a gang in a Pittsburgh steel mill will for a long time remain a thousand Negroes from Mississippi. Under the conditions that prevail in New York they would all within six months become New Yorkers. The rapidity with which Negroes become good New Yorkers is one of the marvels to observers.

These three reasons form a single reason why there is small probability that Harlem will ever be a point of race friction between the races in New York. One of the principal factors in the race riot in Chicago in 1919 was the fact that at that time there were 12,000 Negroes employed in gangs in the stockyards. There was considerable race feeling in Harlem at the time of the hegira of white residents due to the "invasion," but that feeling, of course, is no more. Indeed, a number of the old white residents who didn't go and could not get away before the housing shortage struck New York are now living peacefully side by side with colored residents. In fact, in some cases white and colored tenants occupy apartments in the same house. Many white merchants still do business in thickest Harlem. On the whole, I know of no place in the country where the feeling between the races is so cordial and at the same time so matter-of-fact and taken for granted. One of the surest safeguards against an outbreak in New York such as took place in so many Northern cities in the summer of 1919 is the large proportion of Negro police on duty in Harlem.

To my mind, Harlem is more than a Negro community; it is a large scale laboratory experiment in the race problem. The statement has often been made that if Negroes were transported to the North in large numbers the race problem with all of its acuteness and with new aspects would be transferred with them. Well, 175,000 Negroes live closely together in Harlem, in the heart of New York—75,000 more than live in any Southern city—and do so without any race friction. Nor is there any unusual record of crime. I once heard a captain of the 38th Police Precinct (the Harlem precinct) say that on the whole it was the most law-abiding precinct in the city. New York guarantees its Negro citizens the fundamental rights of American citizenship and protects them in the exercise of those rights. In return the Negro loves New York and is proud of it, and contributes in his way to its greatness. He still meets with discriminations, but possessing the basic rights, he knows that these discriminations will be abolished.

I believe that the Negro's advantages and opportunities are greater in Harlem than in any other place in the country, and that Harlem will become the intellectual, the cultural and the financial center for Negroes of the United States, and will exert a vital influence upon all Negro peoples.

Source: Excerpt from "Harlem: The Culture Capital," originally written in 1925 and published in Alain Locke, ed., *The New Negro* (New York: Albert and Charles Boni, 1925), pp. 301–11.

SELECT BIBLIOGRAPHY:

Robert E. Fleming, *James Weldon Johnson* (Boston: Twayne, 1987).

James Weldon Johnson, *The Autobiography of an Ex-Coloured Man* (Garden City, N.Y.: Garden City Publishing Co., 1912).

———, *Along This Way: The Autobiography of James Weldon Johnson* (New York: Viking, 1933; reprinted, Viking Penguin, 1990).

————, *Complete Poems*, ed. by Sondra K. Wilson (New York: Penguin Books, 2000).

————, ed., *God's Trombones: Seven Negro Sermons in Verse* (New York: Viking, 1927; reprinted, Viking Penguin, 1990).

Eugene Levy, *James Weldon Johnson: Black Leaders, Black Voice* (Chicago: University of Chicago Press, 1973).

Kenneth M. Price, and Lawrence J. Oliver, eds., *Critical Essays on James Weldon Johnson, Critical Essays on American Literature* (New York; London: G. K. Hall; Prentice Hall International, 1997).

⌐ **9** ⌐

Black Workers in the Great Depression

During the depths of the Great Depression nearly half of all African Americans in the labor force was unemployed. The NAACP was slow to respond to the crisis of black labor, and more radical black perspectives from the Communist Party as well as trade unions were gaining greater influence in the African-American community.

Abram L. Harris (1899–1963) earned his Ph.D. in economics from Columbia University in 1930, and was once cited as "the quintessential expert on alternative approaches in economics" during his era. In his early career, Harris professed a deep interest in Marxist thought and paid a good deal of attention to working-class struggles. After his appointment as a professor at the University of Chicago in 1946, however, Harris began to distance himself from his early involvement with leftist politics.

⌐

THE NEGRO WORKER: A PROBLEM OF PROGRESSIVE LABOR ACTION

The task of progressive labor action is the organization of those workers who have been neglected by traditional trade unionism; the rehabilitation of unionism in those industries where it has petered out or failed to establish control because of lethargic and self-satisfied leadership which refuses to recognize the inadequacy of craft unionism in such highly integrated and mechanized industries as packing, steel, rubber and automobiles; the stimulation of an offensive against the open shop, company union, employee welfare capitalism of the trustified industries; and weaning labor of subservience to the two major political parties in order to create independent working-class political action. None of these purposes can be accomplished without first creating a greater degree of solidarity than now exists among the workers.

The two great obstacles to labor solidarity are the psychology of craft unionism and the psychology of race prejudice. White workers both organized and unorganized have sought time and again to prohibit the employment of Negro workers, or to limit it to menial occupations or to those jobs that offered little direct competition. They have tried to reduce Negro labor to a class of non-competitors. The employers although not free from race antipathy themselves have not hesitated to exploit it as a means of carrying out a policy of *Divide and rule*. Thus during the early period of capitalistic development in steel, packing, coal and shipping, the employers used Negro labor only spasmodically, in case of a strike, or in a period of industrial expansion when the supply of foreign labor was insufficient to meet the emergency, or because foreign labor had learned the necessity of unionization. Between 1880 and 1915 southern Negro labor was something of an industrial reserve for many basic industries. This reserve was not chiefly agricultural as is often thought. Its background was agricultural but in the eighties Negroes began to move gradually from the rural sections to the cities of the South, thence to northern industrial centers as occasion warranted.

In 1915 huge waves of this southern Negro labor poured in to northern industries when large numbers of our recent immigrants returned to their former homes to answer the call to arms. More of this labor drifted north when the United States entered the war in response to the demand created by industrial expansion. And after the war it continued to come because of the cessation of foreign immigration, and because employers, traditionally hostile to the employment of Negroes awoke to their value in breaking strikes or in defeating the purposes of unionism. And Negro workers undisciplined in collective bargaining, ignorant of trade union traditions, distrustful of white workers especially when organized, and led by opportunist leaders nurtured upon philanthropy and the doles of the rich, not only accepted struck jobs with impunity, but accepted the employer's terms as to wages and working conditions, chief of which was non-membership in trade unions, as a long denied opportunity for the mitigation of economic thraldom.

These changes of Negro labor from south to north, from domestic and small industrial employment to capitalistic industry occasioned much bitterness between Negro and white workers, as was exhibited in the Chicago and East St. Louis race riots. But one wonders why astute trade union leaders had not foreseen in the sporadic employment of Negro strike-breakers in the early industrial development, the uses to which they might be put at some later time. For example, the once militant but now almost shattered United Mine Workers saw that their ability to control the northern coal fields was dependent upon the degree to which organization was affected among both white and black miners in the southern fields. Although the union failed to accomplish its aim, it recognized the necessity of organizing both white and black miners inasmuch as Negro mine labor was not only employed in West Virginia, Alabama, Kentucky and Tennessee but had a long history dating back to the 80s in the breaking of strikes in Illinois, Pennsylvania and Ohio. Had similar strategy been employed by other unions, it is not at all unlikely that at least the seeds of working-class solidarity would have been sown among Negro and white masses before the exodus to the north.

The fact that Negro labor was chiefly unskilled meant that it had no place in a labor movement that was based upon skilled craftsmanship, despite the fact that it could be used, thanks to the increasing mechanization of heavy industries, to defeat the purposes of unionism. This applies with almost equal force to the organization of the unskilled white workers. Such unions as the machinists, the boilermakers, the blacksmiths, the molders, the plumbers, the sheet metal workers, and the tile workers were never too friendly to their less skilled brother, the white helper. As a matter of fact these unions for a long time opposed the admission of the white helper and sought to confirm his status in order to preserve their monopoly of the job. Some of these unions that were most bitter to the white helper were likewise hostile to the Negro. They sought to forestall Negro competition by excluding Negro mechanics from the union. So clauses were written to that effect in the union's constitution or ritual. And many unions like the carpenters, the bricklayers, the confectionery workers, and the hotel workers, that had no constitutional barriers against Negro membership and that felt keen competition from the traditional employment of Negroes, were forced to organize them into segregated locals; or leave them out of the union as the leaders of the molders did in Nashville, Tennessee, because the white molders objected to the organization of the Negro and because the Negroes were afraid of being discharged once they had joined the union.

Today there were not less than 26 unions whose constitutions or rituals limit membership to white men. They are the Brotherhood of Railway Carmen, the Switchmen of North America, the Brotherhood of Railway and Steamship Clerks and Freight Handlers, the Order of Sleeping Car Conductors, the Order of Railway Telegraphers, the National Organization of Masters, Mates and Pilots of North America, the Railway Mail Association, the Wire Weavers Protective Association, the Commercial Telegraphers, the Boilermakers, Iron Shipbuilders and Helpers Union, the International Association of Machinists, the Brotherhood of Dining Car Conductors, the Order of Railway Expressmen, the American Federation of Express Workers, the American Federation of Railroad Workers, the Brotherhood of Railroad Station Employees and Clerks, the Train Dispatchers, the Railroad Yard Masters of America, the Neptune Association, the Brotherhood of Locomotive Engineers, the Brotherhood of Railway Conductors, the Brotherhood of Locomotive Firemen and Enginemen, and the Brotherhood of Railroad Trainmen.

Ten of the above unions are affiliated with the American Federation of Labor, which has appealed to them to lower the barriers to Negro admission. Those unions that have responded were forced to do so because of increasing Negro competition. But their response has usually taken the form of separate organization characterized by one or all of the following discriminations: Negroes are to be organized into auxiliary locals but only where their employment has become traditional; the auxiliary locals of Negro members are to be subordinate to the nearest white local; Negro members may not transfer to white locals; they are not eligible for office; they may not be promoted to skilled work; or they are represented in conventions or conferences only by white members. This is the kind of response that the Carmen, and the Blacksmiths made to the appeals of the Federation.

The Boilermakers have not as yet decided how they will respond. But in deference to the sacrosanct doctrine of trade autonomy, the Federation officials accepted these half-measures as something of a victory, which firmly established the Federation's claim of organizing all workers regardless of race. At one time the Executive Council was decidedly opposed to the affiliation of unions that openly debarred Negro workers. This attitude delayed the admission of the Machinists. And it has been said that it was also a factor in the Federation's refusal to accept one of the railroad brotherhoods. But the Machinists were admitted and without relinquishing the right to debar Negroes of the craft.

The Federation sought to circumvent the racial discrimination of its affiliated bodies by empowering the Executive Council to charter directly local and federal unions of Negro workers who are debarred from the union of their craft, or who are unskilled and, therefore, unorganizable into craft unions. This moral gesture has not materially improved Negro organization or increased Negro trade union affiliation.

In the first place the responsibility for the members of a Negro local obtaining the prevailing wage is liable to fall upon the very union that denies them admission; and the Federation which is the "international" of such Negro locals, as it has been claimed surely cannot force a local of a national or international union to handle the wage grievances of one of its directly chartered Negro locals. In the second place these locals of Negro workers usually become dues paying entities that are separated from the main currents of the trade union world. In the third place the leaders of the Federation have been very well satisfied with meager results to vigorously push organization among Negroes. And in the fourth place when persons inside and outside of the Federation have called attention to the weakness of its Negro organizational policy, it has merely passed resolutions, or congratulated itself that it could find no fault with its past methods and results. Yet of the hundreds of Negro locals and federal unions organized by the Federation between 1917 and 1924, there are not more than 22 at present.

Instead of merely passing resolutions expressing a desire to see more Negroes in the labor movement, as it did at its recent and previous conventions, the Federation should inquire into the reasons for its past ineffectiveness among the unorganized white and black workers. It should seek to establish some definitive machinery for bringing about greater cooperation among Negroes and whites in the labor movement. A part of such machinery should certainly have been incorporated in its program of workers' education long ago. A proposal of this kind emanated from one of the conventions of the National Association for the Advancement of Colored People a few years back but failed to provoke any response from the A. F. of L. leaders.

To effect a rapprochement between white and black labor is, of course, no simple task. But what the leadership of organized labor needs to be censured for is not its failure to effect greater harmony but its refusal to make some attempt toward a realistic understanding of the problem and the issues involved. If progressives in their turn are to make headway in bringing Negro and white workers into closer alignment for economic and political action they must first understand the difficulties and prepare to remove them. This is what conventional trade unionism has failed to do.

The known Negro trade union membership was about 45,000 in 1926. If the membership of the independent Negro unions, chiefly paper unions, are included the total membership was about 56,000. According to the census for 1930 there were almost 1,300,000 Negroes employed in transportation, extraction of minerals and manufacturing. So Negro workers, including those above ten years of age, were about 4.3 per cent organized. But only 20.8 per cent of all American wage-earners, excluding agricultural workers, are trade union members. The Negro is only about a fifth as well organized as all workers. When skill is made a prerequisite for trade union affiliation, less than 16.6 per cent of the 825,000 Negroes employed in manufacturing industries are available for affiliation, since 68 per cent of them were unskilled and 15.5 per cent semi-skilled.

Moreover those industries where trade unionism is weakest having capitulated to the offensive of welfare capitalism, or where craft unionism can make little headway because of integration and specialization have the greatest number of Negro workers. For example, in iron and steel there were 106,000 unskilled and 24,000 semi-skilled Negroes in 1920; in the food industries, mainly packing, there were 28,000 unskilled and 16,000 semi-skilled; in textiles, there were 18,000 unskilled and 8,000 semi-skilled; in lumber and furniture, 107,000 unskilled; and in tobacco 20,000 semi-skilled and 21,000 unskilled Negroes. A labor movement which avoids the unpleasant job of going into these industries because the workers have manifested no desire for organization or because organization will take time and money, is both timid and reactionary, and will become the victim of its own inertia. It is the task of progressives to precipitate action among the workers in these industries. And effective action cannot ignore the position of Negro labor if for no other reason than that organized white labor is fully protected only when Negro and white workers are equally organized. That there are obstacles in the way of unity between white and black labor, progressives need not deny, but they should deny that these obstacles are insuperable.

This denial should not take the form of the radicals' stock-in-trade generalization about the solidarity of economic interest between white and black workers. It should be embodied in intelligent appraisals of situations where Negroes and whites are being brought or have been brought into industrial relationship. In such situations it would develop upon progessives to show white and black workers how race prejudice defeats their mutual welfare.

In this connection special mention may be made of the situation in the South. It is the opinion of certain white workers there that "the two races should have separate, distinct labor organizations connected by central bodies composed of representatives of both races." It has been remarked that this "is an advance over the short-sighted, opportunistic policy which is still in vogue in most white labor circles," namely, that of excluding negro workers from unions altogether or at any rate being indifferent to the needs of this group.

It will have to be borne in mind that there are dangers connected with anything which may lead to the development of a bi-racial movement. White employers are not actuated by racial interests. They will not hesitate to use white labor versus black, and vice-versa. "Certainly in the long run white and black labor cannot rise to the highest position in the economic order apart from each other." Nevertheless, vague, fine-sounding idealistic phrases are not helpful in solving the problem. We emphasize that intelligent appraisals of concrete situations where Negroes and whites are being brought into industrial relationship are essential.

But this is not all. The sympathy of groups of Negro workers who can lead the masses of their fellows must be won. To do this progressives will have to begin from the bottom and build up. They must carry to the Negro workers some understanding of modern industrialism and the position of the worker under it, remembering that the Negro is of recent industrial experience. Finally, progressives must realize that Negro economic and political leadership is opportunistic and petty bourgeois. On the political side it teaches the masses that their national interest is best protected by the Republican party; and that in local political matters they should follow the policy of rewarding their friends and punishing their enemies. Being economically weak the Negro like all such classes has looked to legislation for the removal of the social and economic disadvantages from which he suffers. A labor party which would connect the Negro's special racial demands with its broader economic and social reforms can in time wean large sections of the Negro workers from the major parties. On the economic side, the Negro masses have been taught that their welfare is best promoted by adopting a conciliatory attitude to those who control industrial and economic opportunity, through subservience to the wealthy and through the establishment of a sort of self-sufficient Negro petty capitalism.

Here the progressives must show the Negro masses that their problem like that of the white masses, is inevitably that of work and wages. For even if the Negro leaders who look upon the creation of Negro financial and business enterprise as the economic salvation of the Negro masses, are successful in realizing their ideal, the institutions that they hope to establish are to be run on the basis of economic individualism and private profit, despite the tendency of these leaders to confuse "racial cooperation in business" with genuine consumers' cooperation. The success of a Negro petty capitalism will merely give economic reality to our contemporary Negro bourgeoisie which is temperamentally detached from the realities of working-class life. But however successful Negro business enterprise may be, and whether it proceeds on a quasi-self-sufficient racial basis or takes its chances for survival in the general competitive arena, it must in the nature of things remain a diminutive force in modern industrialism, which is to say, that its much heralded power for mitigating the stress of Negro unemployment will be inconsequential. The great masses of Negro workers will continue to find their employment with those who now control finance and industry. And the few Negroes who will obtain work at the hands of the black capitalists of the tomorrow will not thereby cease to be wage-earners. Their problem will merely be shifted from the center of modern economic life where white capitalists dominate to the margin where small Negro enterprisers eke out the wages of management.

Thus progressives carry to the Negro masses some realization of the causes of unemployment, low wages, and the need for labor unionism and cooperation, in general; and of the reasons that explain the special severity of industrial disadvantage upon them as a racial group, in particular. But none of these lessons will take root if they are presented spasmodically and, above all, if white workers are unwilling to accept Negroes into working-class fellowship. As great as these difficulties may seem, a policy of letting well enough alone or procrastination will never overcome them. Progressives will therefore do well to begin to grapple with them now.

Source: "The Negro Worker: A Problem of Progressive Labor Action," *Crisis* 37, no. 3 (March 1930), pp. 83–85. The editors wish to thank the Crisis Publishing Co., Inc., the publisher of the magazine of the National Association for the Advancement of Colored People, for the use of the material from *The Crisis*.

SELECT BIBLIOGRAPHY:

Eric Arnesen, *Brotherhoods of Color: Black Railroad Workers and the Struggle for Equality* (Cambridge: Harvard University Press, 2001).

Robert Biles, *The South and the New Deal* (Lexington: University Press of Kentucky, 1994).

Philip Sheldon Foner, *History of the Labor Movement in the United States*, 10 vols. (New York: International Publishers, 1975).

Keith P. Griffler, "The Black Radical Intellectual and the Black Worker the Emergence of a Program for Black Labor, 1918–1938" (Ph.D. diss., Ohio State University, 1993).

Abram L. Harris, *The Negro Worker: A Problem of Vital Concern to the Entire Labor Movement*, Pamphlet No. 3, Progressive Labor Library (New York: Conference for Progressive Labor Action, 1930).

———, *The Social Philosophy of Karl Marx* (Chicago: University of Chicago Press, 1948).

———, *Race, Radicalism and Reform: Selected Papers, Abram L. Harris*, ed. William Darity, Jr. (New Brunswick, N.J.: Transaction Publishers, 1989).

Abram L. Harris and Sterling Shapiro, *The Black Worker: The Negro and the Labor Movement* (New York: Columbia University Press, 1931).

⤚ 10 ⤚

The Scottsboro Trials, *1930s*

The Scottsboro case became an international scandal in the early 1930s, when nine African Americans (some of whom were children) from Scottsboro, Alabama, were charged with raping a white woman on a freight train. Yet both contemporary observers and historians have found that these charges were fraudulent and that there was little possibility the "Scottsboro boys" might receive a fair trial in Alabama's racist, Jim Crow courts. In 1931, eight of the defendants were found guilty and sentenced to death.

The case received attention from various civil rights organizations and the American Communist Party, and appeals on behalf of the Scottsboro boys were twice presented before the U.S. Supreme Court. In 1932, the high court set aside their convictions on grounds that they did not have adequate counsel. Subsequently, two of the original defendants were tried and convicted again. In 1935 the Supreme Court overturned these convictions as well, ruling that African Americans had been arbitrarily excluded from Alabama's jury pools. Thus, in addition to exposing the injustice of Alabama's courts, the Scottsboro case also helped establish important legal precedents for African Americans. However, it was not until the 1950s that all of the Scottsboro boys were freed.

Scottsboro Boys Appeal from Death Cells
to the Toilers of the World

From the death cells in Kilby Prison, where they have been held under conditions of the most ghastly torture ever since the mock trials in the lower court at Scottsboro, Ala., the eight Scottsboro boys send the following appeal to the workers of the whole world to rally to the mass fight to smash the hideous frame-up and lynch murder verdicts:

From the death cell here in Kilby Prison, eight of us Scottsboro boys is writing this to you.

We have been sentenced to die for something we ain't never done. Us poor boys been sentenced to burn up on the electric chair for the reason that we is workers—and the color of our skin is black. We like any one of you workers is none of us older than 20. Two of us is 14 and one is 13 years old.

What we guilty of? Nothing but being out of a job. Nothing but looking for work. Our kinfolk was starving for food. We wanted to help them out. So we hopped a freight—just like any one of you workers might a done—to go down to Mobile to hunt work. We was taken off the train by a mob and framed up on rape charges.

At the trial they give us in Scottsboro we could hear the crowds yelling, "Lynch the Niggers." We could see them toting those big shotguns. Call 'at a fair trial?

And while we lay here in jail, the boss-man make us watch 'em burning up other Negroes on the electric chair. "This is what you'll get," they say to us.

What for? We ain't done nothing to be in here at all. All we done was to look for a job. Anyone of you might have done the same thing—and got framed up on the same charge just like we did.

Only ones helped us down here been the International Labor Defense and the League of Struggle for Negro Rights. We don't put no faith in the National Association for the Advancement of Colored People. They give some of us boys eats to go against the other boys who talked for the I.L.D. But we wouldn't split. Nohow. We know our friends and our enemies.

Working class boys, we asks you to save us from being burnt on the electric chair. We's only poor working class boys whose skin is black. We shouldn't die for that.

We hear about working people holding meetings for us all over the world. We asks for more big meetings. It'll take a lot of big meetings to help the I.L.D. and the L.S.N.R to save us from the boss-man down here.

Help us boys. We ain't done nothing wrong. We are only workers like you are. Only our skin is black.

(Signed) Andy Wright, Olen Montgomery, Ozie Powell, Charlie Weems, Clarence Norris, Haywood Patterson, Eugene Williams, Willie Robertson.

Source: "Scottsboro Boys Appeal from Death Cells to the Toilers of the World," originally published in *The Negro Worker* 2, no. 5 (May 1932), pp. 8–9.

SELECT BIBLIOGRAPHY:

Dan T. Carter, *Scottsboro: A Tragedy of the American South* (Baton Rouge: Louisiana State University Press, 1979).

Gabriel J. Chin, "A White Woman's Word: The Scottsboro Case (1931)," in *Race on Trial: Law and Justice in American History*, ed. by Annette Gordon-Reed (Oxford: Oxford University Press, 2002).

James E. Goodman, *Stories of Scottsboro* (New York: Pantheon Books, 1994).

Kwando M. Kinshasa, *The Man from Scottsboro: Clarence Norris and the Infamous 1931 Alabama Rape Trial, in His Own Words* (Jefferson; London: McFarland, 2003).

Clarence Norris and Sybil Washington, *The Last of the Scottsboro Boys: An Autobiography* (New York: Putnam, 1979).

Lita Sorensen, *The Scottsboro Boys Trial: A Primary Source Account*, 1st ed. (New York: Rosen Pub. Group, 2004).

⌁ 11 ⌁

"You Cannot Kill the Working Class," *Angelo Herndon, 1933*

Angelo Herndon (1913–) was an African-American Communist organizer who, after working on behalf of poor and unemployed blacks and whites in Atlanta, Georgia, was charged with "insurrection" in 1932. In his defense, Herndon spoke directly to the all-white jury and, though he was found guilty, the jurors recommended mercy. Still, the court sentenced Herndon to eighteen to twenty years in prison. However, Herndon was finally released in 1936, after his case drew international attention.

⌁

ANGELO HERNDON'S SPEECH TO THE JURY, JANUARY 17, 1933

Gentlemen of the Jury: I would like to explain in detail the nature of my case and the reason why I was locked up. I recall back about the middle of June 1932, when the Relief Agencies of the City of Atlanta, the County Commission and the city government as a whole, were cutting both Negro and white workers off relief.

We all know that there were citizens who suffered from unemployment. There were hundreds and thousands of Negroes and whites who were each day looking for work, but in those days there was no work to be found.

The Unemployment Council, which has connection with the Unemployed Committees of the United States, after 23,000 families had been dropped from the relief rolls, started to organize the Negro and white workers of Atlanta on the same basis, because we know that their interests are the same. The Unemployment Council understood that in order to get relief, both races would have to organize together and forget about the question whether those born with a white skin are "superior" and those born with a black skin are "inferior." They both were starving and the capitalist class would continue to use this weapon to keep them further divided. The policy of the Unemployment Council is to organize Negroes and whites together on the basis of fighting for unemployment relief and unemployment insurance at the expense of the state. The Unemployment Council of Atlanta issued those leaflets after the relief had been cut off, which meant starvation for thousands of people here in Atlanta. The leaflets called upon the Negro and white workers to attend a meeting at the court house building on a Thursday morning. I forget the exact date. This action was initiated as the result of statements handed out to the local press by County Commissioners who said that there was nobody in the City of Atlanta starving, and if there were, those in need should come to the offices of the Commissioners and the matter would be looked into. That statement was made by Commissioner Hendrix.

The Unemployment Council pointed out in its circulars that there were thousands of unemployed workers in the City of Atlanta who faced hunger and starvation. Therefore, they were called upon to demonstrate in this court house building, about the middle part of June. When the Committee came down to the court house, it so happened that Commissioner Hendrix was not present that morning. There were unemployed white women with their babies almost naked and without shoes to go on their feet, and there were also Negro women with their little babies actually starving for the need of proper nourishment, which had been denied them by the county of Fulton and State of Georgia and City of Atlanta as well.

Well, the Negro and white workers came down to the Commissioners' office to show that there was starvation in the City of Atlanta and that they were in actual need of food and proper nourishment for their kids, which they never did receive. I think Commissioner Stewart was in the office at that time. The white workers were taken into his room and the Negroes had the door shut in their faces. This was done with the hope of creating racial animosity in order that they would be able to block the fight that the Negro and white workers were carrying on—a determined fight to get relief. The white workers were told: "Well, the county hasn't any money, and of course, you realize the depression and all that but we haven't got the money." We knew that the county did have money, but were using it for their own interest, and not for the interest of the Negro workers or white workers, either way. They talked to the white workers some considerable time, but when the white workers came out, they had just about as much results as the Negroes did—only a lot of hot air blown over them by the Commissioners, which didn't put any shoes on their little babies' feet and no milk in their stomachs to give them proper nourishment. No one disputed the fact they did keep the Negroes on the outside, but the white workers were in the same condition that their Negro brothers were in. In spite of the fact that the County Commissioners had published statements to the effect that there was no money in the county treasury to provide unemployment relief for the Negro and white workers, still the next day after the demonstration the County Commissioners voted $6,000 for relief, mainly because it was shown that for the first time in the history of Atlanta and the State of Georgia, Negro and white workers did join together and did go to the Commissioners and demand unemployment insurance. Have not they worked in the City of Atlanta, in different industries, different shops and other industrial concerns located in Atlanta for all their years, doing this work, building up the city where it is at the present time? And now, when they were in actual need of food to hold their bodies together, and when they came before the state and county officials to demand something to hold their bodies together, they were denied it. The policy of the Unemployment Council is to organize these workers and demand those things that are denied them. They have worked as slaves, and are entitled to a decent living standard. And, of course, the workers will get it if you ever organize them.

After the successful demonstration, the solicitor's office had two detectives stationed at the post office to arrest anyone who came to take mail out of box 339. On Monday, July 11, 1932, I went to the post office to get mail from this box and was arrested by detectives, Mr. Watson and Mr. Chester. I had organized unemployed workers, Negro and white, of Atlanta, and forced the County Commissioners to kick in $6,000 for unemployment relief. For this I was locked up in the station house and held eleven days without even any kind of charges booked against me. I was told at the station house that I was being held on "suspicion." Of course, they knew what the charges were going to be, but in order to hold me in jail and give me the dirtiest kind of inhuman treatment that one could describe, they held me there eleven days without any charge whatsoever until my attorney filed a writ of habeas corpus demanding that they place charges against me or turn me loose. It was about the 22nd of July, and I still hadn't been indicted; there had been three sessions of the grand jury, and my case had been up before them each time, but still there was no indictment. This was a deliberate plot to hold me in jail. At the habeas corpus hearing, the judge ordered that if I wasn't indicted by the next day by 2:30, I should be released. Solicitor Hudson assured the judge that there would be an indictment, which, of course, there was. Ever since then I have been cooped up in Fulton County Tower, where I have spent close to six months—I think the exact time was five months and three weeks. . . .

They knew that the workers of Atlanta were starving, and by arresting Angelo Herndon on a charge of attempting to incite insurrection the unity of Negro and white workers that was displayed in the demonstration that forced the County

Commissioners to kick in with $6,000 would be crushed forever. They locked Angelo Herndon up on such charges. But I can say this quite clearly, if the State of Georgia and the City of Atlanta think that by locking up Angelo Herndon, the question of unemployment will be solved, I say you are deadly wrong. If you really want to do anything about the case, you must go out and indict the social system. I am sure that if you would do this, Angelo Herndon would not be on trial here today, but those who are really guilty of insurrection would be here in my stead. But this you will not do, for your role is to defend the system under which the toiling masses are robbed and oppressed. There are thousands of Negro and white workers who, because of unemployment and hunger, are organizing. If the state wants to break up this organization, it cannot do it by arresting people and placing them on trial for insurrection, insurrection laws will not fill empty stomachs. Give the people bread. The officials knew then that the workers were in need of relief, and they know now that the workers are going to organize and get relief. . . .

[I]t is to the interest of the capitalist class that the workers be kept down all of the time so they can make as much profit as they possibly can. So, on the other hand, it is to the interest of Negro and white workers to get as much for their work as they can—that is, if they happen to have any work. Unfortunately, at the present time there are millions of workers in the United States without work, and the capitalist class, the state government, city government and all other governments, have taken no steps to provide relief for those unemployed. And it seems that this question is left up to the Negro and white workers to solve, and they will solve it by organizing and demanding the right to live, a right that they are entitled to. They have built up this country, and are therefore entitled to some of the things that they have produced. Not only are they entitled to such things, but it is their right to demand them. . . .

EXCERPTS FROM *YOU CANNOT KILL THE WORKING CLASS*

They say that once a miner, always a miner. I don't know if that's so, but I do know that my father never followed any other trade. His sons never doubted that they would go down into the mines as soon as they got old enough. The wail of the mine whistle morning and night, and the sight of my father coming home with his lunch-pail, grimy from the day's coating of coal-dust, seemed a natural and eternal part of our lives.

Almost every working-class family, especially in those days, nursed the idea that one of its members, anyway, would get out of the factory, and wear clean clothes all the time and sit at a desk. My family was no exception. They hoped that I would be the one to leave the working-class. They were ready to make almost any sacrifices to send me through high-school and college. They were sure that if a fellow worked hard and had intelligence and grit, he wouldn't have to be a worker all his life.

I haven't seen my mother or most of my family for a long time—but I wonder what they think of that idea now!

My father died of miner's pneumonia when I was very small, and left my mother with a big family to care for. Besides myself, there were six other boys and two girls. We all did what we could. Mother went out to do housework for rich white folks. An older brother got a job in the steel mills. I did odd jobs, working in stores, running errands, for $2 and $3 a week. They still had the idea they could scrimp and save and send me through college. But when I was 13, we saw it wouldn't work.

So one fine morning in 1926, my brother Leo and I started off for Lexington, KY. It was just across the border, and it had mines, and we were miner's kids.

A few miles outside of Lexington, we were taken on at a small mine owned by the powerful DeBardeleben Coal Corporation. . . .

One day the company put up a notice that due to large overhead expenses, they would have to cut our pay from 42 to 31 cents a ton. We were sore as hell. But there wasn't any union in the mine, and practically none of us had any experience at organization, and though we grumbled plenty we didn't take any action. We were disgusted, and some of us quit. Whites and Negroes both.

I was one of those who quit. My contact with unions, and with organization, and the Communist Party, and unity between black and white miners—all that was still in the future. The pay-cut and the rotten conditions got my goat, and I walked off, because as yet I didn't know of anything else to do. . . .

I wish I could remember the exact date when I first attended a meeting of the Unemployment Council, and met up with a couple of members of the Commun¬ist Party. That date means a lot more to me than my birthday, or any other day in my life.

The workers in the South, mostly deprived of reading-matter, have developed a wonderful grapevine system for transmitting news. It was over this grapevine that we first heard that there were "reds" in town.

The foremen—when they talked about it—and the newspapers, and the bigshot Negroes in Birmingham, said that the "reds" were foreigners, and Yankees, and believed in killing people, and would get us in a lot of trouble. But out of all the talk I got a few ideas clear about the Reds. They believed in organizing and sticking together. They believed that we didn't have to have bosses on our backs. They believed that Negroes ought to have equal rights with whites. It all sounded O.K. to me. But I didn't meet any of the Reds for a long time.

One day in June, 1930, walking home from work, I came across some handbills put out by the Unemployment Council in Birmingham. They said: "Would you rather fight—or starve?" They called on the workers to come to a mass meeting at 3 o'clock.

Somehow I never thought of missing that meeting. I said to myself over and over: "It's war! It's war! And I might as well get into it right now!" I got to the meeting while a white fellow was speaking. I didn't get everything he said, but this much hit me and stuck with me: that the workers could only get things by fighting for them, and that the Negro and white workers had to stick together to get results. The speaker described the conditions of the Negroes in Birmingham, and I kept saying to myself: "That's it." Then a Negro spoke from the same platform, and somehow I knew that this was what I'd been looking for all my life.

At the end of the meeting I went up and gave my name. From that day to this, every minute of my life has been tied up with the workers' movement.

I joined the Unemployment Council, and some weeks later the Communist Party. I read all the literature of the movement that I could get my hands on, and began to see my way more clearly.

. . . The Unemployment Council opened a fight for cash relief, and aid for single men, and equal relief for Negro and white. They called for a meeting in Capitol Park, and we gathered about the Confederate Monument, about 500 of us, white and Negro, and then we marched on the Community Chest headquarters. There were about 100 cops there. The officials of the Community Chest spoke, and said that the best thing for the Negroes to do was to go back to the farms. They tried very hard to give the white workers there the idea that if the Negroes went back to the farms, the whites would get a lot more relief.

Of course our leaders pointed out that the small farmers and share-croppers and tenants on the cotton-lands around Birmingham were starving, and losing their land and stock, and hundreds were drifting into the city in the hope of getting work.

Then Oscar Adams spoke up. He was the editor of the Birmingham Reporter, a Negro paper. What he said opened my eyes—but not in the way he expected. He said we shouldn't be misled by the leaders of the Unemployment Council, that we should go politely to the white bosses and officials and ask them for what they wanted, and do as they said.

Adams said: "We Negroes don't want social equality." I was furious. I said inside of myself: "Oscar Adams, we Negroes want social and every other kind of equality. There's no reason on God's green earth why we should be satisfied with anything less."

That was the end of any ideas I had that the big-shots among the recognized Negro leaders would fight for us, or really put up any struggle for equal rights. I knew that Oscar Adams and the people like him were among our worst enemies, especially dangerous because they work from inside our ranks and a lot of us get the idea that they are with us and of us.

I look back over what I've written about those days since I picked up the leaflet of the Unemployment Council, and wonder if I've really said what I mean. I don't know if I can get across to you the feeling that came over me whenever I went to a meeting of the Council, or of the Communist Party, and heard their speakers and read their leaflets. All my life I'd been sweated and stepped on and Jim-Crowed. I lay on my belly in the mines for a few dollars a week, and saw my pay stolen and slashed, and my buddies killed. I lived in the worst section of town, and rode behind the "Colored" signs on streetcars, as though there was something disgusting about me. I heard myself called "nigger" and "darky," and I had to say "Yes, sir" to every white man, whether he had my respect or not.

I had always detested it, but I had never known that anything could be done about it. And here, all of a sudden, I had found organizations in which Negroes and whites sat together, and worked together, and knew no difference of race or color. Here were organizations that weren't scared to come out for equality for the Negro people, and for the rights of the workers. The Jim-Crow system, the wage-slave system, weren't everlasting after all! . . .

We organized a number of block committees of the Unemployment Councils, and got rent and relief for a large number of families. We agitated endlessly for unemployment insurance.

In the middle of June, 1932, the state closed down all the relief stations. A drive was organized to send all the jobless to the farms.

We gave out leaflets calling for a mass demonstration at the courthouse to demand that the relief be continued. About 1000 workers came, 600 of them white. We told the commissioners we didn't intend to starve. We reminded them that $800,000 had been collected in the Community Chest drive. The commissioners said there wasn't a cent to be had.

But the very next day the commission voted $6,000 for relief to the jobless!

On the night of July 11, I went to the Post Office to get my mail. I felt myself grabbed from behind and turned to see a police officer.

I was placed in a cell, and was shown a large electric chair, and told to spill everything I knew about the movement. I refused to talk, and was held incommunicado for eleven days. Finally I smuggled out a letter through another prisoner, and the International Labor Defense got on the job.

Assistant Solicitor John Hudson rigged up the charge against me. . . .

The trial was set for January 16, 1933. The state of Georgia displayed the literature that had been taken from my room, and read passages of it to the jury. They questioned me in great detail. Did I believe that the bosses and government ought to pay insurance to unemployed workers? That Negroes should have complete equality with white people? Did I believe in the demand for the self-determination of the Black Belt—that the Negro people should be allowed to rule the Black Belt territory, kicking out the white landlords and government officials? Did I feel that the working-class could run the mills and mines and government? That it wasn't necessary to have bosses at all?

I told them I believed all of that—and more. . . .

The state held that my membership in the Communist Party, my possession of Communist literature, was enough to send me to the electric chair. They said to the jury: "Stamp this damnable thing out now with a conviction that will automatically carry with it a penalty of electrocution."

And the hand-picked lily-white jury responded:

"We, the jury, find the defendant guilty as charged, but recommend that mercy be shown and fix his sentence at from 18 to 20 years."

I had organized starving workers to demand bread, and I was sentenced to live out my years on the chain-gang for it. But I knew that the movement itself would not stop. I spoke to the court and said:

"They can hold this Angelo Herndon and hundreds of others, but it will never stop these demonstrations on the part of Negro and white workers who demand a decent place to live in and proper food for their kids to eat."

I said: "You may do what you will with Angelo Herndon. You may indict him. You may put him in jail. But there will come thousands of Angelo Herndons. If you really want to do anything about the case, you must go out and indict the social system. But this you will not do, for your role is to defend the system under which the toiling masses are robbed and oppressed.

"You may succeed in killing one, two, even a score of working-class organizers. But you cannot kill the working class." . . .

Sources: (1) Angelo Herndon's Speech to the Jury, January 17, 1933; and (2) excerpt from Angelo Herndon, *You Cannot Kill the Working Class* (New York: International Labor Defense and League of Struggle for Negro Rights, 1937–?).

SELECT BIBLIOGRAPHY:

F. T. Griffiths, "Ralph Ellison, Richard Wright, and the Case of Angelo Herndon," *African American Review* 35, no. 4 (Winter 2001), pp. 615–36.

Elizabeth Lawson, *Twenty Years on the Chain Gang? Angelo Herndon Must Go Free* (New York: International Labor Defense, 1935).

Charles H. Martin, *The Angelo Herndon Case and Southern Justice* (Baton Rouge: Louisiana State University Press, 1976).

———, "Communists and Blacks: The ILD and the Angelo Herndon Case," *Journal of Negro History* 64, no. 2 (Spring 1979), pp. 131–41.

⥤ 12 ⥤

Hosea Hudson, Black Communist Activist

Hosea Hudson (1889–1988) was born in rural Wilkes County, Georgia, and he joined the Communist Party in 1931 in the wake of the Scottsboro and Camp Hill cases. In 1932 his political affiliations caused him to be fired from his job as an iron molder. Hudson subsequently worked on the Works Progress Administration (WPA), served as vice president of the Birmingham and Jefferson County locals of the Workers Alliance, was president of Steel Local 2815, and vice president of the Alabama Political Education Association. Hudson used several aliases and often worked underground, especially during the 1950s when he was a Communist organizer in the South. In 1971 he visited the Soviet Union for the first time. Hudson's moving account of his lifelong involvement in the Communist movement is presented in *Black Worker in the Deep South* (1972), and in Nell Irvin Painter's 1979 book, *The Narrative of Hosea Hudson*.

⥤

I found this Party, a party of the working class, gave me rights equal with all others regardless of color, sex, or age or educational standards. I with my uneducation could express myself, without being made fun of by others who could read well and fast, using big words. I was treated with high respect. I had a right to help make the policy. At every convention, maybe some policy question would change at the convention and we have a discussion from the floor. After a thorough discussion, decisions are arrived at by majority vote. Then all members, including those who disagree, are duty bound to explain, fight for, and carry out such decisions. When that decision is made, everybody got to fall into line.

I've been to many Party conventions. The first one I went to was an extraordinary plenary session called in New York by Earl Browder. That was in 1933, the 4th of July. That was the first time I got out of the South.

We left at night on a Monday, left out of Birmingham in a old piece of car, went over to Atlanta, me and Don and the rest of them. They taken me in the car from Birmingham to Atlanta. When we all got to Atlanta, we put down their car and we all got in Ben Davis' car and pulled out for New York. We went up with Ben Davis. That was the first time I met him. Ben Davis was in Atlanta, he was then involved in the Angelo Herndon case. We drove to New York from Atlanta. I don't know what model of Ford it was, but 'twas seven of us packed up in that Ford. All the way from Atlanta to New York City. It was *hot!* That was the worst trip I ever had in my life. Seven people, seven grown people—wont no children in the crowd—it was seven people. 'twas three Negroes: me, Ben, and Al Murphy. We went up in the front seat together. In the back seat was the D.O. of the time, Don, and his wife, and another guy from Texas name of Lee, and another guy name of Ted Mebber. All four of them was white. Now you know that was some ride. . . .

I didn't get to know Ben Davis too much on the trip. We's going up, riding. I know he was a lawyer, and I felt at that time that he was superior. I wasn't used to being around that kind of people, Negro lawyers. And everybody was talking. Him and Al Murphy, they done a lot of discussing about everything, the country and the conditions. Ben Davis was a friendly guy, he was friendly to me, but he was driving the car, and Murphy sitting between me and him. I'm over on the side and the whites back here talking. Everybody talking and riding, try to keep encouragement. I was just listening, because at that time my development was very low, practically zero. I wont doing no talking.

We went on, got to New York, and we all got off. Some went in different places. Ben didn't go to that extraordinary plenary session. He didn't attend Party conferences. I presume, I never did know, I never questioned, but I presume he was up there to discuss with Patterson and them something about the ILD and the Herndon case in Atlanta, and also the Scottsboro case, which he wasn't involved in, but he did play a part in the Scottsboro case in Alabama.

That was the first big conference, first big meeting of the Party I was in. They had fraternal delegates at that particular meeting. They were there from Chile, and they had fraternal delegates there from Germany. The guy that Hitler killed— I can't think of his name right now—but he was the leader of the Party and Hitler killed him.[1] His name was very familiar with me. He was at that meeting. He spoke. About four or five fraternal delegates was there. I didn't meet them personally, I just was there when they spoke. It was a lot being said I didn't understand. I was still in the learning stage. I was just sitting quiet, listening. Some I understood what they said, and some I didn't.

After the meeting was over, it was a Negro woman there at the convention from North Carolina, and she was living in a big housing project there in New York, call it the Coop. I forgotten her name. She taken me on the trolley down to the waterfront down on Broadway, we rid all the way down there. It was real cold. It was on July 4th, and it was cold enough to have on a overcoat. It was real chilly like the fall of the year. I seen a big ship there with peep holes and they was playing the music and everybody around right there at the water. That was the first time I seen ships.

I didn't see Ben anymore until we got ready to come back to Atlanta, and we all came back in the car together. Murphy stayed in New York, but all the whites came back. Lee sat in the front with us coming back, so it was still a question of I was looking for some one to stop us. It wasn't worse, though, cause Lee was smaller than Murphy was and it wasn't quite as tight up. . . .

The coal miners and the ore miners was the first ones begin to organize in the NRA days. I never did know the whole thing, but in that period, the NRA, it was something worked out between John L. Lewis and Roosevelt, I think. That's my thinking. And whatever the agreement was, when they come out with the NRA, John L. Lewis came out organizing the coal miners.

We began to build the Party among the coal miners and the ore miners when they began to reorganize their UMW locals. Many of the miners were living in Birmingham, particularly the Negroes. We had some big struggles.

The bosses had all the coal mine communities guarded. They had deputy sheriffs in the coal mine areas. We didn't call them deputy sheriffs, we called them company dicks. Now out there in that Sareyton mine, out in North Birmingham, the guy out there, his name was Self. If a guy would be sick and he wouldn't go in to work, Self would go around "shack rousting." He go around, knock on those doors, see who all at home, who all in, who all out. If someone didn't go to work, Self want to know what's wrong. He'd tell the Negroes, "By God, if you ain't sick, when I get through with you, you will be sick." He was the shack rouster hisself, called hisself deputy sheriff of the company. Any stranger going in the mine quarters, especially through the week days, would be questioned, stopped and questioned by the company dicks. . . .

In Birmingham in the month of November of '33, we Party members call a meeting of workers from some of the mines and steel plants and iron foundries one Sunday afternoon, to organize a committee to begin to build rank and file committees in some of the coal and ore mine union locals around Birmingham and Bessemer. What these committees was doing was bombarding some of the unions, the top leaders, calling for industrial unions, *industrial* unions.[2] Because our Party position was the onliest way you going to get out of this present oppression, you got to organize the industrial unions and organize the unorganized workers, organize the Negro. The Negro hadn't been organized in unions before.

They was all lily white unions. They wouldn't take Negroes in. This meeting, we had planned to hold it in the old Negro Penny Saving Bank, down on 2nd Avenue and somewhere between 15th or 16th Street. (Since that time this bank been torn down.)

Some of us had just began to go into that hall and arrange the chairs, early waiting for the other workers to come. Only nine of us had got into that hall, four white and five Negroes. A young white worker, Ward Turner, was to chair that meeting. Ted Welbaum, a young white YCL member from New York, was there with us and two other white workers. (That was the whites.) Then Joe Howard, myself, Homer Martin, and Sol Norman, and another young Negro coal miner by the name of Mosley was there. Mosley and I went down on the next floor below our floor, the third floor, to the men's room. When we got to the second floor, we found city detective Mosley, the head of the Red Squad, and three other police standing down there questioning the Negro who was in charge of that building. The young coal miner Mosley just kept walking on down to the ground floor, right past that group of officers, and I turn around and went back up to our hall and told the rest of the boys that was up there that the police was down on the floor below, asking that Negro a lots of rough questions.

Ward Turner told everybody to get them a seat and sit down, and we sat down in the different places in the hall. Turner took his seat at the table where the chairman was to sit at. After a while, all of that bunch of police began to rush up the stairway, headed for our hall. Detective Mosley walk over to Turner and asked him what kind of meeting is that. Turner told him that this is a Socialist Party meeting. Mosley pick up all of the notes of paper that Turner had on the table and told all of us to get out of this hall. We all headed down to the ground floor. When we got down to the door at the sidewalk, the police had backed a paddy wagon up to the curb and form themselves into a line from that door to that police wagon. And we all walk right straight into that police wagon from that building.

As we were hauled away from that hall we could see several of our people standing on the corner who was headed to the meeting. But by the police hurrying into that hall to break up that meeting as they did, they saved many of those workers their jobs.

The police took us eight to the southside jail and lodged us Negroes there in a cell with other Negroes that was in there for that Sunday night. We didn't know what was going to happen to us, cause it had been the custom when they arrest any of the members of the ILD or the Party to take them out after a certain time of night—so we were told—and whip them. We didn't know whether they was going to whip us or not. We were just there. So I didn't throw my clothes off all that night. I just laid on the bunk, on the old bunk they had there, in my clothes. That was Sunday night.

The next morning the four white workers who was placed in a different cell and all us Negroes was hauled down to the city hall separate and placed into a different room and mugged one by one. Our pictures was taken and we was fingerprinted. They kept all four there until late that afternoon. Then they put us in what they call the "bull pen" where all the misdemeanors was, like you arrested for drunk or something like that. Not no bad crime. Everybody put out here in one big old place together. You sit around, sit on bunks, anywhere you can find. Ain't none of them decent, but you ain't got no particular place to sleep, just bunk up and do the best you can on the cots. That was where I seed a crap game for the first time in my life. A old man there had some dice and playing craps for a penny. He'd take them dice and work his hand around and shake them and "crack, crack, crack!" and throw them dice. When he throw them and the dice turn up, every time they turn up, he'd hit. He was a real dice shooter. He was a old man. We just set there and looked at him.

Didn't nobody bother me, nobody asked anybody what they was there for. We four, me, Sol, Homer Martin, and Joe Howard, we four was together. And quite naturally we sit around together, but we didn't talk. We always was told not to do no talking in jail, cause you never know when the walls are bugged or not, so we didn't talk about none of our affairs. They kept us there till Tuesday.

Now Sol, they tried to hold Sol for a while, cause Sol when they first arrest him, they asked him what his name was, he wouldn't tell them what his name. Old Detective Mosley hit Sol in the face around his eye. He had a red, very bad bruised face. I didn't see him when he got hit. All I seen was afterwards, and he had a big bloody place on the side of his face and his eye was all bloodshot.

Tuesday they taken us back for trial, put us in separate cells, except me and Homer Martin in a cell to ourselves. I don't know what time they had Joe Howard or the white guys' trial.

I had heard that whenever we was arrested that we were not to ever plead guilty when we went before a judge. I had told Homer Martin that we were not to plead guilty when we were asked by the judge. We was all lined up in a long line of Negroes. Some of them had been picked up by the police for drunk that Saturday afternoon. As they march up, they were asked the question by the judge, "You are charge of being drunk, are you guilty or not guilty?"

In most cases these Negroes would say, "Guilty, Judge."

And the judge would say, "$13 or 13 days." Most of them would be led off by the police to jail to begin serve that 13 days.

When Homer Martin and I got up before him, I was in the front of Homer. We were told what our charges was—that was meeting to overthrow the government. "Are you guilty or not guilty?"

I said, "Not guilty, Judge."

He said to me, "Stand aside."

Homer Martin told him the same thing, and he was told to stand aside. We were finally taken back into a room and the door was locked. And we sat there all the rest of that afternoon until just about night, from early that morning without any water or food. Finally they call us out and took us back to the southside jail, and then we were given water and some of that lousy black-eyed peas and hard cornbread with all of the corn husks and other filth in it. But we had to eat it because that was all that we could get until the next morning.

About 1 o'clock Wednesday the key-boy come to the bull pen and call us and told us to get ready, we were wanted down at the warden's desk. We walked out and we all walk down to the desk sergeant. He had a great big double forehead, a great big wide double forehead and smoked a pipe. I guess he might of been a Irishman, he had big feet. (He was called to be the good police among the Negroes there in Birmingham after that time. They said, "He's a good man, that boy, he's a good man." The Negroes called him nice cause when he caught them in their misdemeanors, he'd give them a little break.) This sergeant told the key-boy to unlock the outside iron gate and he said to us four Negroes: "You God damn niggers get out of that gate and get out of town. You damn Reds better not be caught in Birmingham any more. If you do, it will not be good for you."[3] We all walked out and went to our various homes. (Joe Howard passed from this life in Birmingham some time in 1939. I stayed there and built steel local 2815. Homer Martin passed there in 1974.)

Sol Norman left Birmingham. I heard that he went back to Selma, Alabama. That was his home, down Selma. He worked with the sharecroppers union, but something happen to him there in around '35. Down in 19 and 65 I was talking to some people and they was around the area of Selma the time of that terror in 1935. It was a husband and wife, and the husband said they had some rough times down there, "but down in our part, where we live, they didn't never come down there and bother us cause we was so well organized together till they was afraid to try and come in there to mess with us. We was just too hot for them down there." The deputy sheriffs and the Ku Klux and them didn't come in there, but it was up in some other place where they was terrorizing and beating and arresting Negroes. Negroes was coming up missing.

Then I was talking to a preacher in 1953, Reverend Rivers (he's dead now). This preacher was a pastor down there in Selma at that time, and 'twas a white man, a merchant, had a blacksmith shop. He took this preacher out in his yard and showed him eight or nine things that was made out of concrete that looked like bears standing up. They had a solid bottom, and the top was a lid, was a piece of sheet iron with a lock on it, to lock it. They was just the size enough to put a man in.

Reverend Rivers kept asking this white man, talking like a preacher, said, "Boss, what is this? I just like this thing. This is a pretty, pretty thing. I just like to have one of them."

The white man said, "No, Reverend, you don't want that. That's for these people that won't listen at you and won't listen at us. That's made for these kind of people."

Reverend Rivers, he said it made him so sick that he went home and went to bed, had to have a doctor. He could just see all these people he knowed done come up missing, and they done put them in them concrete things and dropped them in the Alabama River. And he couldn't tell nobody. So when he got able, when he got well enough to move out, he left there and come to Birmingham. His wife said, "I bet you that's what happened to Willie Foster." He was one of the local leaders of the ILD there in Birmingham, and they sent him down there to see about some arrests. He never did come back. "They about put him in them barrels and dropped him in the river, cause he turn up missing and we never did hear from him."

We didn't never know what happened to Sol Norman to know the truth about it. It was hard to say if he left out of there or not, because we none of us at that time used our regular names when we went to a new different place. He might of left and used a new name someplace else. Or they might of put him in one of them concrete barrels Reverend Rivers was looking at. . . .

Notes: 1. Ernest Thaelmann. 2. All the unions was craft unions. 3. That was what he had to say to us Negroes knowing that we was considered to be Reds. He showed his real colors with us.

Source: Excerpts, reprinted by permission of the publisher, from *The Narrative of Hosea Hudson: His Life as a Negro Communist in the South*, edited by Neil Irvin Painter (Cambridge, Mass.: Harvard University Press, 1979). Copyright 1979 by the President and Fellows of Harvard College.

SELECT BIBLIOGRAPHY:

Hosea Hudson, *Black Worker in the Deep South: A Personal Record* (New York: International Publishers, 1972).
Robin D.G. Kelley, *Hammer and Hoe: Alabama Communists during the Great Depression* (Chapel Hill: University of North Carolina Press, 1990).
Nell Irvin Painter, *Southern History across the Color Line* (Chapel Hill: University of North Carolina Press, 2002).
Mark Solomon, *The Cry Was Unity: Communists and African Americans, 1917–1936* (Jackson: University Press of Mississippi, 1999).

〜 13 〜

"Breaking the Bars to Brotherhood," *Mary McLeod Bethune, 1935*

Mary McLeod Bethune (1875–1955) was one of seventeen children born to exslave parents in South Carolina. She worked as a teacher in her early adult life and in 1904 founded the Daytona Normal and Industrial School. In 1920 Bethune was elected vice president of the National Urban League. She was active for many years in the National Association of Colored Women, and was elected as its president in 1924. Bethune came to national prominence, however, during the Great Depression. She was the leading African-American figure within the administration of Franklin D. Roosevelt, serving as the director of the Negro Division of the National Youth Administration. In 1935 she was given the NAACP's Springarn Award, and in that same year was named president of the newly formed National

Council of Negro Women. Bethune was an adviser to the U.S. delegation at the 1945 founding conference of the United Nations in San Francisco.

Mr. Chairman, My Fellow Citizens, Members and Officers of the National Association for the Advancement of Colored People: There is a great happiness in my heart tonight—not a selfish, personal happiness, but a happiness and satisfaction that come to one who has labored in the heat of the day for the common good, and now as the shadows of life begin to lengthen comes to receive a "Well Done," a signal of recognition of one's life work. And with this happiness comes a humble gratitude for the distinguished approval of this organization dedicated to the cause of social justice and human welfare. To be worthy of being included in the illustrious group of Spingarn medalists, who by their intelligence, courage, devotion, faith and work have helped to shape and build a better world, one must respond to the stimulus of this occasion with a spirit of rededication to service, of reconsecration to the needs of the people. This spirit of rededication and reconsecration permeates me now as I stand before you.

The National Association for the Advancement of Colored People has for the past twenty-six years accepted the challenge of the times and has ventured forth upon its task, high endeavor for human understanding, and the world has responded to this endeavor. I seem to hear this call, coming from the pioneers of this great movement:

> Come, Clear the way; then, clear the way.
> Blind kings and creeds have had their day.
> Break the dead branches from the path.
> Our hope is in the aftermath.
> Our hope is in heroic man.
> Star-led to build the world again.
> To this event all ages ran;
> Make way for brotherhood;
> Make way for man.

This dauntless organization has spent its efforts almost wholly in clearing the way for a race, in breaking dead branches from the paths of liberty and the pursuit of happiness. The success of the early clearers of the way is but an indication of what is yet to be done by those who follow in their train. The dead branches hewn away by those stalwart pioneers left plain and straight the highway which the youths are travelling. That way brought us hope. That is the song which the past has taught us. Now we keep faith with that hope to sing the song which the present challenges.

If I have merited the honor of receiving the Spingarn medal, it is because my life has been dedicated to the task of breaking the bars to brotherhood. Brotherhood is not an ideal. It is but a state or a condition attendant upon achievement of an ideal. It is one of the components of an ideal. I believe that brotherhood depends upon and follows achievement. In the light of this belief, I wish to indicate and develop briefly those fundamental principles and issues involved in bringing about a state of brotherhood.

The law of life is the law of cooperation, and unless we learn thoroughly this fundamental tenet of social organization I fear that the historian of the future, when he attempts to record the history of the black man in America, will write "a people possessed of tremendous possibilities, potentialities and resources, mental and physical, but a people unable to capitalize [on] them because of their racial non-cohesiveness." If we would make way for social and political justice and a larger brotherhood, we must cooperate. Racial cohesion means making a road of all of the achievements of those who have educational advantages until we reach the lowest man, the lowest strata of the masses; that mass that is standing so helplessly waiting for you and for me to administer the human touch.

Unless the people have vision, they perish. What can we see; and, having seen, are we willing to venture? Do we see our large opportunity for the race to produce? Do we see an intellectual interpretation of our religious thought unhampered by superstitious belief, or limited by too great a satisfaction? Do we see the brotherhood of the peoples of the world working out an abundant life in their activities, of duty, of art, of business, of every day living?

The National Association for the Advancement of Colored People has always sought men of vision to lead the way. Today we pray for the expansion of that vision from a few to an ever increasing group of prepared men and women and of youths of all races to guide and direct the mass. The veil of ignorance and superstition is not yet lifted. Broad vision, zeal and preparedness will do much to lift it. Social group understanding and appreciation are necessary to brotherhood. The dead branches of misunderstanding and lack of appreciation have kept our existence clouded with prejudice. Human understanding is the key to brotherhood. The march of racial advancement is continually hindered by misunderstanding. Misunderstandings clutter up the highways of life which make for true harmonious relations.

But right must triumph and prejudice must be done away with. In this staunch belief, men and women of this organization continue to struggle toward the goal of social justice and to strive for worthy and proper consideration for every man in his right to live, to be, to do, to possess, and to pursue happiness. Now is the time for thinking men and women, for thinking youths of every race, to stand up with those who have labored for years and be counted, in their participation in this great forward march of the National Association for the Advancement of Colored People. No greater crime can there be than that one in which a man should be unfair to his neighbor and interferes with his right to develop harmonious relationships and realize the highest attainment of his abilities. The great unrest in the world today, the great doubts which assail men, the enormous amount of mistrust entangles our lives and makes us look askance at our brothers, all are the products of injustice, wrought by one man upon another.

Equality of opportunity is necessary to brotherhood. We stand in adoration of those who, regardless of the section of the country in which they live, have been big enough, courageous enough, to stand for social justice and equality of opportunity, even at the risk of their lives. The National Association for the Advancement of Colored People has proven the necessity for breaking the bars to brotherhood through their advocacy of the destruction of blind kings and creeds which have been rulers in the lives of humanity. The creeds of selfishness, self-centered ideas, have led to narrow leadership. The creed of over-ambition and self domination has led to unfair publicity. Let us cease to give allegiance to such unmoral kinship in our lives. Above all, let us cease now to render allegiance to the creed of belief in the inherent superiority of white and the inherent inferiority of black. Let us rest with confidence on the creed of larger development in our narrow selves; greater scope of opportunity to work out our ambitions; sure and certain belief in all convictions which are ours; and towering over all, our belief in becoming free men.

The creed of freedom has not yet been written. Humanity is yet a slave to her desires, her fears, her intelligence, her social standing, her craving for power. Let us as workers under this banner make free men spread truth about economic adjustment; truth about moral obligation; truth about segregation; truth about citizenship; truth about home building; yes, truth wherever truth is needed. Then our lives may be lived with freedom and we shall be what ourselves demand us to be.

Who shall disseminate this truth? I would call tonight upon those who are startled, who have clearly in mind a purpose in life; who do not fear the struggle and the work which must needs be the lot of those who dare to live above the cloud of popular thought and limited desires.

My fellow citizens, in the light of this dream, in the light of this firm hope, in the belief that brotherhood is the desired end in life, in accordance with God's plan, and with a rededication to share in the responsibility of rebuilding and inspiring vision, to keep faith with the ideals and purposes of the National Association for the Advancement of Colored People, I, in the name of the womanhood of America, accept this medal. I accept it with gratitude for the opportunity for God-given service. I accept it as a badge which will mark me before all men as an advocate of respect and justice for all mankind. The brightness which we saw so many years ago has become a light, a star. May we challenge ourselves anew and follow in its radiance, ever thoughtful, ever courageous, ever enduring, in molding lives with highest principles. And may those who follow after us gain inspiration because we dare to stand at a time like this.

Mr. Chairman, my fellow citizens, I am grateful.

Source: Excerpts from speech located in the Mary McLeod Bethune Papers, Amistad Research Center, Tulane University, New Orleans.

SELECT BIBLIOGRAPHY:

Mary McLeod Bethune, *Mary McLeod Bethune: Building a Better World: Essays and Selected Documents*, ed. by Audrey T. McCluskey and Elaine M. Smith (Bloomington: Indiana University Press, 1999).

Bettye Collier-Thomas, *N.C.N.W., 1935–1980* (Washington, D.C.: National Council of Negro Women, 1981).

Paula Giddings, *When and Where I Enter: The Impact of Black Women and Sex in America* (New York: William Morrow, 1984).

Eloise Greenfield, *Mary McLeod Bethune* (New York: Crowell, 1977).

Joyce Ann Hanson, *Mary McLeod Bethune & Black Women's Political Activism* (Columbia: University of Missouri Press, 2003).

———, "The Ties that Bind: Mary McLeod Bethune and the Political Mobilization of African-American Women" (Ph.D. dissertation, University of Connecticut, 1997).

Nancy Ann Zrinyi Long, *The Life and Legacy of Mary McLeod Bethune* (Boston: Pearson Custom Pub., 2006).

Elaine Smith, "Mary McLeod Bethune and the National Youth Administration," in *Clio Was a Woman: Studies in the History of American Women*, ed. Mabel E. Deutrich and Virginia C. Purdy (Washington, D.C.: Howard University Press, 1980).

⌐ 14 ⌐

Adam Clayton Powell, Jr., and the Fight for Black Employment in Harlem

Adam Clayton Powell, Jr. (1908–1972) was raised in New York City. He earned his bachelor's degree at Colgate University, and completed advanced studies at the Union Theological Seminary and Columbia University. During the Great Depression, Powell emerged as an important protest figure in Harlem, leading "don't buy where you can't work" campaigns against white-owned businesses. In 1937, Powell assumed his father's post as minister of Harlem's Abyssinian Baptist Church, where he quickly became an influential voice on behalf of civil rights. Powell's flamboyant style and confrontational rhetoric attracted a popular following within the national black community. Serving in Congress for a quarter century, Powell helped to pass major educational and civil rights legislation. Toward the end of Powell's career, his mishandling of public funds and long absences from Congress eroded his base of support in Harlem. Narrowly defeated by Charles Rangel for Harlem's congressional seat, Powell retired in 1970 and died two years later.

⌐

THE FIGHT FOR JOBS

The Coordinating Committee for Employment is beginning a serious business in Harlem. It is beginning a fight for jobs. It has asked for work. It has pleaded for work. It has held work conferences. It has utilized every means at its disposal to get the employers of New York City to stop starving the Negroes of New York. These means have failed.

The Committee is now inaugurating a mass boycott and picketing of every enterprise in Greater New York that refuses to employ Negroes. The Gas and Electric Company has seen the light, the telephone company must also. The big department stores must follow suit. If Negroes can work at Ovington's, Wanamaker's, Macy's and Bloomingdale's, then an appreciable percentage must work at Gimbel's, Klein's, Hearn's, Saks and other stores.

The milk companies are next. No more subterfuges, no more passing the buck, but black faces must appear on Harlem milk wagons immediately or the milk concerns shall be boycotted.

Three hundred and fifty thousand consumers are not anything to be sneezed at and if anyone dares try to sneeze, we are killing him with the worst cold he ever had. The same thing goes for the Metropolitan Life. As long as we have Negro insurance companies there is no reason why Negroes should pay one cent to any other insurance company that refuses to employ Negroes.

PLATFORM FOR JOB CAMPAIGN

1. AIMS: To provide a greater measure of employment for Negro workers in the institutions and establishments which are sustained by the purchasing power of the Negro.

2. All jobs obtained must provide for a standard living wage equal to that prevailing at the time of employment.

3. Wherever Negroes obtain jobs and union conditions prevail, the Negro workers must be, or must become members of the established union.

4. Workers are to be hired on the qualifying standards set by the employer.

5. Applicants for employment shall not be confined to any organization, or individual.

6. Employment of Negroes outside of the Harlem area must not be sacrificed for any possible local increases.

7. Any increase in employment of Negroes in Harlem must be accomplished without the victimization of white for black workers.

8. The Harlem Job Committee shall charge no fee or in any way exact profit of any kind from any employer or employee.

9. In pursuance of the above objectives the Committee will secure and utilize the cooperation and support of all responsible institutions and organizations in Harlem.

10. The Harlem Job Committee will cooperate with those employers recognizing the justice of the Committee's objectives. The Committee will, however, utilize every legal and recognized means to obtain its aims, in cases where employers either fail or are unwilling to cooperate.

Sources: "Soap Box," *Amsterdam News*, May 7, 1938; and "Platform for Job Campaign," *Amsterdam News*, May 14, 1938.

S E L E C T   B I B L I O G R A P H Y :

Charles V. Hamilton, *Adam Clayton Powell, Jr.: The Political Biography of an American Dilemma* (New York: Atheneum, 1991).

Wil Haygood, *King of the Cats: The Life and Times of Adam Clayton Powell, Jr.* (New York: Amistad, 2006).

Neil Hickey and Ed Edwin, *Adam Clayton Powell and the Politics of Race* (New York: Fleet Publishing, 1965).

Adam Clayton Powell, Jr., *The Autobiography of Adam Clayton Powell, Jr.* (New York: Dial Press, 1971).

⌒ 15 ⌒

Black Women Workers during the Great Depression

Throughout the Great Depression, African-American women typically had to work full time and often faced discrimination, poor pay, and oppressive labor conditions. The documents below illustrate the views of black women who worked during this era.

⌒

WOMEN OF THE COTTON FIELDS, ELAINE ELLIS

Another cotton-picking season has opened in the South. On the farms and plantations, tenants and croppers are harvesting the gleaming white crop with the hope that this year they will get enough from their share to live through the winter. In the cities, the relief agencies are following their annual custom of commanding thousands of undernourished families to go to the cotton fields and pick for what they can get, or starve.

Scenes showing pickers at work in these fields can be secured on post-cards throughout the South. Chambers of Commerce and other civic bodies use such pictures quite often in pamphlets which invite the summer tourist to visit Dixie and learn something about the picturesque region that formed the background for "My Old Kentucky Home" and other folk songs that will never be forgotten. The average tourist will drive through some of these states, visit a few capitols, shake hands with a few governors if he gets a chance to see any, and return home. The cotton fields will cease to be of much interest, for he will have seen too many of them.

Tourists are not told by the big-shot advertising agencies that these cotton fields tell the story of what Norman Thomas calls "probably the most depressed body of workers in America." The men, women, and little children who work in these fields under the blazing Southern sun create the great Cotton Kingdom for which this region is famed. In return for their labor, they receive only poverty, ignorance, and disease.

And it is the woman, Negro and white, on whom the burden is heaviest. In every cotton field one can see her type—a stooped woman dragging a heavy cotton sack. Usually she wears a slatted sunbonnet, and her arms and neck are swathed with rags to protect them from the blistering heat.

This is the woman whom civilization has passed by. But it is from her loins, no less than from the earth itself, that the world's greatest cotton industry has sprung. A slave, and a breeder of slaves, hundreds of thousands of her kind have been crushed in its gigantic and merciless machinery. And as long as the tenant system continues, she must be sacrificed to its greed.

In the past, this woman was compelled to reproduce a large number of children because a large labor supply was in demand. Large families also mean a cheaper form of labor; for children, as well as women, generally represent labor that does not have to be paid. Consequently, the "overhead" falls upon the family instead of the landlord. The landlord himself has enforced this monopoly by letting his farm go to the tenant or cropper having the largest family.

Now the tenant-croppers are charged with "over-population" by economists and agriculturists who disregard the unwholesome economic factors that have caused an increase in farm tenancy. This increase has amounted to 60 percent since 1930 despite the fact that the A.A.A. drove approximately 300,000 tenants and sharecroppers from the land.

As one solution to this "over-population," proponents of the sterilization racket are endeavoring to work up an agitation for sterilization of these cotton workers. The now ex-governor of Arkansas, J. M. Futrell, and H. L. Mencken, the writer, have expressed themselves highly in favor of such a measure. Sterilization, one of the tenets of Fascism, makes women its chief victim. One can readily visualize its vicious application as a means of controlling the labor supply.

On the other hand, birth control information has been denied these women, although in some sections of the South there is a plan to introduce it by means of traveling clinics. Now that there is a surplus labor supply, this method that would be such a boon to women is beginning to be viewed in a most favorable light. But the most simple medical attention is still denied them. Even during pregnancy, a woman must work in the field. The fact that she is carrying a child does not excuse her from dragging and lifting the heavy cotton sack. Frequently, when the child is born, she does not have the assistance of a physician. Women in the neighborhood, or a midwife, must help her through her confinement. Very often she does not have even this inadequate aid. It is a common occurrence for a woman who is pregnant to pick cotton until the labor pangs strike her. She may be able to drag herself to the shade of a tree, or to the wagon or car, to give birth to her child. But sometimes it is born among the cotton plants. After it is a few weeks old, it will be taken by its mother to the field. There it will sleep on a pallet with brothers and sisters too young to pick. As soon as it is old enough to carry a sack, it, too, will go into the field.

The mother, in addition to working in the home field, will "hire out" to a neighboring landlord as soon as this crop is harvested. In addition, she has the upkeep of the house, and further outside work. Her hours average from about twelve to fourteen a day, each being one of extreme toil.

There is an equally bad situation existing for young girls. Many have their health ruined for life because they are forced to drag and lift the heavy cotton sacks during puberty. While the landlords' daughters attend universities and join sororities, these daughters of the croppers help to pay the cost of their dinner dances, rush weeks, and dissipations.

In the lives of these illiterate farm women, there is mute evidence of a capacity for creation. During planting time, they will sow the seeds of zinnias along the outer cotton rows. After the day's drudgery, which ends late at night with the housework, they will return with buckets of water for the seeds. Often one of these women can be seen standing idle for a moment during the busiest part of the day to gaze across the even rows to where gaily colored zinnias flame among the white cotton. And the change in her is miraculous. This woman is suddenly straight and clear-eyed, and pushing back her bonnet, she shades her eyes with her hand as she looks across the field shimmering in waves of heat. But just as suddenly, she will droop, and turn again to her task. The cotton must be picked!

But the women of the cotton fields are awakening. It began back in 1931 when Estelle Milner, a young Negro girl, brought the tenants and sharecroppers of Camp Hill, Alabama, a little paper called *The Southern Worker*. The Organization of the Sharecroppers Union that followed, and the bloody battles of Camp Hill and Reeltown will never be forgotten. In the years that have followed, the Sharecroppers Union, Southern Tenant Farmers Union, and the Farmers Union have organized more than 300,000 tenants and sharecroppers throughout the South.

The bloodshed that planters and deputy sheriffs caused at Camp Hill and Reeltown, when mangled croppers were forced to flee for their lives, marked only the beginning of terrorism that breaks out wherever unions of these workers demand better conditions. But undaunted, they struggle on, frequently chalking up victories to their score.

And the women are standing by their men.

I Am a Domestic, Naomi Ward

They just can't be as bad as they seem to me—these women I have worked for as a domestic. After all, I knew many fine women in various capacities before I was forced, as a penniless widow of forty, to go out to service in order to earn a living for my child and myself.

No, she can't be as bad as she seems, this average woman who hires a maid—so overbearing, so much a slavedriver, so unwilling to grant us even a small measure of human dignity. But I have had three years of experience in at least a dozen households to bear eloquent witness to the contrary.

Of course I am speaking of the average woman. There must be many exceptions. But in my experience the only exception I encountered was a woman whose friends thought her a trifle crazy.

It was true that she employed me by way of astrology—that is, of all the many applicants she figured that my date of birth showed that we would get on well together. I cooked for her one week by astrology and by a color chart the next. That is, our dinner would be entirely purple one day—eggplant, purple cabbage, and beets; and next it would consist of golden corn, yellow squash, carrots, and oranges. And sometimes, poor dear, she would ask me to sit by her bed and talk to her all night to keep her awake because she feared dying in her sleep.

Take this matter of inconsiderateness, of downright selfishness. No other women workers have the slave hours we domestics have. We usually work from twelve to fourteen hours a day, seven days a week, except for our pitiful little "Thursday afternoon off." The workday itself is often nerve-racking. Try broiling a steak to a nice turn in the kitchen while a squalling baby in the next room, in need of a dry diaper, tries to protect himself from his brother, aged two, who insists on experimenting on the baby's nose with a hammer. See how your legs can ache after being on them from 7:00 A.M. until 9:00 P.M., when you are finishing that last mountain of dishes in the pantry! Know how little you care for that swell dinner you cooked when it comes to you, cold, from the table at 8:00 P.M.

Our wages are pitifully small. I doubt if wages for domestics average higher anywhere than in New York City; and here $45 a month is good for a "refined woman, good cook, and fond of children." I often wonder just what they mean by "refined." I remember one woman to whom I applied saying: "Say—Wadda ya mean? Usin' better English 'an I do askin' me fer a job! Git out."

Then there was the old lady in "reduced circumstances" whose sick husband tried to earn a living as a door-to-door salesman. I'm sure she could not afford a maid, even a part time one at $6 a week. She was unhappy, had little to do, and took it out by standing over me at each little task.

One day I was glad to see she had borrowed a book from a lending library. I thought that now, engrossed in her book, she would leave me alone. Unwisely I said: "I see you are reading — —. I read it last year and enjoyed it." Mrs. S— looked at me forbiddingly and merely grunted. Later she followed me to the kitchen and whispered: "Naomi, do you read?" I looked at her bewildered. "Read? Why, of course I read!" Then the point of the question dawned on me. I had to laugh. "You mean, Mrs. S—, do I read instead of getting on with my work when you are out? No, I don't do that."

Then there was the grandma in the household of Southern folk, a fat old lady who would call me away from anything I was doing to help her dress. "Naomi, please fasten my garters—I can't reach," or "Tie my shoes—I hate leaning over!" After I had been in that household a week I found the three-year-old calling me "Naomi Noble" instead of my own name. Grandma explained: "Down South we always call our niggers by our own last name, so here we'll call you 'Naomi Noble.'"

These women are so contradictory. They want someone "good with children"; yet when we turn out to be really good—that is, interested, kindly, and intelligent in our handling of their spoiled offspring—they are likely as not to resent the fact that we have succeeded where they failed. They hate the feeling that a "low" domestic worker can do anything better than they.

It is not only the long hours, the small pay, and the lack of privacy—we often have to share a room with the children—that we maids find hardest to bear. It is being treated most of the time as though we are completely lacking in human dignity and self-respect. During my first year at this work I was continually hopeful. But now I know that when I enter that service elevator I should park my self-respect along with the garbage that clutters it. Self-respect is a luxury I cannot retain and still hold my job. My last one was a good example of this.

As such jobs go, it was a good one. It was "part time." That is, I worked as cook nine instead of the customary twelve to fourteen hours per day. My Sundays were free. My wage was $40 per month, and I "slept out." After my last ride down with the garbage I could hurry home to the furnished room I shared with my schoolgirl daughter. My employer, Mrs. B—, was the wife of a fashionable doctor. And another person worked with me as a chambermaid. She was a little French girl, new in America, and just learning our language. We two got along splendidly.

Mrs. B—'s apartment was huge. But Lucille and I together kept it immaculate. However, no matter how much we scoured and dusted on hands and knees Mrs. B— could always find imaginary dust. "Now Naomi," or "Lucille—you know you're lying when you say you cleaned under that settee!" Mrs. B— was a hypochondriac who drank too much. One day she would be maudlin, the next vindictive. "Now you know I'm no slavedriver and you know there's little work to do around here—why can't you do it well instead of just trying to get by?" Or, "What's happened to all that butter I got yesterday?" The idea being that I had stolen some of it. And I would answer respectfully, minutely accounting for the disposal of the butter. We domestics, whatever our background, are supposed to be natural born thieves. "Lucille! You took my box of candy!"

"No, madame!" with a flash of peasant temper, banging open several bureau drawers, "here is your candy where you yourself put it, madame!"

No apology. Why apologize. We needed our jobs, didn't we?

Mrs. B— was forever giving me orders as to just how many minutes to cook a certain dish—corned beef, for instance! Of course the only way to get around this was to listen respectfully, say: "Yes, Mrs. B—," and then go ahead and cook it as it should be cooked. I had learned early that Mrs. B— would tolerate no discussion on such matters. That was "talking back" or "impudence." She was always talking about a legendary Negro cook she had once had for six, eight, or ten years (the time varied according to the low or high of the whisky bottle) who in all that time had never "answered back."

"Mrs. B— is the one beeg liar," Lucille would whisper at such times. Lucille, by the way, in learning English, had also acquired some fine cusswords. She enjoyed muttering, when Mrs. B— had been especially trying: "Son o' de beech! Son o' de beech!"

Healthy Lucille came down with a heavy cold, and finally, after trying to conceal her misery had to go to bed for three days. Mr. B— berated her soundly for not having told her. The truth was Lucille knew that when I had been sick for two days my pay had been docked, and she feared the same thing happening to her. While she was ill I did her work as well as my own; but there was no extra pay in my envelope at the end of the month.

When Mrs. B— had hired me my hours were to be from noon until after dinner. Dinner was to be at seven. But soon dinner was set ahead to seven-thirty and then to eight. Which meant that I did not get through till nine or ten. Mrs. B— would say: "Now, Naomi, don't rush yourself to have dinner just on the dot—it doesn't matter to us whether it's at eight or eight-thirty. We like to sit around and sip our cocktails."

We dared not say: "But it matters a lot to us whether we finish at eight or ten!"

Lucille and I both met our Waterloo in the following fashion. I had cooked a huge dinner for many guests—we always had company besides the ordinary family of five—and it was 9:00 P.M. before we two sat down to our meal, both too tired to eat.

Suddenly the bell rang furiously and Lucille came back, flushed with anger. "She say to put the cake right on the ice!"

Soon the bell rang again. "Is that cake on the ice?" called out Mrs. B—.

I sang out. "We've just started our dinner, Mrs. B—."

Later I said to Lucille: "Does she think we're horses or dogs that we can eat in five minutes—either a coltie or a Kiltie?" (Kiltie was the dog.) Lucille, who loved such infantile jokes, broke into peals of laughter.

In a second Mrs. B— was at our side, very angry. She had been eavesdropping in the pantry. "I heard every word you said!"

"Well, Mrs. B—, we're *not* horses or dogs, and we *have* been eating only five minutes!"

"You've been a disturbing influence in this house ever since you've been here!" Mrs. B— thundered. "Before you came Lucille thought I was a wonderful woman to work for—and tonight you may take your wages and go. Tomorrow, Lucille, your aunt is to come, and we shall see whether you go too!"

I wanted to tell her what I thought of her, but for Lucille's sake I kept quiet. At last at the door I offered my hand to Lucille, saying: "Here is my address."

"I am not interested!" she cried dramatically, throwing the paper to the floor.

I felt suddenly slapped. But from the pleading look in Lucille's eyes, I understood. Mrs. B— was still in the pantry, and poor Lucille was thinking of her stern French aunt and that she would get no references after ten months' work.

They have us there! For a petty whim they can withhold that precious bit of paper without which it is hard for us to obtain another ticket to slavery. I knew, in my case, I would never get a reference from Mrs. B—. So I did not ask for one, but rode on down for the last time with the garbage.

Jobless, and with only $15 between us and starvation, I still felt a wild sense of joy. For just a few days I should be free and self-respecting!

Sources: (1) Elaine Ellis, "Women of the Cotton Fields," *Crisis* 45 (October 1938), pp. 333, 342, reprinted by permission; and (2) Naomi Ward, "I Am a Domestic," *New Masses* 35 (June 25, 1940), pp. 20–21. The editors wish to thank the Crisis Publishing Co., Inc., the publisher of the magazine of the National Association for the Advancement of Colored People, for the use of the material from *The Crisis*.

SELECT BIBLIOGRAPHY:

Sharon Harley and the Black Women and Work Collective, eds., *Sister Circle: Black Women and Work* (New Brunswick: Rutgers University Press, 2002).

Jacqueline Jones, *Labor of Love, Labor of Sorrow: Black Women, Work, and the Family from Slavery to the Present* (New York: Basic Books, 1985).

Harvard Sitkoff, *A New Deal for Blacks: The Emergence of Civil Rights as a National Issue* (New York: Oxford University Press, 1978).

Leslie M. Swann, "African American Women in the World War II Defense Industry" (Ph.D. diss., Temple University, 2004).

ᵏ 16 ᵏ

Southern Negro Youth Conference, *1939*

Foreshadowing the critical role that African-American students played in the modern civil rights movement, Southern Negro Youth Conferences were held in such places as Virginia, Tennessee, and Alabama in the era before World War II. Participants aimed to promote the economic status of African Americans, improve educational opportunities, and agitate on behalf of civil rights causes.

ᵏ

CALL TO THIRD ALL-SOUTHERN NEGRO YOUTH CONFERENCE

"Hands locked together and with heads erect, we march into the future, fearless and unafraid. We are Americans. We are the hope of our people. We have the right to live." With these words 534 young men and women, assembled in Richmond, Virginia for the First All-Southern Negro Youth Conference, concluded their sessions in February, 1937. These youth then set out to improve the conditions under which they and theirs live and labor.

Since that day in February, 1937, when 534 representatives of Negro youth organizations resolved to join their efforts for the achievement of equal opportunities, the Second All-Southern Negro Youth Conference convened in Chattanooga, Tennessee in April, 1938. We could seek no better time than the present to assess the progress we have made and to memorialize ourselves, our friends and our national representatives, of our plans for moving onward with the task we have begun. For this purpose, we invite the Negro youth of the South, and all who love democracy well, to the Third All-Southern Negro Youth Conference, Birmingham, Alabama, April 28, 29, 30, 1939.

At this conference we will have an opportunity to accomplish certain well-defined objectives:

1. To consider the mutual problems and aspirations of Southern Negro Youth.
   a. Our economic status: the National Youth Administration, the Civilian Conservation Corps, vocational guidance, apprenticeship training, Negro business, labor movement.
   b. Citizenship rights: voting, anti-lynching legislation, the national defense program.
   c. Education: equality in educational opportunities, the content of Negro education, federal aid to education.
   d. The role of religion in the life of Negro youth.
   e. The special problems of rural youth.
   f. The development of a cooperative relationship with Southern white youth.
   g. Peace: the preservation of democracy, protection of the rights of racial and religious minorities at home and abroad.
   h. Special problems: marriage and home life, crime and juvenile delinquency, housing, recreation, health.
2. To provide a medium for cooperative planning and action in meeting our problems.
3. To develop a greater appreciation for the contributions of the Negro to our cultural life, through holding an All-Southern Art Exhibit and a Festival of Music in connection with the conference.

As the Third All Southern Negro Youth Conference convenes, we recall that the history of the past few years has been filled with new currents of progress. We have just begun to estimate the importance of the growing movement of organized labor which marches apace with the rapid industrialization of the South. Its presence where feudal conditions once reigned supreme, gives assurance of a rising standard of living for all working men and women.

In addition, the special attention extended by the national administration has lent great impetus to the sober consideration of the South's problems. Not many weeks ago, the Supreme Court rendered a momentous decision. It held that Lloyd Gaines had an inalienable right, which the State must enforce, to enter the law school of the University of Missouri. What new horizons for winning complete equality in educational opportunities does this decision offer to Southern Negro Youth!

Of great significance as a sign of the times have been the recent efforts of Southerners from all walks of life, to think and work unitedly for the advancement of the South. Such an effort has given rise to the historic Southern Conference for Human Welfare.

The low economic status of our youth constantly reminds us of the urgent need of securing decent living standards. Five boys who languish in jail—the Scottsboro boys—call for our help, and are grim witnesses to the fact that our civil liberties are still to be achieved. The growing incidence of crime and delinquency among our youth; their scant educational play facilities; the presence among us of scores of thousands who toil in penury and degradation as tenant-farmers and share-croppers; the denial of our right to vote and participate in the ordinary affairs of government—these conditions fairly cry out for adequate remedy.

We invite Southern men and women to seek a solution to these problems through participating in the Third All-Southern Negro Youth Conference. The youth are the guardians of tomorrow's world. Let us assemble in Birmingham over the week-end of April 28th. Let us achieve the full blessings of true democracy for ourselves, our people and our nation!

Source: "Call to Third All-Southern Negro Youth Conference," issued in March 1939.

SELECT BIBLIOGRAPHY:

Johnetta Richards, "The Southern Negro Youth Conferences" (Ph.D. diss., University of Cincinnati, 1987).

Earl Smith, "Images and Accomplishments of the Southern Negro Nation Youth Conferences," in Gerald McWorter, ed., *Black Liberation Movement: Papers Presented at 6th National Council for Black Studies Conference* (Urbana: Afro-American Studies and Research Program, University of Illinois, 1983).

➳ 17 ➳

A. Philip Randolph and the Negro March on Washington Movement, 1941

Asa Philip Randolph (1889–1979) had a long and controversial career as a civil rights activist. Born in Florida and educated in New York, Randolph began earning his credentials as a radical labor activist when he helped found the Brotherhood of Sleeping Car Porters in 1925. Later he became influential in trade union politics and was a pioneer of nonviolent direct-action protest tactics. In 1940 he was elected to the National Board of Directors of the NAACP and became its vice president in 1946. In 1955 he was elected vice president of the AFL-CIO.

One of Randolph's most notable achievements involved his work on behalf of the March on Washington Movement of 1941. Randolph objected to anti-black discrimination in defense industries and issued a stirring call for a "thundering march on Washington" that would "shake up white America." When massive African-American support began to grow for the march, President Franklin D. Roosevelt agreed to establish a Fair Employment Practices Committee. In response, the march was called off.

➳

CALL TO THE MARCH

We call upon you to fight for jobs in National Defense.

We call upon you to struggle for the integration of Negroes in the armed forces, such as the Air Corps, Navy, Army and Marine Corps of the Nation.

We call upon you to demonstrate for the abolition of Jim-Crowism in all Government departments and defense employment.

This is an hour of crisis. It is a crisis of democracy. It is a crisis of minority groups. It is a crisis of Negro Americans.

What is this crisis?

To American Negroes, it is the denial of jobs in Government defense projects. It is racial discrimination in Government departments. It is widespread Jim-Crowism in the armed forces of the Nation.

While billions of the taxpayers' money are being spent for war weapons, Negro workers are being turned away from the gates of factories, mines and mills— being flatly told, "NOTHING DOING." Some employers refuse to give Negroes jobs when they are without "union cards," and some unions refuse Negro workers union cards when they are "without jobs."

What shall we do?

What a dilemma!

What a runaround!

What a disgrace!

What a blow below the belt!

'Though dark, doubtful and discouraging, all is not lost, all is not hopeless. 'Though battered and bruised, we are not beaten, broken or bewildered.

Verily, the Negroes' deepest disappointments and direst defeats, their tragic trials and outrageous oppressions in these dreadful days of destruction and disaster to democracy and freedom, and the rights of minority peoples, and the dignity and independence of the human spirit, is the Negroes' greatest opportunity to rise to the highest heights of struggle for freedom and justice in Government, in industry, in labor unions, education, social service, religion and culture.

With faith and confidence of the Negro people in their own power for self-liberation, Negroes can break down the barriers of discrimination against employment in National Defense. Negroes can kill the deadly serpent of race hatred in the Army, Navy, Air and Marine Corps, and smash through and blast the Government, business and labor-union red tape to win the right to equal opportunity in vocational training and re-training in defense employment.

Most important and vital to all, Negroes, by the mobilization and coordination of their mass power, can cause PRESIDENT ROOSEVELT TO ISSUE AN EXECUTIVE ORDER ABOLISHING DISCRIMINATIONS IN ALL GOVERNMENT DEPARTMENTS, ARMY, NAVY, AIR CORPS AND NATIONAL DEFENSE JOBS.

Of course, the task is not easy. In very truth, it is big, tremendous and difficult.

It will cost money.

It will require sacrifice.

It will tax the Negroes' courage, determination and will to struggle. But we can, must and will triumph.

The Negroes' stake in national defense is big. It consists of jobs, thousands of jobs. It may represent millions, yes, hundreds of millions of dollars in wages. It consists of new industrial opportunities and hope. This is worth fighting for.

But to win our stakes, it will require an "all-out," bold and total effort and demonstration of colossal proportions.

Negroes can build a mammoth machine of mass action with a terrific and tremendous driving and striking power that can shatter and crush the evil fortress of race prejudice and hate, if they will only resolve to do so and never stop, until victory comes.

Dear fellow Negro Americans, be not dismayed in these terrible times. You possess power, great power. Our problem is to harness and hitch it up for action on the broadest, daring and most gigantic scale.

In this period of power politics, nothing counts but pressure, more pressure, and still more pressure, through the tactic and strategy of broad, organized, aggressive mass action behind the vital and important issues of the Negro. To this end, we propose that ten thousand Negroes MARCH ON WASHINGTON FOR JOBS IN NATIONAL DEFENSE AND EQUAL INTEGRATION IN THE FIGHTING FORCES OF THE UNITED STATES.

An "all-out" thundering march on Washington, ending in a monster and huge demonstration at Lincoln's Monument will shake up white America.

It will shake up official Washington.

It will give encouragement to our white friends to fight all the harder by our side, with us, for our righteous cause.

It will gain respect for the Negro people.

It will create a new sense of self-respect among Negroes.

But what of national unity?

We believe in national unity which recognizes equal opportunity of black and white citizens to jobs in national defense and the armed forces, and in all other institutions and endeavors in America. We condemn all dictatorships, Fascist, Nazi and Communist. We are loyal, patriotic Americans, all.

But, if American democracy will not defend its defenders; if American democracy will not protect its protectors; if American democracy will not give jobs to its toilers because of race or color; if American democracy will not insure equality of opportunity, freedom and justice to its citizens, black and white, it is a hollow mockery and belies the principles for which it is supposed to stand.

To the hard, difficult and trying problem of securing equal participation in national defense, we summon all Negro Americans to march on Washington. We summon Negro Americans to form committees in various cities to recruit and register marchers and raise funds through the sale of buttons and other legitimate means for the expenses of marchers to Washington by buses, train, private automobiles, trucks, and on foot.

We summon Negro Americans to stage marches on their City Halls and Councils in their respective cities and urge them to memorialize the President to issue an executive order to abolish discrimination in the Government and national defense.

However, we sternly counsel against violence and ill-considered and intemperate action and the abuse of power. Mass power, like physical power, when misdirected is more harmful than helpful.

We summon you to mass action that is orderly and lawful, but aggressive and militant, for justice, equality and freedom.

Crispus Attucks marched and died as a martyr for American independence. Nat Turner, Denmark Vesey, Gabriel Prosser, Harriet Tubman and Frederick Douglass fought, bled and died for the emancipation of Negro slaves and the preservation of American democracy.

Abraham Lincoln, in times of the grave emergency of the Civil War, issued the Proclamation of Emancipation for the freedom of Negro slaves and the preservation of American democracy.

Today, we call upon President Roosevelt, a great humanitarian and idealist, to follow in the footsteps of his noble and illustrious predecessor and take the second decisive step in this world and national emergency and free American Negro citizens of the stigma, humiliation and insult of discrimination and Jim-Crowism in Government departments and national defense.

The Federal Government cannot with clear conscience call upon private industry and labor unions to abolish discrimination based upon race and color as long as it practices discrimination itself against Negro Americans.

WHY SHOULD WE MARCH?

Though I have found no Negroes who want to see the United Nations lose this war, I have found many who, before the war ends, want to see the stuffing knocked out of white supremacy and of empire over subject peoples. American Negroes, involved as we are in the general issues of the conflict, are confronted not with a choice but with the challenge both to win democracy for ourselves at home and to help win the war for democracy the world over.

There is no escape from the horns of this dilemma. There ought not to be escape. For if the war for democracy is not won abroad, the fight for democracy cannot be won at home. If this war cannot be won for the white peoples, it will not be won for the darker races.

Conversely, if freedom and equality are not vouchsafed the peoples of color, the war for democracy will not be won. Unless this double-barreled thesis is accepted and applied, the darker races will never wholeheartedly fight for the victory of the United Nations. That is why those familiar with the thinking of the American Negro have sensed his lack of enthusiasm, whether among the educated or uneducated, rich or poor, professional or non-professional, religious or secular, rural or urban, north, south, east or west.

That is why questions are being raised by Negroes in church, labor union and fraternal society; in poolroom, barbershop, schoolroom, hospital, hair-dressing parlor; on college campus, railroad, and bus. One can hear such questions asked as these: What have Negroes to fight for? What's the difference between Hitler and that "cracker" Talmadge of Georgia? Why has a man got to be Jim-Crowed to die for democracy? If you haven't got democracy yourself, how can you carry it to somebody else?

What are the reasons for this state of mind? The answer is: discrimination, segregation, Jim Crow. Witness the navy, the army, the air corps; and also government services at Washington. In many parts of the South, Negroes in Uncle Sam's uniform are being put upon, mobbed, sometimes even shot down by civilian and military police, and on occasion lynched. Vested political interests in race prejudice are so deeply entrenched that to them winning the war against Hitler is secondary to preventing Negroes from winning democracy for themselves. This is worth many divisions to Hitler and Hirohito. While labor, business, and farm are subjected to ceilings and floors and not allowed to carry on as usual, these interests trade in the dangerous business of race hate as usual.

When the defense program began and billions of the taxpayers' money were appropriated for guns, ships, tanks and bombs, Negroes presented themselves for work only to be given the cold shoulder. North as well as South, and despite their qualifications, Negroes were denied skilled employment. Not until their wrath and indignation took the form of a proposed protest march on Washington, scheduled for July 1, 1941, did things begin to move in the form of defense jobs for Negroes. The march was postponed by the timely issuance (June 25, 1941) of the famous Executive Order No. 8802 by President Roosevelt. But this order and the President's Committee on Fair Employment Practice, established thereunder, have as yet only scratched the surface by way of eliminating discriminations on account of race or color in war industry. Both management and labor unions in too many places and in too many ways are still drawing the color line.

It is to meet this situation squarely with direct action that the March on Washington Movement launched its present program of protest mass meetings. Twenty thousand were in attendance at Madison Square Garden, June 16; sixteen thousand in the Coliseum in Chicago, June 26; nine thousand in the City Auditorium of St. Louis, August 14. Meetings of such magnitude were unprecedented among Negroes. The vast throngs were drawn from all walks and levels of Negro life—businessmen, teachers, laundry workers, Pullman porters, waiters, and red caps; preachers, crapshooters, and social workers; jitterbugs and Ph.D.'s. They came and sat in silence, thinking, applauding only when they considered the truth was told, when they felt strongly that something was going to be done about it.

The March on Washington Movement is essentially a movement of the people. It is all Negro and pro-Negro, but not for that reason anti-white or anti-Semitic, or anti-Catholic, or anti-foreign, or anti-labor. Its major weapon is the nonviolent demonstration of Negro mass power. Negro leadership has united back of its drive for jobs and justice. "Whether Negroes should march on Washington, and if so, when?" will be the focus of a forthcoming national conference. For the plan of a protest march has not been abandoned. Its purpose would be to demonstrate that American Negroes are in deadly earnest, and all out for their full rights. No power on earth can cause them today to abandon their fight to wipe out every vestige of second-class citizenship and the dual standards that plague them.

A community is democratic only when the humblest and weakest person can enjoy the highest civil, economic, and social rights that the biggest and most powerful possess. To trample on these rights of both Negroes and poor whites is such a commonplace in the South that it takes readily to anti-social, anti-labor, anti-Semitic and anti-Catholic propaganda. It was because of laxness in enforcing the Weimar constitution in republican Germany that Nazism made headway. Oppression of the Negroes in the United States, like suppression of the Jews in Germany, may open the way for a fascist dictatorship.

By fighting for their rights now, American Negroes are helping to make America a moral and spiritual arsenal of democracy. Their fight against the poll tax, against lynch law, segregation, and Jim Crow, their fight for economic, political, and social equality, thus becomes part of the global war for freedom.

Program of the March on Washington Movement

1. We demand, in the interest of national unity, the abrogation of every law which makes a distinction in treatment between citizens based on religion, creed, color, or national origin. This means an end to Jim Crow in education, in housing, in transportation and in every other social, economic, and political privilege; and especially, we demand, in the capital of the nation, an end to all segregation in public places and in public institutions.

2. We demand legislation to enforce the Fifth and Fourteenth Amendments guaranteeing that no person shall be deprived of life, liberty or property without due process of law, so that the full weight of the national government may be used for the protection of life and thereby may end the disgrace of lynching.

3. We demand the enforcement of the Fourteenth and Fifteenth Amendments and the enactment of the Pepper Poll Tax bill so that all barriers in the exercise of the suffrage are eliminated.

4. We demand the abolition of segregation and discrimination in the army, navy, marine corps, air corps, and all other branches of national defense.

5. We demand an end to discrimination in jobs and job training. Further, we demand that the F.E.P.C. be made a permanent administrative agency of the U.S. Government and that it be given power to enforce its decisions based on its findings.

6. We demand that federal funds be withheld from any agency which practices discrimination in the use of such funds.

7. We demand colored and minority group representation on all administrative agencies so that these groups may have recognition of their democratic right to participate in formulating policies.

8. We demand representation for the colored and minority racial groups on all missions, political and technical, which will be sent to the peace conference so that the interests of all people everywhere may be fully recognized and justly provided for in the post-war settlement.

Sources: (1) Excerpt from "Call to the March, July 1, 1941," originally published in *The Black Worker,* May 1941; and (2) "Why Should We March?" *Survey Graphic* 31 (November 1942), pp. 488–89.

SELECT BIBLIOGRAPHY:

Jervis Anderson, *A. Philip Randolph: A Biographical Portrait* (New York: Harcourt Brace Jovanvich, 1973).

William Harris, *Keeping the Faith: A. Philip Randolph, Milton P. Webster, and the Brotherhood of Sleeping Car Porters, 1925–1937* (Urbana: University of Illinois Press, 1977).

Andrew Edmund Kersten, *A. Philip Randolph: A Life in the Vanguard* (Lanham, MD: Rowman & Littlefield Publishers, 2007).

Manning Marable, *Black American Politics: From the Washington Marches to Jesse Jackson* (London: Verso, 1985).

Paula Pfeffer, *A. Philip Randolph: Pioneer of the Civil Rights Movement* (Baton Rouge: Louisiana State University Press, 1990).

Jack Santino, *Miles of Smiles, Years of Struggle: Stories of Black Pullman Porters* (Urbana: University of Illinois Press, 1989).

Joseph F. Wilson, ed., *Tearing down the Color Bar: An Analysis and Documentary History of the Brotherhood of Sleeping Car Porters* (New York: Columbia University Press, 1989).

⌐ 18 ⌐

Charles Hamilton Houston and the War Effort among African Americans, *1944*

Charles Hamilton Houston (1895–1950) was born in Washington, D.C., and in 1922 he graduated cum laude from Harvard Law School, where he was also the first African American ever elected to be an editor of the Harvard Law Review. Houston later taught at Howard University, where Thurgood Marshall was one of his students, and argued a number of important cases before the U.S. Supreme Court. His primary legacy, however, lay in his work as a key strategist in the legal assault against racial discrimination. Though the Supreme Court's famous *Brown* decision to abolish compulsory segregation in public schools did not occur until four years after Houston's death, he helped shape many of the important legal precedents that led up to this decision. Even a half century after his death, Houston's reputation as the principal architect of the legal campaign against Jim Crow has continued to grow.

⌐

THE NEGRO SOLDIER

I want to speak particularly on the subject of the armed forces. Here, after nearly three years of war, Negroes are still insulted by the Navy's barring all Negro women, except those now passing for white, from the Waves, the Marines, and the Spars. We have officers in the Army and the Navy; but there is still not a single Negro lieutenant in the United States Marines. The Army puts Negroes in uniform, transports them South and then leaves them to be kicked, cuffed and even murdered with impunity by white civilians. In places, Negro service men do not have as many civil rights as prisoners of war. In at least one Army camp down South for a time there was one drinking fountain for white guards and German prisoners, and a segregated fountain for Negro soldiers. And Negroes know that just as soon as the shooting stops many Americans will give the same Germans, Austrians, Italians, Rumanians and others who were trying to kill them preference over Negroes who were defending them, simply because these Germans and others are white.

Many white service men are talking about what they are going to do to put the Negro in his place as soon as they get back home. Many Negroes are getting to the point of disgust and desperation where they had just as soon die fighting one place as another. Meanwhile enemy propaganda is carrying the stories of racial dissension in the United States to all corners of the earth, and the colored peoples of Asia, Africa and India are getting an eyeful of how white Americans act abroad.

I advocate immediate enlistment of Negro women as Waves, Spars and Marines; assignment and promotion of Negroes in all the armed forces strictly according to service, experience and merit; and the organization of non-segregated combat units on a volunteer basis. The administration of the G.I. Bill of Rights and all other veteran rehabilitation programs must be administered impartially with absolutely no discrimination.

The American color bar unless speedily removed will be the rock on which our international Good Neighbor policy and our pious claim to moral leadership will founder. The moment the peoples of Asia, Africa and India become convinced that our true war aims are to perpetuate the old colonial system with the white man's heel on the colored man's neck, and that we are fighting Japan merely to substitute European imperialism in place of Japanese imperialism—that moment we might as well begin preparing for World War III, and World War III will not necessarily be to America's advantage. The Negro problem gives the United States the opportunity to practice what it preaches, and it is time the country awakens to the fact it is guaranteeing its own salvation by making a substantial down payment on the Four Freedoms at home.

Source: "The Negro Soldier," reprinted with permission from the *Nation* 159 (October 21, 1944), pp. 496–97. For subscription information to the Nation, call 1-800-333-8536. Portions of each week's *Nation* magazine can be accessed at www.thenation.com.

SELECT BIBLIOGRAPHY:

Steven H. Hobbs, "From the Shoulders of Houston: A Vision for Social and Economic Justice," *Howard Law Journal* 32 (1989).

Richard Kluger, *Simple Justice: The History of* Brown v. Board of Education *and Black America's Struggle for Equality* (New York: Knopf, 1975).

Genna Rae McNeil, *Groundwork: Charles Hamilton Houston and the Struggle for Civil Rights* (Philadelphia: University of Pennsylvania Press, 1983).

⚊ 19 ⚊

"An End to the Neglect of the Problems of the Negro Woman!"
Claudia Jones, 1949

Claudia Jones (1915–1965) was born in Trinidad and moved to Harlem in 1924. At age eighteen, Jones joined the Young Communist League and by 1940 had risen to become the national chair of the organization. Jones earned the admiration and respect of many groups for her activities concerning issues of civil rights, labor, and gender equality. In 1951 she was found guilty of violating the Smith Act (which made it illegal to advocate Marxism) and was expelled from the United States. Relocating to London, Jones quickly became a major political figure within the black emigrant community. Angela Davis and others cite Jones's writings and political activism as critical in the development of black feminist thought. Her essay below, "An End to the Neglect of the Problems of the Negro Woman," presents an analysis of gender within the African-American community from a Marxist perspective.

⚊

An outstanding feature of the present stage of the Negro liberation movement is the growth in the militant participation of Negro women in all aspects of the struggle for peace, civil rights, and economic security. Symptomatic of this new militancy is the fact that Negro women have become symbols of many present-day struggles of the Negro people. This growth of militancy among Negro women has profound meaning, both for the Negro liberation movement and for the emerging anti-fascist, anti-imperialist coalition.

To understand this militancy correctly, to deepen and extend the role of Negro women in the struggle for peace and for all interests of the working class and the Negro people, means primarily to overcome the gross neglect of the special problems of Negro women. This neglect has too long permeated the ranks of the labor movement generally, of Left-progressives, and also of the Communist Party. The most serious assessment of these shortcomings by progressives, especially by Marxist-Leninists, is vitally necessary if we are to help accelerate this development and integrate Negro women in the progressive and labor movement and in our own Party.

The bourgeoisie is fearful of the militancy of the Negro woman, and for good reason. The capitalists know, far better than many progressives seem to know, that once Negro women undertake action, the militancy of the whole Negro people, and thus of the anti-imperialist coalition, is greatly enhanced.

Historically, the Negro woman has been the guardian, the protector, of the Negro family. From the days of the slave traders down to the present, the Negro woman has had the responsibility of caring for the needs of the family, of militantly shielding it from the blows of Jim-Crow insults, of rearing children in an atmosphere of lynch terror, segregation, and police brutality, and of fighting for an education for the children. The intensified oppression of the Negro people, which has been the hallmark of the postwar reactionary offensive, cannot therefore but lead to an acceleration of the militancy of the Negro woman. As mother, as Negro, and as worker, the Negro woman fights against the wiping out of the Negro family, against the Jim-Crow ghetto existence which destroys the health, morale, and very life of millions of her sisters, brothers, and children.

Viewed in this light, it is not accidental that the American bourgeoisie has intensified its oppression, not only of the Negro people in general, but of Negro women in particular. Nothing so exposes the drive to fascization in the nation as the callous attitude which the bourgeoisie displays and cultivates toward Negro women. The vaunted boast of the ideologist of Big Business that American women possess "the greatest equality" in the world is exposed in all its hypocrisy when one sees that in many parts of the world, particularly in the Soviet Union, the New Democracies, and the formerly oppressed land of China, women are attaining new heights of equality. But above all else, Wall Street's boast stops at the water's edge where Negro and working-class women are concerned. Not equality, but degradation and super-exploitation: this is the actual lot of Negro women!

Consider the hypocrisy of the Truman Administration, which boasts about "exporting democracy throughout the world" while the state of Georgia keeps a widowed Negro mother of twelve children under lock and key. Her crime? She defended her life and dignity—aided by her two sons—from the attacks of a "white supremacist." Or ponder the mute silence with which the Department of Justice has greeted Mrs. Amy Mallard, widowed Negro school teacher, since her husband was lynched in Georgia because he had bought a new Cadillac and become, in the opinion of the "white supremacists," "too uppity." Contrast this with the crocodile tears shed by the U.S. delegation to the United Nations for Cardinal Mindszenty, who collaborated with the enemies of the Hungarian People's Republic and sought to hinder the forward march to fuller democracy by the formerly oppressed workers and peasants of Hungary. Only recently, President Truman spoke solicitously in a Mother's Day Proclamation about the manifestation of "our love and reverence" for all mothers of the land. The so-called "love and reverence" for the mothers of the land by no means includes Negro mothers who, like Rosa Lee Ingram, Amy Mallard, the wives and mothers of the Trenton Six, or the other countless victims, dare to fight back against lynch law and "white supremacy" violence.

ECONOMIC HARDSHIPS

Very much to the contrary, Negro women—as workers, as Negroes, and as women—are the most oppressed stratum of the whole population.

In 1940, two out of every five Negro women, in contrast to two out of every eight white women, worked for a living. By virtue of their majority status among the Negro people, Negro women not only constitute the largest percentage of women heads of families, but are the main breadwinners of the Negro family. The large proportion of Negro women in the labor market is primarily a result of the low-scale earnings of Negro men. This disproportion also has its roots in the treatment and position of Negro women over the centuries.

Following emancipation, and persisting to the present day, a large percentage of Negro women—married as well as single—were forced to work for a living. But despite the shift in employment of Negro women from rural to urban areas, Negro women are still generally confined to the lowest-paying jobs. . . . The super-exploitation of the Negro woman worker is thus revealed not only in that she receives, as woman, less than equal pay for equal work with men, but in that the majority of Negro women get less than half the pay of white women. Little wonder, then, that in Negro communities the conditions of ghetto-living—low salaries, high rents, high prices, etc.—virtually become an iron curtain hemming in the lives of Negro children and undermining their health and spirit! Little wonder that the maternity death rate for Negro women is triple that of white women! Little wonder that one out of every ten Negro children born in the United States does not grow to manhood or womanhood!

The low scale of earnings of the Negro woman is directly related to her almost complete exclusion from virtually all fields of work except the most menial and underpaid, namely, domestic service. . . .

During the anti-Axis war, Negro women for the first time in history had an opportunity to utilize their skills and talents in occupations other than domestic and personal service. They became trail blazers in many fields. Since the end of the war, however, this has given way to growing unemployment, to the wholesale firing of Negro women, particularly in basic industry.

This process has been intensified with the development of the economic crisis. Today, Negro women are being forced back into domestic work in great numbers. . . .

Inherently connected with the question of job opportunities where the Negro woman is concerned, is the special oppression she faces as Negro, as woman, and as worker. She is the victim of the white chauvinist stereotype as to where her place should be. In the film, radio, and press, the Negro woman is not pictured in her real role as breadwinner, mother, and protector of the family, but as a traditional "mammy" who puts the care of children and families of others above her own. This traditional stereotype of the Negro slave mother, which to this day appears in commercial advertisements, must be combatted and rejected as a device of the imperialists to perpetuate the white chauvinist ideology that Negro women are "backward," "inferior," and the "natural slaves" of others.

HISTORICAL ASPECTS

Actually, the history of the Negro woman shows that the Negro mother under slavery held a key position and played a dominant role in her own family grouping. This was due primarily to two factors: the conditions of slavery, under which marriage, as such, was non-existent, and the Negro's social status was derived from the mother and not the father; and the fact that most of the Negro people brought to these shores by the slave traders came from West Africa where the position of women, based on active participation in property control, was relatively higher in the family than that of European women.

Early historians of the slave trade recall the testimony of travelers indicating that the love of the African mother for her child was unsurpassed in any part of the world. There are numerous stories attesting to the self-sacrificial way in which East African mothers offered themselves to the slave traders in order to save their sons, and Hottentot women refused food during famines until after their children were fed.

It is impossible within the confines of this article to relate the terrible sufferings and degradation undergone by Negro mothers and Negro women generally under slavery. Subject to legalized rape by the slaveowners, confined to slave pens, forced to march for eight to fourteen hours with loads on their backs and to perform back-breaking work even during pregnancy, Negro women bore a burning hatred for slavery, and undertook a large share of the responsibility for defending and nurturing the Negro family.

The Negro mother was mistress in the slave cabin, and despite the interference of master or overseer, her wishes in regard to mating and in family matters were paramount. During and after slavery, Negro women had to support themselves and the children. Necessarily playing an important role in the economic and social life of her people, the Negro woman became schooled in self-reliance, in courageous and selfless action.[1]

There is documentary material of great interest which shows that Negro family life and the social and political consciousness of Negro men and women underwent important changes after emancipation. One freedman observed, during the Civil War, that many men were exceedingly jealous of their newly acquired authority in family relations and insisted upon a recognition of their superiority over women. After the Civil War, the slave rows were broken up and the tenant houses scattered all over the plantation in order that each family might carry on an independent existence. The new economic arrangement, the change in the mode of production, placed the Negro man in a position of authority in relation to his family. Purchase of homesteads also helped strengthen the authority of the male.

Thus, a former slave, who began life as a freedman on a "one-horse" farm, with his wife working as a laundress, but who later rented land and hired two men, recalls the pride which he felt because of his new status: "In my humble palace on a hill in the woods beneath the shade of towering pines and sturdy oaks, I felt as a king whose supreme commands were 'law and gospel' to my subjects."

One must see that a double motive was operative here. In regard to his wife and children, the Negro man was now enabled to assume economic and other authority over the family; but he also could fight against violation of women of his group where formerly he was powerless to interfere.

The founding of the Negro church, which from the outset was under the domination of men, also tended to confirm the man's authority in the family. Sanction for male ascendancy was found in the Bible, which for many was the highest authority in such matters.

Through these and other methods, the subordination of Negro women developed. In a few cases, instead of legally emancipating his wife and children, the husband permitted them to continue in their status of slaves. In many cases, state laws forbade a slave emancipated after a certain date to remain in the state. Therefore, the only way for many Negro wives and children to remain in the state was to become "enslaved" to their relatives. Many Negro owners of slaves were really relatives of their slaves.

In some cases, Negro women refused to become subject to the authority of the men. In defiance of the decisions of their husbands to live on the places of their former masters, many Negro women took their children and moved elsewhere.

NEGRO WOMEN IN MASS ORGANIZATIONS

This brief picture of some of the aspects of the history of the Negro woman, seen in the additional light of the fact that a high proportion of Negro women are obliged today to earn all or part of the bread of the family, helps us understand why Negro women play a most active part in the economic, social, and political life of the Negro community today. Approximately 2,500,000 Negro women are organized in social, political, and fraternal clubs and organizations. The most prominent of their organizations are the National Association of Negro Women, the National Council of Negro Women, the National Federation of Women's Clubs, the Women's Division of the Elks' Civil Liberties Committee, the National Association of Colored Beauticians, National Negro Business Women's League, and the National Association of Colored Graduate Nurses. Of these, the National Association of Negro Women, with 75,000 members, is the largest membership organization. There are numerous sororities, church women's committees of all denominations, as well as organizations among women of West Indian descent. In some areas, N.A.A.C.P. chapters have Women's Divisions, and recently the National Urban League established a Women's Division for the first time in history.

Negro women are the real active forces—the organizers and workers—in all the institutions and organizations of the Negro people. These organizations play a many-sided role, concerning themselves with all questions pertaining to the economic, political, and social life of the Negro people, and particularly of the Negro family. Many of these organizations are intimately concerned with the problems of Negro youth, in the form of providing and administering educational scholarships, giving assistance to schools and other institutions, and offering community service. . . .

THE NEGRO WOMAN WORKER

The negligible participation of Negro women in progressive and trade-union circles is thus all the more startling. In union after union, even in those unions where a large concentration of workers are Negro women, few Negro women are to be found as leaders or active workers. The outstanding exceptions to this are the Food and Tobacco Workers' Union and the United Office and Professional Workers' Union.

But why should these be exceptions? Negro women are among the most militant trade unionists. The sharecroppers' strikes of the '30s were sparkplugged by Negro women. Subject to the terror of the landlord and white supremacist, they waged magnificent battles together with Negro men and white progressives in that struggle of great tradition led by the Communist Party. Negro women played a magnificent part in the pre-C.I.O. days in strikes and other struggles, both as workers and as wives of workers, to win recognition of the principle of industrial unionism, in such industries as auto, packing, steel, etc. More recently, the militancy of Negro women unionists is shown in the strike of the packinghouse workers, and even more so, in the tobacco workers' strike—in which such leaders as Moranda Smith and Velma Hopkins emerged as outstanding trade unionists. The struggle of the tobacco workers led by Negro women later merged with the political action of Negro and white which led to the election of the first Negro in the South (in Winston-Salem, N.C.) since Reconstruction days.

It is incumbent on progressive unionists to realize that in the fight for equal rights for Negro workers, it is necessary to have a special approach to Negro women workers, who, far out of proportion to other women workers, are the main breadwinners in their families. The fight to retain the Negro woman in industry and to upgrade her on the job, is a major way of struggling for the basic and special interests of the Negro woman worker. Not to recognize this feature is to miss the special aspects of the effects of the growing economic crisis, which is penalizing Negro workers, particularly Negro women workers, with special severity.

The Domestic Worker

One of the crassest manifestations of trade-union neglect of the problems of the Negro woman worker has been the failure, not only to fight against relegation of the Negro woman to domestic and similar menial work, but to *organize* the domestic worker. It is merely lip-service for progressive unionists to speak of organizing the unorganized without turning their eyes to the serious plight of the domestic worker, who, unprotected by union standards, is also the victim of exclusion from all social and labor legislation. Only about one in ten of all Negro women workers is covered by present minimum-wage legislation, although about one-fourth of all such workers are to be found in states having minimum-wage laws. All of the arguments heretofore projected with regard to the real difficulties of organizing the domestic workers—such as the "casual" nature of their employment, the difficulties of organizing day workers, the problem of organizing people who work in individual households, etc.—must be overcome forthwith. There is a danger that Social-Democratic forces may enter this field to do their work of spreading disunity and demagogy, unless progressives act quickly.

The lot of the domestic worker is one of unbearable misery. Usually, she has no definition of tasks in the household where she works. Domestic workers may have "thrown in," in addition to cleaning and scrubbing, such tasks as washing windows, caring for the children, laundering, cooking, etc., and all at the lowest pay. The Negro domestic worker must suffer the additional indignity, in some areas, of having to seek work in virtual "slave markets" on the streets where bids are made, as from a slave block, for the hardiest workers. Many a domestic worker, on returning to her own household, must begin housework anew to keep her own family together. . . .

It is incumbent on the trade unions to assist the Domestic Workers' Union in every possible way to accomplish the task of organizing the exploited domestic workers, the majority of whom are Negro women. Simultaneously, a legislative fight for the inclusion of domestic workers under the benefits of the Social Security Law is vitally urgent and necessary. Here, too, recurrent questions regarding "administrative problems" of applying the law to domestic workers should be challenged and solutions found.

The continued relegation of Negro women to domestic work has helped to perpetuate and intensify chauvinism directed against all Negro women. Despite the fact that Negro women may be grandmothers or mothers, the use of the chauvinist term "girl" for adult Negro women is a common expression. The very economic relationship of Negro women to white women, which perpetuates "madam –maid" relationships, feeds chauvinist attitudes and makes it incumbent on white women progressives, and particularly Communists, to fight consciously against all manifestations of white chauvinism, open and subtle.

Chauvinism on the part of progressive white women is often expressed in their failure to have close ties of friendship with Negro women and to realize that this fight for equality of Negro women is in their own self-interest, inasmuch as the super-exploitation and oppression of Negro women tends to depress the standards of all women. Too many progressives, and even some Communists, are still guilty of exploiting Negro domestic workers, of refusing to hire them through the Domestic Workers' Union (or of refusing to help in its expansion into those areas where it does not yet exist), and generally of participating in the vilification of "maids" when speaking to their bourgeois neighbors and their own families. Then, there is the expressed "concern" that the exploited Negro domestic worker does not "talk" to, or is not "friendly" with, her employer, or the habit of assuming that the duty of the white progressive employer is to "inform" the Negro woman of her exploitation and her oppression which she undoubtedly knows quite intimately. Persistent challenge to every chauvinist remark as concerns the Negro woman is vitally necessary, if we are to break down the understandable distrust on the part of Negro women who are repelled by the white chauvinism they often find expressed in progressive circles.

MANIFESTATIONS OF WHITE CHAUVINISM

Some of the crassest expressions of chauvinism are to be found at social affairs, where, all too often, white men and women and Negro men participate in dancing, but Negro women are neglected. The acceptance of white ruling-class standards of "desirability" for women (such as light skin), the failure to extend courtesy to Negro women and to integrate Negro women into organizational leadership, are other forms of chauvinism.

Another rabid aspect of the Jim-Crow oppression of the Negro woman is expressed in the numerous laws which are directed against her as regards property rights, intermarriage (originally designed to prevent white men in the South from marrying Negro women)—and laws which hinder and deny the right of choice, not only to Negro women, but Negro and white men and women.

For white progressive women and men, and especially for Communists, the question of social relations with Negro men and women is above all a question of strictly adhering to social equality. This means ridding ourselves of the position which sometimes finds certain progressives and Communists fighting on the economic and political issues facing the Negro people, but "drawing the line" when it comes to social intercourse or intermarriage. To place the question as a "personal" and not a political matter, when such questions arise, is to be guilty of the worst kind of Social-Democratic, bourgeois-liberal thinking as regards the Negro question in American life; it is to be guilty of imbibing the poisonous white-chauvinist "theories" of a Bilbo or a Rankin. Similarly, too, with regard to guaranteeing the "security" of children. This security will be enhanced only through the struggle for the liberation and equality of all nations and peoples, and not by shielding children from the knowledge of this struggle. This means ridding ourselves of the bourgeois-liberal attitudes which "permit" Negro and white children of progressives to play together at camps when young, but draw the line when the children reach teen-age and establish boy–girl relationships.

The bourgeois ideologists have not failed, of course, to develop a special ideological offensive aimed at degrading Negro women, as part and parcel of the general reactionary ideological offensive against women of "kitchen, church, and children." They cannot, however, with equanimity or credibility, speak of the Negro woman's "place" as in the home; for Negro women are in other peoples' kitchens. Hence, their task has been to intensify their theories of male "superiority" as regards the Negro woman by developing introspective attitudes which coincide with the "new school" of "psychological inferiority" of women. The whole intent of a host of articles, books, etc., has been to obscure the main responsibility for the oppression of Negro women by spreading the rotten bourgeois notion about a "battle of the sexes" and "ignoring" the fight of both Negro men and women—the whole Negro people—against their common oppressors, the white ruling class.

Chauvinist expressions also include paternalistic surprise when it is learned that Negroes are professional people. Negro professional women-workers are often confronted with such remarks as "Isn't your family proud of you?" Then, there is the reverse practice of inquiring of Negro women professionals whether "someone in the family" would like to take a job as a domestic worker.

The responsibility for overcoming these special forms of white chauvinism rests, not with the "subjectivity" of Negro women, as it is often put, but squarely on the shoulders of white men and white women. Negro men have a special responsibility particularly in relation to rooting out attitudes of male superiority as regards women in general. There is need to root out all "humanitarian" and patronizing attitudes toward Negro women. In one community, a leading Negro trade unionist, the treasurer of her Party section, would be told by a white progressive woman after every social function: "Let me have the money; something may happen to you." In another instance, a Negro domestic worker who wanted to join the Party was told by her employer, a Communist, that she was "too backward" and "wasn't ready" to join the Party. In yet another community, which since the war has been populated in the proportion of sixty percent Negro to forty percent white, white progressive mothers maneuvered to get their children out of the school in this community. To the credit of the initiative of the Party section organizer, a Negro woman, a struggle was begun which forced a change in arrangements which the school principal, yielding to the mothers' and to his own prejudices, had established. These arrangements involved a special class in which a few white children were isolated with "selected Negro kids" in what was termed an "experimental class in race relations."

These chauvinist attitudes, particularly as expressed toward the Negro woman, are undoubtedly an important reason for the grossly insufficient participation of Negro women in progressive organizations and in our Party as members and leaders.

The American bourgeoisie, we must remember, is aware of the present and even greater potential role of the masses of Negro women, and is therefore not loathe to throw plums to Negroes who betray their people and do the bidding of imperialism.

Faced with the exposure of their callous attitude to Negro women, faced with the growing protests against unpunished lynching and the legal lynchings "Northern style," Wall Street is giving a few token positions to Negro women. Thus, Anna Arnold Hedgeman, who played a key role in the Democratic National Negro Committee to Elect Truman, was rewarded with the appointment as Assistant to Federal Security Administrator Ewing. Thus, too, Governor Dewey appointed Irene Diggs to a high post in the New York State Administration.

Another straw in the wind showing attempts to whittle down the militancy of Negro women was the State Department's invitation to a representative of the National Council of Negro Women—the only Negro organization so designated—to witness the signing of the Atlantic Pact.

KEY ISSUES OF STRUGGLE

There are many key issues facing Negro women around which struggles can and must be waged. . . .

American history is rich in examples of the cost—to the democratic rights of both women and men—of failure to wage this fight. The suffragists, during their first jailings, were purposely placed on cots next to Negro prostitutes to "humiliate" them. They had the wisdom to understand that the intent was to make it so painful, that no woman would dare to fight for her rights if she had to face such consequences. But it was the historic shortcoming of the women's suffrage leaders, predominantly drawn as they were from the bourgeoisie and the petty-bourgeoisie, that they failed to link their own struggles to the struggles for the full democratic rights of the Negro people following emancipation.

A developing consciousness on the woman question today, therefore, must not fail to recognize that the Negro question in the United States is *prior* to, and not equal to, the woman question; that only to the extent that we fight all chauvinist expressions and actions as regards the Negro people and fight for the full equality of the Negro people, can women as a whole advance their struggle for equal rights. For the progressive women's movement, the Negro woman, who combines in her status the worker, the Negro, and the woman, is the vital link to this heightened political consciousness. To the extent, further, that the cause of the Negro woman worker is promoted, she will be enabled to take her rightful place in the Negro proletarian leadership of the national liberation movement, and by her active participation contribute to the entire American working class, whose historic mission is the achievement of a Socialist America—the final and full guarantee of woman's emancipation. . . .

The struggle for jobs for Negro women is a prime issue. The growing economic crisis, with its mounting unemployment and wage-cuts and increasing evictions, is making its impact felt most heavily on the Negro masses. In one Negro community after another, Negro women, the last to be hired and the first to be fired, are the greatest sufferers from unemployment. Struggles must be developed to win jobs for Negro women in basic industry, in the white-collar occupations, in the communities, and in private utilities. . . .

THE STRUGGLE FOR PEACE

Winning the Negro women for the struggle for peace is decisive for all other struggles. Even during the anti-Axis war, Negro women had to weep for their soldier-sons, lynched while serving in a Jim-Crow army. Are they, therefore, not interested in the struggle for peace? . . .

Our Party, based on its Marxist-Leninist principles, stands foursquare on a program of full economic, political, and social equality for the Negro people and of equal rights for women. Who, more than the Negro woman, the most exploited and oppressed, belongs in our Party? Negro women can and must make an enormous contribution to the daily life and work of the Party. Concretely, this means prime responsibility lies with white men and women comrades. Negro men comrades, however, must participate in this task. Negro Communist women must everywhere now take their rightful place in Party leadership on all levels.

The strong capacities, militancy, and organizational talents of Negro women, can, if well utilized by our Party, be a powerful lever for bringing forward Negro workers—men and women—as the leading forces of the Negro people's liberation movement, for cementing Negro and white unity in the struggle against Wall Street imperialism, and for rooting the Party among the most exploited and oppressed sections of the working class and its allies.

In our Party clubs, we must conduct an intensive discussion of the role of the Negro women, so as to equip our Party membership with clear understanding for undertaking the necessary struggles in the shops and communities. We must end the practice, in which many Negro women who join our Party, and who, in their churches, communities, and fraternal groups are leaders of masses, with an invaluable mass experience to give to our Party, suddenly find themselves viewed in our clubs, not as leaders, but as people who have "to get their feet wet" organizationally. We must end this failure to create an atmosphere in our clubs in which new recruits—in this case Negro women—are confronted with the "silent treatment" or with attempts to "blueprint" them into a pattern. In addition to the white-chauvinist implications in such approaches, these practices confuse the basic need for Marxist-Leninist understanding which our Party gives to all workers, and which enhances their political understanding, with chauvinist disdain for the organizational talents of new Negro members, or for the necessity to promote them into leadership.

To win the Negro women for full participation in the anti-fascist, anti-imperialist coalition, to bring her militancy and participation to even greater heights in the current and future struggles against Wall Street imperialism, progressives must acquire political consciousness as regards her special oppressed status.

It is this consciousness, accelerated by struggles, that will convince increasing thousands that only the Communist Party, as the vanguard of the working class, with its ultimate perspective of Socialism, can achieve for the Negro women—for the entire Negro people—the full equality and dignity of their stature in a Socialist society in which contributions to society are measured, not by national origin, or by color, but a society in which men and women contribute according to ability, and ultimately under Communism receive according to their needs.

Note: 1. Today, in the rural sections of the South, especially on the remnants of the old plantations, one finds households where old grandmothers rule their daughters, sons, and grandchildren with a matriarchal authority.

Source: Essay originally published in *Political Affairs* (1949).

SELECT BIBLIOGRAPHY:

Carole Boyce Davies, "Deportable Subjects: U.S. Immigration Laws and the Criminalizing of Communism," *South Atlantic Quarterly* 100, no. 4 (Fall 2001), pp. 949–66.

———, *Left of Karl Marx: The Political Life of Black Communist Claudia Jones* (Durham: Duke University Press, 2007).

Buzz Johnson, *I Think of My Mother: Notes on the Life and Times of Claudia Jones* (London: Karia Press, 1985).

Mark D. Naison, *The Communist Party in Harlem: 1928–1936* (Urbana: University of Illinois Press, 1983).

Marika Sherwood, *Claudia Jones: A Life in Exile* (London: Lawrence & Wishart, 1999).

⌒ 20 ⌒

"The Negro Artist Looks Ahead," *Paul Robeson, 1951*

Born in Princeton, New Jersey, Paul Robeson (1898–1976) studied and played football at Rutgers College (now University), where he was an All-American athlete and valedictorian. In 1923 he earned a degree from Columbia Law School and was admitted to the Bar of New York. Yet Robeson gained most of his fame as an actor and singer and later as a civil rights activist, scholar, and author. Throughout the

1930s and 1940s he was arguably the most popular and influential black public figure in the United States and the world. While living in London during the
Depression, he became involved in a wide variety of progressive networks and organizations, working on behalf of labor, African liberation, and other issues. He traveled to Spain during its Civil War to express solidarity with the republican forces
combating fascism. However, it was Robeson's affinity for the Soviet Union's model
of socialism and for the Russian people that made him a prime target for political
attacks inside the United States during the Cold War. Concert promoters were
pressured to cancel his performances, and his income plummeted to almost nothing. In 1950 the State Department seized his passport, revoking his right to travel
abroad for eight years. Vindicated by the courts after a long legal battle to win back
his passport, Robeson immediately left the country for several years. Poor health
made it difficult for him to revive his acting and singing career. Retiring from public life, Robeson died of a stroke in 1976. Despite the vigorous attempts by the U.S.
government to destroy Robeson's reputation and name, new generations of activists
and artists continue to be inspired by his example of personal courage and integrity.

We are here today to work out ways and means of finding jobs for colored actors
and colored musicians, to see that the pictures and statues made by colored
painters and sculptors are sold, to see that the creations of Negro writers are
made available to the vast American public. We are here to see that colored scientists and professionals are placed in leading schools and universities, to open up
opportunities for Negro technicians, to see that the way is open for colored
lawyers to advance to judgeships—yes, to the Supreme Court of these United
States, if you please.

It is not just a question of jobs, of positions, of commercial sales. No—the
questions at hand cannot be resolved without the resolution of deeper problems
involved here. We are dealing with the position in this society of a great people—
of fifteen million closely-bound human beings, of whom ten millions in the cotton and agricultural belt of the South form a kind of nation based upon common
oppression, upon a magnificent common heritage, upon unified aspiration for full
freedom and full equality in the larger democratic society.

The Negro people today are saying all up and down this nation (when you get
on the streets, into the churches, into the bars to talk to them): "We will not suffer the genocide that might be visited upon us. We are prepared to fight to the
death for our rights."

One great creation, modern popular music, whether it be in theatre, film,
radio, records—wherever it may be—is almost completely based upon the Negro
idiom. There is no leading American singer, performer of popular songs, whether
it be a Crosby, a Sinatra, a Shore, a Judy Garland, an Ella Logan, who has not listened (and learned) by the hour to Holiday, Waters, Florence Mills, to Bert
Williams, to Fitzgerald, and to the greatest of all, Bessie Smith. Without these
models, who would ever have heard of a Tucker, a Jolson, a Cantor?

Go into the field of the dance. Where could there have come an Astaire, an Eleanor Powell and a James Barton without a Bill Robinson, a Bert Williams, an Eddie Rector, a Florence Mills? How could Artie Shaw and Bennie Goodman have appeared but for a Teddy Wilson, Turner Latan, Johnny Dunn, Hall Johnson, Will Marion Cook? Whence stems even Gershwin? From the music of Negro America joined with the ancient Hebrew idiom. Go and listen to some of the great melodies. Here again is a great American composer, deeply rooted, whether he knew it or not, in an African tradition, a tradition very close to his own heritage.

I speak very particularly of this popular form. This is very important to the Negro artists, because billions, literally billions of dollars, have been earned and are being earned from their creation, and the Negro people have received almost nothing.

At another stage of the arts there is no question, as one goes about the world, of the contribution of the Negro folk songs, of the music that sprang from my forefathers in their struggle for freedom—not songs of contentment—but songs like "Go Down, Moses" that inspired Harriet Tubman, John Brown, and Sojourner Truth to the fight for emancipation.

I think of Larry Brown who went abroad, heard Moussorgsky, heard the great folk music of other lands and dedicated himself, as did Harry Burleigh before him, to showing that this was a great music, not just "plantation songs."

One perhaps forgets my own career, and that for five years I would sing nothing but the music of my people. Later, when it was established as a fine folk music, I began to learn of the folk music of other peoples. This has been one of the bonds that have drawn me so close to the peoples of the world, bonds through this likeness in music that made me understand the political growth of many peoples, the struggles of many peoples, and brought me back to you to fight here in this land, as I shall continue to do. . . .

So we are dealing with a people who come from great roots. There is no need to quote the names of an Anderson or a Hayes and many more; or of the great scientists—of a Julian, of a Carver. No need today for the Negro people to prove any more that they have a right to full equality. They have proven it again and again.

The roots of this great outpouring we are talking about today in the cultural expression of my people, is a great culture from a vast continent. If these origins are somewhat blurred in this America of ours, they are clear in Brazil where Villa-Lobos joins Bach with African rhythms and melodies; in Cuba and Haiti a whole culture, musical and poetic, is very deep in the Africa of its origins—an African culture quite comparable to the ancient culture of the Chinese—similar in religious concepts, in language, in poetry, in its sculpture, in its whole esthetic—a culture which has deeply influenced the great artists of our time—a Picasso, a Modigliani, a Brancusi, an Epstein, a deFalla, a Milhaud.

As I have said, in spite of all these contributions to our culture, the fruits have been taken from us. Think of Handy, one of the creators of the Blues; think of Count Basie, playing to half-filled houses at the Apollo; colored arrangers receiving a pittance while white bands reap harvests. What heartbreak for every Negro composer! Publishing houses taking his songs for nothing and making fortunes. Theatres in the heart of the Negro communities dictating to Negro performers what they shall act, arrogantly telling Negro audiences what they shall see. . . .

Let us touch for a moment on radio and television. We all know the difficulties—no major hours with Negro talent, an occasional guest appearance eagerly awaited by the Negro audience. Why this discrimination? Well, these mass media are based on advertising, commercialism at its worst, and the final answer is very simple. It goes to the root of all that has been said. The final answer is: "The South won't take it."

Now, I had a program myself in the '40s, all set up by one of the biggest advertising agencies, a very fine program, a dignified program in which I would have been doing Othello and many other things. One morning they said, "We made some inquiries and the South just won't have it. You can come on once in a while and sing with Mr. Voorhees, and so forth, but no possibility of a Negro artist having his own program." Not *that* dignity. And so we have allowed the South with its patterns to determine for all America how, when and where the Negro will be denied an opportunity.

I think that public opinion could be aroused on this issue. This is a matter of national protest, of national pressure. These media happen to be under the control of Federal Communications. We are dealing here with matters as serious as the passage of an Anti-Lynch Bill, Anti-Poll Tax and Free Voting Legislation, of F.E.P.C., of the whole issue of Federal and States rights. We can demand a change in the public interest in the pursuance of democratic procedures. Added to this, of course, can be pressure on the advertisers who wax fat today from the purchases of Negro customers. These latter, plus their allies, could have very decisive influence.

The films today are of vast significance and influence. Here, too, the South determines the attempts to camouflage, to pass off so-called progressive films, to find new approaches to the treatment of the Negro. They have been very thoroughly analyzed and exposed for what they are by V. J. Jerome in his exhaustive pamphlet on "The Negro in Hollywood Films." Here, too, the mounting of the right kind of campaign could shake Hollywood to its foundations, and help would be forthcoming from all over the world. Their markets everywhere in the world could be seriously affected, if the lead came from here.

The struggle on this front could have been waged with some real measure of success at any time, but today conditions insure the careful heeding of the collective wrath of the Negro people and their allies. For today, in the struggle extending all over the world, all pronouncements of our wonderful democracy ring hollow and clearly false as soon as one points the finger at the oppression of fifteen million second- and third-class citizens of this land. . . .

The Government can be pressured in this time and it certainly can be pressured on this issue. Most important for us here is the recognition of the Negro's rights to all kinds of jobs in the arts, not only the rights of the artists, but technical jobs for engineers, all sorts of opportunities in production, in scenic design, at all levels. I am very much interested in that: I've got a son, Paul, who studied engineering at Cornell, majored in Communications. I'd like to see him get a good job in television.

And so in the case of Actors Equity—we who are members of Equity must fight not only for the rights of Negro actors, we must see that the stagehands are there. We must fight within the AFL, Equity's parent organization, for the right of Negroes to work in *every* field. And so in the American Guild of Musical Artists and in the American Federation of Radio Artists—they are shouting an awful lot these days about how democratic and American they are: Let them show it!

The final problem concerns new ways, new opportunities based upon a deep sense of responsibility in approaching the problem of the Negro people in its totality. There are despoilers abroad in our land, akin to these who attempted to throttle our Republic at its birth. Despoilers who would have kept my beloved people in unending serfdom, a powerful few who blessed Hitler as he destroyed a large segment of a great people. . . .

And let us learn how to bring to the great masses of the American people *our* culture and *our* art. For in the end, what are we talking about when we talk about American culture today? We are talking about a culture that is restricted to the very, very few. How many workers ever get to the theatre? I was in concerts for 20 years, subscription concerts, the two thousand seats gone before any Negro in the community, any worker, could even hear about a seat. Even then, the price was $12.00 for six concerts. How could working people ever hear these concerts? Only by my going into the trade unions and singing on the streets and on the picket lines and in the struggles for the freedom of our people—only in this way could the workers of this land hear me.

We are talking about a culture which as yet has no relationship to the great masses of the American people. I remember an experience in England. I sang not only in Albert Hall, the concert halls, but also in the picture theatres, and one night I came out and a young woman was standing there with her mother, an aged lady. "My grandmother wants to thank you very much. She always wanted to hear you in person. She heard you tonight and she's going home. She just had sixpence above her bus fare." So she was able to hear me. Later, that was so in the Unity Theatre in London—now a theatre which has stretched all over England. Here in America, in 1948 in the Deep South, I remember standing singing to white workers in Memphis, workers who had come out on strike that Negro workers might get equal wages.

In the theatre I felt this years ago and it would interest you to know that the opening night of *Othello* in New York, in Chicago, in San Francisco (I never told this to the Guild), I told Langner he could have just one-third of the house for the elite. I played the opening night of *Othello* to the workers from Fur, from Maritime, from Local 65.

Just the other night I sang at the Rockland Palace in the Bronx, to this people's audience. We speak to them every night. To thousands. Somewhere, with the impetus coming from the arts, sciences and professions, there are literally millions of people in America who would come to hear us, the Negro artists. This can be very important. Marion Anderson, Roland Hayes, all of us started in the Baptist Churches. I'm going right back there very soon. If you want to talk about audiences, I defy any opera singer to take those ball parks like Sister Tharpe or Mahalia Jackson. . . .

Haydn with his folk songs—the people made it up in the first place. The language of Shakespeare—this was the creation of the English-speaking people; the language of Pushkin, the creation of the Russian people, of the Russian peasants. That is where it came from—a little dressed up with some big words now and then which can be broken down into very simple images.

So, in the end, the culture with which we deal comes from the people. We have an obligation to take it back to the people, to make them understand that in fighting for their cultural heritage they fight for peace. They fight for their own rights, for the rights of the Negro people, for the rights of all in this great land. All of this is dependent so much upon our understanding the power of this people, the power of the Negro people, the power of the masses of America, of a world where we can all walk in complete dignity.

Source: Excerpt from "The Negro Artist Looks Ahead," originally published in *Masses and Mainstream* (January 1952), pp. 7–14.

SELECT BIBLIOGRAPHY:

Sheila Tully Boyle and Andrew Bunie, *Paul Robeson. The Years of Promise and Achievement* (Amherst: University of Massachusetts Press, 2001).

Lenwood G. Davis, *A Paul Robeson Research Guide: A Selected, Annotated Bibliography* (Westport, Conn.: Greenwood Press, 1982).

Joseph Dorinson and William Pencak, eds., *Paul Robeson: Essays on His Life and Legacy* (Jefferson: McFarland, 2004).

Martin Duberman, *Paul Robeson* (New York: Knopf, 1988).

Philip S. Foner, *Paul Robeson Speaks: Writings, Speeches, Interviews, 1918–1974* (Larchmont, N.Y.: Bruner/Mazel, 1978).

Paul Robeson, *Here I Stand* (Boston: Beacon Press, 1958).

Paul Robeson, Jr., *The Undiscovered Paul Robeson: An Artist's Journey, 1898–1939* (New York: Wiley, 2001).

⤳ 21 ⤳

Thurgood Marshall: The *Brown* Decision and the Struggle for School Desegregation

Thurgood Marshall (1908–1993) was born in Maryland, and studied at Lincoln University and Howard Law School. In 1938, he joined the staff of the NAACP, where he helped the organization establish its Legal Defense and Education Fund. Marshall rose to national attention when he acted as counsel before the U.S. Supreme Court on the famous *Brown v. Board of Education of Topeka, Kansas* case, which made discrimination in education unconstitutional. The case was monumental because the court held that segregation deprived children of equal protection under the Fourteenth Amendment of the U.S. Constitution, thereby overturning the "separate but equal" doctrine established in *Plessy v. Ferguson*. Marshall then went on to serve as a federal judge and as Solicitor General of the United States, before becoming the first African American to be appointed to the U.S. Supreme Court, in 1967. For more than two decades, Marshall represented the voice of civil rights and social justice on the high court, which had become increasingly conservative due to the judicial appointments under Presidents Nixon and Reagan.

SEGREGATION AND DESEGREGATION

. . . There had been much discussion during recent years concerning the question of the removal in this country of dual citizenship based solely on race and color. The primary emphasis has been on the elimination of racial segregation. No one denies that progress is being made. There are, however, some who say that the progress is too slow and others who say that the progress is too rapid. The important thing to remember is that progress is being made. We are moving ahead. We have passed the crossroads. We are moving toward a completely integrated society, North and South.

Those who doubt this and those who are afraid of complete integration are victims of a background based upon long indoctrination of only one side of the controversy in this country. They know only of one side of the controversy in this country. They know only of one side of slavery. They know only the biased reports about Reconstruction and the long-standing theory which seems to support the "legality" of the separate-but-equal doctrine.

In order to adequately appraise the situation, we must first understand the problem in relation to our history—legal and political. Secondly, we must give proper weight to progress that has been made with and without legal pressure, and thirdly, we must look to the future.

Our government is based on the principle of the equality of man the individual, not the group. All of us can quote the principle that "All men are created equal." Our basic legal document, the Constitution of the United States, guarantees equal protection of the laws to all of us. Many state constitutions have similar provisions. We even have a "Bill of Rights" in the Constitution of Louisiana. These high-sounding principles we preach and teach. However, in the eyes of the world we stand convicted of violating these principles day in and day out.

Today, one hundred and seventy-seven years after the signing of the Declaration of Independence and eighty-six years after the Fourteenth Amendment was adopted, we have a society where, in varying degrees throughout the country, but especially in the South, Negroes, solely because they are Negroes, are segregated, ostracized and set apart from all other Americans. This discrimination extends from the cradle to the graveyard. (And I emphasize grave*yard*, rather than grave.)

Or, to put it even more bluntly, in many areas of this country, a white paroled murderer would be welcome in places which would at the same time exclude such people as Ralph Bunche, Marian Anderson, Jackie Robinson, and many others. Constitutionally protected individual rights have been effectively destroyed by outmoded theories of racial or group inferiority. Why is this true? How long can we afford the luxury of segregation and discrimination?

One reason this condition of dual citizenship exists is because we have been conditioned to an acceptance of this theory as a fact. We are the products of a misunderstanding of history. As a matter of fact, only in recent years have accurate studies of the pre–Civil War period and the Reconstruction period of our history been published.

Our position today is tied up with our past history—at least as far back as the 1820s. At that time the antislavery movement was beginning to take permanent form. It should be borne in mind that those people in New England, Ohio and other areas, who started this movement became dedicated to a principle which has become known as the Judaeo-Christian ethic. This principle was carried forth in their determination to remove slavery from our society, and to remove the badges of caste and inferiority whereby an American could be ostracized or set apart from fellow Americans solely because of race. Of course, slavery per se was the immediate objective—the abolition of slavery—but the ultimate goal was the same as the unfinished business we have before us today, namely, to remove race and caste from the American life.

These people in the 1820 period—1820 to 1865—sought to translate their moral theories and principles into law. They started by pamphleteering and speechmaking. They recognized that equal protection of the laws must always be, in part, an ethical and moral concept, rather than a law. They sought to constitutionalize this moral argument or ideal. Slavery—with its theories of racial damnation, racial inferiority and racial discrimination—was inherently repugnant to the American creed and Christian ethics. They sought to support their moral theories by use of the Declaration of Independence and certain sections of the Constitution as it existed at that time. In so far as public meetings were concerned, speakers were barred from such meetings in the South—brutally beaten or killed, and many were run out of similar meetings in Northern cities and towns. It was, therefore, impossible to get behind the original iron curtain to get public support for much of the program.

In their legal attack they were thwarted by the decision of the United States Supreme Court in the Dred Scott case, which held that no person of African descent, slave or free, had any rights that a white man was bound to respect. The important thing to remember throughout this period is that the opponents of slavery were seeking a Constitutional basis—a legal platform—for the democratic principle of the equality of man.

After the Emancipation Proclamation was signed, many states passed Black Codes and other infamous statutes, effectively returning the emancipated slaves to their inferior status. Consequently, the same people who fought to abolish slavery had to take the lead in Congress in writing the thirteenth, fourteenth and fifteenth amendments.

This short period of intense legislation was followed by the Reconstruction period. Much of that which we have read concerning this period has emphasized, overstated and exaggerated the errors of judgment made in trying to work out the "Negro problem" in such fashion as to give real meaning to these Civil War amendments [but these amendments] were actually thwarted by the conspiracy between Northern capitalists and others to bring "harmony" by leaving the Negro and his problem to the tender mercies of the South. This brought about the separate-but-equal pattern, which spread not only throughout the South but extended and now exists in many Northern and Western areas.

Despite the distortion of this historical background, which has become firmly embedded in our minds, is the "understanding" that racial segregation is legal and valid even if in violation of our moral principles. The fallacy of this reasoning is that the equal protection of the laws was intended to be the constitutionalization of the ethic and moral principle of the absolute equality of man—the right of an individual neither to be circumscribed or conditioned by group, race or color.

It should, therefore, be remembered that our society is the victim of the following periods of history: the period of slavery, when the slaveholders defended slavery by repeating over and over again the myth that slavery was not only a positive good for the nation but was absolutely beneficial and necessary for the Negroes themselves. Consequently, even free Negroes were denied the right of citizenship and subjected to all manner of abuse without legal redress. Immediately following the Civil War, and indeed up to the 1930s, is the period when Negroes were no longer slaves but were certainly not yet full citizens. Having passed through this laissez-faire period in so far as asserting our Constitutional rights is concerned, Negroes began in the thirties the all-out fight to secure the right to vote and at the same time to break down discrimination and segregation.

In so far as securing the right to vote, beginning with the registration cases and the white-primary cases and others, much progress has been made to the end that as of the 1948 national elections, at least 1,300,000 Negroes voted in the deep South. We have seen Negroes elected to the city council in Richmond, Virginia, Nashville, Tennessee, and many cities in North Carolina. We have seen Negroes elected to the governing board of the Democratic party in Atlanta, Georgia. We have also seen Negroes elected to school boards in cities such as Atlanta, Georgia, Lynchburg, Virginia, and Winston-Salem, North Carolina. There are still, however, several small areas in Alabama, Mississippi, and at least four parishes in Louisiana where Negroes are still prevented from registering as qualified voters. (But these are distinctly local problems, which are being attended to and can be pushed aside on that basis.)

In the North we have seen the drive for protection of the right to work without regard to race and color—the drive for F.E.P.C. legislation. We have seen such legislation passed in at least eight states in the North, leaving forty states and the District of Columbia to go, before we have the necessary safeguards to protect man's right not to be deprived of an opportunity to earn a livelihood because of race, religion or ancestry.

We have also seen the breaking-down of the legal barriers to owning and occupying real property without regard to race or color. Today, as a result of several Supreme Court decisions, any American any place in the United States, regardless of race or color, may own and occupy property wherever he can find a willing seller, has the money to purchase the property and courage to live on it. We still, however, have residential segregation throughout the country, not by law, not by the courts, but by a combination of circumstances, such as, the reactionary policies of mortgage companies and real-estate boards, public-housing agencies, including F.H.A., and other governmental agencies. We also find an unwillingness on the part of many Negroes to exercise their rights in this field. In recent years instead of progress toward an integrated community, we find that the Negro ghetto is merely expanding into a larger and more glorified and gilded ghetto. This unwillingness to exercise our own rights is due in part to the long indoctrination that we are different from or inferior to others and therefore should voluntarily segregate ourselves.

As of the present time, the paramount issue in so far as Americanism is concerned is the ending of all racial distinctions in American life. The reasons for this are many. A weighty factor, of course, is the recognition by more and more people in high places that the world situation in regard to the sensitive areas throughout the world depends on how well we can handle our race problem in this country. Our country can no longer tolerate an Achilles heel of discriminatory practices toward its darker citizens. Even more important is the realization that the equality of man as a principle and the equal protection of the laws as a Constitutional concept are both based upon the moral principle of individual responsibility rather than racial identity.

Racial segregation in our country is immoral, costly, and damaging to the nation's prestige. Segregation and discrimination violate the Judaeo-Christian ethic, and the democratic creed on which our national morality is based is soundly established in the minds of most men. But in addition, it has been shown that the costs of segregation and discrimination to the nation are staggering. Elmo Roper, social scientist and pollster of American public opinion, has stated, "The resultant total of the cost of discrimination comes to roughly $10 out of every $75 paycheck, or, in total, $30 billion lost every year." This figure alone would amount to a cost of $2,000 per year to every individual in America. But perhaps even more damaging to the nation is the current effect of America's racial practices on America's role in international affairs and world leadership. According to a recent statement by our State Department experts, nearly half of the recent Russian propaganda about America has been concentrated on race, linking Communist germ-warfare charges with alleged racial brutality in this country. In addition, Americans returning from abroad consistently report having been questioned over and over about racial problems in this country.

This concern about American racial practices seems especially strong among the two-thirds of the world that is darker-skinned. Our former ambassador to

India, Chester Bowles, wrote the following statement, after attending an Indian press conference: "As I later discovered is almost invariably the case in any Asian press conference or forum, the Number One question was, 'What about America's treatment of the Negro?'"

Shortly after returning from a tour of Asian and Pacific areas, Vice-President Nixon made this statement:

> Americans must create a better understanding of American ideals abroad by practicing and thinking tolerance and respect for human rights every day of the year. Every act of racial discrimination or prejudice in the United States hurts Americans as much as an espionage agent who turns over a weapon to a foreign enemy.

Historically, we have to ask whether or not, even as we stand today, our country can afford to continue in practicing *not* what they preach. Historically, the segregation patterns in the United States are carry-overs from the principles of slavery. They are based on the exploded theory of the inferiority of the minority group. Segregation is recognized as resulting from the decision of the majority group without even consulting, less known in seeking, the consent of the segregated group. All of us know that segregation traditionally results in unequal facilities for the segregated group. Duplication of facilities is expensive, diverts funds from the economy which could be utilized to improve facilities for all groups. Finally, segregation leads to the blockage of real communication between the two groups. In turn, this blockage increases mutual suspicion, distrust, hostility, stereotypes and prejudice; and these, all together, result in a social climate of tension favorable to aggressive behavior and social disorganization which sometimes culminate in race riots. Even where we do not have race riots, the seeds of tension are ever present in a segregated system.

The harm done to the individual begins with the child's earliest years, when he becomes aware of status differences among groups in society and begins to react to patterns of segregation. Prejudice and discrimination are potentially damaging to the personalities of all children. The children of the majority group are affected differently from those of the minority group. This potential psychological damage is crystallized by segregation practices sanctioned by public law—and it is the same whether in the North, the East, the West, or the South. Damage to the immediate community is inevitable. This is followed by damage to the state, our federal government and, finally, the world today. The only answer is the complete removal of all racial distinctions that lay at the basis of all this. . . .

. . . Perhaps the most noticeable and the most complete example of desegregation involving millions of persons is found in the armed forces. At the beginning of World War II, the Army policy was one of almost complete segregation of Negro troops, the Air Force was just beginning an "experiment" in the training of Negro flyers in the face of a widespread belief that Negroes could not be taught to fly airplanes, the Navy confined Negroes almost exclusively to the Messmen's Branch, and the Marines excluded Negroes entirely. But soon cracks began to appear in the wall. The Army's Officers Candidate School and a few other service schools became integrated; the Air Forces regarded its experiment with a Negro pursuit squadron as a success and expanded it to a fighter group; the Navy in 1942 allowed Negroes to enlist in branches other than the Messmen's service (although they were still segregated and barred from seagoing vessels); and, in 1942, the Marine Corps admitted its first Negroes, in strictly segregated units, as laborers, antiaircraft gunners and ammunition handlers.

Subsequently, the pressures for integration increased. The armed forces found that they had serious morale problems in some of the segregated Negro units. They also found that the picture of a segregated American Army of Occupation, attempting to teach democracy to the people of Germany and Japan, was a ridiculous experiment. So, in a series of careful and unpublicized moves, the armed forces began a gradual program of racial desegregation. In 1953, the Secretary of the Army reported that at least ninety percent of the Negroes in the Army were serving in nonsegregated units (the number continues to increase), and added: "The Army policy is one of complete integration, and it is to be accomplished as soon as possible."

In the European Army Command, a battalion commander from the deep South is quoted as saying: "We got the order. We got detailed instructions for carrying it out and a time limit to do it in. And that was it."

And in our armed forces all over the globe, Negro servicemen were brought into previously all-white units rapidly and with no trouble by officers who gave white servicemen such terse instructions as these: "Some Negro men are joining our unit. These men are soldiers. Treat them as such."

This is the problem that everybody says is such a "horrible" thing to face up to.

What is the picture today? According to Lee Nichols' exciting new book *Breakthrough on the Color Front*, the Army reports that less than 10,000 Negroes are still serving in all-Negro units out of some 200,000 Negroes in the Army. Assistant Defense Secretary John A. Hannah estimates that by June, 1954, there will be no remaining segregated Army units. The Air Force, which had moved more rapidly, stated that Negro servicemen who were in the Air Force in August, 1953, had been integrated into all of its units throughout the world. Of the 23,000 Negroes serving in the Navy in 1953, about half were still in the Messmen's or Steward's Branch. The rest were integrated and scattered through nearly every job classification that the Navy has. The Marine Corps, last of all the services to take Negroes, reports that its last two all-Negro units were integrated "some time" before the summer of 1952.

Today, Negro and white draftees from the most poverty-stricken parts of the deep South, as well as the rest of the nation, are inducted into a completely integrated command, and the typical report from commanders who had previously held fears was that "the frictions and antagonisms that lay behind previous race conflicts have been substantially reduced, and that so far there has not been a single major incident traceable to integration."

What about segregation in the nation's capital? Many Americans have expressed disgust, and foreign visitors have stated their amazement, at the fact that public and private facilities in the capital of our democracy were almost completely segregated—restaurants, schools, housing projects, theaters, and so forth. Though there is still much to be done in Washington, there have been several recent examples of progress. On June 3, 1953, the National Capital Housing Authority announced the adoption of a policy of opening all present and future public low-rent housing properties in the District of Columbia to low-income families, without regard to race. Around that same time, the Supreme Court handed down a decision preventing discrimination in Washington restaurants. All the restaurants have abided by the decision, and no incident of any kind has been reported. Hotel accommodations now are available to Negroes in most of the larger hotels, although the policy of many smaller hotels is still uncertain. Negroes are now admitted to the three legitimate theaters of Washington, and to at least four—and probably more—of the downtown movie theaters. The majority of the city's private schools have opened their doors to Negroes, and the Catholic parochial schools have also become integrated. A recent bulletin reports that the nation's capital has even agreed to desegregate the jails. Washington is slowly moving toward a position where it can command the respect of the world where race relations are involved.

Why have people decided to desegregate? Members of American communities have tried to integrate their institutions for an extremely varied number of reasons. The pressures to desegregate have come from several forces—sometimes from an aroused Negro community, sometimes from administrative rulings of local authorities, sometimes from rulings by a national body, sometimes from voluntary decision by a majority of concerned community members. It now appears that the success or failure of the desegregation effort is not related to the reason for desegregating, since the reasons are so varied.

The success of racial desegregation has been shown to be related not so much to the type of community that is involved or the prejudice of its members as to the close adherence to a set of specific principles. We have reached the stage where scientists, sociologists and others, have agreed upon rules which when followed bring about smooth desegregation whether in Illinois or Louisiana. The main point is that once the state law preventing intergroup communication in institutional life is removed, it is then up to the local community to work out its own salvation, with the understanding that it must be done within the American framework.

The accomplishment of effective and efficient desegregation with a minimum of social disturbance depends on the following five things:

1. There must be a clear and unequivocal statement of policy by leaders with prestige, and by authority officials.
2. There must be firm enforcement and persistent execution of the nonsegregation policy in the face of initial resistance.
3. Authorities and law enforcement officials must show a willingness to deal with violations, attempted violations or incitement to violations, by applying the law and backing it up with strong enforcement action.

4. Authorities must refuse to employ, engage in or tolerate subterfuges, gerry-mandering or other devices for evading the principle and the fact of deseg-regation.

5. The accomplishment of desegregation must be accompanied by continual interpretation of the reasons for the action, and appealing to the democratic and moral values of all persons involved.

In conclusion, racial segregation is grounded upon the myth of inherent racial superiority. This myth has been completely exploded by all scientific studies. It now stands exposed as a theory which can only be explained as a vehicle for per-petuating racial prejudice. History reveals that racial segregation is a badge of slavery, is just as unscientifically supported, immoral and un-American as slavery. Recent history shows that it can be removed, and that it can be done effectively when approached intelligently.

There is no longer any justification for segregation. There is no longer any excuse for it. There is no longer any reason under the sun why intelligent people should continue to find excuses for not ending segregation in their own commu-nity, in the South as well as in the North.

Source: Excerpt from the Edwin Rogers Embree Memorial Lectures of Thurgood Marshall at Dillard University, New Orleans, Spring 1954.

SELECT BIBLIOGRAPHY:

Howard Ball, *A Defiant Life: Thurgood Marshall and the Persistence of Racism in America* (New York: Crown Publishers, 1999).

Roger Goldman, *Thurgood Marshall: Justice for All* (New York: Carroll and Graf, 1992).

Michael J. Klarman, *Brown V. Board of Education and the Civil Rights Movement* (Oxford: Oxford University Press, 2007).

Thurgood Marshall, *Supreme Justice Speeches and Writings: Thurgood Marshall*, ed. by J. Clay Smith (Philadelphia: University of Pennsylvania Press, 2003).

———, *Thurgood Marshall: His Speeches, Writings, Arguments, Opinions, and Reminis-cences*, ed. by Mark V. Tushnet, *The Library of Black America* (Chicago: Lawrence Hill Books, 2001).

Emma Gleders Sterne, "Hammer of Justice: Thurgood Marshall," in *I Have a Dream* (New York: Knopf, 1965).

Mark V. Tushnet, *Making Civil Rights Law: Thurgood Marshall and the Supreme Court, 1936–1961* (New York: Oxford University Press, 1994).

ADDITIONAL RESOURCES:

"Race and Place—An African-American Community in Jim Crow: Charlottesville, VA," www.vcdh.virginia.edu/afam/raceandplace/index.html.

Jane Elizabeth Dailey, Glenda Elizabeth Gilmore, and Bryant Simon, eds., *Jumpin' Jim Crow: Southern Politics from Civil War to Civil Rights* (Princeton: Princeton University Press, 2000).

William Greaves, *From These Roots*, New York: William Greaves Productions, 2005. DVD Video.

Darlene Clark Hine, *Black Women in the Nursing Profession: A Documentary History*, The History of American Nursing (New York: Garland, 1985).

————, *Black Women in White: Racial Conflict and Cooperation in the Nursing Profession, 1890–1950* (Bloomington: Indiana University Press, 1989).

Gilbert Jonas and with a forward by Julian Bond, *Freedom's Sword: The NAACP and the Struggle against Racism in America, 1909–1969* (London: Routledge, 2007).

Isaac Julien, *Looking for Langston: A Meditation on Langston Hughes (1902–1907)*, New York: Water Bearer Films, 1988. DVD Video.

Michael J. Klarman, *From Jim Crow to Civil Rights: The Supreme Court and the Struggle for Racial Equality* (Oxford; New York: Oxford University Press, 2004).

Christopher Moore, *Fighting for America: Black Soldiers—The Unsung Heroes of World War II* (New York: Presidio Press/Ballantine Books, 2006).

Blaise N'Djehoya, *Africa to America to Paris: The Migration of Black Writers*, Princeton: Films for the Humanities & Sciences 2005. DVD Video.

James T. Patterson, *Brown V. Board of Education: A Civil Rights Milestone and Its Troubled Legacy* (New York: Oxford University Press, 2002).

Nina Rosenblum and William Miles, *Liberators: Fighting on Two Fronts in World War II*, Santa Monica: Direct Cinema Ltd., 2006. DVD Video.

Lorraine Toussaint, Inc Faith Project, and Inc Blackside, *This Far by Faith: African American Spiritual Journeys*, Boston: PBS 2003. DVD Video.

Robert Whitaker, *On the Laps of Gods: The Red Summer of 1919 and the Struggle for Justice That Remade a Nation* (New York: Crown Publishers, 2008).

WE SHALL OVERCOME: THE SECOND RECONSTRUCTION, 1954–1975

INTRODUCTION

With the *Brown vs. Board of Education* decision of May 1954, the Supreme Court unanimously overturned the "separate but equal" policy that had sanctioned racially segregated schools for six decades. This legal victory was the culmination of a long campaign led by the NAACP and liberal integrationist leaders such as A. Philip Randolph and Walter White to outlaw segregation throughout the federal government and in all publicly funded institutions. The long-term goal, however, was the complete dismantling of racial segregation in all aspects of public life—at restaurants and hotels, in transportation, within both organized labor and business, at banks and financial-lending institutions, and with real estate companies. This would require something more than a courtroom victory over the defenders of Jim Crow. It would mean the social and political restructuring of American life, insomuch as its entire structure reflected and perpetuated the ideas of white supremacy and black subordination.

Historians of the Black Freedom movement of 1955–1966—the period between the Montgomery bus boycott and the Meredith march across Mississippi in the summer of 1966—sometimes present these years as a series of public events, mass campaigns, and demonstrations, which inevitably culminated into the successful desegregation of U.S. society. The political victories achieved in Montgomery, Birmingham, and Selma, however, were only one very dramatic aspect of the larger socioeconomic, cultural, and political metamorphosis of American race relations between World War II and the Vietnam War. At first, the racial shifts seemed more symbolic than substantive: the left-wing movement to desegregate professional baseball in 1947, the deracialization of popular music and the growing recognition of jazz as America's true classical music, the popularity of black poets and novelists such as Gwendolyn Brooks, Richard Wright, and Ralph Ellison, and the Nobel Peace Prize awarded to black American diplomat Ralph Bunche.

But the presence of black people in literally all aspects of American life began to become clearly measurable. In the labor force, African Americans represented

over 10 percent of all U.S. workers, and comprised over 20 percent in key manufacturing and industrial areas. Under Randolph's leadership, blacks began exerting greater influence inside organized labor. In local and state politics, black voters became pivotal to Democratic Party organizations. In the presidential
elections of 1948 and 1960, African-American voters were the crucial margin of
victory for Democratic candidates Harry S. Truman and John F. Kennedy, respectively. Perhaps the greatest clout that black Americans began to assert, which
inevitably contributed to destroying the rationale for Jim Crow, was inside the
U.S. economy. By 1960, the black American consumer market—the total amount
of goods and services purchased—exceeded $30 billion annually. Nationally
based corporations with southern subsidiaries and affiliates began to question the
continued utility of legal segregation. Large corporations began to develop marketing strategies specifically for black consumers and began advertising in the
black media. Small numbers of blacks slowly began to be hired in mid-level corporate management. As in the similar case of dismantling South African apartheid
a generation later, the corporate establishment was somewhat more advanced
than the parochial southern white political establishment in recognizing the
inevitability of legal desegregation. All that was needed was massive social pressure from below that would force the state to carry out racial reforms that were
by now long overdue.

From the standpoint of those in power, the American racial dilemma also
began to be considered within a global context. With the establishment of the
United Nations, the United States desperately sought to present itself and its
interests as being supportive of decolonization in the Third World. The newly
independent nations of Asia, Africa, and the Caribbean were both lucrative
potential markets and political allies in the global struggle against communism.
By contrast, the Soviets could point to their long-standing political and material
support for democratic revolutionary movements throughout the world, high-
lighted by the triumph of Fidel Castro in Cuba, and their close relationships with
Patrice Lumumba in the Congo and Kwame Nkrumah in Ghana. Communists
effectively attacked the U.S. political hypocrisy of refusing to grant basic civil
rights and the elective franchise to millions of its citizens. Thus the *ancien régime*
of legal white supremacy was no longer tenable or useful to the geopolitical interests of the U.S. state. By the 1960s Jim Crow policies and practices placed U.S.
corporations at a competitive disadvantage in the pursuit of global markets and
the employment of multinational, multiracial workers. Change had to come. It
was only a question of how much, and how soon.

This section documents the social pressure from mass movements that finally
destroyed the legal apparatus for racial segregation. It may be helpful, however,
to consider that the Black Freedom movement, especially in the decade following the Montgomery bus boycott, was a very broad-based united front. Politics
and ideology, more than personalities, defined the racial and social composition
of each constituency inside the popular coalition. In perhaps overly simplistic
terms, the desegregationist united front had a moderate or conservative wing, a
centrist group, and a left wing. On the right stood the NAACP and the National

Urban League, which in the 1960s were headed, respectively, by Roy Wilkins and Whitney M. Young. Wilkins's 1956 speech cited here (document 2) calls upon the South to recognize "Negro citizenship," and then engage in negotiations "beginning more than half way, with understanding and good will." This moderate approach to integration was combined with a curious attack on communism. Wilkins equates the repressive actions of southern policemen "knocking on doors and taking men away" with "the Soviet Communist method." The real point of Wilkins's argument was to place the interests and objectives of the desegregation movement into a context that was acceptable by the liberal white establishment, corporations, and the national Democratic Party.

The moderate or liberal integrationists were not social revolutionaries. They did not want to destroy the system—they wanted to become fully assimilated within it. They sought full participation for Negroes across the board, in politics, the courts, media, the arts, in business, and all professions. It would not become apparent until some years later that the objectives pursued by liberal integrationists were inherently flawed. On one hand, the political mantra of the NAACP and its Legal Defense Fund was the pursuit of "color blindness": that African Americans should not be treated differently on the basis of their racialized ethnic status. Conversely, there was also the necessity of putting into place corrective measures within the state and civil society that provided minimal guarantees that blacks and other racialized groups would achieve significantly greater opportunities and access to resources, employment, credit, and capital. Hence, these corrective steps or affirmative action, initiated first by presidential executive orders, had to use tools such as quotas and timetables to measure the progress of desegregation within specific universities, companies, or within government agencies. The paradox, of course, is that to abolish race as a social category of significance, one must utilize racial correctives that reduce the historic preferences and privileges that nearly all white Americans have exercised for centuries over black people. The liberal integrationists understood this inherent contradiction. However, they hoped that once Jim Crow was finally outlawed, mainstream middle America would ultimately embrace these racial reforms without a political backlash.

The centrists within the civil rights coalition included the Southern Christian Leadership Conference (SCLC) and the Congress of Racial Equality (CORE). The SCLC had been organized in 1957 by Martin Luther King, Jr., in the aftermath of the Montgomery bus boycott victory. The SCLC's program (document 3) clearly defines its objectives of "achieving full citizenship rights, equality, and the integration of the Negro in all aspects of American life." SCLC's political action "revolves around two main focal points: the use of nonviolent philosophy as a means of creative protest; and securing the right of the ballot for every citizen." Like the NAACP, the SCLC declared itself "firmly opposed to segregation in any form that it takes." But the SCLC's core strategy was much more committed to social protest "even when this means going to jail," and the use of "imaginative, bold constructive action to end the demoralization caused by the legacy of slavery and segregation—inferior schools, slums, and second-class citizenship."

CORE had been founded in 1941 in Chicago and was led by James Farmer. Unlike SCLC, which had a predominantly southern black religious membership, CORE was interracial and largely middle class from the beginning. It was a network of affiliated local organizations that were engaged in protests of all kinds, including civil disobedience, voter-registration efforts, and economic boycotts. CORE inspired and initiated the freedom rides of 1961, the tactic of placing black and white desegregation activists on southern buses to challenge Jim Crow restrictions on public transportation. CORE also initiated a number of important civil rights demonstrations in the North during the early 1960s, effectively making the point that institutional racism was a national problem, not just a southern one.

Although the center of the Black Freedom movement's united front contained a number of influential leaders, including Ralph David Abernathy, Septima Clark, Wyatt T. Walker, Hosea Williams, Ella Baker, Fred Shuttlesworth, and Andrew Young—the charismatic, visionary spokesperson of this group, and indeed for the movement as a whole, was Martin Luther King, Jr. In his 1957 statement reprinted here, "Nonviolence and Racial Justice," King draws parallels between the domestic struggle against segregation with the "quest for freedom and human dignity on the part of people who have long been victims of colonialism" in Africa and Asia. "Privileged groups rarely give up their privileges without strong resistance," King observed. "But when oppressed people rise up against oppression there is no stopping point short of full freedom" (document 7). After Montgomery, King traveled extensively throughout the United States and the world, building the SCLC as a political force and carrying the message of nonviolent social change. Following the outbreak of the student-led sit-in demonstrations, King and the SCLC launched direct-action campaigns at schools, restaurants, department stores, and public transportation facilities throughout the South. There were inevitably some political reverses and defeats for King and the SCLC, notably the failure to pressure law-enforcement and city officials in Albany, Georgia, during 1961–1962 to desegregate that city's public accommodations and services. But the disappointments in Albany yielded invaluable lessons about organizing, which helped build a successful campaign to desegregate Birmingham, Alabama, in 1963. King's famous "I Have a Dream" speech, delivered at the 1963 March on Washington, summarizes his moral philosophy and political goals (document 7).

At the left wing of the Black Freedom movement were the ideological heirs of Henry Highland Garnet, Ida B. Wells-Barnett, William Monroe Trotter, and Paul Robeson—the transformationists, or black radicals. They favored the destruction of Jim Crow, but were intensely critical of the social and economic system that had long perpetuated racial inequality. Integration was a means, not the end, to the realization of black freedom. This radical perspective was most clearly represented by the Student Nonviolent Coordinating Committee (SNCC), several of whose mentors had learned organizing skills in radical movements of the 1930s, such as the Southern Negro Youth Congress. SNCC's "Statement of Purpose," drafted in May 1960 by the Reverend James Lawson, reflects King's general philosophy of embracing nonviolence that "seeks a social order of justice permeated by love" (document 4). However, the steps necessary to achieve that beloved community were radically different from those that King had suggested. First, SNCC saw itself as a catalyst for social change, not as a leadership caste that would enforce its ideas and interests on black communities. As Ella Baker's article of June 1960 suggested, the Black Freedom movement should move "toward *group-centered leadership*, rather than toward a *leader-centered group pattern of organization . . .*" (document 6). The desegregation activists should try to motivate the development of organic, grassroots leadership at local levels, providing them with the tactical weapons and resources necessary to help fight to achieve their own objectives and then move out of their way. In this manner, SNCC refused to see itself as some kind of permanent bureaucracy or well-meaning but controlling political elite. The masses would make history, not charismatic preachers and politicians. John Lewis's censored speech at the 1963 Washington March (document 8) reflects this radical orientation: "The revolution is at hand, and we must free ourselves of the chains of political and economic slavery. . . . We all recognize the fact that if any radical social, political, and economic changes are to take place in our society, the people, the masses must bring them about."

SNCC's militant analysis was complemented by other radical currents dealing with issues of gender and racial oppression. Inside SNCC itself, women activists began to critique the male chauvinism and sexist behavior of their own comrades. The "SNCC Position Paper: Women in the Movement," drafted in November 1964, extensively criticized the systematic gender discrimination at every level of the organization. Perhaps "some women will begin to recognize day-to-day discriminations. And maybe sometime in the future the whole of the women in this movement will become so alert as to force the rest of the movement to stop the discrimination and start the slow process of changing values and ideas so that all of us gradually come to understand that this is no more a man's world than it is a white world" (document 11).

Black nationalists had traditionally stood apart from efforts to achieve integration, specifically because they were convinced that whites lacked either the capacity or interest in ending racism, and that African Americans would be better off concentrating on building their own separate communities. The Nation of Islam, under the direction of Elijah Muhammad, espoused a conservative, separatist creed that condemned all whites as "devils" and favored the establishment of "a state or territory of our own" that was to be exclusively black (document 12). It was from this deeply conservative religious sect that the most influential voice of black radicalism in the 1960s would emerge: Malcolm X.

Even while he was associated with the Nation of Islam, Malcolm X's public attacks against white racism and colonialism won the attention and support of activists in SNCC and CORE. After his break with Elijah Muhammad in March 1964, Malcolm's ideology evolved rapidly toward the left. He embraced Third World revolutions and strongly denounced the Vietnam War. In his "Ballot or the Bullet" speech of April 1964, Malcolm extended his support for the desegregation campaigns throughout the South, stating, "We will work with you against the seg-regated school system because it's criminal, because it is absolutely destructive, in every way imaginable, to the minds of the children. . . ." He advised African Americans to purchase "rifles and shotguns" and to defend themselves "in areas where the government has proven itself either unwilling or unable to defend the lives and the property of Negroes . . ." (document 13). Malcolm also advocated socialism and a fundamental redivision of resources between "the haves vs. the have nots." Although his revolutionary trajectory was brutally cut short when he was assassinated at age thirty-nine on February 21, 1965, Malcolm X left a pow-erful legacy that would at once reconfigure the entire shape and philosophy of the Black Freedom movement.

With the passage of the 1964 Civil Rights and the 1965 Voting Rights Acts, the desegregationist united front had largely achieved its major legislative objectives. But the legislative victories did not transform the fundamental structure of eco-nomic and political inequality. Urban rebellions, began sporadically in the sum-mer of 1964, then spread into the fiery insurrections of Watts in 1965 and Detroit in 1967, indicating that black discontent and rage against racial injustice was a national issue. When the new leader of SNCC, Stokely Carmichael (later Kwame Ture), announced his support for the slogan "Black Power," the conservative and moderate groups within the movement denounced him. In September 1966, Bayard Rustin, the chief organizer of the 1963 March on Washington, character-ized the Black Power debate as "the most bitter the community has experienced since the days of Booker T. Washington and W. E. B. Du Bois, and one which threatens to ravage the entire civil rights movement." Rustin equated Black Power with "affording the same emotional release as 'Back to Africa' and 'Buy Black' did in earlier periods of frustration and hopelessness." Black Power's new-found popularity reflects "in short, the growing conviction that the Negroes can-not win" (document 14).

Rustin correctly predicted that the old desegregationist coalition would come apart over issues like Black Power and the war in Vietnam. But what he could not have anticipated, given his deep ideological and political commitment to liberal integrationism, was how widespread and popular Black Power quickly became across black America, and how profoundly this concept would redefine African-American politics, culture, music, and social relations. Both SNCC and CORE soon ousted their white members. Within the span of two years, "Negroes" would become "black" or "Afro-American"; afros, dashikis, and kente cloth came into fashion; thousands of names were changed to reflect African culture—from LeRoi Jones to Amiri Baraka, from Don L. Lee to Haki Madhubuti, from Arthur Lee Smith to Molefi Asante; in popular music, "We Shall Overcome" gave way to James Brown's "Say it Loud, I'm Black and I'm Proud!"

For nearly a decade, Black Power replaced liberal integrationism as the dom-inant political ideology and discourse for many African Americans. Despite its popularity as a public slogan, however, Black Power never consolidated itself as a coherent social philosophy or strategy. When people engaged in sit-ins and boycotts against Jim Crow, everyone knew what the "goal" was: abolishing legal segregation and removing the obscenity of "colored" and "white" signs that were omnipresent across the South. What was the goal of Black Power? If "power" was, in theory, the capacity of any group to realize its specific interests, then what were the specific interests of the African-American people? Historically, for more than a century, the black nationalists had a standard answer: build separate black institutions, reject alliances with whites, oppose racial assimilation, and develop a culture and value system based on African traditions. But even as the old integrationist coalition unraveled, multiple interpretations for what Black Power was, or should be, exploded on the political scene.

In retrospect, one can identify at least five major, yet overlapping, tendencies that characterized the contradictory movement of Black Power: conservative black nationalism or black capitalism; cultural nationalism; religious nationalism; revolutionary nationalism; and black electoral political activism. Conservative black nationalism was the strategy advanced by CORE's Floyd McKissick and Roy Innis, and by a number of black entrepreneurs and black executives with ties to corporations, foundations, and the Republican Party. Drawing heavily on the earlier ideas of Booker T. Washington, these new black conservatives insisted that African Americans should establish their own businesses, employ other blacks, and sell their goods and services to black consumers. The only racial integration they sought was within the capital markets. Blacks should look toward themselves, not the federal government, to uplift their own communities. McKissick used this approach to develop an all-black planned community located in North Carolina, called "Soul City." The interpretation of Black Power as "Black Capitalism" was so conservative that even Richard M. Nixon endorsed it during his 1968 presidential campaign.

Cultural nationalism focused on the African identity of black Americans, emphasizing the need for African Americans to transform their names, clothing apparel, diet, hairstyles, cultural rituals, and family structures to conform with the imagined reality of the continent. Theorist Maulana Karenga conceived "Kwanzaa," a seven-day celebration of African culture, which was soon observed regularly among millions of black Americans. For a time, the most influential cultural nationalist was poet/playwright Amiri Baraka. From his base in Newark, New Jersey, Baraka was mentor to the "Black Arts Movement," a renaissance of black performing and creative artists. Baraka's Congress of African People called upon African Americans to separate themselves "from assimilation or brainwashing or subjugation by the mind of the white nation. . . . As nationalists and Pan-Africanists we must understand that we must move to have self-determination, self-sufficiency, self-respect, and self-defense wherever we exist in large numbers—whether it is Chicago or Johannesburg" (document 23).

The black religious nationalists were in many ways the protégés of Henry Highland Garnet and Henry McNeal Turner. They sought to merge the rituals of black spirituality and faith with the political movement of African-American empowerment. Black theologians such as James Cone theorized the existence of a black Christ, and the transformation of Christianity into a revolutionary praxis on the side of the oppressed. Reverend Albert Cleage in Detroit established the Church of the Black Madonna, its adherents quickly spreading across the country. The Nation of Islam also experienced something of an organizational rebound, due to the emergence of a charismatic new national spokesman, Louis Farrakhan. Farrakhan had some of the personal qualities and speaking ability that had made Malcolm X so attractive, but he also held deeply conservative beliefs that were radically at odds with building a popular democratic movement within black communities.

The revolutionary nationalist tendency of the Black Power movement was perhaps the most theoretically and politically rich group that emerged in the 1960s. The most prominent and widely studied formation among this group was the Black Panther Party, founded by Huey P. Newton and Bobby Seale in October 1966. At their height, the Panthers probably had fewer than 5,000 formal members. Yet their armed confrontations with the police and the free educational and health-care programs they sponsored for poor urban communities conferred upon the Panthers an almost legendary status. The Black Panther Party Platform and Program reprinted here, "What We Want, What We Believe," is one of the clearest and most elegant statements of the goals of the Black Freedom movement that African-American people have produced throughout their history (document 17). The Panthers developed local organizations across the United States, attracting gifted community activists such as Fred Hampton in Chicago. In his speech excerpted here (document 18), Hampton states forcefully that historically, racism in America was a product of capitalism: "We have to understand very clearly that there's a man in our community called a capitalist. Sometimes he's Black and sometimes he's white. But that man has to be driven out of our community because anybody who comes into the community to make profit off of people by exploiting them can be defined as a capitalist." Speeches such as these may help to explain why the FBI launched a massive and illegal campaign to destroy the Black Panther Party and its supporters.

Politically similar yet independent of the Panthers were the black activists within the Communist Party. After decades of severe government repression and the imprisonment of most of its leaders, the party made significant gains among African Americans by the late 1960s. After his release from prison in 1961, Henry Winston, who became the National Chairman of the Communist Party, was an inspiration to many African Americans (document 24). The formation of the Che-Lumumba club in Los Angeles gave some African-American revolutionaries their own political home within the broader Communist movement, and the youth organization (the Young Workers Liberation League) attracted black youth around the country. The most prominent black American Communist was Angela Y. Davis, who was imprisoned for nearly two years (document 19). A massive international movement calling for her freedom contributed to her legal vindication and release in 1972. *Freedomways*, a journal founded in 1961, amplified the voice of radicalism in the African-American community.

One of the most dynamic expression of Black Power inside the labor movement was the League of Revolutionary Black Workers. The League was a network of working-class organizations created largely in automobile plants in Detroit, and later in other cities. The League's "General Program (Here's Where We're Coming From)" presents a synthesis of Marxism and revolutionary nationalism: "United States society is racist, capitalist, and imperialist by nature. It is aggressively expansive, exploitative, and oppressive . . . the direction of our organization is clear. We're not talking about dealing with a single issue as the only factor, nor are we talking about reforms in the system; but we are talking about the seizure of state power" (document 20).

Finally, the Black Power group with the greatest influence, at least by the mid-1970s, were the black elected officials. The number of black officials grew dramatically in the years after the passage of the Voting Rights Act, from less than 200 in 1965 to 3,500 a decade later. The number of African Americans in Congress tripled, and in 1971 the Congressional Black Caucus was established. Elected officials soon learned the public discourse of black-is-beautiful, and employed the rhetoric of cultural, religious, and even revolutionary nationalism to win elections. Baraka joined the influential Detroit Congressman Charles Diggs and Gary, Indiana, Mayor Richard Hatcher to sponsor the National Black Political Convention in March 1972. The Gary Convention was in many respects the high point of the Black Power movement, a moment when competing versions of black nationalism were largely hegemonic within the national black community. Black politicians were forced to embrace a progressive agenda passed by the convention, which presented a profoundly radical perspective on the future of American society (document 22):

> We come to Gary in an hour of great crisis and tremendous promise for Black America. While the white nation hovers on the brink of chaos, while its politicians offer no hope of real change, we stand on the edge of history and are faced with an amazing and frightening choice: We may choose in 1972 to slip back into the decadent white politics of American life, or we may press forward, moving relentlessly from Gary to the creation of our own Black life. The choice is large, but the time is very short. . . . A Black political convention, indeed all truly Black politics must begin from this truth: *The American system does not work for the masses of our people, and it cannot be made to work without radical fundamental change.*

The aftermath of the Gary convention fell far short of its visionary goals. As more African-American activists went into electoral politics, many became largely disconnected from the social-protest movements and the black nationalist community groups from which they had come. As America staggered through the Watergate scandal and the end of the war in Vietnam, black political aspirations had begun to be fully assimilated into the mainstream. Affirmative action programs and minority economic set-asides helped produce a rapidly growing, affluent, black middle class. Black activists who only fifteen years before had been arrested in civil disobedience demonstrations with King, or for weapons charges with the Panthers, now found themselves inside Congress, state legislatures, or corporate management. The Black Freedom movement in both of its ten-year-long phases—the campaign for desegregation and the struggle for Black Power—had largely transformed the political contours of U.S. society. But much as the first Reconstruction had been defeated, the second Reconstruction's very successes would create new contradictions and unanticipated detours, as African Americans now searched to define new meanings for the concept of freedom.

~ 1 ~

Rosa Parks, Jo Ann Robinson, and the Montgomery Bus Boycott, *1955–1956*

Many historians have dated the beginning of the modern civil rights movement to the Montgomery bus boycott of 1955–1956, which drew national attention and effectively ended segregation on city buses in Montgomery, Alabama. Though this boycott is often remembered because it led to the emergence of Martin Luther King, Jr., more importantly it was a wide-ranging, grassroots protest movement. To a considerable degree, it was initiated by two women in the Montgomery community, Jo Ann Gibson Robinson (1912–1992) and Rosa Parks (1913–2005).

Robinson was born in Georgia and earned an M.A. in English at Atlanta University before she moved to Montgomery and accepted a post as a professor at Alabama State College. Later she joined the Dexter Avenue Baptist Church, and became president of the Women's Political Council of Montgomery. Like many African-American residents of her community, Robinson suffered abuse and humiliation on city buses, and she repeatedly demanded that city authorities rectify the situation. In May 1954—more than a year before most Americans had ever heard of Rosa Parks or Martin Luther King, Jr.—Robinson penned a letter to Montgomery's mayor threatening a large-scale boycott of the city bus system. Later, as an active member of the Montgomery Improvement Association, she played an important role in organizing and sustaining the protest. In the early 1960s Robinson relocated to Los Angeles, where she taught in the public schools until her retirement in 1976.

Rosa Parks was born in Tuskegee, Alabama. She was a well-respected seamstress and an active member of the NAACP when she broke a local segregation ordinance, on December 1, 1955, by refusing to give up her seat on a Montgomery bus to a white man who had boarded after her. Her subsequent arrest helped spark the famous boycott and led her to earn the title "Mother of the Civil Rights Movement." Parks subsequently was employed by the Southern Christian Leadership Conference (SCLC) in Detroit, Michigan, and later worked for Congressman John Conyers, Jr.

~

"To Keep from Being Insulted"

Honorable Mayor W. J. Gayle
City Hall
Montgomery, Alabama

Dear Sir:

The Women's Political Council is very grateful to you and the City Commissioners for the hearing you allowed our representatives during the month of March, 1954, when the "city-bus-fare-increase case" was being reviewed.

There were several things the Council asked for:

1. A city law that would make it possible for Negroes to sit from back toward front, and whites from front toward back until all the seats are taken:
2. That Negroes not be asked or forced to pay fare at front and go to the rear of the bus to enter:
3. That buses stop at every corner in residential sections occupied by Negroes as they do in communities where whites reside.

We are happy to report that busses have begun stopping at more corners now in some sections where Negroes live than previously. However, the same practices seating and boarding the bus continue.

Mayor Gayle, three-fourths of the riders of these public conveyances are Negroes. If Negroes did not patronize them, they could not possibly operate.

More and more of our people are already arranging with neighbors and friends to ride to keep from being insulted and humiliated by bus drivers.

There has been talk from twenty-five or more local organizations of planning a city-wide boycott of busses. We, sir, do not feel that forceful measures are necessary in bargaining for a convenience which is right for all bus passengers. We, the Council, believe that when this matter has been put before you and the Commissioners, that agreeable terms can be met in a quiet and sensible manner to the satisfaction of all concerned.

Many of our Southern cities in neighboring states have practiced the policies we seek without incident whatsoever. Atlanta, Macon and Savannah in Georgia have done this for years. Even Mobile, in our own state, does this and all the passengers are satisfied.

Please consider this plea, and if possible, act favorably upon it, for even now plans are being made to ride less, or not at all, on our busses. We do not want this.

Respectfully yours,
The Women's Political Council
Jo Ann Robinson, President

~

Interview with Rosa Parks

I had left my work at the men's alteration shop, a tailor shop in the Montgomery Fair department store, and as I left work, I crossed the street to a drugstore to pick up a few items instead of trying to go directly to the bus stop. And when I had finished this, I came across the street and looked for a Cleveland Avenue bus that apparently had some seats on it. At that time it was a little hard to get a seat on the bus. But when I did get to the entrance of the bus, I got in line with a number of other people who were getting on the same bus.

As I got up on the bus and walked to the seat I saw there was only one vacancy that was just back of where it was considered the white section. So this was the seat that I took, next to the aisle, and a man was sitting next to me. Across the aisle there were two women, and there were a few seats at this point in the very front of the bus that was called the white section. I went on to one stop and I didn't particularly notice who was getting on the bus, didn't particularly notice the other people getting on. And on the third stop there were some people getting on, and at this point all of the front seats were taken. Now in the beginning, at the very first stop I had got on the bus, the back of the bus was filled up with people standing in the aisle and I don't know why this one vacancy that I took was left, because there were quite a few people already standing toward the back of the bus. The third stop is when all the front seats were taken, and this one man was standing and when the driver looked around and saw he was standing, he asked the four of us, the man in the seat with me and the two women across the aisle, to let him have those front seats.

At his first request, didn't any of us move. Then he spoke again and said, "You'd better make it light on yourselves and let me have those seats." At this point, of course, the passenger who would have taken the seat hadn't said anything. In fact, he never did speak to my knowledge. When the three people, the man who was in the seat with me and the two women, stood up and moved into the aisle, I remained where I was. When the driver saw that I was still sitting there, he asked if I was going to stand up. I told him, no, I wasn't. He said, "Well, if you don't stand up, I'm going to have you arrested." I told him to go on and have me arrested.

He got off the bus and came back shortly. A few minutes later, two policemen got on the bus, and they approached me and asked if the driver had asked me to stand up, and I said yes, and they wanted to know why I didn't. I told them I didn't think I should have to stand up. . . . They placed me under arrest then and had me to get in the police car, and I was taken to jail and booked on suspicion, I believe. . . . They had to determine whether or not the driver wanted to press charges or swear out a warrant, which he did. Then they took me to jail and I was placed in a cell. In a little while I was taken from the cell, and my picture was made and fingerprints taken. I went back to the cell then, and a few minutes later I was called back again, and when this happened I found out that Mr. E. D. Nixon and Attorney and Mrs. Clifford Durr had come to make bond for me.

⌐⌐

EXCERPTS FROM JO ANN ROBINSON'S ACCOUNT OF THE BOYCOTT

In October 1955, Mary Louise Smith, an eighteen-year-old black girl, was arrested and fined for refusing to move to the rear of the bus. Her case was unpublicized and no one knew about it until after her arrest and conviction. She, too, was found guilty; she paid her fine and kept on riding the bus.

Intermittently, twenty to twenty-five thousand black people in Montgomery rode city buses, and I would estimate that, up until the boycott of December 5, 1955, about three out of five had suffered some unhappy experience on the public transit lines. But the straw that broke the camel's back came on Thursday, December 1, 1955, when an incident occurred which was almost a repeat performance of the Claudette Colvin case.

In the afternoon of Thursday, December 1, a prominent black woman named Mrs. Rosa Parks was arrested for refusing to vacate her seat for a white man. Mrs. Parks was a medium-sized, cultured mulatto woman; a civic and religious worker; quiet, unassuming, and pleasant in manner and appearance; dignified and reserved; of high morals and a strong character. She was—and still is, for she lives to tell the story—respected in all black circles. By trade she was a seamstress, adept and competent in her work.

Tired from work, Mrs. Parks boarded a bus. The "reserved seats" were partially filled, but the seats just behind the reserved section were vacant, and Mrs. Parks sat down in one. It was during the busy evening rush hour. More black and white passengers boarded the bus, and soon all the reserved seats were occupied. The driver demanded that Mrs. Parks get up and surrender her seat to a white man, but she was tired from her work. Besides, she was a woman, and the person waiting was a man. She remained seated. In a few minutes, police summoned by the driver appeared, placed Mrs. Parks under arrest, and took her to jail.

It was the first time the soft-spoken, middle-aged woman had been arrested. She maintained decorum and poise, and the word of her arrest spread. Mr. E. D. Nixon, a longtime stalwart of our NAACP branch, along with liberal white attorney Clifford Durr and his wife Virginia, went to jail and obtained Mrs. Parks's release on bond. Her trial was scheduled for Monday, December 5, 1955.

The news traveled like wildfire into every black home. Telephones jangled; people congregated on street corners and in homes and talked. But nothing was done. A numbing helplessness seemed to paralyze everyone. Very few stayed off the buses the rest of that day or the next. There was fear, discontent, and uncertainty. Everyone seemed to wait for someone to *do* something, but nobody made a move. For that day and a half, black Americans rode the buses as before, as if nothing had happened. They were sullen and uncommunicative, but they rode the buses. There was a silent, tension-filled waiting. For blacks were not talking loudly in public places—they were quiet, sullen, waiting. Just waiting! Thursday evening came and went.

Thursday night was far spent, when, at about 11:30 P.M., I sat alone in my peaceful single-family dwelling on a quiet street. I was thinking about the situation. Lost in thought, I was startled by the telephone's ring. Black attorney Fred Gray, who had been out of town all day, had just gotten back and was returning the phone message I had left for him about Mrs. Parks's arrest. Attorney Gray, though a very young man, had been one of my most active colleagues in our previous meetings with bus company officials and Commissioner Birmingham. A Montgomery native who had attended Alabama State and been one of my students, Fred Gray had gone on to law school in Ohio before returning to his home town to open a practice with the only other black lawyer in Montgomery, Charles Langford.

Fred Gray and his wife Bernice were good friends of mine, and we talked often. In addition to being a lawyer, Gray was a trained, ordained minister of the gospel, actively serving as assistant pastor of Holt Street Church of Christ.

Tonight his voice on the phone was very short and to the point. Fred was shocked by the news of Mrs. Parks's arrest. I informed him that I already was thinking that the WPC should distribute thousands of notices calling for all bus riders to stay off the buses on Monday, the day of Mrs. Parks's trial. "Are you ready?" he asked. Without hesitation, I assured him that we were. With that he hung up, and I went to work.

I made some notes on the back of an envelope: "The Women's Political Council will not wait for Mrs. Parks's consent to call for a boycott of city buses. On Friday, December 2, 1955, the women of Montgomery will call for a boycott to take place on Monday, December 5."

Some of the WPC officers previously had discussed plans for distributing thousands of notices announcing a bus boycott. Now the time had come for me to write just such a notice. I sat down and quickly drafted a message and then called a good friend and colleague, John Cannon, chairman of the business department at the college, who had access to the college's mimeograph equipment. When I told him that the WPC was staging a boycott and needed to run off the notices, he told me that he too had suffered embarrassment on the city buses. Like myself, he had been hurt and angry. He said that he would happily assist me. Along with two of my most trusted senior students, we quickly agreed to meet almost immediately, in the middle of the night, at the college's duplicating room. We were able to get three messages to a page, greatly reducing the number of pages that had to be mimeographed in order to produce the tens of thousands of leaflets we knew would be needed. By 4 A.M. Friday, the sheets had been duplicated, cut in thirds, and bundled. Each leaflet read:

> Another Negro woman has been arrested and thrown in jail because she refused to get up out of her seat on the bus for a white person to sit down. It is the second time since the Claudette Colvin case that a Negro woman has been arrested for the same thing. This has to be stopped. Negroes have rights, too, for if Negroes did not ride the buses, they could not operate. Three-fourths of the riders are Negroes, yet we are arrested, or have to stand over empty seats. If we do not do something to stop these arrests, they will continue. The next time it may be you, or your daughter, or mother. This woman's case will come up on Monday. We are, therefore, asking every Negro to stay off the buses Monday in protest of the arrest and trial. Don't ride the buses to work, to town, to school, or anywhere on Monday. You can afford to stay out of school for one day if you have no other way to go except by bus. You can also afford to stay out of town for one day. If you work, take a cab, or walk. But please, children and grown-ups, don't ride the bus at all on Monday. Please stay off of all buses Monday.

Between 4 and 7 A.M., the two students and I mapped out distribution routes for the notices. Some of the WPC officers previously had discussed how and where to deliver thousands of leaflets announcing a boycott, and those plans now stood me in good stead. We outlined our routes, arranged the bundles in sequences, stacked them in our cars, and arrived at my 8 A.M. class, in which both young men were enrolled, with several minutes to spare. We weren't even tired or hungry. Just like me, the two students felt a tremendous sense of satisfaction at being able to contribute to the cause of justice.

After class my two students and I quickly finalized our plans for distributing the thousands of leaflets so that one would reach every black home in Montgomery. I took out the WPC membership roster and called the former president, Dr. Mary Fair Burks, then the Pierces, the Glasses, Mrs. Mary Cross, Mrs. Elizabeth Arrington, Mrs. Josie Lawrence, Mrs. Geraldine Nesbitt, Mrs. H. Councill Trenholm, Mrs. Catherine N. Johnson, and a dozen or more others. I alerted all of them to the forthcoming distribution of the leaflets, and enlisted their aid in speeding and organizing the distribution network. Each would have one person waiting at a certain place to take a package of notices as soon as my car stopped and the young men could hand them a bundle of leaflets.

Then I and my two student helpers set out. Throughout the late morning and early afternoon hours we dropped off tens of thousands of leaflets. Some of our bundles were dropped off at schools, where both students and staff members helped distribute them further and spread the word for people to read the notices and then pass them on to neighbors. Leaflets were also dropped off at business places, storefronts, beauty parlors, beer halls, factories, barber shops, and every other available place. Workers would pass along notices both to other employees as well as to customers.

During those hours of crucial work, nothing went wrong. Suspicion was never raised. The action of all involved was so casual, so unconcerned, so nonchalant, that suspicion was never raised, and neither the city nor its people ever suspected a thing! We never missed a spot. And no one missed a class, a job, or a normal routine. Everything was done by the plan, with perfect timing. By 2 o'clock, thousands of the mimeographed handbills had changed hands many times. Practically every black man, woman, and child in Montgomery knew the plan and was passing the word along. No one knew where the notices had come from or who had arranged for their circulation, and no one cared. Those who passed them on did so efficiently, quietly, and without comment. But deep within the heart of every black person was a joy he or she dared not reveal. . . .

Before Monday was half gone, Negroes had made history. Never before had they united in such a manner. There was open respect and admiration in the eyes of many whites who had looked on before, dubious and amused. Even clerks in dime stores, all white, were more cordial. They were heard to add, after a purchase by a black customer, "Y'all come back to see us," which was a very unusual occurrence. The black customers held their heads higher. They felt reborn, important for the first time. A greater degree of race pride was exhibited. Many were themselves surprised at the response of the masses, and could not explain, if they had wanted to, what had changed them overnight into fearless, courageous, proud people, standing together for human dignity, civil rights, and, yes, self-respect! There was a stick-togetherness that drew them like a magnet. They showed a genuine fondness for one another. They were really free—free inside! They felt it! Acted it! Manifested it in their entire beings! They took great pride in being black.

The Monday Night Meeting at Holt Street Church

Six thousand black people, along with local reporters, packed Holt Street Baptist Church that night, December 5, 1955, for the first mass meeting of the bus boycott. In the main auditorium, the balcony, the basement, the aisles, steps, the front, side, and back yards, and for three blocks up and down Holt Street, people crowded near to hear what was said. Loudspeakers were set up so that crowds who sat in parked cars two blocks away could hear. Police cars patrolling the area warned those inside the church to turn down the volume, which was disturbing the people outside, but no one paid any attention. The volume stayed loud.

White journalists from Montgomery and other nearby places were on hand to report the news of the boycott. Cameras flashed repeatedly, taking pictures of the thousands gathered in the church. So intent were the people on what was being said that the photographers went unnoticed.

The pulpit was jammed with Baptist, Methodist, Congregational, Catholic, and other ministers, and with organization officials. They conducted a spirited devotion of prayer and hymns. Prayers were offered for "endurance, tolerance, faith in God." There were prayers for the city commissioners; for "misguided whites"; for the weak; and for all races and nations. People felt the spirit. Their enthusiasm inundated them, and they overflowed with "powerful emotion."

Reverend Ralph Abernathy, presiding, said the boycott was not a one-man show, nor a preacher's show, but the show of 45,000 black Montgomerians. It was also a show of black Americans all over America and all over the world and of freedom-loving people everywhere. When one ministerial spokesman after another told of the tremendous success of the one-day boycott, cries of joy and thunderous applause pealed forth and "ascended the heavens to God Almighty," as one present was heard to say.

The leaders reiterated that the protest had been and would be kept Christian, non-violent, legal. Even Joe Azbell, city editor of the *Montgomery Advertiser*, seemed impressed, for in his article on Wednesday, December 7, he confessed that "there was discipline among Negroes which whites were not aware of."

When the question was posed as to whether the people would end the one-day bus boycott, thousands of voices shouted the same word, "No! No!" One lone voice cried out in clear tones, "This is just the beginning!" Thunderous applause was the response.

Those on the podium agreed, without one dissenting vote, that the protest must continue. Ministers pledged themselves and their congregations to remain off the buses until legal steps were taken that would insure fair, unbiased, equal treatment of all bus passengers. Mr. E. D. Nixon received an ovation when he observed that "Negroes stopped riding the bus because they were arrested, and now they are being arrested for not riding them."

As the *Alabama Journal* reported the next day, the Negroes passed a four-part resolution urging:

1. All citizens of Montgomery "regardless of race, color, or creed" to refrain from riding buses owned and operated by the City Lines Bus Company "until some arrangement has been worked out between said citizens and the bus company."

2. That every person owning or who has access to automobiles will use them in assisting other persons to get to work "without charge."

3. That employers of persons who live a great distance from their work, "as much as possible" provide transportation for them.

4. That the Negro citizens of Montgomery are ready and willing to send a delegation to the bus company to discuss their grievances and to work out a solution for the same.

At these times, after almost two months had passed and with no end in sight, groups of widely-read pedestrians, picked up along the way and carried home, would get into deep conversations when their faith wavered in the balance. Indeed, one must wonder about the peculiar turns that things take sometimes, and about the controlling force that may compel them. Call it fate, destiny, a trick of nature, or the will of God, there is an inexplicable something, a force or power that seems to direct men's lives and twist them into some particular shape. Sometimes that shape is good, sometimes not so good.

During such periods of intense suffering—and people did suffer, mentally, spiritually, and financially—there were those weary souls who began to question God's presence, to wonder where God was and if God was really with the whites on segregation. Even the white man's religion, some said, seemed to be based to a great extent on segregation and white supremacy. Then some mused, "Is God white?"

So they would reason as we drove along, going home from a hard day's work. "Whites were born into, and have lived a lifetime enjoying the role of the superior, feasting their egos on the belief in racial supremacy. To these people, blacks are not equal."

"Yes, those folks don't believe in racial equality, and because of that belief, they think that black people can exist on less than the whites can."

"Separate but equal is right, but it's this separate but unequal that is killing us."

"In the separate schools, libraries, recreational parks, types of employment, salaries, waiting rooms, drinking fountains—no matter what—there has not been equality."

Many of these people had become disillusioned with life itself and wondered at the hypocrisy of it all. How could one set of human beings be so cruel and inhuman to another set, just because of the color of their skin and the texture of their hair? Was it because the side in control was superior? Or were whites afraid that, if the other side was given a chance, *it* would prove superior? Was the white man really afraid of the black man?

Most of the drivers who picked up pedestrians as they walked along, tired and hungry, would find a way to bring them out of such moods. We would tell a joke on "whitey" that showed him in a less exalted position than someone had just pictured him in, and everybody would laugh. In no time they would have forgotten the ugly mood they were in and begin all over again. . . .

The Last Mile

Almost four months had passed since December 5, 1955. Every plan the City Fathers had proposed to end the boycott had failed. Most of Montgomery's buses stood dusty and empty where they had been parked at Christmas. The MIA had developed its own free transportation service. There was a general belief that the situation could and would go on indefinitely.

The MIA continued to receive funds from all parts of the U.S. and many places abroad. People from across the world still came to see and write about the situation.

Each Monday night thousands of people attended the weekly mass meetings. Collections were always taken, and every person who could contributed religiously and generously of her or his earnings to operate the transportation services. All of us who had steady jobs continued to give a percentage of our earnings each week, as we had since the beginning of the boycott. Drivers were paid regularly and were satisfied with their salaries. The station wagons had to be kept in good repair; fuel bills were enormous. The more money we needed, the more people, locally and elsewhere, seemed to give. The giving, the sharing, the serving continued on throughout the spring, summer, and fall of 1956. By April it was clear that the bus company and Montgomery's City Fathers had realized that black Americans meant it when they said they would never return to the buses except on an integrated basis, for all other efforts to get city buses rolling again had failed. Then our case in the federal courts began to move forward.

On May 11, a three-judge federal court, sitting in the federal courthouse in downtown Montgomery, heard arguments in the MIA's suit seeking a declaration that racially segregated seating on city buses violated the 14th Amendment's guarantee of equal government treatment of all citizens, irrespective of race, as the Supreme Court already had ruled on with regard to schools in its 1954 landmark opinion in *Brown v. Board of Education of Topeka*.

Several weeks later, on June 5, the judges announced that they had voted two to one against the constitutionality of segregated seating on Montgomery's city buses. Relegating black riders to the rear of city buses, or forcing them to stand over empty seats reserved for whites, or making them surrender seats to white passengers, were all unconstitutional practices.

Judge Richard T. Rives wrote the 2-to-1 majority decision. U.S. District Court Judge Frank M. Johnson joined him in the majority opinion. Their opinion struck down as unconstitutional the statutes requiring racially segregated seating on city buses.

After their opinion, the two judges were deluged for months with hate mail, abusive telephone calls, and threats from segregationists for the stand they took and the opinion they gave that helped to wipe out segregation. Old friends no longer spoke to them. Black Montgomerians, however, will never forget either Rives or Johnson.

Montgomery city officials, though, did not celebrate or welcome Rives' and

Johnson's ruling. Instead, they announced they would appeal the decision to the U.S. Supreme Court. Five months passed without any resolution of the matter. The city's buses remained segregated, and the MIA's transportation system continued to function most effectively. Then, in mid-November, just as the City Commission, under prodding from local segregationists, moved in state court to enjoin the operation of our carpool system, the U.S. Supreme Court issued a brief but decisive order, upholding Rives' and Johnson's ruling that Montgomery's buses had to be integrated. We thought at first that the change would take effect immediately, but then learned, to our dismay, that the order would be effective only when formally served on Montgomery officials. The City Commission, however, seeking to postpone as long as possible the arrival of that order, petitioned the Supreme Court to reconsider its ruling. The court rejected that request, but the legal maneuvering delayed matters for several weeks, and it was not until Thursday, December 20, that U.S. marshals formally served the Supreme Court order on city officials. That night the MIA held two mass meetings, and the next morning Montgomery City Lines resumed full service on all routes. Among its first passengers of the day were Mrs. Parks, Dr. King, and Reverend Abernathy, who boarded an early morning bus and took seats in what had once been the reserved, whites-only section as news photographers snapped pictures of the historic event. . . .

Sources: (1) Letter from Jo Ann Robinson to W.J. Gayle, May 21, 1954, reprinted by permission of the University of Tennessee Press. From *The Montgomery Bus Boycott and the Women Who Made It: The Memoir of Jo Ann Gibson Robinson*, edited, with a foreword, by David J. Garrow (Knoxville: University of Tennessee Press, 1987). Copyright 1987 by the University of Tennessee Press; (2) interview with Rosa L. Parks *My Soul is Rested: Movement Days in the Deep South Remembered* by Howell Raines (New York: Putnam's, 1977). Copyright 1977 by Howell Raines. Used by permission of Putnam/Berkley, a division of Penguin/Putnam Inc.; and (3) excerpts from an account by Jo Ann Robinson, from David J. Garrow, ed., *The Montgomery Bus Boycott and the Women Who Made It: The Memoir of Jo Ann Gibson Robinson*. Copyright 1987 by the University of Tennessee Press, pp. 43–47, 61–63, 112–13, 161–63.

SELECT BIBLIOGRAPHY:

Douglas Brinkley, *Rosa Parks* (New York: Viking, 2000).
Stewart Burns, ed., *Daybreak of Freedom: The Montgomery Bus Boycott* (Chapel Hill: University of North Carolina Press, 1997).
Vicki L. Crawford, Jacqueline Anne Rouse, and Burton Woods, *Women in the Civil Rights Movement, 1941–1965* (Brooklyn: Carlson Publishing, 1990).
David J. Garrow, *The Montgomery Bus Boycott and the Women Who Made It: The Memoir of Jo Ann Gibson Robinson* (Knoxville: University of Tennessee Press, 1987).
———, ed., *The Walking City: The Montgomery Bus Boycott, 1955–1956* (Brooklyn: Carlson Publishing, 1989).
Martin Luther King, Jr., *Stride toward Freedom: The Montgomery Story* (New York: Harpers, 1958).
Brian Ward and Tony Badger, *The Making of Martin Luther King and the Civil Rights Movement* (New York: New York University Press, 1996).
Donnie Williams and Wayne Greenhaw, *The Thunder of Angels: The Montgomery Bus Boycott and the People Who Broke the Back of Jim Crow* (Chicago: Lawrence Hill Books, 2006).

~~ **2** ~~

Roy Wilkins and the NAACP

Roy Wilkins (1901–1981) was born in St. Louis, Missouri, and educated at the University of Minnesota, where he helped edit the school's paper, the *Minnesota Daily*. In 1931, Wilkins began working under Walter White as the assistant executive secretary of the NAACP. Wilkins also succeeded W. E. B. Du Bois as editor of the organization's official journal, *Crisis*, and in 1955 he became executive secretary of the NAACP. In this capacity, Wilkins became an important voice in the modern civil rights movement. With the eruption of Black Power in the mid-1960s, both Wilkins and the NAACP began to lose touch with a new generation of black militancy. The emergence of the Congressional Black Caucus and the newly elected black mayors of major cities in the 1970s also reduced Wilkins's influence. Wilkins subsequently served as chairman of the Leadership Council on Civil Rights and as a trustee and board member of many important organizations.

~~

It is a pleasure to greet again our members and friends in the Southeast region of the NAACP, and particularly those in South Carolina.

There were some signs last summer that the traditional Southern hospitality would no longer be extended to me as executive secretary of the NAACP. Federal Judge Ashton Williams took special pains to suggest from his bench that I should not be permitted to speak again in South Carolina.

But of course he did not mean that. Judge Williams believes, like all good Americans—and certainly all federal judges—in freedom of speech. We may not like what a man has to say, but we have not yet got to the place where we bar him from speaking, as long as he observes the proprieties.

Personally, I don't like what Senator James Eastland of Mississippi and Senator Strom Thurmond of South Carolina say in their speeches but I would not bar either of them from speaking. In fact it would not be exaggerating too much to say that the more such men speak, the more aid they render our cause.

Nevertheless, I *am* sorry, indeed, that my Columbia speech struck Judge Williams as such a poor one—even though it is a difficult task for an NAACP speaker to please a listener who thinks of the NAACP in the same way he thinks of the Ku Klux Klan. The NAACP, after all, has always proceeded according to the law and has always obeyed the rulings of the courts, even when we thought those rulings were unfair. This is in conspicuous contrast to the Klan which, as everyone is aware, has made its own laws, put itself up as judge and carried out its own punishments, while at the same time ignoring the U.S. Supreme Court and all the other courts.

In these respects the Klan has a resemblance to some organizations recently formed in South Carolina and elsewhere in the South, but no resemblance to the

NAACP. I could agree heartily with Judge Williams if he were to declare that South Carolina would benefit if all those organizations did not exist here.

For South Carolina and the South are faced with a problem requiring sober, honest, fair, and sincere consideration.

Basic Question

Here is the big, basic question for Southerners: Shall we obey the law as to our race relations, or shall we defy the law and insist that our 1856 philosophy be the pattern for 1956? Specifically, shall we comply with the Court's opinion on public schools?

On all sides we hear that tensions between the races have increased and that conditions have worsened.

I suggest that if this is true, the underlying bedrock cause is the refusal on the part of the Southern whites to recognize the Negro as a citizen.

The millions of words that have been written and spoken on the Negro, the public schools, the Supreme Court, and the host of other items in the race relations picture have ignored completely this fundamental issue of status.

Consciously and subconsciously, Southern Whites have treated our people as wards, to be done with as they in their wisdom see fit. It comes as a great shock to them to have the highest court in the land hear, evaluate, and uphold the Negro's claims *as a citizen*.

In the southern scheme of things, Negroes were to do as they were told, regardless of their own desires, or any laws to the contrary. This is the "tradition" of which so much is now being made.

The result is that most white Southerners have come to believe, deeply, sincerely and completely, that they have a God-given right to control Negroes. They are bewildered, frustrated, angry, and defiant when this system is challenged.

Editor Thomas Waring, of the *News and Courier*, has complained to the world that the press, radio, television and national magazines are "against" the South, and that they refuse to give its spokesmen a hearing.

In its January issue, *Harper's Magazine* published an article by Mr. Waring which concerned itself principally with assertions that Negroes *as a race* are immoral, criminal, diseased and mentally retarded.

Antiquated Arguments

These "arguments" are strikingly similar to those made in slavery debates more than a hundred years ago. In the light of what has happened to the Negro and the rest of the world since 1860, the Waring contentions, even if sincerely held by scores of thousands of persons, are nonetheless invalid. Because most people once thought the world flat did not make it a fact.

The Waring article, like so much of the talk out of the South, blandly brushes aside the clear responsibility of the South itself for the present "statistics" on Negroes. People who are held to a substandard economic level, barred almost completely from your textile industry, for example, cheated year after weary year as sharecroppers, paid a pittance as domestic servants, denied hospital care, and until five years ago barred from state medical schools—still barred in South Carolina—these people are supposed to be healthy, happy, thrifty, educated, well-housed, responsible, dedicated citizens.

For eighty years Negroes have gone to school in shacks, while whites had the best the government could afford; yet they are now supposed to be the scholastic equals of whites.

Why doesn't Editor Waring compare the Negro students in Boston or Hartford or Pittsburgh or Toledo or Minneapolis with the white students in Charleston or Columbia or Spartanburg or Memphis or Atlanta?

A two-legged man can always out-run a cripple; the point is, how would he do against other two-legged men?

But even if it had any validity, the Waring thesis would astound and disgust thoughtful people inside and outside the South. For they ask: What has all this to do with *equality as a citizens under the law?*

And this is the question our opponents persistently refuse to discuss. Instead, they have chosen to chase down a hundred emotional and unrelated by-paths, some of them ridiculous in the extreme.

They have gone "hog wild and pig crazy" passing laws against the NAACP and desegregation. But on February 18, Attorney General Eugene Cook of Georgia admitted in a speech that most of the laws just passed by his legislature would be "stricken down in due course." The same holds true for what the South Carolina legislature is doing. Its members are merely exercising themselves.

The South Carolina state legislature, for example, in February, called upon the Attorney General of the United States to place the NAACP on his subversive list. Well, if the NAACP were truly a Communist-front organization we would have been on the list long ago. The Communist charge against us is a feeble lie being used throughout the South to excite the gullible and the ignorant.

Assault on NAACP

The assault upon the NAACP, of course, is only one of the methods being employed to intimidate the Negro population, create tension and bypass the basic issue.

There are the White Citizens Councils. More than a year ago the *Montgomery Advertiser* called them "manicured Ku Klux Klans" and it is still a good description.

The Councils constitute a conspiracy to defy the Supreme Court's school ruling and maintain white supremacy. Although they repeat over and over that they do not sanction violence, their public and private statements, mass meetings, and hate literature have been creating the climate in which violence has occurred. The hoodlums have been given the green light.

The murders in Mississippi, the bombings in Montgomery, Alabama, the violence directed at Rev. M. DeLaine, the gunshots into the home of Rev. M. Hinton, our state president, in Columbia, and the disgraceful rioting at the University of Alabama, may all be traced directly to the hysterical atmosphere whipped up by the Citizens Councils and their spokesmen.

United States Senators cannot go about the country preaching lawless defiance of courts and constitutional government without sharing the responsibility for the violence that may ensue.

Governors of states who preach nullification by means of the fancy word, "interposition," are also encouraging more direct violation of law and personal rights.

At the University of Alabama under pitiful hypnosis of the whiteness cult, 1000 young white men demonstrated their superiority over Negroes by throwing eggs and rocks at one lone Negro girl.

In admiration for this 1,000-to-1 battle, a group of men in Lake City, S.C., is reported to have sent a case of eggs to the University.

This, then, is what we are offered as proper and credible debate of a constitutional question; this is the type of mentality for which Editor Waring seeks a hearing in the forums of the rest of the nation.

Violence Encouraged

But the encouragement of violence by innuendo—Senator Eastland, addressing White Councils at Montgomery, Alabama, following the University riot said: "I know you people of Alabama are not going to let the NAACP take over your schools"—is not the only sin of the Councils.

For cowardly and reprehensible economic pressures are the primary weapon of this organization. Sharecroppers, day laborers, home and farm owners, small retail business men and even domestic servants have been "squeezed" if they signed a petition or otherwise spoke up for their rights.

To appreciate the scope of the cowardice, one must remember that none of the victims threatens the power structure of the South. Negroes own no great industries publish no daily papers, sit in no legislatures, have only a fingernail hold in financial circles, are not sheriffs, sit on no court benches, and hold only a few scattered and minor political offices. Their industrial employment is limited to unskilled categories.

What threat do they pose? Are these Citizen Council members, these industrial executives, bankers, educators, editors, ministers of the gospel and other respectable white community leaders any safer or happier because some Negro family is made to face sudden disaster? Does it make a textile executive more secure to know that a Negro widow with four children over in Clarendon county is thrown off the land and has to beg bread and milk for the "sin" of assuming she is a human being?

Is this the thinking, are these the acts, which Editor Waring claims should be "understood" by the North?

Problem of South

Probably nothing illustrates the problem of the South so well as the Montgomery bus protest. And Montgomery city officials, all of whom belong to the White Citizens Councils, have met the situation in the customary southern manner. The police state has come out in the open at Montgomery. The grand jury has indicted

115 persons under a state antiboycott law. This is the Soviet communism method. Here we have the police knocking on doors and taking men away. Here we have mass arrests. Here we have a grand jury delivering a lecture on observance of the segregation line. Precisely like the Communists. Its report said:

"Segregation laws and the NAACP attack on segregation are the primary cause of the unrest and increasing tension between whites and Negroes in Montgomery. In this state we are committed to segregation by custom and by law; we intend to maintain it.

"The settlement of differences over school attendance, public transportation and other public facilities must be made within those laws which reflect our way of life."

What the grand jury said, my friends, is: Here in Montgomery we don't care a hoot about any law except *our* law; don't get any notions about the Supreme Court or the Constitution, or the United States; this is Montgomery, Alabama, and this is what we say black people must do—or else. So 115 people, including practically all the leading ministers among Negroes, are subject to fines and jail sentences.

Understanding Negroes

Montgomery whites claim not to be able to understand "their" Negroes. Well, I'll be glad to explain. "Their" Negroes are sick and tired of segregation, of the daily insults and mistreatment and daily humiliations. It is that simple. Their cups have run over.

The grand jury to the contrary, there was no "outside interference" at Montgomery. Negro ministers there took the lead and guided their flocks toward dignity. The entire nation has been inspired by their quiet Christian courage.

If these men of God go to jail there is a good chance that thousands over the country will follow them to similar jails for similar "crimes."

The time has come for freedom. We have been patient—God knows!—but the time is here. Who can say with truth that we want to go too fast? Ninety years is a long time to wait—no man who waits that long is going too fast.

Certainly, as far as education is concerned, there has been ample warning of the changes to be expected. A Maryland court in 1935 ordered a Negro student admitted to the law school of the University of Maryland. In 1938 the United States Supreme Court put the handwriting on the wall with its decision in the Gaines case at the University of Missouri. Now, twenty years from the Maryland signal and seventeen years from the Missouri notice they tell us we are trying to "force" something "overnight."

Moreover, up to the present, every advance has had to be fought for; almost nothing has been voluntarily given. We won what we now have; the South gave none of the major items in good will and fairness. And what do we ask when we say the time is here? We ask the acknowledgement of our status as citizens. We ask the rights and privileges and responsibilities of citizenship. We ask equality with other citizens under the law.

Desegregation Problem

The school desegregation problem can be solved if the South will begin by recognizing Negro citizenship—unreserved citizenship. This is the first requisite.

From that point plans can be made for a "good faith" beginning on desegregation. Negro citizens will meet any such beginning more than half way, with understanding and good will.

Nothing stands in the way of the easing of tensions except the flat refusal of Southern Whites to make a start. Surely, Negroes cannot be expected to bargain when they are presented with nothing but a "never, never" proposition to bargain over; and when they refrain from discussion on such a basis, they surely cannot be accused fairly of creating or maintaining tension.

In 1857—99 years ago—the Supreme Court declared a Negro had no rights which a white man was bound to respect. That decision was reversed by the Civil War, yet today many whites are following the Dred Scott decision and ignoring all that has happened since. The present situation is squarely in the hands of the leaders of opinion in the South. Condemnation of the NAACP is a smokescreen. A plea for understanding based on considerations of timing is understandable; a plea for understanding based on defiance of constitutional government is a plea for anarchy and secession.

The white people of the South must face up to the basic questions of law and citizenship under law. I, for one, do not for a minute underestimate the difficulties, real or imagined, which confront them in their soul searching. But in every question there are right and wrong sides, profitable ones and unprofitable ones, comfortable ones and uncomfortable ones, easy and difficult ones.

The choice for them is not easy, but it must be made. Our people and our Association stand ready, as always, to help them arrive at a just decision.

It is long past time to begin.

Source: Excerpt from an address delivered on February 24, 1956, NAACP Southeast Regional Convention, Charleston, South Carolina, originally published in *Crisis* 46 (April 1956), pp. 197–201, 254–55, reprinted with permission.

SELECT BIBLIOGRAPHY:

Minnie Finch, *The NAACP: Its Fight for Justice* (Metuchen, N.J.: Scarecrow Press, 1981).
Charles F. Kellogg, *NAACP: A History of the National Association for the Advancement of Colored People* (Baltimore: Johns Hopkins University Press, 1967).
Roy Wilkins and William T. Ingersoll, *The Reminiscences of Roy Wilkins: Interviewed by William Ingersoll* (Alexandria: Alexander Street press, 2003).
Roy Wilkins, with Tom Mathews, *Standing Fast: The Autobiography of Roy Wilkins* (New York: Da Capo Press, 1994).

～ 3 ～

The Southern Christian Leadership Conference, *1957*

The Southern Christian Leadership Conference (SCLC) was established in 1957 by Martin Luther King, Jr., as an off-shoot of the Montgomery Improvement

Association, the organizing coalition that helped coordinate the 1955–1956 Montgomery bus boycott. During the Black Freedom movement of the 1960s, the SCLC was in many respects situated ideologically and politically at the center of the broad desegregationist coalition. It was to the left of the NAACP and National Urban League in its use of civil disobedience tactics and nonviolent grassroots organizing. But it was frequently more moderate and programmatic than the activists in the Student Nonviolent Coordinating Committee and the Congress of Racial Equality. King led the SCLC until his assassination in 1968, and the organization continues to operate out of Atlanta, Georgia. Though the SCLC is interracial and nonsectarian, its board is largely made up of African-American ministers and is presently led by the Rev. Joseph Lowery.

PROGRAM OF THE SOUTHERN CHRISTIAN LEADERSHIP CONFERENCE

Aims and Purposes of SCLC

The Southern Christian Leadership Conference has the basic aim of achieving full citizenship rights, equality, and the integration of the Negro in all aspects of American life. SCLC is a service agency to facilitate coordinated action of local community groups within the frame of their indigenous organizations and natural leadership. SCLC activity revolves around two main focal points: the use of nonviolent philosophy as a means of creative protest; and securing the right of the ballot for every citizen.

Philosophy of SCLC

The basic tenets of Hebraic-Christian tradition, coupled with the Gandhian concept of *satyagraha*—truth force—is at the heart of SCLC's philosophy. Christian nonviolence actively resists evil in any form. It never seeks to humiliate the opponent, only to win him. Suffering is accepted without retaliation. Internal violence of the spirit is as much to be rejected as external physical violence. At the center of nonviolence is redemptive love. Creatively used, the philosophy of nonviolence can restore the broken community in America. SCLC is convinced that nonviolence is the most potent force available to an oppressed people in their struggle for freedom and dignity.

SCLC and Nonviolent Mass Direct Action

SCLC believes that the American dilemma in race relations can best and most quickly be resolved through the action of thousands of people, committed to the philosophy of nonviolence, who will physically identify themselves in a just and moral struggle. It is not enough to be intellectually dissatisfied with an evil system. The true nonviolent resister presents his physical body as an instrument to defeat the system. Through nonviolent mass direct action, the evil system is creatively dramatized in order that the conscience of the community may grapple with the rightness or wrongness of the issue at hand. . . .

SCLC and Voter-Registration

The right of the ballot is basic to the exercise of full citizenship rights. All across the South, subtle and flagrant obstacles confront the Negro when he seeks to register and vote. Poll taxes, long form questionnaires, harassment, economic reprisal, and sometimes death, meet those who dare to seek this exercise of the ballot. In areas where there is little or no attempt to block the voting attempts of the Negro, apathy generally is deeply etched upon the habits of the community. SCLC, with its specialized staff, works on both fronts: aiding local communities through every means available to secure the right to vote (e.g., filing complaints with the Civil Rights Commission) and arousing interest through voter-registration workshops to point up the importance of the ballot. Periodically, SCLC, upon invitation, conducts a voter-registration drive to enhance a community's opportunity to free itself from economic and political servitude. SCLC believes that the most important step the Negro can take is that short walk to the voting booth.

SCLC and Civil Disobedience

SCLC sees civil disobedience as a natural consequence of nonviolence when the resister is confronted by unjust and immoral laws. This does not imply that SCLC advocates either anarchy or lawlessness. The Conference firmly believes that all people have a moral responsibility to obey laws that are just. It recognizes, however, that there also are unjust laws. From a purely moral point of view, an unjust law is one that is out of harmony with the moral law of the universe, or as the religionist would say, out of harmony with the Law of God. More concretely, an unjust law is one in which the minority is compelled to observe a code which is not binding on the majority. An unjust law is one in which people are required to obey a code that they had no part in making because they were denied the right to vote. In the face of such obvious inequality, where difference is made legal, the nonviolent resister has no alternative but to disobey the unjust law. In disobeying such a law, he does so peacefully, openly and nonviolently. Most important, he *willingly* accepts the penalty for breaking the law. This distinguishes SCLC's position on civil disobedience from the "uncivil disobedience" of the racist opposition in the South. In the face of laws they consider unjust, they seek to defy, evade, and circumvent the law. BUT they are *unwilling* to accept the penalty for breaking the law. The end result of their defiance is anarchy and disrespect for the law. SCLC, on the other hand, believes that civil disobedience involves the highest respect for the law. He who openly disobeys a law that conscience tells him is unjust and willingly accepts the penalty is giving evidence that he so respects the law that he belongs in jail until it is changed. . . .

SCLC and Segregation

SCLC is firmly opposed to segregation in any form that it takes and pledges itself to work unrelentingly to rid every vestige of its scars from our nation through nonviolent means. Segregation is an evil and its presence in our nation has blighted our larger destiny as a leader in world affairs. Segregation does as much harm to the *segregator* as it does to the *segregated*. The *segregated* develops a false sense of inferiority and the *segregator* develops a false sense of superiority, both contrary to the American ideal of democracy. America must rid herself of segregation not alone because it is politically expedient, but because it is morally right!

SCLC and Constructive Program

SCLC's basic program fosters nonviolent resistance to all forms of racial injustice, including state and local laws and practices, even when this means going to jail; and imaginative, bold constructive action to end the demoralization caused by the legacy of slavery and segregation—inferior schools, slums, and second-class citizenship. Thus, the Conference works on two fronts. On the one hand it resists continuously the system of segregation which is the basic cause of flagging standards; on the other hand, it works constructively to improve the standards themselves. There MUST be a balance between attacking the causes and healing the effects of segregation.

SCLC and the Beloved Community

The ultimate aim of SCLC is to foster and create the "beloved community" in America where brotherhood is a reality. It rejects any doctrine of black supremacy for this merely substitutes one kind of tyranny for another. The Conference does not foster moving the Negro from a position of disadvantage to one of advantage for this would thereby subvert justice. SCLC works for integration. Our ultimate goal is genuine intergroup and interpersonal living— *integration*. Only through nonviolence can reconciliation and the creation of the beloved community be effected. The international focus on America and her internal problems against the dread prospect of a hot war, demand our seeking this end.

Source: "This is SCLC," pamphlet printed as mimeograph by the SCLC in Atlanta, Georgia, in 1957.

SELECT BIBLIOGRAPHY:

Randolph H. Boehm, *Records of the SCLC: 1954–1970* (Bethesda, Md.: University Publications of America, 1995).

Adam Fairclough, *To Redeem the Soul of America: The Southern Christian Leadership Conference and Martin Luther King, Jr.* (Athens: University of Georgia Press, 1978).

David Garrow, *Bearing the Cross: Martin Luther King, Jr., and the Southern Christian Leadership Conference* (New York: Morrow, 1986).

Thomas R. Peake, *Keeping the Dream Alive: A History of the Southern Christian Leadership Conference from King to the Nineteen-Eighties* (New York: Lang, 1987).

Emilie Schmeidler, "Shaping Ideas and Actions: CORE, SCLC, and SNCC in the Struggle for Equality, 1960–1966" (Ph.D. diss., University of Michigan, 1980).

⟿ 4 ⟿

Student Nonviolent Coordinating Committee and the Sit-In Movement, *1960*

The Student Nonviolent Coordinating Committee (SNCC) emerged in 1960 at Shaw University in Raleigh, North Carolina, with the aid of one of the SCLC's most important leaders, Ella Baker. Initially, the group was closely affiliated with the SCLC, and they focused primarily on voter-registration drives. Though the organization experienced success in this capacity, many SNCC workers also grew disenchanted with both the organized white violence they encountered and the lack of federal support for their efforts. By the middle of the decade many SNCC leaders began to rethink the philosophy of racial integration, and they questioned the continuing viability of tactical nonviolence. Whites were largely forced out of the organization in 1966, and many of the group's early leaders—including Julian Bond, Diane Nash, James Lawson, and John Lewis—were replaced by more outspoken, militant activists such as Stokely Carmichael and H. Rap Brown, who identified with the emerging Black Power movement. SNCC was the smallest of the major desegregation organizations in the 1960s, but in many respects left a greater legacy than any other civil rights group. The "True Believers" or dedicated activists within SNCC were deeply idealistic and sought through their personal sacrifices and collective struggles to dismantle the institutions of racial inequality and social injustice.

⟿

STUDENT NONVIOLENT COORDINATING COMMITTEE STATEMENT OF PURPOSE
We affirm the philosophical or religious ideal of nonviolence as the foundation of our purpose, the pre-supposition of our faith, and the manner of our action. Nonviolence as it grows from Judaic-Christian traditions seeks a social order of justice permeated by love. Integration of human endeavor represents the crucial first step towards such a society.

Through nonviolence, courage displaces fear; love transforms hate. Acceptance dissipates prejudice; hope ends despair. Peace dominates war; faith reconciles doubt. Mutual regard cancels enmity. Justice for all overthrows injustice. The redemptive community supersedes systems of gross social immorality.

Love is the central motif of nonviolence. Love is the force by which God binds man to himself and man to man. Such love goes to the extreme; it remains loving and forgiving even in the midst of hostility. It matches the capacity of evil to inflict suffering with an even more enduring capacity to absorb evil, all the while persisting in love.

By appealing to conscience and standing on the moral nature of human existence, nonviolence nurtures the atmosphere in which reconciliation and justice become actual possibilities.

Source: "Statement of Purpose," drafted for the Student Nonviolent Coordinating Committee by the Rev. James Lawson, May 14, 1960, mimeographed document.

SELECT BIBLIOGRAPHY:

Clayborne Carson, *In Struggle: SNCC and the Black Awakening of the 1960s* (Cambridge, Mass.: Harvard University Press, 1981).

Cynthia Griggs Fleming, *Soon We Will Not Cry: The Liberation of Ruby Doris Smith Robinson* (Lanham: Rowman & Littlefield, 2000).

Cheryl Lynn Greenberg, *A Circle of Trust: Remembering SNCC* (New Brunswick, N.J.: Rutgers University Press, 1998).

Wesley C. Hogan, *Many Minds, One Heart: SNCC's Dream for a New America* (Chapel Hill: University of North Carolina Press, 2007).

John Lewis and Michael D'Orso, *Walking with the Wind: A Memoir of the Movement* (New York: Simon & Schuster, 1998).

Cleveland Sellers, *The River of No Return: The Autobiography of a Black Militant and the Life and Death of SNCC* (New York: William and Morrow, 1973).

Emily Stoper, *The Student Nonviolent Coordinating Committee: The Growth of Radicalism in a Civil Rights Organization* (Brooklyn, N.Y.: Carlson Publishing, 1989).

Miles Wolff, *Lunch at the Five and Ten, the Greensboro Sit-Ins: A Contemporary History* (New York: Stein and Day, 1970).

Howard Zinn, *SNCC: The New Abolitionists* (Boston: Beacon Press, 1964).

5

Freedom Songs, *1960s*

Music, folklore, and poetry have always been important windows in understanding the political culture and history of African Americans. During the civil rights movement of the 1950s and 1960s, "freedom songs" served many functions: they promoted solidarity, increased faith, expressed sorrow, and strengthened the wills of movement activists. Many of these songs were traditional songs of protest, whereas others were adaptations of spirituals or labor union songs. Marchers adopted "We Shall Overcome" as the unofficial theme song for the movement, and "Ain't Gonna Let Nobody Turn Me 'Round" was widely sung, in slightly different versions, across the terrain of the Black Freedom movement.

"We Shall Overcome"

> We shall overcome, we shall overcome,
> We shall overcome someday.
> Oh, deep in my heart, I do believe,
> We shall overcome someday.
>
> We are not afraid, we are not afraid,
> We are not afraid today.

Oh, deep in my heart, I do believe,
We shall overcome someday.

We are not alone, we are not alone,
We are not alone today.
Oh, deep in my heart, I do believe,
We are not alone today.

The truth will make us free, the truth will make us free,
The truth will make us free someday.
Oh, deep in my heart, I do believe,
We shall overcome someday.

We'll walk hand in hand, we'll walk hand in hand,
We'll walk hand in hand someday.
Oh, deep in my heart, I do believe,
We shall overcome someday.

The Lord will see us through, the Lord will see us through,
The Lord will see us through someday.
Oh, deep in my heart, I do believe,
We shall overcome someday.

Black and white together, black and white together,
Black and white together now.
Oh, deep in my heart, I do believe,
We shall overcome someday.

We shall all be free, we shall all be free,
We shall all be free someday.
Oh, deep in my heart, I do believe,
We shall overcome someday.

***

"Ain't Gonna Let Nobody Turn Me 'Round"

Ain't gonna let nobody turn me 'round,
    turn me 'round, turn me 'round,
Ain't gonna let nobody turn me 'round,
I'm gonna keep on a walkin', keep on a talkin',
Marching up to freedom land.

Ain't gonna let Nervous Nelly turn me 'round,
    turn me 'round, turn me 'round,
Ain't gonna let Nervous Nelly turn me 'round,
I'm gonna keep on a walkin', keep on a talkin',
Marching up to freedom land.

Ain't gonna let Chief Pritchett turn me 'round,
    turn me 'round, turn me 'round,
Ain't gonna let Chief Pritchett turn me 'round,
I'm gonna keep on a walkin', keep on a talkin',
Marching up to freedom land.

Ain't gonna let Mayor Kelly turn me 'round,
    turn me 'round, turn me 'round,
Ain't gonna let Mayor Kelly turn me 'round,
I'm gonna keep on a walkin', keep on a talkin',
Marching up to freedom land.

Ain't gonna let segregation turn me 'round,
    turn me 'round, turn me 'round,
Ain't gonna let segregation turn me 'round,
I'm gonna keep on a walkin', keep on a talkin',
Marching up to freedom land.

Ain't gonna let Z. T. turn me 'round,
    turn me 'round, turn me 'round,
Ain't gonna let Z. T. turn me 'round,
I'm gonna keep on a walkin', keep on a talkin',
Marching up to freedom land.

Ain't gonna let no jailhouse turn me 'round,
    turn me 'round, turn me 'round,
Ain't gonna let no jailhouse turn me 'round,
I'm gonna keep on a walkin', keep on a talkin',
Marching up to freedom land.

Ain't gonna let no injunction turn me 'round,
    turn me 'round, turn me 'round,
Ain't gonna let no injunction turn me 'round,
I'm gonna keep on a walkin', keep on a talkin',
Marching up to freedom land.

Source: Traditional songs: "We Shall Overcome" and "Ain't Gonna Let Nobody Turn Me 'Round."

SELECT BIBLIOGRAPHY:

Guy and Candie Carawan, *Sing for Freedom: The Story of the Civil Rights Movement Through Its Songs* (Bethlehem, Pa.: A Sing Out Publication, 1990).

Tom Glazer, *Songs of Peace, Freedom, and Protest* (New York: McKay, 1970).

Movement Soul: Sounds of the Freedom Movement in the South, 1963–1964, Washington, D.C.: Folkways, 2000. Sound Recording.

Kerran L. Sanger, *"When the Spirit Says Sing!": The Role of Freedom Songs in the Civil Rights Movement* (New York: Garland, 1995).

Voices of the Civil Rights Movement: Black American Freedom Songs, 1960–1966, Washington, D.C.: Smithsonian Folkways, 1997. Sound Recording.

⚊ **6** ⚊

"We Need Group-Centered Leadership," *Ella Baker*

Ella Baker (1903–1986) played an instrumental role in the development of the civil rights movement of the 1950s and 1960s. Baker was born in Norfolk, Virginia, and grew up in rural Littleton, North Carolina. After graduating from Shaw University, she organized consumer cooperatives in New York and worked on consumer affairs for the Works Progress Administration (WPA). In the 1940s Baker became a national field secretary of the NAACP, traveling throughout the country organizing branches and developing membership drives. Increasingly, Baker became disaffected with the NAACP's leadership, because decision-making occurred primarily in the national office rather than in the branch organizations. In 1957 Baker joined King to help found the SCLC. She directed the SCLC national office and was instrumental in coordinating major civil disobedience actions. She became critical of the SCLC because of its emphasis on charismatic leadership. In 1960 Baker was the principal organizer in helping student protesters establish the SNCC. She solicited funds for SNCC and assisted in planning strategies for voter registration drives and desegregation campaigns. Baker eventually broke with the SCLC after she disagreed with ministers who felt that SNCC should simply be an arm of the SCLC, rather than an independent organization. Although she preferred working behind the scenes to playing a public leadership role, she is widely regarded by scholars as one of the central leaders in the Black Freedom movement.

⚊

"BIGGER THAN A HAMBURGER"

Raleigh, N.C.—The Student Leadership Conference made it crystal clear that current sit-ins and other demonstrations are concerned with something much bigger than a hamburger or even a giant-sized Coke.

Whatever may be the difference in approach to their goal, the Negro and white students, North and South, are seeking to rid America of the scourge of racial segregation and discrimination—not only at lunch counters, but in every aspect of life.

In reports, casual conversations, discussion groups, and speeches, the sense and the spirit of the following statement that appeared in the initial newsletter of the students at Barber-Scotia College, Concord, N.C., were re-echoed time and again:

> We want the world to know that we no longer accept the inferior position of second-class citizenship. We are willing to go to jail, be ridiculed, spat upon and even suffer physical violence to obtain First Class Citizenship.

By and large, this feeling that they have a destined date with freedom, was not limited to a drive for personal freedom, or even freedom for the Negro in the South.

Repeatedly it was emphasized that the movement was concerned with the moral implications of racial discrimination for the "whole world" and the "Human Race."

This universality of approach was linked with a perceptive recognition that "it is important to keep the movement democratic and to avoid struggles for personal leadership."

It was further evident that desire for supportive cooperation from adult leaders and the adult community was also tempered by apprehension that adults might try to "capture" the student movement. The students showed willingness to be met on the basis of equality, but were intolerant of anything that smacked of manipulation or domination.

This inclination toward *group-centered leadership*, rather than toward a *leader-centered group pattern of organization*, was refreshing indeed to those of the older group who bear the scars of the battle, the frustrations and the disillusionment that come when the prophetic leader turns out to have heavy feet of clay.

However hopeful might be the signs in the direction of group-centeredness, the fact that many schools and communities, especially in the South, have not provided adequate experience for young Negroes to assume initiative and think and act independently accentuated the need for guarding the student movement against well-meaning, but nevertheless unhealthy, over-protectiveness.

Here is an opportunity for adult and youth to work together and provide genuine leadership—the development of the individual to his highest potential for the benefit of the group.

Many adults and youth characterized the Raleigh meeting as the greatest or most significant conference of our period.

Whether it lives up to this high evaluation or not will, in a large measure, be determined by the extent to which there is more effective training in and understanding of non-violent principles and practices, in group dynamics, and in the redirection into creative channels of the normal frustrations and hostilities that result from second-class citizenship.

Source: "Bigger than a Hamburger," *Southern Patriot* 18 (June 1960).

SELECT BIBLIOGRAPHY:

Ellen Cantarow, *Moving the Mountain: Women Working for Social Change* (Old Westbury, N.Y.: Feminist Press, 1980).

Clayborne Carson, *In Struggle: SNCC and the Black Awakening of the 1960s* (Cambridge, Mass.: Harvard University Press, 1981).

Joanne Grant, *Ella Baker: Freedom Bound* (New York: Wiley, 1998).

Joy James, "Ella Baker, 'Black Women's Work' and Activist Intellectuals," *Black Scholar* 24, no. 2 (1994), pp. 8–15.

Peter J. Ling and Sharon Monteith, eds., *Gender and the Civil Rights Movement* (New Brunswick: Rutgers University Press, 2004).

Shyrlee Pallard, *Ella Baker: A Leader behind the Scenes* (Englewood Cliffs, N.J.: Silver Burdett Press, 1990).

Joanne Grant, *Ella Baker: Freedom Bound* (New York: Wiley, 1999).

Barbara Ransby, *Ella Baker and the Black Freedom Movement: A Radical Democratic Vision* (Chapel Hill: University of North Carolina Press, 2005).

~ 7 ~

Martin Luther King, Jr., and Nonviolence, *1957 and 1963*

Martin Luther King, Jr. (1929–1968) was *the* political and moral leader of the Black Freedom movement in the mid-twentieth century. King graduated from Moorhouse College in 1948, and received an M.A. from Crozier Theological Seminary in 1951 and a doctorate from Boston University in 1955. King emerged as an important voice for civil rights during the Montgomery bus boycott in 1955, and he was the founding president of the Southern Christian Leadership Conference (SCLC) in 1957. Drawing inspiration from Mohandas Gandhi, the black church, and various theologians, King advocated an ethic of nonviolence, not simply as an organizing tactic but as a way of life. In addition to helping organize several major campaigns of civil disobedience in such diverse places as Albany, Birmingham, Selma, and Chicago, King won the Nobel Peace Prize in 1964. Although he was subjected to illegal surveillance and harassment by the FBI, King became increasingly radical in his critique of U.S. society. On economic issues King gravitated toward democratic socialism, advocating full-employment and social-welfare legislation. At the time of his death in April 1968 he was planning to launch a major Poor People's Campaign in Washington, D.C. King was assassinated in Memphis, Tennessee.

~

EXCERPT FROM NONVIOLENCE AND RACIAL JUSTICE

It is commonly observed that the crisis in race relations dominates the arena of American life. This crisis has been precipitated by two factors: the determined resistance of reactionary elements in the south to the Supreme Court's momentous decision outlawing segregation in the public schools, and the radical change in the Negro's evaluation of himself. While southern legislative halls ring with open defiance through "interposition" and "nullification," while a modern version of the Ku Klux Klan has arisen in the form of "respectable" white citizens' councils, a revolutionary change has taken place in the Negro's conception of his own nature and destiny, once he thought of himself as an inferior and patiently accepted injustice and exploitation. Those days are gone.

This new self-respect and sense of dignity on the part of the Negro undermined the south's negative peace, since the white man refused to accept the change. The tension we are witnessing in race relations today can be explained in part by this revolutionary change in the Negro's evaluation of himself and his determination to struggle and sacrifice until the walls of segregation have been finally crushed by the battering rams of justice.

The determination of Negro Americans to win freedom from every form of oppression springs from the same profound longing for freedom that motivates oppressed peoples all over the world. The rhythmic beat of deep discontent in Africa and Asia is at the bottom a quest for freedom and human dignity on the part of people who have long been victims of colonialism. The struggle for freedom on the part of oppressed people in general and of the American Negro in particular has developed slowly and is not going to end suddenly. Privileged groups rarely give up their privileges without strong resistance. But when oppressed people rise up against oppression there is no stopping point short of full freedom. Realism compels us to admit that the struggle will continue until freedom is a reality for all the oppressed peoples of the world.

Hence the basic question which confronts the world's oppressed is: How is the struggle against the forces of injustice to be waged? There are two possible answers. One is resort to the all too prevalent method of physical violence and corroding hatred. The danger of this method is its futility. Violence solves no social problems; it merely creates new and more complicated ones. Through the vistas of time a voice still cries to every potential Peter, "Put up your sword!" The shores of history are white with the bleached bones of nations and communities that failed to follow this command. If the American Negro and other victims of oppression succumb to the temptation of using violence in the struggle for justice, unborn generations will live in a desolate night of bitterness, and their chief legacy will be an endless reign of chaos.

The alternative to violence is nonviolent resistance. This method was made famous in our generation by Mohandas K. Gandhi, who used it to free India from the domination of the British empire. Five points can be made concerning nonviolence as a method in bringing about better racial conditions.

First, this is not a method for cowards; it *does* resist. The nonviolent resister is just as strongly opposed to the evil against which he protests as is the person who uses violence. His method is passive or nonaggressive in the sense that he is not physically aggressive toward his opponent. But his mind and emotions are always active, constantly seeking to persuade the opponent that he is mistaken. This method is passive physically but strongly active spiritually; it is nonaggressive physically but dynamically aggressive spiritually.

A second point is that nonviolent resistance does not seek to defeat or humiliate the opponent, but to win his friendship and understanding. The nonviolent resister must often express his protest through noncooperation or boycotts, but he realizes that noncooperation and boycotts are not ends themselves; they are merely means to awaken a sense of moral shame in the opponent. The end is redemption and reconciliation. The aftermath of nonviolence is the creation of the beloved community, while the aftermath of violence is tragic bitterness.

A third characteristic of this method is that the attack is directed against forces of evil rather than against persons who are caught in those forces. It is evil we are seeking to defeat, not the persons victimized by evil. Those of us who struggle against racial injustice must come to see that the basic tension is not between races. As I like to say to the people in Montgomery, Alabama: "The tension in this city is not between white people and Negro people. The tension is at bottom between justice and injustice, between the forces of light and the forces of darkness. And if there is a victory it will be a victory not merely for 50,000 Negroes, but a victory for justice and the forces of light. We are out to defeat injustice and not white persons who may happen to be unjust."

A fourth point that must be brought out concerning nonviolent resistance is that it avoids not only external physical violence but also internal violence of spirit. At the center of nonviolence stands the principle of love. In struggling for human dignity the oppressed people of the world must not allow themselves to become bitter or indulge in hate campaigns. To retaliate with hate and bitterness would do nothing but intensify the hate in the world. Along the way of life, someone must have sense enough and morality enough to cut off the chain of hate. This can be done only by projecting the ethics of love to the center of our lives.

In speaking of love at this point, we are not referring to some sentimental emotion. It would be nonsense to urge men to love their oppressors in an affectionate sense. "Love" in this connection means understanding good will. There are three words for love in the Greek New Testament. First, there is *eros*. In Platonic philosophy *eros* meant the yearning of the soul for the realm of the divine. It has come now to mean a sort of aesthetic or romantic love. Second, there is *philia*. It meant intimate affectionateness between friends. *Philia* denotes a sort of reciprocal love: the person loves because he is loved. When we speak of loving those who oppose us we refer to neither *eros* nor *philia*; we speak of a love which is expressed in the Greek word *agape*. *Agape* means nothing sentimental or basically affectionate; it means understanding, redeeming good will for all men, an overflowing love which seeks nothing in return. It is the love of God working in the lives of men. When we love on the *agape* level we love men not because we like them, not because their attitudes and ways appeal to us, but because God loves them. Here we rise to the position of loving the person who does the evil deed while hating the deed he does.

Finally, the method of nonviolence is based on the conviction that the universe is on the side of justice. It is this deep faith in the future that causes the nonviolent resister to accept suffering without retaliation. He knows that in his struggle for justice he has cosmic companionship. This belief that God is on the side of truth and justice comes down to us from the long tradition of our Christian faith. There is something at the very center of our faith which reminds us that Good Friday may reign for a day, but ultimately it must give way to the triumphant beat of the Easter drums. Evil may so shape events that Caesar will occupy a palace and Christ a cross, but one day that same Christ will rise up and split history into A.D. and B.C., so that even the life of Caesar must be dated by his name. So in Montgomery we can walk and never get weary, because we know that there will be a great camp meeting in the promised land of freedom and justice.

This, in brief, is the method of nonviolent resistance. It is a method that challenges all people struggling for justice and freedom. God grant that we wage the struggle with dignity and discipline. May all who suffer oppression in this world reject the self-defeating method of retaliatory violence and choose the method that seeks to redeem. Through using this method wisely and courageously we will emerge from the bleak and desolate midnight of man's inhumanity to man into the bright daybreak of freedom and justice.

I HAVE A DREAM

Five score years ago a great American, in whose symbolic shadow we stand, signed the Emancipation Proclamation. This momentous decree came as a great beacon light of hope to millions of Negro slaves who had been seared in the flames of withering injustice. It came as a joyous daybreak to end the long night of captivity.

But one hundred years later, we must face the tragic fact that the Negro is still not free. One hundred years later, the life of the Negro is still sadly crippled by the manacles of segregation and the chains of discrimination. One hundred years later, the Negro lives on a lonely island of poverty in the midst of a vast ocean of material prosperity. One hundred years later the Negro still languishes in the corners of American society and finds himself an exile in his own land. So we have come here today to dramatize an appalling condition.

In a sense we have come to our nation's capital to cash a check. When the architects of our republic wrote the magnificent words of the Constitution and the Declaration of Independence, they were signing a promissory note to which every American was to fall heir. This note was a promise that all men would be guaranteed the unalienable rights of life, liberty, and the pursuit of happiness.

It is obvious today that America has defaulted on this promissory note insofar as her citizens of color are concerned. Instead of honoring this sacred obligation, America has given the Negro people a bad check; a check which has come back marked "insufficient funds." But we refuse to believe that the bank of justice is bankrupt. We refuse to believe that there are insufficient funds in the great vaults of opportunity of this nation. So we have come to cash this check—a check that will give us upon demand the riches of freedom and the security of justice. We have also come to this hallowed spot to remind America of the fierce urgency of *now*. This is no time to engage in the luxury of cooling off or to take the tranquilizing drug of gradualism. *Now* is the time to make real the promises of democracy. *Now* is the time to rise from the dark and desolate valley of segregation to the sunlit path of racial justice. *Now* is the time to open the doors of opportunity to all of God's children. *Now* is the time to lift our nation from the quicksands of racial injustice to the solid rock of brotherhood.

It would be fatal for the nation to overlook the urgency of the moment and to underestimate the determination of the Negro. This sweltering summer of the Negro's legitimate discontent will not pass until there is an invigorating autumn of freedom and equality. Nineteen sixty-three is not an end, but a beginning. Those who hope that the Negro needed to blow off steam and will now be content will have a rude awakening if the nation returns to business as usual. There will be neither rest nor tranquillity in America until the Negro is granted his citizenship rights. The whirlwinds of revolt will continue to shake the foundations of our nation until the bright day of justice emerges.

But there is something that I must say to my people who stand on the warm threshold which leads into the palace of justice. In the process of gaining our rightful place we must not be guilty of wrongful deeds. Let us not seek to satisfy our thirst for freedom by drinking from the cup of bitterness and hatred. We must forever conduct our struggle on the high plane of dignity and discipline. We must not allow our creative protest to degenerate into physical violence. Again and again we must rise to the majestic heights of meeting physical force with soul force. The marvelous new militancy which has engulfed the Negro community must not lead us to a distrust of all white people, for many of our white brothers, as evidenced by their presence here today, have come to realize that their destiny is tied up with our destiny and their freedom is inextricably bound to our freedom. We cannot walk alone.

And as we walk, we must make the pledge that we shall march ahead. We cannot turn back. There are those who are asking the devotees of civil rights, "When will you be satisfied?" We can never be satisfied as long as the Negro is the victim of the unspeakable horrors of police brutality. We can never be satisfied as long as our bodies, heavy with the fatigue of travel, cannot gain lodging in the motels of the highways and the hotels of the cities. We cannot be satisfied as long as the Negro's basic mobility is from a smaller ghetto to a larger one. We can never be satisfied as long as a Negro in Mississippi cannot vote and a Negro in New York believes he has nothing for which to vote. No, no, we are not satisfied, and we will not be satisfied until justice rolls down like waters and righteousness like a mighty stream.

I am not unmindful that some of you have come here out of great trials and tribulations. Some of you have come fresh from narrow jail cells. Some of you have come from areas where your quest for freedom left you battered by the storms of persecution and staggered by the winds of police brutality. You have been the veterans of creative suffering. Continue to work with the faith that unearned suffering is redemptive.

Go back to Mississippi, go back to Alabama, go back to South Carolina, go back to Georgia, go back to Louisiana, go back to the slums and ghettos of our modern cities, knowing that somehow this situation can and will be changed. Let us not wallow in the valley of despair.

I say to you today, my friends, that in spite of the difficulties and frustrations of the moment I still have a dream. It is a dream deeply rooted in the American dream.

I have a dream that one day this nation will rise up and live out the true meaning of its creed: "We hold these truths to be self-evident; that all men are created equal."

I have a dream that one day on the red hills of Georgia the sons of former slaves and the sons of former slaveowners will be able to sit down together at the table of brotherhood.

I have a dream that one day even the state of Mississippi, a desert state sweltering with the heat of injustice and oppression, will be transformed into an oasis of freedom and justice.

I have a dream that my four little children will one day live in a nation where they will not be judged by the color of their skin but by the content of their character.

I have a dream today.

I have a dream that one day the state of Alabama, whose governor's lips are presently dripping with the words of interposition and nullification, will be transformed into a situation where little black boys and black girls will be able to join hands with little white boys and white girls and walk together as sisters and brothers.

I have a dream today.

I have a dream that one day every valley shall be exalted, every hill and mountain shall be made low, the rough places will be made plains, and the crooked places will be made straight, and the glory of the Lord shall be revealed, and all flesh shall see it together.

This is our hope. This is the faith with which I return to the South. With this faith we will be able to hew out of the mountain of despair a stone of hope. With this faith we will be able to transform the jangling discords of our nation into a beautiful symphony of brotherhood. With this faith we will be able to work together, to pray together, to struggle together, to go to jail together, to stand up for freedom together, knowing that we will be free one day.

This will be the day when all of God's children will be able to sing with new meaning, "My country 'tis of thee, sweet land of liberty, of thee I sing. Land where my fathers died, land of the pilgrim's pride, from every mountainside, let freedom ring."

And if America is to be a great nation this must become true. So let freedom ring from the prodigious hilltops of New Hampshire. Let freedom ring from the mighty mountains of New York. Let freedom ring from the heightening Alleghenies of Pennsylvania!

Let freedom ring from the snowcapped Rockies of Colorado!

Let freedom ring from the curvaceous peaks of California!

But not only that; let freedom ring from Stone Mountain of Georgia!

Let freedom ring from Lookout Mountain of Tennessee!

Let freedom ring from every hill and molehill of Mississippi. From every mountainside, let freedom ring.

When we let freedom ring, when we let it ring from every village and every hamlet, from every state and every city, we will be able to speed up that day when all of God's children, black men and white men, Jews and Gentiles, Protestants and Catholics, will be able to join hands and sing in the words of the old Negro spiritual, "Free at last! Free at last! Thank God Almighty, we are free at last!"

Sources: (1) Excerpts from "Nonviolence and Racial Justice," copyright 1957 by Martin Luther King, Jr., copyright renewed 1985 by Coretta Scott King; and (2) "I Have a Dream" speech delivered at the March on Washington, August 28, 1963, copyright 1963 by Martin Luther King, Jr., copyright renewed 1991 by Coretta Scott King. Both are reprinted by arrangement with The Heirs to the Estate of Martin Luther King, Jr., c/o Writers House, Inc., as agent for the proprietor.

SELECT BIBLIOGRAPHY:

Taylor Branch, *At Canaan's Edge: America in the King Years, 1965–1968* (New York: Simon & Schuster Paperbacks, 2007).

————, *Parting the Waters: America in the King Years, 1954–1963* (New York: Simon & Schuster Paperbacks, 2005).

————, *Pillar of Fire: America in the King Years, 1963–1965* (New York: Simon & Schuster, 1999).

Clayborne Carson, ed., *The Papers of Martin Luther King, Jr.*, 6 vols. (Berkeley: University of California Press, 1992).

David Garrow, *Bearing the Cross: Martin Luther King and the Southern Christian Leadership Conference* (New York: Morrow, 1988).

Martin Luther King, Jr., *Stride toward Freedom: The Montgomery Story* (New York: Harper and Row, 1958).

————, *Strength to Love* (New York: Harper and Row, 1964).

————, *Where Do We Go from Here: Chaos or Community?* (New York: Harper and Row, 1967).

David L. Lewis, *King: A Critical Biography* (New York: Praeger, 1970).

James Melvin Washington, ed., *A Testament of Hope: The Essential Writings of Martin Luther King, Jr.* (San Francisco: Harper and Row, 1968).

⌁ 8 ⌁

"The Revolution Is at Hand," *John R. Lewis, 1963*

John R. Lewis (1940–) was born in poverty in Troy, Alabama, and received a bachelor's degree from Fisk University in 1963. As a student in Nashville, Lewis firmly believed in nonviolent social protest, and was involved in a wide array of sit-ins, freedom rides, and marches. He also served as chairman of SNCC from 1963 to 1966. In 1963, Lewis gave an address at the March on Washington that stirred controversy when some of the march organizers insisted that aspects of his speech that forcefully criticized the Kennedy administration be deleted at the last minute. (The passage below reprints the original text, before it was censored.) In the 1970s, Lewis launched a successful political career in Atlanta. In 1986 Lewis upset the highly favored candidacy of Julian Bond to become a Democratic congressman from Georgia in the U.S. House of Representatives. In 1991 Lewis was appointed as one of three chief deputy whips in the House, thereby becoming one of the most influential politicians in Congress. Lewis's long history within the Black Freedom movement has given him a moral authority that many other elected officials lack.

⌁

We march today for jobs and freedom, but we have nothing to be proud of, for hundreds and thousands of our brothers are not here—for they have no money for their transportation, for they are receiving starvation wages . . . or no wages at all.

In good conscience, we cannot support the administration's civil-rights bill, for it is too little, and too late. There's not one thing in the bill that will protect our people from police brutality.[1]

The voting section of this bill will not help the thousands of citizens who want to vote; will not help the citizens of Mississippi, of Alabama and Georgia who are qualified to vote, who are without a sixth-grade education. "One Man, One Vote," is the African cry. It is ours, too.

People have been forced to move for they have exercised their right to register to vote. What is in the bill that will protect the homeless and starving people of this nation? What is there in this bill to insure the equality of a maid who earns five dollars a week in the home of a family whose income is a hundred thousand dollars a year?

This bill will not protect young children and old women from police dogs and fire hoses for engaging in peaceful demonstrations. This bill will not protect the citizens in Danville, Virginia, who must live in constant fear in a police state.[2] This bill will not protect the hundreds of people who have been arrested on trumped-up charges, like those in Americus, Georgia, where four young men are in jail, facing a death penalty, for engaging in peaceful protest.

For the first time in a hundred years this nation is being awakened to the fact that segregation is evil and it must be destroyed in all forms. Our presence today proves that we have been aroused to the point of action.

We are now involved in a serious revolution. This nation is still a place of cheap political leaders allying themselves with open forms of political, economic and social exploitation.

In some parts of the South we have worked in the fields from sun-up to sun-down for twelve dollars a week. In Albany, Georgia, we have seen our people indicted by the federal government for peaceful protest, while the Deputy Sheriff beat Attorney C. B. King and left him half-dead; while local police officials kicked and assaulted the pregnant wife of Slater King, and she lost her baby.

It seems to me that the Albany indictment is part of a conspiracy on the part of the federal government and local politicians for political expediency.

I want to know, Which side is the federal government on?

The revolution is at hand, and we must free ourselves of the chains of political and economic slavery. The nonviolent revolution is saying, "We will not wait for the courts to act, for we have been waiting hundreds of years. We will not wait for the President, nor the Justice Department, nor Congress, but we will take matters into our own hands, and create a great source of power, outside of any national structure that could and would assure us victory." For those who have said, "Be patient and wait!" we must say, "Patience is a dirty and nasty word." We cannot be patient, we do not want to be free gradually, we want our freedom, and we want it now. We cannot depend on any political party, for both the Democrats and the Republicans have betrayed the basic principles of the Declaration of Independence.

We all recognize the fact that if any radical social, political and economic changes are to take place in our society, the people, the masses must bring them about. In the struggle we must seek more than mere civil rights; we must work for the community of love, peace and true brotherhood. Our minds, souls and hearts cannot rest until freedom and justice exist for *all the people*.

The revolution is a serious one. Mr. Kennedy is trying to take the revolution out of the streets and put it in the courts. Listen, Mr. Kennedy, listen, Mr. Congressman, listen, fellow citizens—the black masses are on the march for jobs and freedom, and we must say to the politicians that there won't be a "cooling-off period."

We won't stop now. All of the forces of Eastland, Barnett and Wallace won't stop this revolution. The next time we march, we won't march on Washington, but we will march through the South, through the Heart of Dixie, the way Sherman did. We will make the action of the past few months look petty. And I say to you, *Wake up America!!*

All of us must get in the revolution—get in and stay in the streets of every city, village and hamlet of this nation, until true freedom comes, until the revolution is complete. The black masses in the Delta of Mississippi, in Southwest Georgia, Alabama, Harlem, Chicago, Philadelphia and all over this nation are on the march.

Notes: 1. This was changed to read: "True, we support the administration's civil-rights bill, but this bill will not protect young children and old women from police dogs and fire hoses. . . ." 2. In Danville, Virginia, policemen, armed with submachine guns and in armored cars, regularly broke up mass demonstrations by Negroes. After each demonstration, scores of Negroes were taken to hospitals with fractured skulls and lacerations.

Source: Speech by John Lewis, delivered at the March on Washington, August 28, 1963, courtesy of U.S. Representative John Lewis.

SELECT BIBLIOGRAPHY:

Taylor Branch, *Parting the Waters: America in the King Years, 1954–1963* (New York: Simon and Schuster, 1988).
Clayborne Carson, *In Struggle: SNCC and the Black Awakening of the 1960s* (Cambridge: Harvard University Press, 1981).
John Lewis, *Walking with the Wind: A Memoir of the Movement* (New York: Simon and Schuster, 1998).

⚊ 9 ⚊

"The Salvation of American Negroes Lies in Socialism," *W. E. B. Du Bois*

For two generations, Du Bois was the premier voice of reform within the Black Freedom movement. In the early 1930s he began to study Marxism seriously for the first time. He visited the Soviet Union and was generally impressed with its cultural and socioeconomic gains under socialism. In 1944, Du Bois returned to the NAACP as the director of research, but was dismissed from the organization four years later, largely because of his increasingly radical political views. During the Cold War Du Bois was subjected to intense political harassment and surveillance by the U.S. government. His passport was seized and his ability to earn a living virtually disappeared. Du Bois's books were deemed subversive, and even the NAACP national leadership isolated itself from his plight.

Du Bois courageously fought against McCarthyism and challenged the censorship of radical ideas inside the United States. By the 1950s he had long since rejected the concept of the "Talented Tenth" as the vanguard for social change within the black community. An extensive visit to the People's Republic of China in 1959 profoundly influenced Du Bois, and he came to the conclusion that "capitalism cannot reform itself; it is doomed to self-destruction." Four days after he formally applied for admission to join the Communist Party, he left the United States to live and work in Ghana. Less than two years later, on the eve of the 1963 March on Washington, D.C., Du Bois died at the age of ninety-five.

～

THE NEGRO AND SOCIALISM

The United States, which would like to be regarded as a democracy devoted to peace, finds itself today making the greatest preparations for war of any nation on earth and holding elections where citizens have no opportunity to vote for the policies which they prefer.

What are the causes of this contradictory situation? First, we know that our main reason in preparing for war is the fact that slowly but surely socialism has spread over the world and become a workable form of government. Today for the first time in history the majority of mankind live under socialist regimes, either complete socialism as in the Soviet Union and China, or partial socialism as in India and Scandinavia. Most Americans profess to believe that this spread of socialism is mainly the result of a conspiracy led by the Soviet Union and abetted by a section of American citizens. For fear of this group, we have curtailed democratic government, limited civil liberties, and planned war on a gigantic scale.

The spread of socialism in the last one hundred years is unquestionably a fact. It stemmed from growing protest against that tremendous expansion of business enterprise which followed the French revolution. This private initiative and economic anarchy resulted in the factory system, which stemmed from the American slave trade, the sugar empire and the cotton kingdom. All this was concurrent with such suffering and degradation among the laboring masses that by the end of the nineteenth century there was hardly a man of thought and feeling, scarcely a scientist nor an artist, who did not believe that socialism must eventually supplant unbridled private capitalism, or civilization would die.

All over the earth since the Civil War in America, socialism has grown and spread and become more and more definite. It has emerged from dream and doctrinaire fantasy such as characterized Fourier and St. Simon into the rounded doctrine of Karl Marx and finally into the socialist states of Lenin and Mao Tse-tung. In all this struggling advance lay the central idea that men must work for a living, but that the results of their work must not mainly be to support privileged persons and concentrate power in the hands of the owners of wealth; that the welfare of the mass of people should be the main object of government.

To ensure this end the conviction grew that government must increasingly be controlled by the governed: that the mass of people, increasing in intelligence, with incomes sufficient to live a good and healthy life, should control all government, and that they would be able to do this by the spread of science and scientific technique, access to truth, the use of reason, and freedom of thought and of creative impulse in art and literature.

The difficulty of accomplishing this lay in the current culture patterns—in repressive religious dogmas, and in the long inculcated belief that nothing better than private ownership and control of capital could be planned, with human nature as it is.

Democratic control, therefore, while it increased, tended to be narrowly political rather than economic. It had to do with the selection of officials rather than with work and income. Discovery of new natural forces and of increased use of machines with intricate industrial techniques tended to put land, labor, and the ownership of capital and wealth into control of the few who were fortunate or aggressive or unscrupulous and to emphasize a belief that, while the mass of citizens might share in government by electing officials to administer law, and legislators might make laws in certain areas of government, the people could not control industry or limit income.

As science increased its mastery of nature and as industry began to use world trade to expand markets, an entirely new problem of government arose. Industry realized that, unless industrial organization largely controlled government, it could not control land and labor, monopolize materials, set prices in the world market, and regulate credit and currency. For this purpose new and integrated world industry arose called "Big Business"—a misleading misnomer. Its significance lay not simply in its size. It was not just little shops grown larger. It was an organized super-government of mankind in matters of work and wages, directed with science and skill for the private profit of individuals. It could not be controlled by popular vote unless that vote was intelligent, experienced, and cast by persons essentially equal in income and power. The overwhelming majority of mankind was still ignorant, sick and poverty stricken.

Repeated and varying devices for keeping and increasing democratic control over industry and wealth were regularly rendered useless by the superior training and moral unscrupulousness of the owners of wealth, as against the ignorance and inexperience of the voters. Bribery of the poorer voters; threats and even violence; fear of the future and organized conspiracy of the interested few against the unorganized many; lying and deftly spread propaganda used race hate, religious dogma and differing family and class interests to ruin democracy. In our own day we have seen that the income tax, designed to place the burden of government expense on property owners in ratio to income, actually lays the heaviest weight of taxation on the low income classes, while the rich individuals and corporations escape with the least proportion of taxes.

When the American farmers and workers revolted against the beginnings of the British colonial system and set out to establish a republic of free and equal citizens, it seemed to most thinking people that a new era in the development of western civilization had begun. Here, beyond the privilege of titled Europe, beyond the deep-seated conditioning of the masses to hereditary inequality and subservience to luxury and display, was to arise a nation of equal men. That equality was to be based on economic opportunity, which, as Karl Marx later preached, was the only real equality.

But unfortunately while the United States proclaimed, it never adopted complete equality. First, it prolonged the European recognition of property as more significant than manhood. Then it discovered that theft of land from the Indians was not murder but a method of progress. Next, America reduced the African labor, which rising British commerce had forced on her, to slave status and gained thereby such fabulous income from tobacco, sugar and cotton that Europe became the center of triumphant private capitalism, and the United States its handmaid to furnish free land and cheap labor.

This nation had to fight a Civil War to prevent all American labor from becoming half enslaved. Thus, from 1620 when the Puritans landed until 1865 when slavery was abolished, there was no complete democracy in the United States. This was not only because a large part of the laboring class was enslaved, but also because white labor was in competition with slaves and thus itself not really free.

In the late nineteenth and twentieth centuries, while socialism advanced in the leading European nations and in North America, in most of the world European monopoly of wealth and technique—strengthened by theories of the natural inferiority of most human beings—led to the assumed right of western Europe to rule the world for the benefit and amusement of white people. This theory of world domination was hidden behind the rise of the western working classes, and helped keep democracy and social progress from eastern Europe, Asia, and Africa; from Central and South America, and the islands of the seven seas.

In Western Europe a labor movement, and popular education kept forcing increasing numbers of the workers and of the middle classes into a larger share of economic power. But on the other hand, the mass of colored labor, and white labor in backward Latin and Slavic lands, were reduced to subordinate social status so that increased profit from their land and labor helped to maintain the high profits and high wages of industry in Western Europe and North America. Also it was easy there to hire white soldiers to keep "niggers," "chinks," "dagoes," and "hunkies" in their places. This was the essence of colonial imperialism. It was industry organized on a world scale, and holding most of mankind in such economic subjection as would return the largest profit to the owners of wealth.

Meantime, the new effort to achieve socialism, fathered by Karl Marx and his successors, increased. It declared that even before the mass of workers were intelligent and experienced enough themselves to conduct modern industry, industrial guidance might be furnished them by a dictatorship of their own intelligent and devoted leaders. As knowledge and efficiency increased, democracy would spread among the masses and they would become capable of conducting a modern welfare state. This social program the world governed by owners of capital regarded as impossible without the dictatorship falling out of their well-meaning hands and into the hands of demagogues. Every sort of force was employed to stop even the attempt to set up such states. Yet the first World War, caused by rivalry over the ownership of colonies, resulted in the effort to start a complete socialist state in Russia; and after the second World War, arising from the same causes as the first, a similar attempt was made in China.

Despite wide and repeated opposition, which used every despicable and criminal method possible, both of these states have become so successful and strong that their overthrow by outside force or inner revolt does not today seem at all likely. Also and meantime, in all leading countries, socialistic legislation steadily increased. It did not creep. It advanced with powerful strides.

This development has emphasized the fight between beleaguered private capitalism and advancing socialism, the Communists pointing out the unnecessary lag of socialization in western lands and the capitalists accusing communism of undemocratic dictatorship.

In order to fight socialism, super Big Business, as contrasted with ordinary small business enterprise, had to become itself socialism in reverse. If public welfare instead of private profit became its object, if public officials supplanted private owners, socialistic government would be in control of industry. However, those Americans who hope that the welfare state will thus be realized under a system of private capital are today having the carpet pulled from beneath their feet by the recession of democracy in the United States. This has come about by the repudiation of socialism by organized labor and the consequent refusal of the labor vote to follow even the goals of the New Deal. This surrender of labor has been led by the new industrial South, with favorable climate, cheap labor, and half that labor disfranchised and most of it unorganized. The mass of Southerners do not vote. In the Congressional District where the black boy [Emmett] Till was murdered, there live 400,000 Negroes and 300,000 whites. Yet only 7,000 voters went to the polls to elect the present Congressman. The disfranchisement of the black half of the labor vote in the South keeps Negroes poor, sick, and ignorant. But it also hurts white labor by making democratic government unworkable so long as the South has from three to ten times the voting power of the North and West.

Because of this systematic and illegal disfranchisement, a majority of American voters can often be outvoted by a minority. Laws like the McCarran and Smith Acts can become illegal statutes, because a minority of voters can prevail over a majority. Figures to prove this are easy to adduce, but I only mention now the fact that former Senator Lehman of New York represented the vote of 5 million citizens who went to the polls, while Senator Eastland of Mississippi represented less than 150 thousand voters. Yet Eastland was far more powerful than Lehman.

This loss of democratic control of the government of our nation can be even more clearly demonstrated. There was no effective candidate for the Presidency in the last national election who stood pledged for peace, disarmament, abolition of the draft, lower taxes, recognition of the right of the Soviet Union and China to have the government which they choose and for stopping our effort to force other nations to do as we want them to do. Not only did we have no chance to decide our foreign policy, but we were equally helpless in deciding our course in domestic affairs. Our system of education is falling to pieces. We need teachers and school houses by the millions, but we cannot have them if we continue making weapons at the present rate and setting our youth to learning death and destruction instead of building, healing, and teaching.

Is this curtailment of democracy the result of knowledge and discussion? On the contrary, knowledge and discussion are today so far curtailed that most men do not even attempt to express their opinions, lest they be accused of treason or conspiracy.

Why is this?

At the very time when the colonial peoples were trying desperately to have food and freedom, powerful Americans became obsessed by the ambition to have North America replace Britain as the empire upon which the sun never dared to set. They demanded high profits and high wages even if the rest of the world starved. In order to restore world rule of organized industry, shaken by war and depression, the United States prefers preparation for universal and continuous world war, until a colonial imperialism in some form is restored under our leadership.

To this program most people of the United States have submitted. How was such submission brought about? Such a national policy found unexpected support in our long encouraged prejudice against people with black or colored skins and against all groups of foreign-born who were not of Anglo-Saxon descent. This provincial point of view, repudiated by science and religion, still remains in America a living and powerful motive guiding our lives and likes. This support of the colonial system by American race prejudice has resulted in our present program of war. How was this accomplished? How have the majority of American people been convinced that preparation for war, suspension of civil liberties and curtailment of democracy are our best paths to progress?

America is an intelligent nation, despite large illiterate groups and the lack of an integrated background of culture. We still have large numbers of the poor and sick, but our average income is far higher than that of most nations. This nation wants to do right, as evidenced by a plethora of churches and a wide and loud profession of religion. If any country is ready for increase of democracy, it is the United States. Yet we are preparing our sons for war, because we actually have been induced to believe that the Soviet Union is behind a world-wide criminal conspiracy to destroy the United States and that socialism is the result. The statement is so fantastic that most foreign peoples cannot conceive how it can be true that we really accept this fairy tale.

To restore our lost opportunity to make huge profit on private investment in Russia, the Balkans, and particularly in China, Big Business has restricted and guided public access to truth. It has dominated news gathering, monopolized the press and limited publishing. By fear of losing employment, by secret police and high pay to informers, often confessed liars; by control of education and limitation of radio and television and censorship of the drama—by all these methods and others, the public opinion of the nation has been forced into one iron channel of disaster.

In order to let the nation return to normal sanity we must realize that socialism is not a crime nor a conspiracy, but the path of progress toward which the feet of all mankind are set. Some of the greatest intellectual leaders of our era have been advocates of socialism: Charles Kingsley, Leo Tolstoi, Edward Bellamy, William Morris, Henry George, Robert Owen, Bernard Shaw, Sidney and Beatrice Webb, Kier Hardie, H. G. Wells, Harold Laski. The footsteps of the long oppressed and staggering masses are not always straight and sure, but their mistakes can never cause the misery and distress which the factory system caused in Europe, colonial imperialism caused in Asia and Africa, and which slavery, lynching, disfranchisement, and Jim Crow legislation have caused in the United States.

Our way out of this impasse is straight and clear and as old as the struggle of freedom for the mind of man: Americans must face the facts at all costs. Walking with determination through a morass of deliberate distortion, we must insist on the right to know the truth, to discuss it and to listen to its interpretation by men of intelligence and honesty; we must restore to all citizens their civil rights and the right to vote, no matter whether they are Negroes, Communists, or naturalized foreign-born. We must insist that our foreign policy as well as our domestic problems and especially our problem of industry, be subjects on which we shall have the right to vote.

Meantime, we are prisoners of propaganda. The people of the United States have become completely sold to that method of conducting industry which has been so powerful and triumphant in the world for two centuries that Americans regard it as the only normal way of life. We regard the making of things and their purchase and sale for private profit as the chief end of living. We look on painting and poetry as harmless play. We regard literature as valuable only as handmaiden to industry. We teach Business as a science when it is only an art of legal theft. We regard advertising as a profession even when it teaches the best way to lie. We consider the unselfish sacrifice of one to the progress of all as wasted effort. Wealth is the height of human ambition even when we have no idea of how to spend it, except to make more wealth or to waste it in harmful or useless ostentation. We want high profits and high wages even if most of the world starves.

Putting aside questions of right, and suspecting all our neighbors of being as selfish as we ourselves are, we have adopted a creed of wholesale selfishness. We believe that, if all people work for their own selfish advantage, the whole world will be the best of possible worlds. This is the rat race upon which we are set, and we are suspicious and afraid of folk who oppose this program and plead for the old kindliness, the new use of power and machine for the good of the unfortunate and the welfare of all the world of every race and color. We can and do give charity abundantly, particularly when we are giving away money or things which we cannot ourselves use. We give to beggars but we hate the beggars who recoil from begging. This is what stands back of our murderous war preparation as well as back of our endless itch to be rich. At any cost, or in any way, this is our reason for living, gambling on radio, on stock exchange or on race track is our way of life.

The power of wealth and private industry extends itself over education, literature and art and we live in fear, with a deliberately low standard of culture, lest democracy displace monopoly of wealth in the control of the state.

One of the devastating effects of our current education on our youth is the training of them by military officials. They are indoctrinated by propaganda against socialism, by ridicule for their attachment to their mothers, and with disrespect for all women. They learn to kill and destroy, and force as a social method of progress is extolled. Small wonder that what we call "juvenile delinquency" increases among us.

One of the contradictions of our day is our argument about the distribution of property and the relative size of incomes, at a time when secrecy as to the truth about these matters is a matter of official compulsion, and most carefully guarded on the ground that a man's income is his private business and the ownership of property concerns the owner primarily. These propositions are false and ridiculous. The distribution of income is a public affair since it is increasingly the result of public function. Property is a matter of state control, permitted to rest in private hands only so long as it is of public benefit that it should so rest. For any reasonable thought or action concerning property, there should come first open information as to its ownership. Without that, no science or ethic of wealth is possible. We can only guess madly and conclude erroneously. Taking the meager guesswork of the United States census, as some approximation of the truth: it is clear that the poor are still with us in this rich land.

There are nearly 40 percent of our families who receive less than $2,000 a year and over six million of our 46 1/2 million families receive less than $500. In addition to this there is a psychological poverty, in some ways more frightening than actual lack of income: there is the great number of artisans, white-collar workers and professional men who could live plainly on their incomes but who skimp and borrow and gamble, and sometimes steal to "keep up with the Joneses"; who drive a car and spend too little on food and medicine; who buy fur coats and crowd into one room. American culture is made uneasy and insane by the millions among us who expect in some way to get flamboyantly rich and cannot be satisfied with that simple life which all experience teaches is the finest and best.

Especially must American Negroes, awaking from their present fear and lethargy, reassert that leadership in the American world of culture which Phillis Wheatly began in the eighteenth century, Frederick Douglass led in the nineteenth, and James Weldon Johnson and Carter Woodson advanced in the twentieth. American Negroes must study socialism, its rise in Europe and Asia, and its peculiar suitability for the emancipation of Africa. They must realize that no system of reform offers the American Negro such real emancipation as socialism. The capitalism which so long ruled Europe and North America was founded on

Negro slavery in America, and that slavery will never completely disappear so long as private capitalism continues to survive.

The fight to preserve racial segregation along the color line in the United States only helps to drive the American Negro that much faster into the arms of socialism. The movement of the whole nation toward the welfare state, and away from the concept of private profit as the only object of industry, is bound to show itself sooner or later in the whole nation. But if the Negro tenth of the nation is forced ahead by color discrimination, the socialization of the nation will come that much sooner. Consider the situation: there are today about 16 million Americans of admitted Negro descent. They are by reason of this descent subjected to public insult, loss of opportunity to work according to ability or to receive wages level with white workers; most of these people are disfranchised and segregated in education, travel, civil rights and public recreation. Ten million of these Negroes are poor, receiving less than $50 a week per family. Half of them cannot read or write. They live mostly in the rural districts and small towns of the former slave states, whence their efforts to escape are hindered by law, mob violence, and scarcity of places of refuge which welcome or give them work or places to live.

Above this depressed 10 million are 4 million Negroes who are economically insecure and on the edge of poverty. They work as laborers and servants in the towns and cities. They can read and write, but among them are a class of criminals. Next come 1 1/2 million middle-class Negroes living in cities. They have education and property and are engaged in semiskilled work and white-collar jobs. Many are trained in the better-paid work of personal service, some are teachers and ministers of religion. Out of this group have come the leading intelligentsia. At the economic apex of this middle economic group are a half million Negroes who are well-to-do, receiving at least $10,000 a year. They are professional and business men, civil servants and public entertainers. They have good, sometimes elaborate homes, motor cars and servants. They live mostly in the larger cities.

When discussing American Negroes, one must distinguish among these classes. Southerners raving about the degradation of Negroes are usually talking about their disfranchised and exploited serfs. Negroes talking of their progress are usually referring to their bourgeoisie. But the Negro intelligentsia must ask how it happens that in free, rich America so many Negroes must be poor, sick and ignorant while in Communist Russia, peasants who were emancipated at nearly the same time as Negroes, live without poverty, with universal education and with national attack on disease? Why is it that the Chinese coolie, who recently was as low as the Negro slave, is today a man in his own country, with the blood-sucking whites driven out? Every effort is made in America to suppress this line of thought among Negroes; but as thought in America regains its lost freedom, as democracy begins to replace plutocracy, the social thought of the nation will find increasing support from Negroes.

Even before such freedom comes, the segregated Negro group will increasingly be forced toward socialistic methods to solve their inner problems. They will unite in boycotts as in Montgomery, Alabama; they will turn to consumers' cooperation;

a new Negro literature must soon burst out of prison bonds and it will find in socialism practically its only voice. Negro schools and colleges, so long as students are excluded from public education, will become centers of thought where the Soviet Union and China cannot escape intelligent discussion.

The modern rise of Africans in the twentieth century to self-expression and organized demand for autonomy and freedom was due in large part to the Pan-African movement started by American Negroes. Today every part of Africa has a national congress fighting for the ends which the Pan-American movement started in 1919. Further leadership of Africa by black America has been stopped —but too late. Already the Africans have their own leaders, and these leaders like Nkrumah and Azikiwe are quite aware of the Soviet Union and China and are building their new nations on socialist lines.

Moreover as the mass of the colored peoples of the world move toward socialism in Asia and Africa, it is inevitable that they influence American Negroes. I had long hoped that American Negroes would lead this procession because of their chances for education. But "philanthropy," disguised in bribes, and "religion" cloaked in hypocrisy, strangled Negro education and stilled the voices of prophets. The yellow, brown and black thinkers of Asia have forged ahead. But nevertheless the black folk of America will hear their voices and, what is more compelling, will see their outstanding success. On March 6, 1957, when ancient Ghana was reborn in West Africa, American Negroes realized how far toward socialism this group of black folk had gone. Soon, too, socialism in the black Sudan, in East Africa, the Belgian Congo and South Africa will place the Black world in the train of Soviet Russia, China, and India and tear loose from the allegiance, which American Negroes try now to profess, to the dictatorship of wealth in the United States.

One thing and one alone keeps socialism from growing even more rapidly than it is—that is fear of war and especially of attack by the Soviet Union and China. Most of our vast national income is being spent for preparation for such war and we have but small funds left for education, health and water development and control which we so sorely need. The frantic and continual cultivation of the national fear goes on just as the danger of war decreases. The class structure of our nation grows tremendously at the very time that our propagandists are fiercely denying it. We have a privileged class of men with more income than they can possibly spend and more power than they can hire brains to use. In the guise of idle rich, with trained executives and with a vast and useless military organization throwing away the taxes piled on the workers, this ruling clique outrivals the aristocracy of George III or Louis XIV. We have a middle class of white-collar workers, technicians, artisans, artists, professional men and teachers able to live in comfort so long as they restrict their thought and planning, and deceive themselves in thinking they will sometime join the "independently" rich.

Our last presidential election was a farce. We had no chance to vote for the questions in which we were really interested: Peace, Disarmament, the Draft, unfair taxation, race bias, education, social medicine, and flood control. On the contrary we had before us one ticket under two names and the nominees shadow-boxed with false fanfare and advertisement for the same policies, with infinitesimal shades of difference and with spurious earnestness. Small wonder that half of the American voters stayed home.

Thus it is clear today that the salvation of American Negroes lies in socialism. They should support all measures and men who favor the welfare state; they should vote for government ownership of capital in industry; they should favor strict regulation of corporations or their public ownership; they should vote to prevent monopoly from controlling the press and the publishing of opinions. They should favor public ownership and control of water, electric, and atomic power; they should stand for a clean ballot, the encouragement of third parties, independent candidates, and the elimination of graft and gambling on television and even in churches.

The question of the method by which the socialist state can be achieved must be worked out by experiment and reason and not by dogma. Whether or not methods which were right and clear in Russia and China fit our circumstances is for our intelligence to decide. The atom bomb has revolutionized our thought. Peace is not only preferable today, it is increasingly inevitable. Passive resistance is not the end of action, but the beginning. After refusing to fight, there is the question how to live. The Negro church which stops discrimination against bus riders must next see how those riders can earn a decent living and not remain helplessly exploited by those who own busses and make Jim Crow laws. This may well be a difficult program, but it is the only one.

Sources: Excerpt from "The Negro and Socialism," in Helen Alfred, ed., *Toward a Socialist America* (New York: Peace Publications, 1958), pp. 179–91.

⁓ 10 ⁓

"The Special Plight and the Role of Black Women," *Fannie Lou Hamer*

Born Fannie Lou Townsend (1917–1977), Hamer was the youngest of twenty children in a family of sharecroppers, and she left school in the sixth grade in order to work full time on a Mississippi plantation. She toiled for most of her life in rural poverty and became involved in civil rights activism, when she began working with the SNCC in 1962. As an SNCC organizer in Sunflower County, Mississippi, she assisted local black residents in registering to vote. Hamer became vice chair of the insurgent Mississippi Freedom Democratic Party (MFDP) in 1964, and campaigned for Congress from Mississippi's second congressional district. As a leader of the MFDP, Hamer participated in a widely publicized challenge to the all-white Mississippi delegation at the 1964 National Democratic Convention in Atlantic City, New Jersey. In a moving public presentation, Hamer testified before the convention's credentials committee about how she had been severely beaten when she and other civil rights activists attempted to challenge Jim Crow laws in Winona, Mississippi. Hamer subsequently established the Freedom Farm Cooperative and was instrumental in building a low-income daycare center and two hundred units of low-income housing for her Mississippi community. Hamer consistently fought for women's rights, economic justice, and black empowerment, and her deep influence among a generation of black activists cannot be overemphasized.

The special plight and the role of black women is not something that just happened three years ago. We've had a special plight for 350 years. My grandmother had it. My grandmother was a slave. She died in 1960. She was 136 years old. She died in Mount Bayou, Mississippi.

It's been a special plight for the black woman. I remember my uncles and some of my aunts—and that's why it really tickled me when you talked about integration. Because I'm very black, but I remember some of my uncles and some of my aunts was as white as anybody in here, and blue-eyed, and some kind of green-eyed—and my grandfather didn't do it, you know. So what the folks is fighting at this point is what they started. They started unloading the slave ships of Africa, that's when they started. And right now, sometimes, you know I work for the liberation of all people, because when I liberate myself, I'm liberating other people. But you know, sometimes I really feel more sorrier for the white woman than I feel for ourselves because she been caught up in this thing, caught up feeling very special, and folks, I'm going to put it on the line, because my job is not to make people feel comfortable—[drowned out by applause]. You've been caught up in this thing because, you know, you worked my grandmother, and after that you worked my mother, and then finally you got hold of me. And you really thought, people—you might try and cool it now, but I been watching you, baby. You thought that you was *more* because you was a woman, and especially a white woman, you had this kind of angel feeling that you were untouchable. You know that? There's nothing under the sun that made you believe that you was just like me, that under this white pigment of skin is red blood, just like under this black skin of mine. So we was used as black women over and over and over. You know, I remember a time when I was working around white people's house, and one thing that would make me mad as hell, after I would be done slaved all day long, this white woman would get on the phone, calling some of her friends, and said, "You know, I'm tired, because *we* have been working," and I said, "That's a damn lie." You're not used to that kind of language, honey, but I'm gone tell you where it's *at*. So all of these things was happening because you *had* more. You had been put on a pedestal, and then not only put on a pedestal, but you had been put in something like a ivory castle. So what happened to you, we have busted the castle open and whacking like hell for the pedestal. And when you hit the ground, you're gone have to fight like hell, like we've been fighting all this time.

In the past, I don't care how poor this white woman was, in the South she still felt like she was more than us. In the North, I don't care how poor or how rich this white woman has been, she still felt like she was more than us. But coming to the realization of the thing, her freedom is shackled in chains to mine, and she realizes for the first time that she is not free until I am free. The point about it, the male influence in this country—you know the white male, he didn't go and brainwash the black man and the black woman, he brainwashed his wife too. . . . He made her think that she was a angel. You know the reason I can say it, folks, I been watching. And there's a lot of people been watching. That's why it's such a shock wherever we go throughout this country, it's a great blow. White Americans today don't know what in the world to do because when they put us *behind* them, that's where they made their mistake. If they had put us in front, they wouldn't have *let* us look back. But they put us behind them, and we watched every move they made. . . .

And this is the reason I tell the world, as I travel to and fro, I'm not fighting for equal rights. What do I want to be equal to [Senator] Eastland for? Just tell me that. But we are not only going to liberate ourselves. I think it's a responsibility. I think we're special people, God's children is going to help in the survival of this country if it's not too late. We're a lot sicker than people realize we are. And what we are doing now in the South, in politics, in gaining seats for black people and concerned whites in the state of Mississippi, is going to have an effect on what happens throughout this country. You know, I used to think that if I could go North and tell people about the plight of the black folk in the state of Mississippi, everything would be all right. But traveling around, I found one thing for sure: it's up-South and down-South, and it's no different. The man shoot me in the face in Mississippi, and you turn around he'll shoot you in the back here [in New York]. We have a problem, folks, and we want to try to deal with the problem in the only way that we can deal with the problem as far as black women. And you know, I'm not hung up on this about liberating myself from the black man, I'm not going to try that thing. I got a black husband, six feet three, two hundred and forty pounds, with a 14 shoe, that I don't *want* to be liberated from. But we are here to work side by side with this black man in trying to bring liberation to all people.

Sunflower County is one of the poorest counties, one of the poorest counties on earth, while Senator James O. Eastland—you know, people tells you, don't talk politics, but the air you breathe is polluted air, it's political polluted air. The air you breathe is politics. So you have to be involved. You have to be involved in trying to elect people that's going to help do something about the liberation of all people.

Sunflower County, the county where I'm from, is Senator Eastland's county that owns 5,800 acres of some of the richest black fertile soil in Mississippi, and where kids, there in Sunflower County, suffer from malnutrition. But I want to tell you one of the things that we're doing, right now in Sunflower County. In 1969 I founded the Freedom Farm Coop. We started off with 40 acres of land. Nineteen-seventy in Sunflower County, we fed 1,500 people from this 40 acres of land. Nineteen-seventy I've become involved with Y.W.D.—Young World Developers. On the 14th of January 1971, we put $85,400 on 640 acres of land, giving us the total of 680 acres of land. We also have 68 houses. We hope sometime in '71 we will build another hundred houses on a hundred of the 640 acres.

This coming Saturday . . . young people will be walking throughout the world against hunger and poverty. It will be forty countries walking, millions of people throughout the world. In the United States it will be over 377 walks. These walkers are young people that really care about what's going on. . . . And out of this walk—people will pay so much per mile for the kids that'll be walking—and out of this walk we hope to get a million dollars for Sunflower County. . . . If we get the kind of economic support that we need in Sunflower County, in two more years . . . we'll have the tools to produce food ourselves.

A couple of weeks ago, we moved the first poor white family into Freedom Farm in the history of the state of Mississippi. A white man came to me and said, "I got five children and I don't have nowhere to live. I don't have food. I don't have anything. And my children, some of them, is sick." And we gave this man a house. . . .

We have a job as black women, to support whatever is right, and to bring in justice where we've had so much injustice. Some people say, well, I work for $24 per week. That's not true in my case, I work sometimes for $15 per week. I remember my mother working for 25 and 30 cents per day. But we are organizing ourselves now, because we don't have any other choice. Sunflower County is one of the few counties in the state of Mississippi where in that particular area we didn't lose one black teacher. Because . . . I went in and told the judge, I said, "Judge, we're not going to stand by and see you take a man with a master's degree and bring him down to janitor help. So if we don't have the principal . . . there ain't gonna *be* no school, private or public." These are the kinds of roles.

A few years ago throughout the country the middle-class black woman—I used to say not really black women, but the middle-class colored women, c-u-l-l-u-d, didn't even respect the kind of work that I was doing. But you see now, baby, whether you have a Ph.D., D.D., or no D, we're in this bag together. And whether you're from Morehouse or Nohouse, we're still in this bag together. Not to fight to try to liberate ourselves from the men—this is another trick to get us fighting among ourselves—but to work together with the black man, then we will have a better chance to just act as human beings, and to be treated as human beings in our sick society.

I would like to tell you in closing a story of an old man. This old man was very wise, and he could answer questions that was almost impossible for people to answer. So some people went to him one day, two young people, and said, "We're going to trick this guy today. We're going to catch a bird, and we're going to carry it to this old man. And we're going to ask him, 'This that we hold in our hands today, is it alive or is it dead?' If he says 'Dead,' we're going to turn it loose and let it fly. But if he says, 'Alive,' we're going to crush it." So they walked up to this old man, and they said, "This that we hold in our hands today, is it alive or is it dead?" He looked at the young people and he smiled. And he said, "It's in your hands."

Source: Excerpt from a speech delivered at the NAACP Legal Defense Fund Institute, New York City, May 7, 1971, pp. 609–14.

SELECT BIBLIOGRAPHY:

Christopher Myers Asch, "No Compromise: The Freedom Struggles of James O. Eastland and Fannie Lou Hamer" (Ph.D. diss., University of North Carolina at Chapel Hill, 2005).

Vicki L. Crawford, Jacqueline Anne Rouse, and Barbara Woods, *Women in the Civil Rights Movement: Trailblazers and Torchbearers, 1941–1965* (Brooklyn, N.Y.: Carlson Publishing, 1990).

Chana Kai Lee, *For Freedom's Sake: The Life of Fannie Lou Hamer, Women in American History* (Urbana: University of Illinois Press, 2000).

Kay Mills, *This Little Light of Mine: The Life of Fannie Lou Hamer* (New York: Dutton, 1993).

～ 11 ～

"SNCC Position Paper: Women in the Movement," *1964*

Women activists were central to the entire work of SNCC, but they were subjected to the practices of gender subordination that unfortunately were evident throughout the Black Freedom movement. By 1964 a number of SNCC women had begun to criticize the sexist behaviors and policies of the organization's mostly male leadership. This statement was written in November 1964 by two white members of the SNCC.

1. Staff was involved in crucial constitutional revisions at the Atlanta staff meeting in October. A large committee was appointed to present revisions to the staff. The committee was all men.

2. Two organizers were working together to form a farmers league. Without asking any questions, the male organizer immediately assigned the clerical work to the female organizer although both had had equal experience in organizing campaigns.

3. Although there are some women in Mississippi project who have been working as long as some of the men, the leadership group in COFO is all men.

4. A woman in a field office wondered why she was held responsible for day-to-day decisions, only to find out later that she had been appointed project director but not told.

5. A fall 1964 personnel and resources report on Mississippi projects lists the number of people on each project. The section on Laurel, however, lists not the number of persons, but "three girls."

6. One of SNCC's main administrative officers apologizes for appointment of a woman as interim project director in a key Mississippi project area.

7. A veteran of two years' work for SNCC in two states spends her day typing and doing clerical work for other people in her project.

8. Any woman in SNCC, no matter what her position or experience, has been asked to take minutes in a meeting when she and other women are outnumbered by men.

9. The names of several new attorneys entering a state project this past summer were posted in a central movement office. The first initial and last name of each lawyer was listed. Next to one name was written: (girl).

10. Capable, responsible, and experienced women who are in leadership positions can expect to have to defer to a man on their project for final decision-making.

11. A session at the recent October staff meeting in Atlanta was the first large meeting in the past couple of years where a woman was asked to chair.

Undoubtedly this list will seem strange to some, petty to others, laughable to most. The list could continue as far as there are women in the movement. Except that most women don't talk about these kinds of incidents, because the whole subject is [not] discussible—strange to some, petty to others, laughable to most. The average white person finds it difficult to understand why the Negro resents being called "boy," or being thought of as "musical" and "athletic," because the average white person doesn't realize that *he assumes he is superior*. And naturally he doesn't understand the problem of paternalism. So too the average SNCC worker finds it difficult to discuss the woman problem because of the assumptions of male superiority. Assumptions of male superiority are as widespread and deep rooted and every much as crippling to the woman as the assumptions of white supremacy are to the Negro. Consider why it is in SNCC that women who are competent, qualified, and experienced, are automatically assigned to the "female" kinds of jobs such as typing, desk work, telephone work, filing, library work, cooking, and the assistant kind of administrative work but rarely the "executive" kind.

The woman in SNCC is often in the same position as that token Negro hired in a corporation. The management thinks that it has done its bit. Yet, every day the Negro bears an atmosphere, attitudes and actions which are tinged with condescension and paternalism, the most telling of which are when he is not promoted as the equally or less-skilled whites are. This paper is anonymous. Think about the kinds of things the author, if made known, would have to suffer because of raising this kind of discussion. Nothing so final as being fired or outright exclusion, but the kinds of things which are killing to the insides—insinuations, ridicule, over-exaggerated compensations.

This paper is presented anyway because it needs to be made know[n] that many women in the movement are not "happy and contented" with their status. It needs to be made known that much talent and experience are being wasted by this movement when women are not given jobs commensurate with their abilities. It needs to be known that just as Negroes were the crucial factor in the economy of the cotton South, so too in SNCC are women the crucial factor that keeps the movement running on a day-to-day basis. Yet they are not given equal say-so when it comes to day-to-day decisionmaking. What can be done? Probably nothing right away. Most men in this movement are probably too threatened by the possibility of serious discussion on this subject. Perhaps this is because they have recently broken away from a matriarchal framework under which they may have grown up. Then too, many women are as unaware and insensitive to this subject as men, just as there are many Negroes who don't understand they are not free or who want to be part of white America. They don't understand that they have to give up their souls and stay in their place to be accepted. So too, many women, in order to be accepted by men, on men's terms, give themselves up to that caricature of what a woman is—unthinking, pliable, an ornament to please the man.

Maybe the only thing that can come out of this paper is discussion—amidst the laughter—but still discussion. (Those who laugh the hardest are often those who need the crutch of male supremacy the most.) And maybe some women will begin to recognize day-to-day discriminations. And maybe sometime in the future the whole of the women in this movement will become so alert as to force the rest of the movement to stop the discrimination and start the slow process of changing values and ideas so that all of us gradually come to understand that this is no more a man's world than it is a white world.

November, 1964

Source: "Student Nonviolent Coordinating Committee Position Paper: Women in the Movement," text made available through the Institute of Advanced Technology in the Humanities, University of Virginia at Charlottesville, April 18, 1998.

SELECT BIBLIOGRAPHY:

Sara Evans, *Personal Politics: The Roots of Women's Liberation in the Civil Rights Movement and the New Left* (New York: Knopf, 1979).

Peter J. Ling and Sharon Monteith, eds., *Gender and the Civil Rights Movement* (New Brunswick: Rutgers University Press, 2004).

Doug McAdam, *Freedom Summer* (New York: Oxford University Press, 1988).

⚊ 12 ⚊

Elijah Muhammad and the Nation of Islam

Born Elijah Poole, Elijah Muhammad (1897–1975) changed his name sometime around 1931, after he came under the influence of Wallace D. Fard, the founder and charismatic leader of the Nation of Islam (NOI). After Fard disappeared in 1934, Muhammad claimed leadership of the group and set up a new headquarters for the NOI in Chicago.

The NOI became the most prominent conservative black-nationalist formation from World War II until the emergence of Black Power. According to Muhammad's teachings, black people were the descendants of the original race of humankind, and the white race was a genetic mutation created by an evil scientist named Yakub. The NOI preached strict standards of discipline, obedience of authority, and patriarchy. The Fruit of Islam, an internal security force within the sect, was fiercely loyal to Muhammad, who was termed the "Messenger of Allah." The explosive growth of the NOI in the 1950s and early 1960s was chiefly due to Malcolm X, who at this time was the national spokesman of the religious sect and a devoted follower of Muhammad. After Malcolm X's break with the NOI and his subsequent assassination, Muhammad's influence among black nationalists sharply declined. Following Muhammad's death in 1975, his son Wallace came into the leadership of the NOI and soon repudiated many of the central tenets and separatist policies of his father.

PROGRAM AND POSITION

What Muslims Want:

1) We want freedom. We want a full, complete freedom.
2) We want justice, equal justice under the law. We want justice applied equally regardless of creed, class or color.
3) We want equality of opportunity.
4) We want our people in America whose parents or grandparents were descendants from slaves to be allowed to establish a separate state or territory of their own.
5) We want freedom of all believers of Islam now held in federal prison.
6) We want an immediate end to the police brutality and mob attacks against the so-called Negroes throughout the United States.
7) As long as we are not allowed to establish a state or territory of our own, we demand not only equal justice under the laws of the United States, but equal employment opportunities now!
8) We want the government of the United States to exempt our people from all taxation as long as we are deprived of equal justice under the laws of the land.
9) We want equal education—but separate schools, up to sixteen for boys and eighteen for girls on the condition that the girls be sent to women's colleges and universities. We want all black children educated, taught and trained by their own teachers.

What Muslims Believe:

1) We believe in the one God whose proper name is Allah.
2) We believe in the Holy Koran and in the scriptures of all the prophets of God.
3) We believe in the truth of the Bible, but we believe that it has been tampered with and must be reinterpreted so that mankind will not be snared by the falsehoods that have been added to it.

4) We believe in Allah's prophets and the scriptures they brought to the people.

5) We believe in the resurrection of the dead—not in physical resurrection—but in mental resurrection. We believe that the so-called Negroes are most in need of mental resurrection. Therefore, they will be resurrected first. Furthermore, we believe we are the people of God's choice.

6) We believe in the judgment, we believe this first judgment will take place as God revealed, in America.

7) We believe this is the time in history for the separation of the so-called Negroes and the so-called white Americans.

8) We believe in justice for all, whether in God or not; we believe as others, that we are due equal justice as human beings. We believe in equality—as a nation—of equals. We do not believe that we are equal with our slave masters in the status of "freed slaves." We recognize and respect American citizens as independent people and we respect their laws which govern this nation.

9) We believe that the offer of integration is hypocritical and is made by those who are trying to deceive the black people into believing that their 400-year-old open enemies of freedom, justice, and equality are, all of a sudden, their "friends."

10) We believe that intermarriage or race-mixing should be prohibited.

11) We believe that we who declared ourselves to be righteous Muslims should not participate in wars which take the lives of humans.

12) We believe our women should be respected and protected as the women of other nationalities are respected and protected.

13) We believe that Allah (God) appeared in the person of Master W. Fard Muhammad, July 1930; the long awaited "Messiah" of the Christians and the "Mahdi" of the Muslims.

Source: Excerpt from "Program and Position" of the Nation of Islam, in Clifton E. Marsh, *From Black Muslims to Muslims: The Transition from Separatism to Islam, 1930–1980* (Metuchen, N.J.: Scarecrow Press, 1984), pp. 62–64.

SELECT BIBLIOGRAPHY:

Claude Andrew Clegg, *An Original Man: The Life and Times of Elijah Muhammad* (New York: St. Martin's Press, 1997).

Edward E. Curtis, *Black Muslim Religion in the Nation of Islam, 1960–1975* (Chapel Hill: University of North Carolina Press, 2006).

———, *Islam in Black America: Identity, Liberation, and Difference in African-American Islamic Thought* (Albany: State University of New York Press, 2002).

Karl Evanzz, *The Messenger: The Rise and Fall of Elijah Muhammad* (New York: Pantheon Books, 1999).

C. Eric Lincoln, *The Black Muslims in America*, 3d ed. (Trenton, N.J.: Africa World Press, 1994).

Louis E. Lomax, *When the Word Is Given: A Report on Elijah Muhammad, Malcolm X, and the Black Muslim World* (Westport, Conn.: Greenwood Press, 1963).

Clifton Marsh, *From Black Muslims to Muslims: The Resurrection, Transformation, and Change of the Lost-Found Nation of Islam in America, 1930–1995* (Lanham, Md.: Scarecrow Press, 1996).

~ 13 ~

Malcolm X and Revolutionary Black Nationalism

Born Malcolm Little, Malcolm X (1925–1965) grew up in Michigan under difficult circumstances after his father was murdered by racists. He then worked as a small-time hustler and drug dealer in Boston and Harlem until he was arrested for robbery in 1946. Malcolm converted to the Nation of Islam (NOI) in 1948. Following his release, he quickly established his reputation as a brilliant, fiery-tongued orator, and through his tenure as an NOI minister in Harlem the organization enjoyed a marked increase in its membership. By 1962, however, Elijah Muhammad and other prominent NOI leaders had become privately critical of Malcolm and jealous of his growing national prominence outside their organization. After a controversial remark made by Malcolm following the assassination of President John F. Kennedy, Muhammad seized the opportunity to "silence" his protégé. Malcolm left the NOI in March 1964, first establishing the religious Muslim Mosque, Inc., and several months later, the Organization of Afro-American Unity. In his last year of life, Malcolm made a well-publicized pilgrimage to Mecca and traveled extensively throughout Africa. Politically and ideologically, he was rapidly changing, embracing a revolutionary black nationalist, internationalist perspective. Malcolm's close identification with socialism and Third World liberation led to his extensive surveillance by the FBI. On February 21, 1965, Malcolm was assassinated in the Audubon Ballroom in Harlem. In death, his influence within the black world became far greater than his political stature during his own lifetime.

~

"THE BALLOT OR THE BULLET"
Mr. Moderator, brothers and sisters, friends and enemies: I just can't believe everyone in here is a friend and I don't want to leave anybody out. The question tonight, as I understand it, is "The Negro Revolt, and Where Do We Go from Here?" or "What Next?" In my little humble way of understanding it, it points toward either the ballot or the bullet.

Before we try and explain what is meant by the ballot or the bullet, I would like to clarify something concerning myself. I'm still a Muslim, my religion is still Islam. That's my personal belief. Just as Adam Clayton Powell is a Christian minister who heads the Abyssinian Baptist Church in New York, but at the same time takes part in the political struggles to try and bring about rights to the black people in this country; and Dr. Martin Luther King is a Christian minister down in Atlanta, Georgia, who heads another organization fighting for the civil rights of black people in this country; and Reverend Galamison—I guess you've heard of him—is another Christian minister in New York who has been deeply involved in the school boycotts to eliminate segregated education; well, I myself am a minister, not a Christian minister, but a Muslim minister; and I believe in action on all fronts by whatever means necessary.

Although I'm still a Muslim, I'm not here tonight to discuss my religion. I'm not here to try and change your religion. I'm not here to argue or discuss anything that we differ about, because it's time for us to submerge our differences and realize that it is best for us to first see that we have the same problem, a common problem—a problem that will make you catch hell whether you're a Baptist, or a Methodist, or a Muslim, or a nationalist. Whether you're educated or illiterate, whether you live on the boulevard or in the alley, you're going to catch hell just like I am. We're all in the same boat and we all are going to catch the same hell from the same man. He just happens to be a white man. All of us have suffered here, in this country, political oppression at the hands of the white man, economic exploitation at at the hands of the white man, and social degradation at the hands of the white man.

Now in speaking like this, it doesn't mean that we're anti-white, but it does mean we're anti-exploitation, we're antidegradation, we're antioppression. And if the white man doesn't want us to be anti-*him*, let him stop oppressing and exploiting and degrading us. Whether we are Christians or Muslims or nationalists or agnostics or atheists, we must first learn to forget our differences. If we have differences, let us differ in the closet; when we come out in front, let us not have anything to argue about until we get finished arguing with the man. If the late President Kennedy could get together with Khrushchev and exchange some wheat, we certainly have more in common with each other than Kennedy and Khrushchev had with each other.

If we don't do something real soon, I think you'll have to agree that we're going to be forced either to use the ballot or the bullet. It's one or the other in 1964. It isn't that time is running out—time has run out! Nineteen sixty-four threatens to be the most explosive year America has ever witnessed. The most explosive year. Why? It's also a political year. It's the year when all of the white politicians will be back in the so-called Negro community jiving you and me for some votes. The year when all of the white political crooks will be right back in your and my community with their false promises, building up our hopes for a letdown, with their trickery and their treachery, with their false promises which they don't intend to keep. As they nourish these dissatisfactions, it can only lead to one thing, an explosion; and now we have the type of black man on the scene in America today—I'm sorry, Brother Lomax[1]—who just doesn't intend to turn the other cheek any longer.

Don't let anybody tell you anything about the odds are against you. If they draft you, they send you to Korea and make you face 800 million Chinese. If you can be brave over there, you can be brave right here. These odds aren't as great as those odds. And if you fight here, you will at least know what you're fighting for.

I'm not a politician, not even a student of politics; in fact, I'm not a student of much of anything. I'm not a Democrat, I'm not a Republican, and I don't even consider myself an American. If you and I were Americans, there'd be no problem. Those Hunkies that just got off the boat, they're already Americans; Polacks are already Americans; the Italian refugees are already Americans. Everything that came out of Europe, every blue-eyed thing, is already an American. And as long as you and I have been over here, we aren't Americans yet.

Well, I am one who doesn't believe in deluding myself. I'm not going to sit at your table and watch you eat, with nothing on my plate, and call myself a diner. Sitting at the table doesn't make you a diner, unless you eat some of what's on that plate. Being here in America doesn't make you an American. Being born here in America doesn't make you an American. Why, if birth made you American, you wouldn't need any legislation, you wouldn't need any amendments to the Constitution, you wouldn't be faced with civil-rights filibustering in Washington, D.C., right now. They don't have to pass civil-rights legislation to make a Polack an American.

No, I'm not an American. I'm one of the twenty-two million black people who are the victims of democracy, nothing but disguised hypocrisy. So, I'm not standing here speaking to you as an American, or a patriot, or a flag-saluter, or a flag-waver— no, not I. I'm speaking as a victim of this American system. And I see America through the eyes of the victim. I don't see any American dream; I see an American nightmare.

These twenty-two million victims are waking up. Their eyes are coming open. They're beginning to see what they used to only look at. They're becoming politically mature. They are realizing that there are new political trends from coast to coast. As they see these new political trends, it's possible for them to see that every time there's an election the races are so close that they have to have a recount. They had to recount in Massachusetts to see who was going to be governor, it was so close. It was the same way in Rhode Island, in Minnesota, and in many other parts of the country. And the same with Kennedy and Nixon when they ran for President. It was so close they had to count all over again. Well, what does this mean? It means that when white people are evenly divided, and black people have a bloc of votes of their own, it is left up to them to determine who's going to sit in the White House and who's going to be in the dog house.

It was the black man's vote that put the present administration in Washington, D.C. Your vote, your dumb vote, your ignorant vote, your wasted vote put in an administration in Washington, D.C., that has seen fit to pass every kind of legislation imaginable, saving you until last, then filibustering on top of that. And your and my leaders have the audacity to run around clapping their hands and talk about how much progress we're making. And what a good President we have. If he wasn't good in Texas, he sure can't be good in Washington, D.C. Because Texas is a lynch state. It is in the same breath as Mississippi, no different; only they lynch you in Texas with a Texas accent and lynch you in Mississippi with a Mississippi accent. And these Negro leaders have the audacity to go and have some coffee in the White House with a Texan, a Southern cracker—that's all he is—and then come out and tell you and me that he's going to be better for us because, since he's from the South, he knows how to deal with the Southerners. What kind of logic is that? Let Eastland be President, he's from the South too. He should be better able to deal with them than Johnson.[2]

In this present administration they have in the House of Representatives 257 Democrats to only 177 Republicans. They control two-thirds of the House vote. Why can't they pass something that will help you and me? In the Senate, there are 67 Senators who are of the Democratic party. Only 33 of them are Republicans. Why, the Democrats have got the government sewed up, and you're the one who sewed it up for them. And what have they given you for it? Four years in office, and just now getting around to some civil-rights legislation. Just now, after everything else is gone, out of the way, they're going to sit down now and play with you all summer long—the same old giant con game that they call filibuster.[3] All those are in cahoots together. Don't you ever think they're not in cahoots together, for the man that is heading the civil-rights filibuster is a man from Georgia named Richard Russell. When Johnson became President, the first man he asked for when he got back to Washington, D.C., was "Dicky"—that's how tight they are. That's his boy, that's his pal, that's his buddy. But they're playing that old con game. One of them makes believe he's for you, and he's got it fixed where the other one is so tight against you, he never has to keep his promise.

So it's time in 1964 to wake up. And when you see them coming up with that kind of conspiracy, let them know your eyes are open. And let them know you got something else that's wide open too. It's got to be the ballot or the bullet. The ballot or the bullet. If you're afraid to use an expression like that, you should get on out of the country, you should get back in the cotton patch, you should get back in the alley. They get all the Negro vote, and after they get it, the Negro gets nothing in return. All they did when they got to Washington was give a few big Negroes big jobs. Those big Negroes didn't need big jobs, they already had jobs. That's camouflage, that's trickery, that's treachery, window-dressing. I'm not trying to knock out the Democrats for the Republicans, we'll get to them in a minute. But it is true—you put the Democrats first and the Democrats put you last.

Look at it the way it is. What alibis do they use, since they control Congress and the Senate? What alibi do they use when you and I ask, "Well, when are you going to keep your promise?" They blame the Dixiecrats. What is a Dixiecrat? A Democrat. A Dixiecrat is nothing but a Democrat in disguise. The titular head of the Democrats is also the head of the Dixiecrats, because the Dixiecrats are a part of the Democratic Party. The Democrats have never kicked the Dixiecrats out of the party. The Dixiecrats bolted themselves once, but the Democrats didn't put them out. Imagine, these low-down Southern segregationists put the Northern Democrats down. But the Northern Democrats have never put the Dixiecrats down. No, look at that thing the way it is. They have got a con game going on, a political con game, and you and I are in the middle. It's time for you and me to wake up and start looking at it like it is, and trying to understand it like it is; and then we can deal with it like it is. . . .

So, what I'm trying to impress upon you, in essence, is this: You and I in America are faced not with a segregationist conspiracy, we're faced with a government conspiracy. Everyone who's filibustering is a Senator—that's the government. Everyone who's finagling in Washington, D.C., is a Congressman—that's the government. You don't have anybody putting blocks in your path but people who are a part of the government. The same government that you go abroad to fight for and die for is the government that is in a conspiracy to deprive you of your voting rights, deprive you of your economic opportunities, deprive you of decent housing, deprive you of decent education. You don't need to go to the employer alone, it is the government itself, the government of America, that is responsible for the oppression and exploitation and degradation of black people in this country. And you should drop it in their lap. This government has failed the Negro. This so-called democracy has failed the Negro. And all these white liberals have definitely failed the Negro.

So, where do we go from here? First, we need some friends. We need some new allies. The entire civil-rights struggle needs a new interpretation, a broader interpretation. We need to look at this civil-rights thing from another angle— from the inside as well as from the outside. To those of us whose philosophy is black nationalism, the only way you can get involved in the civil-rights struggle is to give it a new interpretation. That old interpretation excluded us. It kept us out. So, we're giving a new interpretation to the civil-rights struggle, an interpretation that will enable us to come into it, take part in it. And these handkerchief-heads who have been dillydallying and pussyfooting and compromising—we don't intend to let them pussyfoot and dillydally and compromise any longer.

How can you thank a man for giving you what's already yours? How then can you thank him for giving you only part of what's already yours? You haven't even made progress, if what's being given to you, you should have had already. That's not progress. And I love my Brother Lomax, the way he pointed out we're right back where we were in 1954. We're not even as far up as we were in 1954. We're behind where we were in 1954. There's more segregation now than there was in 1954. There's more racial animosity, more racial hatred, more racial violence today in 1964, than there was in 1954. Where is the progress?

And now you're facing a situation where the young Negro's coming up. They don't want to hear that "turn-the-other-cheek" stuff, no. In Jacksonville, those were teenagers, they were throwing Molotov cocktails. Negroes have never done that before. But it shows you there's a new deal coming in. There's new thinking coming in. There's new strategy coming in. It'll be Molotov cocktails this month, hand grenades next month, and something else next month. It'll be ballots, or it'll be bullets. It'll be liberty, or it will be death. The only difference about this kind of death—it'll be reciprocal. You know what is meant by "reciprocal"? That's one of Brother Lomax's words, I stole it from him. I don't usually deal with those big words because I don't usually deal with big people. I deal with small people. I find you can get a whole lot of small people and whip hell out of a whole lot of big people. They haven't got anything to lose, and they've got everything to gain. And they'll let you know in a minute: "It takes two to tango; when I go, you go."

The black nationalists, those whose philosophy is black nationalism, in bringing about this new interpretation of the entire meaning of civil rights, look upon it as meaning, as Brother Lomax has pointed out, equality of opportunity. Well, we're justified in seeking civil rights, if it means equality of opportunity, because all we're doing there is trying to collect for our investment. Our mothers and fathers invested sweat and blood. Three hundred and ten years we worked in this country without a dime in return—I mean without a *dime* in return. You let the white man walk around here talking about how rich this country is, but you never stop to think how it got rich so quick. It got rich because you made it rich.

You take the people who are in this audience right now. They're poor, we're all poor as individuals. Our weekly salary individually amounts to hardly anything. But if you take the salary of everyone in here collectively it'll fill up a whole lot of baskets. It's a lot of wealth. If you can collect the wages of just these people right here for a year, you'll be rich—richer than rich. When you look at it like that, think how rich Uncle Sam had to become, not with this handful, but millions of black people. Your and my mother and father, who didn't work an eight-hour shift, but worked from "can't see" in the morning until "can't see" at night, and worked for nothing, making the white man rich, making Uncle Sam rich. . . .

By ballot I only mean freedom. Don't you know—I disagree with Lomax on this issue—that the ballot is more important than the dollar? Can I prove it? Yes. Look in the U.N. There are poor nations in the U.N.; yet those poor nations can get together with their voting power and keep the rich nations from making a move. They have one nation, one vote—everyone has an equal vote. And when those brothers from Asia, and Africa and the darker parts of this earth get together, their voting power is sufficient to hold Sam in check. Or Russia in check. Or some other section of the earth in check. So, the ballot is most important.

Right now, in this country, if you and I, twenty-two million African-Americans—that's what we are—Africans who are in America. In fact, you'd get farther calling yourself African instead of Negro. Africans don't catch hell. You're the only one catching hell. They don't have to pass civil-rights bills for Africans. An African can go anywhere he wants right now. All you've got to do is tie your head up. That's right, go anywhere you want. Just stop being a Negro. Change your name to Hoogagagooba. That'll show you how silly the white man is. You're dealing with a silly man. A friend of mine who's very dark put a turban on his head and went into a restaurant in Atlanta before they called themselves desegregated. He went into a white restaurant, he sat down, they served him, and he said, "What would happen if a Negro came in here?" And there he's sitting, black as night, but because he had his head wrapped up the waitress looked back at him and says, "Why, there wouldn't no nigger dare come in here."

So, you're dealing with a man whose bias and prejudice are making him lose his mind, his intelligence, every day. He's frightened. He looks around and sees what's taking place on this earth, and he sees that the pendulum of time is swinging in your direction. The dark people are waking up. They're losing their fear of the white man. No place where he's fighting right now is he winning. Everywhere he's fighting, he's fighting someone your and my complexion. And they're beating him. He can't win any more. He's won his last battle. He failed to win the Korean War. He couldn't win it. He had to sign a truce. That's a loss. Any time Uncle Sam, with all his machinery for warfare, is held to a draw by some rice-eaters, he's lost the battle. He had to sign a truce. America's not supposed to sign a truce. She's supposed to be bad. But she's not bad any more. She's bad as long as she can use her hydrogen bomb, but she can't use hers for fear Russia might use hers. Russia can't use hers, for fear that Sam might use his. So, both of them are weaponless. They can't use the weapon, because each's weapon nullifies the other's. So the only place where action can take place is on the ground. And the white man can't win another war fighting on the ground. Those days are over. The black man knows it, the brown man knows it, the red man knows it, and the yellow man knows it. So they engage him in guerrilla warfare. That's not his style. You've got to have heart to be a guerrilla warrior, and he hasn't got any heart. I'm telling you now. . . .

The political philosophy of black nationalism means that the black man should control the politics and the politicians in his own community; no more. The black man in the black community has to be reeducated into the science of politics so he will know what politics is supposed to bring him in return. Don't be throwing out any ballots. A ballot is like a bullet. You don't throw your ballots until you see a target, and if that target is not within your reach, keep your ballot in your pocket. The political philosophy of black nationalism is being taught in the Christian church. It's being taught in the N.A.A.C.P. It's being taught in CORE meetings. It's being taught in S.N.C.C. meetings. It's being taught in Muslim meetings. It's being taught where nothing but atheists and agnostics come together. It's being taught everywhere. Black people are fed up with the dillydal-lying, pussyfooting, compromising approach that we've been using toward getting our freedom. We want freedom now, but we're not going to get it saying "We Shall Overcome." We've got to fight until we overcome.

The economic philosophy of black nationalism is pure and simple. It only means that we should control the economy of our community. Why should white people be running all the stores in our community? Why should white people be running the banks of our community? Why should the economy of our community be in the hands of the white man? Why? If a black man can't move his store into a white community, you tell me why a white man should move his store into a black community. The philosophy of black nationalism involves a reeducation program in the black community in regard to economics. Our people have to be made to see that any time you take your dollar out of your community and spend it in a community where you don't live, the community where you live will get poorer and poorer, and the community where you spend your money will get richer and richer. Then you wonder why where you live is always a ghetto or a slum area. And where you and I are concerned, not only do we lose it when we spend it out of the community, but the white man has got all our stores in the community tied up; so that though we spend it in the community, at sundown the man who runs the store takes it over across town somewhere. He's got us in a vise.

So the economic philosophy of black nationalism means in every church, in every civic organization, in every fraternal order, it's time now for our people to become conscious of the importance of controlling the economy of our community. If we own the stores, if we operate the businesses, if we try and establish some industry in our own community, then we're developing to the position where we are creating employment for our own kind. Once you gain control of the economy of your own community, then you don't have to picket and boycott and beg some cracker downtown for a job in his business.

The social philosophy of black nationalism only means that we have to get together and remove the evils, the vices, alcoholism, drug addiction, and other evils that are destroying the moral fiber of our community. We ourselves have to lift the level of our community, the standard of our community to a higher level, make our own society beautiful so that we will be satisfied in our own social circles and won't be running around here trying to knock our way into a social circle where we're not wanted.

So I say, in spreading a gospel such as black nationalism, it is not designed to make the black man reevaluate the white man—you know him already—but to make the black man reevaluate himself. Don't change the white man's mind; you can't change his mind. And that whole thing about appealing to the moral conscience of America—America's conscience is bankrupt. She lost all conscience a long time ago. Uncle Sam has no conscience. They don't know what morals are. They don't try and eliminate an evil because it's evil, or because it's illegal, or because it's immoral; they eliminate it only when it threatens their existence. So you're wasting your time appealing to the moral conscience of a bankrupt man like Uncle Sam. If he had a conscience, he'd straighten this thing out with no more pressure being put upon him. So it is not necessary to change the white man's mind. We have to change our own mind. You can't change his mind about us. We've got to change our own minds about each other. We have to see each other with new eyes. We have to see each other as brothers and sisters. We have to come together with warmth so we can develop unity and harmony that's necessary to get this problem solved ourselves. How can we do this? How can we avoid jealousy? How can we avoid the suspicion and the divisions that exist in the community? I'll tell you how. . . .

Our gospel is black nationalism. We're not trying to threaten the existence of any organization, but we're spreading the gospel of black nationalism. Anywhere there's a church that is also preaching and practicing the gospel of black nationalism, join that church. If the N.A.A.C.P. is preaching and practicing the gospel of black nationalism, join the N.A.A.C.P. If CORE is spreading and practicing the gospel of black nationalism, join CORE. Join any organization that has a gospel that's for the uplift of the black man. And when you get into it and see them pussyfooting or compromising, pull out of it because that's not black nationalism. We'll find another one. . . .

It's time for you and me to stop sitting in this country, letting some cracker Senators, Northern crackers and Southern crackers, sit there in Washington, D.C., and come to a conclusion in their mind that you and I are supposed to have civil rights. There's no white man going to tell me anything about *my* rights. Brothers and sisters, always remember, if it doesn't take Senators and Congressmen and Presidential proclamations to give freedom to the white man, it is not necessary for legislation or proclamation or Supreme Court decisions to give freedom to the black man. You let that white man know, if this is a country of freedom, let it be a country of freedom; and if it's not a country of freedom, change it.

We will work with anybody, anywhere, at any time, who is genuinely interested in tackling the problem head-on, nonviolently as long as the enemy is nonviolent, but violent when the enemy gets violent. We'll work with you on the voter-registration drive, we'll work with you on rent strikes, we'll work with you on school boycotts—I don't believe in any kind of integration; I'm not even worried about it because I know you're not going to get it anyway; you're not going to get it because you're afraid to die; you've got to be ready to die if you try and force yourself on the white man, because he'll get just as violent as those crackers in Mississippi, right here in Cleveland. But we will work with you on the school boycotts, because we're against a segregated school system. A segregated school system produces children who, when they graduate, graduate with crippled minds. But this does not mean that a school is segregated because it's all black. A segregated school means a school that is controlled by people who have no real interest in it whatsoever.

Let me explain what I mean. A segregated district or community is a community in which people live, but outsiders control the politics and the economy of that community. They never refer to the white section as a segregated community. It's the all-Negro section that's a segregated community. Why? The white man controls his own school, his own bank, his own economy, his own politics, his own everything, his own community—but he also controls yours. When you're under someone else's control, you're segregated. They'll always give you the lowest or the worst that there is to offer, but it doesn't mean you're segregated just because you have your own. You've got to *control* your own. Just like the white man has control of his, you need to control yours.

You know the best way to get rid of segregation? The white man is more afraid of separation than he is of integration. Segregation means that he puts you away from him, but not far enough for you to be out of his jurisdiction; separation means you're gone. And the white man will integrate faster than he'll let you separate. So we will work with you against the segregated school system because it's criminal, because it is absolutely destructive, in every way imaginable, to the minds of the children who have to be exposed to that type of crippling education.

Last but not least, I must say this concerning the great controversy over rifles and shotguns. The only thing that I've ever said is that in areas where the government has proven itself either unwilling or unable to defend the lives and the property of Negroes, it's time for Negroes to defend themselves. Article number two of the Constitutional amendments provides you and me the right to own a rifle or a shotgun.[4] It is constitutionally legal to own a shotgun or a rifle. This doesn't mean you're going to get a rifle and form battalions and go out looking for white folks, although you'd be within your rights—I mean, you'd be justified; but that would be illegal and we don't do anything illegal. If the white man doesn't want the black man buying rifles and shotguns, then let the government do its job. That's all. And don't let the white man come to you and ask you what you think about what Malcolm says—why, you old Uncle Tom. He would never ask you if he thought you were going to say, "Oh, man!" No, he is making a Tom out of you.

So, this doesn't mean forming rifle clubs and going out looking for people, but it is time, in 1964, if you are a man, to let that man know. If he's not going to do his job in running the government and providing you and me with the protection that our taxes are supposed to be for, since he spends all those billions for his defense budget, he certainly can't begrudge you and me spending $12 or $15 for a single-shot, or double-action. I hope you understand. Don't go out shooting people, but any time, brothers and sisters, and especially the men in this audience—some of you wearing Congressional Medals of Honor, with shoulders this wide, chests this big, muscles that big—any time you and I sit around and read where they bomb a church and murder in cold blood, not some grownups, but four little girls while they were praying . . . if you never see me another time in your life, if I die in the morning, I'll die saying one thing: the ballot or the bullet, the ballot or the bullet.

If a Negro in 1964 has to sit around and wait for some cracker Senator to filibuster when it comes to the rights of black people, why, you and I should hang our heads in shame. You talk about a march on Washington in 1963, you haven't seen anything. There's some more going down in '64. And this time they're not going like they went last year. They're not going singing "We Shall Overcome." They're not going with white friends. They're not going with placards already painted for them. They're not going with round-trip tickets. They're going with one-way tickets.

And if they don't want that non-nonviolent army going down there, tell them to bring the filibuster to a halt. The black nationalists aren't going to wait. Lyndon B. Johnson is the head of the Democratic party. If he's for civil rights, let him go into the Senate next week and declare himself. Let him go in there right now and declare himself. Let him go in there and denounce the Southern branch of his party. Let him go in there right now and take a moral stand—right now, not later. Tell him, don't wait until election time. If he waits too long, brothers and sisters, he will be responsible for letting a condition develop in this country which will create a climate that will bring seeds up out of the ground with vegetation on the end of them looking like something these people never dreamed of. In 1964, it's the ballot or the bullet. Thank you.

꧂

STATEMENT OF THE ORGANIZATION OF AFRO-AMERICAN UNITY

The Organization of Afro-American Unity, organized and structured by a cross-section of the Afro-American people living in the U.S.A., has been patterned after the letter and spirit of the Organization of African Unity established at Addis Ababa, Ethiopia, May, 1963.

We, the members of the Organization of Afro-American Unity gathered together in Harlem, New York:

Convinced that it is the inalienable right of all people to control their own destiny;

Conscious of the fact that freedom, equality, justice and dignity are essential objectives for the achievement of the legitimate aspirations of the people of African descent here in the Western Hemisphere, we will endeavor to build a bridge of understanding and create the basis for Afro-American unity;

Conscious of our responsibility to harness the natural and human resources of our people for their total advancement in all spheres of human endeavor;

Inspired by a common determination to promote understanding among our people and co-operation in all matters pertaining to their survival and advancement, we will support the aspirations of our people for brotherhood and solidarity in a larger unity transcending all organizational differences;

Convinced that, in order to translate this determination into a dynamic force in the cause of human progress, conditions of peace and security must be established and maintained;

Determined to unify the Americans of African descent in their fight for human rights and dignity, and being fully aware that this is not possible in the present atmosphere and condition of oppression, we dedicate ourselves to the building of a political, economic, and social system of justice and peace;

Dedicated to the unification of all people of African descent in this hemisphere and to the utilization of that unity to bring into being the organizational structure that will project the black people's contributions to the world;

Persuaded that the Charter of the United Nations, the Universal Declaration of Human Rights, the Constitution of the U.S.A. and the Bill of Rights are the principles in which we believe and these documents if put into practice represent the essence of mankind's hopes and good intentions;

Desirous that all Afro-American people and organizations should henceforth unite so that the welfare and well-being of our people will be assured;

Resolved to reinforce the common bond of purpose between our people by submerging all of our differences and establishing a non-religious and non-sectarian constructive program for human rights;

Do hereby present this charter.

I. Establishment

The Organization of Afro-American Unity shall include all people of African descent in the Western Hemisphere, as well as our brothers and sisters on the African Continent.

II. Self-Defense

Since self-preservation is the first law of nature, we assert the Afro-American's right of self-defense.

The Constitution of the U.S.A. clearly affirms the right of every American citizen to bear arms. And as Americans, we will not give up a single right guaranteed under the Constitution. The history of the unpublished violence against our people clearly indicates that we must be prepared to defend ourselves or we will continue to be a defenseless people at the mercy of a ruthless and violent racist mob.

We assert that in those areas where the government is either unable or unwilling to protect the lives and property of our people, that our people are within their rights to protect themselves by whatever means necessary. A man with a rifle or club can only be stopped by a person who defends himself with a rifle or club.

Tactics based solely on morality can only succeed when you are dealing with basically moral people or a moral system. A man or system which oppresses a man because of his color is not moral. It is the duty of every Afro-American and every Afro-American community throughout this country to protect its people against mass murderers, bombers, lynchers, floggers, brutalizers and exploiters.

III. Education

Education is an important element in the struggle for human rights. It is the means to help our children and people rediscover their identity and thereby increase self-respect. Education is our passport to the future, for tomorrow belongs to the people who prepare for it today.

Our children are being criminally shortchanged in the public school system of America. The Afro-American schools are the poorest run schools in New York City. Principals and teachers fail to understand the nature of the problems with which they work and as a result they cannot do the job of teaching our children. The textbooks tell our children nothing about the great contributions of Afro-Americans to the growth and development of this country.

The Board of Education's integration program is expensive and unworkable; and the organization of principals and supervisors in the New York City school system has refused to support the Board's plan to integrate the schools, thus dooming it to failure. The Board of Education has said that even with its plan there are 10 percent of the schools in the Harlem-Bedford-Stuyvesant community they cannot improve. This means that the Organization of Afro-American Unity must make the Afro-American community a more potent force for educational self-improvement.

A first step in the program to end the existing system of racist education is to demand that the 10 percent of the schools the Board of Education will not include in its plan be turned over to and run by the Afro-American community. We want Afro-American principals to head these schools. We want Afro-American teachers in these schools. We want textbooks written by Afro-Americans that are acceptable to us to be used in these schools.

The Organization of Afro-American Unity will select and recommend people to serve on local school boards where school policy is made and passed on to the Board of Education.

Through these steps we will make the 10 percent of schools we take over educational showplaces that will attract the attention of people all over the nation.

If these proposals are not met, we will ask Afro-American parents to keep their children out of the present inferior schools they attend. When these schools in our neighborhood are controlled by Afro-Americans, we will return to them.

The Organization of Afro-American Unity recognizes the tremendous importance of the complete involvement of Afro-American parents in every phase of school life. Afro-American parents must be willing and able to go into the schools and see that the job of educating our children is done properly.

We call on all Afro-Americans around the nation to be aware that the conditions that exist in the New York City public school system are as deplorable in their cities as they are here. We must unite our effort and spread our program of self-improvement through education to every Afro-American community in America.

We must establish all over the country schools of our own to train our children to become scientists and mathematicians. We must realize the need for adult education and for job retraining programs that will emphasize a changing society in which automation plays the key role. We intend to use the tools of education to help raise our people to an unprecedented level of excellence and self-respect through their own efforts.

IV. Politics—Economics

Basically, there are two kinds of power that count in America: economic and political, with social power deriving from the two. In order for the Afro-Americans to control their destiny, they must be able to control and affect the decisions which control their destiny: economic, political and social. This can only be done through organization.

The Organization of Afro-American Unity will organize the Afro-American community block by block to make the community aware of its power and potential; we will start immediately a voter-registration drive to make every unregistered voter in the Afro-American community an independent voter; we propose to support and/or organize political clubs, to run independent candidates for office, and to support any Afro-American already in office who answers to and is responsible to the Afro-American community.

Economic exploitation in the Afro-American community is the most vicious form practiced on any people in America; twice as much rent for rat-infested, roach-crawling, rotting tenements; the Afro-American pays more for foods, clothing, insurance rates and so forth. The Organization of Afro-American Unity will wage an unrelenting struggle against these evils in our community. There shall be organizers to work with the people to solve these problems, and start a housing self-improvement program. We propose to support rent strikes and other activities designed to better the community.

V. Social

This organization is responsible only to the Afro-American people and community and will function only with their support, both financially and numerically. We believe that our communities must be the sources of their own strength politically, economically, intellectually and culturally in the struggle for human rights and dignity.

The community must reinforce its moral responsibility to rid itself of the effects of years of exploitation, neglect and apathy, and wage an unrelenting struggle against police brutality.

The Afro-American community must accept the responsibility for regaining our people who have lost their place in society. We must declare an all-out war on organized crime in our community; a vice that is controlled by policemen who accept bribes and graft, and who must be exposed. We must establish a clinic, whereby one can get aid and cure for drug addiction; and create meaningful, creative, useful activities for those who were led astray down the avenues of vice.

The people of the Afro-American community must be prepared to help each other in all ways possible; we must establish a place where unwed mothers can get help and advice; a home for the aged in Harlem and an orphanage in Harlem.

We must set up a guardian system that will help our youth who get into trouble and also provide constructive activities for our children. We must set a good example for our children and must teach them to always be ready to accept the responsibilities that are necessary for building good communities and nations. We must teach them that their greatest responsibilities are to themselves, to their families and to their communities.

The Organization of Afro-American Unity believes that the Afro-American community must endeavor to do the major part of all charity work from within the community. Charity, however, does not mean that to which we are legally entitled in the form of government benefits. The Afro-American veteran must be made aware of all the benefits due him and the procedure for obtaining them. These veterans must be encouraged to go into business together, using G.I. loans, etc.

Afro-Americans must unite and work together. We must take pride in the Afro-American community, for it is home and it is power.

What we do here in regaining our self-respect, manhood, dignity and freedom helps all people everywhere who are fighting against oppression.

VI. *Culture*

"A race of people is like an individual man; until it uses its own talent, takes pride in its own history, expresses its own culture, affirms its own selfhood, it can never fulfill itself."

Our history and our culture were completely destroyed when we were forcibly brought to America in chains. And now it is important for us to know that our history did not begin with slavery's scars. We come from Africa, a great continent and a proud and varied people, a land which is the new world and was the cradle of civilization. Our culture and our history are as old as man himself and yet we know almost nothing of it. We must recapture our heritage and our identity if we are ever to liberate ourselves from the bonds of white supremacy. We must launch a cultural revolution to unbrainwash an entire people.

Our cultural revolution must be the means of bringing us closer to our African brothers and sisters. It must begin in the community and be based on community participation. Afro-Americans will be free to create only when they can depend on the Afro-American community for support and Afro-American artists must realize that they depend on the Afro-American for inspiration. We must work toward the establishment of a cultural center in Harlem, which will include people of all ages, and will conduct workshops in all the arts, such as film, creative writing, painting, theater, music, Afro-American history, etc.

This cultural revolution will be the journey to our rediscovery of ourselves. History is a people's memory, and without a memory man is demoted to the lower animals.

Armed with the knowledge of the past, we can with confidence charter a course for our future. Culture is an indispensable weapon in the freedom struggle. We must take hold of it and forge the future with the past.

When the battle is won, let history be able to say to each one of us: "He was a dedicated patriot: *Dignity* was his country, *Manhood* was his government, and *Freedom* was his land" (from *And Then We Heard the Thunder*, by John Oliver Killens).

Notes: 1. The reference is to Louis E. Lomax, author of *The Negro Revolt*, published in 1962. 2. President Johnson was from Texas and had represented the state in the Senate. 3. To prevent passage of a civil rights bill in 1964, southerners in Congress began a long filibuster. The bill was finally passed in a modified form. 4. The reference is to the Second Amendment of the Constitution. The first ten amendments, known collectively as the Bill of Rights, were ratified December 15, 1791. The Second Amendment reads: "A well-regulated militia being necessary to the security of a free State, the right of the people to keep and bear arms, shall not be infringed."

Sources: (1) "The Ballot or the Bullet" speech delivered in Cleveland, Ohio, April 3, 1964, reprinted in *Malcolm X Speaks* (New York: Merit Publishers, 1965), pp. 23–44. Copyright 1965, 1989 by Betty Shabazz and Pathfinder Press, reprinted by permission; and (2) "Statement of the Basic Aims and Objectives of the Organization of Afro-American Unity," June 28, 1964, reprinted in George Breitman, ed., *The Last Year of Malcolm X: The Evolution of a Revolutionary* (New York: Merit Publishers, 1967), pp. 105–11. Copyright Pathfinder Press, reprinted by permission.

SELECT BIBLIOGRAPHY:

George Breitman, *The Last Year of Malcolm X* (New York: Merit Publishers, 1967).
John Hendrick Clarke, *Malcolm X: The Man and His Times* (New York: Macmillan, 1970).
James Cone, *Martin and Malcolm: A Dream or a Nightmare?* (Maryknoll, N.Y.: Orbis Books, 1991).
Michael Eric Dyson, *The Myth and Meaning of Malcolm X* (New York: Oxford University Press, 1995).
Peter R. Goldman, *The Death and Life of Malcolm X* (New York: Harper and Row, 1973).
Robert L. Jenkins and Mfanya Donald Tryman, eds., *The Malcolm X Encyclopedia* (Westport: Greenwood Press, 2002).
Malcolm X, *Malcolm X Speaks: Selected Speeches and Statements*, ed. George Breitman (New York: Merit Publishers, 1965).

∼ 14 ∼

Black Power

When "Black Power" suddenly emerged as a controversial slogan in the summer of 1966, it reflected the growing dissatisfaction of the more militant wing of the Black Freedom movement that had lost its faith in nonviolent direct action and the politics of the white liberal establishment. The most prominent and charismatic spokesperson for this new expression of black nationalism was Stokely Carmichael (1941–1998). Born in Trinidad, Carmichael moved to New York when he was eleven. He received a B.A. in philosophy from Howard University in 1964 and throughout the early 1960s maintained a high level of activism. In 1966 he replaced John Lewis as head of the SNCC and began to push the slogan "Black Power," which argued that integration was not, by itself, an adequate solution to the problems of African Americans. In 1967, Carmichael expanded on his philosophy with his important primer, coauthored with Charles Hamilton, *Black Power: The Politics of Liberation in America.* By the early 1970s Carmichael had become profoundly influenced by revolutionary Pan-Africanist thought, represented by African leaders such as Kwame Nkrumah. Changing his name to Kwame Ture, he created the All-African Peoples Revolutionary Party, a small, radical black formation inside the United States. Ture was widely respected and admired even by those who did not share his political perspectives for his life-long dedication to the struggle for black freedom.

Bayard Rustin (1910–1987) was born in West Chester, Pennsylvania, and studied at Wilberforce University, Cheney State Teacher's College, and the City College of New York. A member of the Young Communist League in the mid-1930s and a conscientious objector during World War II, Rustin became one of the principal organizers within the Black Freedom movement. He helped establish the SCLC, worked as a special assistant to Dr. King for seven years, and was the primary architect behind the 1963 March on Washington. Like many of the older, more moderate black leaders of the 1960s, Rustin was disconcerted by the Black Power slogan and was concerned about the backlash it caused among many whites. Rustin's politics increasingly became conservative, even criticizing King for his vigorous opposition to the Vietnam War. Toward the end of his life Rustin publicly acknowledged his homosexuality and openly supported the struggle for lesbian and gay rights.

⌒

"What We Want"
By Stokely Carmichael

One of the tragedies of the struggle against racism is that up to now there has been no national organization which could speak to the growing militancy of young black people in the urban ghetto. There has been only a civil rights movement, whose tone of voice was adapted to an audience of liberal whites. It served as a sort of buffer zone between them and angry young blacks. None of its so-called leaders could go into a rioting community and be listened to. In a sense, I blame ourselves—together with the mass media—for what has happened in Watts, Harlem, Chicago, Cleveland, Omaha. Each time the people in those cities saw Martin Luther King get slapped, they became angry; when they saw four little black girls bombed to death, they were angrier; and when nothing happened, they were steaming. We had nothing to offer that they could see, except to go out and be beaten again. We helped to build their frustration.

For too many years, black Americans marched and had their heads broken and got shot. They were saying to the country, "Look, you guys are supposed to be nice guys and we are only going to do what we are supposed to do—why do you beat us up, why don't you give us what we ask, why don't you straighten yourselves out?" After years of this, we are at almost the same point—because we demonstrated from a position of weakness. We cannot be expected any longer to march and have our heads broken in order to say to whites: come on, you're nice guys. For you are not nice guys. We have found you out.

An organization which claims to speak for the needs of a community—as does the Student Nonviolent Coordinating Committee—must speak in the tone of that community, not as somebody else's buffer zone. This is the significance of black power as a slogan. For once, black people are going to use the words they want to use—not just the words whites want to hear. And they will do this no matter how often the press tries to stop the use of the slogan by equating it with racism or separatism.

An organization which claims to be working for the needs of a community—as SNCC does—must work to provide that community with a position of strength from which to make its voice heard. This is the significance of black power beyond the slogan.

Black power can be clearly defined for those who do not attach the fears of white America to their questions about it. We should begin with the basic fact that black Americans have two problems: they are poor and they are black. All other problems arise from this two-sided reality: lack of education, the so-called apathy of black men. Any program to end racism must address itself to that double reality.

Almost from its beginning, SNCC sought to address itself to both conditions with a program aimed at winning political power for impoverished Southern blacks. We had to begin with politics because black Americans are a propertyless people in a country where property is valued above all. We had to work for power, because this country does not function by morality, love, and nonviolence, but by power. Thus we determined to win political power, with the idea of moving on from there into activity that would have economic effects. With power, the masses could *make or participate in making* the decisions which govern their destinies, and thus create basic change in their day-to-day lives.

But if political power seemed to be the key to self-determination, it was also obvious that the key had been thrown down a deep well many years earlier. Disenfranchisement, maintained by racist terror, makes it impossible to talk about organizing for political power in 1960. The right to vote had to be won, and SNCC workers devoted their energies to this from 1961 to 1965. They set up voter registration drives in the Deep South. They created pressure for the vote by holding mock elections in Mississippi in 1963 and by helping to establish the Mississippi Freedom Democratic Party (MFDP) in 1964. That struggle was eased, though not won, with the passage of the 1965 Voting Rights Act. SNCC workers could then address themselves to the question: "Who can we vote for, to have our needs met—how do we make our vote meaningful?"

SNCC had already gone to Atlantic City for recognition of the Mississippi Freedom Democratic Party by the Democratic convention and been rejected; it had gone with the MFDP to Washington for recognition by Congress and been rejected. In Arkansas, SNCC helped thirty Negroes to run for School Board elections; all but one were defeated, and there was evidence of fraud and intimidation sufficient to cause their defeat. In Atlanta, Julian Bond ran for the state legislature and was elected—twice—and unseated—twice. In several states, black farmers ran in elections for agricultural committees which make crucial decisions concerning land use, loans, etc. Although they won places on a number of committees, they never gained the majorities needed to control them.

All of the efforts were attempts to win black power. Then, in Alabama, the opportunity came to see how blacks could be organized on an independent party basis. An unusual Alabama law provides that any group of citizens can nominate candidates for county office and, if they win 20 percent of the vote, may be recognized as a county political party. The same then applies on a state level. SNCC went to organize in several counties such as Lowndes, where black people—who form 80 per cent of the population and have an average annual income of $943—felt they could accomplish nothing within the framework of the Alabama Democratic Party because of its racism and because the qualifying fee for this year's elections was raised from $50 to $500 in order to prevent most Negroes from becoming candidates. On May 3, five new county "freedom organizations" convened and nominated candidates for the offices of sheriff, tax assessor, members of the school boards. These men and women are up for election in November—if they live until then. Their ballot symbol is the black panther: a bold, beautiful animal, representing the strength and dignity of black demands today. A man needs a black panther on his side when he and his family must endure—as hundreds of Alabamians have endured—loss of job, eviction, starvation, and sometimes death, for political activity. He may also need a gun and SNCC reaffirms the right of black men everywhere to defend themselves when threatened or attacked. As for initiating the use of violence, we hope that such programs as ours will make that unnecessary; but it is not for us to tell black communities whether they can or cannot use any particular form of action to resolve their problems. Responsibility for the use of violence by black men, whether in self-defense or initiated by them, lies with the white community.

This is the specific historical experience from which SNCC's call for "black power" emerged on the Mississippi march last July. But the concept of "black power" is not a recent or isolated phenomenon: It has grown out of the ferment of agitation and activity by different people and organizations in many black communities over the years. Our last year of work in Alabama added a new concrete possibility. In Lowndes County, for example, black power will mean that if a Negro is elected sheriff, he can end police brutality. If a black man is elected tax assessor, he can collect and channel funds for the building of better roads and schools serving black people—thus advancing the move from political power into the economic arena. In such areas as Lowndes, where black men have a majority, they will attempt to use it to exercise control. This is what they seek: control. Where Negroes lack a majority, black power means proper representation and sharing of control. It means the creation of power bases from which black people can work to change statewide or nationwide patterns of oppression through pressure from strength—instead of weakness. Politically, black power means what it has always meant to SNCC: the coming-together of black people to elect representatives and *to force those representatives to speak to their needs.* It does not mean merely putting black faces into office. A man or woman who is black and from the slums cannot be automatically expected to speak to the needs of black people. Most of the black politicians we see around the country today are not what SNCC means by black power. The power must be that of a community, and emanate from there.

SNCC today is working in both North and South on programs of voter registration and independent political organizing. In some places, such as Alabama, Los Angeles, New York, Philadelphia, and New Jersey, independent organizing under the black panther symbol is in progress. The creation of a national "black panther party" must come about: it will take time to build, and it is much too early to predict its success. We have no infallible master plan and we make no claim to exclusive knowledge of how to end racism; different groups will work in their own different ways. SNCC cannot spell out the full logistics of self-determination but it can address itself to the problem by helping black communities define their needs, realize their strength, and go into action along a variety of lines which they must choose for themselves. Without knowing all the answers, it can address itself to the basic problem of poverty: to the fact that in Lowndes County, 86 white families own 90 percent of the land. What are black people in that county going to do for jobs, where are they going to get money? There must be reallocation of land and money.

Ultimately, the economic foundations of this country must be shared if black people are to control their lives. The colonies of the United States—and this includes the black ghettoes within its borders, north and south—must be liberated. For a century, this nation has been like an octopus of exploitation, its tentacles stretching from Mississippi and Harlem to South America, the Middle East, southern Africa, and Vietnam; the form of exploitation varies from area to area but the essential result has been the same—a powerful few have been maintained and enriched at the expense of the poor and voiceless colored masses. This pattern must be broken. As its grip loosens here and there around the world, the hopes of black Americans become more realistic. For racism to die, a totally different America must be born.

This is what the white society does not wish to face; this is why that society prefers to talk about integration. But integration speaks not at all to the problem of poverty, only to the problem of blackness. Integration today means the man who "makes it," leaving his black brothers behind in the ghetto as fast as his new sports car will take him. It has no relevance to the Harlem wino or to the cotton-picker making three dollars a day. As a lady I know in Alabama once said, "the food that Ralph Bunche eats doesn't fill my stomach."

Integration, moreover, speaks to the problem of blackness in a despicable way. As a goal, it has been based on complete acceptance of the fact that *in order to have* a decent house or education, blacks must move into a white neighborhood or send their children to a white school. This reinforces, among both black and white, the idea that "white" is automatically better and "black" is by definition inferior. This is why integration is a subterfuge for the maintenance of white supremacy. It allows the nation to focus on a handful of Southern children who get into white schools, at great price, and to ignore the 94 percent who are left behind in unimproved all-black schools. Such situations will not change until black people have power—to control their own school boards, in this case. Then Negroes become equal in a way that means something, and integration ceases to be a one-way street. Then integration doesn't mean draining skills and energies from the ghetto into white neighborhoods; then it can mean white people moving from Beverly Hills into Watts, white people joining the Lowndes County Freedom Organization. Then integration becomes relevant. . . .

To most whites, black power seems to mean that the Mau Mau are coming to the suburbs at night. The Mau Mau are coming, and whites must stop them. Articles appear about plots to "get Whitey," creating an atmosphere in which "law and order must be maintained." Once again, responsibility is shifted from the oppressor to the oppressed. Other whites chide, "Don't forget—you're only 10 percent of the population; if you get too smart, we'll wipe you out." If they are liberals, they complain, "what about me?—don't you want my help any more?" These are people supposedly concerned about black Americans, but today they think first of themselves, of their feelings of rejection. Or they admonish, "you can't get anywhere without coalitions," without considering the problems of coalition with whom?; on what terms (coalescing from weakness can mean absorption, betrayal)?; when? Or they accuse us of "polarizing the races" by our calls for black unity, when the true responsibility for polarization lies with whites who will not accept their responsibility as the majority power for making the democratic process work. . . .

Whites will not see that I, for example, as a person oppressed because of my blackness, have common cause with other blacks who are oppressed because of blackness. This is not to say that there are no white people who see things as I do, but that it is black people I must speak to first. It must be the oppressed to whom SNCC addresses itself primarily, not to friends from the oppressing group.

From birth, black people are told a set of lies about themselves. We are told that we are lazy—yet I drive through the Delta area of Mississippi and watch black people picking cotton in the hot sun for fourteen hours. We are told, "If you work hard, you'll succeed"—but if that were true, black people would own this country. We are oppressed because we are black—not because we are ignorant, not because we are lazy, not because we're stupid (and got good rhythm), but because we're black. . . .

The need for psychological equality is the reason why SNCC today believes that blacks must organize in the black community. Only black people can convey the revolutionary idea that black people are able to do things themselves. Only they can help create in the community an aroused and continuing black consciousness that will provide the basis for political strength. In the past, white allies have furthered white supremacy without the whites involved realizing it—or wanting it, I think. Black people must do things for themselves; they must get poverty money they will control and spend themselves, they must conduct tutorial programs themselves so that black children can identify with black people. This is one reason Africa has such importance: The reality of black men ruling their own nations gives blacks elsewhere a sense of possibility, of power, which they do not now have.

This does not mean we don't welcome help, or friends. But we want the right to decide whether anyone is, in fact, our friend. In the past, black Americans have been almost the only people whom everybody and his momma could jump up and call their friends. We have been tokens, symbols, objects—as I was in high school to many young whites, who liked having "a Negro friend." We want to decide who is our friend, and we will not accept someone who comes to us and says: "If you do X, Y, and Z, then I'll help you." We will not be told whom we should choose as allies. We will not be isolated from any group or nation except by our own choice. We cannot have the oppressors telling the oppressed how to rid themselves of the oppressor. . . .

There is a vital job to be done among poor whites. We hope to see, eventually, a coalition between poor blacks and poor whites. That is the only coalition which seems acceptable to us, and we see such a coalition as the major internal instrument of change in American society. SNCC has tried several times to organize poor whites; we are trying again now, with an initial training program in Tennessee. It is purely academic today to talk about bringing poor blacks and whites together, but the job of creating a poor-white power bloc must be attempted. The main responsibility for it falls upon whites. Black and white can work together in the white community where possible; it is not possible, however, to go into a poor Southern town and talk about integration. Poor whites everywhere are becoming more hostile—not less—partly because they see the nation's attention focussed on black poverty and nobody coming to them. Too many young middle-class Americans, like some sort of Pepsi generation, have wanted to come alive through the black community; they've wanted to be where the action is— and the action has been in the black community.

Black people do not want to "take over" this country. They don't want to "get whitey"; they just want to get him off their backs, as the saying goes. It was for example the exploitation by Jewish landlords and merchants which first created black resentment toward Jews—not Judaism. The white man is irrelevant to blacks, except as an oppressive force. Blacks want to be in his place, yes, but not in order to terrorize and lynch and starve him. They want to be in his place because that is where a decent life can be had. . . .

As for white America, perhaps it can stop crying out against "black supremacy," "black nationalism," "racism in reverse," and begin facing reality. The reality is that this nation, from top to bottom, is racist; that racism is not primarily a problem of "human relations" but of an exploitation maintained—either actively or through silence—by the society as a whole. Camus and Sartre have asked, can a man condemn himself? Can whites, particularly liberal whites, condemn themselves? Can they stop blaming us, and blame their own system? Are they capable of the shame which might become a revolutionary emotion?

We have found that they usually cannot condemn themselves, and so we have done it. But the rebuilding of this society, if at all possible, is basically the responsibility of whites—not blacks. We won't fight to save the present society, in Vietnam or anywhere else. We are just going to work, in the way we see fit, and on goals we define, not for civil rights but for all our human rights.

Position Paper on Black Power
Student Nonviolent Coordinating Committee

The myth that the Negro is somehow incapable of liberating himself, is lazy, etc., came out of the American experience. In the books that children read, whites are always "good" (good symbols are white), blacks are "evil" or seen as savages in movies, their language is referred to as a "dialect," and black people in this country are supposedly descended from savages.

Any white person who comes into the movement has these concepts in his mind about black people if only subconsciously. He cannot escape them because the whole society has geared his subconscious in that direction.

Miss America coming from Mississippi has a chance to represent all of America, but a black person from either Mississippi or New York will never represent America. So that white people coming into the movement cannot relate to the black experience, cannot relate to the word "black," cannot relate to the "nitty gritty," cannot relate to the experience that brought such a word into being, cannot relate to chitterlings, hog's head cheese, pig feet, hamhocks, and cannot relate to slavery, because these things are not a part of their experience. They also cannot relate to the black religious experience, nor to the black church unless, of course, this church has taken on white manifestations.

Negroes in this country have never been allowed to organize themselves because of white interference. As a result of this, the stereotype has been reinforced that blacks cannot organize themselves. The white psychology that blacks have to be watched, also reinforces the stereotype. Blacks, in fact, feel intimidated by the presence of whites, because of their knowledge of the power that whites have over their lives. One white person can come into a meeting of black people and change the complexion of that meeting, whereas one black person would not change the complexion of that meeting unless he was an obvious Uncle Tom. People would immediately start talking about "brotherhood," "love," etc.; race would not be discussed.

If people must express themselves freely, there has to be a climate in which they can do this. If blacks feel intimidated by whites, then they are not liable to vent the rage that they feel about whites in the presence of whites—especially not the black people whom we are trying to organize, i.e., the broad masses of black people. A climate has to be created whereby blacks can express themselves. The reason that whites must be excluded is not that one is anti-white, but because the efforts that one is trying to achieve cannot succeed because whites have an intimidating effect. Ofttimes the intimidating effect is in direct proportion to the amount of degradation that black people have suffered at the hands of white people.

It must be offered that white people who desire change in this country should go where that problem (of racism) is most manifest. The problem is not in the black community. The white people should go into white communities where the whites have created power for the express [purpose] of denying blacks human dignity and self-determination. Whites who come into the black community with ideas of change seem to want to absolve the power structure of its responsibility of what it is doing, and saying that change can come only through black unity, which is only the worst kind of paternalism. This is not to say that whites have not had an important role in the movement. In the case of Mississippi, their role was very key in that they helped give blacks the right to organize, that role is now over, and it should be.

People now have the right to picket, the right to give out leaflets, the right to vote, the right to demonstrate, the right to print.

These things which revolve around the right to organize have been accomplished mainly because of the entrance of white people into Mississippi, in the summer of '64. Since these goals have now been accomplished, their (whites') role in the movement has now ended. What does it mean if black people, once having the right to organize, are not allowed to organize themselves? It means that blacks' ideas about inferiority are being reinforced. Shouldn't people be able to organize themselves? Blacks should be given this right. Further (white participation) means in the eyes of the black community that whites are the "brains" behind the movement and blacks cannot function without whites. This only serves to perpetuate existing attitudes within the existing society, i.e., blacks are "dumb," "unable to take care of business," etc. Whites are "smart," the "brains" behind everything.

How do blacks relate to other blacks as such? How do we react to Willie Mays as against Mickey Mantle? What is our response to Mays hitting a home run against Mantle performing the same deed? One has to come to the conclusion that it is because of black participation in baseball. Negroes still identify with the Dodgers because of Jackie Robinson's efforts with the Dodgers. Negroes would instinctively champion all-black teams if they opposed all-white or predominantly white teams. The same principle operates for the movement as it does for baseball: a mystique must be created whereby Negroes can identify with the movement.

Thus an all-black project is needed in order for the people to free themselves. This has to exist from the beginning. This relates to what can be called "coalition politics." There is no doubt in our minds that some whites are just as disgusted with this system as we are. But it is meaningless to talk about coalition if there is no one to align ourselves with, because of the lack of organization in the white communities. There can be no talk of "hooking up" unless black people organize blacks and white people organize whites. If these conditions are met then perhaps at some later date—and if we are going in the same direction—talks about exchange of personnel, coalition, and other meaningful alliances can be discussed.

In the beginning of the movement, we had fallen into a trap whereby we thought that our problems revolved around the right to eat at certain lunch counters or the right to vote or to organize our communities. We have seen, however, that the problem is much deeper. The problem of this country, as we had seen it, concerned all blacks and all whites (and therefore) if decisions were left to the young people, then solutions would be arrived at. But this negates the history of black people and whites. We have dealt stringently with the problem of "Uncle Tom," but we have not yet gotten around to Simon Legree. We must ask ourselves who is the real villain? Uncle Tom or Simon Legree? Everybody knows Uncle Tom but who knows Simon Legree?

So what we have now (in S.N.C.C.) is a closed society. A clique. Black people cannot relate to S.N.C.C., because of its unrealistic, nonracial atmosphere; denying their experiences of America as a racist society. In contrast, S.C.L.C. [the Rev. Dr. Martin Luther King Jr.'s Southern Christian Leadership Conference] has a staff that at least maintains a black facade. The front office is virtually all black, but nobody accuses S.C.L.C. of being racist.

If we are to proceed toward true liberation, we must cut ourselves off from white people. We must form our own institutions, credit unions, co-ops, political parties, write our own histories.

To proceed further, let us make some comparisons between the Black movement of the (early) 1900s and the movement of the 1960s—the N.A.A.C.P. [the National Association for the Advancement of Colored People] with S.N.C.C. Whites subverted the Niagara movement [the fore-runner of the N.A.A.C.P.] which, at the outset, was an all-black movement. The name of the new organization was also very revealing, in that it pre-supposed blacks have to be advanced to the level of whites. We are now aware that the N.A.A.C.P. has grown reactionary, is controlled by the black power structure itself, and stands as one of the main roadblocks to black freedom. S.N.C.C., by allowing the whites to remain in the organization, can have its efforts subverted in the same manner, i.e., through having them play important roles such as community organizers, etc. Indigenous leadership cannot be built with whites in the positions they now hold.

These facts do not mean that whites cannot help. They can participate on a voluntary basis. We can contract work out to them, but in no way can they participate on a policy-making level.

The charge may be made that we are "racists," but whites who are sensitive to our problems will realize that we must determine our own destiny.

In an attempt to find a solution to our dilemma, we propose that our organization (S.N.C.C.) should be black-staffed, black-controlled and black-financed. We do not want to fall into a similar dilemma that other civil rights organizations have fallen. If we continue to rely upon white financial support we will find ourselves entwined in the tentacles of the white power complex that controls this country. It is also important that a black organization (devoid of cultism) be projected to our people, so that it can be demonstrated that such organizations are viable.

More and more, we see black people in this country being used as a tool of the white liberal establishment. Liberal whites have not begun to address themselves to the real problem of black people in this country; witness their bewilderment, fear and anxiety when nationalism is mentioned concerning black people. An analysis of their (white liberal) reaction to the word alone (nationalism) reveals a very meaningful attitude of whites of any ideological persuasion toward blacks in this country. It means previous solutions to black problems in this country have been made in the interests of those whites dealing with these problems and not in the best interests of black people in this country. Whites can only subvert our true search and struggle for self-determination, self-identification, and liberation in this country. Re-evaluation of the white and black roles must NOW take place so that whites no longer designate roles that black people play but rather black people define white people's roles.

Too long have we allowed white people to interpret the importance and meaning of the cultural aspects of our society. We have allowed them to tell us what was good about our Afro-American music, art and literature. How many black critics do we have on the "jazz" scene? How can a white person who is not a part of the black psyche (except in the oppressor's role) interpret the meaning of the blues to us who are manifestations of the songs themselves?

It must also be pointed out that on whatever level of contact that blacks and whites come together, that meeting or confrontation is not on the level of the blacks but always on the level of the whites. This only means that our everyday contact with whites is a reinforcement of the myth of white supremacy. Whites are the ones who must try to raise themselves to our humanistic level. We are not, after all, the ones who are responsible for a genocidal war in Vietnam; we are not the ones who are responsible for neocolonialism in Africa and Latin America; we are not the ones who held a people in animalistic bondage over 400 years. We reject the American dream as defined by white people and must work to construct an American reality defined by Afro-Americans.

One of the criticisms of white militants and radicals is that when we view the masses of white people we view the over-all reality of America, we view the racism, the bigotry, and the distortion of personality, we view man's inhumanity to man: we view in reality 180 million racists. The sensitive white intellectual and radical who is fighting to bring about change is conscious of this fact but does not have the courage to admit this. When he admits this reality, then he must also admit his involvement because he is a part of the collective white America. It is only to the extent that he recognizes this that he will be able to change this reality.

Another concern is how does the white radical view the black community and how does he view the poor white community in terms of organizing. So far, we have found that most white radicals have sought to escape the horrible reality of America by going into the black community and attempting to organize black people while neglecting the organization of their own people's racist communities. How can one clean up someone else's yard when one's own yard is untidy? Again we feel that S.N.C.C. and the civil-rights movement in general is in many aspects similar to the anticolonial situations in the African and Asian countries. We have the whites in the movement corresponding to the white civil servants and missionaries in the colonial countries who have worked with the colonial people for a long period of time and have developed a paternalistic attitude toward them. The reality of the colonial people taking over their own lives and controlling their own destiny must be faced. Having to move aside and letting this natural process of growth and development take place must be faced.

These views should not be equated with outside influence or outside agitation but should be viewed as the natural process of growth and development within a movement; so that the move by the black militants and S.N.C.C. in this direction should be viewed as a turn toward self-determination.

It is very ironic and curious how aware whites in this country can champion anticolonialism in other countries in Africa, Asia, and Latin America, but when black people move toward similar goals of self-determination in this country they are viewed as racists and anti-white by these same progressive whites. In proceeding further, it can be said that this attitude derives from the overall point of view of the white psyche as it concerns the black people. This attitude stems from the era of the slave revolts when every white man was a potential deputy or sheriff or guardian of the state. Because when black people got together among themselves to work out their problems, it became a threat to white people, because such meetings were potential slave revolts.

It can be maintained that this attitude or way of thinking has perpetuated itself to this current period and that it is part of the psyche of white people in this country whatever their political persuasion might be. It is part of the white fear-guilt complex resulting from the slave revolts. There have been examples of whites who stated that they can deal with black fellows on an individual basis but become threatened or menaced by the presence of groups of blacks. It can be maintained that this attitude is held by the majority of progressive whites in this country.

A thorough re-examination must be made by black people concerning the contributions that we have made in shaping this country. If this re-examination and re-evaluation is not made, and black people are not given their proper due and respect, then the antagonisms and contradictions are going to become more and more glaring, more and more intense until a national explosion may result.

When people attempt to move from these conclusions it would be faulty reasoning to say they are ordered by racism, because, in this country and in the West, racism has functioned as a type of white nationalism when dealing with black people. We all know the habit that this has created throughout the world and particularly among nonwhite people in this country.

Therefore any re-evaluation that we must make will, for the most part, deal with identification. Who are black people, what are black people; what is their relationship to America and the world?

It must be repeated that the whole myth of "Negro citizenship," perpetuated by the white elite, has confused the thinking of radical and progressive blacks and whites in this country. The broad masses of black people react to American society in the same manner as colonial peoples react to the West in Africa, and Latin America, and had the same relationship—that of the colonized toward the colonizer.

"BLACK POWER" AND COALITION POLITICS
By Bayard Rustin

There are two Americas—black and white—and nothing has more clearly revealed the divisions between them than the debate currently raging around the slogan of "black power." Despite—or perhaps because of—the fact that this slogan lacks any clear definition, it has succeeded in galvanizing emotions on all sides, with many whites seeing it as the expression of a new racism and many Negroes taking it as a warning to white people that Negroes will no longer tolerate brutality and violence. But even within the Negro community itself, "black power" has touched off a major debate—the most bitter the community has experienced since the days of Booker T. Washington and W. E. B. Du Bois, and one which threatens to ravage the entire civil-rights movement. Indeed, a serious split has already developed between advocates of "black power" like Floyd McKissick of CORE and Stokely Carmichael of SNCC on the one hand, and Dr. Martin Luther King of SCLC, Roy Wilkins of the NAACP, and Whitney Young of the Urban League on the other.

There is no question, then, that great passions are involved in the debate over the idea of "black power"; nor, as we shall see, is there any question that these passions have their roots in the psychological and political frustrations of the Negro community. Nevertheless, I would contend that "black power" not only lacks any real value for the civil-rights movement, but that its propagation is positively harmful. It diverts the movement from a meaningful debate over strategy and tactics, it isolates the Negro community, and it encourages the growth of anti-Negro forces.

In its simplest and most innocent guise, "black power" merely means the effort to elect Negroes to office in proportion to Negro strength within the population. There is, of course, nothing wrong with such an objective in itself, and nothing inherently radical in the idea of pursuing it. But in Stokely Carmichael's extravagant rhetoric about "taking over" in districts of the South where Negroes are in the majority, it is important to recognize that Southern Negroes are only in a position to win a maximum of two congressional seats and control of eighty local counties. (Carmichael, incidentally, is in the paradoxical position of screaming at liberals—wanting only to "get whitey off my back"—and simultaneously needing their support: after all, he can talk about Negroes taking over Lowndes County only because there is a fairly liberal federal government to protect him should Governor Wallace decide to eliminate this pocket of black power.) Now there might be a certain value in having two Negro congressmen from the South, but obviously they could do nothing by themselves to reconstruct the face of America. Eighty sheriffs, eighty tax assessors, and eighty school-board members might ease the tension for a while in their communities, but they alone could not create jobs and build low-cost housing; they alone could not supply quality integrated education.

The relevant question, moreover, is not whether a politician is black or white, but what forces he represents. Manhattan has had a succession of Negro borough presidents, and yet the schools are increasingly segregated. Adam Clayton Powell and William Dawson have both been in Congress for many years; the former is responsible for a rider on school integration that never gets passed, and the latter is responsible for keeping the Negroes of Chicago tied to a mayor who had to see riots and death before he would put eight-dollar sprinklers on water hydrants in the summer. I am not for one minute arguing that Powell, Dawson, and Mrs. Motley should be impeached. What I am saying is that if a politician is elected because he is black and is deemed to be entitled to a "slice of the pie," he will behave in one way; if he is elected by a constituency pressing for social reform, he will, whether he is white or black, behave in another way.

Southern Negroes, despite exhortations from SNCC to organize themselves into a Black Panther party, are going to stay in the Democratic party—to them it is the party of progress, the New Deal, the New Frontier, and the Great Society—and they are right to stay. For SNCC's Black Panther perspective is simultaneously utopian and reactionary—the former for the by now obvious reason that one-tenth of the population cannot accomplish much by itself, the latter because such a party would remove Negroes from the main area of political struggle in this country (particularly in the one-party South, where the decisive battles are fought out in Democratic primaries), and would give priority to the issue of race precisely at a time when the fundamental questions facing the Negro and American society alike are economic and social. . . .

The winning of the right of Negroes to vote in the South insures the eventual transformation of the Democratic party, now controlled primarily by Northern machine politicians and Southern Dixiecrats. The Negro vote will eliminate the Dixiecrats from the party and from Congress, which means that the crucial question facing us today is who will replace them in the South. Unless civil-rights leaders (in such towns as Jackson, Mississippi; Birmingham, Alabama; and even to a certain extent Atlanta) can organize grass-roots clubs whose members will have a genuine political voice, the Dixiecrats might well be succeeded by black moderates and black Southern-style machine politicians, who would do little to push for needed legislation in Congress and little to improve local conditions in the South. While I myself would prefer Negro machines to a situation in which Negroes have no power at all, it seems to me that there is a better alternative today—a liberal–labor–civil-rights coalition which would work to make the Democratic party truly responsive to the aspirations of the poor, and which would develop support for programs (specifically those outlined in A. Philip Randolph's $100 billion Freedom Budget) aimed at the reconstruction of American society in the interests of greater social justice. The advocates of "black power" have no such programs in mind; what they are in fact arguing for (perhaps unconsciously) is the creation of a *new black establishment*.

Nor, it might be added, are they leading the Negro people along the same road which they imagine immigrant groups traveled so successfully in the past. Proponents of "black power"—accepting a historical myth perpetrated by moderates—like to say that the Irish and the Jews and the Italians, by sticking together and demanding their share, finally won enough power to overcome their initial disabilities. But the truth is that it was through alliances with other groups (in political machines or as part of the trade-union movement) that the Irish and the Jews and the Italians acquired the power to win their rightful place in American society. They did not "pull themselves up by their own boot-straps"—no group in American society has ever done so; and they most certainly did not make isolation their primary tactic. . . .

"Black power" is, of course, a somewhat nationalistic slogan and its sudden rise to popularity among Negroes signifies a concomitant rise in nationalist sentiment (Malcolm X's autobiography is quoted nowadays in Grenada, Mississippi, as well as in Harlem). We have seen such nationalistic turns and withdrawals back into the ghetto before, and when we look at the conditions which brought them about, we find that they have much in common with the conditions of Negro life at the present moment: conditions which lead to despair over the goal of integration and to the belief that the ghetto will last forever.

It may, in the light of the many juridical and legislative victories which have been achieved in the past few years, seem strange that despair should be so widespread among Negroes today. But anyone to whom it seems strange should reflect on the fact that despite these victories *Negroes today are in worse economic shape, live in worse slums, and attend more highly segregated schools than in 1954*. Thus—to recite the appalling, and appallingly familiar, statistical litany once again—more Negroes are unemployed today than in 1954; the gap between the wages of the Negro worker and the white worker is wider; while the unemployment rate among white youths is decreasing, the rate among Negro youths has increased to *32 percent* (and among Negro girls the rise is even more startling). Even the one gain which has been registered, a decrease in the unemployment rate among Negro adults, is deceptive, for it represents men who have been called back to work after a period of being laid off. In any event, unemployment among Negro men is still twice that of whites, and no new jobs have been created.

So too with housing, which is deteriorating in the North (and yet the housing provisions of the 1966 civil-rights bill are weaker than the anti-discrimination laws in several states which contain the worst ghettos even with these laws on their books). And so too with schools: according to figures issued recently by the Department of Health, Education and Welfare, 65 percent of first-grade Negro students in this country attend schools that are from 90 to 100 percent black. (If in 1954, when the Supreme Court handed down the desegregation decision, you had been the Negro parent of a first-grade child, the chances are that this past June you would have attended that child's graduation from a segregated high school).

To put all this in the simplest and most concrete terms: the day-to-day lot of the ghetto Negro has not been improved by the various judicial and legislative measures of the past decade. . . .

Then there is the war in Vietnam, which poses many ironies for the Negro community. On the one hand, Negroes are bitterly aware of the fact that more and more money is being spent on the war, while the anti-poverty program is being cut, on the other hand, Negro youths are enlisting in great numbers, as though to say that it is worth the risk of being killed to learn a trade, to leave a dead-end situation, and to join the only institution in this society which seems really to be integrated. . . .

The Vietnam war is also partly responsible for the growing disillusion with non-violence among Negroes. The ghetto Negro does not in general ask whether the United States is right or wrong to be in Southeast Asia. He does, however, wonder why he is exhorted to non-violence when the United States has been waging a fantastically brutal war, and it puzzles him to be told that he must turn the other cheek in our own South while we must fight for freedom in South Vietnam.

Thus, as in roughly similar circumstances in the past—circumstances, I repeat, which in the aggregate foster the belief that the ghetto is destined to last forever—Negroes are once again turning to nationalistic slogans, with "black power" affording the same emotional release as "Back to Africa" and "Buy Black" did in earlier periods of frustration and hopelessness. This is not only the case with the ordinary Negro in the ghetto; it is also the case with leaders like McKissick and Carmichael, neither of whom began as a nationalist or was at first cynical about the possibilities of integration. It took countless beatings and 24 jailings—that, and the absence of strong and continual support from the liberal community—to persuade Carmichael that his earlier faith in coalition politics was mistaken, that nothing was to be gained from working with whites, and that an alliance with the black nationalists was desirable. In the areas of the South where SNCC has been working so nobly, implementation of the Civil Rights Acts of 1964 and 1965 has been slow and ineffective. Negroes in many rural areas cannot walk into the courthouse and register to vote. Despite the voting-rights bill, they must file complaints and the Justice Department must be called to send federal registrars. Nor do children attend integrated schools as a matter of course. There, too, complaints must be filed and the Department of Health, Education and Welfare must be notified. Neither department has been doing an effective job of enforcing the bills. The feeling of isolation increases among SNCC workers as each legislative victory turns out to be only a token victory—significant on the national level, but not affecting the day-to-day lives of Negroes. Carmichael and his colleagues are wrong in refusing to support the 1966 bill, but one can understand why they feel as they do.

It is, in short, the growing conviction that the Negroes cannot win—a conviction with much grounding in experience—which accounts for the new popularity of "black power." So far as the ghetto Negro is concerned, this conviction expresses itself in hostility first toward the people closest to him who have held out the most promise and failed to deliver (Martin Luther King, Roy Wilkins, etc.), then toward those who have proclaimed themselves his friends (the liberals and the labor movement), and finally toward the only oppressors he can see (the local storekeeper and the policeman on the corner). On the leadership level, the conviction that the Negroes cannot win takes other forms, principally the adoption of what I have called a "no-win" policy. Why bother with programs when their enactment results only in "sham"? Why concern ourselves with the image of the movement when nothing significant has been gained for all the sacrifices made by SNCC and CORE? Why compromise with reluctant white allies when nothing of consequence can be achieved anyway? Why indeed have anything to do with whites at all?

On this last point, it is extremely important for white liberals to understand—as, one gathers from their references to "racism in reverse," the President and the Vice President of the United States do not—that there is all the difference in the world between saying, "If you don't want me, I don't want you" (which is what some proponents of "black power" have in effect been saying) and the statement, "Whatever you do, I don't want you" (which is what racism declares). It is, in other words, both absurd and immoral to equate the despairing response of the victim with the contemptuous assertion of the oppressor. It would, moreover, be tragic if white liberals allowed verbal hostility on the part of Negroes to drive them out of the movement or to curtail their support for civil rights. The issue was injustice before "black power" became popular, and the issue is still injustice.

In any event, even if "black power" had not emerged as a slogan, problems would have arisen in the relation between whites and Negroes in the civil-rights movement. In the North, it was inevitable that Negroes would eventually wish to run their own movement and would rebel against the presence of whites in positions of leadership as yet another sign of white supremacy. In the South, the well-intentioned white volunteer had the cards stacked against him from the beginning. Not only could he leave the struggle any time he chose to do so, but a higher value was set on his safety by the press and the government—apparent in the differing degrees of excitement generated by the imprisonment or murder of whites and Negroes. The white person's importance to the movement in the South was thus an ironic outgrowth of racism and was therefore bound to create resentment. . . .

Nevertheless, pride, confidence, and a new identity cannot be won by glorifying blackness or attacking whites; they can only come from meaningful action, from good jobs, and from real victories such as were achieved on the streets of Montgomery, Birmingham, and Selma. When SNCC and CORE went into the South, they awakened the country, but now they emerge isolated and demoralized, shouting a slogan that may afford a momentary satisfaction but that is calculated to destroy them and their movement. Already their frustrated call is being answered with counter-demands for law and order and with opposition to police-review boards. Already they have diverted the entire civil-rights movement from the hard task of developing strategies to realign the major parties of this country, and embroiled it in a debate that can only lead more and more to politics by frustration. . . .

We must see, therefore, in the current debate over "black power," a fantastic challenge to American society to live up to its proclaimed principles in the area of race by transforming itself so that all men may live equally and under justice. We must see to it that in rejecting "black power," we do not also reject the principle of Negro equality. Those people who would use the current debate and/or the riots to abandon the civil-rights movement leave us no choice but to question their original motivation. . . .

Sources: (1) Stokely Carmichael, excerpt from "What We Want," *New York Review of Books* 7, no. 4 (September 22, 1966), pp. 5–6, 8; (2) SNCC, "Position Paper on Black Power," published in the *New York Times*, August 5, 1966; and (3) Bayard Rustin, excerpt from "'Black Power' and Coalition Politics," *Commentary* 42 (September 1966), pp. 35–40.

SELECT BIBLIOGRAPHY:

Jervis Anderson, *Bayard Rustin: Troubles I've Seen: A Biography* (New York: HarperCollins, 1997).

Stokely Carmichael, *Stokely Speaks: Black Power Back to Pan-Africanism* (New York: Random House, 1971).

Stokely Carmichael and Charles Hamilton, *Black Power: The Politics of Liberation in America* (New York: Random House, 1967).

Stokely Carmichael, with Ekwueme Michael Thelwell, *Ready for Revolution: The Life and Struggles of Stokely Carmichael (Kwame Ture)* (New York: Scribner, 2005).

Clayborne Carson, *In Struggle: SNCC and the Black Awakening of the 1960s* (Cambridge, Mass.: Harvard University Press, 1981).

John D'Emilio, *Lost Prophet: The Life and Times of Bayard Rustin* (Chicago: University of Chicago Press, 2004).

Peniel E. Joseph, ed., *Black Power Movement: Rethinking the Civil Rights-Black Power Era* (London: Routledge, 2006).

———, *Waiting 'Til the Midnight Hour: A Narrative History of Black Power in America* (New York: Henry Holt and Co., 2006).

William Van DeBurg, *New Day in Babylon: The Black Power Movement and American Culture, 1965–1975* (Chicago: University of Chicago Press, 1992).

∼ 15 ∼

"CORE Endorses Black Power," *Floyd McKissick, 1967*

Floyd McKissick (1922–1991) was born in Asheville, North Carolina. He was denied admission into the University of North Carolina Law School because of his race, and with the aid of NAACP lawyer Thurgood Marshall he successfully sued the university. Upon gaining admission, he became the first African American to earn an L.L.B. there. McKissick became active in the Congress of Racial Equality (CORE) and replaced James Farmer as the head of the organization in 1966. Under his influence, CORE began to closely identify with the Black Power movement. In 1968, McKissick left CORE and moved to Warren County, North Carolina, where he attempted to launch "Soul City," an all-black, planned community. Through the Nixon administration, McKissick successfully secured a $14- million bond issue guarantee from the Department of Housing and Urban Development. The quid pro quo for federal backing, however, was that McKissick had to publicly endorse Nixon for reelection to the presidency in 1972. McKissick's strategy of "Black Capitalism" inevitably collapsed, and with it so did the dream of Soul City. McKissick died of lung cancer in April 1991.

⌒

WHY THE NEGRO MUST REBEL

We are given rhetoric about power sharing: "The Land of the Free. Home of the Brave." "With liberty and justice for all." I could name dozens of others that sound beautiful, but mean absolutely nothing for black people, here or on any other continent.

They were never intended to mean anything for black people. They were written when we were still slaves.

There are black people starving in Mississippi, millions of colored people starving in India while white Americans bask in luxury, spending millions to go to the moon, billions on a war in Vietnam which pits yellow people against yellow people.

There are rebellions throughout the United States—black people demanding that they no longer be exploited, that they be free—free to live in dignity. . . .

In America, as we have seen, the belief in white superiority runs deep. It was a dominant factor in the slave trade. The black African wasn't recognized as a human being.

A belief ferocious enough to allow human slavery cannot be dissipated by a mere century and, in America, it has been quietly reinforced.

Although slavery as a recognized legal institution has been abolished, economic slavery, economic exploitation, has not. Black people in this country have never been allowed to share in the economic riches of America. A few get in— here and there—a few get rich, but their success has no effect on the masses of black people.

White landlords, white storekeepers, white corporate managers and a white, Anglo-Saxon Wall Street, conspire to keep the black man in his place.

As whites quietly exit to the comfortable suburbs, they do not relinquish the economic control of the ghetto; they maintain control of the city agencies and the political scene. They determine what opportunities will be available and what will be reserved for whites only—and, occasionally, one or two good "Negroes."

With the climate existing in the United States, we would be foolish, as leaders, to think that black people are not being politically oppressed. If black people got political power, they might be able to merge their values with the values of the dominant culture. And the white man wants to protect his values—particularly his economic values. The materialism which has distorted his dealings with the entire world. . . .

Placing the Blame

And who is to blame for the rebellions? This point we need not argue. The white man is the judge, jury and the executioner in his system and he first made the law so as to control us. We are called the violators of his "law and order"— "criminals."

Yet he knows that the white racist society is to blame for all of the conditions which force a man to rebel. His concept of "law and order" means the legal methods of exploiting blacks. We object and we resist.

Some so-called Negro leaders even have the audacity to join the man—by calling a liberation struggle a riot—his brothers hoodlums and criminals—and damning his brothers who seek to overthrow the yoke of oppression. . . .

In this country, the ghetto is not defined by barbed wire: the ghetto follows the black man wherever he goes. . . .

Yes, black people know fear and live with it each and every day of their lives—in deadly fear of the white man's potential. We know he can kill, we know he will—because of his hurt pride—we know that his personality demands that he control whatever he sees, we know that normal dissent is treason in his blue eyes.

"He Will Kill Us"

In fact, we know the man better than he knows himself. We know him for what he is. We know he will kill us if he can—one by one or all at once. . . .

Even our friends in the peace movement find it too easy to look thousands of miles away from home and, with much indignation, see the extermination of the Vietnamese.

On the other hand, they cannot see 10 blocks away, where many black people are the walking dead—dead in mind and spirit, because of lack of hope and lack of chance.

We cannot look elsewhere for help. We cannot lean on the crutch of religion. We cannot depend on phony "coalitions." We must work out our own methods. We must draw our own conclusions.

To those queasy individuals who are afraid of the resolutions presented here, let me state my unequivocal opinion: The right of revolution is a constitutional right, condoned by the creation of the American Constitution itself. When we assert the right of revolution, we are asserting a constitutional right.

Revolution in America is justified by all standards of morality—religious and ethical: It is required to fulfill the basic, natural rights of man.

Even white men recognized the need for revolution when, in 1776, they revolted because they were oppressed. And today—1967—black people are more oppressed than any white man has ever been—in the history of the world.

This is the time when we must unite—brothers and sisters. We must join in making plans. . . .

Source: Excerpts from speech delivered at the "National Conference of Black Power," Newark, New Jersey, July 20–23, 1967. Originally published in the *New York Times*, July 30, 1967.

SELECT BIBLIOGRAPHY:

Inge Powell Bell, *CORE and the Strategy of Nonviolence* (New York: Random House, 1968).

Floyd B. McKissick, *Three-Fifths of a Man* (New York: Macmillan, 1969).

August Meier and Elliott Rudwick, *CORE: A Study in the Civil Rights Movement* (New York: Oxford University Press, 1973).

～ 16 ～

"To Atone for Our Sins and Errors in Vietnam," *Martin Luther King, Jr., 1967*

Though Martin Luther King, Jr. (1929–1968) is frequently remembered for his "I Have a Dream" speech at the 1963 March on Washington, in the last several years of his life his politics moved to the left and he began to focus greater attention on entrenched patterns of economic exploitation inside U.S. society. America, he said, needed a "revolution in values," and on many occasions he suggested that there must be a fundamental change in the way that society was organized. King also spoke out against U.S. militarism in Vietnam—a move for which he was widely criticized in the mainstream press. However, given King's long-standing commitment to nonviolence and the fact that he held a Nobel Peace Prize, his condemnation of the war carried a great deal of moral authority and was a great boost to the antiwar movement. In the aftermath of the creation of a federal holiday celebrating King's birthday, there has been a tendency within popular culture to concentrate almost exclusively on his pre-1966 public career. This is not only historically dishonest, but an attempt to "mainstream" King to conform to more conservative standards. If we listen to his words delivered at New York City's Riverside Church exactly one year before his assassination, a strikingly different and more radical King emerges from the text.

～

I come to this magnificent house of worship tonight, because my conscience leaves me no other choice. I join with you in this meeting because I am in deepest agreement with the aims and work of the organization which has brought us together: Clergy and Laymen Concerned About Vietnam. The recent statement of your executive committee is the sentiment of my own heart, and I found myself in full accord when I read its opening lines: "A time comes when silence is betrayal." That time has come for us in relation to Vietnam.

The truth of these words is beyond doubt, but the mission to which they call us is a most difficult one. Even when pressed by the demands of inner truth, men do not easily assume the task of opposing their government's policy, especially in time of war. Nor does the human spirit move without great difficulty against all the apathy of conformist thought within one's own bosom and in the surrounding world. Moreover, when the issues at hand seem as perplexed as they often do in the case of this dreadful conflict, we are always on the verge of being mesmerized by uncertainty; but we must move on.

Some of us who have already begun to break the silence of the night have found that the calling to speak is often a vocation of agony, but we must speak. We must speak with all the humility that is appropriate to our limited vision, but we must speak. And we must rejoice as well, for surely this is the first time in our nation's history that a significant number of its religious leaders have chosen to move beyond the prophesying of smooth patriotism to the high grounds of a firm dissent based upon the mandates of conscience and the reading of history. Perhaps a new spirit is rising among us. If it is, let us trace its movements well and pray that our own inner being may be sensitive to its guidance, for we are deeply in need of a new way beyond the darkness that seems so close around us.

Over the past two years, as I have moved to break the betrayal of my own silences and to speak the burnings of my own heart, as I have called for radical departures from the destruction of Vietnam, many persons have questioned me about the wisdom of my path. At the heart of their concerns this query has often loomed large and loud: Why are *you* speaking about the war, Dr. King? Why are you joining the voices of dissent? Peace and civil rights don't mix, they say. Aren't you hurting the cause of your people? they ask. And when I hear them, though I often understand the source of their concern, I am nevertheless greatly saddened, for such questions mean that the inquirers have not really known me, my commitment or my calling. Indeed, their questions suggest that they do not know the world in which they live.

In the light of such tragic misunderstanding, I deem it of signal importance to try to state clearly, and I trust concisely, why I believe that the path from Dexter Avenue Baptist Church—the church in Montgomery, Alabama, where I began my pastorate—leads clearly to this sanctuary tonight.

I come to this platform tonight to make a passionate plea to my beloved nation. This speech is not addressed to Hanoi or to the National Liberation Front. It is not addressed to China or to Russia.

Nor is it an attempt to overlook the ambiguity of the total situation and the need for a collective solution to the tragedy of Vietnam. Neither is it an attempt to make North Vietnam or the National Liberation Front paragons of virtue, nor to overlook the role they can play in a successful resolution of the problem. While they both may have justifiable reason to be suspicious of the good faith of the United States, life and history give eloquent testimony to the fact that conflicts are never resolved without trustful give and take on both sides.

Tonight, however, I wish not to speak with Hanoi and the N.L.F., but rather to my fellow Americans who, with me, bear the greatest responsibility in ending a conflict that has exacted a heavy price on both continents.

Since I am a preacher by trade, I suppose it is not surprising that I have seven major reasons for bringing Vietnam into the field of my moral vision. There is at the outset a very obvious and almost facile connection between the war in Vietnam and the struggle I and others have been waging in America. A few years ago there was a shining moment in that struggle. It seemed as if there was a real promise of hope for the poor—both black and white—through the Poverty Program. There were experiments, hopes, new beginnings. Then came the buildup in Vietnam and I watched the program broken and eviscerated as if it were some idle political plaything of a society gone mad on war, and I knew that America would never invest the necessary funds or energies in rehabilitation of its poor so long as adventures like Vietnam continued to draw men and skills and money like some demonic destructive suction tube. So I was increasingly compelled to see the war as an enemy of the poor and to attack it as such.

Perhaps the more tragic recognition of reality took place when it became clear to me that the war was doing far more than devastating the hopes of the poor at home. It was sending their sons and their brothers and their husbands to fight and to die in extraordinarily high proportions relative to the rest of the population. We were taking the black young men who had been crippled by our society and sending them eight thousand miles away to guarantee liberties in Southeast Asia which they had not found in Southwest Georgia and East Harlem. So we have been repeatedly faced with the cruel irony of watching Negro and white boys on TV screens as they kill and die together for a nation that has been unable to seat them together in the same schools. So we watch them in brutal solidarity burning the huts of a poor village, but we realize that they would never live on the same block in Detroit. I could not be silent in the face of such cruel manipulation of the poor.

My third reason moves to an even deeper level of awareness, for it grows out of my experience in the ghettos of the North over the last three years—especially the last three summers. As I have walked among the desperate, rejected and angry young men I have told them that Molotov cocktails and rifles would not solve their problems. I have tried to offer them my deepest compassion while maintaining my conviction that social change comes most meaningfully through nonviolent action. But they asked—and rightly so—what about Vietnam? They asked if our own nation wasn't using massive doses of violence to solve its problems, to bring about the changes it wanted. Their questions hit home, and I knew that I could never again raise my voice against the violence of the oppressed in the ghettos without having first spoken clearly to the greatest purveyor of violence in the world today—my own government. For the sake of those boys, for the sake of this government, for the sake of the hundreds of thousands trembling under our violence, I cannot be silent.

For those who ask the question, "Aren't you a civil-rights leader?" and thereby mean to exclude me from the movement for peace, I have this further answer. In 1957 when a group of us formed the Southern Christian Leadership Conference, we chose as our motto: "To save the soul of America." We were convinced that we could not limit our vision to certain rights for black people, but instead affirmed the conviction that America would never be free or saved from itself unless the descendants of its slaves were loosed completely from the shackles they still wear. . . .

Now, it should be incandescently clear that no one who has any concern for the integrity and life of America today can ignore the present war. If America's soul becomes totally poisoned, part of the autopsy must read Vietnam. It can never be saved so long as it destroys the deepest hopes of men the world over. So it is that those of us who are yet determined that America *will* be are led down the path of protest and dissent, working for the health of our land. . . .

. . . [A]s I ponder the madness of Vietnam and search within myself for ways to understand and respond to compassion my mind goes constantly to the people of that peninsula. I speak now not of the soldiers of each side, not of the junta in

Saigon, but simply of the people who have been living under the curse of war for almost three continuous decades now. I think of them too because it is clear to me that there will be no meaningful solution there until some attempt is made to know them and hear their broken cries.

They must see Americans as strange liberators. The Vietnamese people proclaimed their own independence in 1945 after a combined French and Japanese occupation, and before the Communist revolution in China. They were led by Ho Chi Minh. Even though they quoted the American Declaration of Independence in their own document of freedom, we refused to recognize them.[1] Instead, we decided to support France in its reconquest of her former colony.

Our government felt then that the Vietnamese people were not "ready" for independence, and we again fell victim to the deadly Western arrogance that has poisoned the international atmosphere for so long. With that tragic decision we rejected a revolutionary government seeking self-determination, and a government that had been established not by China (for whom the Vietnamese have no great love) but by clearly indigenous forces that included some Communists. For the peasants this new government meant real land reform, one of the most important needs in their lives.

For nine years following 1945 we denied the people of Vietnam the right of independence. For nine years we vigorously supported the French in their abortive effort to recolonize Vietnam.

Before the end of the war we were meeting 80 percent of the French war costs. Even before the French were defeated at Dien Bien Phu, they began to despair of the reckless action, but we did not. We encouraged them with our huge financial and military supplies to continue the war even after they had lost the will. Soon we would be paying almost the full costs of this tragic attempt at recolonization.

After the French were defeated it looked as if independence and land reform would come again through the Geneva agreements.[2] But instead there came the United States, determined that Ho should not unify the temporarily divided nation, and the peasants watched again as we supported one of the most vicious modern dictators—our chosen man, Premier Diem. The peasants watched and cringed as Diem ruthlessly routed out all opposition, supported their extortionist landlords and refused even to discuss reunification with the North. The peasants watched as all this was presided over by United States influence and then by increasing numbers of United States troops who came to help quell the insurgency that Diem's methods had aroused. When Diem was overthrown they may have been happy, but the long line of military dictatorships seemed to offer no real change—especially in terms of their need for land and peace.

The only change came from America as we increased our troop commitments in support of governments which were singularly corrupt, inept and without popular support. All the while the people read our leaflets and received regular promises of peace and democracy—and land reform. Now they languish under our bombs and consider *us*—not their fellow Vietnamese—the real enemy. They move sadly and apathetically as we herd them off the land of their fathers into concentration camps where minimal social needs are rarely met. They know they must move or be destroyed by our bombs. So they go—primarily women and children and the aged.

They watch as we poison their water, as we kill a million acres of their crops. They must weep as the bulldozers roar through their areas preparing to destroy the precious trees. They wander into the hospitals, with at least twenty casualties from American firepower for one Vietcong-inflicted injury. So far we may have killed a million of them—mostly children. They wander into the towns and see thousands of the children, homeless, without clothes, running in packs on the streets like animals. They see the children degraded by our soldiers as they beg for food. They see the children selling their sisters to our soldiers, soliciting for their mothers.

What do the peasants think as we ally ourselves with the landlords and as we refuse to put any action into our many words concerning land reform? What do they think as we test out our latest weapons on them, just as the Germans tested out new medicine and new tortures in the concentration camps of Europe? Where are the roots of the independent Vietnam we claim to be building? Is it among these voiceless ones?

We have destroyed their two most cherished institutions: the family and the village. We have destroyed their land and their crops. We have cooperated in the crushing of the nation's only non-Communist revolutionary political force—the unified Buddhist Church. We have supported the enemies of the peasants of Saigon. We have corrupted their women and children and killed their men. What liberators!

Now there is little left to build on—save bitterness. Soon the only solid physical foundations remaining will be found at our military bases and in the concrete of the concentration camps we call fortified hamlets. The peasants may well wonder if we plan to build our new Vietnam on such grounds as these? Could we blame them for such thoughts? We must speak for them and raise the questions they cannot raise. These too are our brothers.

Perhaps the more difficult, but no less necessary, task is to speak for those who have been designated as our enemies. What of the National Liberation Front—that strangely anonymous group we call V.C. or Communists? What must they think of us in America when they realize that we permitted the repression and cruelty of Diem which helped to bring them into being as a resistance group in the South? What do they think of our condoning the violence which led to their own taking-up of arms? How can they believe in our integrity when now we speak of "aggression from the North" as if there were nothing more essential to the war? How can they trust us when now we charge them with violence after the murderous reign of Diem and charge them with violence while we pour every new weapon of death into their land? Surely we must understand their feelings even if we do not condone their actions. Surely we must see that the men we supported pressed them to their violence. Surely we must see that our own computerized plans of destruction simply dwarf their greatest acts.

How do they judge us when our officials know that their membership is less than 25 percent Communist and yet insist on giving them the blanket name? What must they be thinking when they know that we are aware of their control of major sections of Vietnam and yet we appear to allow national elections in which this highly organized political parallel government will have no part? They ask how we can speak of free elections when the Saigon press is censored and controlled by the military junta. And they are surely right to wonder what kind of new government we plan to help form without them—the only party in real touch with the peasants. They question our political goals and they deny the reality of a peace settlement from which they will be excluded. Their questions are frighteningly relevant. Is our nation planning to build on political myth again and then shore it up with the power of new violence?

Here is the true meaning and value of compassion and nonviolence when it helps us to see the enemy's point of view, to hear his questions, to know his assessment of ourselves. For from his view we may indeed see the basic weaknesses of our own condition, and if we are mature, we may learn and grow and profit from the wisdom of the brothers who are called the opposition.

So, too, with Hanoi. In the North, where our bombs now pummel the land and our mines endanger the waterways, we are met by a deep but understandable mistrust. To speak for them is to explain this lack of confidence in Western words, and especially their distrust of American intentions now. In Hanoi are the men who led the nation to independence against the Japanese and the French, the men who sought membership in the French commonwealth and were betrayed by the weakness of Paris and the willfulness of the colonial armies. It was they who led a second struggle against French domination at tremendous costs, and then were persuaded to give up the land they controlled between the 13th and 17th parallels as a temporary measure at Geneva. After 1954 they watched us conspire with Diem to prevent elections which would have surely brought Ho Chi Minh to power over a United Vietnam,[3] and they realized they had been betrayed again. . . .

At this point I should make it clear that while I have tried in these last few minutes to give a voice to the voiceless on Vietnam and to understand the arguments of those who are called enemy, I am as deeply concerned about our own troops there as anything else. For it occurs to me that what we are submitting them to in Vietnam is not simply the brutalizing process that goes on in any war where armies face each other and seek to destroy. We are adding cynicism to the process of death, for they must know after a short period there that none of the things we claim to be fighting for are really involved. Before long they must know that their government has sent them into a struggle among Vietnamese, and the more sophisticated surely realize that we are on the side of the wealthy and the secure, while we create a hell for the poor.

Somehow this madness must cease. We must stop now. I speak as a child of God and brother to the suffering poor of Vietnam. I speak for those whose land is

being laid waste, whose homes are being destroyed, whose culture is being sub-
verted. I speak for the poor of America who are paying the double price of
smashed hopes at home and death and corruption in Vietnam. I speak as a citizen
of the world, for the world as it stands aghast at the path we have taken. I speak
as an American to the leaders of my own nation. The great initiative in this war
is ours. The initiative to stop it must be ours. . . .

If we continue there will be no doubt in my mind and in the mind of the
world that we have no honorable intentions in Vietnam. It will become clear
that our minimal expectation is to occupy it as an American colony and men will
not refrain from thinking that our maximum hope is to goad China into a war so
that we may bomb her nuclear installations. If we do not stop our war against
the people of Vietnam immediately the world will be left with no other alternative than to see this as some horribly clumsy and deadly game we have decided
to play.

The world now demands a maturity of America that we may not be able to
achieve. It demands that we admit that we have been wrong from the beginning
of our adventure in Vietnam, that we have been detrimental to the life of the
Vietnamese people. The situation is one in which we must be ready to turn
sharply from our present ways.

In order to atone for our sins and errors in Vietnam, we should take the initiative in bringing a halt to this tragic war. I would like to suggest five concrete things
that our government should do immediately to begin the long and difficult
process of extricating ourselves from this nightmarish conflict. . . .

Meanwhile we in the churches and synagogues have a continuing task while we
urge our government to disengage itself from a disgraceful commitment. We
must continue to raise our voices if our nation persists in its perverse ways in
Vietnam. We must be prepared to match actions with words by seeking out every
creative means of protest possible.

Notes: 1. In September 1945, the Republic of Vietnam was established. The Constitution
proclaimed its independence from all colonial rule and incorporated the famous principle of the American Declaration of Independence—the "self-evident" truths that "all
men are created equal," and are endowed with "certain inalienable rights; that among
these are life, liberty, and the pursuit of happiness." 2. The Geneva Conference ended the
war between France and the Republic of Vietnam. At Geneva, Vietnam was clearly established as a single sovereign nation, temporarily divided into regrouping zones for truce
purposes. While the United States refused to sign the Agreement, it did pledge that it
would "refrain from use of force to upset the agreement," and it acknowledged its U.N.
obligation to respect Vietnam's territorial integrity and independence. 3. With the backing of the United States, President Ngo Dihn Diem of South Vietnam refused to allow
the people of South Vietnam to vote in the elections scheduled under the Geneva
Agreement to be held in 1956. The reason was clear to all. As President Eisenhower later
conceded, "possibly 80 percent of the population would have voted for the Communist
Ho Chi Minh."

Source: Excerpt from "Testament of Hope" speech delivered at Riverside Church, New York City, April 4, 1967, copyright 1967 by Martin Luther King, Jr., copyright renewed by the Martin Luther King, Jr. Estate. Reprinted by arrangement with The Heirs to the Estate of Martin Luther King, Jr., c/o Writers House, Inc., as agent for the proprietor.

SELECT BIBLIOGRAPHY:

Taylor Branch, *At Canaan's Edge: America in the King Years, 1965–1968* (New York: Simon & Schuster, 2007).

David J. Garrow, *Bearing the Cross: Martin Luther King, Jr., and the Southern Christian Leadership Conference* (New York: Morrow, 1986).

Vincent Harding, *Martin Luther King: The Inconvenient Hero* (Maryknoll, N.Y.: Orbis Books, 1996).

Michael K. Honey, *Going Down Jericho Road: The Memphis Strike, Martin Luther King's Last Campaign* (New York: W. W. Norton & Co., 2007).

Thomas F. Jackson, *From Civil Rights to Human Rights: Martin Luther King, Jr. and the Struggle for Economic Justice* (Philadelphia: University of Pennsylvania Press, 2007).

Martin Luther King, Jr., *Where Do We Go from Here: Chaos or Community?* (New York: Harper and Row, 1967).

———, *The Measure of a Man* (Philadelphia: Pilgrim Press, 1968).

⚊ 17 ⚊

Huey P. Newton and the Black Panther Party for Self-Defense

Along with Bobby Seale, Huey P. Newton (1942–1989) helped found the Black Panther Party for Self-Defense in October 1966, in Oakland, California, and he quickly became known as the organization's chief theoretician. To many, Newton represented the revolutionary vanguard of the Black Liberation movement. The Panthers gained widespread support within black urban communities for their free breakfast programs for children and their public health services. The group came to national attention when they marched onto the floor of the California state legislature carrying arms. The Black Panthers patrolled Oakland streets to safeguard black residents against police brutality. In October 1967, Newton was involved in an altercation in which a police officer was shot and killed. Newton was charged with the killing and his case quickly became a *cause célèbre*. He was found guilty of involuntary manslaughter, but his case was eventually overturned. Yet by the time of his release the Black Panthers had already begun to decline as a political formation, largely due to the systematic repression by local law-enforcement agencies and coordinated through COINTELPRO (the Counter-Intelligence Program) of the FBI. Newton successfully continued his education, achieving a doctorate from the University of California at Santa Cruz in 1980.

However, Newton increasingly fell victim to a series of personal demons, including drug dependency and violently antisocial behavior. In 1989 Newton was murdered in Oakland by a member of a local street gang.

OCTOBER 1966 BLACK PANTHER PARTY PLATFORM AND PROGRAM
What We Want, What We Believe

1. *We want freedom. We want power to determine the destiny of our Black Community.*

We believe that black people will not be free until we are able to determine our destiny.

2. *We want full employment for our people.*

We believe that the federal government is responsible and obligated to give every man employment or a guaranteed income. We believe that if the white American businessmen will not give full employment, then the means of production should be taken from the businessmen and placed in the community so that the people of the community can organize and employ all of its people and give a high standard of living.

3. *We want an end to the robbery by the white man of our Black Community.*

We believe that this racist government has robbed us and now we are demanding the overdue debt of forty acres and two mules. Forty acres and two mules was promised 100 years ago as restitution for slave labor and mass murder of black people. We will accept the payment in currency which will be distributed to our many communities. The Germans are now aiding the Jews in Israel for the genocide of the Jewish people. The Germans murdered six million Jews. The American racist has taken part in the slaughter of over fifty million black people; therefore, we feel that this is a modest demand that we make.

4. *We want decent housing, fit for shelter of human beings.*

We believe that if the white landlords will not give decent housing to our black community, then the housing and the land should be made into cooperatives so that our community, with government aid, can build and make decent housing for its people.

5. *We want education for our people that exposes the true nature of this decadent American society. We want education that teaches us our true history and our role in the present-day society.*

We believe in an educational system that will give to our people a knowledge of self. If a man does not have knowledge of himself and his position in society and the world, then he has little chance to relate to anything else.

6. *We want all black men to be exempt from military service.*

We believe that Black people should not be forced to fight in the military service to defend a racist government that does not protect us. We will not fight and kill other people of color in the world who, like black people, are being victimized by the white racist government of America. We will protect ourselves from the force and violence of the racist police and the racist military, by whatever means necessary.

7. *We want an immediate end to POLICE BRUTALITY and MURDER of black people.*

We believe we can end police brutality in our black community by organizing black self-defense groups that are dedicated to defending our black community from racist police oppression and brutality. The Second Amendment to the Constitution of the United States gives a right to bear arms. We therefore believe that all black people should arm themselves for self-defense.

8. *We want freedom for all black men held in federal, state, county and city prisons and jails.*

We believe that all black people should be released from the many jails and prisons because they have not received a fair and impartial trial.

9. *We want all black people when brought to trial to be tried in court by a jury of their peer group or people from their black communities, as defined by the Constitution of the United States.*

We believe that the courts should follow the United States Constitution so that black people will receive fair trials. The 14th Amendment of the U.S. Constitution gives a man a right to be tried by his peer group. A peer is a person from a similar economic, social, religious, geographical, environmental, historical and racial background. To do this the court will be forced to select a jury from the black community from which the black defendant came. We have been, and are being tried by all-white juries that have no understanding of the "average reasoning man" of the black community.

10. *We want land, bread, housing, education, clothing, justice and peace. And as our major political objective, a United Nations–supervised plebiscite to be held throughout the black colony in which only black colonial subjects will be allowed to participate, for the purpose of determining the will of black people as to their national destiny.*

When, in the course of human events, it becomes necessary for one people to dissolve the political bands which have connected them with another, and to assume, among the powers of the earth, the separate and equal station to which the laws of nature and nature's God entitle them, a decent respect to the opinions of mankind requires that they should declare the causes which impel them to the separation.

We hold these truths to be self-evident, that all men are created equal; that they are endowed by their Creator with certain unalienable rights; that among these are life, liberty, and the pursuit of happiness. *That, to secure these rights, governments are instituted among men, deriving their just powers from the consent of the governed; that, whenever any form of government becomes destructive of these ends, it is the right of the people to alter or to abolish it, and to institute a new government, laying its foundation on such principles, and organizing its powers in such form, as to them shall seem most likely to effect their safety and happiness.* Prudence, indeed, will dictate that governments long established should not be changed for light and transient causes; and, accordingly, all experience hath shown, that mankind are more disposed to suffer, while evils are sufferable, than to right themselves by abolishing the forms to which they are accustomed. *But, when a long train of abuses and usurpations, pursuing invariably the same object, evinces a design to reduce them under absolute despotism, it is their right, it is their duty, to throw off such government, and to provide new guards for their future security.*

⟿

RULES OF THE BLACK PANTHER PARTY

Every member of the BLACK PANTHER PARTY throughout this country of racist America must abide by these rules as functional members of this party. CENTRAL COMMITTEE members, CENTRAL STAFFS, and LOCAL STAFFS, including all captains subordinate to either national, state, and local leadership of the BLACK PANTHER PARTY will enforce these rules. Length of suspension or other disciplinary action necessary for violation of these rules will depend on national decisions by national, state or state area, and local committees and staffs where said rule or rules of the BLACK PANTHER PARTY WERE VIOLATED.

Every member of the party must know these verbatim by heart. And apply them daily. Each member must report any violation of these rules to their leadership or they are counter-revolutionary and are also subjected to suspension by the BLACK PANTHER PARTY.

The rules are:

1. No party member can have narcotics or weed in his possession while doing party work.

2. Any party member found shooting narcotics will be expelled from this party.

3. No party member can be DRUNK while doing daily party work.

4. No party member will violate rules relating to office work, general meetings of the BLACK PANTHER PARTY, and meetings of the BLACK PANTHER PARTY ANYWHERE.

5. No party member will USE, POINT, or FIRE a weapon of any kind unnecessarily or accidentally at anyone.

6. No party member can join any other army force other than the BLACK LIBERATION ARMY.

7. No party member can have a weapon in his possession while DRUNK or loaded off narcotics or weed.

8. No party member will commit any crimes against other party members or BLACK people at all, and cannot steal or take from the people, not even a needle or a piece of thread.

9. When arrested BLACK PANTHER MEMBERS will give only name, address, and will sign nothing. Legal first aid must be understood by all Party members.

10. The Ten-Point Program and platform of the BLACK PANTHER PARTY must be known and understood by each Party member.

11. Party Communications must be National and Local.

12. The 10-10-10 program should be known by all members and also understood by all members.

13. All Finance officers will operate under the jurisdiction of the Ministry of Finance.

14. Each person will submit a report of daily work.

15. Each Sub-Section Leaders, Section Leaders, and Lieutenants, Captains must submit Daily reports of work.

16. All Panthers must learn to operate and service weapons correctly.

17. All Leadership personnel who expel a member must submit this information to the Editor of the Newspaper, so that it will be published in the paper and will be known by all chapters and branches.

18. Political Education Classes are mandatory for general membership.

19. Only office personnel assigned to respective offices each day should be there. All others are to sell papers and do Political work out in the community, including Captains, Section Leaders, etc.

20. COMMUNICATIONS—all chapters must submit weekly reports in writing to the National Headquarters.

21. All Branches must implement First Aid and/or Medical Cadres.

22. All Chapters, Branches, and components of the BLACK PANTHER PARTY must submit a monthly Financial Report to the Ministry of Finance, and also the Central Committee.

23. Everyone in a leadership position must read no less than two hours per day to keep abreast of the changing political situation.

24. No chapter or branch shall accept grants, poverty funds, money or any other aid from any government agency without contacting the National Headquarters.

25. All chapters must adhere to the policy and the ideology laid down by the CENTRAL COMMITTEE of the BLACK PANTHER PARTY.

26. All Branches must submit weekly reports in writing to their respective Chapters.

8 Points of Attention

1) Speak politely.
2) Pay fairly for what you buy.
3) Return everything you borrow.
4) Pay for anything you damage.
5) Do not hit or swear at people.
6) Do not damage property or crops of the poor, oppressed masses.
7) Do not take liberties with women.
8) If we ever have to take captives do not ill-treat them.

3 Main Rules of Discipline

1) Obey orders in all your actions.
2) Do not take a single needle or a piece of thread from the poor and oppressed masses.
3) Turn in everything captured from the attacking enemy.

~~~

ON THE DEFECTION OF ELDRIDGE CLEAVER
FROM THE BLACK PANTHER PARTY AND THE DEFECTION
OF THE BLACK PANTHER PARTY FROM THE BLACK COMMUNITY

By Huey P. Newton

The Black Panther Party bases its ideology and philosophy on a concrete analysis of concrete conditions, using dialectical materialism as our analytical method. As dialectical materialists we recognize that contradictions can lead to development. The internal struggle of opposites based upon their unity causes matter to have motion as a part of the process of development. We recognize that nothing in nature stands outside of dialectics, even the Black Panther Party. But we welcome these contradictions, because they clarify and advance our struggle. We had a contradiction with our former Minister of Information, Eldridge Cleaver. But we understand this as necessary to our growth. Out of this contradiction has come new growth and a new return to the original vision of the Party.

Early in the development of the Black Panther Party I wrote an essay titled "The Correct Handling of a Revolution." This was in response to another contradiction—the criticisms raised against the Party by the Revolutionary Action Movement (RAM). At that time RAM criticized us for our above-ground action—openly displaying weapons and talking about the necessity for the community to arm itself for its own self-defense. RAM said that they were underground, and saw this as the correct way to handle a revolution. I responded to them by pointing out that you must establish your organization above ground so that the people will relate to it in a way that will be positive and progressive to them. When you go underground without doing this, you bury yourself so deeply that the people can neither relate to nor contact you. Then the terrorism of the underground organization will be just that—striking fear into the hearts of the very people whose interest the organization claims to be defending—because the people cannot relate to them and there is nobody there to interpret their actions. You have to set up a program of practical action and be a model for the community to follow and appreciate.

The original vision of the Party was to develop a lifeline to the people, by serving their needs and defending them against their oppressors who come to the community in many forms—from armed police to capitalist exploiters. We knew that this strategy would raise the consciousness of the people and also give us their support. Then, if we were driven underground by the oppressors, the people would support us and defend us. They would know that, in spite of the oppressor's interpretations, that our only desire was to serve their true interests; and they would defend us. In this manner we might be forced underground, but there would be a lifeline to the community which would always sustain us, because the people would identify with us and not with our common enemy.

For a time the Black Panther Party lost its vision and defected from the community. With the defection of Eldridge Cleaver, however, we can move again to a full-scale development of our original vision and come out of the twilight zone which the Party has been in during the recent past.

The only reason that the Party is still in existence at this time, and the only reason that we have been able to survive the repression of the Party and murders of some of our most advanced comrades is because of the Ten-Point Program—our survival program. Our programs would be meaningless and insignificant if they were not community programs. This is why it is my opinion that as long as the Black community and oppressed people are found in North America the Black Panther Party will last. The Party will survive as a structured vehicle, because it serves the true interests of oppressed people and administers to their needs—this was the original vision of the Party. The original vision was not structured by rhetoric nor by ideology. It was structured by the practical needs of the people, and its dreamers were armed with an ideology which provided a systematic method of analysis of how best to meet those needs.

When Bobby Seale and I came together to launch the Black Panther Party, we had been through many groups. Most of them were so dedicated to rhetoric and artistic rituals that they had withdrawn from living in the Twentieth Century. Sometimes their analyses were beautiful, but they had no practical programs which would deliver their understandings to the people. When they did try to develop practical programs, they often failed, because they lacked a systematic ideology which would help them do concrete analyses of concrete conditions to gain a full understanding of the community and its needs. When I was in Donald Warden's Afro-American Association, I watched him try to make a reality of community control through Black Capitalism. But Warden did not have a systematic ideology, and his attempts to initiate his program continually frustrated him and the community too. They did not know why capitalism would not work for them, even though it had worked for other ethnic groups.

When we formed the Party, we did so because we wanted to put theory and practice together, in a systematic manner. We did this through our basic Ten Point Program. In actuality it was a 20-Point Program, with the practice expressed in "What We Want" and the theory expressed in "What We Believe." This program was designed to serve as a basis for a structured political vehicle.

The actions we engaged in at that time were strictly strategic actions, for political purposes. They were designed to mobilize the community. Any action which does not mobilize the community toward the goal is not a revolutionary action. The action might be a marvelous statement of courage, but if it does not mobilize the people toward the goal of a higher manifestation of freedom, it is not making a political statement and could even be counter-revolutionary.

We realized at a very early point in our development, that revolution is a process. It is not a particular action, nor is it a conclusion. It is a process. This is why when feudalism wiped out slavery, feudalism was revolutionary. This is why when capitalism wiped out feudalism, capitalism was revolutionary. The concrete analysis of concrete conditions will reveal the true nature of the situation and increase our understanding. This process moves in a dialectical manner and we understand the struggle of the opposites based upon their unity.

Many times people say that our Ten-Point Program is reformist; but they ignore the fact that revolution is a process. We left the program open-ended, so that it could develop and people could identify with it. We did not offer it to them as a conclusion; we offered it as a vehicle to move them to a higher level. In their quest for freedom, and in their attempts to prevent the oppressor from stripping them of all the things they need to exist, the people see things as moving from A to B to C; they do not see things as moving from A to Z. In other words they have to see first some basic accomplishments, in order to realize that major successes are possible. Much of the time the revolutionary will have to guide them into this understanding. But he can never take them from A to Z in one jump, because it is too far ahead. Therefore, when the revolutionary begins to indulge in Z, or final conclusions, the people do not relate to him. Therefore he is no longer a revolutionary, if revolution is a process. This makes any action or function which does not promote the process—non-revolutionary.

When the Party went to Sacramento, when the Party faced down the policemen in front of the office of *Ramparts* magazine, and when the Party patrolled the police with arms, we were acting (in 1966) at a time when the people had given up the philosophy of non-violent direct action and were beginning to deal with sterner stuff. We wanted them to see the virtues of disciplined and organized armed self-defense, rather than spontaneous and disorganized outbreaks and riots. There were Police Alert Patrols all over the country, but we were the first *armed* police patrol. We called ourselves the Black Panther Party for Self-Defense. In all of this we had political and revolutionary objectives in mind, but we knew that we could not succeed without the support of the people.

Our strategy was based on a consistent ideology, which helped us to understand the conditions around us. We knew that the law was not prepared for what we were doing and policemen were so shocked that they didn't know what to do. We saw that the people felt a new pride and strength because of the example we set for them; and they began to look toward the vehicle we were building for answers.

Later we dropped the term "Self-Defense" from our name and just became the Black Panther Party. We discouraged actions like Sacramento and police observations because we recognized that these were not the things to do in every situation or on every occasion. We never called these revolutionary actions. The only time an action is revolutionary is when the people relate to it in a revolutionary way. If they will not use the example you set, then no matter how many guns you have, your action is not revolutionary.

The gun itself is not necessarily revolutionary, because the fascists carry guns—in fact they have more guns. A lot of so-called revolutionaries simply do not understand the statement by Chairman Mao that "Political power grows out of the barrel of a gun." They thought Chairman Mao said political power is the gun, but the emphasis is on grows. The culmination of political power is the ownership and control of the land and the institutions thereon, so that you can then get rid of the gun. That is why Chairman Mao makes the statement that, "We are advocates of the abolition of war, we do not want war; but war can only be abolished through war, and in order to get rid of the gun, it is necessary to take up the gun." He is always speaking of getting rid of it. If he did not look at it in those terms, then he surely would not be revolutionary. In other words, the gun by all revolutionary principles is a tool to be used in our strategy; it is not an end in itself. This was a part of the original vision of the Black Panther Party.

I had asked Eldridge Cleaver to join the Party a number of times. But he did not join until after the confrontation with the police in front of the office of *Ramparts* magazine, where the police were afraid to go for their guns. Without my knowledge, he took this as *the* Revolution and *the* Party. But in our basic program it was not until Point 7 that we mentioned the gun, and this was intentional. We were trying to build a political vehicle through which the people could express their revolutionary desires. We recognized that no party or organization can make the revolution, only the people can. All we could do was act as a guide to the people. Because revolution is a process, and because the process moves in a dialectical manner. At one point one thing might be proper, but the same action could be improper at another point. We always emphasized a concrete analysis of concrete conditions, and then an appropriate response to these conditions as a way of mobilizing the people and leading them to higher levels of consciousness.

People constantly thought that we were security guards and community police or something like this. This is why we dropped the term "Self-Defense" from our name and directed the attention of the people to the fact that the only way *they* would get salvation is through *their* control of the institutions which serve the community. This would require that they organize a political vehicle which would keep their support and endorsement through its survival programs of service. They would look to it for answers and guidance. It would not be an organization which runs candidates for political office, but it would serve as a watchman over the administrators whom the people have placed in office.

Because the Black Panther Party grows out of the conditions and needs of oppressed people, we are interested in everything the people are interested in, even though we may not see these particular concerns as the final answers to our problems. We will never run for political office, but we will endorse and support those candidates who are acting in the true interests of the people. We may even provide campaign workers for them and do voter registration and basic precinct work. This would not be out of a commitment to electoral politics, however. It would be our way of bringing the will of the people to bear on situations in which they are interested. We will also hold such candidates responsible to the community, no matter how far removed their offices may be from the community. So we lead the people by following their interests, with a view toward raising their consciousness to see beyond particular goals.

When Eldridge joined the Party it was after the police confrontation, which left him fixated with the "either-or" attitude. This was that either the community picked up the gun with the Party or else they were cowards and there was no place for them. He did not realize that if the people did not relate to the Party, then there was no way that the Black Panther Party could make any revolution, because the record shows that the people are the makers of the revolution and of world history.

Sometimes there are those who express personal problems in political terms, and if they are eloquent, then these personal problems can sound very political. We charge Eldridge Cleaver with this. Much of it is probably beyond his control, because it is so personal. But we did not know that when he joined the Party, he was doing so only because of that act in front of *Ramparts*. We weren't trying to prove anything to ourselves, all we were trying to do, at that particular point, was defend Betty Shabazz. But we were praised by the people.

Under the influence of Eldridge Cleaver the Party gave the community no alternative for dealing with us, except by picking up the gun. This move was reactionary simply because the community was not at that point. Instead of being a cultural cult group, we became, by that act, a revolutionary cult group. But this is a basic contradiction, because revolution is a process, and if the acts you commit do not fall within the scope of the process then they are non-revolutionary.

What the revolutionary movement and the Black community needs is a very strong structure. This structure can only exist with the support of the people and it can only get its support through serving them. This is why we have the service to the people program—the most important thing in the Party. We will serve their needs, so that they can survive through this oppression. Then when they are ready to pick up the gun, serious business will happen. Eldridge Cleaver influenced us to isolate ourselves from the Black community, so that it was war between the oppressor and the Black Panther Party, not war between the oppressor and the oppressed community.

The Black Panther Party defected from the community long before Eldridge defected from the Party. Our hook-up with white radicals did not give us access to the white community, because they do not guide the white community. The Black community does not relate to them, so we were left in a twilight zone, where we could not enter the community with any real political education programs; yet we were not doing anything to mobilize whites. We had no influence in raising the consciousness of the Black community and that is the point where we defected.

We went through a free-speech movement in the Party, which was not necessary, and only further isolated us from the Black community. We had all sorts of profanity in our paper and every other word which dropped from our lips was profane. This did not happen before I was jailed, because I would not stand for it. But Eldridge's influence brought this about. I do not blame him altogether; I blame the Party because the Party accepted it.

Eldridge was never fully in the leadership of the Party. Even after Bobby was snatched away from us, I did not place Eldridge in a position of leadership, because he was not interested in that. I made David Hilliard administrator of programs. I knew that Eldridge would not do anything to lift the consciousness of the comrades in the Party. But I knew that he could make a contribution; and I pressed him to do so. I pressed him to write and edit the paper, but he wouldn't do it. The paper did not even come out every week until after Eldridge went to jail. But Eldridge Cleaver did make great contributions to the Black Panther Party with his writing and speaking. We want to keep this in mind, because there is a positive and negative side to everything.

The correct handling of a revolution is not to offer the people an "either-or" ultimatum. We must instead gain the support of the people through serving their needs. Then when the police or any other agency of repression tries to destroy the program, the people will move to a higher level of consciousness and action. Then the organized structure can guide the people to the point where they are prepared to deal in many ways. This was the strategy we used in 1966 when we were related to in a positive way.

So the Black Panther Party has reached a contradiction with Eldridge Cleaver and he has defected from the Party, because we would not order everyone into the streets tomorrow to make a revolution. We recognize that this is impossible because our dialectics or ideology, our concrete analysis of concrete conditions say that it is a fantasy, because the people are not at that point now. This contradiction and conflict may seem unfortunate to some, but it is a part of the dialectical process. The resolution of this contradiction has freed us from incorrect analyses and emphases.

We are now free to move toward the building of a community structure which will become a true voice of the people, promoting their interests in many ways. We can continue to push our basic survival program. We can continue to serve the people as advocates of their true interests. We can truly become a political revolutionary vehicle which will lead the people to a higher level of consciousness, so that they will know what they must really do in their quest for freedom, and they will have the courage to adopt any means necessary to seize the time and obtain that freedom.

Huey P. Newton
Minister of Defense
Black Panther Party
Servant of the People

Sources: (1) "The Black Panther Program: What We Want, What We Believe," October 1966; (2) "Rules of the Black Panther Party," Central Headquarters, Oakland, California; and (3) Excerpt from Huey P. Newton, "On the Defection of Eldridge Cleaver from the Black Panther Party and the Defection of the Black Panther Party from the Black Community," *Black Panther Intercommunal News Service*, April 17, 1971.

SELECT BIBLIOGRAPHY:

Paul Alkebulan, *Survival Pending Revolution: The History of the Black Panther Party* (Tuscaloosa: University of Alabama Press, 2007).
Elaine Brown, *A Taste of Power: A Black Woman's Story* (New York: Pantheon Books, 1992).
Philip S. Foner, ed., *The Black Panthers Speak* (Philadelphia: Lippincott, 1970).

David Hilliard and Lewis Cole, *This Side of Glory: The Autobiography of David Hilliard and the Story of the Black Panther Party* (Boston: Little, Brown, 1993).

David Hilliard and Donald Weise, eds., *The Huey P. Newton Reader* (New York: Seven Stories Press, 2002).

J. L. Jeffries, *Huey P. Newton: The Radical Theorist* (Jackson: University Press of Mississippi, 2002).

Jama Lazerow and Yohuru R. Williams, eds., *In Search of the Black Panther Party: New Perspectives on a Revolutionary Movement* (Durham: Duke University Press, 2006).

Huey P. Newton, *To Die for the People: The Writings of Huey P. Newton*, Intro. Franz Schurmann (New York: Random House, 1972).

———, *Revolutionary Suicide* (New York: Harcourt Brace Jovanovich, 1973).

Hugh Pearson, *The Shadow of the Panther: Huey Newton and the Price of Black Power in America* (Reading, Mass.: Addison-Wesley, 1994).

Jane Rhodes, *Framing the Black Panthers: The Spectacular Rise of a Black Power Icon* (New York: New Press, 2007).

Bobby Seale, *Seize the Time: The Story of the Black Panther Party and Huey Newton* (New York: Random House, 1970).

~ 18 ~

"The People Have to Have the Power," *Fred Hampton*

By 1969, Black Panther chapters had been established throughout the United States, from North Carolina to Nebraska. That same year, 27 Panthers were killed by local police and law-enforcement agencies and 749 members were arrested. Perhaps the most influential chapter outside of the Bay Area was headed by activist Fred Hampton (1948–1969) in Chicago. Hampton was an outstanding organizer and charismatic speaker. In 1969, the Chicago police launched a carefully planned raid against the Panther headquarters and murdered Hampton. In this excerpt, Hampton presents in a popular style a synthesis of Marxian theory within the framework of Black Power.

~

A lot of people get the word revolution mixed up and they think revolution's a bad word. Revolution is nothing but like having a sore on your body and then you put something on that sore to cure that infection. I'm telling you that we're living in a sick society. We're involved in a society that produces ADC victims. We're involved in a society that produces criminals, thieves and robbers and rapers. Whenever you are in a society like that, that is a sick society.

. . . We're gonna organize and dedicate ourselves to revolutionary political power and teach ourselves the specific needs of resisting the power structure, arm ourselves, and we're gonna fight reactionary pigs with international proletarian revolution. That's what it has to be. The people have to have the power—it belongs to the people.

. . . Unless people show us through their social practice that they relate to the struggle in Babylon, that means that they're not internationalists, that means that they're not revolutionaries. And when you're marchin' on this cruel war in Washington, all you radicals . . . we need to have some moratoriums on Babylon. We need to have some moratoriums on the Black community in Babylon and all oppressed communities in Babylon.

. . . We have to understand very clearly that there's a man in our community called a capitalist. Sometimes he's Black and sometimes he's white. But that man has to be driven out of our community because anybody who comes into the community to make profit off of people by exploiting them can be defined as a capitalist.

Any program that's brought into our community should be analyzed by the people of that community. It should be analyzed to see that it meets the relevant needs of that community.

. . . That's what the Breakfast for Children Program is. A lot of people think it's charity. But what does it do? It takes people from a stage to a stage to another stage. Any program that's revolutionary is an advancing program. Revolution is change.

. . . We say that the Breakfast for Children Program is a socialistic program. It teaches the people basically that—by practice. We thought up and let them practice that theory and inspect that theory. What's more important?

. . . And a woman said, "I don't know if I like communism, and I don't know if I like socialism. But I know that the Breakfast for Children Program feeds my kids. And if you put your hands on that Breakfast for Children Program . . ."

. . . You know, a lot of people have hang-ups with the Party because the Party talks about a class struggle. . . . We say primarily that the priority of this struggle is class. That Marx and Lenin and Che Guevara and Mao Tse-tung and anybody else that has ever said or knew or practiced anything about revolution always said that a revolution is a class struggle. It was one class—the oppressed, and that other class—the oppressor. And it's got to be a universal fact. Those that don't admit to that are those that don't want to get involved in a revolution, because they know as long as they're dealing with a race thing, they'll never be involved in a revolution.

. . . We never negated the fact that there was racism in America, but we said that the by-product, what comes off of capitalism, that happens to be racism . . . that capitalism comes first and next is racism. That when they brought slaves over here, it was to make money. So first the idea came that we want to make money, then the slaves came in order to make that money. That means, through historical fact, that racism had to come from capitalism. It had to be capitalism first and racism was a by-product of that.

. . . We may be in the minority, but this minority is gonna keep on shouting loud and clear: We're not gonna fight fire with fire, we're gonna fight fire with water. We're not gonna fight racism with racism, we're gonna fight racism with solidarity. We're not gonna fight capitalism with Black capitalism . . . we're gonna fight capitalism with socialism.

. . . We know that Black people are most oppressed. And if we didn't know that, then why in the hell would we be running around talking about the Black liberation struggle has to be the vanguard for all liberation struggles?

Any theory you got, practice it. And when you practice it, you make some mistakes. When you make a mistake, you correct that theory, and then it will be corrected theory that will be able to be applied and used in any situation. That's what we've got to be able to do.

. . . A lot of us read and read and read, but we don't get any practice. We have a lot of knowledge in our heads, but we've never practiced it; and made any mistakes and corrected those mistakes so that we will be able to do something properly. So we come up with, like we say, more degrees than a thermometer but we are not able to walk across the street and chew gum at the same time. Because we have all that knowledge but it's never been exercised, it's never been practiced. We never tested it with what's really happening. We call it testing it with objective reality. You might have any kind of thought in your mind, but you've got to test it with what's out there. You see what I mean?

. . . The only way that anybody can tell you the taste of a pear is if he himself has tasted it. That's the only way. That's objective reality. That's what the Black Panther Party deals with. We're not into metaphysics, we're not idealists, we're dialectical materialists. And we deal with what reality is, whether we like it or not. A lot of people can't relate to that because everything they do is gauged by the way they like things to be. We say that's incorrect. You look and see how things are, and then you deal with that.

. . . We some Marxist-Leninist cussin' niggers. And we gonna continue to cuss, goddammit. 'Cause that's what we relate to. That's what's happening in Babylon. That's objective reality.

. . . You're dealing in subjectivity, because you're not testing it with objective reality. And what's wrong is that you don't go test it. Because if you test it, you'll get objective. Because as soon as you walk out there, a whole lot of objective reality will vamp down upon your ass. . . .

. . . You can jail a revolutionary, but you can't jail the revolution. You can lock up a freedom fighter like Huey P. Newton, but you can't lock up freedom fighting. . . . Because if you do, you come up with answers that don't answer, explanations that don't explain, conclusions that don't conclude.

If you think about me and you think about me, niggers, and you ain't gonna do no revolutionary act, then forget about me. I don't want myself on your mind if you're not going to work for the people.

Like I always said, if you're asked to make a commitment at the age of 20, and you say I don't want to make no commitment only because of the simple reason that I'm too young to die, I want to live a little bit longer. What you did is . . . you're dead already.

You have to understand that people have to pay the price for peace. You dare to struggle, you dare to win. If you dare not struggle, then goddammit you don't deserve to win. Let me say to you peace if you're willing to fight for it.

Let me say in the spirit of liberation—I been gone for a little while, at least my body's been gone for a little while. But I'm back now, and I believe I'm back to stay.

I believe I'm going to do my job. I believe I was born not to die in a car wreck. I don't believe I'm going to die in a car wreck. I don't believe I going to die slipping on a piece of ice. I don't believe I going to die because I have a bad heart. I don't believe I'm going to die because I have lung cancer.

I believe I'm going to be able to die doing the things I was born for. I believe I'm going to die high off the people. I believe I'm going to die a revolutionary in the international revolutionary proletarian struggle. I hope each one of you will be able to die [in] the international revolutionary proletarian struggle, or you'll be able to live in it. And I think that struggle's going to come.

Why don't you live for the people.

Why don't you struggle for the people.

Why don't you die for the people.

Source: Excerpts from *"Fred Speaks": Fred Hampton 20th Commemoration* (Chicago: December 4th Committee, 1989).

SELECT BIBLIOGRAPHY:

Artists United, *When One of Us Falls, a Thousand Will Take His Place* (Chicago: Artists United, 1970).

Ward Churchill and Jim Vander Wall, *Agents of Repression: The FBI's Secret Wars Against the Black Panther Party and the American Indian Movement* (Boston: South End Press, 1988).

Commission of Inquiry into Black Panthers and the Police, Ramsey Clark and Roy Wilkins, chairmen, *Search and Destroy: A Report* (New York: Metropolitan Applied Research Center, 1973).

⟿ 19 ⟿

"I Am a Revolutionary Black Woman," *Angela Y. Davis, 1970*

Born in Birmingham, Alabama, Angela Y. Davis (1944–) studied at the Sorbonne in Paris, graduated *magna cum laude* from Brandeis, and did graduate work at both the University of Frankfurt in Germany and University of California at San Diego. In 1969, Davis was subject to a gross violation of academic freedom when she was fired from her professorship at the University of California at Los Angeles after her membership in the Communist Party came to the attention of then-governor Ronald Reagan. When guns she had purchased for self-defense were used by the Black Panthers in a courtroom shooting in San Marino County, California, the FBI placed her on its "Ten Most Wanted" list. She was captured in New York, jailed for two years and tried for kidnapping, conspiracy, and murder. The Communist Party and the National Alliance Against Racist and Political Repression organized a mass international struggle to win her freedom, and a jury finally acquitted her of the charges. Since her release in 1972 Davis has continued to struggle on behalf of numerous progressive causes, including gender and racial equality, the eradication of the prison-industrial complex, and socialism. Davis's 1981 book *Women, Race and Class* was pivotal in the development of the political and social criticism termed "black feminist thought." In the early 1990s

Davis left the U.S. Communist Party and helped to found the Committees of Correspondence, a national organization committed to socialism and democracy. In her most recent books, *Are Prisons Obsolete?* (2003) and *Abolition Democracy: Beyond Empire, Prisons, and Torture* (2005), Davis continues her critique of the prison-industrial complex. Davis is currently a professor in the History of Consciousness program at the University of California at Santa Cruz and holds a distinguished appointment as the University of California Presidential Chair in African-American and Feminist Studies.

Before anything else I am a black woman. I dedicated my life to the struggle for the liberation of black people—my enslaved, imprisoned people.

I am a Communist because I am convinced that the reason we have been forcefully compelled to eke out an existence at the very lowest level of American society has to do with the nature of capitalism. If we are going to rise out of our oppression, our poverty, if we are going to cease being the targets of the racist-minded mentality of racist policemen, we will have to destroy the American capitalist system. We will have to obliterate a system in which a few wealthy capitalists are guaranteed the privilege of becoming richer and richer, whereas the people who are forced to work for the rich, and especially Black people, never take any significant step forward.

I am a Communist because I believe that black people, with whose labor and blood this country was built, have a right to a great deal of wealth that has been hoarded in the hands of the Hugheses, the Rockefellers, the Kennedys, the DuPonts, all the superpowerful white capitalists of America.

Further, I am a Communist because I believe Black men should not be coerced into fighting a racist, imperialist war in Southeast Asia, where the United States government is violently denying a nonwhite people the right to control their own lives, just as they violently suppressed us for hundreds of years.

My decision to join the Communist party emanated from my belief that the only true path of liberation for black people is the one that leads toward a complete and total overthrow of the capitalist class in this country and all its manifold institutional appendages which insure its ability to exploit the masses and enslave black people. Convinced of the need to employ Marxist-Leninist principles in the struggle for liberation, I joined the Che-Lumumba Club, which is a militant, all-black collective of the Communist party in Los Angeles committed to the task of rendering Marxism-Leninism relevant to black people. But mindful of the fact that once we as black people set out to destroy the capitalist system we would be heading in a suicidal direction if we attempted to go at it alone. The whole question of allies was crucial. And furthermore aside from students, we need important allies at the point of production. I do not feel that all white workers are going to be inveterate conservatives. Black leadership in working-class struggles is needed to radicalize necessary sectors of the working class.

The practical perspective of the Che-Lumumba Club is based on an awareness of the need to emphasize the national character of our people's struggle and to struggle around the specific forms of oppression which have kept us at the very lowest levels of American society for hundreds of years, but at the same time to place ourselves as black people in the forefront of a revolution involving masses of people to destroy capitalism, to eventually build a socialist society and thus to liberate not only our own people but all the downtrodden in this country. And further, recognizing the international character of the revolution especially in this period when the battle against our home-grown capitalists is being carried out all over the world, in Indochina, Africa and Latin America. My decision to join the Communist party was predicated in part on the ties the party has established with revolutionary movements throughout the world. . . .

The American judicial system is bankrupt. In so far as black people are concerned, it has proven itself to be one more arm of a system carrying out the systematic oppression of our people. We are the victims, not the recipients of justice.

It is obvious that democracy in America is hopelessly deteriorated, when the courts, allegedly guardians of the rights of the people, have been enlisted to play an active role in the genocidal war against black people.

We must reject the right of the courts to further oppress us. The only way we can get justice is demand it and to create a mass movement which will give notice to our enemy that we will use all means at our disposal to secure justice for our people. This is the only way we can expect to free all our brothers and sisters held captive in America's dungeons. This is the only way we can expect to ultimately gain total liberation.

. . . no revolutionary should fail to understand the underlying significance of the dictum that the success or failure of a revolution can almost always be gauged by the degree to which the status of women is altered in a radical, progressive direction. After all, Marx and Engels contended that there are two basic facts around which the history of mankind revolves: production and reproduction. The way in which people obtain their means of subsistence on one hand, and the way in which the family is organized on the other hand.

Further, if it is true the outcome of a revolution will reflect the manner in which it is waged, we must unremittingly challenge anachronistic bourgeois family structures and also the oppressive character of women's role in American society in general. Of course, this struggle is part and parcel of a total revolution. Led by women, the fight for the liberation of women must be embraced by men as well. The battle for women's liberation is especially critical with respect to the effort to build an effective black liberation movement. For there is no question about the fact that as a group, black women constitute the most oppressed sector of society.

Historically we were constrained not only to survive on an economic level as slaves, but our sexual status was that of a breeder of property for the white slave master as well as being the object of his perverse sexual desires. Our enemies have attempted to mesmerize us, to mesmerize black people, by propounding a whole assortment of myths with respect to the black woman. We are inveterate matriarchs, implying we have worked in collusion with the white oppressor to insure the emasculation of our men. Unfortunately, some black women have accepted these myths without questioning their origin and without being aware of the counter-revolutionary content and effect. They're consequently falling into behind-the-scenes positions in the movement and refuse to be aggressive and take leadership in our struggle for fear of contributing to the oppression of the black male.

As black women, we must liberate ourselves and provide the impetus for the liberation of black men from this whole network of lies around the oppression of black women, which serve only to divide us, thus impeding the advance of our total liberation struggle. . . .

I think it is important to link up the struggle for my freedom with the fight to free other black political prisoners . . . I maintain that the fight should call for the freedom of all black men and women. For few of us have received fair trials. We certainly have not been judged by juries from among our peers.

Even if I am eventually allowed to leave the dungeon, I will not consider myself free. My freedom will become a reality when we as a people have destroyed our enemies, when we black people have broken the yokes of our oppression and can freely erect a society which reflects our needs and our dreams. I will not be free until all black people are free.

As a preface to my brief remarks I now declare publicly before the court, before the people of this country that I am innocent of all charges which have been leveled against me by the State of California. I am innocent and therefore maintain that my presence in this courtroom today is unrelated to any criminal act.

I stand before this court as a target of a political frame-up which, far from pointing to my culpability, implicates the State of California as an agent of political repression. Indeed the state reveals its own role by introducing as evidence against me my participation in the struggles of my people—black people—against the many injustices of society. Specifically my involvement with the "Soledad Brothers Defense Committee." The American people have been led to believe that such involvement is Constitutionally protected.

In order to insure that these political questions are not obscured, I feel compelled to play an active role in my own defense as the defendant, as a black woman and as a Communist. It is my duty to assist all those directly involved in the proceedings, as well as the people of this state and the American people in general, to thoroughly comprehend the substantive issues at stake in my case. These have to do with my political beliefs, affiliations and my day-to-day efforts to fight all the conditions which have economically and politically paralyzed black America.

No one can better represent my political beliefs and activities than I. A system of justice which virtually condemns to silence the one person who stands to lose most would seem to be self-defeating.

It is particularly crucial to black people to combat this contradiction inherent in the judicial system, for we have accumulated a wealth of historical experience which confirms our belief that the scales of American justice are out of balance.

In order to enhance the possibility of being granted a fair trial, of which at present I am extremely doubtful, it is imperative that I be allowed to represent myself. I might add that my request is not without legal precedent.

If this court denies our motion to include me as co-counsel in this case, it will be aligning itself with the forces of racism and reaction which threaten to push this country into the throes of fascism, and the many people who have become increasingly disillusioned with the court system in this country will have a further reason to solidify their contention that it is no longer possible to get a fair trial in America.

Source: Excerpts from "I Am a Revolutionary Black Woman," published originally in *Muhammad Speaks* (December 1970).

SELECT BIBLIOGRAPHY:

Bettina Aptheker, *The Morning Breaks: The Trial of Angela Davis* (New York: International Publishers, 1975).
Angela Y. Davis, *If They Come in the Morning* (New York: Okpaku, 1971).
———, *Angela Davis: An Autobiography* (New York: Random House, 1988).
———, *Women, Culture and Politics* (New York: Random House, 1989).
———, *Women, Race and Class* (New York: Random House, 1989).
Joy James, ed., *The Angela Y. Davis Reader* (Malden: Blackwell, 1998).

~ 20 ~

"Our Thing Is DRUM!" *The League of Revolutionary Black Workers*

The most important Black Power group to emerge with a working-class constituency was the League of Revolutionary Black Workers. The League was a network of independent black militant workers' organizations including Detroit's DRUM (Dodge Revolutionary Union Movement), FRUM (Ford Revolutionary Union Movement), and the United Black Brothers of Mahwah, New Jersey. Although the League had disappeared by the mid-1970s, it left a vibrant political legacy that merged Marxist theory with the black militancy of industrial factory workers.

~

GENERAL PROGRAM (HERE'S WHERE WE'RE COMING FROM)
The League of Revolutionary Black Workers is dedicated to waging a relentless struggle against racism, capitalism, and imperialism. We are struggling for the liberation of black people in the confines of the United States as well as to play a major revolutionary role in the liberation of all oppressed people in the world.

In U.S. society, a small class owns the basic means of production. There aren't any black people in this class, nor are the masses of whites; however, they are not in the same position as blacks.

Our black community is virtually a black working class, because of our relationship to the basic means of production. Black workers comprise the backbone of the productive process in this country. Since slavery, we have been the major producers of goods and services. In addition, we've produced goods under the most inhumane conditions. Our black community is comprised of industrial workers, social service workers, our gallant youth, and many ad hoc community groups.

The racist subordination of black people and black workers creates a privileged status for white people and white workers. While the imperialist oppression and exploitation of the world creates a privileged status for the people and workers of the U.S., the white labor movement has failed to deal with the worsening conditions of black workers and the key role of black workers in the economy and the working class. The white labor movement has turned its back on black worker problems such as less job security, speed-up, less pay, bad health (silicosis, in particular), the worst kind of jobs, and in most cases, exclusion from skilled trades.

These two systems of privilege become the basis for the aristocracy of white labor which gives white labor a huge stake in the imperialist system and renders white labor unable and unfit to lead the working class in the U.S.

United States society is racist, capitalist, and imperialist by nature. It is aggressively expansive, exploitative, and oppressive. The expansion of U.S. imperialism is primarily by means of worldwide financial penetration, backed up by a worldwide military regime. This gives a monopoly control of the resources, wealth and labor of the capitalist world to U.S. finance capital. They use the most barbarous methods of warfare and subversion to maintain its billions of dollars in profit.

U.S. imperialism supports every reactionary and fascist regime in the world by means of subversion, CIA assassinations, invasions, terror bombings, and criminal means of warfare. U.S. imperialism also resorts to nuclear blackmail, to intimidate the revolutionary peoples of the world. Imperialism faces its inevitable destruction as the national liberation struggles, currently focused in Southeast Asia, become worldwide. This involves the rest of Asia, including populous India, along with the emerging struggles in Latin America and the developing struggles in Africa. The workers and peoples of Europe are also drawn into the anti-imperialist struggle as the grip of U.S. imperialism loosens on Europe as the result of the struggles waged in the rest of the world.

The oppressive, imperialist nature of U.S. society is evidenced at home in the suppression of the black liberation struggle, workers' struggles, and anti-war struggles, in an increasingly militaristic fashion. One of the essential domestic props of U.S. imperialism is the white labor aristocracy which shares in the spoils of the plunder of the world and is based in the domestic subordination of black workers.

The white labor aristocracy collaborates with the U.S. imperialist government in its aggressive wars, its CIA subversion and supports its political line. It also colludes with monopoly corporations at home to allow speed-up and unsafe working conditions, inflation that outstrips any wage gains, leaves most workers unorganized, and supports the brutal subordination of black workers.

The League of Revolutionary Black Workers emerged specifically, out of the failure of the white labor movement to address itself to the racist work conditions and to the general inhumane conditions of black people.

Our strength comes from the historical and heroic struggles of our people, our inspiration comes from the revolutionary upsurges of the international struggles, and our convictions are guided by the principles of Marxism-Leninism.

The League of Revolutionary Black Workers is a political organization. We relate to the total black community. Our actual practice involves us with industrial and service workers, youth, and several ad hoc groups; these categories make up the League of Revolutionary Black Workers. Our duty is to plan the most feasible means to insure freedom and justice for the liberation of black people based on the concrete conditions we relate to. In addition, we have the task of training our people for leadership and other special capacities that make a viable organization. Most importantly, the direction of our organization is clear. We're not talking about dealing with a single issue as the only factor, nor are we talking about reforms in the system; but we are talking about the seizure of state power.

It is clear to us that the development of our struggle based on concrete realities, dictates the need for black peoples' liberation political party. We state, unequivocally, that this must be a black Marxist-Leninist party, designed to liberate black people, dedicated to leading the workers' struggles in this country, and resolved to wage a relentless struggle against imperialism.

The League's program for building a black Marxist-Leninist party is as follows:

1. Organizing of black workers on the broadest possible scale into the League and its component parts.
2. Politicizing and educating the masses of black people to the nature of racism, capitalism, and imperialism, to further outline the solution to these problems in League programs and documents.
3. Supporting the efforts of our people to develop a broad economic base within the community to aid the revolutionary struggle.
4. Developing a broad based self-defense organization in the community.
5. Carrying on unceasing struggles on behalf of black workers and the total community.
6. Forming principled alliances and coalitions, on the broadest possible base, with other oppressed minorities, organizations, movements, and forces, black or white, which struggle against the evils of racism, capitalism and imperialism.

Our short-range objective is to secure state power with the control of the means of production in the hands of the workers under the leadership of the most advanced section of the working class, the black working-class vanguard.

Our long-range objective is to create a society free of race, sex, class, and national oppression, founded on the humanitarian principle of from each according to his ability, to each according to his needs. . . .

Deep in the gloom
of the firefilled pit
Where the Dodge rolls down the line,
We challenge the doom
of dying in shit
While strangled by a swine. . . .

. . . For hours and years
we've sweated tears
Trying to break our chain—
But we broke our backs
and died in packs
To find our manhood slain. . . .
But now we stand—
For DRUM's at hand
To lead our Freedom fight,
and from now til then
we'll unite like men—
For now we know our might—
and damn the plantation
and the whole Dodge nation
For DRUM has dried our tears. . . .
and now as we die
we've a different cry—
For now we hold our spears!
U.A.W. is scum—
OUR THING IS DRUM!!!!!

Source: "General Program (Here's Where We're Coming From)," *General Policy Statement and Labor Program* (Highland Park, MI: League of Revolutionary Black Workers, 1970).

SELECT BIBLIOGRAPHY:

Dan Georgakas and Marvin Surkin, *Detroit: I Do Mind Dying?* (New York: St. Martin's Press, 1975); Updated ed. (Boston: South End Press, 1998).
James A. Geschwender, *Class, Race, and Worker Insurgency: The League of Revolutionary Black Workers* (New York: Cambridge University Press, 1977).
Jim Jacobs, *"Our Thing Is DRUM!"* (Boston: New England Free Press, 1970).

∽ 21 ∽

Attica: "The Fury of Those Who Are Oppressed," *1971*

In September 1971, African-American and Latino prisoners in the maximum-security correctional facility located in Attica, New York, seized control of the prison. Despite efforts to reach a negotiated settlement, New York Governor Nelson Rockefeller authorized law-enforcement agencies to storm the prison, leaving scores of inmates and captive guards dead or seriously injured. The demands cited below express the political objectives of Attica's prisoners.

~~~

The Five Demands
To the people of America

The incident that has erupted here at Attica is not a result of the dastardly bushwacking of the two prisoners Sept. 8, 1971 but of the unmitigated oppression wrought by the racist administration network of the prison, throughout the year.

WE are MEN! We are not beasts and do not intend to be beaten or driven as such. The entire prison populace has set forth to change forever the ruthless brutalization and disregard for the lives of the prisoners here and throughout the United States. What has happened here is but the sound before the fury of those who are oppressed.

We will not compromise on any terms except those that are agreeable to us. We call upon all the conscientious citizens of America to assist us in putting an end to this situation that threatens the lives of not only us, but each and everyone of us as well.

We have set forth demands that will bring closer to reality the demise of these prisons, institutions that serve no useful purpose to the People of America but to those who would enslave and exploit the People of America.

Our Demands Are Such:

1. We want complete amnesty, meaning freedom from any physical, mental and legal reprisals.
2. We want now, speedy and safe transportation out of confinement, to a non-imperialistic country.
3. We demand that the FEDERAL GOVERNMENT intervene, so that we will be under direct FEDERAL JURISDICTION.
4. We demand the reconstruction of ATTICA PRISON to be done by inmates and/or inmate supervision.
5. We urgently demand immediate negotiation thru Wm. M. Kunstler, Attorney-at-Law, 588 Ninth Ave., NYC, Assemblyman Arthur O. Eve, of Buffalo, the Solidarity Committee, Minister Farrakhan of MUHAMMAD SPEAKS, *Palante, The Young Lord's Party Paper*, the Black Panther Party, Clarence Jones of the *Amsterdam News*, Tom Wicker of *NY Times*, Richard Roth of the *Courier Express*, the Fortune Society, David Anderson of the Urban League of Rochester, Blond-Eva Bond of NICAP, and Jim Ingram of *Democrat Chronicle* of Detroit, Mich. We guarantee the safe passage of all people to and from this institution. We invite *all the people* to come here and witness this degradation, so that they can better know how to bring this degradation to an end.

The Inmates of Attica Prison

THE FIFTEEN PRACTICAL PROPOSALS

Practical Proposals:

1. Apply the New York State minimum wage law to all state institutions. STOP SLAVE LABOR.
2. Allow all New York State prisoners to be politically active, without intimidation or reprisals.
3. Give us true religious freedom.
4. End all censorship of newspapers, magazines, letters and other publications coming from the publisher.
5. Allow all inmates, at their own expense, to communicate with anyone they please.
6. When an inmate reaches conditional release date, give him a full release without parole.
7. Cease administrative resentencing of inmates returned for parole violations.
8. Institute realistic rehabilitation programs for all inmates according to their offense and personal needs.
9. Educate all correctional officers to the needs of the inmates, i.e., understanding rather than punishment.
10. Give us a healthy diet, stop feeding us so much pork, and give us some fresh fruit daily.
11. Modernize the inmate education system.
12. Give us a doctor that will examine and treat all inmates that request treatment.
13. Have an institutional delegation comprised of one inmate from each company authorized to speak to the institution administration concerning grievances (QUARTERLY).
14. Give us less cell time and more recreation with better recreational equipment and facilities.
15. Remove inside walls, making one open yard, and no more segregation or punishment.

Source: "The Five Demands: To the people of America," reprinted from *A Time to Die: The Attica Prison Revolt* by Tom Wicker by permission of the University of Nebraska Press. Copyright 1975 by Tom Wicker.

SELECT BIBLIOGRAPHY:

Malcolm Bell, *The Turkey Shoot: Tracking the Attica Cover-Up* (New York: Grove Press, 1985).

New York State Special Commission on Attica, *The Official Report of the New York State Special Commission on Attica* (New York: Bantam Books, 1972).

Russell G. Oswald, *Attica: My Story* (Garden City, N.Y.: Doubleday, 1972).

Tom Wicker, *A Time to Die: The Attica Prison Revolt* (Lincoln: University of Nebraska Press, 1994).

Richard Andrew Featherstone, and Stephen H. Paschen, *Narratives from the 1971 Attica Prison Riot: Toward a New Theory of Correctional Disturbances* (Lewiston: Edwin Mellen Press, 2005).

⟿ 22 ⟿

The National Black Political Convention, Gary, Indiana, *March 1972*

By the early 1970s, more than one thousand African Americans had been elected to public office, and Black Power formations and community-based activist groups flourished in hundreds of cities and towns. The attempt to consolidate these diverse currents into a national political force led to the National Black Political Convention, held in March 1972 in Gary, Indiana. The principal organizers of the convention were Gary Mayor Richard Hatcher, Detroit Congressman Charles Diggs, and then-cultural nationalist and Black Arts Movement founder Amiri Baraka, formerly LeRoi Jones. The meeting attracted nearly three thousand delegates and more than four thousand observers and was in many respects the zenith of the Black Power movement. Speakers at the convention aimed to increase blacks' political power in a number of arenas, demanding a government response to the pressing need for child care, a guaranteed annual wage, increased funds for community development, the creation of new public-service jobs, and the end of the death penalty.

⟿

The Gary Declaration: Black Politics at the Crossroads

Introduction

The Black Agenda is addressed primarily to Black people in America. It rises naturally out of the bloody decades and centuries of our people's struggle on these shores. It flows from the most recent surgings of our own cultural and political consciousness. It is our attempt to define some of the essential changes which must take place in this land as we and our children move to self-determination and true independence.

The Black Agenda assumes that no truly basic change for our benefit takes place in Black or white America unless we Black people organize to initiate that change. It assumes that we must have some essential agreement on overall goals, even though we may differ on many specific strategies.

Therefore, this is an initial statement of goals and directions for our own generation, some first definitions of crucial issues around which Black people must organize and move in 1972 and beyond. Anyone who claims to be serious about the survival and liberation of Black people must be serious about the implementation of the Black Agenda.

What Time Is It?

We come to Gary in an hour of great crisis and tremendous promise for Black America. While the white nation hovers on the brink of chaos, while its politicians offer no hope of real change, we stand on the edge of history and are faced with an amazing and frightening choice: We may choose in 1972 to slip back into the decadent white politics of American life, or we may press forward, moving relentlessly from Gary to the creation of our own Black life. The choice is large, but the time is very short.

Let there be no mistake. We come to Gary in a time of unrelieved crisis for our people. From every rural community in Alabama to the high-rise compounds of Chicago, we bring to this Convention the agonies of the masses of our people. From the sprawling Black cities of Watts and Nairobi in the West to the decay of Harlem and Roxbury in the East, the testimony we bear is the same. We are the witnesses to social disaster.

Our cities are crime-haunted dying grounds. Huge sectors of our youth—and countless others—face permanent unemployment. Those of us who work find our paychecks able to purchase less and less. Neither the courts nor the prisons contribute to anything resembling justice or reformation. The schools are unable—or unwilling—to educate our children for the real world of our struggles. Meanwhile, the officially approved epidemic of drugs threatens to wipe out the minds and strength of our best young warriors.

Economic, cultural, and spiritual depression stalk Black America, and the price for survival often appears to be more than we are able to pay. On every side, in every area of our lives, the American institutions in which we have placed our trust are unable to cope with the crises they have created by their single-minded dedication to profits for some and white supremacy above all.

Beyond These Shores

And beyond these shores there is more of the same. For while we are pressed down under all the dying weight of a bloated, inwardly decaying white civilization, many of our brothers in Africa and the rest of the Third World have fallen prey to the same powers of exploitation and deceit. Wherever America faces the unorganized, politically powerless forces of the non-white world, its goal is domination by any means necessary—as if to hide from itself the crumbling of its own systems of life and work.

But Americans cannot hide. They can run to China and the moon and to the edges of consciousness, but they cannot hide. The crises we face as Black people are the crises of the entire society. They go deep, to the very bones and marrow, to the essential nature of America's economic, political, and cultural systems. They are the natural end-product of a society built on the twin foundations of white racism and white capitalism.

So, let it be clear to us now: The desperation of our people, the agonies of our cities, the desolation of our countryside, the pollution of the air and the water—these things will not be significantly affected by new faces in the old places in Washington, D.C. This is the truth we must face here in Gary if we are to join our people everywhere in the movement forward toward liberation.

White Realities, Black Choice

A Black political convention, indeed all truly Black politics must begin from this truth: *The American system does not work for the masses of our people, and it cannot be made to work without radical fundamental change.* (Indeed, this system does not really work in favor of the humanity of anyone in America.)

In light of such realities, we come to Gary and are confronted with a choice. Will we believe the truth that history presses into our face—or will we, too, try to hide? Will the small favors some of us have received blind us to the larger sufferings of our people, or open our eyes to the testimony of our history in America?

For more than a century we have followed the path of political dependence on white men and their systems. From the Liberty Party in the decades before the Civil War to the Republican Party of Abraham Lincoln, we trusted in white men and white politics as our deliverers. Sixty years ago, W. E. B. Du Bois said he would give the Democrats their "last chance" to prove their sincere commitment to equality for Black people—and he was given white riots and official segregation in peace and in war.

Nevertheless, some twenty years later we became Democrats in the name of Franklin Roosevelt, then supported his successor Harry Truman, and even tried a "non-partisan" Republican General of the Army named Eisenhower. We were wooed like many others by the superficial liberalism of John F. Kennedy and the make-believe populism of Lyndon Johnson. Let there be no more of that.

Both Parties Have Betrayed Us

Here at Gary, let us never forget that while the times and the names and the parties have continually changed, one truth has faced us insistently, never changing: Both parties have betrayed us whenever their interests conflicted with ours (which was most of the time), and whenever our forces were unorganized and dependent, quiescent and compliant. Nor should this be surprising, for by now we must know that the American political system, like all other white institutions in America, was designed to operate for the benefit of the white race: It was never meant to do anything else.

That is the truth that we must face at Gary. If white "liberalism" could have solved our problems, then Lincoln and Roosevelt and Kennedy would have done so. But they did not solve ours nor the rest of the nation's. If America's problems could have been solved by forceful, politically skilled and aggressive individuals, then Lyndon Johnson would have retained the presidency. If the true "American Way" of unbridled monopoly capitalism, combined with a ruthless military imperialism could do it, then Nixon would not be running around the world, or making speeches comparing his nation's decadence to that of Greece and Rome.

If we have never faced it before, let us face it at Gary: The profound crisis of Black people and the disaster of America are not simply caused by men nor will they be solved by men alone. These crises are the crises of basically flawed economics and politics, and of cultural degradation. None of the Democratic candidates and none of the Republican candidates—regardless of their vague promises to us or to their white constituencies—can solve our problems or the problems of this country without radically changing the systems by which it operates.

The Politics of Social Transformation

So we come to Gary confronted with a choice. But it is not the old convention question of which candidate shall we support, the pointless question of who is to preside over a decaying and unsalvageable system. No, if we come to Gary out of the realities of the Black communities of this land, then the only real choice for us is whether or not we will live by the truth we know, whether we will move to organize independently, move to struggle for fundamental transformation, for the creation of new directions, towards a concern for the life and the meaning of Man. Social transformation or social destruction, those are our only real choices.

If we have come to Gary on behalf of our people in America, in the rest of this hemisphere, and in the Homeland—if we have come for our own best ambitions—then a new Black Politics must come to birth. If we are serious, the Black Politics of Gary must accept major responsibility for creating both the atmosphere and the program for fundamental, far-ranging change in America. Such responsibility is ours because it is our people who are most deeply hurt and ravaged by the present systems of society. That responsibility for leading the change is ours because we live in a society where few other men really believe in the responsibility of a truly humane society for anyone anywhere.

We Are the Vanguard

The challenge is thrown to us here in Gary. It is the challenge to consolidate and organize our own Black role as the vanguard in the struggle for a new society. To accept that challenge is to move independent Black politics. There can be no equivocation on that issue. History leaves us no other choice. White politics has not and cannot bring the changes we need.

We come to Gary and are faced with a challenge. The challenge is to transform ourselves from favor-seeking vassals and loud-talking, "militant" pawns, and to take up the role that the organized masses of our people have attempted to play ever since we came to these shores: That of harbingers of true justice and humanity, leaders in the struggle for liberation.

A major part of the challenge we must accept is that of redefining the functions and operations of all levels of American government, for the existing governing structures—from Washington to the smallest county—are obsolescent. That is part of the reason why nothing works and why corruption rages throughout public life. For white politics seeks not to serve but to dominate and manipulate.

We will have joined the true movement of history if at Gary we grasp the opportunity to press Man forward as the first consideration of politics. Here at Gary we are faithful to the best hopes of our fathers and our people if we move for nothing less than a politics which places community before individualism, love before sexual exploitation, a living environment before profits, peace before war, justice before unjust "order," and morality before expediency.

This is the society we need, but we delude ourselves here at Gary if we think that change can be achieved without organizing the power, the determined national Black power, which is necessary to insist upon such change, to create such change, to seize change.

Towards a Black Agenda

So when we turn to a Black Agenda for the seventies, we move in the truth of history, in the reality of the moment. We move recognizing that no one else is going to represent our interests but ourselves. *The society we seek cannot come unless Black people organize to advance its coming.* We lift up a Black Agenda recognizing that white America moves towards the abyss created by its own racist arrogance, misplaced priorities, rampant materialism, and ethical bankruptcy. Therefore, we are certain that the Agenda we now press for in Gary is not only for the future of Black humanity, but is probably the only way the rest of America can save itself from the harvest of its criminal past.

So, Brothers and Sisters of our developing Black nation, we now stand at Gary as people whose time has come. From every corner of Black America, from all liberation movements of the Third World, from the graves of our fathers and the coming world of our children, we are faced with a challenge and a call: Though the moment is perilous we must not despair. We must seize the time, for the time is ours.

We begin here and now in Gary. We begin with an independent Black political movement, an independent Black Political Agenda, an independent Black spirit. Nothing less will do. We must build for our people. We must build for our world. We stand on the edge of history. We cannot turn back.

Source: "The Gary Declaration," from "The National Black Political Agenda" (Washington, D.C.: National Black Political Convention, 1972).

SELECT BIBLIOGRAPHY:

Manning Marable, *Race, Reform and Rebellion: The Second Reconstruction in Black America, 1945–1990* (Jackson: University Press of Mississippi, 1991).
Komozi Woodard, *A Nation within a Nation: Amiri Baraka (LeRoi Jones) and Black Power Politics* (Chapel Hill: University of North Carolina Press, 1999).

⌒ 23 ⌒

"There Is No Revolution Without the People," *Amiri Baraka, 1972*

Amiri Baraka (1934–), born Everett Leroi Jones, was one of the most gifted and influential African-American artists and writers of the twentieth century. Born in Newark, New Jersey, he briefly attended Howard University. In the late 1950s, Baraka became part of the "Beat" literary and countercultural movement in Greenwich Village. Baraka soon established himself as a prominent poet, playwright, and music critic. With the rise of Black Power, Baraka transformed himself and his art, relocating first to Harlem and subsequently back to Newark. He was the central leader of the Black Arts Movement in the 1960s and 1970s, as well as a powerful voice for the politics of black cultural nationalism. Baraka was the founder of the Congress of African People in 1970, and one of the key organizers of the Gary Black Political Convention held in March 1972. In the mid-1970s,

Baraka experienced another ideological transformation, identifying himself with a Maoist interpretation of Marxism. In recent years, Baraka has continued to be highly productive, challenging institutions of power and privilege artistically and politically.

~

THE PAN-AFRICAN PARTY AND THE BLACK NATION

. . . The Congress of African People should be used not only as a formulator of the theoretical structure of such a party, but also as an initiating element and the actual beginning of the party itself. Even though we are representatives of many different, fragmented understandings of nationalist and quasi-nationalist, as well as varieties of Pan-Africanist, ideologies, still the Congress must begin to put the process of operational unity into motion, for Africans of any persuasion. That is, we must understand through achievement of practical projects that theoretical ideology must be subservient to the commonality of our experience, and by working together the gap between so-called ideologies will disappear and strong working relationships will develop among black people of seemingly widely divergent theoretical political ideologies.

Among three of the most common ideas relating to Nationalism and Pan-Africanism are what can be called:

1—Back to Africa (or Repatriation)
2—Separation (to another part of America)
3—Instant Revolution

We feel that repatriation people must understand and to a certain extent the separation (meaning to remove to Africa or another part of U.S.) people must understand that black people, circa 1970, ain't going anywhere. It is very difficult, as you well know, to get them to go up the street to a meeting. Garvey's thought is best interpreted as a movement to re-create the power of the African State, but finally, as a precursor to contemporary Pan-Africanism, along with brothers like Blyden, Padmore, Nkrumah and others.

To create Africa as a unified power base to demand respect for black people the world over—this is Pan-Africanism, because wherever we are we have a commonality based on our common struggle.

But "Back to Africa" for certain, in all our ways we can re-establish contact, since we understand our connection racially, historically, culturally, politically and emotionally. But it is necessary to raise the level of our people's political consciousness, so that all of us are aware of our commonality and readied to consciously wage a common struggle.

The South may be the great strategic battleground of the African in America, perhaps; it has the food and space to allow a people to survive against great odds, but whatever we would do with the people, with ourselves, actually we must first organize. And if the struggle is raised and of such a nature that we must all go into the South, or that we migrate constantly because of the mounting pressures that force people to that action, then it will still be a raised level of political consciousness that permits that move.

In the meantime, we must *separate the mind*, win the mind, wage the revolution to win the black man's mind so we will begin to move *together* as a people conscious that we are a people, struggling for national liberation. Separation must come *mentally* before any *physical* movement can begin—separation away from assimilation or brainwashing or subjugation by the mind of the white nation. And that separation from white control must be a prerequisite for the mental and emotional trip "Back to Africa," i.e., to realization that we are an African people, meaning black, of a common color, culture and consciousness. And whether we call ourselves Arabs, Saudis, Sudanese, Ethiopians, Egyptians, Kamites, Hamitic, we have only said black a number of different ways.

As nationalists and Pan-Africanists we must understand that we must move to have self-determination, self-sufficiency, self-respect and self-defense wherever we exist in large numbers—whether it is Chicago or Johannesburg. And the process of "gaining, maintaining and using power" is basically connected, whatever the specific local method.

A political party is an organ of consciousness. It must bring consciousness to black people in whatever context is necessary. All the different ways men express their lives must be understood and shaped by the party, which is the nation *becoming*. Whether it is religion or history or economics, social organization, arts, or the national ethos, and of course politics, the community organization of significance and potential in the struggle for national liberation will be able to make ideological input in *all the areas of black people's lives*, and hence give direction. A people's way of life gives them *Identity, Purpose and Direction. Identity:* who you are and therefore who your enemy is. *Purpose:* what is to be done in relationship to that identity, i.e., nation building. *Direction:* how it is to be done, by any means necessary. A black-skinned man living a cracker way of life has for all intents and purposes the identity, purpose and direction of a cracker. The political party must have an ideology that provides the mass of black people with alternatives to the *Identity, Purpose* and *Direction* of the white boy.

There is no revolution without the people. It is the organized community that is our only chance of self-defense or self-determination. The larger the community involvement, the quicker change will come. No so-called vanguard organization can bring a revolution, only the people themselves can do this. An organization moving without the community or alienating the community will soon be isolated, and very soon eliminated.

The United States is not China or nineteenth-century Russia, or even Cuba or Vietnam. It is the most highly industrialized nation ever to exist, a place where the slaves ride in Cadillacs and worship their master's image, as God. American power over Africans around the world must be broken before the other colonial powers are completely broken. Also, it should never be forgotten that we are a different people, want a different nation, than our slavemasters. In the Lenin revolution, the masses, the majority, theoretically[1] overthrew the minority, almost overnight. In America the "minority," i.e., oppressors, are the majority, or think they benefit by oppression.

We must think of our struggle as one for national liberation just as colored people are fighting wars of *national liberation* all around the world. We are fighting alien colonialists and enslavers, we are not making "revolution" against our own people. It is important to understand this. We must not be coopted by talk of instant revolution, into being the peasant army, the first slaughtered wave, for *another people's* rise to political power.

An organization for world African liberation, the developing prototype for the much-needed national/international political party, must be an organic manifestation of that people's determination to struggle. It must have an ideology based on its own history and ethos, on its traditions and the immediate contemporary context in which it finds itself.

We are not the Chinese. Mao raised an army, a state within a state, then separated from the main and waged war on it until it capitulated. (But they were *all* Chinese!) But even today the Chinese are just emerging from the almost constantly continuing *cultural revolution*, which seeks to win the minds of the people, so that the overall development of the Chinese nation can continue without being interrupted by externally and internally inspired coups such as toppled Kwame Nkrumah!

But the American situation offers only few usable parallels. We are controlled largely by the ideas of our oppressors. The political party must build *alternative* systems, values, institutions that will move us and raise us. How we build such alternative forms is what the Congress of African People is about.

It seems obvious that the only places the developing prototype vehicle-organization for the national/international African political party can exist healthily or with any relevance is in areas of the most intense black population, wherever in the world. In the U.S., the cities of major black population and the black intensely populated rural areas in the South must be the first areas of organization.

The community organization is always the kernel for the political party. Thus, because of a structure like the Congress of African People, it is possible to set up offices to begin organizing on the level of a political party more directly.

The areas of political power should be in the areas of organization: Public Office (elected or appointed)—the local C.A.P. offices must be prepared to conduct voter registration. Money can be raised for "voter registration" from national political parties and other groups interested in the black vote. The reason for voter registration drives is twofold; first, obviously to try to move on local political power and try to get hold of the goods and services that can accrue to even the smallest political office. These goods and services, and the monies available because of them, become the energizing elements of a growing local party structure. This is very important because in the rush of fantasy-producing revolutionary talk, it is not understood that whatever the level of the struggle, goods and services and, of course, finances will be needed.

The other obvious use of voter registration is voter education, which becomes *financed projects for raising the African political consciousness*. Getting into the homes of black people every day, organizing from strictly local, to regional, to state, while the C.A.P. superstructure works to create the national and international cohesion and development.

But the local C.A.P. organization must not only conduct voter registration, actually voter education, drives but also *run candidates* in all elections. Again, it is a basic level of political power! Goods, services, finances and two other important ingredients, the *gradual development of a sympathetic area in which to work*, and hopefully expand, and the *"legitimate" areas of political* (and gradually through an association with *actual*, rather than rhetorical) *power*.

When the most conscious black activists do not move in "electoral" politics, the area is left to stooges, thieves and toms. They become the local power figures and, like it or not, have some allegiance from the community, based on their ability to supply goods and services (e.g., jobs) and their association with legitimate areas of power. (When we say "legitimate," we mean association with symbols given legitimacy by white people, who, we should not forget, still control the symbolism and imagery in most black areas and, of course, the power which is the reason for the so-called legitimacy in the first place.) We must get beyond idle neophyte militancy to effective political organizing and build allegiance from our people by coopting all so-called or seemingly legitimate political processes in the black communities.

All political candidates *must* run against nationalists in the black community, and finally nationalists, Pan-Africanists, must organize sufficiently to win. The nationalist Pan-Africanist political party must begin to represent some degree of *actual* power, not just frustrated rhetoric, and the local political area is one clear way in which to move. It is one level of political consciousness, and the African community's mind must be moved *from where it is*. That is, you can talk about black mayors to black people with more credibility than you can talk about black nations, where we believe it must finally get. But you must build where you are, and through such building and continuous development through association and acquisition of some actual power, finally make talk of nation *legitimate*.

Community organization is necessary even if the base of any so-called community organization is the local party office. This means that the C.A.P. office must offer a wide divergence of community programs, or at least see to their initiation: health, welfare, education, arts, and any programs that are needed in black communities around the world. Free health-care programs in the community move black people into it who might never come into anything "political." As such, the community organization is a clear area of political power. Also any kind of antipoverty money must be controlled by the local party office. All monies used against black people must be diverted into the hands of the actual builders of the community and the money used to expand the development of Nationalist Pan-Africanist ideas. This means moving to control the local community organizations by merely mastering the numbers and nonsense (actually by being better organizers) that go with so-called democratic processes in the election of community organization officials, etc.

In other words, whatever funds or potential power is available in the African community must be controlled by the nationalist Pan-Africanist political party.

Alliances and coalitions are another area of political power. We can make alliances with all peoples of color (and certainly our brothers), developing as we said a certain level of operational unity, however diverse we might seem. But this whole area of political power must be approached formally and consistently as an important area of political organization. Alliances must be made with other black organizations, with black student groups, professionals, church, community, business men, politicians, but also Third World alliances, so that actually we will all be fighting the same battle at the same time to liberate ourselves, concentrating on our own areas while providing one another with a cross-fertilization of ideas and resources. The truly Pan-African international organization has yet to come into existence, and this is precisely what world Africans need—an international Pan-Africanist party capable of dealing not only with the international problems of Africans by means of international alliances and international exchange of information and resources, but also a party able to function on the lowest level: to win municipal elections. Many times bloods want to deal internationally or Pan-Africanistically and cannot even win a local councilmanic election. To do the large you must learn by doing the small. . . .

There is no instant revolution probable in America. What must be done by Africans in America and around the world is to organize actual systems capable of surviving America and its white domination of the world. "Murder mouthing" will only get you murdered. The military aspect of national liberation is important, make no mistake. But to speak of self-defense without being able to put it into practice is not revolutionary, it is slave-stupid.

The process of organizing in all the areas of political power is the one constant of our survival. All areas! But we must be really organized, really trained, and practice a value system that will constantly remind us who our real enemies are.

In the last area of political power, survival techniques are desperately needed, and these must be exchanged. Just as brothers in Angola need those Green Beret boots, we in the United States with access to those boots need things the Angolan troops possess. Where is the political structure to put this kind of exchange in motion?

We cannot be so ready to die that we forget that the purpose of our struggle is life! We must train to live, we must study and work to *live*. We must train in all the areas of gaining political power and become as skilled at voter registration and canvassing as we must become at disruption. But we must really become experts at both. We are not fighting a child, but the strongest nation on the planet. One reason it is the strongest is that many of our own brothers and sisters are part of its mind and muscle.

The first step is the creation of the organization (party) that can move on all levels, with a value system (morality) superior to the one that enslaves us. . . .

<hr />

"A Poem for Black Hearts"

> For Malcolm's eyes, when they broke
> the face of some dumb white man, For

Malcolm's hands raised to bless us
all black and strong in his image
of ourselves, For Malcolm's words
fire darts, the victor's tireless
thrusts, words hung above the world
change as it may, he said it, and
for this he was killed, for saying,
and feeling, and being///change, all
collected hot in his heart, For Malcolm's
heart, raising us above our filthy cities,
for his stride, and his beat, and his address
to the grey monsters of the world, For Malcolm's
pleas for your dignity, black men, for your life,
black man, for the filling of your minds
with righteousness, For all of him dead and
gone and vanished from us, and all of him which
clings to our speech black god of our time.
For all of him, and all of yourself, look up,
black man, quit stuttering and shuffling, look up,
black man, quit whining and stooping, for all of him,
For Great Malcolm a prince of the earth, let nothing in us rest
until we avenge ourselves for his death, stupid animals
that killed him, let us never breathe a pure breath if
we fail, and white men call us faggots till the end of
the earth.

1969

Note: 1. And what happened to the Asian masses in "Russia" because of the Russian revolution? Or the black masses in Cuba because of the Cuban revolution?

Sources: (1) Excerpt from Baraka, "The Pan-African Party and the Black Nation," in Robert Chrisman and Nathan Hare, *Pan-Africanism* (Indianapolis: Bobbs-Merrill, 1974), pp. 114–26; and (2) "A Poem for Black Hearts" reprinted by permission of Sterling Lord Literistic, as agents for the author. Copyright by Amiri Baraka.

SELECT BIBLIOGRAPHY:

Amiri Baraka, *The Autobiography of Leroi Jones* (Chicago: Lawrence Hill Books, 1997).
———, *Blues People: Negro Music in White America* (New York: Morrow, 1963).
———, *The Dead Lecturer* (New York: Grove Press, 1964).
———, *It's Nation Time* (Chicago: Third World Press, 1970).
Kimberly W. Benston, *Imamu Amiri Baraka (LeRoi Jones): A Collection of Critical Essays* (Englewood Cliffs, N.J.: Prentice-Hall, 1978).
William Harris, *The Poetry and Politics of Amiri Baraka: The Jazz Aesthetic* (Columbia: University of Missouri Press, 1985).
Werner Sollors, *Amiri Baraka/LeRoi Jones: The Quest for a "Populist Modernism"* (New York: Columbia University Press, 1978).
Jerry Gafio Watts, *Amiri Baraka: The Politics and Art of a Black Intellectual* (New York: New York University Press, 2001).

K. Komozi Woodard, *A Nation within a Nation: Amiri Baraka (Leroi Jones) and Black Power Politics* (Chapel Hill: University of North Carolina Press, 1999).

⌇ **24** ⌇

"My Sight Is Gone But My Vision Remains," *Henry Winston*

Henry Winston (1911–1986) played an important role in the Communist Party of the United States (CPUSA) and in the U.S. anti-imperialist movement. Winston grew up in Hattiesburg, Mississippi, and Kansas City, Missouri, and although his family's economic situation forced him to leave high school early, his precocious intellect and outstanding organizational skills were evident when he began working, at age nineteen, for Kansas City's Unemployed Council. Later, he joined the Young Communist League (YCL) and the CPUSA and by 1936 he was the YCL's national organizational secretary and a member of the CPUSA's central committee. During World War II Winston helped to enlist thousands of Communists into the armed forces, and he himself fought in Europe and earned an honorable discharge. In 1947, however, he was handed a five-year jail sentence under the Smith Act, which prohibited advocating Marxism. Winston first went underground, but later surrendered and served his time in the federal penitentiary in Terre Haute, Indiana. While incarcerated, Winston developed a brain tumor but prison officials refused to give him proper medical treatment, thereby causing him to go blind. In 1966 Winston was voted CPUSA chairman, and in this capacity helped defend Angela Davis, opposed the Vietnam War, and wrote two books, *Strategy for a Black Agenda* and *Class, Race, and Black Liberation*. Winston died in Moscow in 1986.

⌇

"ON RETURNING TO THE STRUGGLE"

Upon my release by Presidential order on Friday, June 30, from the U.S. Public Health Hospital at Staten Island after serving most of my time, I promised newspapermen answers to their questions later. I am glad to answer those questions today.

I am, of course, happy to be free and once more to be with my family and friends. My joy is marred, however, by the fact that my good comrade and friend, Gilbert Green, is still imprisoned in Leavenworth Prison, a victim, like myself and others, of a political frameup under the viciously undemocratic thought control law known as the Smith Act. He is due to be released July 29.

I want to thank publicly all those who fought so hard for my release—my family and my friends, and many, many others in various walks of life. I am deeply grateful to the many Negro leaders in the ministry and elsewhere, who spoke up for my freedom. I am deeply appreciative of the efforts of the Rev. Edler P. Hawkins, moderator of the Presbyterian Church, Roger Baldwin and Norman Thomas, who never permitted their political disagreement with me to stop their fight for justice and humanity.

My present plans call for some rest and then a lengthy visit with my mother and sisters who live in the Midwest.

Subsequently I plan to return to New York where I shall further retrain myself to activity under the handicap of blindness—a disability brought on by callous and criminal neglect of Federal officials. Had I been paroled in 1958, when I was eligible for parole, I would not have had to undergo surgery in 1960 and would not today be suffering from my affliction. Had prison officials and governmental authorities, even as late as 1959, heeded my complaints, I might not be blind today.

However, despite my handicap, I intend to resume my part in the fight for an America and a world of peace and security, free of poverty, disease, and race discrimination.

In prison I followed with special pride the accounts of the magnificent struggle of my people. I regard the Freedom Riders as heroes of our time who are making a contribution not only to the cause of Negro freedom but of democratic rights for all Americans.

I return from prison with the unshaken conviction that the people of our great land, Negro and white, need a Communist Party fighting for the unity of the people for peace, democracy, security, and socialism. I take my place in it again with deep pride. My sight is gone but my vision remains.

~~

"A LETTER TO MY BROTHERS AND SISTERS"

My Brothers and Sisters:

Pan-Africanism has become for us an all pervasive question. It has become the subject of discussion at the breakfast table, the lunch counter and at dinner. The fact is that wherever our folk gather—on the job, on the campus, the church and trade unions—Pan-Africanism is talked about. The public media have brought this subject into every home. The healthy feelings of our people for justice in the U.S.A. and in Africa are distorted. The purveyors of this concept wrongly pose the question. They consciously direct the discussion into one of Pan-Africanism versus Communism, Pan-Africanism and reforms in the imperialist system, one world government on the continent of Africa and many different variations of the same theme: not struggle against fascism, not struggle against classical colonialism or neo-colonialism, and certainly not revolutionary struggle to oust imperialism. They do everything to prevent our people from discerning the main enemy of freedom and the forces necessary to win that freedom.

These are times in which the souls of Black people are seriously being tried. Black men and women, and especially Black youth, rightly declare that a correct strategy must be put into operation to achieve unconditional equality in their economic, political and social life.

The kind of equality the Black people demand in the United States must embody in practice the actual exercise of that right which is characterized by opportunities fully realized, free of discrimination on the job, in housing, education, health, culture and unrestricted in their struggles in any area of democratic and social advancement.

Imperialist Oppression

Our people seek complete freedom from imperialist oppression for our brothers and sisters on the continent of Africa. The white imperialist minority from the United States, Britain, France, Portugal, Belgium and increasingly West Germany and Japan are doing everything to maintain imperialist domination. They strive to maintain classical colonialism like that in the Portuguese colonies. Powerful monopoly circles in the U.S. support the fascist imperialist regime of Vorster in South Africa, who keeps the Black majority of Africans under conditions of classical colonialism.

These same monopoly and banking interests are trying everything to halt and turn back the wheels of history in Africa, where our brothers and sisters in the majority of African countries have achieved political independence. They consciously organize military coups against any anti-imperialist tendencies in African governments. In the former Belgian Congo they murdered Patrice Lumumba and overthrew his anti-imperialist government.

Perhaps the prime example of imperialist machinations in this respect was the overthrow of the Nkrumah Government in Ghana. They did this at a time when Ghana had taken steps to strengthen its economic ties with socialist countries. If Ghana had been given a chance she would have been in a better position to advance to the goal of full economic independence. That would have meant the ouster of foreign imperialism from the soil of Ghana. The destiny of the country would have been fully in the hands of the Ghanaian people and self-determination would have existed in fact.

Imperialism cannot use the same old methods in dominating Africa. They are compelled to take into account the new world reality. What is this new world reality? It is the fact that in October 1917, the great October Socialist Revolution took place in Russia. This powerful development was a mighty blow against imperialism, and placed on a new level the struggle for emancipation not alone of the working class, peasants and oppressed nationalities of Russia. It was also an achievement which exerted and was increasingly to exert profound influence among the oppressed peoples on all continents, against imperialism. . . .

U.S. Imperialism and Africa

Let us ponder this fact. Let us look at U.S. imperialism and its relations with Africa. The dictates of the ruling class in the U.S. are followed; not only in spirit but to the letter, by the Nixon Administration. U.S. imperialism will step up all activities in the coming period to strengthen military; economic and political relations with Israel for basically three reasons: 1. To maintain imperialist control over oil in the Middle East. 2. To retard the movement for political and economic independence in the Arab countries. 3. To control the Mediterranean and use this part of the world as a base of operations against the national liberation movements and the Soviet Union.

U.S. imperialist policies also include economic and military support to the Portuguese colonial regime and the maintenance of classical colonialism in the colonies of Mozambique, Angola, Guinea-Bissau, etc. Of central importance for U.S. imperialism will be its growing economic and military support of the Vorster fascist regime in South Africa. The present government of South Africa is guided by the following: "A people that fails to preserve the purity of its racial blood thereby destroys the unity of the soul of the nation in all its manifestations." (From *Mein Kampf* by Adolf Hitler.)

This is the essence of apartheid. That is why the Black African majority in the country lives under conditions of classical colonialism. The imperialists in the U.S. will strive to use South Africa as a base to extend its control over the entire continent of Africa. The prototype for the whole of Black Africa would then become like the lot of the Black African majority in South Africa.

New Tactics of Oppression

Let us remember the following: Imperialism of yesterday needed missionaries to fasten classical colonialism upon the people of Africa. They fought among themselves for spheres of influence and simultaneously waged bloody and genocidal wars against the people of Africa, heroically fighting for their land and their independence. Black people in the U.S. have been fighting for their equality since 1619. We cannot forget that our brothers and sisters on the continent of Africa have been fighting for their freedom for hundreds of years earlier. They have come a long way in unison with all anti-imperialist forces. They see the possibilities of victory. They understand that neo-colonialism cannot use the same old deceit, that it must make certain concessions and find new kinds of "missionaries" if it is to defeat the cause of freedom and retain imperialist domination.

I would urge that you think deeply. It is important, if your hopes and dreams are to be realized. It is especially important to examine carefully every theory that is put forward and presented as being the answer. It seems to me that it is of great importance to study carefully the many different concepts of Pan-Africanism. It is necessary also to examine such propositions as "one world government," as well as the new call for mass migration, and the alleged panacea of an "All African People's Party."

This is very important because of the tremendous riches in Africa. Consider the following from *African Progress*, Magazine of African Political, Business and Economic Affairs, July–August, 1972: "Africa is the world's principal producer of gold, manganese, radium, scandium, cesium, corundum, graphite. It also dominates the world market in certain strategic minerals: cobalt, chrome, lithium, beryllium, tantalum, germanium, iron ore, coal, nickel, vanadium, copper, zinc, lead, bauxite, silver, platinum, columbium, cadmium, phosphates, tin, uranium, etc."

The fight for self-determination in each African country is a struggle to guarantee that these riches become the property of Africans, that the profits from these riches are not taken out of Africa and find their way into the banks of Wall Street, London, Paris and other imperialist states. The acquisition of these riches by Africans is the only way that guarantees can be established for Africans to be able to determine their own relationships to other states and determine their own destiny. The Africans fight for, and we must support them in this effort, to guarantee that science and technology be made available to Africans for the development of their countries.

It is against this effort of Africans that an expanding barrage of propaganda is being consciously developed to win our people to support neo-colonialism. Why is this so? If South Africa alone is considered, the following picture indicates the importance attached to South Africa by U.S. corporations. Some of them are: Ford, General Motors, Chrysler, Union Carbide, U.S. Steel, Standard Oil, Mobil, Esso, Chase Manhattan Bank, First National City Bank. *Fortune* magazine, in its July 1972 issue, notes that 292 corporations have established subsidiaries or affiliates there.

Black folk well know the discriminatory policies of these firms towards our people in the U.S. It is clear that neo-colonialism in South Africa can only be a support to imperialist oppression of the Black majority.

African Liberation and the U.S.A.

The national liberation movement of South Africa tells us that imperialism finds the road against them easier to travel if their reactionary policies can be cloaked and brought to them by successful Black men and women. They ask us not to fall for this kind of trap. They appeal to us to do all in our power to bring about sanctions against South Africa. Such international support will help them. If this is done the possibilities exist for ending colonial rule in South Africa and helping this Black majority to take its rightful place as the leading force in the nation.

Let us therefore examine every program that is put forward from the standpoint of whether it assists this kind of struggle. If it does, it is a contribution to the continent-wide struggle against imperialism. What then may be some points for guidance? They can be summarized as follows:

1. No economic, political or military relations whatsoever with the Vorster regime in the Republic of South Africa.

2. Congress shall tax and the Treasury shall collect taxes on all profits made in South Africa at maximum rates without deductions for local taxes paid.

3. The Overseas Private Investment Corporation shall refuse to insure any new investments in South Africa and cancel all outstanding insurance on investments in the Republic of South Africa.

4. The President shall instruct the Export-Import Bank and all other U.S. credit agencies to refuse all credits for business with the Republic of South Africa and instruct U.S. representatives of international lending agencies to oppose all credits to the Republic of South Africa or companies operating therein.

5. The State Department shall denounce all existing investment, trade and commercial treaties with the Union of South Africa and the President shall remove most favored nation treatment from South African goods.

6. The immediate withdrawal of the sugar quota to the Republic of South Africa.

I think that the reaction among African leaders on the firing line will be of benefit. You will find in the pages of this booklet the greetings of many of them to the Twenty-Fourth Congress of the Communist Party of the Soviet Union, held in March–April, 1971.

Their views will be extremely helpful in understanding why we must give all-out support to their liberation struggles.

May I extend to you a firm handshake in the struggle to achieve victory for our people in the struggle against imperialism, in the U.S.A., in Africa, and throughout the world.

Sincerely,
Henry Winston
National Chairman, C.P.U.S.A.

Sources: (1) "On Returning to the Struggle" published with permission from *Political Affairs* 40, no. 8 (August 1961), pp. 1–2; and (2) excerpt from "A Letter to my Brothers and Sisters" with permission from *Political Affairs* 52, no. 2 (February 1973), pp. 13–21.

SELECT BIBLIOGRAPHY:

Gilbert Green, *Cold War Fugitive: A Personal Story of the McCarthy Years* (New York: International Publishers, 1984).

Henry Winston, *Strategy for a Black Agenda: A Critique of New Theories of Liberation in the United States and Africa* (New York: International Publishers, 1973).

———, *Class, Race, and Black Liberation* (New York: International Publishers, 1977).

Nikolai Mostovets, *Henry Winston, Profile of a U.S. Communist* (Moscow: Progress Publishers, 1983).

ADDITIONAL RESOURCES:

Raymond Arsenault, *Freedom Riders: 1961 and the Struggle for Racial Justice, Pivotal Moments in American History* (Oxford: Oxford University Press, 2006).

Kevin A. Beauchamp, *The Untold Story of Emmett Louis Till*, New York: Thinkfilm 2005. DVD Video.

Winifred Breines, *The Trouble between Us: An Uneasy History of White and Black Women in the Feminist Movement* (Oxford: Oxford University Press, 2006).

"The Civil Rights in Mississippi Digital Archive," www.lib.usm.edu/legacy/spcol/crda/.

C-SPAN; National Cable Satellite Corp.; organized by the Georgetown University African American Studies Program; cosponsored by the Georgetown University Women's Center,

Black Women in the Civil Rights Movement, West Lafayette: C-SPAN Archives, 2006. DVD Video.

Vicki L. Crawford, Jacqueline Anne Rouse, and Barbara Woods, eds., *Women in the Civil Rights Movement: Trailblazers and Torchbearers, 1941–1965*. 1st pbk ed., Blacks in the Diaspora (Bloomington: Indiana University Press, 1993).

Eddie S. Glaude, ed., *Is It Nation Time?: Contemporary Essays on Black Power and Black Nationalism* (Chicago: University of Chicago Press, 2002).

Horace Huntley and David Montgomery, eds., *Black Workers' Struggle for Equality in Birmingham, The Working Class in American History* (Urbana: University of Illinois Press, 2007).

Gilbert Jonas and with a forward by Julian Bond, *Freedom's Sword: The NAACP and the Struggle against Racism in America, 1909–1969* (London: Routledge, 2007).

Michael J. Klarman, *From Jim Crow to Civil Rights : The Supreme Court and the Struggle for Racial Equality* (Oxford; New York: Oxford University Press, 2004).

"The Malcolm X Project at Columbia University," www.columbia.edu/cu/ccbh/mxp/courses .html.

Charles M. Payne, *I've Got the Light of Freedom: The Organizing Tradition and the Mississippi Freedom Struggle* (Berkeley: University of California Press, 2007).

THE FUTURE IN THE PRESENT: CONTEMPORARY AFRICAN-AMERICAN THOUGHT, 1975 TO THE PRESENT

INTRODUCTION

The successes of the modern Black Freedom Movement were largely accomplished by the existence of a strong black working class. In 1970, for example, almost 40 percent of all African Americans in the paid labor force were employed in blue-collar jobs, many in heavy industries such as steel, automobile production, food and tobacco manufacturing, and electrical and nonelectrical machinery. Most of these jobs were unionized, which provided pensions and healthcare for workers and their families. The bulk of the well-paid workers were located in the industrial heartland of the U.S. Midwest and Northeast. Blacks had also significantly narrowed the historic wage gap they experienced with whites, as their percentage of medium incomes compared to white incomes rose from about 50 percent in 1958 to 63 percent in 1973. For African Americans with college degrees, under age thirty-five, the historic income gap between blacks and whites virtually disappeared. The number of African Americans attending colleges and professional schools soared, from about 400,000 in 1970 to 1.1 million only 10 years later. Policies such as affirmative action, combined with the enforcement of equal opportunity laws established by the federal government, directly contributed to the creation of the modern black middle class.

The economic foundations for black advancement began to change in the 1970s, due to the destructive processes of what economists termed "deindustrialization." Between 1973 and 1980, over 4 million jobs disappeared in the United States, as hundreds of American corporations moved their operations outside the country. New York City alone lost 40,000 to 50,000 jobs in the apparel and textile industries. Corporations increasingly divested their profits from U.S.-based subsidiaries and reinvested in operations abroad. In the 1970s, over 30 million total jobs were eliminated through factory closings, relocations, and then phased elimination of operations. The shrinking of U.S.-based industries had a deep impact on labor unions, as the percentage of union members within the American labor force decreased by half in only two decades. Hardest hit were African-American blue-collar workers, because in 1983, over 27 percent of all blacks in the U.S. labor force were union members, a significantly higher percentage than for white workers.

Concurrent with the restructuring of the capitalist economy was a worldwide trend to dismantle the welfare state. Beginning with the 1979 election of Margaret Thatcher in the United Kingdom and the triumph of mass conservation in the United States under Ronald Reagan the following year, an antistalist philosophy began to exert hegemony affecting the ways in which governments functioned all over the world. With the shift to the right, the government significantly reduced or eliminated support for many of the liberal welfare programs that had been instituted during the previous half-century: public housing, public education, job training, food stamps and child nutrition, and support for the indigent and disabled. As President Reagan succinctly put the matter, government was "not the solution, government was the problem." The difficulty confronting black Americans here was twofold. Historically, for all of its limitations, as a result of mass pressure the federal government has been the chief public guarantor of civil rights and has at times even forced the abolition of the most extreme forms of racial domination; for example, the adoption of the Thirteenth Amendment to the Constitution outlawing slavery and the passage of the Civil Rights Act and Voting Rights Act ending Jim Crow segregation. Reducing federal power and bringing about a return to "states rights" were, at face value, potentially damaging to blacks' interests. Secondly, African Americans in the 1980s were heavily overrepresented as employees of the public sector. Reducing the size of the state inevitably would mean that African Americans would experience significantly higher levels of unemployment. Black women were especially vulnerable to the conservative assault on the public sector. Eighty-five percent of all professional African-American women by the early 1990s, for example, worked in three major industries dominated by government and nonprofit employment: social services, health care, and education.

Another factor that had an impact on black politics was the collapse of the Soviet Union and the international Communist movement during 1989–1991. Since the end of World War II, international politics had been defined by the Cold War struggle between the United States and the Soviet Union. The dissolution of the Soviet model instantly meant that the political space for a Third World—those non-Western states strategically positioned between capitalism and communism—also ceased to exist. In the 1980s the United States invaded Grenada and installed its own puppet regime, and the leftist Sandinistas lost power in Nicaragua. By the early 1990s, Asian, African, and Caribbean states with long histories of socialist politics were pressured to adopt "neoliberal," market-oriented policies and austerity measures. Social-democratic parties worldwide shifted significantly to the right. Although no widespread movement for communism or socialism existed in the United States, these global political developments were profoundly felt within African-American politics. With few models to point to, some argued that socialism, however defined, no longer represented a viable alternative to capitalism. If black people had any future, it was argued, it was to be found in the capitalist marketplace. The traditional discourse of the black left—"socialism," "anti-imperialism," "cooperative economics"— began to lose ground to the gospel of wealth, entrepreneurship, and black capitalism. The conservative ideology of Booker T. Washington resurfaced in the age of cyberspace.

The erosion of the public sector and the loss of millions of urban jobs contributed to a significant increase in class stratification within the national black community. The African-American community was overwhelmingly working class in composition in the 1970s. By the late 1990s, the socioeconomic profile of black America had changed considerably. About 51 percent of all black employees sixteen years old and over were classified as white-collar workers. Approximately 60 percent of these were white-collar sales and clerical personnel; many in this group were nonunion workers with limited or nonexistent benefits and wages. However, another 20 percent of the black labor force, nearly 3 million workers, was classified as professional and technical workers and administrators. The percentage of blue-collar workers had declined to 28 percent of the black labor force. Black farm laborers, farmers, and agricultural managers, who in 1940 had represented one-third of the entire black workforce, had virtually disappeared, with only about 80,000 jobs remaining. During this period, the black business sector had mushroomed.

By 1992 the number of black-owned businesses had grown to 621,000. The number of black-owned real estate, insurance, and financial lending companies had quadrupled in only fifteen years, and this sector's total gross receipts had increased sixfold. By the late 1990s, a small number of African-American executives had become chief executive officers and presidents of major corporations, such as Time Warner and American Express. An even smaller number of black celebrities—such as television personalities Oprah Winfrey and Bill Cosby, pop star Michael Jackson, and superstar athletes such as golfer Tiger Woods, and basketball stars Michael Jordan and Earvin "Magic" Johnson—were each worth hundreds of millions of dollars. For the first time in U.S. history, a "black bourgeoisie" had come to exist.

These economic changes had profound consequences for African Americans. Deprived of their tax revenues from industries and manufacturing companies, city governments reduced expenditures for public institutions of all kinds—schools, hospitals, parks, libraries, public universities, and public housing. With the election of Ronald Reagan as president in 1980, the new conservative administration quickly moved to reduce federal government spending on urban development and social services. The Reagan administration terminated the Comprehensive Employment and Training Act program, a successful job training program that had been funded in 1982 at $3.1 billion; eliminated $2 billion from the federal food stamps program; reduced federal support for child nutrition programs by $1.7 billion over a two-year period; and closed down the Neighborhood Self Help and Planning Assistance programs, which provided technical and financial help to inner cities. In the first year of the Reagan administration, the real median income of all black families fell by 5.2 percent.

Also in the 1980s, a strong white backlash against civil rights expressed itself in opposition to school desegregation in the North and growing hostility to increased racial integration in higher education and professional occupations through affirmative action. Millions of white Americans became convinced that "too much" had been given to blacks in recent years. Middle-class African Americans also encountered more subtle, yet unmistakable, patterns of racial discrimination that severely restricted their upward mobility. Sociologist Lawrence Bobo has described this racial ceiling on group advancement as "laissez faire racism." The examples of "laissez faire racism," which have been documented by numerous studies, are almost endless: white car dealerships that charge blacks hundreds of dollars more for automobiles than they do whites; hospitals that routinely provide substandard treatment for minorities; insurance companies that systematically charge black consumers higher rates than whites to insure homes of identical market value; grocery store chains that transport older produce from white suburban shopping-mall markets to groceries in predominantly black communities; the denial of employment opportunities to blacks at senior levels of management and administration in large companies and institutions.

Many middle-class blacks, confronted with the steady deterioration of public services, schools, and the elimination of jobs in central cities, relocated to the suburbs. However, because white real estate firms, banks, and financial lending institutions continued informal policies of residential discrimination, many upper- to middle-income blacks found themselves moving from segregated ghettoes to racially segregated suburbs or planned communities. Black working-class families without the material resources or credit to purchase homes outside economically depressed areas found themselves living in what, at times, had become almost urban wastelands.

In huge districts of America's major cities, neighborhoods had become desperately poor—Chicago's South Side, East New York in Brooklyn, the South Bronx, South Central Los Angeles, East Oakland, and nearly all of Detroit. Families attempting to upgrade their residences or start businesses in these neighborhoods were forced to rely on "predatory lenders," finance companies charging outrageously high interest rates on borrowed money. In such inner city communities, businesses of nearly every type, other than personal services such as restaurants, barber shops, beauty salons, and funeral homes largely disappeared. By the 1990s in many inner cities, between one-third to one-half of a neighborhood's total adult population was no longer in the paid labor force. Millions survived in the informal economy, generating a subsistence income through activities as diverse as braiding hair, childcare, collecting and selling recyclable bottles and cans, catering food, auto repair, moving, producing and selling crafts, and so on. For many who had once held stable blue-color jobs, low-wage service jobs, such as in the fast-food industry, were among the few alternatives.

Such widespread poverty, such intense patterns of unemployment, hunger and homelessness, as well as the growth of global markets in drugs and arms, fostered the trafficking in illegal drugs. In the early 1980s, a new addictive product, "crack," a rock-type of cocaine, was introduced into inner-city neighborhoods. Unlike powdered cocaine, the fashionable drug of choice of the wealthy, crack was very inexpensive, readily available, and highly addictive. Within a few years, several hundred thousand African Americans had become addicted to crack, and relatively few drug treatment centers were available. With the decline in employment and educational opportunities, some young people saw selling drugs as the only way to make a decent income, and violence, once relatively rare in black working-class communities, increased significantly. Although several inner-city communities became the marketplace for the lucrative international traffic in illegal substances, the overwhelming bulk of the profits were reaped by those outside these communities, such as international crime cartels and the banks that launder their money. Inner-city communities became the targets of police sweeps and searches. Though a minority of young men were actively involved in criminal activities connected with the drug traffic, virtually all black male youth were subject to being stigmatized as criminals by the police and media.

Federal and state governments responded by making the penalties for drug sale and possession more severe, by eliminating parole, and by constructing a vast network of new prisons. Legislatures passed new mandatory minimum sentencing laws, requiring convicted felons to serve lengthy prison terms before becoming eligible for release. Juveniles were increasingly treated as adults, and were subjected to many of the same penalties. Developments in New York State during these years were typical of what occurred throughout the nation. Between 1817 and 1981, the state had constructed thirty-three prisons; between 1981 and 1999, it built thirty-eight new correctional facilities. New York's prison population grew in two decades from 13,500 to 74,000.

Throughout the country, the total population of prisoners reached 650,000 in 1983, 1 million in 1990, and 2 million by 2001. One-half of these prisoners were African Americans. By 2000, one-third of all black males in their twenties were under the control of the criminal justice system, either in prison or jail, on parole, probation, or awaiting trial. The major reason for this disproportion in incarceration was the stark racism that pervaded the criminal justice system. Though African Americans in 2002 constituted approximately 14 percent of all illegal drug users, they comprised approximately one-third of all drug arrests and over 50 percent of all drug convictions in federal and state courts. The socioeconomic and political consequences of mass incarceration for the black community have been profound. Several million black households have been destroyed; tens of thousands of black children separated from their parents and raised in foster care. In seven states as of 2005, convicted felons lost the right to vote for life, and as a result, by 2000 over 1.4 million African Americans had been permanently disenfranchised. For several million blacks with criminal records, better paying jobs were no longer available even years after their release and rehabilitation. Inside prisons, however, incarcerated African Americans organized a wide variety of resistance activities (document 15).

Despite these unprecedented challenges, African Americans in the 1980s collectively initiated a series of highly successful resistance movements. In electoral politics at the local level, the most significant of these was represented by Harold

Washington. For nearly fifty years the Cook County Democratic Party machine had controlled municipal government in Chicago by manipulating votes and using corrupt patronage and graft. Under Chicago political boss Mayor Richard Daley the black community was severely disadvantaged; schools were underfunded and public services were unequally distributed. In 1982 a coalition of largely black community organizations convinced Congressman Washington to challenge the Democratic machine. Washington forged an unprecedented coalition of blacks, Latinos, labor, progressive whites, and other constituencies, sometimes referred to as a "rainbow coalition," and, in a three-way race, Washington defeated incumbent mayor Jane Byrne, and Richard M. Daley, the son of the former mayor, to win the Democratic Party's nomination. In the general election on April 12, 1983, Washington defeated Republican challenger Bernard Upton to become the first African-American mayor of Chicago (see document 3). As mayor, Washington tried to eliminate corruption, made city government more transparent, forged coalitions with neighborhood groups, expanded city services in minority neighborhoods, and restored the city's financial health through a property tax increase. Reelected in 1987, Washington died of a heart attack on November 25 of that same year.

The advances achieved by politicians like Washington pressured local and national politics to give greater priority to African-American issues, and set the stage for the 1984 presidential campaign of Jesse Jackson. Becoming involved in the civil rights movement first through CORE, Jackson had joined the SCLC and soon became a protégé of Dr. Martin Luther King Jr. After King's assassination, Jackson launched Operation PUSH (People United to Save Humanity), which created "corporate covenants" and other business-related partnerships that produced jobs and expanded black entrepreneurship.

In 1983, Jackson announced his candidacy for the Democratic Party's presidential nomination. Many black elected officials and prominent civil rights leaders, including Coretta Scott King and Andrew Young, opposed Jackson's candidacy. However, he successfully built an interracial coalition similar to Harold Washington's, which included blacks, Latinos, lesbians and gays, environmentalists, peace activists, progressives from organized labor, and many others. In 1984, Jackson lost the three-way Democratic primary to Walter F. Mondale, but his "Rainbow Coalition" won him 3.5 million popular votes, making him the first serious African-American challenger for the presidency.

The success of Jackson's 1984 presidential campaign created widespread support for his second effort to capture the Democratic Party's nomination four years later. Jackson's Rainbow Coalition called for federal initiatives to address unemployment, health, education, housing, and urban problems. The campaign mobilized an unprecedented interracial coalition and prompted hundreds of thousands of new black voters to register. Jackson received over 7 million popular votes—from 4 million African Americans and an additional 3 million whites, Asians, and Latinos, and won a series of primary contests. Jackson narrowly lost the nomination, however, to Massachusetts Governor Michael Dukakis, who was subsequently defeated in the general election by Republican candidate George H. W. Bush (document 7).

Another issue central to black activism in the 1980s and early 1990s was South Africa. The Reagan administration initiated a policy of "constructive engagement" with the apartheid regime of South Africa, encouraging American investment in the country, thus providing economic support for the white-minority state. This prompted demonstrations against apartheid and U.S. investment in South Africa. Following Reagan's reelection in 1984, several groups of black progressive— nationalists, integrationists, and transformationalists—mapped out strategies to attack the administration's links with apartheid South Africa. The best known of these groups was led by Randall Robinson, executive director of TransAfrica; Mary Frances Berry, a civil rights commissioner; and District of Columbia congressman Walter Fauntroy. The coalition leaders staged a small, symbolic demonstration in front of the South African embassy in late November 1984, and they were "pleasantly surprised" when officials panicked and called the police. Their arrests sparked hundreds of nonviolent demonstrations across the United States. Within two weeks, protests involving hundreds of thousands of people were staged at South African consulates in more than one dozen cities, including Salt Lake City, Boston, Chicago, and Houston (see document 6).

On college campuses, hundreds of thousands of students demonstrated against universities and corporations that did business inside South Africa. Divestment legislation amounting to $400 million in public funds was secured in Massachusetts, Connecticut, Michigan, Maryland, Philadelphia, and a dozen other smaller cities in 1985. Jesse Jackson challenged the Democratic leadership to demand immediate freedom for Nelson Mandela, the political spokesperson for the African National Congress (ANC) and future South African president, who had been imprisoned on Robben's Island for over two decades. Other black congressmen pressured for the release of other political prisoners as well.

Successful models of black political resistance also emerged from African-American popular culture. In the 1970s a new urban-based cultural movement popularly termed hip-hop emerged. The core elements of hip-hop culture include graffiti, break dancing, emceeing, deejaying, and rap music, which is based on the spoken word and its interplay with the musical beat. To many, rap's jarring style and frequent use of profanity was difficult to understand. However, for many young blacks and Latinos born after the civil rights and Black Power period, hip-hop embodied their own feelings and expressions about the nature of contemporary society. Created in the context of poverty, high unemployment, and the drug epidemic in inner cities, rap was a means through which to give voice to a generation's critique of their own marginalization from mainstream society. Militant, edgy, and radical in their lyrics, hip-hop artists used their records as a platform to address the inequities of the establishment. Such artists as Afrika Bambataa and the Zulu Nation, Grandmaster Flash and the Furious Five, who were later termed "old school rap" artists, were unscrupulously exploited by managers and music business executives. In 1982, twenty-two-year-old rapper Chuck

D. (Clareton Ridenhower) formed the group Public Enemy, which signed a contract with Def Jam Records. Public Enemy's second album, *It Takes a Nation of Millions to Hold Us Back*, was a bold and provocative statement of revolutionary politics.

In the 1990s, progressive artists such as Public Enemy, KRS One, a Tribe Called Quest, and Mos Def spoke about AIDS/HIV awareness, called for an end to black-on-black violence, encouraged voter registration, and campaigned against budget cuts in public schools. Black female rap artists such as Sister Souljah, Salt-n-Pepa, and Queen Latifah provided powerful images of self-confidence and activism for millions of young African-American women. Successful hip-hop entrepreneur Russell Simmons, cofounder of Def Jam records, initiated campaigns to promote voting among black youth and to oppose the privatization of public schools and a public educational effort to debate the issue of "black reparations," the question of whether African Americans should finally be compensated for centuries of enslavement and Jim Crow segregation (document 18).

By the mid-1990s, in response to the escalating prison industrial complex and epidemic of police brutality, many African Americans concluded that a new kind of social protest was necessary, to promote black pride, personal responsibility, and collective empowerment. These efforts crystallized in 1994–1995 around Nation of Islam leader Louis Farrakhan's call for a "Million Man March." On October 16, 1995, approximately one million participants poured into the Washington Mall from all over the United States. It was without question the largest single gathering of black people in U.S. history. Studies indicated that the participants were mostly of the middle class, older, and had a proportionally higher level of education than black men in general. The march was, for many, an emotional event that symbolized the coming together of black men across generations, rededicated to a common social and political project of atonement, personal responsibility, and collective empowerment. Speakers who ranged from religious leaders to community activists, addressed issues of education, racism, welfare, and other community issues. This perhaps explains the popular slogan in support of the mobilization: "Farrakhan may have called the March, but the March belongs to us (document 13)."

Black feminists condemned the patriarchy and homophobia prevalent in much of the mobilization's literature. Others praised the objective of the March but criticized Farrakhan for anti-Semitism and racism. Still others objected to the emphasis on "atonement" at a time when the Republican-controlled Congress was eliminating programs designed to help the black community. Nevertheless, it had an important impact on raising awareness about the continued struggle against structural inequalities. Within the next year, over 1.5 million additional black men had registered to vote.

As the conservative nationalists briefly took center stage, the revolutionary nationalists had become largely marginalized. With the government-sponsored destruction of the Black Panthers and the demise of radical groups such as the League of Revolutionary Black Workers, the revolutionary nationalists sought to reconstitute themselves as a viable political force. In 1980, two progressive nationalist groups emerged: in Brooklyn, the National Black United Front (NBLU), led by the Reverend Herbert Daughtry, and in Philadelphia, the National Black Independent Political Party (NBIPP), which included activists Ronald Daniels and Benjamin Chavis. After attracting several thousand supporters but only achieving modest success, NBIPP disappeared in the mid-1980s, and NBUF largely declined as a political force several years later. The two most prominent revolutionary nationalists in this period were political prisoners who had become internationally known. Assata Shakur, a former activist in the Black Panther Party, escaped from prison and in the early 1980s found political asylum in Cuba. Her moving portrait of the plight of African-American women prisoners presented here gives some insights into her radical political philosophy (document 2).

America's most celebrated and controversial prisoner on death row in the 1990s was unquestionably Mumia Abu-Jamal. Also a former member of the Black Panther Party, Jamal was convicted of the murder of a Philadelphia police officer. Despite substantial evidence of witness tampering and illegal activities by prosecutors and police, Jamal was denied a new trial. Yet from the isolation of his prison cell on death row, Jamal's articulate voice and powerful prose found an international audience (document 14).

Some of the most powerful and original critiques of racialized inequality during these years were produced by African-American feminists. The Combahee River Collective statement, originally written in the spring of 1977, reflected the core ideas behind this new feminist movement. The statement envisioned a politics of black liberation that simultaneously challenged sexism, homophobia, racism, and class exploitation at every level of society (document 1). The Combahee River Collective Statement was soon followed by a series of black feminist theoretical works and collections of social essays that powerfully reshaped the entire black left. Some of the major works included Michele Wallace's *Black Macho and the Myth of the Superwoman*, bell hooks's *Ain't I a Woman* and *Feminist Theory: From Margin to Center* (see document 5), Patricia Hill Collins's *Black Feminist Thought*, Barbara Smith's wonderfully titled anthology, *All the Women Are White, All the Blacks are Men, But Some of Us Are Brave: Black Women's Studies*, and Angela Davis's *Women, Race and Class*. One of the most popular black feminist intellectuals was Audre Lorde. A lesbian, feminist, and revolutionary, Lorde wrote poetry and social essays with such grace and clarity that she motivated and appealed to very diverse audiences (document 4). The development of black feminist thought in universities was paralleled by the growth of black women's leadership in thousands of community-based, grassroots-oriented organizations at the neighborhood level throughout the United States.

The transformationist, black-radical tradition had not disappeared, despite the political defeats and losses in previous years. It has been evident in the militant role played by African-American workers in bringing about significant changes in the AFL-CIO, as well as in the successful struggle for a free South Africa. In the late 1990s, it attempted to reconstitute itself as a vital political force once again. In the aftermath of the Million Man March, a small group of African-American political activists, intellectuals, and leaders from labor, lesbian-gay, feminist, revolutionary nationalist, and Marxist organizations initiated a call for a Black Radical Congress (BRC), a national gathering of black progressive forces. At the Congress, which was held in Chicago on June 19–21, 1998, more than 2,000 activists who self-identified with radical anticapitalist politics came together. A nationwide network of BRC local organizing committees was formed, involving members in various local and national campaigns against police brutality, for full employment, and in efforts to halt the execution of Mumia Abu-Jamal. The BRC's "Call to the Congress," "Principles of Unity," and "Freedom Agenda" presented the basic political beliefs that could unify a broadly diverse group of activists (document 16).

As the twenty-first century dawned, American politics took a sharp turn to the right with two events: the narrow electoral victory of Republican George W. Bush as president in 2000 (see document 17), and the terrorist attacks on the World Trade Center in New York City and the Pentagon, on September 11, 2001 (see document 20). The attacks on 9/11 prompted the U.S. government to pass laws severely restricting civil liberties and constitutional rights. Many Americans who were of Middle Eastern descent, or were identified as Muslims, were subjected to harassment, surveillance, and even arrest. As the United States launched its military invasion of Iraq in 2003, African-American opposition quickly became overwhelming (document 20). In terms of racial relations, the campaign in Iraq provoked waves of American xenophobia and intolerance. The "war on terror" had created in the United States a new "Racialized Other"—who was Muslim or Middle Eastern in background.

As many African Americans fought to end U.S. military involvement in Iraq and to remove the Republican-controlled Congress, there continued to be reminders that the United States remained a structurally racist society. The most vivid example of this was provided by the Hurricane Katrina crisis of August–September 2005. The areas most devastated by Hurricane Katrina were Louisiana, Mississippi, and southwestern Alabama. By any standard, in terms of tens of billions of dollars in property damage and over one thousand lives lost, it was the largest natural disaster in U.S. history. The most heavily damaged major urban center that the storm affected was New Orleans, a city with an unrivaled historical tradition of black music and culture.

After the disaster struck New Orleans, President George W. Bush defensively argued that no one could have possibly anticipated the flooding experienced throughout much of the city, despite the fact that a number of scientists and investigative reporters had, for years, predicted that such a catastrophe was inevitable. But what made the New Orleans tragedy an "unnatural disaster" was the federal government's gross incompetence and indifference in taking the necessary measures to preserve the lives and property of hundreds of thousands of its citizens.

Even before Hurricane Katrina struck, it was obvious that the overwhelming majority of New Orleans residents who would be trapped inside the city to face the deluge would be poor and working-class African Americans, who comprised nearly 70 percent of the city's population. As the levees collapsed and the city's predominantly black Ninth Ward flooded, thousands of evacuees were herded into the Superdome and Convention Center, where they were forced to endure days without toilets and running water, food, electricity, and medical help. Hundreds of black evacuees seeking escape on a bridge across the Mississippi River were confronted and forcibly pushed back into the city. Much of the media coverage cruelly manipulated racist stereotypes in its reports. The barrage of racialized images of a terrorized crime-engulfed city prompted hundreds of white ambulance drivers and emergency personnel to refuse to enter the New Orleans disaster zone. Television reports locally and nationally quickly proliferated false exposés about "babies in the Convention Center who got their throats cut" and "armed hordes" hijacking ambulances and trucks.

Nationally, most African-American leaders, public officials, and intellectuals were overwhelmed and outraged by the flood of racist stereotypes in the media, and their government's appalling inaction in the rescuing of poor black people. African Americans were stunned and perplexed by white America's general apathy and denial about the racial implications of the Katrina catastrophe. But the racial stigmatization of New Orleans's outcasts forced many African Americans to ponder whether their government and white institutions had become incapable of expressing true compassion for the suffering of their people (document 23).

In 2007–2008, the presidential campaign of Democratic Illinois senator Barack Obama represented one of the innovative challenges by people of African descent to the structure of white privilege and power in America. Unlike Jackson's protest-oriented presidential campaigns of 1984 and 1988, the Obama campaign was from the beginning both pragmatic and ideologically liberal-progressive. Along with a new generation of African-American leaders—such as Massachusetts governor Deval Patrick and Newark, New Jersey, mayor Corey Booker—Obama espoused a race-neutral politics, minimizing discussions about blacks' grievances while emphasizing the common ground shared by Americans regardless of race, ethnicity, class, or gender. Despite Obama's relatively moderate politics, many conservative pundits sought to exploit Islamophobia and racial bigotry from the beginning of his campaign. Because Obama's father had been a Kenyan of Muslim descent, critics falsely charged that Obama, a Christian, was secretly a Muslim, and even a possible terrorist. Another controversy that nearly destroyed Obama's campaign was the provocative statements of the candidate's former pastor, the Reverend Jeremiah Wright. Obama's response to the Wright controversy was a brilliant address, "A More Perfect Union," which critics praised as the most powerful and thoughtful statement about the meaning of race in American life since Dr. Martin Luther King Jr.'s, "I Have A Dream" speech, delivered at the March on Washington, D.C. (document 25).

Defeating his major opponent, New York senator Hillary Rodham Clinton, Obama captured the Democratic Party's presidential nomination in August 2008.

Many still doubted the ability of an African American to be elected to the U.S. presidency, citing previous gubernatorial and mayoral elections in which African-American candidates received far fewer votes from whites than voter surveys had predicted. However, on November 4, 2008, the U.S. electorate made history by electing the first African American, Barack Obama, as the nation's chief executive. Winning with a margin of nearly 53 percent—the largest vote of any Democratic presidential candidate since Lyndon Johnson in 1964—Obama's triumph was produced by a combination of old-fashioned coalition building and new age technology. He captured between 95 and 97 percent of all African-American voters, as well as a substantial share of the vote from other racialized minorities, including 67 percent of Latinos and 62 percent of Asian Americans. Jewish voters overwhelmingly backed Obama with 78 percent of their votes. The charismatic candidate won 62 percent from young voters (ages 18–29) and 58 percent from women voters. Supported by the major trade unions, Obama also appealed as well to more educated affluent voters. He won a majority of voters earning over $250,000 annually and held an 18-point margin over his Republican opponent, senator John McCain, among voters with advanced academic and professional degrees. Obama's electoral victory sparked hundreds, and probably thousands, of spontaneous celebrations and street parties across the country.

Less widely recognized was that a crucial dimension of Obama's victory was his ability to appeal to moderate Republicans and independents. Roughly one-sixth of Americans who had voted for George W. Bush in 2000 and/or 2004 voted for Obama in 2008. Throughout his presidential campaign, Obama explicitly refused to attack the Republican Party, per se, focusing criticisms on either McCain, the Republican right wing, or Republican policies. Obama's campaign recognized that in the wake of political disasters such as the unpopular Iraq War, and the federal mishandling of Hurricane Katrina in 2005, many voters longed for a politics that transcended partisan divisions. Obama's race-neutrality and demeanor of cool competency reassured millions of white Americans, allowing them to vote for a "black candidate."

Does the emergence of Barack Obama represent the possibility of a "post-racial America," a society that transcends its historic racial divide of structural inequality? Despite this extraordinary accomplishment, it is imperative to distinguish between the elevation of individuals and the material realities of black daily life in twenty-first-century America. In addition to support from a mass movement, Obama's victory was made possible, in part, by his brilliant oratory and his ability to reframe issues in ways that brought diverse constituencies together. This was clearly represented by Obama's keynote address at the 2004 Democratic Party National Convention, as well as his later address, "A More Perfect Union" (document 25). Obama has assumed a historic role similar to that of Nelson Mandela of South Africa, an inspirational, charismatic leader of African descent who advances a politics of racial reconciliation, human rights, and color-blind cooperation. One major concern is whether the extraordinary hopes and expectations of Obama's millions of admirers can be addressed by an administration challenged by a severe economic recession and wars abroad.

It is sometimes stated that the only constant in politics is change. The African-American people, now numbering over 42 million, represent a virtual nation within a nation, possessing its own rich traditions of culture, social organization, rituals and beliefs, and modes of political struggle. The history of black American social and political thought is a history of vast change and transformation through slavery, segregation, and ghettoization. Yet it is also a story of long memory, of political cultures of continuity and institutional developments transcending generations. The ideologies of integration, black nationalism, and radical transformation have in different ways and over time spoken to a common project—the achievement of full and unconditional freedom for black people. Throughout each phase of struggle, through long storms of oppression, black folk have found courage in the enduring belief that they would never be turned around, that the struggle for freedom would continue, and that it could one day be won.

— 1 —

Black Feminisms: Combahee River Collective Statement, *1977*

The Combahee River Collective was formed by a group of black feminists in Boston in 1974, and the organization lasted until about 1980. The following statement was a reflection of collective thinking, drafted by Barbara Smith, a prominent black lesbian feminist author and activist, with help from Demita Frazier and Beverly Smith. Although the statement originally appeared in Zilla Eisenstein's anthology, *Capitalist Patriarchy and the Case for Socialist Feminism* (1977), it has been reprinted on several other occasions and remains among the most important articulations of black feminist theory and practice. The Combahee River Collective addressed the ways that racism, sexism, classism, and heterosexism all work to perpetuate each other and much of their work reflected the goals of other black feminist groups such as the National Black Feminist Organization (NBFO) and Black Women Organized for Action (BWOFA).

—

We are a collective of black feminists who have been meeting together since 1974. During that time we have been involved in the process of defining and clarifying our politics, while at the same time doing political work within our own group and in coalition with other progressive organizations and movements. The most general statement of our politics at the present time would be that we are actively committed to struggling against racial, sexual, heterosexual, and class oppression and see as our particular task the development of integrated analysis and practice based upon the fact that the major systems of oppression are interlocking. The synthesis of these oppressions creates the conditions of our lives. As black women we see black feminism as the logical political movement to combat the manifold and simultaneous oppressions that all women of color face.

We will discuss four major topics in the paper that follows: (1) The genesis of contemporary black feminism; (2) what we believe, i.e., the specific province of our politics; (3) the problems in organizing black feminists, including a brief herstory of our collective; and (4) black feminist issues and practice.

1. The Genesis of Contemporary Black Feminism

Before looking at the recent development of black feminism, we would like to affirm that we find our origins in the historical reality of Afro-American women's continuous life-and-death struggle for survival and liberation. Black women's extremely negative relationship to the American political system (a system of white male rule) has always been determined by our membership in two oppressed racial and sexual castes. As Angela Davis points out in "Reflections on the Black Woman's Role in the Community of Slaves," black women have always embodied, if only in their physical manifestation, an adversary stance to white male rule and have actively resisted its inroads upon them and their communities in both dramatic and subtle ways. There have always been black women activists—some known, like Sojourner Truth, Harriet Tubman, Frances E. W. Harper, Ida B. Wells-Barnett, and Mary Church Terrell, and thousands upon thousands unknown—who had a shared awareness of how their sexual identity combined with their racial identity to make their whole life situation and the focus of their political struggles unique. Contemporary black feminism is the outgrowth of countless generations of personal sacrifice, militancy, and work by our mothers and sisters.

A black feminist presence has evolved most obviously in connection with the second wave of the American women's movement beginning in the late 1960s. Black, other Third World, and working women have been involved in the feminist movement from its start, but both outside reactionary forces and racism and elitism within the movement itself have served to obscure our participation. In 1973 black feminists, primarily located in New York, felt the necessity of forming a separate black feminist group. This became the National Black Feminist Organization (NBFO).

Black feminist politics also have an obvious connection to movements for black liberation, particularly those of the 1960s and 1970s. Many of us were active in those movements (civil rights, black nationalism, the Black Panthers), and all of our lives were greatly affected and changed by their ideology, their goals, and the tactics used to achieve their goals. It was our experience and disillusionment within these liberation movements, as well as experience on the periphery of the white male left, that led to the need to develop a politics that was antiracist, unlike those of white women, and antisexist, unlike those of black and white men.

There is also undeniably a personal genesis for black feminism, that is, the political realization that comes from the seemingly personal experiences of individual black women's lives. Black feminists and many more black women who do not define themselves as feminists have all experienced sexual oppression as a constant factor in our day-to-day existence.

Black feminists often talk about their feelings of craziness before becoming conscious of the concepts of sexual politics, patriarchal rule, and, most importantly, feminism, the political analysis and practice that we women use to struggle against our oppression. The fact that racial politics and indeed racism are pervasive factors in our lives did not allow us, and still does not allow most black women, to look more deeply into our own experiences and define those things that make our lives what they are and our oppression specific to us. In the process of consciousness-raising, actually life-sharing, we began to recognize the commonality of our experiences and, from that sharing and growing consciousness, to build a politics that will change our lives and inevitably end our oppression.

Our development also must be tied to the contemporary economic and political position of black people. The post–World War II generation of black youth was the first to be able to minimally partake of certain educational and employment options, previously closed completely to black people. Although our economic position is still at the very bottom of the American capitalist economy, a handful of us have been able to gain certain tools as a result of tokenism in education and employment which potentially enable us to more effectively fight our oppression.

A combined antiracist and antisexist position drew us together initially, and as we developed politically we addressed ourselves to heterosexism and economic oppression under capitalism.

2. What We Believe

Above all else, our politics initially sprang from the shared belief that black women are inherently valuable, that our liberation is a necessity not as an adjunct to somebody else's but because of our need as human persons for autonomy. This may seem so obvious as to sound simplistic, but it is apparent that no other ostensibly progressive movement has ever considered our specific oppression a priority or worked seriously for the ending of that oppression. Merely naming the pejorative stereotypes attributed to black women (e.g., mammy, matriarch, Sapphire, whore, bulldagger), let alone cataloguing the cruel, often murderous, treatment we receive, indicates how little value has been placed upon our lives during four centuries of bondage in the Western hemisphere. We realize that the only people who care enough about us to work consistently for our liberation is us. Our politics evolve from a healthy love for ourselves, our sisters, and our community which allows us to continue our struggle and work.

This focusing upon our own oppression is embodied in the concept of identity politics. We believe that the most profound and potentially the most radical politics come directly out of our own identity, as opposed to working to end somebody else's oppression. In the case of black women this is a particularly repugnant, dangerous, threatening, and therefore revolutionary concept because it is obvious from looking at all the political movements that have preceded us that anyone is more worthy of liberation than ourselves. We reject pedestals, queenhood, and walking ten paces behind. To be recognized as human, levelly human, is enough.

We believe that sexual politics under patriarchy is as pervasive in black women's lives as are the politics of class and race. We also often find it difficult to separate race from class from sex oppression because in our lives they are most often experienced simultaneously. We know that there is such a thing as racial-sexual oppression which is neither solely racial nor solely sexual, e.g., the history of rape of black women by white men as a weapon of political repression.

Although we are feminists and lesbians, we feel solidarity with progressive black men and do not advocate the fractionalization that white women who are separatists demand. Our situation as black people necessitates that we have solidarity around the fact of race, which white women of course do not need to have with white men, unless it is their negative solidarity as racial oppressors. We struggle together with black men against racism, while we also struggle with black men about sexism.

We realize that the liberation of all oppressed peoples necessitates the destruction of the political-economic systems of capitalism and imperialism as well as patriarchy. We are socialists because we believe the work must be organized for the collective benefit of those who do the work and create the products and not for the profit of the bosses. Material resources must be equally distributed among those who create these resources. We are not convinced, however, that a socialist revolution that is not also a feminist and antiracist revolution will guarantee our liberation. We have arrived at the necessity for developing an understanding of class relationships that takes into account the specific class position of black women who are generally marginal in the labor force, while at this particular time some of us are temporarily viewed as doubly desirable tokens at white-collar and professional levels. We need to articulate the real class situation of persons who are not merely raceless, sexless workers, but for whom racial and sexual oppression are significant determinants in their working/economic lives. Although we are in essential agreement with Marx's theory as it applied to the very specific economic relationships he analyzed, we know that this analysis must be extended further in order for us to understand our specific economic situation as black women.

A political contribution which we feel we have already made is the expansion of the feminist principle that the personal is political. In our consciousness-raising sessions, for example, we have in many ways gone beyond white women's revelations because we are dealing with the implications of race and class as well as sex. Even our black women's style of talking/testifying in black language about what we have experienced has a resonance that is both cultural and political. We have spent a great deal of energy delving into the cultural and experiential nature of our oppression out of necessity because none of these matters have ever been looked at before. No one before has ever examined the multilayered texture of black women's lives.

As we have already stated, we reject the stance of lesbian separatism because it is not a viable political analysis or strategy for us. It leaves out far too much and far too many people, particularly black men, women, and children. We have a great deal of criticism and loathing for what men have been socialized to be in this society: what they support, how they act, and how they oppress. But we do not have the misguided notion that it is their maleness, per se—i.e., their biological maleness—that makes them what they are. As black women we find any type of biological determinism a particularly dangerous and reactionary basis upon which to build a politic. We must also question whether lesbian separatism is an adequate and progressive political analysis and strategy, even for those who practice it, since it so completely denies any but the sexual sources of women's oppression, negating the facts of class and race.

3. Problems in Organizing Black Feminists

During our years together as a black feminist collective we have experienced success and defeat, joy and pain, victory and failure. We have found that it is very difficult to organize around black feminist issues, difficult even to announce in certain contexts that we *are* black feminists. We have tried to think about the reasons for our difficulties, particularly since the white women's movement continues to be strong and to grow in many directions. In this section we will discuss some of the general reasons for the organizing problems we face and also talk specifically about the stages in organizing our own collective.

The major source of difficulty in our political work is that we are not just trying to fight oppression on one front or even two, but instead to address a whole range of oppressions. We do not have racial, sexual, heterosexual, or class privilege to rely upon, nor do we have even the minimal access to resources and power that groups who possess any one of these types of privilege have. . . .

Feminism is, nevertheless, very threatening to the majority of black people because it calls into question some of the most basic assumptions about our existence, i.e., that gender should be a determinant of power relationships. Here is the way male and female roles were defined in a black nationalist pamphlet from the early 1970s.

> We understand that it is and has been traditional that the man is the head of the house. He is the leader of the house/nation because his knowledge of the world is broader, his awareness is greater, his understanding is fuller and his application of this information is wiser. . . . After all, it is only reasonable that the man be the head of the house because he is able to defend and protect the development of his home. . . . Women cannot do the same things as men—they are made by nature to function differently. Equality of men and women is something that cannot happen even in the abstract world. Men are not equal to other men, i.e., ability, experience, or even understanding. The value of men and women can be seen as in the value of gold and silver—they are not equal but both have great value. We must realize that men and women are a complement to each other because there is no house/family without a man and his wife. Both are essential to the development of any life.

The material conditions of most black women would hardly lead them to upset both economic and sexual arrangements that seem to represent some stability in their lives. Many black women have a good understanding of both sexism and racism, but because of the everyday constrictions of their lives cannot risk struggling against them both.

The reaction of black men to feminism has been notoriously negative. They are, of course, even more threatened than black women by the possibility that black feminists might organize around our own needs. They realize that they might not only lose valuable and hard-working allies in their struggles but that they might also be forced to change their habitually sexist ways of interacting with and oppressing black women. Accusations that black feminism divides the black struggle are powerful deterrents to the growth of an autonomous black women's movement.

Still, hundreds of women have been active at different times during the three-year existence of our group. And every black woman who came, came out of a strongly felt need for some level of possibility that did not previously exist in her life. . . .

4. Black Feminist Issues and Practice

During our time together we have identified and worked on many issues of particular relevance to black women. The inclusiveness of our politics makes us concerned with any situation that impinges upon the lives of women, Third World, and working people. We are of course particularly committed to working on those struggles in which race, sex, and class are simultaneously factors in oppression. We might, for example, become involved in workplace organizing at a factory that employs Third World women or picket a hospital that is cutting back on already inadequate health care to a Third World community, or set up a rape crisis center in a black neighborhood. Organizing around welfare or daycare concerns might also be a focus. The work to be done and the countless issues that this work represents merely reflect the pervasiveness of our oppression.

Issues and projects that collective members have actually worked on are sterilization abuse, abortion rights, battered women, rape, and health care. We have also done many workshops and educationals on black feminism on college campuses, at women's conferences, and most recently for high school women.

One issue that is of major concern to us and that we have begun to publicly address is racism in the white women's movement. As black feminists we are made constantly and painfully aware of how little effort white women have made to understand and combat their racism, which requires among other things that they have a more than superficial comprehension of race, color, and black history and culture. Eliminating racism in the white women's movement is by definition work for white women to do, but we will continue to speak to and demand accountability on this issue.

In the practice of our politics we do not believe that the end always justifies the means. Many reactionary and destructive acts have been done in the name of achieving "correct" political goals. As feminists we do not want to mess over people in the name of politics. We believe in collective process and a nonhierarchical distribution of power within our own group and in our vision of a revolutionary society. We are committed to a continual examination of our politics as they develop through criticism and self-criticism as an essential aspect of our practice. As black feminists and lesbians we know that we have a very definite revolutionary task to perform and we are ready for the lifetime of work and struggle before us.

Source: "Combahee River Collective: A Black Feminist Statement," copyright 1979 by Zilla R. Eisenstein. Reprinted by permission of the Monthly Review Foundation.

⚬ 2 ⚬

"Women in Prison: How We Are," *Assata Shakur, 1978*

Born Joanne Chesimard, Assata Shakur (1947–) was a Black Panther and a leader in the Black Liberation Army (BLA) during the early 1970s. As a result, she was subject to systematic surveillance, harassment, and attack by the Federal Bureau of Investigation's infamous COINTELPRO operation. Between 1971 and 1973 she was arraigned and tried seven different times for alleged crimes, ranging from bank robbery to kidnapping to murder, and yet none of the charges led to conviction. In 1973, however, she was captured on the New Jersey State Turnpike after a shootout in which a state trooper and a Black Panther were killed. In 1977 she was convicted of murder by an all-white jury in a highly disputed trial and handed a life sentence. Shakur has always maintained her innocence. She escaped from prison in 1979 and has been living in Cuba since 1986.

⚬

We sit in the bull pen. We are all black. All restless. And we are all freezing. When we ask, the matron tells us that the heating system cannot be adjusted. All of us, with the exception of a woman, tall and gaunt, who looks naked and ravished, have refused the bologna sandwiches. The rest of us sit drinking bitter, syrupy tea. . . .

There are no criminals here at Riker's Island Correctional Institution for Women, (New York), only victims. Most of the women (over 95 percent) are black and Puerto Rican. Many were abused children. Most have been abused by men and all have been abused by "the system."

There are no big-time gangsters here, no premeditated mass murderers, no godmothers. There are no big-time dope dealers, no kidnappers, no Watergate women. There are virtually no women here charged with white-collar crimes like embezzling or fraud. Most of the women have drug-related cases. Many are charged as accessories to crimes committed by men. The major crimes that women here are charged with are prostitution, pickpocketing, shoplifting, robbery and drugs. Women who have prostitution cases or who are doing "fine" time make up a substantial part of the short-term population. The women see stealing or hustling as necessary for the survival of themselves or their children because jobs are scarce and welfare is impossible to live on. One thing is clear: amerikan capitalism is in no way threatened by the women in prison on Riker's Island.

One gets the impression, when first coming to Riker's Island, that the architects conceived of it as a prison modeled after a juvenile center. In the areas where visitors usually pass there is plenty of glass and plenty of plants and flowers. The cell blocks consist of two long corridors with cells on each side connected by a watch room where the guards are stationed, called a bubble. Each corridor has a day room with a TV, tables, multi-colored chairs, a stove that doesn't work and a refrigerator. There's a utility room with a sink and a washer and dryer that do not work.

Instead of bars the cells have doors which are painted bright, optimistic colors with slim glass observation panels. The doors are controlled electronically by the guards in the bubble. The cells are called rooms by everybody. They are furnished with a cot, a closet, a desk, a chair, a plastic upholstered headboard that opens for storage, a small book case, a mirror, a sink and a toilet. The prison distributes brightly colored bedspreads and throw rugs for a homey effect. There is a school area, a gym, a carpeted auditorium, two inmate cafeterias and outside recreation areas that are used during the summer months only.

The guards have successfully convinced most of the women that Riker's Island is a country club. They say that it is a playhouse compared to some other prisons (especially male): a statement whose partial veracity is not predicated upon the humanity of correction officials at Riker's Island, but, rather, by contrast to the unbelievably barbaric conditions of other prisons. Many women are convinced that they are, somehow, "getting over." Some go so far as to reason that because they are not doing hard time, they are not really in prison.

This image is further reinforced by the pseudo-motherly attitude of many of the guards; a deception which all too often successfully reverts women to children. The guards call the women inmates by their first names. The women address the guards either as Officer, Miss —— or by nicknames (Teddy Bear, Spanky, Aunt Louise, Squeeze, Sarge, Black Beauty, Nutty Mahogany, etc.). Frequently, when a woman returns to Riker's she will make rounds, gleefully embracing her favorite guard: the prodigal daughter returns.

If two women are having a debate about any given topic the argument will often be resolved by "asking the officer." The guards are forever telling the women to "grow up," to "act like ladies," to "behave" and to be "good girls." If an inmate is breaking some minor rule like coming to say "hi" to her friend on another floor or locking in a few minutes late, a guard will say, jokingly, "don't let me have to come down there and beat your butt." It is not unusual to hear a guard tell a woman, "what you need is a good spanking." The tone is often motherly, "didn't I tell you, young lady, to. . . ."; or, "you know better than that"; or, "that's a good girl." And the women respond accordingly. Some guards and inmates "play" together. One officer's favorite "game" is taking off her belt and chasing her "girls" down the hall with it, smacking them on the butt.

But beneath the motherly veneer, the reality of guard life is ever present. Most of the guards are black, usually from working-class, upward-bound, civil-service-oriented backgrounds. They identify with the middle class, have middle-class values and are extremely materialistic. They are not the most intelligent women in the world and many are extremely limited. Most are aware that there is no justice in the amerikan judicial system and that blacks and Puerto Ricans are discriminated against in every facet of amerikan life. But, at the same time, they are convinced that the system is somehow "lenient." To them, the women in prison are "losers" who don't have enough sense to stay out of jail. Most believe in the bootstrap theory—anybody can "make it" if they try hard enough. They congratulate themselves on their great accomplishments. In contrast to themselves they see the inmate as ignorant, uncultured, self-destructive, weak-minded and stupid. They ignore the fact that their dubious accomplishments are not based on superior intelligence or effort, but only on chance and a civil service list.

Many guards hate and feel trapped by their jobs. The guard is exposed to a certain amount of abuse from co-workers, from the brass as well as from inmates, ass kissing, robotizing and mandatory overtime. (It is common practice for guards to work a double shift at least once a week.) But no matter how much they hate the military structure, the infighting, the ugliness of their tasks, they are very aware of how close they are to the welfare lines. If they were not working as guards most would be underpaid or unemployed. Many would miss the feeling of superiority and power as much as they would miss the money, especially the cruel, sadistic ones.

The guards are usually defensive about their jobs and indicate by their behavior that they are not at all free from guilt. They repeatedly, compulsively say, as if to convince themselves, "This is a job just like any other job." The more they say that the more preposterous it seems. . . .

The black liberation struggle is equally removed from the lives of women at Riker's. While they verbalize acute recognition that amerika is a racist country where the poor are treated like dirt they, nevertheless, feel responsible for the filth of their lives. The air at Riker's is permeated with self-hatred. Many women bear marks on their arms, legs and wrists from suicide attempts or self-mutilation. They speak about themselves in self-deprecating terms. They consider themselves failures.

While most women contend that whitey is responsible for their oppression they do not examine the cause or source of that oppression. There is no sense of class struggle. They have no sense of communism, no definition of it, but they consider it a bad thing. They do not want to destroy Rockefella. They want to be just like him. Nicky Barnes, a major black dope seller, is discussed with reverence. When he was convicted practically everyone was sad. Many gave speeches about how kind, smart and generous he was. No one spoke about the sale of drugs to our children.

Politicians are considered liars and crooks. The police are hated. Yet, during cop and robber movies, some cheer loudly for the cops. One woman pasted photographs of Farrah Fawcett Majors all over her cell because she "is a baad police bitch." Kojak and Barretta get their share of admiration.

A striking difference between women and men prisoners at Riker's Island is the absence of revolutionary rhetoric among the women. We have no study groups. We have no revolutionary literature floating around. There are no groups of militants attempting to "get their heads together." The women at Riker's seem vaguely aware of what a revolution is but generally regard it as an impossible dream. Not at all practical.

While men in prison struggle to maintain their manhood there is no comparable struggle by women to preserve their womanhood. One frequently hears women say, "Put a bunch of bitches together and you've got nothin but trouble"; and, "Women don't stick together, that's why we don't have nothin." Men prisoners constantly refer to each other as brother. Women prisoners rarely refer to each other as sister. Instead, "bitch" and "whore" are the common terms of reference. Women, however, are much kinder to each other than men, and any form of violence other than a fist fight is virtually unknown. Rape, murder and stabbings at the women's prison are non-existent.

For many, prison is not that much different from the street. It is, for some, a place to rest and recuperate. For the prostitute prison is a vacation from turning tricks in the rain and snow. A vacation from brutal pimps. Prison for the addict is a place to get clean, get medical work done and gain weight. Often, when the habit becomes too expensive, the addict gets herself busted (usually subconsciously), so she can get back in shape, leave with a clean system ready to start all over again. One woman claims that for a month or two every year she either goes to jail or to the crazy house to get away from her husband.

For many the cells are not much different from the tenements, the shooting galleries and the welfare hotels they live in on the street. Sick call is no different from the clinic or the hospital emergency room. The fights are the same except they are less dangerous. The police are the same. The poverty is the same. The alienation is the same. The racism is the same. The sexism is the same. The drugs are the same and the system is the same. Riker's Island is just another institution. In childhood school was their prison, or youth houses or reform schools or children shelters or foster homes or mental hospitals or drug programs and they see all institutions as indifferent to their needs, yet necessary to their survival.

The women at Riker's Island come there from places like Harlem, Brownsville, Bedford-Stuyvesant, South Bronx and South Jamaica. They come from places where dreams have been abandoned like the buildings. Where there is no more sense of community. Where neighborhoods are transient. Where isolated people run from one fire trap to another. The cities have removed us from our strengths, from our roots, from our traditions. They have taken away our gardens and our sweet potato pies and given us McDonald's. They have become our prisons, locking us into the futility and decay of pissy hallways that lead nowhere. They have alienated us from each other and made us fear each other. They have given us dope and television as a culture.

There are no politicians to trust. No roads to follow. No popular progressive culture to relate to. There are no new deals, no more promises of golden streets and no place else to migrate. My sisters in the streets, like my sisters at Riker's Island, see no way out. "Where can I go?" said a woman on the day she was going home. "If there's nothing to believe in," she said, "I can't do nothin except try to find cloud nine."

What of our Past? What of our History? What of our Future?

I can imagine the pain and the strength of my great great grandmothers who were slaves and my great great grandmothers who were Cherokee Indians trapped on reservations. I remembered my great grandmother who walked everywhere rather than sit in the back of the bus. I think about North Carolina and my home town and I remember the women of my grandmother's generation: strong, fierce women who could stop you with a look out the corners of their eyes. Women who walked with majesty; who could wring a chicken's neck and scale a fish. Who could pick cotton, plant a garden and sew without a pattern. Women who boiled clothes white in big black cauldrons and who hummed work songs and lullabys. Women who visited the elderly, made soup for the sick and shortnin bread for the babies.

Women who delivered babies, searched for healing roots and brewed medicines. Women who darned sox and chopped wood and layed bricks. Women who could swim rivers and shoot the head off a snake. Women who took passionate responsibility for their children and for their neighbors' children too.

The women in my grandmother's generation made giving an art form. "Here, gal, take this pot of collards to Sister Sue"; "Take this bag of pecans to school for the teacher"; "Stay here while I go tend Mister Johnson's leg." Every child in the neighborhood ate in their kitchens. They called each other sister because of feeling rather than as the result of a movement. They supported each other through the lean times, sharing the little they had.

The women of my grandmother's generation in my home town trained their daughters for womanhood. They taught them to give respect and to demand respect. They taught their daughters how to churn butter; how to use elbow grease. They taught their daughters to respect the strength of their bodies, to lift boulders and how to kill a hog; what to do for colic, how to break a fever and how to make a poultice, patchwork quilts, plait hair and how to hum and sing. They taught their daughters to take care, to take charge and to take responsibility. They would not tolerate a "lazy heifer" or a "gal with her head in the clouds." Their daughters had to learn how to get their lessons, how to survive, how to be strong. The women of my grandmother's generation were the glue that held family and the community together. They were the backbone of the church. And of the school. They regarded outside institutions with dislike and distrust. They were determined that their children should survive and they were committed to a better future.

I think about my sisters in the movement. I remember the days when, draped in African garb, we rejected our foremothers and ourselves as castrators. We did penance for robbing the brother of his manhood, as if we were the oppressor. I remember the days of the Panther Party when we were "moderately liberated." When we were allowed to wear pants and expected to pick up the gun. The days when we gave doe-eyed looks to our leaders. The days when we worked like dogs and struggled desperately for the respect which they struggled desperately not to give us. I remember the black history classes that did mention women and the posters of our "leaders" where women were conspicuously absent. We visited our sisters who bore the complete responsibility of the children while the Brotha was doing his thing. Or had moved on to bigger and better things.

Most of us rejected the white women's movement. Miss ann was still Miss ann to us whether she burned her bras or not. We could not muster sympathy for the fact that she was trapped in her mansion and oppressed by her husband. We were, and still are, in a much more terrible jail. We knew that our experiences as black women were completely different from those of our sisters in the white women's movement. And we had no desire to sit in some consciousness-raising group with white women and bare our souls.

Women can never be free in a country that is not free. We can never be liberated in a country where the institutions that control our lives are oppressive. We can never be free while our men are oppressed. Or while the amerikan government and amerikan capitalism remain intact.

But it is imperative to our struggle that we build a strong black women's movement. It is imperative that we, as black women, talk about the experiences that shaped us; that we assess our strengths and weaknesses and define our own history. It is imperative that we discuss positive ways to teach and socialize our children.

The poison and pollution of capitalist cities is choking us. We need the strong medicine of our foremothers to make us well again. We need their medicines to give us strength to fight and the drive to win. Under the guidance of Harriet Tubman and Fannie Lou Hamer and all of our foremothers, let us rebuild a sense of community. Let us rebuild the culture of giving and carry on the tradition of fierce determination to move on closer to freedom.

Source: Excerpt from "Women in Prison: How We Are" with permission from *Black Scholar* 9, no. 7 (April 1978), pp. 50–57.

SELECT BIBLIOGRAPHY:
Assata Shakur, *Assata: An Autobiography* (Westport, Conn.: Lawrence Hill, 1987).
———, "The Continuity of Struggle," *Souls* 1, no. 2 (Spring 1999), pp. 93–101.
Evelyn Williams, *Inadmissible Evidence: The Story of the African-American Trial Lawyer Who Defended the Black Liberation Army* (Chicago: Lawrence Hill Books, 1993).

⟿ **3** ⟿

"It's Our Turn," *Harold Washington, 1983*

Harold Washington (1922–1987) grew up in Chicago, studied at Roosevelt University and Northwestern University Law School, held various local political offices, and served in the U.S. House of Representatives before he finally became the first African-American mayor of Chicago in 1983. Washington's campaign was waged outside of the political mainstream, and in vowing to clean up the corruption left over from Richard J. Daly's political machine, he forged a successful political coalition among black, liberal white, and Latino voters. Yet the strident opposition he faced also helped to expose the racism of many ethnic whites in what is often considered to be the most segregated city in the United States. As mayor, Washington faced legendary battles with Chicago's city council, although he still implemented many reforms. Partially as a result of stress, overwork, and exhaustion, Washington died suddenly in office in late 1987.

⟿

Chicago is a divided city. Chicago is a city where citizens are treated unequally and unfairly. Chicago is a city in decline. Each year for the last decade, we have lost 11,500 jobs, 3,500 housing units and nearly 36,000 people.

Since 1955, women, Latinos, Blacks, youth and progressive whites have been left out of the Chicago government. Since 1979, the business, labor and intellectual communities have been allowed but token involvement in Chicago government.

Sadly, we have learned what happens when there is no governmental stability—and when the few rule over us. The results are that more people don't have jobs, more are out of food, out of their homes and out of hope.

Our businesses are failing at the highest rate since the Depression, in part from high interest rates, and the only answer the city government provides is fat consultant contracts for a few politically connected firms and jobs for a few patronage workers.

We have a school system which does not educate, in which students continue to lag far behind the rest of the country in tests of reading and math ability.

We have a continuing crime problem in the city. Despite a drop in crime statistics, it's still not safe to walk the streets or run a business. Even at home, Chicagoans are robbed, mugged and beaten.

We no longer have dependable housing in this city. There has been an epidemic of abandoned buildings and rents have skyrocketed. Subsidized housing is no longer being built. And, with interest rates as they are, no one can afford to buy their own home anymore.

Finally, "the city that works" doesn't work anymore. City services cost more than in any other city in America, and yet they just aren't there—sewers are in disrepair, streets are marred with giant potholes. We have one of the highest infant mortality rates in the country, and traffic appears to be permanently snarled.

We have these terrible problems in Chicago, partly because leadership has not striven for unity and pointed boldly to the new directions. Instead, it has perpetuated outdated politics and pie-in-the-sky financing.

I have compassion for the terrible plight of people and a vision for its future: I honestly believe that of those candidates mentioned, only I can rebuild Chicago by rallying Chicagoans to create a city in which every individual will receive his or her full measure of dignity. In the future, I see a Chicago of compassion; a city where no one has to live with rats, where the sick can be cured and where no one is overtaxed on property and burdened with other hidden taxes.

All the other candidates who have declared and who will be running for mayor would perpetuate politics as usual. Those candidates will continue the shell game of city financing at a time of crisis.

I would prefer not to run. But, there is a sense of urgency which moves me. Chicago can only be rebuilt if all the people of Chicago and her leaders work together. I was born, raised and educated in this city, and I have served it on three levels of government. I love representing Chicago in Washington, where we need courageous voices to speak out and act against Reagan and Reaganomics. But I can't watch the city of Chicago be destroyed by petty politics and bad government.

I have heard the earnest pleas of thousands of people to enter the race. Therefore, I declare that I am a candidate for the mayor of Chicago. Not to do so would be a mockery of my longstanding dedication to public service.

I see a Chicago that runs well, in which services are provided as a right, not as a political favor.

I see a Chicago of educational excellence and equality of treatment in which all children can learn to function in this evermore-complex society, in which jobs and contracts are dispensed fairly to those that want and qualify for them, and in which justice rains down like water.

Some may say this is visionary—I say *they* lack vision.

Already, a new day is dawning. The unprecedented voter registration and voter turnout in Chicago in the last week is evidence of this. The people of Chicago who have been neglected by the political bosses have announced their willingness to become involved, to unify and to act. I invite them to join my campaign. If I'm to be mayor, it would be as the spokesperson of this new movement —not the mayor of just a political faction, but mayor of all Chicago. We devoutly search for unity.

As mayor of this city, I would open the doors of City Hall. I would dig into that untapped reservoir of talented whites, Latinos, women and Blacks and unleash that ability for the benefit of this city.

Fairness will be our standard. On my first day in office, I will sign a freedom of information order to open the secret files of City Hall to inspection by all citizens. We seek *accountability*. As mayor, I shall gather the best talent of the city to tackle the record of problems I have outlined. We shall strive for excellence.

Thousands of Chicagoans have beseeched me to undertake this task. Their faith is not misplaced. . . .

Source: "Harold Washington's Announcement of Candidacy for the Democratic Nomination for Mayor of Chicago," from Dempsey J. Travis, *Harold: The People's Mayor* (Chicago: Urban Research Press, 1989), used by permission of Ramon Price for the Washington Estate.

SELECT BIBLIOGRAPHY:

Paul Kleppner, *Chicago Divided: The Making of a Black Mayor* (Dekalb: Northern Illinois University Press, 1985).
Manning Marable, "Harold Washington and the Politics of Race in Chicago," *Black Scholar* 17, no. 6 (November–December 1986), pp. 14–23.
Alton Miller, *Harold Washington: The Mayor, the Man* (Chicago: Bonus Books, 1989).

4

"I Am Your Sister," *Audre Lorde, 1984*

Audre Lorde (1934–1992) was one of the key intellectuals in the feminist movement in the late twentieth century. Born in New York City, Lorde studied at Hunter College and Columbia University, where she earned an M.A. in library science. Later, she worked as a college lecturer, founded the Kitchen Table–Women of Color Press, and served on the editorial committee of the *Black Scholar*, but she was most widely known as a lesbian feminist, political activist, and poet. Some of her most important works are *Uses of the Erotic* (1978), which has become a staple of feminist literature, and *Sister Outsider* (1984), a collection of essays and speeches that traces the development of many of her ideas. Lorde died of lung cancer in 1992. Since her death, the beauty and the expressive power of her writings have become even more widely recognized by an international audience.

AGE, RACE, CLASS, AND SEX: WOMEN REDEFINING DIFFERENCE

Much of Western European history conditions us to see human differences in simplistic opposition to each other: dominant/subordinate, good/bad, up/down, superior/inferior. In a society where the good is defined in terms of profit rather than in terms of human need, there must always be some group of people who, through systematized oppression, can be made to feel surplus, to occupy the place of the dehumanized inferior. Within this society, that group is made up of black and Third-World people, working-class people, older people, and women.

As a forty-nine-year-old black lesbian feminist socialist mother of two, including one boy, and a member of an interracial couple, I usually find myself a part of some group defined as other, deviant, inferior, or just plain wrong. Traditionally, in American society, it is the members of oppressed, objectified groups who are expected to stretch out and bridge the gap between the actualities of our lives and the consciousness of our oppressor. For in order to survive, those of us for whom oppression is as American as apple pie have always had to be watchers, to become familiar with the language and manners of the oppressor, even sometimes adopting them for some illusion of protection. Whenever the need for some pretense of communication arises, those who profit from our oppression call upon us to share our knowledge with them. In other words, it is the responsibility of the oppressed to teach the oppressors their mistakes. I am responsible for educating teachers who dismiss my children's culture in school. Black and Third-World people are expected to educate white people as to our humanity. Women are expected to educate men. Lesbians and gay men are expected to educate the heterosexual world. The oppressors maintain their position and evade responsibility for their own actions. There is a constant drain of energy, which might be better used in redefining ourselves and devising realistic scenarios for altering the present and constructing the future.

Institutionalized rejection of difference is an absolute necessity in a profit economy which needs outsiders as surplus people. As members of such an economy, we have *all* been programmed to respond to the human differences between us with fear and loathing and to handle that difference in one of three ways: ignore it, and if that is not possible, copy it if we think it is dominant, or destroy it if we think it is subordinate. But we have no patterns for relating across our human differences as equals. As a result, those differences have been misnamed and misused in the service of separation and confusion.

Certainly there are very real differences between us of race, age, and sex. But it is not those differences between us that are separating us. It is rather our refusal to recognize those differences, and to examine the distortions that result from our misnaming them and their effects upon human behavior and expectation.

Racism, the belief in the inherent superiority of one race over all others and thereby the right to dominance. Sexism, the belief in the inherent superiority of one sex over the other and thereby the right to dominance. Ageism. Heterosexism. Elitism. Classism.

It is a lifetime pursuit for each one of us to extract these distortions from our living at the same time as we recognize, reclaim, and define those differences upon which they are imposed. For we have all been raised in a society where those distortions were endemic within our living. Too often, we pour the energy needed for recognizing and exploring difference into pretending those differences are insurmountable barriers, or that they do not exist at all. This results in a voluntary isolation, or false and treacherous connections. Either way, we do not develop tools for using human difference as a springboard for creative change within our lives. We speak not of human difference, but of human deviance.

Somewhere, on the edge of consciousness, there is what I call a *mythical norm*, which each one of us within our hearts knows "that is not me." In America, this norm is usually defined as *white, thin, male, young, heterosexual, Christian, and financially secure.* It is with this mythical norm that the trappings of power reside within this society. Those of us who stand outside that power often identify one way in which we are different, and we assume that to be the primary cause of all oppression, forgetting other distortions around difference, some of which we ourselves may be practicing. By and large within the women's movement today, white women focus upon their oppression as women and ignore differences of race, sexual preference, class, and age. There is a pretense to a homogeneity of experience covered by the word *sisterhood* that does not in fact exist.

Unacknowledged class differences rob women of each others' energy and creative insight. Recently a women's magazine collective made the decision for one issue to print only prose, saying poetry was a less "rigorous" or "serious" art form. Yet even the form our creativity takes is often a class issue. Of all the art forms, poetry is the most economical. It is the one that is the most secret, that requires the least physical labor, the least material, and the one that can be done between shifts, in the hospital pantry, on the subway, and on scraps of surplus paper. Over the last few years, writing a novel on tight finances, I came to appreciate the enormous differences in the material demands between poetry and prose. As we reclaim our literature, poetry has been the major voice of poor, working-class, and colored women. A room of one's own may be a necessity for writing prose, but so are reams of paper, a typewriter, and plenty of time. The actual requirements to produce the visual arts also help determine, along class lines, whose art is whose. In this day of inflated prices for material, who are our sculptors, our painters, our photographers? When we speak of a broadly based women's culture, we need to be aware of the effect of class and economic differences on the supplies available for producing art.

As we move toward creating a society within which we can each flourish, ageism is another distortion of relationship that interferes without vision. By ignoring the past, we are encouraged to repeat its mistakes. The "generation gap" is an important social tool for any repressive society. If the younger members of a community view the older members as contemptible or suspect or excess, they will never be able to join hands and examine the living memories of the community, nor ask the all important question, "Why?" This gives rise to a historical amnesia that keeps us working to invent the wheel every time we have to go to the store for bread.

We find ourselves having to repeat and relearn the same old lessons over and over that our mothers did because we do not pass on what we have learned, or because we are unable to listen. For instance, how many times has this all been said before? For another, who would have believed that once again our daughters are allowing their bodies to be hampered and purgatoried by girdles and high heels and hobble skirts?

Ignoring the differences of race between women and the implications of those differences presents the most serious threat to the mobilization of women's joint power.

As white women ignore their built-in privilege of whiteness and define *woman* in terms of their own experience alone, then women of color become "other," the outsider whose experience and tradition is too "alien" to comprehend. An example of this is the signal absence of the experience of women of color as a resource for women's studies courses. The literature of women of color is seldom included in women's literature courses and almost never in other literature courses, nor in women's studies as a whole. All too often, the excuse given is that the literatures of women of color can only be taught by colored women, or that they are too difficult to understand, or that classes cannot "get into" them because they come out of experiences that are "too different." I have heard this argument presented by white women of otherwise quite clear intelligence, women who seem to have no trouble at all teaching and reviewing work that comes out of the vastly different experiences of Shakespeare, Molière, Dostoyevski, and Aristophanes. Surely there must be some other explanation.

This is a very complex question, but I believe one of the reasons white women have such difficulty reading black women's work is because of their reluctance to see black women as women and different from themselves. To examine black women's literature effectively requires that we be seen as whole people in our actual complexities—as individuals, as women, as human—rather than as one of those problematic but familiar stereotypes provided in this society in place of genuine images of black women. And I believe this holds true for the literatures of other women of color who are not black.

The literatures of all women of color recreate the textures of our lives, and many white women are heavily invested in ignoring the real differences. For as long as any difference between us means one of us must be inferior, then the recognition of any difference must be fraught with guilt. To allow women of color to step out of stereotypes is too guilt-provoking, for it threatens the complacency of those women who view oppression only in terms of sex.

Refusing to recognize difference makes it impossible to see the different problems and pitfalls facing us as women.

Thus, in a patriarchal power system where white skin privilege is a major prop, the entrapments used to neutralize black women and white women are not the same. For example, it is easy for black women to be used by the power structure against black men, not because they are men, but because they are black. Therefore, for black women, it is necessary at all times to separate the needs of the oppressor from our own legitimate conflicts within our communities. This same problem does not exist for white women. Black women and men have shared racist oppression and still share it, although in different ways. Out of that shared oppression we have developed joint defenses and joint vulnerabilities to each other that are not duplicated in the white community, with the exception of the relationship between Jewish women and Jewish men.

On the other hand, white women face the pitfall of being seduced into join-ing the oppressor under the pretense of sharing power. This possibility does not exist in the same way for women of color. The tokenism that is sometimes extended to us is not an invitation to join power; our racial "otherness" is a visi-ble reality that makes that quite clear. For white women there is a wider range of pretended choices and rewards for identifying with patriarchal power and its tools.

Today, with the defeat of ERA, the tightening economy, and increased conser-vatism, it is easier once again for white women to believe the dangerous fantasy that if you are good enough, pretty enough, sweet enough, quiet enough, teach the children to behave, hate the right people, and marry the right men, then you will be allowed to coexist with patriarchy in relative peace, at least until a man needs your job or the neighborhood rapist happens along. And true, unless one lives and loves in the trenches it is difficult to remember that the war against dehumanization is ceaseless.

But black women and our children know the fabric of our lives is stitched with violence and with hatred, that there is no rest. We do not deal with it only on the picket lines, or in dark midnight alleys, or in the places where we dare to verbal-ize our resistance. For us, increasingly, violence weaves through the daily tissues of our living—in the supermarket, in the classroom, in the elevator, in the clinic and the school yard, from the plumber, the baker, the saleswoman, the bus driver, the bank teller, the waitress who does not serve us.

Some problems we share as women, some we do not. You fear your children will grow up to join the patriarchy and testify against you; we fear our children will be dragged from a car and shot down in the street, and you will turn your backs upon the reasons they are dying.

The threat of difference has been no less blinding to people of color. Those of us who are black must see that the reality of our lives and our struggle does not make us immune to the errors of ignoring and misnaming difference. Within black communities, where racism is a living reality, differences among us often seem dangerous and suspect. The need for unity is often misnamed as a need for homogeneity, and a black feminist vision mistaken for betrayal of our common interests as a people. Because of the continuous battle against racial erasure that black women and black men share, some black women still refuse to recognize that we are also oppressed as women, and that sexual hostility against black women is practiced not only by the white racist society, but implemented within our black communities as well. It is a disease striking the heart of black nation-hood, and silence will not make it disappear. Exacerbated by racism and the pressures of powerlessness, violence against black women and children often becomes a standard within our communities, one by which manliness can be measured. But these woman-hating acts are rarely discussed as crimes against black women.

As a group, women of color are the lowest-paid wage earners in America. We are the primary targets of abortion and sterilization abuse, here and abroad. In certain parts of Africa, small girls are still being sewed shut between their legs to keep them docile and for men's pleasure. This is known as female circumcision, and it is not a cultural affair as the late Jomo Kenyatta insisted, it is a crime against black women.

Black women's literature is full of the pain of frequent assault, not only by a racist patriarchy, but also by black men. Yet the necessity for and history of shared battle have made us, black women, particularly vulnerable to the false accusation that anti-sexist is anti-black. Meanwhile, womanhating as a recourse of the powerless is sapping strength from black communities, and our very lives. Rape is on the increase, reported and unreported, and rape is not aggressive sexuality, it is sexualized aggression. As Kalamu ya Salaam, a black male writer points out, "As long as male domination exists, rape will exist. Only women revolting and men made conscious of their responsibility to fight sexism can collectively stop rape."

Differences between ourselves as black women are also being misnamed and used to separate us from one another. As a black lesbian feminist comfortable with the many different ingredients of my identity, and a woman committed to racial and sexual freedom from oppression, I find I am constantly being encouraged to pluck out some one aspect of myself and present this as the meaningful whole, eclipsing or denying the other parts of self. But this is a destructive and fragmenting way to live. My fullest concentration of energy is available to me only when I integrate all the parts of who I am, openly, allowing power from particular sources of my living to flow back and forth freely through all my different selves, without the restrictions of externally imposed definition. Only then can I bring myself and my energies as a whole to the service of those struggles which I embrace as part of my living.

A fear of lesbians, or of being accused of being a lesbian, has led many black women into testifying against themselves. It has led some of us into destructive alliances, and others into despair and isolation. In the white women's communities, heterosexism is sometimes a result of identifying with the white patriarchy, a rejection of that interdependence between women-identified women that allows the self to be, rather than to be used in the service of men. Sometimes it reflects a die-hard belief in the protective coloration of heterosexual relationships, sometimes a self-hate, which all women have to fight against, taught us from birth.

Although elements of these attitudes exist for all women, there are particular resonances of heterosexism and homophobia among black women. Despite the fact that woman-bonding has a long and honorable history in the African and African-American communities, and despite the knowledge and accomplishments of many strong and creative women-identified black women in the political, social and cultural fields, heterosexual black women often tend to ignore or discount the existence and work of black lesbians. Part of this attitude has come from an understandable terror of black male attack within the close confines of black society, where the punishment for any female self-assertion is still to be accused of being a lesbian and therefore unworthy of the attention or support of the scarce black male. But part of this need to *misname and ignore black lesbians comes from a very real fear that openly women-identified black women who are no longer dependent upon men for their self-definition may well reorder our whole concept of social relationships.*

Black women who once insisted that lesbianism was a white woman's problem now insist that black lesbians are a threat to black nationhood, are consorting with the enemy, are basically unblack. These accusations, coming from the very women to whom we look for deep and real understanding, have served to keep many black lesbians in hiding, caught between the racism of white women and the homophobia of their sisters. Often, their work has been ignored, trivialized, or misnamed, as with the work of Angelina Grimké, Alice Dunbar-Nelson, Lorraine Hansberry. Yet women-bonded women have always been some part of the power of black communities, from our unmarried aunts to the amazons of Dahomey.

And it is certainly *not black lesbians who are assaulting women and raping children and grandmothers on the streets of our communities.*

Across this country, as in Boston during the spring of 1979 following the unsolved murders of twelve black women, black lesbians are spearheading movements against violence against black women.

What are the particular details within each of our lives that can be scrutinized and altered to help bring about change? How do we redefine difference for all women? It is not our differences that separate women, but our reluctance to recognize those differences and to deal effectively with the distortions that have resulted from the ignoring and misnaming of those differences.

As a tool of *social control*, women have been encouraged to recognize only one area of human difference as legitimate, those differences that exist between women and men. And we have learned to deal across those differences with the urgency of all oppressed subordinates. All of us have had to learn to live or work or coexist with men, from our fathers on. We have recognized and negotiated these differences, even when this recognition only continued the old dominant/subordinate mode of human relationship, where the oppressed must recognize the masters' difference in order to survive.

But our future survival is predicated upon our ability to relate within equality. As women, we must root out internalized patterns of oppression within ourselves if we are to move beyond the most superficial aspects of social change. Now we must recognize differences among women who are our equals, neither inferior nor superior, and devise ways to use each others' difference to enrich our visions and our joint struggles.

The future of our earth may depend upon the ability of all women to identify and develop new definitions of power and new patterns of relating across difference. The old definitions have not served us, nor the earth that supports us. The old patterns, no matter how cleverly rearranged to imitate progress, still condemn us to cosmetically altered repetitions of the same old exchanges, the same old guilt, hatred, recrimination, lamentation, and suspicion.

For we have, built into all of us, old blueprints of expectation and response, old structures of oppression, and these must be altered at the same time as we alter the living conditions which are a result of those structures. For the master's tools will never dismantle the master's house.

As Paulo Freire shows so well in *The Pedagogy of the Oppressed*, the true focus of revolutionary change is never merely the oppressive situations that we seek to escape, but that piece of the oppressor that is planted deep within each of us, and that knows only the oppressors' tactics, the oppressors' relationships.

Change means growth, and growth can be painful. But we sharpen self-definition by exposing the self in work and struggle together with those whom we define as different from ourselves, although sharing the same goals. For black and white, old and young, lesbian and heterosexual women alike, this can mean new paths to our survival.

Source: Reprinted by permission from *Sister Outsider*, by Audre Lorde. Copyright 1984, 2007 by Audre Lorde. Berkeley, Calif.: Crossing Press, www.tenspeed.com.

SELECT BIBLIOGRAPHY:

Toni Cade, ed., *The Black Woman: An Anthology* (New York: Mentor/New American Library, 1970).

Alexis De Veaux, *Warrior Poet: A Biography of Audre Lorde* (New York: W. W. Norton, 2004).

Joan Wylie Hall, ed., *Conversations with Audre Lorde* (Jackson: University Press of Mississippi, 2004).

Audre Lorde, *The Collected Poems of Audre Lorde* (New York: Norton, 1997).

———, *Uses of the Erotic: The Erotic as Power* (Brooklyn, N.Y.: Out and Out Books, 1978).

———, *Zami: A New Spelling of My Name* (Trumansberg, N.Y.: Crossing Press, 1982).

———, *Sister Outsider: Essays and Speeches* (Trumansberg, N.Y.: Crossing Press, 1984).

———, *A Burst of Light: Essays* (Ithaca, N.Y.: Firebrand Books, 1988).

⤳ 5 ⤳

"Shaping Feminist Theory," bell hooks, 1984

Born Gloria Jean Watkins, bell hooks (1952–) is a social critic, professor, and writer who publishes under the name of her great-grandmother as a means of paying homage to the "unlettered wisdom" of her female ancestors. She earned her Ph.D. at the University of California at Santa Cruz in 1983, and she has taught African-American studies and English at Yale University, Oberlin College, and City College of New York (CUNY). A prominent public intellectual, hooks describes an elaborate web of racism, sexism, and classism that oppresses black women, and much of her work is concerned with dismantling these hierarchical structures. She has also discussed the sometimes tense relations between black female activists and mainstream feminists, and she is presently writing a three-volume memoir.

Feminism in the United States has never emerged from the women who are most victimized by sexist oppression; women who are daily beaten down, mentally, physically, and spiritually—women who are powerless to change their condition in life. They are a silent majority. A mark of their victimization is that they accept their lot in life without visible question, without organized protest, without collective anger or rage. Betty Friedan's *The Feminine Mystique* is still heralded as having paved the way for contemporary feminist movement—it was written as if these women did not exist. Friedan's famous phrase, "the problem that has no name," often quoted to describe the condition of women in this society, actually referred to the plight of a select group of college-educated, middle- and upper-class, married white women—housewives bored with leisure, with the home, with children, with buying products, who wanted more out of life. Friedan concludes her first chapter by stating: "We can no longer ignore that voice within women that says: 'I want something more than my husband and my children and my house.'" That "more" she defined as careers. She did not discuss who would be called in to take care of the children and maintain the home if more women like herself were freed from their house labor and given equal access with white men to the professions. She did not speak of the needs of women without men, without children, without homes. She ignored the existence of all nonwhite women and poor white women. She did not tell readers whether it was more fulfilling to be a maid, a babysitter, a factory worker, a clerk, or a prostitute, than to be a leisure-class housewife.

She made her plight and the plight of white women like herself synonymous with a condition affecting all American women. In so doing, she deflected attention away from her classism, her racism, her sexist attitudes towards the masses of American women. In the context of her book, Friedan makes clear that the women she saw as victimized by sexism were college-educated, white women who were compelled by sexist conditioning to remain in the home. She contends:

> It is urgent to understand how the very condition of being a housewife can create a sense of emptiness, nonexistence, nothingness in women. There are aspects of the housewife role that make it almost impossible for a woman of adult intelligence to retain a sense of human identity, the firm core of self or "I" without which a human

being, man or woman, is not truly alive. For women of ability, in America today, I am convinced that there is something about the housewife state itself that is dangerous.

Specific problems and dilemmas of leisure-class white housewives were real concerns that merited consideration and change but they were not the pressing political concerns of masses of women. Masses of women were concerned about economic survival, ethnic and racial discrimination, etc. When Friedan wrote *The Feminine Mystique*, more than one-third of all women were in the work force. Although many women longed to be housewives, only women with leisure time and money could actually shape their identities on the model of the feminine mystique. They were women who, in Friedan's words, were "told by the most advanced thinkers of our time to go back and live their lives as if they were Noras, restricted to the doll's house by Victorian prejudices.". . .

Friedan was a principal shaper of contemporary feminist thought. Significantly, the one-dimensional perspective on women's reality presented in her book became a marked feature of the contemporary feminist movement. Like Friedan before them, white women who dominate feminist discourse today rarely question whether or not their perspective on women's reality is true to the lived experiences of women as a collective group. Nor are they aware of the extent to which their perspectives reflect race and class biases, although there has been a greater awareness of biases in recent years. Racism abounds in the writings of white feminists, reinforcing white supremacy and negating the possibility that women will bond politically across ethnic and racial boundaries. Past feminist refusal to draw attention to and attack racial hierarchies suppressed the link between race and class. Yet class structure in American society has been shaped by the racial politic of white supremacy; it is only by analyzing racism and its function in capitalist society that a thorough understanding of class relationships can emerge. Class struggle is inextricably bound to the struggle to end racism. . . .

A central tenet of modern feminist thought has been the assertion that "all women are oppressed." This assertion implies that women share a common lot, that factors like class, race, religion, sexual preference, etc., do not create a diversity of experience that determines the extent to which sexism will be an oppressive force in the lives of individual women. Sexism as a system of domination is institutionalized, but it has never determined in an absolute way the fate of all women in this society. Being oppressed means the *absence of choices*. It is the primary point of contact between the oppressed and the oppressor. Many women in this society do have choices (as inadequate as they are), therefore exploitation and discrimination are words that more accurately describe the lot of women collectively in the United States. Many women do not join organized resistance against sexism precisely because sexism has not meant an absolute lack of choices. They may know they are discriminated against on the basis of sex, but they do not equate this with oppression. Under capitalism, patriarchy is structured so that sexism restricts women's behavior in some realms even as freedom from limitations is allowed in other spheres. The absence of extreme restrictions leads many women to ignore the areas in which they are exploited or discriminated against; it may even lead them to imagine that no women are oppressed.

There are oppressed women in the United States, and it is both appropriate and necessary that we speak against such oppression. . . .

However, feminist emphasis on "common oppression" in the United States was less a strategy for politicization than an appropriation by conservative and liberal women of a radical political vocabulary that masked the extent to which they shaped the movement so that it addressed and promoted their class interests.

Although the impulse towards unity and empathy that informed the notion of common oppression was directed at building solidarity, slogans like "organize around your own oppression" provided the excuse many privileged women needed to ignore the differences between their social status and the status of masses of women. It was a mark of race and class privilege, as well as the expression of freedom from the many constraints sexism places on working-class women, that middle-class white women were able to make their interests the primary focus of feminist movement and employ a rhetoric of commonality that made their condition synonymous with "oppression." Who was there to demand a change in vocabulary? What other group of women in the United States had the same access to universities, publishing houses, mass media, money? Had middle-class black women begun a movement in which they had labeled themselves "oppressed," no one would have taken them seriously. Had they established public forums and given speeches about their "oppression," they would have been criticized and attacked from all sides. This was not the case with white bourgeois feminists for they could appeal to a large audience of women, like themselves, who were eager to change their lot in life. Their isolation from women of other class and race groups provided no immediate comparative base by which to test their assumptions of common oppression. . . .

We resist hegemonic dominance of feminist thought by insisting that it is a theory in the making, that we must necessarily criticize, question, reexamine, and explore new possibilities. My persistent critique has been informed by my status as a member of an oppressed group, experience of sexist exploitation and discrimination, and the sense that prevailing feminist analysis has not been the force shaping my feminist consciousness. This is true for many women. There are white women who had never considered resisting male dominance until the feminist movement created an awareness that they could and should. My awareness of feminist struggle was stimulated by social circumstance. Growing up in a Southern, black, father-dominated, working-class household, I experienced (as did my mother, my sisters, and my brother) varying degrees of patriarchal tyranny and it made me angry—it made us all angry. Anger led me to question the politics of male dominance and enabled me to resist sexist socialization. Frequently, white feminists act as if black women did not know sexist oppression existed until they voiced feminist sentiment. They believe they are providing black women with "the" analysis and "the" program for liberation. They do not understand, cannot even imagine, that black women, as well as other groups of women who live daily in oppressive situations, often acquire an awareness of patriarchal politics from their lived experience, just as they develop strategies of resistance (even though they may not resist on a sustained or organized basis).

These black women observed white feminist focus on male tyranny and women's oppression as if it were a "new" revelation and felt such a focus had little impact on their lives. To them it was just another indication of the privileged living conditions of middle- and upper-class white women that they would need a theory to inform them that they were "oppressed." The implication being that people who are truly oppressed know it even though they may not be engaged in organized resistance or are unable to articulate in written form the nature of their oppression. These black women saw nothing liberatory in party-line analyses of women's oppression. Neither the fact that black women have not organized collectively in huge numbers around the issues of "feminism" (many of us do not know or use the term) nor the fact that we have not had access to the machinery of power that would allow us to share our analyses or theories about gender with the American public negate its presence in our lives or place us in a position of dependency in relationship to those white and nonwhite feminists who address a larger audience. . . .

Attempts by white feminists to silence black women are rarely written about. All too often they have taken place in conference rooms, classrooms, or the privacy of cozy living-room settings, where one lone black woman faces the racist hostility of a group of white women. From the time the women's liberation movement began, individual black women went to groups. Many never returned after a first meeting. Anita Cornwall is correct in "Three for the Price of One: Notes from a Gay Black Feminist," when she states, ". . . sadly enough, fear of encountering racism seems to be one of the main reasons that so many black womyn refuse to join the women's movement." Recent focus on the issue of racism has generated discourse but has had little impact on the behavior of white feminists towards black women. Often the white women who are busy publishing papers and books on "unlearning racism" remain patronizing and condescending when they relate to black women. This is not surprising given that frequently their discourse is aimed solely in the direction of a white audience and the focus solely on changing attitudes rather than addressing racism in a historical and political context. They make us the "objects" of their privileged discourse on race. As "objects," we remain unequals, inferiors. Even though they may be sincerely concerned about racism, their methodology suggests they are not yet free of the type of paternalism endemic to white supremacist ideology. Some of these women place themselves in the position of "authorities" who must mediate communication between racist white women (naturally they see themselves as having come to terms with their racism) and angry black women whom they believe are incapable of rational discourse. Of course, the system of racism, classism, and educational elitism remain intact if they are to maintain their authoritative positions. . . .

Racist stereotypes of the strong, superhuman black woman are operative myths in the minds of many white women, allowing them to ignore the extent to which black women are likely to be victimized in this society and the role white women may play in the maintenance and perpetuation of that victimization. In Lillian Hellman's autobiographical work *Pentiment*, she writes, "All my life, beginning at birth, I have taken orders from black women, wanting them and resenting them, being superstitious the few times I disobeyed." The black women Hellman describes worked in her household as family servants, and their status was never that of an equal. Even as a child, she was always in the dominant position as they questioned, advised, or guided her; they were free to exercise these rights because she or another white authority figure allowed it. Hellman places power in the hands of these black women rather than acknowledge her own power over them; hence she mystifies the true nature of their relationship. By projecting onto black women a mythical power and strength, white women both promote a false image of themselves as powerless, passive victims and deflect attention away from their aggressiveness, their power (however limited in a white supremacist, male-dominated state), their willingness to dominate and control others. These unacknowledged aspects of the social status of many white women prevent them from transcending racism and limit the scope of their understanding of women's overall social status in the United States.

Privileged feminists have largely been unable to speak to, with, and for diverse groups of women because they either do not understand fully the interrelatedness of sex, race, and class oppression or refuse to take this interrelatedness seriously. Feminist analyses of woman's lot tend to focus exclusively on gender and do not provide a solid foundation on which to construct feminist theory. They reflect the dominant tendency in Western patriarchal minds to mystify woman's reality by insisting that gender is the sole determinant of woman's fate. Certainly it has been easier for women who do not experience race or class oppression to focus exclusively on gender. Although socialist feminists focus on class and gender, they tend to dismiss race or they make a point of acknowledging that race is important and then proceed to offer an analysis in which race is not considered.

As a group, black women are in an unusual position in this society, for not only are we collectively at the bottom of the occupational ladder, but our overall social status is lower than that of any other group. Occupying such a position, we bear the brunt of sexist, racist, and classist oppression. At the same time, we are the group that has not been socialized to assume the role of exploiter/oppressor in that we are allowed no institutionalized "other" that we can exploit or oppress. (Children do not represent an institutionalized other even though they may be oppressed by parents.) White women and black men have it both ways. They can act as oppressor or be oppressed. Black men may be victimized by racism, but sexism allows them to act as exploiters and oppressors of women. White women may be victimized by sexism, but racism enables them to act as exploiters and oppressors of black people. Both groups have led liberation movements that favor their interests and support the continued oppression of other groups. Black male sexism has undermined struggles to eradicate racism just as white female racism undermines feminist struggle. As long as these two groups or any group defines liberation as gaining social equality with ruling-class white men, they have a vested interest in the continued exploitation and oppression of others.

Black women with no institutionalized "other" that we may discriminate against, exploit, or oppress often have a lived experience that directly challenges the prevailing classist, sexist, racist social structure and its concomitant ideology. This lived experience may shape our consciousness in such a way that our worldview differs from those who have a degree of privilege (however relative within the existing system). It is essential for continued feminist struggle that black women recognize the special vantage point our marginality gives us and make use of this perspective to criticize the dominant racist, classist, sexist hegemony as well as to envision and create a counterhegemony. I am suggesting that we have a central role to play in the making of feminist theory and a contribution to offer that is unique and valuable. The formation of a liberatory feminist theory and praxis is a collective responsibility, one that must be shared. Though I criticize aspects of feminist movement as we have known it so far, a critique that is sometimes harsh and unrelenting, I do so not in an attempt to diminish feminist struggle but to enrich, to share in the work of making a liberatory ideology and a liberatory movement.

Source: Excerpt from "Black Women: Shaping Feminist Theory," from bell hooks, *Feminist Theory: From Margin to Center* (Boston: South End Press, 1984), pp. 1–15.

SELECT BIBLIOGRAPHY:

bell hooks, *Ain't I a Woman: Black Women and Feminism* (Boston: South End Press, 1981).
———, *Feminist Theory: From Margin to Center* (Boston: South End Press, 1984).
———, *Yearning: Race, Gender, and Cultural Politics* (Boston: South End Press, 1990).
———, *Black Looks: Race and Representation* (Boston: South End Press, 1992).
———, *Sisters of the Yam: Black Women and Self Recovery* (Boston: South End Press, 1993).

⚊ 6 ⚊

The Movement against Apartheid: Jesse Jackson and Randall Robinson

The single most important international issue confronting black America after the end of the Vietnam War was apartheid. For nearly forty years, the white-minority regime in South Africa had imposed a rigidly authoritarian form of racial oppression on millions of African people. Thousands of South Africans were executed, imprisoned, or exiled. Mass organizations that led the movement against apartheid, such as the African National Congress and the South African Communist Party, were banned.

In the 1980s, President Ronald Reagan initiated a cordial bilateral policy toward South Africa, termed "constructive engagement." African Americans, outraged by the Reagan administration's friendly initiatives toward apartheid, began to mobilize a mass protest movement to pressure U.S. firms to "divest" their holdings from South Africa. Many protest organizations mobilized black opposition to apartheid. One of the coordinators of the anti-apartheid movement in the United States during the 1980s was Randall Robinson, head of TransAfrica, a black American lobbying agency for Africa and the Caribbean.

Robinson (1941–), born in Richmond Virginia, graduated from Virginia Union University and earned a law degree from Harvard Law School. Robinson has published numerous books whose subjects range from critiques of poverty and crime in America to the demand for black reparations. After his departure from TransAfrica, Robinson continued efforts to address the socioeconomic and political problems of Africa and the Caribbean.

In the first document below, civil rights activist Reverend Jesse Jackson addressed an antiapartheid conference held at the United Nations in 1984. In the second document, political scientist and journalist Clarence Lusane interviewed Robinson in October 1985.

⚊

DON'T ADJUST TO APARTHEID

. . . A great Afro-American, Dr. W. E. B. Du Bois, long ago called attention to "The African Roots of War," as he revealed how the policies of plunder and exploitation of the African continent led to war between the European and American Powers who had developed at the Expense of Africa, and who often went to war between themselves over a redivision of the spoils.

Our Africa policy in the United States, our relations and attitudes towards the countries of the African continent, have always been in distinct contrast to our policy and attitudes towards the nation-states of Europe. Europe, in our perception, has historically been seen as a source of immigrants and culture. While

Africa is perceived in our country as a source of cheap labor and raw materials to be exploited for the benefit of a privileged class of European settlers.

This stereotype of Africa, as being without culture and civilization, a continent to be subjugated by the advocates of "master race" politics, has led to a kind of Tarzan, Jane, Boy relationship between the United States and Africa. This not only reflects racial chauvinism, but a grossly unreal attitude which underplays the significance of Africa to the world in general and to the United States in particular.

One of the tragedies of our own times that this history of negative attitudes has produced, is the massive starvation and drought in huge areas of the African continent. We live in a scientific age that recognizes that what are viewed as natural disasters are often the by-product of years of neglect and plunder. The hunger and death that stalks wide areas of the African continent today must become the concern of the entire international community because it is a threat to the human family.

Poverty and injustice anywhere is a threat to justice everywhere. We, in North America, blessed with one of the most fertile and productive agricultural lands in the world, must cease being insensitive to the current suffering in Africa. We must mobilize our abundant resources, through both government and non-governmental organizations, to bring assistance and relief to our brothers and sisters that are in Africa.

It is a measure of the callousness of the present administration in the United States that it would pull 82 million acres of arable land out of production, while 5,000,000 people a year die of starvation in the Third World. This, too, is a dimension of United States Africa policy, when we, who have such abundant capacity to feed the hungry, deny members of the human family access to this relief from hunger and starvation.

This policy of cynicism and callousness has the United States in an official partnership with the racist *apartheid* regime in South Africa. Corporate greed, in the search for the maximum return on investments, has found in the racist *apartheid* system, with its brutal denial of human rights, a favorable climate guaranteeing the highest profits in the world. An American government that pretends to be outraged by the human rights situation in Poland is apparently quite satisfied with the brutal denial of human rights in Pretoria.

This is measured in part by the deafening official silence in our country concerning the plight of 8,000,000 Black Africans who have been stripped of their South African citizenship and forcibly removed from the cities of South Africa and relocated into Bantustans, thereby made refugees and aliens in their own country. In the language of the *apartheid* regime, this is called "separate development" and the United States southern Africa policy which supports this barbarism is called "constructive engagement."

In the service of this policy, the Reagan administration has given the green light for loans to South Africa from the International Monetary Fund. It has allowed more South African consulates to open in the United States; expanded military ties with the *apartheid* regime, which includes training the South African

Coast Guard; it has encouraged South Africa's repeated military invasions in Angola by withholding diplomatic recognition to the Angolan People's Republic; and has generally created a climate of official endorsement that has made the United States South Africa's number one trading partner.

It must be remembered that the flow of foreign capital into South Africa, from the United States, Britain and other allies, is essential to the *apartheid* regime's economic growth, and economic growth in South Africa, as elsewhere, is essential to political stability.

Double Standard

In order to promote the political stability of the *apartheid* regime, United States policy invariably adopts a double standard in matters of human rights. For example, when a solidarity union in Poland is suppressed and a leader is jailed, our official policy is to implement an economic boycott against Poland in response to this violation of human rights. When the ANC in South Africa and the trade unions affiliated to it are suppressed and abolished, and leaders like Nelson Mandela are jailed, we respond to this violation of human rights by expanding economic, diplomatic and military ties with the regime.

Furthermore, the United States veto is repeatedly used in the United Nations Security Council to frustrate every effort by the international community to effect economic sanctions against South Africa. We, in the United States, must measure human rights by one yardstick and free ourselves of this hypocrisy that increasingly alienates us from the peoples of the world struggling for human dignity and self-determination. Our national view of southern Africa must radically change from seeing it as essentially a piece of geopolitical real estate to be used by the United States for selfish ends, without regard to the aspirations of the people of southern Africa.

This purely geopolitical approach has led to a dangerous situation in which American nuclear technology has been made accessible to the *apartheid* regime. Now that regime has acquired the technical capability of producing atomic weapons. In this way, our Africa policy, together with that of Israel, has helped to create a situation that is a threat to the sovereignty of every nation on the African continent. The disarmament movement in our country must give far more attention to this particular nuclear threat than it has in the past.

Constructive Engagement

The Reagan administration's "constructive engagement" policy is a multi-pronged strategy designed to help South Africa gain acceptance and respectability in the West and thereby break out of the isolation it has experienced in the international community since the late 1960s. This support from the United States has emboldened the *apartheid* regime and encouraged its military aggressions.

This places a particularly heavy burden on the frontline States, who have courageously maintained a principled opposition to *apartheid* in the face of ever-mounting military and diplomatic pressures upon them to accommodate to South Africa's wishes. All of us have been inspired by the courageous struggles and sacrifices being made by these newly-emancipated countries, in an effort to overcome generations of economic and cultural deprivation that are the legacy of colonialism. The fruits of these sacrifices are now being threatened by a new form of subjugation coming from the most brutally racist regime on earth.

I need not tell you that we live in perilous times. I need not tell you that the vast majority of humankind wants peace, economic and social justice and the right of self-determination. This very institution was designed and built by the nations of the world, including the United States, to implement these goals. We in the United States have had a very special interest and mission in creating the United Nations.

Our people have come from all corners of the globe, from Africa, Europe, Asia and the Americas. Our nation indeed is a mini–United Nations. I want to assure you that as I travel around this country and talk to the people in the towns, cities and factories, they tell me how important it is that we learn to live with the rest of the world especially because we are fast becoming a genuinely interdependent world.

The electronic media brings to our living rooms the wars in El Salvador, Lebanon and Angola. The people of this country know and want a continuing dialogue with the rest of the world and they see the United Nations as a forum where this dialogue can take place. I would like to assure you that the political gimmicks to punish this or that international organization are nothing more than political gimmickry. After all, it is somewhat humorous when a major power like ours begins to punish an international organization devoted to uplifting the small farmers of the world. The real American tradition is to stand by the seashore and wave people to come in and share our bounty and not to wave them goodbye. . . .

⌇

STATE OF THE U.S. ANTI-APARTHEID MOVEMENT

The following interview with Randall Robinson of TransAfrica and the Free South Africa movement was conducted for *The Black Scholar* on October 17, 1985.—Clarence Lusane

SCHOLAR: *Approximately one year has passed since the U.S. anti-apartheid movement surged forward. What is your assessment of the major achievement over this period?*
ROBINSON: We started the campaign with three major objectives to be pursued in sequence. The first objective was to more broadly educate the American people on South Africa, and to do that through civil disobedience and broad demonstrations that would provoke the kind of press coverage that the issue has gotten in the United States over the last eleven months.

The second objective growing out of that was to begin a dramatic change in American policy toward South Africa. As a result, the Congress and the administration found themselves in a posture of having to account to a newly informed and invigorated American public. The Congress responded with legislation and President Reagan with an inadequate Executive Order that nonetheless repudiated his own policy of constructive engagement, but does little else in moving us signif-icantly towards the kind of sanctions that the situation in South Africa warrants.

The third objective—yet to be realized, and that's what we have to work on—is that when American policy changes as substantially as it ought to, it begins to influence policy in other Western countries. Then we will have South Africa in a position to do nothing but respond to Western pressure and to negotiate with the real leadership in South Africa. Now, progress toward that objective has been made inasmuch as the unrest in South Africa, coupled with heightening pressure and concern around the world, has produced a hemorrhage of money leaving South Africa both in investment and in bank commitments, and that has caused the South African government an unprecedented kind of concern about the tra-ditional commitment of the West to support the regime.

So we are moving in the right direction and when the Congress comes back, we're going to push for tougher legislation in the next session of Congress. In the meantime, we have to sustain the campaign with thoughtful projects and sustain it with a pace, understanding that we have to have the resources to go for a long, long period of time. It was with that thought that the demonstrations were launched in the first place.

That kind of planning and that kind of expectation have given us the capacity to have daily demonstrations at the South African Embassy and around the country since November 21 of last year—demonstrations that have resulted in the arrest of almost 5,000 people nationally, and over 3,500 at the embassy in Washington.

And we have every capacity to sustain and build on this kind of long-term process of pressure application so that we are now beginning to reap fruit in the middle of the country, since there is divestment legislation virtually under con-sideration at every level of government, even in cities and towns and states that previously had never even considered South Africa to be a major issue. So, this issue has now reached every university; it has become an issue in supermarkets selling goods and in winestores selling wines imported from South Africa. It has become an issue that really has permeated the entire American society.

SCHOLAR: *What have been the main problems and outstanding weaknesses of the campaign?*
ROBINSON: The problems are that the administration, along with the South Africans, is attempting to counterattack by the use of the coarsest tactics, charac-terizing leadership as Marxist; further, instead of frontally attempting to defend apartheid, they are attacking the countries that South Africa would want to desta-bilize—Angola, Mozambique—and the whole issue of American-Soviet contain-ment in the region is being raised in a way that would have the American public believe unrelated to the South Africa issue.

But it is very much related and is a part of South Africa's strategy, taken with right-wing conservatives here in the United States, to weaken the anti-apartheid movement by mustering support for Jonas Savimbi's UNITA in Angola and the MNR in Mozambique, thereby buying South Africa time in Namibia, buying their resources at home to be used in their repression at home. If America will materially support Savimbi and others like him, it is really joining the South African conspiracy to destabilize the region and to cement apartheid at home.

So I think that the counterattack is being waged in that way because they've had diminishing success in their efforts to defend the domestic application of apartheid in South Africa itself.

SCHOLAR: *As you note, Botha and Reagan are attempting to buy time, but what are their real options over the next couple of years since the anti-apartheid movement in South Africa doesn't seem to be abating at all?*
ROBINSON: First of all, I think this upsurge has to be distinguished from Sharpeville or even from Soweto. Since 1982, we've seen an unprecedented increase in resistance to apartheid that is broad and deep all across South Africa. The government's State of Emergency has done nothing to diminish the black commitment to destroy the apartheid system altogether. Nothing short of one person, one vote in a unitary state will be favorably received by the black majority and the black leaders in South Africa. So the South African government now finds the ball in its court; it must decide how to respond.

Our job here is to make certain that the United States, in its private and public sectors, no longer gives encouragement to whites to try to tough it out. So, we have our work cut out for us in making sure that America is removed as a major component of the underpinnings of that system and for white intransigence in general.

SCHOLAR: *How do you see the role of the Free South Africa Movement over the next year and what are some of your plans?*
ROBINSON: Right now we are working on a Freedom Letter Campaign. We are sending a letter from the American people to Bishop Desmond Tutu signed by a million Americans saying that we stand with black South Africans in their struggle for justice. We are going to try to take that letter to Bishop Tutu in Soweto and deliver it personally in December with as many as want to go in the delegation to do that.

This is part of a continuing, consciousness-raising campaign that leads us into next year where we will seek passage in the Congress of stronger legislation; reintroduction of Ronald Dellums' bill calling for disinvestment of American investment so that we will ask for tougher sanctions.

We will also take our campaign to the private sector by giving Americans a better sense of the extent to which American corporations are pivotally involved in the repression of 22 million black South Africans, hopefully mustering enough pressure on those corporations to accelerate their departure from South Africa. All of this will be a part of the 1986 FSAM campaign.

SCHOLAR: *What is your assessment on how soon change will come in South Africa and is there any possibility for peaceful change?*
ROBINSON: It's hard to put a timetable on social change as a general rule since it's difficult to forecast with any accuracy. The thing of which one is certain is that

change is inevitable and that it will come in the foreseeable future, whether that is five years, or ten years, or fifteen years, one can't say. It could be within the next few months.

You have variables that come together in combination to make the force for change simply irresistible and have a lot to do with the continued development of urban military capacity on the part of the African National Congress, the continued growth and political strength of black labor unions in South Africa; the continued deepening of consciousness and activity of young people throughout South Africa, all coupled with increased pressure from without.

When these come together in a kind of requisite chemistry; then you will see South Africa fundamentally changed. One can't say with any preciseness when that will happen. I'm confident having said that that we will see change in the foreseeable future. We are closer to it now than we have ever been.

Sources: (1) Jesse L. Jackson, "Don't Adjust to Apartheid," with permission from *Black Scholar* 16, no. 6 (November/December 1984), pp. 39–43; and (2) Clarence Lusane, "State of the U.S. Anti-Apartheid Movement: An Interview with Randall Robinson," with permission from *Black Scholar* 17, no. 6 (November/December 1985), pp. 40–42.

SELECT BIBLIOGRAPHY:

Kevin Danaher, "South Africa, U.S. Policy, and the Anti-Apartheid Movement," *Review of Radical Political Economics* 11, no. 3 (1997), pp. 42–59.
Janice Love, *The U.S. Anti-Apartheid Movement: Local Activism in Global Politics* (New York: Praeger, 1995).

⁓ 7 ⁓

"Keep Hope Alive," *Jesse Jackson, 1988*

Born Jesse Burns in South Carolina, Jesse Jackson (1941–) took his stepfather's surname in 1956. While he was an undergraduate at North Carolina Agricultural and Technical College, Jackson emerged as a leader of the civil rights demonstrations in Greensboro, North Carolina. Jackson graduated from college in 1964, and in the spring of 1966 he became head of the Chicago chapter of the Southern Christian Leadership Conference's (SCLC) Operation Breadbasket. A confidant of Martin Luther King Jr., Jackson became an ordained minister in 1968. In the 1970s, Jackson created Operation PUSH (People United to Save Humanity), a civil rights organization focusing on economic empowerment and social protest in impoverished, urban areas. In 1983, Jackson announced his candidacy for the Democratic Party's presidential nomination, a decision that generated widespread African-American support. Running under the slogan, "Rainbow Coalition," the civil rights leader attracted significant support from Latinos, Asian

Americans, and many whites around a liberal-left public policy agenda. By the end of the 1984 Democratic primaries, Jackson's efforts had received 3.5 million popular votes. Four years later, Jackson revived his Rainbow Coalition campaign for the presidency, this time winning over 7 million popular votes. Jackson's presidential campaigns illustrated that an African-American candidate could in principle successfully compete for the nation's highest office. Jackson's 1988 address, "Keep Hope Alive," captures the idealism and the spirit behind his unsuccessful presidential campaigns. Since the 1990s, Jackson has been extensively involved in human rights efforts throughout the world, as well as social justice and antiracist struggles in the United States as well.

⌐⌐

COMMON GROUND AND COMMON SENSE

Tonight we pause and give praise and honor to God for being good enough to allow us to be at this place at this time. When I look out at this convention, I see the face of America, red, yellow, brown, black and white, we're all precious in God's sight—the real rainbow coalition. All of us, all of us who are here and think that we are seated. But we're really standing on someone's shoulders. Ladies and gentlemen. Mrs. Rosa Parks.

The mother of the civil-rights movement.

I want to express my deep love and appreciation for the support my family has given me over these past months.

They have endured pain, anxiety, threat and fear.

But they have been strengthened and made secure by a faith in God, in America and in you.

Your love has protected us and made us strong.

To my wife, Jackie, the foundation of our family; to our five children whom you met tonight; to my mother, Mrs. Helen Jackson, who is present tonight; and to my grandmother, Mrs. Maltilda Burns; my brother Chuck and his family; my mother-in-law, Mrs. Gertrude Brown, who just last month at age 61 graduated from Hampton Institute, a marvelous achievement; I offer my appreciation to Mayor Andrew Young who has provided such gracious hospitality to all of us this week.

And a special salute to President Jimmy Carter.

President Carter restored honor to the White House after Watergate. He gave many of us a special opportunity to grow. For his kind words, for his unwavering commitment to peace in the world and the voters that came from his family, every member of his family, led by Billy and Amy, I offer him my special thanks, special thanks to the Carter family.

My right and my privilege to stand here before you has been won—in my lifetime—by the blood and the sweat of the innocent.

Twenty-four years ago, the late Fanny Lou Hamer and Aaron Henry—who sits here tonight from Mississippi—were locked out on the streets of Atlantic City, the head of the Mississippi Freedom Democratic Party.

But tonight, a black and white delegation from Mississippi is headed by Ed Cole, a black man, from Mississippi, twenty-four years later.

Many were lost in the struggle for the right to vote. Jimmy Lee Jackson, a young student, gave his life. Viola Luizzo, a white mother from Detroit, called nigger lover, and brains blown out at point blank range.

Schwerner, Goodman and Chaney—two Jews and a black—found in a common grave, bodies riddled with bullets in Mississippi. The four darling little girls in the church in Birmingham, Ala. They died that we might have a right to live.

Dr. Martin Luther King Jr. lies only a few miles from us tonight.

Tonight he must feel good as he looks down upon us. We sit here together, a rainbow, a coalition—the sons and daughters of slave masters and the sons and daughters of slaves sitting together around a common table, to decide the direction of our party and our country. His heart would be full tonight.

As a testament to the struggles of those who have gone before; as a legacy for those who will come after; as a tribute to the endurance, the patience, the courage of our forefathers and mothers; as an assurance that their prayers are being answered, their work has not been in vain, and hope is eternal; tomorrow night my name will go into nomination for the presidency of the United States of America.

We meet tonight at a crossroads, a point of decision.

Shall we expand, be inclusive, find unity and power; or suffer division and impotence.

We come to Atlanta, the cradle of the old south, the crucible of the new South.

Tonight there is a sense of celebration because we are moved, fundamentally moved, from racial battlegrounds by law, to economic common ground, tomorrow we will challenge to move to higher ground.

Common ground!

Think of Jerusalem—the intersection where many trails met. A small village that became the birthplace for three great religions—Judaism, Christianity and Islam.

Why was this village so blessed? Because it provided a crossroads where different people met, different cultures, and different civilizations could meet and find common ground.

When people come together, flowers always flourish and the air is rich with the aroma of a new spring.

Take New York, the dynamic metropolis. What makes New York so special?

It is the invitation of the Statue of Liberty—give me your tired, your poor, your huddled masses who yearn to breathe free.

Not restricted to English only.

Many people, many cultures, many languages—with one thing in common, the yearn to breathe free.

Common ground!

Tonight in Atlanta, for the first time in this century we convene in the South.

A state where governors once stood in school-house doors. Where Julian Bond was denied his seat in the state legislature because of his conscientious objection to the Vietnam War.

A city that, through its five black universities, has graduated more black students than any city in the world.

Atlanta, now a modern intersection of the new South.

Common ground!

That is the challenge to our party tonight.

Left wing. Right wing. Progress will not come through boundless liberalism nor static conservatism, but at the critical mass of mutual survival. It takes two wings to fly.

Whether you're a hawk or a dove, you're just a bird living in the same environment, in the same world.

The Bible teaches that when lions and lambs lie down together, none will be afraid and there will be peace in the valley. It sounds impossible. Lions eat lambs. Lambs sensibly flee from lions. But even lions and lambs find common ground. Why?

Because neither lions nor lambs want the forest to catch on fire. Neither lions nor lambs want acid rain to fall. Neither lions nor lambs can survive nuclear war. If lions and lambs can find common ground, surely, we can as well, as civilized people.

The only time that we win is when we come together. In 1960, John Kennedy, the late John Kennedy, beat Richard Nixon by only 112,000 votes—less than one vote per precinct. He won by the margin of our hope. He brought us together. He reached out. He had the courage to defy his advisors and inquire about Dr. King's jailing in Albany, Georgia. We won by the margin of our hope, inspired by courageous leadership.

In 1964, Lyndon Johnson brought both wings together. The thesis, the antithesis and to create a synthesis and together we won.

In 1976, Jimmy Carter unified us again and we won. When we do not come together, we never win.

In 1968, division and despair in July led to our defeat in November.

In 1980, rancor in the spring and the summer led to Reagan in the fall. When we divide, we cannot win. We must find common ground as a basis for survival and development and change and growth.

Today when we debated, differed, deliberated, agreed to agree, agreed to disagree, when we had the good judgment to argue our case and then not self-destruct, George Bush was just a little further away from the White House and a little closer to private life.

Tonight, I salute Governor Michael Dukakis.

He has run a well-managed and a dignified campaign. No matter how tired or how tried, he always resisted the temptation to stoop to demagoguery.

I've watched a good mind fast at work, with steel nerves, guiding his campaign out of the crowded field without appeal to the worst in us. I've watched his perspective grow as his environment has expanded. I've seen his toughness and tenacity close up. I know his commitment to public service.

Mike Dukakis's parents were a doctor and a teacher; my parents, a maid, a beautician and a janitor.

There's a great gap between Brookline, Massachusetts, and Haney Street, the Fieldcrest Village housing projects in Greenville, South Carolina.

He studied law; I studied theology. There are differences of religion, region, and race; differences in experiences and perspectives. But the genius of America is that out of the many, we become one.

Providence has enabled our paths to intersect. His foreparents came to America on immigrant ships; my foreparents came to America on slave ships. But whatever the original ships, we're in the same boat tonight.

Our ships could pass in the night if we have a false sense of independence, or they could collide and crash. We would lose our passengers. But we can seek a higher reality and a greater good apart. We can drift on the broken pieces of Reaganomics, satisfy our baser instincts, and exploit the fears of our people. At our highest, we can call upon noble instincts and navigate this vessel to safety. The greater good is the common good.

As Jesus said, "Not my will, but thine be done." It was his way of saying there's a higher good beyond personal comfort or position.

The good of our nation is at stake—its commitment to working men and women, to the poor and the vulnerable, to the many in the world. With so many guided missiles, and so much misguided leadership, the stakes are exceedingly high. Our choice, full participation in a Democratic government, or more abandonment and neglect. And so this night, we choose not a false sense of independence, not our capacity to survive and endure.

Tonight we choose interdependency in our capacity to act and unite for the greater good. The common good is finding commitment to new priorities, to expansion and inclusion. A commitment to expanded participation in the Democratic Party at every level. A commitment to a shared national campaign strategy and involvement at every level. A commitment to new priorities that ensure that hope will be kept alive. A common-ground commitment for a legislative agenda by empowerment for the John Conyers bill, universal, on-site, same-day registration everywhere—and commitment to D.C. statehood and empowerment—D.C. deserves statehood. A commitment to economic set-asides, a commitment to the Dellums bill for comprehensive sanctions against South Africa, a shared commitment to a common direction.

Common ground. Easier said than done. Where do you find common ground at the point of challenge? This campaign has shown that politics need not be marketed by politicians, packaged by pollsters and pundits. Politics can be a marvel arena where people come together, define common ground.

We find common ground at the plant gate that closes on workers without notice. We find common ground at the farm auction where a good farmer loses his or her land to bad loans or diminishing markets. Common ground at the schoolyard where teachers cannot get adequate pay, and students cannot get a scholarship and can't make a loan. Common ground, at the hospital admitting room where somebody tonight is dying because they cannot afford to go upstairs to a bed that's empty, waiting for someone with insurance to get sick. We are a better nation than that. We must do better.

Common ground. What is leadership if not present help in a time of crisis? And so I met you at the point of challenge in Jay, Maine where paper workers were striking for fair wages; in Greenfield, Iowa, where family farmers struggle for a fair price; in Cleveland, Ohio, where working women seek comparable worth; in McFarland, California, where the children of Hispanic farm workers may be dying from poison land, dying in clusters with cancer; in the AIDS hospice in Houston, Texas, where the sick support one another, twelve are rejected by their own parents and friends.

Common ground.

America's not a blanket woven from one thread, one color, one cloth. When I was a child growing up in Greenville, S.C., and grandmother could not afford a blanket, she didn't complain and we did not freeze. Instead, she took pieces of old cloth—patches, wool, silk, gabardine, crockersack on the patches—barely good enough to wipe your shoes with.

But they didn't stay that way very long. With sturdy hands and a strong cord, she sewed them together into a quilt, a thing of beauty and power and culture.

Now, Democrats, we must build such a quilt. Farmers, you seek fair prices and you are right, but you cannot stand alone. Your patch is not big enough. Workers, you fight for fair wages. You are right. But your labor patch is not big enough. Women, you seek comparable worth and pay equity. You are right. But your patch is not big enough. Women, mothers, who seek Head Start and day care and pre-natal care on the front side of life, rather than jail care and welfare on the back side of life, you're right, but your patch is not big enough.

Students, you seek scholarships. You are right. But your patch is not big enough. Blacks and Hispanics, when we fight for civil rights, we are right, but our patch is not big enough. Gays and lesbians, when you fight against discrimination and a cure for AIDS, you are right, but your patch is not big enough. Conservatives and progressives, when you fight for what you believe, right wing, left wing, hawk, dove—you are right, from your point of view, but your point of view is not enough.

But don't despair. Be as wise as my grandmama. Pool the patches and the pieces together, bound by a common thread. When we form a great quilt of unity and common ground we'll have the power to bring about health care and housing and jobs and education and hope to our nation.

We the people can win. We stand at the end of a long dark night of reaction. We stand tonight united in a commitment to a new direction. For almost eight years, we've been led by those who view social good coming from private interest, who viewed public life as a means to increase private wealth. They have been prepared to sacrifice the common good of the many to satisfy the private interest and the wealth of a few.

We believe in a government that's a tool of our democracy in service to the public, not an instrument of the aristocracy in search of private wealth. We believe in government with the consent of the governed of, for, and by the people. We must not emerge into a new day with a new direction. Reaganomics, based on the belief that the rich had too much money—too little money, and the poor had too much.

That's classic Reaganomics. It believes that the poor had too much money and the rich had too little money.

So, they engaged in reverse Robin Hood—took from the poor, gave to the rich, paid for by the middle class. We cannot stand four more years of Reaganomics in any version, in any disguise.

How do I document that case? Seven years later, the richest 1 percent of our society pays 20 percent less in taxes; the poorest 10 percent pay 20 percent more. Reaganomics.

Reagan gave the rich and the powerful a multibillion-dollar party. Now, the party is over. He expects the people to pay for the damage. I take this principled position—convention, let us not raise taxes on the poor and the middle class, but those who had the party, the rich and the powerful, must pay for the party!

I just want to take common sense to high places. We're spending $150 billion a year defending Europe and Japan forty-three years after the war is over. We have more troops in Europe tonight than we had seven years ago, yet the threat of war is ever more remote. Germany and Japan are now creditor nations—that means they've got a surplus. We are a debtor nation—it means we are in debt.

Let them share more of the burden of their own defense—use some of that money to build decent housing!

Use some of that money to educate our children!

Use some of that money for long-term health care!

Use some of that money to wipe out these slums and put America back to work!

I just want to take common sense to high places. If we can bail out Europe and Japan, if we can bail out Continental Bank and Chrysler—and Mr. Iacocca makes $8,000 an hour, we can bail out the family farmer.

I just want to make common sense. It does not make sense to close down 650,000 family farms in this country while importing food from abroad subsidized by the U.S. government.

Let's make sense. It does not make sense to be escorting oil tankers up and down the Persian Gulf paying $2.50 for every $1.00 worth of oil we bring out while oil wells are capped in Texas, Oklahoma and Louisiana. I just want to make sense.

Leadership must meet the moral challenge of its day. What's the moral challenge of our day? We have public accommodations. We have the right to vote. We have open housing.

What's the fundamental challenge of our day? It is to end economic violence. Plant closing without notice, economic violence. Even the greedy do not profit long from greed. Economic violence. Most poor people are not lazy. They're not black. They're not brown. They're mostly white, and female and young.

But whether white, black or brown, the hungry baby's belly turned inside out is the same color. Call it pain. Call it hurt. Call it agony. Most poor people are not on welfare.

Some of them are illiterate and can't read the want-ad sections. And when they can, they can't find a job that matches their address. They work hard every day, I know. I live amongst them. I'm one of them.

I know they work. I'm a witness. They catch the early bus. They work every day. They raise other people's children. They work every day. They clean the streets. They work every day. They drive vans with cabs. They work every day. They change the beds you slept in these hotels last night and can't get a union contract. They work every day.

No more. They're not lazy. Someone must defend them because it's right, and they cannot speak for themselves. They work in hospitals. I know they do. They wipe the bodies of those who are sick with fever and pain. They empty their bed-pans. They clean out their commode. No job is beneath them, and yet when they get sick, they cannot lie in the bed they made up every day. America, that is not right. We are a better nation than that. We are a better nation than that.

We need a real war on drugs. You can't just say no. It's deeper than that. You can't just get a palm reader or an astrologer; it's more profound than that. We're spending $150 billion on drugs a year. We've gone from ignoring it to focusing on the children. Children cannot buy $150 billion worth of drugs a year. A few high-profile athletes—athletes are not laundering $150 billion a year—bankers are.

I met the children in Watts who are unfortunate in their despair. Their grapes of hope have become raisins of despair, and they're turning to each other and they're self-destructing—but I stayed with them all night long. I wanted to hear their case. They said, "Jesse Jackson, as you challenge us to say no to drugs, you're right. And to not sell them, you're right. And to not use these guns, you're right."

And, by the way, the promise of CETA—they displaced CETA. They did not replace CETA. We have neither jobs nor houses nor services nor training—no way out. Some of us take drugs as anesthesia for our pain. Some take drugs as a way of pleasure—both short-term pleasure and long-term pain. Some sell drugs to make money. It's wrong, we know. But you need to know that we know. We can go and buy the drugs by the boxes at the port. If we can buy the drugs at the port, don't you believe the federal government can stop it if they want to?

They say, "We don't have Saturday-night specials any more." They say, "We buy AK-47s and Uzis, the latest lethal weapons. We buy them across the counter on Long Beach Boulevard." You cannot fight a war on drugs unless and until you are going to challenge the bankers and the gun sellers and those who grow them. Don't just focus on the children, let's stop drugs at the level of supply and demand. We must end the scourge on the American culture.

Leadership. What difference will we make? Leadership cannot just go along to get along. We must do more than change presidents. We must change direction. Leadership must face the moral challenge of our day. The nuclear war build-up is irrational. Strong leadership cannot desire to look tough, and let that stand in the way of the pursuit of peace. Leadership must reverse the arms race.

At least we should pledge no first use. Why? Because first use begat first retal-iation, and that's mutual annihilation. That's not a rational way out. No use at all—

let's think it out, and not fight it out, because it's an unwinnable fight. Why hold a card that you can never drop? Let's give peace a chance.

Leadership—we now have this marvelous opportunity to have a breakthrough with the Soviets. Last year, 200,000 Americans visited the Soviet Union. There's a chance for joint ventures into space, not Star Wars and the war arms escalation, but a space defense initiative. Let's build in space together, and demilitarize the heavens. There's a way out.

America, let us expand. When Mr. Reagan and Mr. Gorbachev met, there was a big meeting. They represented together one-eighth of the human race. Seven-eighths of the human race was locked out of that room. Most people in the world tonight—half are Asian, one-half of them are Chinese. There are twenty-two nations in the Middle East. There's Europe; forty million Latin Americans next door to us; the Caribbean; Africa—a half-billion people. Most people in the world today are yellow or brown or black, non-Christian, poor, female, young, and don't speak English—in the real world.

This generation must offer leadership to the real world. We're losing ground in Latin America, the Middle East, South Africa, because we're not focusing on the real world, that real world. We must use basic principles, support international law. We stand the most to gain from it. Support human rights; we believe in that. Support self-determination; we'll build on that. Support economic development; you know it's right. Be consistent, and gain our moral authority in the world.

I challenge you tonight, my friends, let's be bigger and better as a nation and as a party. We have basic challenges. Freedom in South Africa—we've already agreed as Democrats to declare South Africa to be a terrorist state. But don't just stop there. Get South Africa out of Angola. Free Namibia. Support the front-line states. We must have a new, humane human-rights assistance policy in Africa.

I'm often asked, "Jesse, why do you take on these tough issues? They're not very political. We can't win that way."

If an issue is morally right, it will eventually be political. It may be political and never be right. Fannie Lou Hamer didn't have the most votes in Atlantic City, but her principles have outlasted every delegate who voted to lock her out. Rosa Parks did not have the most votes, but she was morally right. Dr. King didn't have the most votes about the Vietnam war, but he was morally right. If we're principled first, our politics will fall in place.

Jesse, why did you take these big bold initiatives? A poem by an unknown author went something like this: We mastered the air, we've conquered the sea, and annihilated distance and prolonged life, we were not wise enough to live on this earth without war and without hate.

As for Jesse Jackson, I'm tired of sailing by little boat, far inside the harbor bar. I want to go out where the big ships float, out on the deep where the great ones are. And should my frail craft prove too slight, the waves that sweep those billows o'er, I'd rather go down in a stirring fight than drown to death in the sheltered shore.

We've got to go out, my friends, where the big boats are.

And then, for our children, young America, hold your head high now. We can win. We must not lose you to drugs and violence, premature pregnancy, suicide, cynicism, pessimism and despair. We can win.

Wherever you are tonight, I challenge you to hope and to dream. Don't submerge your dreams. Exercise above all else, even on drugs, dream of the day you're drug-free. Even in the gutter, dream of the day that you'll be up on your feet again. You must never stop dreaming. Face reality, yes. But don't stop with the way things are; dream of things as they ought to be. Dream. Face pain, but love, hope, faith, and dreams will help you rise above the pain.

Use hope and imagination as weapons of survival and progress, but you keep on dreaming, young America. Dream of peace. Peace is rational and reasonable. War is irrational in this age and unwinnable.

Dream of teachers who teach for life and not for living. Dream of doctors who are concerned more about public health than private wealth. Dream of lawyers more concerned about justice than a judgeship. Dream of preachers who are concerned more about prophecy than profiteering. Dream on the high road of sound values.

And in America, as we go forth to September, October and November and then beyond, America must never surrender to a high moral challenge.

Do not surrender to drugs. The best drug policy is a no first use. Don't surrender with needles and cynicism. Let's have no first use on the one hand, or clinics on the other. Never surrender, young America.

Go forward. America must never surrender to malnutrition. We can feed the hungry and clothe the naked. We must never surrender. We must go forward. We must never surrender to illiteracy. Invest in our children. Never surrender; and go forward.

We must never surrender to inequality. Women cannot compromise ERA or comparable worth. Women are making 60 cents on the dollar to what a man makes. Women cannot buy meat cheaper. Women cannot buy bread cheaper. Women cannot buy milk cheaper. Women deserve to get paid for the work that you do. It's right and it's fair.

Don't surrender, my friends. Those who have AIDS tonight, you deserve our compassion. Even with AIDS you must not surrender in your wheelchairs. I see you sitting here tonight in those wheelchairs. I've stayed with you. I've reached out to you across our nation. Don't you give up. I know it's tough sometimes. People look down on you. It took you a little more effort to get here tonight.

And no one should look down on you, but sometimes mean people do. The only justification we have for looking down on someone is that we're going to stop and pick them up. But even in your wheelchairs, don't you give up. We cannot forget fifty years ago when our backs were against the wall, Roosevelt was in a wheelchair. I would rather have Roosevelt in a wheelchair than Reagan and Bush on a horse. Don't you surrender and don't you give up.

Don't surrender and don't give up. Why can I challenge you this way? Jesse Jackson, you don't understand my situation. You be on television. You don't understand. I see you with the big people. You don't understand my situation. I understand. You're seeing me on TV but you don't know the me that makes me, me. They wonder why does Jesse run, because they see me running for the White House. They don't see the house I'm running from.

I have a story. I wasn't always on television. Writers were not always outside my door. When I was born late one afternoon, October 8th, in Greenville, S.C., no writers asked my mother her name. Nobody chose to write down our address. My mama was not supposed to make it. And I was not supposed to make it. You see, I was born to a teen-age mother who was born to a teen-age mother.

I understand. I know abandonment and people being mean to you, and saying you're nothing and nobody, and can never be anything. I understand. Jesse Jackson is my third name. I'm adopted. When I had no name, my grandmother gave me her name. My name was Jesse Burns until I was 12. So I wouldn't have a blank space, she gave me a name to hold me over. I understand when nobody knows your name. I understand when you have no name.

I understand. I wasn't born in the hospital. Mama didn't have insurance. I was born in the bed at home. I really do understand. Born in a three-room house, bathroom in the backyard, slop jar by the bed, no hot and cold running water. I understand. Wallpaper used for decoration? No. For a windbreaker. I understand. I'm a working person's person, that's why I understand you whether you're black or white.

I understand work. I was not born with a silver spoon in my mouth. I had a shovel programmed for my hand. My mother, a working woman. So many days she went to work early with runs in her stockings. She knew better, but she wore runs in her stockings so that my brother and I could have matching socks and not be laughed at at school.

I understand. At 3 o'clock on Thanksgiving Day we couldn't eat turkey because mama was preparing someone else's turkey at 3 o'clock. We had to play football to entertain ourselves and then around 6 o'clock she would get off the Alta Vista bus; then we would bring up the leftovers and eat our turkey—leftovers, the carcass, the cranberries around 8 o'clock at night. I really do understand.

Every one of these funny labels they put on you, those of you who are watching this broadcast tonight in the projects, on the corners, I understand. Call you outcast, low down, you can't make it, you're nothing, you're from nobody, subclass, underclass—when you see Jesse Jackson, when my name goes in nomination, your name goes in nomination.

I was born in the slum, but the slum was not born in me. And it wasn't born in you, and you can make it. Wherever you are tonight you can make it. Hold your head high, stick your chest out. You can make it. It gets dark sometimes, but the morning comes. Don't you surrender. Suffering breeds character. Character breeds faith. In the end faith will not disappoint.

You must not surrender. You may or may not get there, but just know that you're qualified and you hold on and hold out. We must never surrender. America will get better and better. Keep hope alive. Keep hope alive. Keep hope alive. On tomorrow night and beyond, keep hope alive.

I love you very much. I love you very much.

Source: "Common Ground and Common Sense," address delivered July 20, 1988, reprinted in *Vital Speeches* 54, no. 21 (August 15, 1988), pp. 649–53.

SELECT BIBLIOGRAPHY:

Lucius Barker and Ronald W. Walters, eds., *Jesse Jackson's 1984 Presidential Campaign: Challenge and Change in American Politics* (Urbana: University of Illinois Press, 1989).

Sheila D. Collins, *The Rainbow Challenge: The Jackson Campaign and the Future of U.S. Politics* (New York: Monthly Review Press, 1986).

Elizabeth O. Colton, *The Jackson Phenomenon: The Man, the Power, the Message* (New York: Doubleday, 1989).

Marshall Frady, *Jesse: The Life and Pilgrimage of Jesse Jackson* (New York: Random House, 1996).

Roger D. Hatch, *Beyond Opportunity: Jesse Jackson's Vision for America* (Philadelphia: Fortress Press, 1988).

Manning Marable, *Black American Politics: From the Washington Marches to Jesse Jackson* (London: Verso, 1985).

Adolph Reed, *The Jesse Jackson Phenomenon and the Crisis of Purpose in African-American Politics* (New Haven, Conn.: Yale University Press, 1986).

Barbara A. Reynolds, *Jesse Jackson: America's David* (Washington, D.C.: JFJ Associates, 1985).

⸏ 8 ⸏

"Afrocentricity," *Molefi Asante, 1991*

Born Arthur Smith in Valdosta, Georgia, Molefi Kete Asante (1942–) holds a Ph.D. from UCLA and is currently professor of African-American studies at Temple University. Asante chaired the Department of African-American Studies at Temple for many years, and was responsible for making the program one of the most influential of its kind in the United States. A prolific author, Asante was founding editor of the *Journal of Black Studies* (1969). Asante's lasting influence as an intellectual is chiefly derived from his theory of "Afrocentricity." Asante's ideas about culture, education, and philosophy have had a profound impact on the scholarship of black studies. In this essay, Asante discusses the differences between what he describes as "Eurocentric education" versus multiculturalism.

⸏

THE AFROCENTRIC IDEA IN EDUCATION

Introduction

Many of the principles that govern the development of the Afrocentric idea in education were first established by Carter G. Woodson in *The Mis-education of the Negro* (1933). Indeed, Woodson's classic reveals the fundamental problems pertaining to the education of the African person in America. As Woodson contends, African Americans have been educated away from their own culture and traditions and attached to the fringes of European culture; thus dislocated from themselves, Woodson asserts that African Americans often valorize European culture to the detriment of their own heritage (p. 7). Although Woodson does not advocate rejection of American citizenship or nationality, he believed that assuming African Americans hold the same position as European Americans vis-à-vis the realities of America would lead to the psychological and cultural death of the African-American population. Furthermore, if education is ever to be substantive and meaningful within the context of American society, Woodson argues, it must first address the African's historical experiences, both in Africa and America (p. 7). That is why he places on education, and particularly on the traditionally African-American colleges, the burden of teaching the African American to be responsive to the long traditions and history of Africa as well as America. Woodson's alert recognition, more than 50 years ago, that something is severely wrong with the way African Americans are educated provides the principal impetus for the Afrocentric approach to American education.

. . . I will examine the nature and scope of this approach, establish its necessity, and suggest ways to develop and disseminate it throughout all levels of education. Two propositions stand in the background of the theoretical and philosophical issues I will present. These ideas represent the core presuppositions on which I have based most of my work in the field of education, and they suggest the direction of my own thinking about what education is capable of doing to and for an already politically and economically marginalized people—African Americans.

1. Education is fundamentally a social phenomenon whose ultimate purpose is to socialize the learner; to send a child to school is to prepare that child to become part of a social group.
2. Schools are reflective of the societies that develop them (i.e., a White-supremacist–dominated society will develop a White-supremacist educational system).

Definitions

. . . *Afrocentricity* is a frame of reference wherein phenomena are viewed from the perspective of the African person. The Afrocentric approach seeks in every situation the appropriate centrality of the African person (Asante, 1987). In education this means that teachers provide students the opportunity to study the world and its people, concepts, and history from an African world view. In most classrooms, whatever the subject, Whites are located in the center perspective position. How alien the African-American child must feel, how like an outsider! The little African-American child who sits in a classroom and is taught to accept as heroes and heroines individuals who defamed African people is being actively de-centered, dislocated, and made into a nonperson, one whose aim in life might be to one day shed that "badge of inferiority": his or her Blackness. In Afrocentric educational settings, however, teachers do not marginalize African-American children by causing them to question their own self-worth because their people's story is seldom told. By seeing themselves as the subjects rather than the objects of education—be the discipline biology, medicine, literature, or social studies—African-American students come to see themselves not merely as seekers of knowledge but as integral participants in it. Because all content areas are adaptable to an Afrocentric approach, African-American students can be made to see themselves as centered in the reality of any discipline.

It must be emphasized that Afrocentricity is *not* a Black version of Eurocentricity (Asante, 1987). Eurocentricity is based on White-supremacist notions whose purposes are to protect White privilege and advantage in education, economics, politics, and so forth. Unlike Eurocentricity, Afrocentricity does not condone ethnocentric valorization at the expense of degrading other groups' perspectives. Moreover, Eurocentricity presents the particular historical reality of Europeans as the sum total of the human experience (Asante, 1987). It imposes Eurocentric realities as "universal"; i.e., that which is White is presented as applying to the human condition in general, while that which is non-White is viewed as group-specific and therefore not "human." This explains why some scholars and artists of African descent rush to deny their Blackness; they believe that to exist as a Black person is not to exist as a universal human being. They are the individuals Woodson identified as preferring European art, language, and culture over African art, language, and culture; they believe that anything of European origin is inherently better than anything produced by or issuing from their own people. Naturally, the person of African descent should be centered in his or her historical experiences as an African, but Eurocentric curricula produce such aberrations of perspective among persons of color.

Multiculturalism in education is a nonhierarchical approach that respects and celebrates a variety of cultural perspectives on world phenomena (Asante, 1991). The multicultural approach holds that although European culture is the majority culture in the United States, that is not sufficient reason for it to be imposed on diverse student populations as "universal." Multiculturalists assert that education, to have integrity, must begin with the proposition that all humans have contributed to world development and the flow of knowledge and information, and that most human achievements are the result of mutually interactive, international effort. Without a multicultural education, students remain essentially ignorant of the contributions of a major portion of the world's people. A multicultural education is thus a fundamental necessity for anyone who wishes to achieve competency in almost any subject.

The Afrocentric idea must be the stepping-stone from which the multicultural idea is launched. A truly authentic multicultural education, therefore, must be based upon the Afrocentric initiative. If this step is skipped, multicultural curricula, as they are increasingly being defined by White "resisters" (to be discussed below) will evolve without any substantive infusion of African-American content, and the African-American child will continue to be lost in the Eurocentric framework of education. In other words, the African-American child will neither be confirmed nor affirmed in his or her own cultural information. For the mutual benefit of all Americans, this tragedy, which leads to the psychological and cultural dislocation of African-American children, can and should be avoided.

The Revolutionary Challenge

Because it centers African-American students inside history, culture, science, and so forth rather than outside these subjects, the Afrocentric idea presents the most revolutionary challenge to the ideology of White supremacy in education during the past decade. No other theoretical position stated by African Americans has ever captured the imagination of such a wide range of scholars and students of history, sociology, communications, anthropology, and psychology. The Afrocentric challenge has been posed in three critical ways:

1. It questions the imposition of the White-supremacist view as universal and/or classical (Asante, 1990).
2. It demonstrates the indefensibility of racist theories that assault multiculturalism and pluralism.
3. It projects a humanistic and pluralistic viewpoint by articulating Afrocentricity as a valid, nonhegemonic perspective.

Suppression and Distortion: Symbols of Resistance

. . . Naturally, different adherents to a theory will have different views on its meaning. While two discourses presently are circulating about multiculturalism, only one is relevant to the liberation of the minds of African and White people in the United States. That discourse is Afrocentricity: the acceptance of Africa as central to African people. Yet, rather than getting on board with Afrocentrists to fight against White hegemonic education, some Whites (and some Blacks as well) have opted to plead for a return to the educational plantation. Unfortunately for them, however, those days are gone, and such misinformation can never be packaged as accurate, correct education again.

Ravitch (1990), who argues that there are two kinds of multiculturalism—*pluralist multiculturalism* and *particularist multiculturalism*—is the leader of those professors whom I call "resisters" or opponents to Afrocentricity and multiculturalism. Indeed, Ravitch advances the imaginary divisions in multicultural perspectives to conceal her true identity as a defender of White supremacy. Her tactics are the tactics of those who prefer Africans and other non-Whites to remain on the mental and psychological plantation of Western civilization. In their arrogance the resisters accuse Afrocentrists and multiculturalists of creating "fantasy history" and "bizarre theories" of non-White people's contributions to civilization. What they prove, however, is their own ignorance. Additionally, Ravitch and others (Nicholson, 1990) assert that multiculturalism will bring about the "tribalization" of America, but in reality America has always been a nation of ethnic diversity. When one reads their works on multiculturalism, one realizes that they are really advocating the imposition of a White perspective on everybody else's culture. Believing that the Eurocentric position is indisputable, they attempt to resist and impede the progressive transformation of the monoethnic curriculum. Indeed, the closets of bigotry have opened to reveal various attempts by White scholars (joined by some Blacks) to defend White privilege in the curriculum in much the same way as it has been so staunchly defended in the larger society. It was perhaps inevitable that the introduction of the Afrocentric idea would open up the discussion of the American school curriculum in a profound way. . . .

The Condition of Eurocentric Education

Institutions such as schools are conditioned by the character of the nation in which they are developed. Just as crime and politics are different in different nations, so, too, is education. In the United States a "Whites-only" orientation has predominated in education. This has had a profound impact on the quality of education for children of all races and ethnic groups. The African-American child has suffered disproportionately, but White children are also the victims of monoculturally diseased curricula. . . .

Afrocentricity and History. Most of America's teaching force are victims of the same system that victimizes today's young. Thus, American children are not taught the names of the African ethnic groups from which the majority of the African-American population are derived; few are taught the names of any of the sacred sites in Africa. Few teachers can discuss with their students the significance of the Middle Passage or describe what it meant or means to Africans. Little mention is made in American classrooms of either the brutality of slavery or the ex-slaves' celebration of freedom. American children have little or no understanding of the nature of the capture, transport, and enslavement of Africans. Few have been taught the true horrors of being taken, shipped naked across twenty-five days of ocean, broken by abuse and indignities of all kinds, and dehumanized into a beast of burden, a thing without a name. If our students only knew the truth, if they were taught the Afrocentric perspective on the Great Enslavement, and if they knew the full story about the events since slavery that have served to constantly dislocate African Americans, their behavior would perhaps be different. . . .

Enslavement was truly a living death. While the ontological onslaught caused some Africans to opt for suicide, the most widespread results were dislocation, disorientation, and misorientation—all of which are the consequences of the African person being actively de-centered. The "Jim Crow" period of second-class citizenship, from 1877 to 1954, saw only slight improvement in the lot of African Americans. This era was characterized by the sharecropper system, disenfranchisement, enforced segregation, internal migration, lynchings, unemployment, poor housing conditions, and separate and unequal educational facilities. Inequitable policies and practices veritably plagued the race.

No wonder many persons of African descent attempt to shed their race and become "raceless." One's basic identity is one's self-identity, which is ultimately one's cultural identity; without a strong cultural identity, one is lost. Black children do not know their people's story and White children do not know the story, but remembrance is a vital requisite for understanding and humility. This is why the Jews have campaigned (and rightly so) to have the story of the European Holocaust taught in schools and colleges. Teaching about such a monstrous human brutality should forever remind the world of the ways in which humans have often violated each other. Teaching about the African Holocaust is just as important for many of the same reasons. Additionally, it underscores the enormity of the effects of physical, psychological, and economic dislocation on the African population in America and throughout the African diaspora. Without an understanding of the historical experiences of African people, American children cannot make any real headway in addressing the problems of the present. . . .

Conclusion
The reigning initiative for total curricular change is the movement that is being proposed and led by Africans, namely, the Afrocentric idea. When I wrote the first book on Afrocentricity (Asante, 1980), now in its fifth printing, I had no idea that in ten years the idea would both shake up and shape discussions in education, art, fashion, and politics. Since the publication of my subsequent works, The Afrocentric Idea (Asante, 1987) and Kemet, Afrocentricity, and Knowledge (Asante, 1990) the debate has been joined in earnest. Still, for many White Americans (and some African Americans) the most unsettling aspect of the discussion about Afrocentricity is that its intellectual source lies in the research and writings of African-American scholars. Whites are accustomed to being in charge of the major ideas circulating in the American academy. Deconstructionism, Gestalt psychology, Marxism, structuralism, Piagetian theory, and so forth have all been developed, articulated, and elaborated upon at length, generally by White scholars. On the other hand, Afrocentricity is the product of scholars such as Nobles (1986), Hilliard (1978), Karenga (1986), Keto (1990), Richards (1991), and Myers (1989). There are also increasing numbers of young, impressively credentialed African-American scholars who have begun to write in the Afrocentric vein (Jean, 1991). They, and even some young White scholars, have emerged with ideas about how to change the curriculum Afrocentrically.

Afrocentricity provides all Americans an opportunity to examine the perspective of the African person in this society and the world. The resisters claim that Afrocentricity is anti-White; yet, if Afrocentricity as a theory is against anything it is against racism, ignorance, and monoethnic hegemony in the curriculum. Afrocentricity is not anti-White; it is, however, pro-human. Further, the aim of the Afrocentric curriculum is not to divide America, it is to make America flourish as it ought to flourish. This nation has long been divided with regard to the educational opportunities afforded to children. By virtue of the protection provided by society and reinforced by the Eurocentric curriculum, the White child is already ahead of the African American child by first grade. Our efforts thus must concentrate on giving the African-American child greater opportunities for learning at the kindergarten level. However, the kind of assistance the African-American child needs is as much cultural as it is academic. If the proper cultural information is provided, the academic performance will surely follow suit.

When it comes to educating African-American children, the American educational system does not need a tune-up, it needs an overhaul. Black children have been maligned by this system. Black teachers have been maligned. Black history has been maligned. Africa has been maligned. Nonetheless, two truisms can be stated about education in America. First, some teachers can and do effectively teach African-American children; secondly, if some teachers can do it, others can, too. We must learn all we can about what makes these teachers' attitudes and approaches successful, and then work diligently to see that their successes are replicated on a broad scale. By raising the same questions that Woodson posed more than fifty years ago, Afrocentric education, along with a significant reorientation of the American educational enterprise, seeks to respond to the African person's psychological and cultural dislocation. By providing philosophical and theoretical guidelines and criteria that are centered in an African perception of reality and by placing the African-American child in his or her proper historical context and setting, Afrocentricity may be just the "escape hatch" African Americans so desperately need to facilitate academic success and "steal away" from the cycle of miseducation and dislocation.

Source: "The Afrocentric Idea in Education," *Journal of Negro Education* 60, no. 2 (Spring 1991), pp. 170–80. Copyright 1991 by Howard University.

SELECT BIBLIOGRAPHY:
Molefi Asante, *Afrocentricity: The Theory of Social Change* (Buffalo, N.Y.: Amulefi Publishing Company, 1980).
———, *The Afrocentric Idea*, rev. and expanded ed. (Philadelphia: Temple University Press, 1998).
Molefi Asante, Eileen Newmar, and Cecil A. Blake, eds., *Handbook of Intercultural Communication* (Beverly Hills, Ca.: Sage Publications, 1979).
Molefi Asante and Abdulani S. Vandi, eds., *Contemporary Black Thought: Alternative Analyses in Social and Behavioral Science* (Beverly Hills, Ca.: Sage Publications, 1980).
Molefi Asante and Mark T. Mattson, eds., *The African-American Atlas: Black History and Culture: An Illustrated Reference* (New York: Macmillan, 1998).

⟿ 9 ⟿

The Anita Hill–Clarence Thomas Controversy, *1991*

In 1991, President George Bush nominated Clarence Thomas, a conservative black Republican who was at the time a judge on the United States Court of

Appeals for the District of Columbia, to replace Thurgood Marshall as Associate Judge on the U.S. Supreme Court. Thomas had previously served as the head of the Equal Employment Opportunity Commission during the Reagan administration. Anita Hill, an African-American attorney and law professor, charged that Thomas had sexually harassed and abused her when she worked as his assistant in the federal government. In highly publicized hearings held by the Senate judiciary committee, Hill outlined her charges against Thomas, which he vigorously denied. Despite major opposition from many African Americans and liberal organizations, Thomas was confirmed by the Senate for a seat on the Supreme Court.

The first document below was issued by a group of African-American female scholars and activists who were outraged by the sexist and reactionary rhetoric surrounding the media's and political establishment's defense of Thomas. The statement was first published in an advertisement in the *New York Times*, and was conceived and organized by black-feminist scholars Barbara Ransby, Elsa Barkley Brown, and Deborah King. The second document is an excerpt from an essay by scholar and poet June Jordan, which discusses the failure of many African-American political organizations and leaders to support Hill and to oppose both the sexist personal behavior and conservative political agenda of Thomas.

～

AFRICAN-AMERICAN WOMEN IN DEFENSE OF OURSELVES

As women of African descent, we are deeply troubled by the recent nomination, confirmation and seating of Clarence Thomas as an Associate Justice of the U.S. Supreme Court. We know that the presence of Clarence Thomas on the Court will be continually used to divert attention from historic struggles for social justice through suggestions that the presence of a Black man on the Supreme Court constitutes an assurance that the rights of African Americans will be protected. Clarence Thomas' public record is ample evidence this will not be true. Further, the consolidation of a conservative majority on the Supreme Court seriously endangers the rights of all women, poor and working-class people and the elderly. The seating of Clarence Thomas is an affront not only to African-American women and men, but to all people concerned with social justice.

We are particularly outraged by the racist and sexist treatment of Professor Anita Hill, an African-American woman who was maligned and castigated for daring to speak publicly of her own experience of sexual abuse. The malicious defamation of Professor Hill insulted all women of African descent and sent a dangerous message to any woman who might contemplate a sexual harassment complaint.

We speak here because we recognize that the media are now portraying the Black community as prepared to tolerate both the dismantling of affirmative action and the evil of sexual harassment in order to have any Black man on the Supreme Court. We want to make clear that the media have ignored or distorted many African-American voices. We will not be silenced.

Many have erroneously portrayed the allegations against Clarence Thomas as an issue of either gender or race. As women of African descent, we understand sexual harassment as both. We further understand that Clarence Thomas outrageously manipulated the legacy of lynching in order to shelter himself from Anita Hill's allegations. To deflect attention away from the reality of sexual abuse in African-American women's lives, he trivialized and misrepresented this painful part of African-American people's history. This country, which has a long legacy of racism and sexism, has never taken the sexual abuse of Black women seriously. Throughout U.S. history Black women have been sexually stereotyped as immoral, insatiable, perverse; the initiators in all sexual contacts—abusive or otherwise. The common assumption in legal proceedings as well as in the larger society has been that Black women cannot be raped or otherwise sexually abused. As Anita Hill's experience demonstrates, Black women who speak of these matters are not likely to be believed.

In 1991, we cannot tolerate this type of dismissal of any one Black woman's experience or this attack upon our collective character without protest, outrage, and resistance. As women of African descent, we express our vehement opposition to the policies represented by the placement of Clarence Thomas on the Supreme Court. The Bush administration, having obstructed the passage of civil-rights legislation, impeded the extension of unemployment compensation, cut student aid and dismantled social welfare programs, has continually demonstrated that it is not operating in our best interests. Nor is this appointee. We pledge ourselves to continue to speak out in defense of one another, in defense of the African-American community and against those who are hostile to social justice no matter what color they are. No one will speak for us but ourselves.

~

CAN I GET A WITNESS?

I wanted to write a letter to Anita Hill. I wanted to say thanks. I wanted to convey the sorrow and the bitterness I feel on her behalf. I wanted to explode the history that twisted itself around the innocence of her fate. I wanted to assail the brutal ironies, the cruel consistencies that left her—at the moment of her utmost vulnerability and public power—isolated, betrayed, abused, and not nearly as powerful as those who sought and who seek to besmirch, ridicule, and condemn the truth of her important and perishable human being. I wanted to reassure her of her rights, her sanity, and the African beauty of her earnest commitment to do right and to be a good woman: a good black woman in this America.

But tonight I am still too furious, I am still too hurt, I am still too astounded and nauseated by the enemies of Anita Hill. Tonight my heart pounds with shame.

Is there no way to interdict and terminate the traditional abusive loneliness of black women in this savage country?

From those slavery times when African men could not dare to defend their sisters, their mothers, their sweethearts, their wives, and their daughters—except at the risk of their lives—from those times until today: Has nothing changed?

How is it possible that only John Carr—a young black corporate lawyer who maintained a friendship with Anita Hill ten years ago ("It didn't go but so far," he testified, with an engaging, handsome trace of a smile)—how is it possible that he, alone among black men, stood tall and strong and righteous as a witness for her defense?

What about spokesmen for the NAACP or the National Urban League?

What about spokesmen for the U.S. Congressional Black Caucus?

All of the organizational and elected black men who spoke aloud against a wrong black man, Clarence Thomas, for the sake of principles resting upon decency and concerns for fair play, equal protection, and affirmative action—where did they go when, suddenly, a good black woman arose among us, trying to tell the truth?

Where did they go? And why?

Is it conceivable that a young white woman could be tricked into appearing before twelve black men of the U.S. Senate?

Is it conceivable that a young white woman could be tricked into appearing before a lineup of incredibly powerful and hypocritical and sneering and hellbent black men freely insinuating and freely hypothesizing whatever lurid scenario came into their heads?

Is it conceivable that such a young woman—such a flower of white womanhood—would, by herself, have to withstand the calumny and unabashed, unlawful bullying that was heaped upon Anita Hill?

Is it conceivable that this flower would not be swiftly surrounded by white knights rallying—with ropes, or guns, or whatever—to defend her honor and the honor, the legal and civilized rights, of white people, *per se*?

Anita Hill was tricked. She was set up. She had been minding her business at the University of Oklahoma Law School when the Senators asked her to describe her relationship with Clarence Thomas. Anita Hill's dutiful answers disclosed that Thomas had violated the trust of his office as head of the Equal Employment Opportunity Commission. Sitting in that office of ultimate recourse for women suffering from sexual harassment, Thomas himself harassed Anita Hill, repeatedly, with unwanted sexual advances and remarks.

Although Anita Hill had not volunteered this information and only supplied it in response to direct, specific inquiries from the FBI,

And although Anita Hill was promised the protection of confidentiality as regards her sworn statement of allegations,

And despite the fact that four witnesses—two men and two women, two black and two white distinguished Americans, including a Federal judge and a professor of law—testified, under oath, that Anita Hill had told each of them about these sordid carryings on by Thomas at the time of their occurrence or in the years that followed,

And despite the fact that Anita Hill sustained a remarkably fastidious display of exact recall and never alleged, for example, that Thomas actually touched her,

And despite the unpardonable decision by the U.S. Senate Judiciary Committee to prohibit expert testimony on sexual harassment,

Anita Hill, a young black woman born and raised within a black farm family of thirteen children, a graduate of an Oklahoma public high school who later earned honors and graduated from Yale Law School, a political conservative and, now, a professor of law,

Anita Hill, a young black woman who suffered sexual harassment once in ten years and, therefore, never reported sexual harassment to any of her friends except for that once in ten years,

Anita Hill, whose public calm and dispassionate sincerity refreshed America's eyes and ears with her persuasive example of what somebody looks like and sounds like when she's simply trying to tell the truth,

Anita Hill was subpoenaed by the U.S. Senate Judiciary Committee of fourteen white men and made to testify and to tolerate interrogation on national television.

1. Why didn't she "do something" when Thomas allegedly harassed her?

The Senators didn't seem to notice or to care that Thomas occupied the office of last recourse for victims of sexual harassment. And had the Committee allowed any expert on the subject to testify, we would have learned that it is absolutely typical for victims to keep silent.

2. Wasn't it the case that she had/has fantasies and is delusional?

Remarkably, not a single psychiatrist or licensed psychologist was allowed to testify. These slanderous suppositions about the psychic functionings of Anita Hill were never more than malevolent speculations invited by one or another of the fourteen white Senators as they sat above an assortment of character witnesses hand-picked by White House staffers eager to protect the President's nominee.

One loathsomely memorable item: John Doggett, a self-infatuated black attorney and a friend of Clarence Thomas, declared that Thomas would not have jeopardized his career for Anita Hill because Doggett, a black man, explained to the Senate Committee of fourteen white men, "She is not worth it."

3. Why was she "lying"?

It should be noted that Anita Hill readily agreed to a lie-detector test and that, according to the test, she was telling the truth. It should also be noted that Clarence Thomas refused even to consider taking such a test and that, furthermore, he had already established himself as a liar when, earlier in the Senate hearings, he insisted that he had never discussed *Roe* v. *Wade*, and didn't know much about this paramount legal dispute.

Meanwhile, Clarence Thomas—who has nodded and grinned his way to glory and power by denying systemic American realities of racism, on the one hand, and by publicly castigating and lying about his own sister, a poor black woman, on the other—this Thomas, this Uncle Tom calamity of mediocre abilities, at best, this bootstrap miracle of egomaniacal myth and self-pity, this choice of the very same President who has vetoed two civil-rights bills and boasted about that, how did he respond to the testimony of Anita Hill?

Clarence Thomas thundered and he shook. Clarence Thomas glowered and he growled. "God is my judge!" he cried, at one especially disgusting low point in the Senate proceedings. "God is my judge, Senator. And not you!" This candidate for the Supreme Court evidently believes himself exempt from the judgments of mere men.

This Clarence Thomas—about whom an African-American young man in my freshman composition class exclaimed, "He's an Uncle Tom. He's a hypocritical Uncle Tom. And I don't care what happens to his punk ass"—this Thomas vilified the hearings as a "high-tech lynching."

When he got into hot water for the first time (on public record, at any rate), he attempted to identify himself as a regular black man. What a peculiar reaction to the charge of sexual harassment!

And where was the laughter that should have embarrassed him out of that chamber?

And where were the tears?

When and where was there ever a black man lynched because he was bothering a black woman?

When and where was there ever a white man jailed or tarred and feathered because he was bothering a black woman?

When a black woman is raped or beaten or mutilated by a black man or a white man, what happens?

To be a black woman in this savage country: Is that to be nothing and no one beautiful and precious and exquisitely compelling?

To be a black woman in this savage country: Is that to be nothing and no one revered and defended and given our help and our gratitude?

The only powerful man to utter and to level the appropriate word of revulsion as a charge against his peers—the word was "SHAME"—that man was U.S. Senator Ted Kennedy, a white man whose ongoing, successful career illuminates the unequal privileges of male gender, white race, and millionaire-class identity.

But Ted Kennedy was not on trial. He has never been on trial.

Clarence Thomas was supposed to be on trial but he was not: He is more powerful than Anita Hill. And his bedfellows, from Senator Strom Thurmond to President George Bush, persist—way more powerful than Clarence Thomas and Anita Hill combined.

And so, at the last, it was she, Anita Hill, who stood alone, trying to tell the truth in an arena of snakes and hyenas and dinosaurs and power-mad dogs. And with this televised victimization of Anita Hill, the American war of violence against women moved from the streets, moved from hip hop, moved from multi-million-dollar movies into the highest chambers of the U.S. Government.

And what is anybody going to do about it?

I, for one, am going to write a letter to Anita Hill. I am going to tell her that, thank God, she is a black woman who is somebody and something beautiful and precious and exquisitely compelling.

And I am going to say that if this Government will not protect and defend her, and all black women, and all women, period, in this savage country—if this Government will not defend us from poverty and violence and contempt—then we will change the Government. We have the numbers to deliver on this warning.

And, as for those brothers who disappeared when a black woman rose up to tell the truth, listen: It's getting to be payback time. I have been speaking on behalf of a good black woman. Can you hear me?

Can I get a witness?

Sources: (1) "African-American Women in Defense of Ourselves"; and (2) June Jordan, "Can I Get a Witness?" Both are reprinted with permission from *Black Scholar* 22, nos. 1 and 2 (Winter/Spring 1991), pp. 56–58, 155.

SELECT BIBLIOGRAPHY:

Anita F. Hill and Emma C. Jordan, eds., *Race, Gender and Power in America: The Legacy of the Hill–Thomas Hearings* (New York: Oxford University Press, 1995).

Toni Morrison, ed., *Race-ing Justice, En-gendering Power: Essays on Anita Hill, Clarence Thomas, and the Construction of Social Reality* (New York: Pantheon, 1992).

10

"Race Matters," *Cornel West, 1991*

Cornel West (1953–) was born in Tulsa, Oklahoma, and raised in Sacramento, California. He graduated *magna cum laude* from Harvard College and received his doctorate from Princeton University in 1980. He quickly produced a series of theoretically engaging texts in the fields of theology, philosophy, and Marxist thought. West joined the Democratic Socialists of America in 1982, and for many years served as its honorary chairperson. From 1989 to 1994 he was professor of African-American studies at Princeton, and subsequently joined the faculty of African-American Studies at Harvard University. After a public conflict with Harvard's president, West rejoined the faculty of Princeton University as a University Professor. Considered one of the most influential intellectuals in America, West published the widely read book, *Race Matters* (1991). In subsequent works such as *Democracy Matters* (2004), West advocates a fundamental redistribution of wealth and resources, the reduction of the power of the market, and the creation of a more equitable society in the United States.

NIHILISM IN BLACK AMERICA

Recent discussions about the plight of African Americans—especially those at the bottom of the social ladder—tend to divide into two camps. On the one hand, there are those who highlight the *structural* constraints on the life chances of black people. This point of view involves a subtle historical and sociological analysis of slavery, Jim Crowism, job and residential discrimination, skewed unemployment rates, inadequate health care, and poor education. On the other hand, there are those who stress the *behavioral* impediments to black upward mobility. They focus on the waning of the Protestant ethic—hard work, deferred gratification, frugality, and responsibility—in much of black America.

Those in the first camp—the liberal structuralists—call for full employment, health, education and child-care programs, and broad affirmative-action practices. In short, a new, more sober version of the best of the New Deal and the Great Society: more government money, better bureaucrats, and an active citizenry. Those in the second camp—the conservative behaviorists—promote self-help programs, black business expansion, and non-preferential job practices. They support vigorous "free market" strategies that depend on fundamental changes in how black people act and live. To put it bluntly, their projects rest largely upon a cultural revival of the Protestant ethic in black America.

Unfortunately, these two camps have nearly suffocated the crucial debate that should be taking place about the prospects for black America. This debate must go far beyond the liberal and conservative positions in three fundamental ways. First, we must acknowledge that structures and behavior are inseparable, that institutions and values go hand in hand. How people act and live is shaped—though in no way dictated or determined—by the larger circumstances in which they find themselves. These circumstances can be changed, their limits attenuated, by positive actions to elevate living conditions.

Second, we should reject the idea that structures are primarily economic and political creatures—an idea that sees culture as an ephemeral set of behavioral attitudes and values. Culture is quite as structural as the economy or politics; it is rooted in institutions like families, schools, churches, synagogues, mosques, and communication industries (television, radio, video, music). Similarly, the economy and politics are not only influenced by values, they also promote particular cultural ideals of the good life and good society.

Third, and most important, we must delve into the depths where neither liberals nor conservatives dare to tread, namely, into the murky waters of despair and dread that now flood the streets of black America. To talk about the depressing statistics of unemployment, infant mortality, incarceration, teenage pregnancy, and violent crime is one thing. But to face up to the monumental eclipse of hope, the unprecedented collapse of meaning, the incredible disregard for human (especially black) life and property in much of black America is something else.

The liberal-conservative discussion conceals the most basic issue now facing black America: *the nihilistic threat to its very existence.* This threat is not simply a matter of relative economic deprivation and political powerlessness—though economic well-being and political clout are requisites for meaningful black progress. It is primarily a question of speaking to the profound sense of psychological depression, personal worthlessness, and social despair so widespread in black America.

The liberal structuralists fail to grapple with this threat for two reasons. First, their focus on structural constraints relates almost exclusively to the economy and politics. They show no understanding of the structural character of culture. Why? Because they tend to view people in egoistic and rationalist terms, according to which they are motivated primarily by self-interest and self-preservation. Needless to say, this is partly true about most of us. Yet, people, especially degraded and oppressed people, are also hungry for identity, meaning, and self-worth.

The second reason liberal structuralists overlook the nihilistic threat is a sheer failure of nerve. They hesitate to talk honestly about culture, the realm of meanings and values, because to do so may seem to lend itself too readily to conservative conclusions in the narrow way Americans discuss race. If there is a hidden taboo among liberals, it is to resist talking about values *too much* because it takes the focus away from structures, especially the positive role of government. But this failure leaves the existential and psychological realities of black people in the lurch. In this way, liberal structuralists neglect the battered identities rampant in black America.

As for the conservative behaviorists, they not only misconstrue the nihilistic threat, but inadvertently contribute to it. This is a serious charge, and it rests upon three claims. First, conservative behaviorists talk about values and attitudes as if political and economic structures hardly exist. They rarely, if ever, examine the innumerable cases in which black people do act on the Protestant ethic and still remain at the bottom of the social ladder. Instead, they highlight the few instances in which blacks ascend to the top, as if such success is available to all blacks, regardless of circumstances. Such a vulgar rendition of Horatio Alger in blackface may serve as a source of inspiration to some—a kind of model for those already on the right track. But it cannot serve as a substitute for serious historical and social analysis of the predicaments of and prospects for all black people, especially the grossly disadvantaged ones.

Second, conservative behaviorists discuss black culture as if acknowledging one's obvious victimization by white-supremacist practices (compounded by sexism and class condition) is taboo. They tell black people to see themselves as agents, not victims. And on the surface, this is comforting advice, a nice cliche for downtrodden people. But inspirational slogans cannot substitute for substantive historical and social analysis. Although black people have never been simply victims, wallowing in self-pity and begging for white giveaways, they have been— and are—*victimized*. Therefore, to call on black people to be agents makes sense only if we also examine the dynamics of this victimization against which their agency will, in part, be exercised. What is particularly naive and peculiarly vicious about the conservative behavioral outlook is that it tends to deny the lingering effect of black history—a history inseparable from though not reducible to victimization. In this way, crucial and indispensable themes of self-help and personal responsibility are wrenched out of historical context and contemporary circumstances—as if it is all a matter of personal will.

This ahistorical perspective contributes to the nihilistic threat within black America in that it can be used to justify right-wing cutbacks for poor people struggling for decent housing, child care, health care, and education. And, as I pointed out earlier, although liberals are deficient in important ways, they are right on target in their critique of conservative government cutbacks for services to the poor. These ghastly cutbacks are one cause of the nihilistic threat to black America.

The proper starting point for the crucial debate about the prospects for black America is the nihilism that increasingly pervades black communities. *Nihilism is to be understood here not as a philosophic doctrine that there are no rational grounds for legitimate standards or authority; it is, far more, the lived experience of coping with a life of horrifying meaninglessness, hopelessness, and (most important) lovelessness.* This usually results in a numbing detachment from others and a self-destructive disposition toward the world. Life without meaning, hope, and love breeds a coldhearted, mean-spirited-outlook that destroys both the individual and others.

Nihilism is not new in black America. The first African encounter with the New World was an encounter with a distinctive form of the Absurd. The initial black struggle against degradation and devaluation in the enslaved circumstances of the New World was, in part, a struggle against nihilism. In fact, the major enemy of black survival in America has been, and is, neither oppression nor exploitation but rather the nihilistic threat—that is, loss of hope and absence of meaning. For as long as hope remains and meaning is preserved, the possibility of overcoming oppression stays alive. The self-fulfilling prophecy of the nihilistic threat is that without hope there can be no struggle.

The genius of our black foremothers and forefathers was to create powerful buffers to ward off the nihilistic threat, to equip black folk with cultural armor to beat back the demons of hopelessness, meaninglessness, and lovelessness. These buffers consisted of cultural structures of meaning and feeling that created and sustained communities; this armor constituted ways of life and struggle that embodied values of service and sacrifice, love and care, discipline and excellence. In other words, traditions for black surviving and thriving under usually adverse New World conditions were major barriers against the nihilistic threat. These traditions consist primarily of black religious and civic institutions that sustained familial and communal networks of support. If cultures are, in part, what human beings create (out of antecedent fragments of other cultures) in order to convince themselves not to commit suicide, then black foremothers and forefathers are to be applauded. In fact, until the early seventies black Americans had the lowest suicide rate in the United States. But, now young black people lead the nation in suicides.

What has changed? What went wrong? The bitter irony of integration? The cumulative effects of a genocidal conspiracy? The virtual collapse of rising expectations after the optimistic sixties? None of us fully understands why the nihilistic threat is mor powerful now than ever before. I believe that the commodification of black life and the crisis of black leadership are two basic reasons. The recent shattering of black civil society—black families, neighborhoods, schools, churches, mosques—leaves more and more black people vulnerable to the nihilistic threat. This shattering spawns a deracinated and denuded people with little sense of self and few existential moorings.

Black people have always been in America's wilderness in search of a promised land. Yet many black folk now reside in a jungle with a cutthroat morality devoid of any faith in deliverance or hope for freedom. Contrary to the superficial claims of conservative behaviorists, these jungles are not primarily the result of pathological behavior. Rather, this behavior is the tragic response of a people bereft of resources to confront the workings of U.S. capitalist society. This does not mean that individual black people are not responsible for their actions—black murderers and rapists should go to jail. But it does mean that the nihilistic threat contributes to criminal behavior—a threat that feeds on poverty *and* shattered cultural institutions. The nihilistic threat is now more powerful than ever before because the armor to ward against it is weaker.

But why this shattering of black civil society, this weakening of black cultural institutions in asphalt jungles? *Corporate market institutions* have contributed greatly to this situation. By corporate market institutions I mean that complex set of interlocking enterprises that have a disproportionate amount of capital, power, and influence on how our society is shaped. Needless to say, the primary motivation of these institutions is to make profits, and their basic strategy is to convince the public to consume. These institutions have helped create a seductive way of life, a culture of consumption that capitalizes on every opportunity to make money. Market calculations and cost-benefit analyses hold sway in almost every sphere of U.S. society.

The common denominator in these calculations and analyses is usually the provision, expansion, and intensification of *pleasure*. Pleasure is a multivalent term; it means different things to many people. In our way of life it involves comfort, convenience, and sexual stimulation. This mentality pays little heed to the past, and views the future as no more than a repetition of a hedonistically driven present. This market morality stigmatizes others as objects for personal pleasure or bodily stimulation. In this view, traditional morality is not undermined by radical feminists, cultural radicals in the sixties, or libertarians, as alleged by conservative behaviorists. Rather, corporate market institutions have greatly contributed to undermining traditional morality in order to stay in business and make a profit. This is especially evident in the culture industries—television, radio, video, music—in which gestures of foreplay and orgiastic pleasure flood the marketplace.

Like all Americans, African Americans are influenced greatly by the images of comfort, convenience, machismo, femininity, violence, and sexual stimulation that bombard consumers. These seductive images contribute to the predominance of the market-inspired way of life over all others—and thereby edge out nonmarket values—love, care, service to others—handed down by preceding generations. The predominance of this way of life among those living in poverty-ridden conditions, with a limited capacity to ward off self-contempt and self-hatred, results in the possible triumph of the nihilistic threat in black America.

A major contemporary strategy for holding the nihilistic threat at bay is to attack directly the sense of worthlessness and self-loathing in black America. The angst resembles a kind of collective clinical depression in significant pockets of black America. The eclipse of hope and collapse of meaning in much of black

America is linked to the structural dynamics of corporate market institutions that affect all Americans. Under these circumstances, black existential angst derives from the lived experience of ontological wounds and emotional scars inflicted by white-supremacist beliefs and images permeating U.S. society and culture. These wounds and scars attack black intelligence, black ability, black beauty, and black character daily in subtle and not-so-subtle ways.

The accumulated effect of these wounds and scars produces a deep-seated anger, a boiling sense of rage, and a passionate pessimism regarding America's will to justice. Under conditions of slavery and Jim Crow segregation, this anger, rage, and pessimism remained relatively muted because of a well-justified fear of brutal white retaliation. The major breakthroughs of the sixties—more psychically than politically—swept this fear away. Sadly, the combination of the market way of life, poverty-ridden conditions, black existential angst, and the lessening of fear toward white authorities has directed most of the anger, rage, and despair toward fellow black citizens, especially black women. Only recently has this nihilistic threat—and its ugly inhumane outlook and actions—surfaced in the larger American society. And it surely reveals one of the many instances of cultural decay in a declining empire.

What is to be done about this nihilistic threat? Is there really any hope, given our shattered civil society, market-driven corporate enterprises, and white supremacism? If one begins with the threat of concrete nihilism, then one must talk about some kind of *politics of conversion*. New models of collective black leadership must promote a version of this politics. Like alcoholism and drug addiction, nihilism is a disease of the soul. It can never be completely cured, and there is always the possibility of relapse. But there is always a chance for conversion—a chance for people to believe that there is hope for the future and a meaning to struggle. This chance rests neither on an agreement about what justice consists of nor on an analysis of how racism, sexism, or class subordination operate. Such arguments and analyses are indispensable, but a politics of conversion requires more. Nihilism is not overcome by arguments or analyses; it is tamed by love and care. Any disease of the soul must be conquered by a turning of one's soul. This turning is done by one's own affirmation of one's worth—an affirmation fueled by the concern of others. This is why a love ethic must be at the center of a politics of conversion.

This love ethic has nothing to do with sentimental feelings or tribal connections. Rather it is a last attempt at generating a sense of agency among a downtrodden people. The best exemplar of this love ethic is depicted on a number of levels in Toni Morrison's novel *Beloved*. Self-love and love of others are both modes toward increasing self-valuation and encouraging political resistance in one's community. These modes of valuation and resistance are rooted in a subversive memory—the best of one's past without romantic nostalgia—and guided by a universal love ethic. For my purposes here, *Beloved* can be construed as bringing together the loving yet critical affirmation of black humanity found in the best of black nationalist movements, the perennial hope against hope for transracial coalition in progressive movements, and the painful struggle for self-affirming sanity in a history in which the nihilistic threat seems insurmountable.

The politics of conversion proceed principally on the local level—in those institutions in civil society still vital enough to promote self-worth and self-affirmation. It surfaces on the state and national levels only when grass-roots democratic organizations put forward a collective leadership that has earned the love and respect of and, most important, that has proved itself *accountable* to these organizations. This collective leadership must exemplify moral integrity, character, and democratic statesmanship within itself and within its organizations.

Like liberal structuralists, the advocates of a politics of conversion never lose sight of the structural conditions that shape the sufferings and lives of people. Yet, unlike liberal structuralism, the politics of conversion meet the nihilistic threat head-on. Like conservative behaviorism, the politics of conversion openly confronts the self-destructive and inhumane actions of black people. Unlike conservative behaviorists, the politics of conversion situates (not exonerates) these actions within inhumane circumstances. The politics of conversion shuns the limelight—a limelight that solicits status seekers and ingratiates egomaniacs. Instead, it stays on the ground among the toiling everyday people, ushering forth humble freedom fighters—both followers and leaders—who have the audacity to take the nihilistic threat by the neck and turn back its deadly assaults.

The nihilistic threat to black America is inseparable from a crisis in black leadership. This crisis is threefold. First, at the national level, the courageous yet problematic example of Jesse Jackson looms large. On the one hand, his presidential campaigns based on a progressive multiracial coalition were *the* major left-liberal response to Reagan's conservative policies. For the first time since the last days of Martin Luther King, Jr.—with the grand exception of Harold Washington—the nearly de facto segregation in U.S. progressive politics was confronted and surmounted. On the other hand, Jackson's televisual style resists grass-roots organizing and, most important, democratic accountability. His brilliance, energy, and charisma sustain his public visibility—but at the expense of programmatic follow-through. We are approaching the moment in which this style exhausts its progressive potential.

Other national nonelectoral black leaders—like Benjamin Hooks of the NAACP and John Jacobs of the National Urban League—rightly highlight the traditional problems of racial discrimination, racial violence, and slow racial progress. Yet their preoccupation with race—the mandate from their organizations—downplays the crucial class, environmental, and patriarchal determinants of black life chances. Black politicians—especially new victors like Mayor David Dinkins of New York City and Governor Douglas Wilder of Virginia—are part of a larger, lethargic electoral system riddled with decreasing revenues, loss of public confidence, self-perpetuating mediocrity, and pervasive corruption. Like most American elected officials, few black politicians can sidestep these seductive traps. So black leadership at the national level tends to lack a moral vision that can organize (not just periodically energize) subtle analyses that enlighten (not simply intermittently awaken), and exemplary practices that uplift (not merely convey status that awes), black people.

Second, this relative failure in leadership creates vacuums to be filled by bold and defiant black nationalist figures with even narrower visions, one-note racial analyses, and sensationalist practices. Louis Farrakhan, Al Sharpton, and others vigorously attempt to be protest leaders in this myopic mode—a mode often, though not always, reeking of immoral xenophobia. This kind of black leadership not only is symptomatic of black alienation and desperation in a country more and more indifferent or hostile to the quality of life among black working and poor people, it also reinforces the fragmentation of U.S. progressive efforts that could reverse this deplorable plight. In this way, black nationalist leaders often inadvertently contribute to the very impasse they are trying to overcome: inadequate social attention and action to change the plight of America's "invisible people," especially disadvantaged black people.

Third, this crisis of black leadership contributes to political cynicism among black people; it encourages the idea that we cannot really make a difference in changing our society. This cynicism—already promoted by the larger political culture—dampens the fire of engaged *local* activists who have made a difference, yet who also have little interest in being in the national limelight. Rather they engage in protracted grass-roots organizing in principled coalitions that bring power and pressure to bear on specific issues.

Without such activists there can be no progressive politics. Yet state, regional, and national networks are also required for an effective progressive politics. That is why local-based collective (and especially multigendered) models of black leadership are needed. These models must shun the idea of one black national leader; they also should put a premium on critical dialogue and democratic accountability in black organizations.

Work must get done. Decisions must be made. But charismatic presence is no legitimate substitute for collective responsibility. Only a charisma of humility and accountability is worthy of a leadership grounded in a genuine democratic struggle for greater freedom and equality. This indeed may be the best—and last—hope to hold back the nihilistic threat to black America.

Source: Cornel West, "Nihilism in Black America," *Dissent* (Spring 1991).

SELECT BIBLIOGRAPHY:

Henry Louis Gates, Jr., and Cornel West, *The Future of the Race* (New York: Knopf, 1996).

Cornel West, *The American Evasion of Philosophy: A Genealogy of Pragmatism* (Madison: University of Wisconsin Press, 1989).

———, *The Ethical Dimensions of Marxist Thought* (New York: Monthly Review Press, 1991).

———, *Keeping Faith: Philosophy and Race in America* (New York: Routledge, 1993).

———, *Race Matters* (Boston: Beacon Press, 1993).

———, *Democracy Matters: Winning the Fight against Imperialism* (New York: Penguin Books, 2005).

———, and bell hooks, *Breaking Bread: Insurgent Black Intellectual Life* (Boston: South End Press, 1992).

⤖ 11 ⤖

"Black Anti-Semitism," Henry Louis Gates, Jr., 1992

Henry Louis Gates Jr. (1950–) was born and raised in West Virginia, and graduated Phi Beta Kappa and *summa cum laude* from Yale University. Currently the W. E. B. Du Bois Professor of the Humanities and Director of the W. E. B. Du Bois Institute for African and African American Research at Harvard University, Gates is one of America's most influential public intellectuals. Gates won a MacArthur Fellowship in 1981, and in 1983 earned acclaim with his rediscovery of Harriet E. Wilson's 1859 novel, *Our Nig*. Gates also gained prominence as an advocate of a black literary cannon to complement the traditional, Eurocentric cannon. Perhaps Gates's greatest scholarly achievement was the development of *Encarta Africana*, a massive research project that, in some respects, completed the unfinished *Encyclopedia Africana* project initiated by Du Bois almost a century earlier. In this essay, originally published in the *New York Times*, Gates sharply condemns expressions of anti-Semitism and social intolerance within the African-American community.

⤖

BLACK DEMAGOGUES AND PSEUDO-SCHOLARS

During the past decade, the historic relationship between African Americans and Jewish Americans—a relationship that sponsored so many of the concrete advances of the civil rights era—showed another and less attractive face.

While anti-Semitism is generally on the wane in this country, it has been on the rise among black Americans. A recent survey finds not only that blacks are twice as likely as whites to hold anti-Semitic views but—significantly—that it is among the younger and more educated blacks that anti-Semitism is most pronounced.

The trend has been deeply disquieting for many black intellectuals. But it is something most of us, as if by unstated agreement, simply choose not to talk about. At a time when black America is beleaguered on all sides, there is a strong temptation simply to ignore the phenomenon or treat it as something strictly marginal. And yet to do so would be a serious mistake. As the African-American philosopher Cornel West has insisted, attention to black anti-Semitism is crucial, however discomfiting, in no small part because the moral credibility of our struggle against racism hangs in the balance.

When the Rev. Jesse Jackson, in an impassioned address at a conference of the World Jewish Congress on July 7, condemned the sordid history of anti-Semitism, he not only went some distance toward retrieving the once abandoned mantle of the Rev. Dr. Martin Luther King Jr.'s humane statesmanship, he also delivered a stern rebuke—while not specifically citing black anti-Semitism—to those black leaders who have sought to bolster their own strength through division. Mr. Jackson and others have learned that we must not allow these demagogues to turn the wellspring of memory into a renewable resource of enmity everlasting.

We must begin by recognizing what is new about the new anti-Semitism. Make no mistake: This is anti-Semitism from the top down, engineered and promoted by leaders who affect to be speaking for a larger resentment. This top-down anti-Semitism, in large part the province of the better educated classes, can thus be contrasted with the anti-Semitism from below common among African-American urban communities in the 1930s and 40s, which followed in many ways a familiar pattern of clientelistic hostility toward the neighborhood vendor or landlord.

In our cities, hostility of this sort is now commonly directed toward Korean shop owners. But "minority" traders and shopkeepers elsewhere in the world—such as the Indians of East Africa and the Chinese of Southeast Asia—have experienced similar ethnic antagonism. Anti-Jewish sentiment can also be traced to Christian anti-Semitism, given the historic importance of Christianity in the black community.

Unfortunately, the old paradigms will not serve to explain the new bigotry and its role in black America. For one thing, its preferred currency is not the mumbled epithet or curse but the densely argued treatise; it belongs as much to the repertory of campus lecturers as community activists. And it comes in wildly different packages.

A book popular with some in the "Afrocentric" movement, *The Iceman Inheritance: Prehistoric Sources of Western Man's Racism, Sexism, and Aggression*, by Michael Bradley, argues that white people are so vicious because they, unlike the rest of mankind, are descended from the brutish Neanderthals. More to the point, it speculates that the Jews may have been the "'purest' and oldest Neanderthal-Caucasoids," the iciest of the ice people; hence (he explains) the singularly odious character of ancient Jewish culture.

Crackpot as it sounds, the book has lately been reissued with endorsements from two members of the Africana Studies Department of the City College of New York, as well as an introduction by Dr. John Henrik Clarke, professor emeritus of Hunter College and the great paterfamilias of the Afrocentric movement.

Dr. Clarke recently attacked multiculturalism as the product of what he called the "Jewish educational Mafia." And while Dr. Leonard Jeffries's views on supposed Jewish complicity in the subjugation of blacks captured headlines, his intellectual cohorts such as Conrad Muhammad and Khallid Muhammad address community gatherings and college students across the country purveying a similar doctrine. College speakers and publications have played a disturbing role in legitimating the new creed. Last year, U.C.L.A.'s black newspaper, *Nommo*, defended the importance of The Protocols of the Elders of Zion, the notorious Czarist canard that portrays a Jewish conspiracy to rule the world. (Those who took issue were rebuked with an article headlined: "Anti-Semitic? Ridiculous—Chill.") Speaking at Harvard University earlier this year, Conrad Muhammad, the New York representative of the Nation of Islam, neatly annexed environmentalism to anti-Semitism, when he blamed the Jews for despoiling the environment and destroying the ozone layer.

But the bible of the new anti-Semitism is *The Secret Relationship Between Blacks and Jews*, an official publication of the Nation of Islam that boasts 1,275 footnotes in the course of 334 pages.

Sober and scholarly looking, it may well be one of the most influential books published in the black community in the last twelve months. It is available in black-oriented shops in cities across the nation, even those that specialize in Kente cloth and beads rather than books. It can also can be ordered over the phone, by dialing 1-800-48-TRUTH. Meanwhile, the book's conclusions are, in many circles, increasingly treated as damning historical fact. The book, one of the most sophisticated instances of hate literature yet compiled, was prepared by the historical research department of the Nation of Islam. It charges that the Jews were "key operatives" in the historic crime of slavery, playing an "inordi-nate" and "disproportionate" role and "carv[ing] out for themselves a monu-mental culpability in slavery—and the black holocaust." Among significant sec-tors of the black community, this brief has become a credo of a new philosophy of black self-affirmation.

To be sure, the book massively misrepresents the historical record, largely through a process of cunningly selective quotation of often reputable sources. But its authors could be confident that few of its readers would go to the trouble of actually hunting down the works cited. For if readers actually did so, they might discover a rather different picture.

They might find out—from the book's own vaunted authorities—that, for example, of all the African slaves imported into the New World, American Jewish merchants accounted for less than 2 percent, a finding sharply at odds with the Nation's of Islam's claim of Jewish "predominance" in this traffic.

They might find out that in the domestic trade it appears that all of the Jewish slave traders combined bought and sold fewer slaves than the single gentile firm of Franklin and Armfield. In short, they might learn what the historian Harold Brackman has documented—that the book's repeated insistence that the Jews dominated the slave trade depends on an unscrupulous distortion of the historic record. But the most ominous words in the book are found on the cover: "Volume One." More have been promised, to carry on the saga of Jewish iniquity to the present day.

However shoddy the scholarship of works like *The Secret Relationship*, under-lying it is something even more troubling: the tacit conviction that culpability is heritable. For it suggests a doctrine of racial continuity, in which the racial evil of a people is merely manifest (rather than constituted) by their historical misdeeds. The reported misdeeds are thus the signs of an essential nature that is evil.

How does this theology of guilt surface in our everyday moral discourse? In New York, earlier this spring, a forum was held at the Church of St. Paul and Andrew to provide an occasion for blacks and Jews to engage in dialogue on such issues as slavery and social injustice. Both Jewish and black panelists found common ground and common causes. But a tone-setting contingent of blacks in the audience took strong issue with the proceedings. Outraged, they demanded to know why the Jews, those historic malefactors, had not apologized to the "descendants of African kings and queens."

And so the organizer of the event, Melanie Kaye Kantrowitz, did. Her voice quavering with emotion, she said: "I think I speak for a lot of people in this room when I say 'I'm sorry.' We're ashamed of it, we hate it, and that's why we organized this event." Should the Melanie Kantrowitzes of the world, whose ancestors survived Czarist pogroms and, latterly, the Nazi Holocaust, be the primary object of our wrath? And what is yielded by this hateful sport of victimology, save the conversion of a tragic past into a game of recrimination? Perhaps that was on the mind of another audience member. "I don't want an apology," a dreadlocked woman told her angrily. "I want reparations. Forty acres and a mule, plus interest."

These are times that try the spirit of liberal outreach. In fact, Louis Farrakhan, leader of the Nation of Islam, himself explained the real agenda behind his campaign, speaking before an audience of 15,000 at the University of Illinois last fall. The purpose of "The Secret Relationship," he said, was to "rearrange a relationship" that "has been detrimental to us."

"Rearrange" is a curiously elliptical term here. If a relation with another group has been detrimental, it only makes sense to sever it as quickly and unequivocally as possible. In short, by "rearrange," he means to convert a relation of friendship, alliance and uplift into one of enmity, distrust and hatred. But why target the Jews? Using the same historical methodology, after all, the researchers of the book could have produced a damning treatise on the involvement of left-handers in the "black holocaust." The answer requires us to go beyond the usual shibboleths about bigotry and view the matter, from the demagogues' perspective, strategically: as the bid of one black elite to supplant another. It requires us, in short, to see anti-Semitism as a weapon in the raging battle of who will speak for black America—those who have sought common cause with others or those who preach a barricaded withdrawal into racial authenticity. The strategy of these apostles of hate, I believe, is best understood as ethnic isolationism—they know that the more isolated black America becomes, the greater their power. And what's the most efficient way to begin to sever black America from its allies? Bash the Jews, these demagogues apparently calculate, and you're halfway there.

I myself think that an aphorist put his finger on something germane when he observed, "We can rarely bring ourselves to forgive those who have helped us." For sometimes it seems that the trajectory of black-Jewish relations is a protracted enactment of this paradox.

Many Jews are puzzled by the recrudescence of black anti-Semitism, in view of the historic alliance. The brutal truth has escaped them that the new anti-

Semitism arises not in spite of the black-Jewish alliance but because of it. For precisely such trans-racial cooperation—epitomized by the historic partnership between blacks and Jews—is what poses the greatest threat to the isolationist movement.

In short, for the tacticians of the new anti-Semitism, the original sin of American Jews was their involvement—truly "inordinate," truly "disproportionate"—not in slavery, but in the front ranks of the civil rights struggle.

For decent and principled reasons, many black intellectuals are loath to criticize "oppositional" black leaders. Yet it has become apparent that to continue to maintain a comradely silence may be, in effect, to capitulate to the isolationist agenda, to betray our charge and trust. And, to be sure, many black writers, intellectuals, and religious leaders have taken an unequivocal stand on this issue.

Cornel West aptly describes black anti-Semitism as "the bitter fruit of a profound self-destructive impulse, nurtured on the vines of hopelessness and concealed by empty gestures of black unity."

After twelve years of conservative indifference, those political figures who acquiesced, by malign neglect, to the deepening crisis of black America should not feign surprise that we should prove so vulnerable to the demagogues rousing messages of hate, their manipulation of the past and present.

Bigotry, as a tragic century has taught us, is an opportunistic infection, attacking most virulently when the body politic is in a weakened state. Yet neither should those who are about black America gloss over what cannot be condoned: That much respect we owe to ourselves. For surely it falls to all of us to recapture the basic insight that Dr. King so insistently expounded. "We are caught in an inescapable network of mutuality," he told us. "Whatever affects one directly affects all indirectly." How easy to forget this—and how vital to remember.

Source: "Black Demogogues and Pseudo-Scholars," by Henry Louis Gates, Jr. Copyright 1992 by Henry Louis Gates, Jr. Originally published in the *New York Times*. Reprinted by permission of the author.

SELECT BIBLIOGRAPHY:

Henry Louis Gates, Jr., "Race," in *Writing, and Difference* (Chicago: University of Chicago Press, 1986).

———, *The Signifying Monkey: Towards a Theory of Afro-American Literary Criticism* (New York: Oxford University Press, 1988).

———, *Colored People: A Memoir* (New York: Knopf, 1994).

———, *America Behind the Color Line: Dialogues with African Americans* (New York: Warner Books, 2005).

———, and Nellie Y. McKay, eds., *The Norton Anthology of Afro-American Literature* (New York: Norton, 1996).

━ **12** ━

"Crime—Causes and Cures," *Jarvis Tyner, 1994*

━

Jarvis Tyner (1941–) is the national vice chairman of the Communist Party, USA. He was the founding chairman of the Young Workers Liberation League (YWLL) in 1970 and has been active in struggles concerning civil rights, labor, peace, and anti-imperialism. He has written extensively on political action, civil rights, the struggle for peace, the fight against racism, and many other subjects. Tyner ran for vice president on the Communist Party ticket in both 1972 and 1976. He is currently a member of the Coordinating Committee of the Black Radical Congress. In this essay, Tyner presents a Marxian analysis for the reasons for crime in U.S. society.

━

The growing problem of crime and violence in our country has reached epidemic proportions, as have demands that the government find real solutions.

It is a serious problem indeed. There were over 14 million crimes committed in the U.S. in 1992. While 12 million of these were crimes of property, 1.9 million were violent crimes, including 1.1 million aggravated assaults and 22,760 murders.

Over the past decade the number of violent crimes has grown dramatically. There are over 200 million guns in the hands of civilian Americans. The odds of getting murdered in the U.S. are one in 12,000—which is high by any standard. The streets are not safe. Even children are carrying guns and many of the innocent victims of violence are children and the elderly. Some senior citizens dare not venture out of doors at night.

The growth of crime is one of the most dramatic examples of the general decay of U.S. capitalism. While our government goes around the world boasting of a "stable," "democratic" and "free" technologically advanced society, the tragic presence of so many guns and drugs and the accompanying crime and violence show that our country is facing a deep social and political crisis. We are a nation that is technologically advanced but moving backward in terms of social relations and stability. The country is headed for greater chaos and suffering if the problem of crime and violence is not addressed in an honest, humane and democratic way.

Sickness or Symptom?

Over the last decade there has been a massive campaign around the crime issue. The mass media has spared no effort in sensationalizing this issue. Listening to the evening news is like reading a police rap sheet. The sensationalized journalism of the cheap supermarket tabloids is becoming the dominant style of U.S. journalism—it is news designed to promote hysteria and panic. It is also designed to promote racism, male supremacy and other anti-working-class sentiments so as to rationalize repressive policies and sow greater division among the people. It is news designed to lower the confidence among the masses in humanity, and thereby promote hopelessness and powerlessness.

While the problem is very serious, and must be addressed, the U.S. ruling class has been projecting it as the central issue confronting the country. Many voters in the last elections said that crime is their main concern. This issue has to be carefully considered for it can divide and confuse more than any other. Clearly the answer does not lie in simple calls to "get tough." It is necessary to understand the real source of the problem and act in a way that does not further victimize those already victimized.

Crime presents a danger to society, but it must be understood as a symptom of much bigger ailments.

Our nation is experiencing a prolonged, deep-going structural and systemic crisis of its capitalist system. This is the main sickness which must be addressed if crime and violence are to be seriously reduced.

While there has been a growth in the number of wealthy Americans over the past two decades, the most dramatic growth has been in the number of people living in poverty. Since 1970, 14 million have joined the ranks of the poor. We are a nation where even by modest count, 37 million people live in poverty—one out of every six persons.

Over 20 million are unemployed and underemployed. Millions of people have never had a steady job. These are the long-term unemployed, including the homeless and the millions who are hungry and without health care. With the closing down of many basic industrial plants in the '70s and '80s and the downsizing of major corporations in the '90s, millions of working people have been locked out of better-paying jobs and reduced to permanent unemployment and underemployment. For most working people there is no job security. There is a major decline in the standard of living of the entire working class. Most families need two or more wage earners to make ends meet today.

Economic Racism

Hit hardest of all are the racially oppressed, the African American, Mexican American, Puerto Rican, Asian and Pacific Island and Native American working people. They are victims of economic racism.

The pro-corporate, racist policies of big business and government have led to a situation where the racially and nationally oppressed experience more than double the unemployment and poverty rates of white people. Forty percent of African Americans and Latinos now live in poverty. And linked to the growth in extreme poverty is the resurgence of super segregation.

The crisis is particularly sharp for African American and Latino youth who are confined to the hard life in the cities—a life of drugs, bad housing, underfunded schools, few recreation facilities and no jobs. These are youth whose unemployment rates range from 60 to 80 percent. Many have never worked, and if there is no basic change in the economy and the political situation, most have no future.

At the bottom of this crisis lies the historic decline of U.S. capitalism. This situation has created many hopeless and desperate people who see no honest way of surviving. Feeling that society has abandoned them, too many have concluded, "Why not abandon society?"

Because of the systemic crisis, despite the ups and downs in the business cycle, the economy has been going qualitatively downward. We now have a national emergency of the most urgent kind requiring government action to provide jobs and massive funding to rebuild cities and meet human needs. But the policy has been building jails instead of providing jobs. This situation is a breeding ground for unstable family life, drug addiction, street crime and many other serious problems. The crisis of capitalism is also breeding extreme greed, corruption and thievery in government and industry. This is part of the crime problem as well.

Along with economic conditions, the factor that has driven crime figures drastically up over the past decade has been the massive growth of drug abuse. Sixty-two percent of all street crime is drug-related; most random shootings and "drive-by" killings of innocent victims are related to the drug trade.

The drug epidemic has grown so severe because in fact the government's policy is not to stop it. In fact, the government is part of the problem—it has allowed the massive importation of narcotics and other drugs. This can be seen in the Iran-contra conspiracy and in many new reports that show the CIA has for years been working with drug smugglers, and is even importing drugs itself.

Role of Government and Police

On the community level, local police practice a policy called "selective enforcement"—which is really a form of drug legalization. Selective enforcement has been the chief law enforcement tactic on the nation's streets, especially in low-income Black and Brown communities.

Selective enforcement allows drugs to be sold openly; it is responsible for the streets being turned into war zones where people in hundreds of communities dare not go outside for fear of being caught in the crossfire. Any 12-year-old can tell you where drugs are being sold. Certainly the police know, yet they allow it to go on and only periodically arrest the pushers. The government's complicity can also be seen in the many examples of direct involvement by local police in dealing drugs and shaking down dealers. The authorities not only know where drugs are coming from and are being sold—they are part of the process.

The drug problem did not start in the ghettos and barrios, contrary to what is said in the media. The importation and distribution of drugs goes all the way up to the high councils of the CIA, the government, the military, organized crime and the banking industry.

African-American and Latino youth who are the prime victims of the drug epidemic are being arrested and jailed more than any other group. The prisons are full to the point of overflowing. We live in a society where millions of youth—in a special way African American youth—are tragically cast aside, oppressed and neglected, then imprisoned and criminalized. It is the shame of our nation that, by a wide margin, there are more African-American youth in jail or under the jurisdiction of the courts than are in college. This is a basic failure of the U.S. capitalist system.

However there are other types of crime to which scant attention is paid. White-collar crimes cost billions of dollars annually and cause massive human suffering because the dollars stolen could be spent to benefit the people. The S&L bailout—a multi-billion-dollar scandal that cost the American people dearly—is an example.

Studies show that crime—not to mention drug use—is also high amongst the upper-middle class and the rich. One study showed that the amount of money embezzled from banks was 6,000 times the amount robbed from banks (as cited by A. Monteiro in 4/91 *Political Affairs*). If one were to add up the amount of money lost because the rich, who are the biggest tax cheaters, are not paying their share of taxes, including wealthy bankers laundering drug money, the sum comes to hundreds of billions in cost to society, in effect many times more than the cost of petty crime on the streets. As a rule, the rich steal larger amounts, more often, and are punished less severely and less often.

In addition, the federal government is guilty of political crimes, like crimes against the cities. Over the past decade, 50 percent of the aid to cities has been cut—at a time when corruption in government has risen to an all-time high. There is no major city that is not in financial straits. Almost every state faces cutbacks and retrenchment as they try to avoid bankruptcy.

To this can be added the cost in human suffering and death caused by long-term unemployment, homelessness and hunger, and the fact that the denial of health care to 37 million is cause for a shorter life span and higher mortality rates. These are crimes too—crimes rooted in capitalist greed, racism and anti-working-class policies of government and big business. They are of a political and social character but are crimes nonetheless.

These are all reasons why crime is growing and will continue to grow unless the basic ailments of our society are addressed.

Anti-Crime Hysteria

Rather than addressing the social and economic roots of crime, drugs and violence, the government, over the past decade especially, continues to put its emphasis on more cops, increased police brutality, more prisons, longer sentences and expanding the death penalty.

The mass media, government and most capitalist politicians are creating a hysteria—mainly a racist hysteria—about crime. This was most clearly revealed with the Willie Horton ads that the Republicans used in the 1988 elections. This policy continues under Clinton.

Typically the reason given for the rise in crime is that America has become too lenient on criminals. The view is often expressed that "criminals are getting away with crimes, and if arrested are given too short a sentence." It is argued that the absence of the death penalty, lenient sentencing and the parole system have made committing crimes less risky. Similarly, it is alleged that the police are outgunned.

Most capitalist politicians are quick to blame crime on the criminal mind, lack of character, etc., of individuals, while they do nothing about the prison system, one of the most brutal and the worst in terms of rehabilitation.

Ignored by these views are the economic roots of crime. This school of thought, which is dominant in government, media and industry, is based on the notion that there is nothing basically wrong with the economic system but that there is something wrong with the American people. The victims of poverty and drugs are blamed rather than trying to eliminate the real causes.

Crime, Racism, and Male Supremacy

Linking crime with race and gender is the most prominent form of this anti-people line of argument. Such ideas were very prominent in Pat Buchanan's "family values" speech at the 1992 Republican Convention and the campaign rhetoric of ex-Vice President Dan Quayle during the presidential campaign.

Part of the move to the right by the Clinton Administration and other Democrats can be seen precisely around these issues. President Clinton's speeches in Memphis and Los Angeles (November '93) to promote his anti-crime bill had much of the same message as Quayle and Buchanan. In fact, Clinton has been promoting the right-wing "family values" issue openly, while heaping praise on the likes of Dan Quayle.

Senator Daniel Patrick Moynihan has built his career around attacking female-headed households, especially African American, as the prime causes of crime and violence. He insists that poverty is not the reason for crime. In an article in the winter 1993–94 issue of the *American Educator*, published by the American Federation of Teachers, he writes

> A community that allows a large number of young men to grow up in broken families, dominated by women, never acquiring any stable relationship to male authority, never acquiring any set of rational expectations about the future—that community asks for and gets chaos.

Former New York City Mayor Edward Koch has for a long time put most of his political energy into attacking non-whites. He has consistently raised the question of "Black and minority crime." In his column which appeared in the New York *Daily News* (November 16, 1993), he hailed the Memphis and Los Angeles speeches of Clinton as a breakthrough because Clinton was willing to attack "minority crime." Koch felt that the "dam of political correctness has been broken" and now one can discuss the question without being called a racist. To identify the African-American people with crime, according to Koch, is to honestly deal with the problem. In a bare-faced defense of racist oppression and injustice Koch put it this way: ". . . [the] lack of personal responsibility is the single most important factor contributing to escalating minority crime rather than white racism in all its manifestations."

A widespread example of this approach is the chorus of blame directed at rap artists for crime and violence among youth. Whether or not one agrees with the content of the music, blaming the rappers takes the government and the corporations off the hook. It is the highly profitable record companies who are the main promoters, and beneficiaries—making millions upon millions by promoting violence. . . .

Capitalism without Entitlements

Capitalism without entitlements means greater use of police state methods to control the enormous social problems that will result; it means more jails, not jobs.

When considered in light of Clinton's pledge to arbitrarily throw people off welfare, a picture emerges of an administration that actually plans to force new hundreds of thousands into extreme destitution and ultimately prison—in order to contain their dissatisfaction, anger and rebellion.

Like NAFTA, this bill is strongly supported by big business. They see it as necessary for maintaining control over the victims of poverty and unemployment in an era where they want to eliminate entitlements.

Basically, the anti-crime bill is designed to control poor folks and curb possible political rebellion. It is not designed to stop crime—it's designed to stop the people. It is first and foremost an attack on the rights of the unemployed and underemployed, primarily aimed at the ghettos and barrios, at the victims of economic racism. The thinking that motivates this kind of draconian legislative assault on democratic rights is racist and anti-working-class. It's basically a defense of U.S. capitalism on the decline. And it shows that Clinton is continuing the same thinking and policies of the capitalist class that Reagan and Bush promoted.

It is important to understand that despite the fact that organized crime is behind much of the importation and the distribution of drugs, the proposed anti-crime legislation is not aimed at them at all. This shows that the ruling class has no intention of really attacking crime. There is a conscious racial, anti-working-class political bias behind the entire effort.

It is necessary to fight against this bill and demand instead that the government come up with a serious program that attacks the root causes of crime. Unless there is a strong protest from the people, this bill will be made into law in the early part of this year.

A Monumental Failure

While in 1992 the people voted to defeat George Bush and his policies, the new crime bill is actually a continuation of the same old reactionary policies and worse. The fact that the Clinton Administration is staying the course shows that the capitalist class is unified and the new repressive policy transcends the two main capitalist political parties.

During the Reagan–Bush administrations, record numbers were arrested and imprisoned. The demand for prison space could not keep up with the rate of convictions. And the '80s brought a new phenomenon: prisons for profit. Privately owned and run prisons is now one of America's biggest growth industries. Lucrative profits are being made in this industry, over the misery of so many. And there are even different levels of prison accommodations based on one's ability to pay—a new level of class differentiation in the prison system: horrible medieval-type prisons for the poor and country club prisons for the rich.

During the 1980s, African Americans and Latinos were jailed at unprecedented rates. Under the cover of these policies, the government criminalized hundreds of thousands, especially non-white youth. The United States has achieved the dubious distinction of being the number one nation on the earth when it comes to incarcerating its own population. By 1990 the inmate population, according to the ACLU study, *Americans Behind Bars: One Year Later*, had reached 1,139,803, which is a rate of 455 per 100,000 population—considerably higher than apartheid South Africa which is the second jailer-nation on earth with 311 per 100,000 population.

For African-American men, the rate is 3,370 per 100,000, which is ten times the overall U.S. rate and five times the rate for African males in South Africa. While the South African figures have gone down from 1989, the U.S. overall rate of incarceration increased by 6.8 percent. With the U.S. population at 250 million, by the end of the Reagan era 1 out of every 220 persons in the U.S. were in jail and 2,600 people were on death row. For African-American men that's 1 out of every 28. The Reagan–Bush years were one of the worst periods of racist repression in U.S. history.

If measured by its impact on lowering crime and violence—which after all was the stated intent—this policy was a monumental failure. According to recent studies, even after doubling the number of people put in prison, the crime rate only dropped slightly and may actually have increased by 7 percent.

It is argued that the country cannot afford a federal jobs bill because the "money is not there." However, incarceration presently costs the federal, state and local governments $20.3 billion a year. The absurdity and senselessness of this waste is mind-boggling: it costs about $40,000 a year to send a youth to prison but only $20,000 to send them to college.

The use of the death penalty has not worked either. Murder rates in states with the death penalty are usually slightly higher than in non-death penalty states. Reducing crime by increasing incarceration and through capital punishment has been a costly failure.

An increase in the prison population, use of mandatory sentencing, the death penalty, more cops with more lethal weapons and less rights for the people will lead us in the direction of a police state and do further harm to public safety and democratic rights. Based on the present policies, with more police there will be more police brutality. Communities, especially inner-city communities need real protection but that's not what they get—bitter experience shows they get more repression.

This will all negatively affect thousands of working-class people, their families and their communities. And it won't work. Any anti-crime bill that does not have a strong massive job creation component is no anti-crime bill at all.

A Job: A Constitutional Right

Rather than eliminating entitlements, what is needed is a federal jobs bill to rebuild the country and create millions of jobs. Offering free treatment to the massive numbers of drug-addicted people and taking dangerous weapons out of the hands of the population is the way to reduce crime. Strong gun control is needed, starting with outlawing automatic weapons. Safe streets are possible only with less access to firearms and greater economic security of the working class. Jobs not jails has to be the starting point in attacking all of the problems that contribute to the high crime rates; be they medical, social, cultural, psychological, etc.

A job should be a constitutional right. It should be guaranteed by the government. When the private sector fails to provide the needed jobs, the government should be required to provide them. Rather than cutting back on government services and aid to the cities, the government should tax the rich and cut the military budget to provide funding to meet those vital human needs. Rather than throwing people off of welfare into starvation and homelessness, more welfare should be provided until a decent good-paying job can be created. "Jobs or income" needs to be the birthright of every American.

Rather than boot camps, what is needed is more money for education and massive job creation with union wages and affirmative action, and training. Rather than jailing people addicted to drugs, there needs to be a massive effort to set up free drug rehabilitation facilities all across the country.

A Stake in Society

When so many have been pushed into long-term joblessness and the depths of poverty, it is understandable that some would reach the point of despair, the sense of being defeated, without any hope. Lacking the necessary experience of work, many develop total alienation from family, friends and, of course, from society as a whole. When you add the ingredients of drug addiction, police brutality and racism, that alienation can take on a dangerous dimension. Many have been pushed to the limits of despair as a result of the crisis of capitalism and turn to crime and violence. This system has created conditions that are forcing hundreds of thousands down the path of self destruction; it is a form of entrapment, socioeconomic entrapment.

Some will argue that many have been so dehumanized that a job won't be enough to bring them back. In some cases that is true. But every person must be fought for. We must keep in mind that this situation can be reversed. Most poor people are not criminal. Most youth who live in severe poverty do not turn to crime and drugs.

People are looking for real solutions. Many of them can be won to struggle and indeed can be changed through struggle. The overwhelming majority want to work and want to do the right thing. They have not lost all hope and can be won to a healthy, contributing relationship to society. Instead of pacification they need higher levels of class consciousness.

The first thing needed is to reverse the policies of government that are responsible for putting millions of young people, especially African American and Latino youth, into such horrible circumstances. Providing jobs is the first step in the many steps needed to bring hundreds of thousands out of despair. Health care is needed, plus counseling, sports and recreation—experiences that foster a healthy outlook toward one's fellow human beings.

Ironically, those who demonstrate total alienation actually reflect in a stark way the attitudes of the corporate world: complete selfishness, total greed, not caring who you hurt as long as you get what you want. These are considered "virtuous" in the dog-eat-dog business world. Anything to make a buck is an accurate motto of big business. These ideas didn't start with the drug pusher on the street corner, they started in the corporate suites and are alive and prominent in the media and on Wall Street today. There must be a total fight against such ideas, including exposing their source in the capitalist system, if we are to win.

How to Win

After NAFTA and the many other rebuffs to the people's agenda, it's clear now that Clinton, left on his own, will not deliver progressive change. It is therefore necessary to build a multi-racial grassroots movement, of working people first and foremost, that can force change. And that is what the Communist Party USA is working for. We have a long history of participating in the building of such movements.

In our view, there is a new militancy in the ranks of labor and a new level of unity of labor and the racially oppressed. There is renewed militancy in the ranks of the racially oppressed and those desiring peace and equality. Among all progressive forces there is a greater willingness to build independent politics, including third-party movements, and to support candidates who are ready to fight for jobs and equality.

Our starting point is that there is a way out. Taxing the rich and slashing the military budgets are among the most popular slogans of our day. The goal of the Communist Party program is to bring these slogans to life. Our program would provide an additional one trillion dollars per year to finance people's needs while reducing the tax burden on the majority. It would do more than provide the conditions for lowering crime drastically. It would upgrade the national spirit and social and cultural well-being of the people. It would provide the means for greater unity of all races and nationalities. It would make the streets safer and homes more livable for the people—working people in the first place.

This program is based on affirmative action, which means it would make a special effort where the problem is especially critical, in regards to the victims of discrimination. We are for a special effort to uplift those especially held back: African Americans, Latinos, other racially oppressed, and women.

Our country needs a different approach that protects people from crime but also gets more to the causes of crime, an approach that provides a humane and democratic solution. It must be a solution that rejects police state methods, that will unite the people across racial lines and move our country forward, not backward.

The death penalty does not deter crime and is mainly applied to poor people. What we need is not more prisons but more schools, free and accessible drug-treatment facilities, more recreation and health centers, decent housing for all and a guaranteed future for the youth. What is needed are tough laws against discrimination and racism and a commitment to provide for children and families, assuring a more stable home life. What is needed is a government, and a political-economic system based on the principle of putting people before profits.

And ultimately, what is needed is "Bill of Rights" socialism here in our country, if not today, then tomorrow.

Source: "Crime—Causes and Cures." Reprinted by the courtesy of Jarvis Tyner, Vice Chairman, Communist Party USA.

⚊ 13 ⚊

Louis Farrakhan: The Million Man March, *1995*

Louis Farrakhan (1933–) for more than a generation, has been one of the most influential, although controversial, leaders within the African-American community. Born Louis Walcott in Bronx, New York, he was raised in Boston, Massachusetts. As a youth, he learned to play the violin and guitar, and became a talented and popular singer. In 1955, Walcott attended the Nation of Islam's annual Savior's Day Convention in Chicago, where he first encountered Elijah Muhammad and Malcolm X. Joining the NOI later that year, and becoming Louis X, he quickly rose to leadership. In 1956 Louis X became the assistant minister to Malcolm X at Harlem's Mosque 7. Two years later, Louis X was named minister of the NOI's mosque in Boston. Following the assassination of Malcolm X in 1965, Louis X became the minister of Harlem's Mosque 7 for the next decade. Renamed Louis Farrakhan by Elijah Muhammad, in the 1970s, he became a powerful force within black American society. With the death of Elijah Muhammad in 1975, the leadership of the NOI passed to Elijah's son, Wallace Muhammad, ultimately leading Farrakhan to break from the Nation of Islam. In 1981 he reconstituted the "new" Nation of Islam around the conservative patriarchal principles of Elijah Muhammad. On October 16, 1995, Farrakhan organized the "Million Man March" in Washington, D.C., which was the largest public gathering of African Americans in U.S. history. Ten years later, in 2005, Farrakhan returned to Washington, D.C., to convene the "Million Family March."

⚊

"STILL 2 AMERICAS, ONE BLACK, ONE WHITE"

Right here on this mall where we are standing, according to books written on Washington, D.C., slaves used to be brought right here on this Mall in chains to be sold up and down the eastern seaboard. Right along this mall, going over to the White House, our fathers were sold into slavery. But, George Washington, the first president of the United States, said he feared that before too many years passed over his head, this slave would prove to become a most troublesome species of property.

Thomas Jefferson said, he trembled for this country when he reflected that God was just and that his justice could not sleep forever. Well, the day that these presidents feared has now come to pass, for on this mall, here we stand in the capital of America, and the layout of this great city, laid out by a Black man, Benjamin Banneker. This is all placed and based in a secret Masonic ritual. And at the core of the secret of that ritual is the Black man, not far from here is the White House.

And the first president of this land, George Washington, who was a grand master of the Masonic order laid the foundation, the cornerstone of this capitol building where we stand. George was a slave owner. George was a slave owner. Now, the President spoke today and he wanted to heal the great divide. But I respectfully suggest to the President, you did not dig deep enough at the malady that divides Black and White in order affect a solution to the problem.

And so, today, we have to deal with the root so that perhaps a healing can take place. . .

You came not at the call of Louis Farrakhan, but you have gathered here at the call of God. For it is only the call of Almighty God, no matter through whom that call came, that could generate this kind of outpouring. God called us here to this place. At this time. For a very specific reason.

And now, I want to say, my brothers — this is a very pregnant moment. Pregnant with the possibility of tremendous change in our status in America and in the world. And although the call was made through me, many have tried to distance the beauty of this idea from the person through whom the idea and the call was made.

Some have done it mistakenly. And others have done it in a malicious and vicious manner. Brothers and sisters, there is no human being through whom God brings an idea that history doesn't marry the idea with that human being no matter what defect was that human being's character.

You can't separate Newton from the law that Newton discovered, nor can you separate Einstein from the theory of relativity. It would be silly to try to separate Moses from the Torah or Jesus from the Gospel or Muhammad from the Koran.

When you say Farrakhan, you ain't no Moses, you ain't no Jesus, and you're not no Muhammad. You have a defect in your character.

Well, that certainly may be so, however, according to the way the Bible reads, there is no prophet of God written of in the Bible that did not have a defect in his character. But, I have never heard any member of the faith of Judaism separate David from the Psalms, because of what happened in David's life and you're never separated Solomon from the building of the Temple because they say he had a thousand concubines, and you never separated any of the Great Servants of God.

So today, whether you like it or not, God brought the idea through me and he didn't bring it through me because my heart was dark with hatred and anti-semitism, he didn't bring it through me because my heart was dark and I'm filled with hatred for White people and for the human family of the planet. If my heart were that dark, how is the message so bright, the message so clear, the response so magnificent?

So, we stand here today at this historic moment. We are standing in the place of those who couldn't make it here today. We are standing on the blood of our ancestors. We are standing on the blood of those who died in the middle passage, who died in the fields and swamps of America, who died hanging from trees in the South, who died in the cells of their jailers, who died on the highways and who died in the fratricidal conflict that rages within our community. We are standing on the sacrifice of the lives of those heroes, our great men and women that we today may accept the responsibility that life imposes upon each traveler who comes this way.

We must accept the responsibility that God has put upon us, not only to be good husbands and fathers and builders of our community, but God is now calling upon the despised and the rejected to become the cornerstone and the builders of a new world.

And so, our brief subject today is taken from the American Constitution. In these words, Toward a more union. Toward a more perfect union.

Now, when you use the word more with perfect, that which is perfect is that which has been brought to completion. So, when you use more perfect, you're either saying that what you call perfect is perfect for that stage of its development but not yet complete. When Jefferson said, "toward a more perfect union," he was admitting that the union was not perfect, that it was not finished, that work had to be done. And so we are gathered here today not to bash somebody else.

We're not gathered here to say, all of the evils of this nation. But we are gathered here to collect ourselves for a responsibility that God is placing on our shoulders to move this nation toward a more perfect union. Now, when you look at the word toward, toward, it means in the direction of, in furtherance or partial fulfillment of, with the view to obtaining or having shortly before coming soon, eminent, going on in progress. Well, that's right. We're in progress toward a perfect union. Union means bringing elements or components into unity.

It is something formed by uniting two or more things. It is a number of persons, states, etcetera, which are joined or associated together for some common purpose. We're not here to tear down America. America is tearing itself down. We are here to rebuild the wasted cities. . .

White supremacy is the enemy of both White people and Black people because the idea of White supremacy means you should rule because you're White, that makes you sick. And you've produced a sick society and a sick world. The founding fathers meant well, but they said, "toward a more perfect union." So, the Bible says, we know in part, we prophesy in part, but when that which is perfect is come, that which is in part shall be done away with.

So either, Mr. Clinton, we're going to do away with the mind-set of the founding fathers. You don't have to repudiate them like you've asked my brothers to do me. You don't have to say they were malicious, hate filled people. But you must evolve out of their mind-set. You see their minds was limited to those six European nations out of which this country was founded. But you've got Asians here. How are you going to handle that? You've got children of Africa here. How are you going to handle that?

You've got Arabs here. You've got Hispanics here. I know you call them illegal aliens, but hell, you took Texas from them by flooding Texas with people that got your mind. And now they're coming back across the border to what is Northern Mexico, Texas, Arizona, New Mexico, and California. They don't see themselves as illegal aliens. I think they might see you as an illegal alien. You have to be careful how you talk to people. You have to be careful how you deal with people. The Native American is suffering today. He's suffering almost complete extinction. Now, he learned about bingo. You taught him. He learned about black jack. You taught him. He learned about playing roulette. You taught him. Now, he's making a lot of money. You're upset with him because he's adopted your ways. What makes you like this? See, you're like this because you're not well. You're not well. And in the light of today's global village, you can never harmonize with the Asians. You can't harmonize with the islands of the Pacific.

You can't harmonize with the dark people of the world who out number you 11 to 1, if you're going to stand in the mind of white supremacy. White supremacy has to die in order for humanity to live. . .

Now, brothers, moral and spiritual renewal is a necessity. Every one of you must go back home and join some church, synagogue or temple or mosque that is teaching spiritual and moral uplift. I want you, brothers, there's no men in the church, in the mosque.

The men are in the streets and we got to get back to the houses of God. But preachers we have to revive religion in America.

He have to revive the houses of God that they're not personal chiefdoms of those of us who are their preachers and pastors. But we got to be more like Jesus, more like Mohammed, more like Moses and become servants of the people in fulfilling their needs.

Brothers, when you go home, we've got to register eight million, eligible but unregistered brothers, sisters. So you go home and find eight more like yourself. You register and get them to register. I register as Democrat? Should I register as a Republican? Should I register as independent?

If you're an independent, that's fine. If you're a Democrat, that's fine. If you're a Republican, that's OK. Because in local elections you have to do that which is in the best interest of your local community. But what we want is not necessarily a third party, but a third force.

Which means that we're going to collect Democrats, Republicans and independents around an agenda that is in the best interest of our people. And then all of us can stand on that agenda and in 1996, whoever the standard bearer is for the Democratic, the Republican, or the independent party should one come into existence. They've got to speak to our agenda. . . . .

Now, brothers, I want you to take this pledge. When I say I, I want you to say I, and I'll say your name. I know that there's so many names, but I want you to shout your name out so that the ancestors can hear it.

Take this pledge with me. Say with me please, I, say your name, pledge that from this day forward I will strive to love my brother as I love myself. I, say your name, from this day forward will strive to improve myself spiritually, morally, mentally, socially, politically, and economically for the benefit of myself, my family, and my people. I, say your name, pledge that I will strive to build business, build houses, build hospitals, build factories, and then to enter international trade for the good of myself, my family, and my people. I, say your name, pledge that from this day forward I will never raise my hand with a knife or a gun to beat, cut, or shoot any member of my family or any human being, except in self-defense.

I, say your name, pledge from this day forward I will never abuse my wife by striking here, disrespecting her for she is the mother of my children and the producer of my future. I, say your name, pledge that from this day forward I will never engage in the abuse of children, little boys, or little girls for sexual gratification. But I will let them grow in peace to be strong men and women for the future of our people. I, say your name, will never again use the B word to describe my female, but particularly my own Black sister.

I, say your name, pledge from this day forward that I will not poison my body with drugs or that which is destructive to my health and my well being. I, say your name, pledge from this day forward, I will support Black newspapers, Black radio, Black television. I will support Black artists, who clean up their acts to show respect for themselves and respect for their people, and respect for the ears of the human family.

I, say your name, will do all of this so help me God

Source: Excerpt from Farrakhan's speech at the Million Man March, Washington, D.C., October 16, 1995 as recorded by CNN. www-cgi.cnn.com/US/9510/megamarch/10-16 /transcript/index.html

SELECT BIBLIOGRAPHY:

Mattias Gardell, *In the Name of Elijah Muhammad: Louis Farrakhan and the Nation of Islam* (Durham, N.C.: Duke University Press, 1996).
Arthur J. Magida, *Prophet of Rage: A Life of Louis Farrakhan and His Nation* (New York: Basic Books, 1996).

〜 14 〜

"A Voice from Death Row," *Mumia Abu-Jamal*

Born Wesley Cook, Mumia Abu-Jamal (1954–) grew up in Philadelphia and at age fifteen served as the Minister of Information for the Philadelphia chapter of the Black Panther Party. After the destruction of the Panthers, he turned to radio broadcasting, where he became a local celebrity. He served as president of the Philadelphia Association of Black Journalists, and became an outspoken advocate of the local radical MOVE organization. In 1981, while he was moonlighting as a cab driver, Jamal was involved in a late-night altercation in which a police officer,

Daniel Faulkner, was shot and killed. Jamal had a registered .38 handgun, but it was never decisively linked to Faulkner's wounds. Nevertheless, Jamal was convicted of murder and sentenced to death. After more than twenty years on death row, a federal district court found that instructions to jury members had been unconstitutional, and as a result, in 2001 Jamal's sentenced was commuted to life imprisonment. Jamal's case has attracted worldwide attention as a possible human rights violation.

⌒

CAPITAL PUNISHMENT

The death penalty is a creation of the State, and politicians justify it by using it as a stepping stone to higher political office. It's very popular to use isolated cases—always the most gruesome ones—to make generalizations about inmates on death row and justify their sentences. Yet it is deceitful; it is untrue, unreal. Politicians talk about people on death row as if they are the worst of the worst, monsters and so forth. But they will not talk about the thousands of men and women in our country serving lesser sentences for similar and even identical crimes. Or others who, by virtue of their wealth and their ability to retain a good private lawyer, are not convicted at all. The criminal court system calls itself a justice system, but it measures privilege, wealth, power, social status, and—last but not least—race to determine who goes to death row.

Why is it that Pennsylvania's African-Americans, who make up only 9% of its population, comprise close to two-thirds of its death row population? It is because its largest city, Philadelphia, like Houston and Miami and other cities, is a place where politicians have built their careers on sending people to death row. They are not making their constituents any safer. They are not administering justice by their example. They are simply revealing the partiality of justice.

Let us never forget that the overwhelming majority of people on death row are poor. Most of them cannot afford the resources to develop an adequate defense to compete with the forces of the State, let alone money to buy a decent suit to wear in court. As the O. J. Simpson case illustrated once again, the kind of defense you get is the kind of defense you can afford. In Pennsylvania, New Jersey, and New York, in Florida, in Texas, in Illinois, in California—most of the people on death row are there because they could not afford what O. J. could afford, which is the best defense.

One of the most widespread arguments in favor of the death penalty is that it deters crime. Study after study has shown that it does not. If capital punishment deters anything at all, it is rational thinking. How else would it be conceivable in a supposedly enlightened, democratic society? Until we recognize the evil irrationality of capital punishment, we will only add, brick by brick, execution by execution, to the dark temple of Fear. How many more lives will be sacrificed on its altar?

Source: Jamal News Service, 1998.

SELECT BIBLIOGRAPHY:

Mumia Abu-Jamal, *Live from Death Row* (Reading, Mass.: Addison-Wesley, 1995).
———, *Death Blossoms: Reflections from a Prisoner of Conscience* (Plough Publishing House, 1997).
J. Patrick O'Connor, *The Framing of Mumia Abu-Jamal* (Chicago: Lawrence Hill Books, 2008).
Leonard Weinglass, *Race for Justice: Mumia Abu-Jamal's Fight against the Death Penalty* (Monroe, Maine: Common Courage Press, 1995).
Daniel R. Williams, *Executing Justice: An Inside Account of the Case of Mumia Abu-Jamal* (New York: St. Martin's Press, 2002).

~ 15 ~

"Let Justice Roll Down Like Waters," *African-American Prisoners in Sing Sing, 1998*

By the end of the twentieth century, about one in three black males in their twenties was imprisoned, on probation or parole, or awaiting trial in the United States. Nearly one million black Americans were incarcerated in federal prisons, state correctional facilities, and local jails. Prisons have become, in effect, the principal means for extending social control over the lives of millions of African Americans. We have selected excerpts from three essays written by prisoners who in 1998 were enrolled in a Master's of Professional Studies Program in the infamous Sing Sing Prison, one of the oldest correctional facilities in the United States.

~

STATEMENT BY SING SING PRISONERS

We are seventeen theology students currently in exile within the bowels of a New York state prison. Mostly from the five boroughs of New York City, we are from various ethnic groups, mainly Black and Latino. Our faith traditions are primarily Christianity and Islam. We are believers striving to live out our faith in all that we say and do each day. We were transferred to Sing Sing Correctional Facility to study as a group toward a master's degree in professional studies.

There are seventy prisons in New York state and approximately seventy thousand prisoners. According to the New York State Department of Correctional Services figures for 1995, the New York state prison population is made up of 85 percent Blacks and Latinos, with 75 percent coming from the inner-city areas of New York City. Upon release 98 percent of us will return to our neighborhoods.

It is clear that Black and Latino communities are most impacted by the policies of the criminal justice system. Yet our communities have the least to say about what goes on in prison. Those establishing and enforcing criminal justice policies are seldom from our urban communities, and their policies are out of step with the needs of Blacks and Latinos. The policy makers are commonly vociferous and consistently diligent with regard to their "tough-on-crime" stance. But they are eerily silent when it comes to the issues of poverty, education, housing, and health care for the marginalized.

Correctional facilities have become big businesses. With 98 percent of state prisons located in rural districts, the prison-industrial complex reflects the interests of those communities. It costs taxpayers approximately $30,000 a year to incarcerate a prisoner; by contrast it costs $11,215 to send an undergraduate to the State University of New York for a year. The crime rate has actually declined, but they continue to build more prisons. As the educational system in our communities continues to deteriorate, prison construction escalates. The high school dropout rate is alarmingly high in our communities, yet educational budgets are slashed and remedial education is eliminated.

We are prepared to make the best of our time and the necessary adjustments for a successful reentry into society, but facing the parole board is like returning to court and having the judge sentence you again for the same crime. There is a double standard of justice and a double jeopardy in judgment.

There is a public outcry against the parole system. To listen only to government officials one would conclude that most of the crimes committed in New York City are committed by individuals on parole. However, 1995 statistics compiled by the NYPD indicate that only 4.5 percent of crimes were committed by parolees.

Many of the churches and other faith communities in the Black and Latino neighborhoods from which we have come have abandoned us. The silence of Black and Latino Christian, Jewish, and Islamic congregations in urban communities makes them unwilling accomplices to the plight of prisoners.

We feel trapped and cut off by a system that seems to have no capacity for love or compassion and refuses to recognize that people can change. Increasingly, politicians and the media manipulate public sentiment toward vengefulness instead of redemption, and that makes the public slow to understand the social causes of wrong behavior. Prison: easy to get in and difficult to get out—even when you are eligible for parole. Prison is a branding method tantamount to modern slavery; it totally rejects any possibility of rehabilitation. . . .

A message needs to be sent to those in power to stop penalizing every prisoner for the criminal acts of a few parolees. We should be judged by what we have done to change our own lives and should be held accountable for our own actions, not somebody else's.

As a measure to deter crime and to keep urban youth out of prison, adequate and effective education should be the focal point for government, churches, and recreation centers. Education builds a sound and safe society, while illiteracy contributes to the destruction of humanity, perpetuating the poverty that too easily leads to prison. We know first-hand the benefits of education and pledge ourselves to share those benefits both in prison and when we return to our communities.

We ask in the Spirit of Righteousness and the One, True, and Living God, that you take this document to heart, remembering always to consider the good that is inherent in all of creation and the struggle of the despised and imprisoned throughout our nation. Let us "believe and do good works, and exhort one another to truth and exhort one another to endurance" (Qur'an 103.3). Seek God's Spirit and Righteousness with us in every endeavor. In the words of Amos, "Let justice roll down like waters, and righteousness like an ever-flowing stream" (Amos 5:24).

THE PRISON-INDUSTRIAL COMPLEX: AN INVESTMENT IN FAILURE

Bliss as a consequence of profound ignorance is a far-reaching, all-encompassing and enduring lie. This nation generally perceives quality education as a privilege and has greatly erred in embracing this obsolete and futile socio-political stance. In 1995, when elitist policy makers and the media contrived to eradicate post-secondary education from prisons, they hustled and beguiled the public with the premise that higher education is a privilege, and prisoners should not have access to it.

It was irrelevant that only a few prisoners participated in post-secondary education. In fact fewer than 1 percent received government grants. The fact that higher education had proved to be the most dramatic recidivism-reducing program within prisons and saved taxpayers more in the long run was lost in the hullabaloo and "get-tough" rhetoric. New York State prisons only provide an eighth-grade education for its captives. Who benefits from ignorant, inter-personally and managerially incompetent prisoners? No one but the Prison-Industrial Complex.

The Prison-Industrial Complex is a national phenomenon with a vested interest in economic and political power. This multi-billion-dollar industry targets African Americans and Latinos, primarily within socially, economically and politically destitute communities. The criminal justice system is the complex machine that devours African-American and Latino men, women and children as the raw material to sustain the Prison-Industrial Complex under the moral banner of "the war on crime." This is more accurately a war on "street crime," revealed as a war on people of color, the marginalized. Historically, this country has always misused its power against its marginalized. The method has not changed. Mass media works with elitist policy makers to shape and create public misperceptions which so desensitize citizens to the real issues that the targeted group is held with contempt or indifference. The Prison-Industrial Complex is unequivocally "an institutionally racist mechanism, which is neutralizing generations of Black and Latino males in New York and across the nation and is devastating communities of color that comprise America's inner cities," according to John Flateau.

In 1995, 150 new prisons were built in the United States alone, and 171 existing prisons were expanded. New York State Department of Correctional Services (DOCS) is moving forward with the largest prison expansion in 70 years, and residents in New York State are more likely to be victims of crime than in 1981. State and federal governments have mobilized massive resources and demonized, criminalized, and incarcerated African Americans and Latinos. Policy makers are quite vociferous when it comes to "street crime"; they are reticent and less vocal when it comes to poverty, meeting children's needs in such areas as education, health and child care, housing, substance abuse treatment, college tuition, recreation and jobs.

The propensity for this nation to take reactionary measures seems more often than not to benefit the ruling class. It is easier to declare war on "street crime" than it is to declare war on poverty, inferior education in dilapidated schools, and substandard housing. It is easier to build prisons than it is to build people up with hope and a sense of purpose.

Jim Wallis highlights this contradiction well in his book, *The Soul of Politics*. Wallis writes, "Washington is the most powerful city in the nation, and D.C. is the most powerless, without control even over its own affairs and destiny. Considered by many to be a colony, the District of Columbia didn't obtain partial home rule until 1974. To this day, District residents (more than 606,000 people) have no voting representation in Congress, and all actions taken by elected city government are subject to congressional veto. As the 'last colony,' D.C. symbolizes the relationship that many parts of the world have with official Washington."

This national symbolism is illustrated in Albany and City Hall. It is not subtle, but blatant. With about 70,000 prisoners in New York State and about 63,000 ex-offenders on parole at any given time, it is not hard to conclude that current criminal justice policies are more geared toward investment in recidivism, and keeping non-violent offenders for bizarre and lengthy sentences only as financial pawns. If we expect prisoners to return to their communities, why are post-secondary education and effective therapeutic programs scarce, and obsolete in their application? If we desire men and women to return to society with civil interpersonal skills, why relegate them to repositories of violent rage? If we expect men and women to return to their communities as assets, and with respect for the law, why do we ignore brutal and corrupt prison guards/police officers who abuse those in their custody with impunity?

We must honestly question what we expect and how our ideology drives the Prison-Industrial Complex. Young men entering the criminal justice system are asphyxiated by despair and banality. They are fatalistic in their reasoning, and angry. Their escalating negativism and sense of dejection make them ideal fuel for the Prison-Industrial Complex.

America could not let go of slavery, so she inserted a clause in the 13th Amendment which made slavery legal for those who were locked up, and convicted of a crime. Prior to the Civil War, the Slave Codes governed all African-American slaves in the South. Once slavery was abolished America merely rewrote the Slave

Codes, and called it the Black Codes. African Americans were arrested and locked up on trumped-up charges and became a captive labor force. They were leased out to white plantations and other private businesses. The State of Georgia illustrated this well in 1878 when it leased out 1,239 convicts. Not surprisingly, 1,124 were African Americans. Brutality abounded unchecked for decades before reform took place in the 1930s. But where carte blanche control over another human being's life is allowed, exploitation and abuse will continue unabated, especially where the prisoner is held with the lowest regard.

In conclusion, higher education has proven to be a critical therapeutic device for me. Others saw deeper qualities within me that I could not see myself. As my horizons expanded, and I was reconciled with my humanity, the possibilities of what I could become exploded before me. It takes courage and perseverance to honestly acknowledge your deficiencies and work earnestly to correct them. My ignorance was not blissful. I have caused a lot of pain for others, and for myself. While I am still incarcerated, critical education has liberated and empowered me. I will be an asset to others, no matter where I am. Unfortunately, many in prison will not have that opportunity, though they desperately need it.

RIVER HUDSON

The River Hudson, what a wonderful sight for me, even from what is such a negative place behind prison fences and walls. Nonetheless, akin to every other place in time, life is what you and I make it. I close my eyes then, and dream, not of faraway places but of places up the river and down. It is during these times that I am free, if only in my mind. Prison bars, cells, fences and walls can never take away my true freedom inside, for I am free to go sailing up and down the River Hudson through every corner of my mind. As I stand at my prison window facing north, in my mind's eye I see the Boulderberg Manor, a wonderful restaurant from days of old; then, my mind goes south to pier 91 where the Queen Elizabeth II (QE II) sits docked in all her majesty. These thoughts signify freedom for me; the River Hudson, what a wonderful place to be.

As I stand staring into the waves of the river from my window, I think of days my wife and I made countless trips to and from the Palisades Parkway via Annsville Circle, the Bear Mountain Bridge, and the breathtaking scenery along the way. We awoke to frost some days, sunshine on others, but always with a heartwarming view of the River Hudson as we made our way to and from work or leisure. There were never better days in my life. What a blessing to be able to close my eyes and see the gracefulness and peace the River Hudson holds for me. I stay the course behind these fences and walls, drifting, sailing, hoping—little gentle breezes engulfing me—in the corners of my mind.

On yet another day, though they all seem the same from here, I sit looking out across the River Hudson to Rockland County facing me. For the life of me I cannot stop my mind from drifting up the river as I wonder—I see it as clear as if it were yesterday—the Boulderberg Manor Restaurant, overlooking the River Hudson from Tompkins Cove, NY. Again the River Hudson: what a breathtaking view even from the Rockland County side, I recall, during a delectable dining experience. Fresh grilled salmon, asparagus covered with hollandaise sauce, yellow rice pilaf, freshly baked sweet potato bread (I can almost smell that warm fresh baked aroma!); and, lest I forget the view, the River Hudson. Whether facing north, south, or simply east from the gazebo on the restaurant lawn, the view was always the absolute best, as we gazed contentedly across to Westchester. Thus, I truly believe one day in the future, perhaps not the Boulderberg with the impeccable service and delightful hospitality we grew so accustomed to, but some place facing the River Hudson awaits Christine and me when these present days, too, will be thoughts of the past.

Still, some days I lay in my Sing Sing bunk, and I reminisce on my love for driving. There is nothing quite like driving along the River Hudson from Westchester County, going south through small towns and quaint villages like Croton on the Hudson, Ossining, Tarrytown, and Dobbs Ferry. Once I make my way to Riverdale, I prepare to cross the Henry Hudson Bridge. Upon approaching the West Side Highway along the riverside, I see the distinctive reddish-orange and black smokestack of Cunard's QE II luxury cruiseliner perched at New York City's Pier 91. It is something again to draw closer to that seafaring vessel, leave the car, and embark upon the ship itself. The view driving alongside the river is calming, but the view from the ship is something I shall never forget, even as I lie here in my bunk. I think of the vessel moving away from the pier and cruising slowly down the River Hudson—New Jersey on the right, New York City on the left—an unbelievable sight! And as these thoughts rest with me now and again, I know one day I will move away from these banks of Sing Sing and move down the River Hudson to my freedom and joys untold.

Freedom rings bright in the halls of my mind, and yet I know that one day again, freedom will truly be mine. Like a cool breeze that passes across the prison yard I admire the gentle—sometimes choppy—waves of the River Hudson. I think of it now, I'll think of it then—what a pleasure; but such freedom will never elude me again. For me, the River Hudson has been a wonderful source of inspiration, it reminds me I have a better life to come. There are bars, fences, and walls that separate me from some experiences anew, but never from the hopes and dreams of my heart and my mind too. Freedom, that inevitable freedom, is yet to come to release me from this time, but physically, not just in the corners of my mind.

Sources: (1) Statement by Sing Sing Prisoners, May 1998, pp. 36–38; (2) Michael J. Love, "The Prison-Industrial Complex: An Investment in Failure," pp. 24–25; and (3) Willis L. Steele, Jr., "River Hudson," in Pamphlet, *Voices of the Class of 1998: Master of Professional Studies Program at Sing Sing Correctional Facility* (New York: New York Theological Seminary, 1998), pp. 34–35.

～ 16 ～

Black Radical Congress, *1998*

On March 1, 1997, a group of thirty-five veteran political activists met in Chicago to discuss the state of the black-American left and the future of progressive U.S. politics. They decided to plan a large national meeting to be called the "Black Radical Congress," bringing together a broad range of progressive organizations and individuals who were involved in socialist, Communist, lesbian and gay, feminist, and revolutionary black-nationalist political work. The Black Radical Congress (BRC) was held in Chicago on June 19–21, 1998, and attracted more than two thousand African-American activists. The BRC established a network of local organizing committees, and its members became involved in a variety of political activities, including anti–police-brutality cases, economic-justice campaigns, and the struggle to defend public education. The documents below are the "Principles of Unity" that were approved at the initial 1997 Chicago organizing meeting, and served as the basis for the BRC's national mobilization; the "Call to the Congress" issued in the fall of 1997 and circulated nationally; and the major policy document of the BRC, the "Black Freedom Agenda." The "Freedom Agenda" was the product of several drafts and intense discussion over eighteen months. The version presented below was approved by the BRC's national council in April 1999. The Freedom Agenda was largely inspired by the African National Congress's "Freedom Charter," the Black Panther Party's "Ten-Point Program," and the Combahee River Collective Statement of 1977.

～

PRINCIPLES OF UNITY

The Black Radical Congress will convene to establish a "center without walls" for transformative politics that will focus on the conditions of Black working and poor people. Recognizing contributions from diverse tendencies within Black Radicalism—including socialism, revolutionary nationalism and feminism—we are united in opposition to all forms of oppression, including class exploitation, racism, patriarchy, homophobia, anti-immigration prejudice and imperialism. We will begin with a gathering on June 19–21, 1998. From there we will identify proposals for action and establish paths forward. The Black Radical Congress does not intend to replace or displace existing organizations, parties or campaigns but will contribute to mobilizing unaffiliated individuals, as well as organizations, around common concerns.

1. We recognize the diverse historical tendencies in the Black radical tradition including revolutionary nationalism, feminism and socialism.
2. The technological revolution and capitalist globalization have changed the economy, labor force and class formations that need to inform our analysis and strategies. The increased class polarization created by these develop-

ments demands that we, as Black radicals, ally ourselves with the most oppressed sectors of our communities and society.

3. Gender and sexuality can no longer be viewed solely as personal issues but must be a basic part of our analyses, politics and struggles.

4. We reject racial and biological determinism, Black patriarchy and Black capitalism as solutions to problems facing Black people.

5. We must see the struggle in global terms.

6. We need to meet people where they are, taking seriously identity politics and single-issue reform groups, at the same time that we push for a larger vision that links these struggles.

7. We must be democratic and inclusive in our dealings with one another, making room for constructive criticism and honest dissent within our ranks. There must be open venues for civil and comradely debates to occur.

8. Our discussions should be informed not only by a critique of what now exists, but by serious efforts to forge a creative vision of a new society.

9. We cannot limit ourselves to electoral politics—we must identify multiple sites of struggle.

10. We must overcome divisions within the Black radical forces, such as those of generation, region and occupation. We must forge a common language that is accessible and relevant.

11. Black radicals must build a national congress of radical forces in the Black community to strengthen radicalism as the legitimate voice of Black working and poor people, and to build organized resistance.

THE STRUGGLE CONTINUES:
SETTING A BLACK LIBERATION AGENDA FOR THE 21ST CENTURY
CHICAGO, ILLINOIS—JUNE 19–21, 1998

Black people face a deep crisis. Finding a way out of this mess requires new thinking, new vision, and a new spirit of resistance. We need a new movement of Black radicalism.

We know that America's capitalist economy has completely failed us. Every day more of us are unemployed and imprisoned, homeless and hungry. Police brutality, violence and the international drug trade threaten our children with the greatest dangers since slavery. The politicians build more prisons but cut budgets for public schools, day care and health care. They slash welfare yet hire more cops. The government says working people must pay more taxes and receive fewer services, while the rich and the corporations grow fat. Black people and other oppressed people have the power to change the way things are today. But first we must unite against the real enemy.

Now is the time for a revival of the militant spirit of resistance that our people have always possessed, from the Abolitionist Movement to outlaw slavery to the Civil Rights Movement of the 1950s, from Black Power to the anti-apartheid campaign of the 1980s. Now is the time to rebuild a strong, uncompromising movement for human rights, full employment and self-determination. Now is the time for a new Black radicalism.

If you believe in the politics of Black liberation, join us in Chicago in 1998 at the Black Radical Congress. If you hate what capitalism has done to our community—widespread joblessness, drugs, violence and poverty—come to the Congress. If you are fed up with the corruption of the two-party system and want to develop a plan for real political change, come to the Congress. If you want to struggle against class exploitation, racism, sexism and homophobia, come to the Congress. The Black Radical Congress is for everyone ready to fight back: trade unionists and workers, youth and students, women, welfare recipients, lesbians and gays, public-housing tenants and the homeless, the elderly and people on fixed incomes, veterans, cultural workers and immigrants. You!

Sisters and Brothers, we stand at the edge of a new century. The moment for a new militancy and a new commitment to the liberation of all Black people, at home and abroad, has arrived. Let us build a national campaign toward the Black Radical Congress, setting in motion a renewed struggle to reclaim our historic role as the real voice of democracy in this country. Spread the word: "Without struggle, there is no progress!" Now's the time!

THE FREEDOM AGENDA

Preamble

During the last 500 years, humanity has displayed on a colossal scale its capacity for creative genius and ruthless destruction, for brutal oppression and indomitable survival, for rigid tradition and rapid change. The Americas evolved to their present state of development at great cost to their original, indigenous peoples, and at great cost to those whose labor enabled modernization under the yoke of that protracted crime against humanity, slavery. Even so, a good idea is implicit in the Declaration of Independence of the United States that all people are "endowed with certain inalienable rights, and among these are life, liberty and the pursuit of happiness." That the idea of a just society, contained in those words, remains unrealized is what compels this declaration.

Not only has the idea not been realized, but we are moving further away from its realization by the hour. Global capitalism, both the cause and effect of neo-liberal and Reaganist policies, has facilitated the transfer of enormous wealth from the bottom to the top of society in recent years, concentrating the control of abundant resources in ever fewer hands. As a result, the working people who constitute the vast majority of people have confronted a steady decline in their prospects for earning a decent living and controlling their lives. In the U.S., the threat of sudden unemployment hangs over most households. We pay unfair taxes and receive fewer services, while multibillion-dollar fortunes accumulate in the private sector. Prisons proliferate as budgets are slashed for public schools, day care, healthcare and welfare. The grip of big money on the two-party electoral process has robbed us of control over the political institutions that are mandated to serve us. We are losing ground, and democracy is more and more elusive.

As for people of African descent, most of whose ancestors were among the shackled millions who helped build the edifices and culture of the Americas, we carry an enormously disproportionate burden. In the U.S., the living legacy of slavery, and the pervasiveness of institutional white supremacy, have placed us on all-too-familiar terms with poverty, urban and rural, exploitative conditions of employment; disproportionately high rates of unemployment and underemployment; inferior health care; substandard education; the corrosive drug trade, with its accompanying gun violence; police brutality and its partner, excessive incarceration; hate-inspired terrorism; a biased legal system, and discrimination of every kind—persistent even after the end of legal segregation.

Resistance is in our marrow as Black people, given our history in this place. From the Haitian revolution, to the U.S. abolitionist movement against slavery, to the twentieth-century movement for civil rights and empowerment, we have struggled and died for justice. We believe that struggle must continue, and with renewed vigor. Our historical experiences suggest to us, by negative example, what a truly just and democratic society should look like: It should be democratic, not just in myth but in practice, a society in which all people—regardless of color, ethnicity, religion, nationality, national origin, sex, sexual orientation, age, family structure, or mental or physical capability—enjoy full human rights, the fruits of their labor, and the freedom to realize their full human potential. If you agree, and if you are committed to helping achieve justice and democracy in the twenty-first century, please sign your name and/or the name of your organization to this 15-point Freedom Agenda.

The Freedom Agenda

I. We will fight for the human rights of Black people and all people.

We will struggle for a society and world in which every individual enjoys full human rights, full protection of the United Nations Declaration of Human Rights, and in the United States equal protection of the Constitution and of all the laws. We seek a society in which every individual—regardless of color, nationality, national origin, ethnicity, religion, sex, sexual orientation, age, family structure, or mental or physical capability—is free to experience "life, liberty and the pursuit of happiness." We affirm that all people are entitled to:

    a. a safe and secure home;

    b. employment at a living wage—that is, compensation for the full value of their labor;

    c. free, quality health care, including full reproductive freedom with the right to choose when or whether to bear children, and free, quality child care;

    d. free, quality public education.

We oppose the Human Genome Project in its current form and with its current leadership, and we oppose all sociobiological or genetic experiments that are spurred by, and help perpetuate, scientific racism. We will fight for a society and world in which every individual and all social groups can live secure, dignified lives.

II. We will fight for political democracy.

We will struggle to expand political democracy to ensure the people's greater participation in decision-making. In the U.S., we will work to replace the current two-party, winner-take-all electoral system with a more democratic multiparty system based on proportional representation, and we will fight to abolish all registration procedures that restrict the number of eligible voters. We oppose private financing of electoral campaigns, especially corporate contributions; we will work to replace the present corrupt system with public financing.

III. We will fight to advance beyond capitalism, which has demonstrated its structural incapacity to address basic human needs worldwide and, in particular, the needs of Black people.

Guided by our belief that people should come before profits, we will fight to maximize economic democracy and economic justice.

> a. We seek full employment at livable wages, public control of private-sector financial operations, worker control of production decisions, and a guaranteed annual income for the needy;
> b. we will fight to end racial discrimination by capitalist enterprises, especially banks, insurance companies and other financial institutions;
> c. we seek a society in which working people enjoy safe working conditions and flexible hours to accommodate family responsibilities, leisure and vacations;
> d. we seek laws mandating public ownership of utilities, and mandating federal and local budgetary emphases on programs for the general welfare—health care, education, public transportation, recreation and infrastructure;
> e. we will struggle for laws that regulate private-sector business practices, especially regarding prices, fees, plant shutdowns and job relocations—where shutdowns are permitted, adequate compensation to workers shall be required;
> f. we support the historical mission of trade unions to represent workers' interests and to negotiate on their behalf;
> g. we seek a fair, equitable, highly progressive tax system that places the heaviest taxes on the wealthiest sector, and we seek expansion of the earned income tax credit.

IV. We will fight to end the super-exploitation of Southern workers.

More than 50 percent of people of African descent residing in the U.S. live in the South, where workers' earnings and general welfare are besieged by corporate practices, and where "right to work" laws undermine union organizing. Thus, we seek relief for Southern workers from corporate oppression, and we will struggle to repeal anti-union laws. We will also fight for aid to Black farmers, and for the restoration of farm land seized from them by agribusiness, speculators and real-estate developers.

V. We will struggle to ensure that all people in society receive free public education.

We affirm that all are entitled to free, quality public education throughout their lifetime. Free education should include adult education and retraining for occupational and career changes. We will fight to ensure that curricula in U.S. schools, colleges and universities are anti-racist, anti-sexist and anti-homophobic, and for curricula that adequately accommodate students' needs to express and develop their artistic, musical or other creative potential.

VI. We will struggle against state terrorism.

We will fight for a society in which every person and every community is free from state repression, including freedom from state-sponsored surveillance. We seek amnesty for, and the release of, all political prisoners. We will struggle to repeal all legislation that expands the police power of the state and undermines the U.S. Constitution's First and Fourth Amendments. We will fight to eliminate the deliberate trafficking in drugs and weapons in our communities by organized crime, and by institutions of the state such as the Central Intelligence Agency.

VII. We will struggle for a clean and healthy environment.

We will fight for a society in which the welfare of people and the natural environment takes precedence over commercial profits and political expediency. We will work to protect, preserve and enhance society's and the planet's natural heritage— forests, lakes, rivers, oceans, mountain ranges, animal life, flora and fauna. In the U.S., we will struggle against environmental racism by fighting for laws that strictly regulate the disposal of hazardous industrial waste, and that forbid both the discriminatory targeting of poor and non-white communities for dumping and despoilment of the natural environment.

VIII. We will fight to abolish police brutality, unwarranted incarceration and the death penalty.

We are determined to end police brutality and murder:

> a. We will fight for strong civilian oversight of police work by elected civilian review boards that are empowered to discipline police misconduct and enforce residency requirements for police officers;
> b. we seek fundamental changes in police training and education to emphasize public service over social control as the context in which law enforcement occurs, and to stress respect for the histories and cultures of the U.S.-born and immigrant communities served;
> c. we seek to limit incarceration to the most violent criminals, only those who have clearly demonstrated their danger to the lives and limbs of others;

    d. regarding non-violent offenders, we demand that they be released and provided with appropriate medical, rehabilitative and educative assistance without incarceration;

    e. we will struggle for abolition of the death penalty, which has been abolished in the majority of developed nations. In the U.S., the history of the death penalty's application is inextricable from the nation's origins as a slave state. Since Emancipation, it has been a white-supremacist tool intended to maintain control over a population perceived as an alien, ongoing threat to the social order. Application of the death penalty, which is highly discriminatory on the basis of color and class, violates international human-rights law and must be eliminated.

IX. We will fight for gender equality, for women's liberation, and for women's rights to be recognized as human rights in all areas of personal, social, economic and political life.

We will work to create a society and world in which women of African descent, along with their sisters of other colors, nationalities and backgrounds, shall enjoy non-discriminatory access to the education, training and occupations of their choice. We will struggle to ensure that all women enjoy equal access to quality health care and full reproductive rights, including the right to determine when or whether they will bear children and the right to a safe, legal abortion. We will fight to end domestic abuse and sexual harassment in the workplace.

X. We recognize lesbian, gay, bisexual and transgender people as full and equal members of society, and of our communities.

We affirm the right of all people to love whom they choose, to openly express their sexuality, and to live in the family units that meet their needs. We will fight against homophobia, and we support anti-homophobic instruction in public schools. We will fight for effective legal protections for the civil rights and civil liberties of lesbian, gay, bisexual and transgender people, and we demand that violence and murder committed against such people be prosecuted as hate crimes. We will also fight to end discrimination against this sector in employment, health care, social welfare and other areas.

XI. We support affirmative action.

We will fight to retain and expand affirmative-action policies in education, employment, the awarding of government contracts and all other areas affected by historical and contemporary injustices. Affirmative action, with goals and timetables, is indispensable for achieving equal opportunity, justice and fairness for the members of all historically oppressed groups.

XII. We will fight for reparations.

Reparations is a well-established principle of international law that should be applied in the U.S. Historically, the U.S. has been both the recipient and disburser of reparations. As the descendants of enslaved Africans, we have the legal and moral right to receive just compensation for the oppression, systematic brutality and economic exploitation Black people have suffered historically and continue to experience today. Thus, we seek reparations from the U.S. for

> a. its illegal assault on African peoples during the slave trade;
> b. its exploitation of Black labor during slavery; and
> c. its systematic and totalitarian physical, economic and cultural violence against people of African descent over the last four centuries.

XIII. We will struggle to build multicultural solidarity and alliances among all people of color.

We will fight against white-supremacist tactics aimed at dividing people of color. We seek alliances with other people of color to develop unified strategies for achieving multicultural democracy, and for overcoming the divisions that exist around such issues as immigration, bilingual education, political representation and allocation of resources.

XIV. We will uphold the right of the African-American people to self-determination.

The formation of the Black Radical Congress in June 1998 was an act of African-American self-determination, a principle which is codified in the United Nations Declaration of Human Rights. The African-American people are entitled to define the direction, priorities, allies and goals of our struggle against national and racial oppression. Building the power to exercise these prerogatives is central to our struggle against all the systems of oppression confronting our people. Therefore, we will fight for both a national program of liberation and for a mass base of power in the social sectors, institutions, all levels of government, communities and territories of society that affect the lives of our people.

XV. We support the liberation struggles of all oppressed people.

We affirm our solidarity with peoples of African descent throughout the African diaspora. We support their struggles against imperialism and neo-colonialism from without, as well as against governmental corruption, exploitation and human-rights abuses from within. We especially support struggles against transnational corporations, whose global market practices gravely exploit all workers, abuse workers' rights and threaten all workers' welfare. We affirm our solidarity with all oppressed people around the world, whatever their color, nation or religion—none of us is free unless all are free. We believe that all people everywhere should enjoy the right to self-determination and the right to pursue their dreams, unfettered by exploitation and discrimination.

Sources: (1) "BRC Principles of Unity"; (2) The "Call to Congress"; and (3) "The Freedom Agenda of the BRC." Copies in possession of the editors.

⚬ 17 ⚬

2000 Presidential Election

The 2000 presidential election was one of the closest and most bitterly contested in American history. Vice president Al Gore, the Democratic Party's presidential candidate, received over 500,000 more popular votes than his Republican challenger, Texas governor George W. Bush. However, as in the contested election of 1876, an extremely close race in Florida placed that state's electoral votes into question. Florida officials led by Bush's brother, governor Jeb Bush, halted the count of ballots and proclaimed the Republican candidate the victor by several hundred votes. There was widespread evidence that tens of thousands of poor and African-American voters had been denied access to voting. The U.S. Supreme Court in its decision, *Bush v. Gore*, declared the Florida ballot recount unconstitutional, and in effect named Bush the winner of the presidency.

At the U.S. Congressional tally of the Electoral College vote on January 6, 2001, the Congressional Black Caucus objected to awarding Florida's twenty-five contested electoral votes to George W. Bush. Though just one vote from a senator was required to put a stop to the count and adjourn the session, not one senator stepped forward to cast the necessary vote. The Caucus walked out of the session in protest, and Bush was declared president of the United Sates.

In a subsequent investigation of voting rights violations, the Commission on Civil Rights concluded that there were gross violations of the Voting Rights Act in Florida during the 2000 presidential election, preventing thousands of residents from voting and discarding the votes of others. In addition, the Commission found that African-American voters were significantly more likely than whites to be barred from voting.

⚬

LETTER TO GOVERNOR BUSH FROM CHAIRPERSON MARY FRANCES BERRY

March 8, 2001

Via Facsimile and U.S. Mail

The Honorable John Ellis Bush
Governor
Office of the Governor
The Florida Capitol
Tallahassee, FL 32399-0001

Dear Governor Bush:

I am writing to express my deep disappointment with your statement of priorities that was presented during the opening of the Florida legislative session, in which you did not address the most serious problems that occurred in Florida during the 2000 elections. My disappointment is based on my preliminary assessment that these problems would not be resolved even if the legislature approved your request that new technology for recording votes be acquired and put into place. Voting technology reforms are necessary and your support of them is a step in the right direction. These measures standing alone, however, are insufficient to address the significant and distressing issues and barriers that prevented qualified voters from participating in the recent Presidential election.

As you know, the Commission has undertaken a formal investigation into allegations by Floridians of voting irregularities arising out of the November 7, 2000 Presidential election. The Commission has held two fact-finding hearings in Florida to examine whether eligible voters faced avoidable barriers that undermined their ability to cast ballots and have their ballots counted in this closely contested election.

In total, over 100 witnesses testified under oath before the Commission, including approximately 65 scheduled witnesses who were selected for the two hearings due to their knowledge of and/or experience with the issues under investigation. The Commission heard testimony from top elected and appointed state officials, including your own testimony, that of the Secretary of State, the Attorney General, the Director of the Florida Division of Elections and other Florida state and county officials. A representative of Database Technologies, Inc. [Choicepoint], a firm involved in the controversial, state-sponsored removal of felons from the voter registration rolls also testified.

We also heard the sworn testimony of registered voters and experts on election reform issues, election laws and procedures and voting rights. Also, the Chair and Executive Director of the Select Task Force on Election Reforms that you established testified before the Commission. Testimony was also received from the supervisors of elections for several counties, county commission officials, law enforcement personnel, and a states attorney. In addition to the scheduled witnesses, the Commission extended an opportunity for concerned persons, including Members of Congress and members of the Florida State Legislature, to submit testimony under oath that was germane to the issues under investigation. Significantly, the Commission subpoenaed scores of relevant documents to assist with this investigation.

The evidence points to an array of problems. These problems cry out for solutions, for example, a process for insuring the equitable allocation of resources to insure that poor and or people of color areas are not disproportionately affected. They also include a better process for identifying felons who are ineligible to vote, insuring coordination between the DMV and election boards to make sure registrations are actually filed and on a timely basis, funds for better training of poll workers, improved and updated communication systems, funds for voter education, and clarifications in the law to permit provisional ballots to be cast, when appropriate. As you know, counties have uneven funding bases and priorities.

Because I believe the need to address these problems is serious, I have determined that the Commission should hold additional hearings in Florida after the conclusion of the legislative session to bring state and local officials before us to assess what changes have been legislated or enacted at the state and local level and to report to the public on what progress has been made.

I expect the Commission to formally endorse the new hearings at our meeting on March 9, 2001. We intend to keep a steady focus on these developments to ensure that the voting rights of all eligible persons are protected.

Respectfully,

Mary Frances Berry
Chairperson

Source: Mary Frances Berry, "Letter to Governor Bush from Chairperson Mary Frances Berry," U.S. Commission on Civil Rights, (2001) www.usccr.gov/pubs/vote2000/Berry .htm.

SELECT BIBLIOGRAPHY:

Douglas Brinkley, "The Great Election 2000 Media Debacle," *Harvard International Journal of Press/ Politics* 6, no. 2 (March 1, 2001), pp. 82–88.

Corrine Brown, "On Voting Rights," House of Representatives (2004) www.house .gov/corrinebrown/ccorner108/cc_041007_votingrights.htm.

John Conyers and United States Congress House Committee on the Judiciary, *How to Make over One Million Votes Disappear: Electoral Sleight of Hand in the 2000 Presidential Election: A Fifty-State Report* (Washington, DC: U.S. House of Representatives, 2001).

Hermon George Jr., "Putting Election 2000 in Perspective: A Declaration of War," *Black Scholar* 31, no. 2 (June 2001), pp. 11–13.

Lani Guinier, "What We Must Overcome," *American Prospect* 12, no. 5 (March 12, 2001), pp. 26–31.

Revathi I. Hines, "The Silent Voices: 2000 Presidential Election and the Minority Vote in Florida," *Western Journal of Black Studies* 26, no. 2 (Summer 2002), pp. 71–74.

Jack N. Rakove, ed., *The Unfinished Election of 2000* (New York: Basic Books, 2001).

United States Commission on Civil Rights, "Voting Irregularities in Florida During the 2000 Presidential Election," The Commission (2001) www.usccr.gov/pubs/vote 2000/report/main.htm.

Hanes Walton Jr., "The Disenfranchisement of the African American Voter in the 2000 Presidential Election: The Silence of the Winner and Loser," *Black Scholar* 31, no. 2 (June 2001), pp. 21–24.

Jerry White, "Why Did the U.S. Media Black out the Civil Commission Report on the Florida Vote?," *Black Scholar* 31, no. 2 (June 2001), pp. 8–10.

~ 18 ~

Hip-Hop Activism

Hip-hop emerged in the Bronx during the mid-1970s as a challenge to structural racism. One element of hip-hop—rap music—became a mainstream multimillion-dollar business. However, a more progressive strand of hip-hop is typically associated with activism. The term hip-hop activism, which became popular in the 1980s, drew attention to hip-hop as a social critique of injustice. Young organizers, scholars, activists, artists and cultural workers have used hip-hop to address the serious issues confronting their generation, including poverty, police brutality, massive incarceration of juveniles, felony disenfranchisement, and the HIV/HIV pandemic. The Hip-Hop Summit Action Network (HSAN), founded in 2001 by Russell Simmons, was one of many organizations to use hip-hop music as a framework for activism.

~

"WHAT WE WANT"

1. We want freedom and the social, political and economic development and empowerment of our families and communities; and for all women, men and children throughout the world.

2. We want equal justice for all without discrimination based on race, color, ethnicity, nationality, gender, sexual orientation, age, creed or class.

3. We want the total elimination of poverty.

4. We want the highest quality public education equally for all.

5. We want the total elimination of racism and racial profiling, violence, hatred and bigotry.

6. We want universal access and delivery of the highest quality health care for all.

7. We want the total elimination of police brutality and the unjust incarceration of people of color and all others.

8. We want the end and repeal of all repressive legislations, laws, regulations and ordinances such as "three strikes" laws; federal and state mandatory minimum sentencing; trying and sentencing juveniles as adults; sentencing disparities between crack and powdered cocaine use; capitol punishment; the Media Marketing Accountability Act; and hip-hop censorship fines by the FCC.

9. We want reparations to help repair the lingering vestiges; damages and suffering of African Americans as a result of the brutal enslavement of generations of Africans in America.

10. We want the progressive transformation of American society into a Nu America as a result of organizing and mobilizing the energy, activism and resources of the hip-hop community at the grassroots level throughout the United States.

11. We want greater unity, mutual dialogue, program development and a prioritizing of national issues for collective action within the hip-hop community through summits, conferences, workshops, issue task force and joint projects.

12. We want advocacy of public policies that are in the interests of hip-hop before Congress, state legislatures, municipal governments, the media and the entertainment industry.

13. We want the recertification and restoration of voting rights for the 10 million persons who have loss their right to vote as a result of a felony conviction. Although these persons have served time in prison, their voting rights have not been restored in 40 states in the U.S.

14. We want to tremendously increase public awareness and education on the pandemic of HIV/AIDS.

15. We want a clean environment and an end to communities in which poor and minorities reside being deliberately targeted for toxic waste dumps, facilities and other environmental hazards.

THE TOOKIE PROTOCOL FOR PEACE
Point I:
Proclamation

A-1: WE THE INVOLVED PARTIES WILL immediately cease fire and end any verbal, written, or physical violence against one another.

A-2: WE THE INVOLVED PARTIES WILL cease and desist the perpetuation of drive-by shootings, walk-up shootings, set-up shootings, ambushes, murder, drug deals, robbery, vandalism, kidnapping, rape, extortion, female and child abuse, illegal profiteering, or any other kind of violence or criminality.

A-3: WE THE INVOLVED PARTIES WILL use every nonviolent measure to resolve all past, present, or future conflicts between us.

A-4: WE THE INVOLVED PARTIES WILL learn to respect one another and co-exist in peace within the community and elsewhere.

A-5: WE THE INVOLVED PARTIES WILL help to restore order and to rebuild the community.

A-6: WE THE INVOLVED PARTIES WILL not disrespect, instigate, or taunt each other or family members, relatives, wives, girlfriends, and acquaintances of the opposite parties.

A-7: WE THE INVOLVED PARTIES WILL not encroach upon each other's community or neighborhood without prior notice, to avoid suspicion or conflict.

A-8: WE THE INVOLVED PARTIES WILL help individually and collectively to keep the community safe from any improprieties.

A-9: WE THE INVOLVED PARTIES WILL not use the Peace Accord as camouflage to commit mayhem against each other.

A-10: WE THE INVOLVED PARTIES WILL neither seek out nor plot with acquaintances or outsiders (defined as parties not obligated to this Proclamation) to carry out vendettas against each other.

A-11: WE THE INVOLVED PARTIES WILL not allow mistreatment or harm to befall any individuals appointed as Peacekeepers or others involved in the peace process.

A-12: WE THE INVOLVED PARTIES will put forth effort to become educated, computer-literate, and to learn a trade that will enable us to become productive in the reconstruction of our community.

A-13: WE THE INVOLVED PARTIES WILL eliminate any self-destructive behavior and personal vices—illicit drug usage, drug dealing, abuse of alcohol, inhalants, etc.—that would intoxicate our minds, impair our judgment and jeopardize the peace negotiations.

A-14: WE THE INVOLVED PARTIES will work side by side to do whatever is ethical to uphold the Peace Accord and Proclamation, and we vow to live in harmony.

A-15: WE THE INVOLVED PARTIES recognize both the Peace Accord and Proclamation as being fair and attainable. We agree to its entire contents.

Sources: Hip-Hop Summit Action Network, "What We Want," www.hsan.org /content/main.aspx?pageid=27.
Stan "Tookie" William, "Tookie Protocol for Peace," www.tookie.com/protocol /index.html.

SELECT BIBLIOGRAPHY:

Jeff Chang, *Can't Stop, Won't Stop: A History of the Hip-Hop Generation* (New York: St. Martin's Press, 2005).
Raymond Codrington, "Hip-Hop Beyond Appropriation: An Introduction to the Series," *Transforming Anthropology* 15, no. 2 (October 2007), pp. 138–140.
Michael Eric Dyson, *Know What I Mean? Reflections on Hip-Hop* (New York: Basic Civitas, 2007).
Bakari Kitwana, *The Hip Hop Generation: Young Blacks and the Crisis in African American Culture* (New York: Basic Civitas Books, 2002).
Tony Mitchell, ed., *Global Noise: Rap and Hip-Hop Outside the USA, Music/Culture* (Middletown: Wesleyan University Press, 2001).
Mark Anthony Neal and Murray Forman, eds., *That's the Joint!: The Hip-Hop Studies Reader* (New York: Routledge, 2004).
Tricia Rose, *Black Noise: Rap Music and Black Culture in Contemporary America, Music/Culture* (Hanover: University Press of New England, 1994).
Andrew Ross and Tricia Rose, eds., *Microphone Fiends: Youth Music & Youth Culture* (New York: Routledge, 1994).
Simmons Russell and Chavis Benjamin, "Hip-Hop Summit Action Network Calls for End to 'Bitch,' 'Ho' and 'Nigger' in Music," *Michigan Chronicle* (April 25, 2007), p. A1.
Timothy Francis Strode and Tim Wood, eds., *The Hip Hop Reader* (New York: Pearson/ Longman, 2008).
S. Craig Watkins, *Hip Hop Matters: Politics, Pop Culture, and the Struggle for the Soul of a Movement* (Boston: Beacon Press, 2005).

⚊ 19 ⚊

World Conference Against Racism—Durban, South Africa

The World Conference Against Racism, Racial Discrimination, Xenophobia and other Forms of Intolerance was held in Durban, South Africa, from August 31 to September 8, 2001. The conference and its Non-Governmental Organizations Forum was attended by 8,000 people including delegates, activists, and scholars from more than 160 countries. Though there were more than 1,500 black Americans who participated in preconference panels and in the official proceedings, official representatives from the U.S. State Department walked out of the meeting in protest with the Israeli delegation.

Among other important topics, conference participants discussed reparations for slavery and colonialism. Conference participants endorsed a document that recognized the negative effects of racism and globalization; the connections between racial discrimination, xenophobia, and class oppression; and called upon Western governments to acknowledge slavery as "a crime against humanity." The conference dramatically escalated social movements by people of African descent in many Third World countries, especially across Latin America.

⚊

THE VIENNA DECLARATION AND PLAN OF ACTION, 2001[1]

Acknowledging the Black Holocausts
Whereas, African Slave Trade and Slavery exploited the motherland of Africa; Forced the brutal displacement or removal of over one hundred million of its people (the largest forced migration in history); Directly caused the death of millions [of] Africans; Destroyed African civilizations which were among the most advanced societies of the world; Impoverished African economies which had prospered up to that time; and launched a period of African under-development and marginalization which continues to this day—five hundred years later;

Whereas, Africa was dismembered and divided among European powers, which created Western monopolies for the continued exploitation of vital African natural resource riches for Western industries; and

Whereas, African Slavery was imposed by and for the benefit of major European and

American states to satisfy their appetites for free labor; and the exploitation of Africans and African descendants by these States continued unabated for over three hundred years; and

Whereas, After the Slave Trade, Africa was subjected to another form of enslavement, namely, Colonization in which the exploitation of Africa's rich natural resource heritage continued unabated by the European powers; and, Eliminating Anti-Black Racism

Whereas, Africans and African descendants are commonly victims of anti-Black racism and of multiple forms of overt and covert discrimination. The most pernicious are institutional, systemic, structural and cultural discrimination. The impact of institutional, structural and cultural racism is felt in every aspect of life: housing, employment, education, health, civil and criminal justice, economic development. Many of these policies and practices are perpetrated by the states themselves; and,

Whereas, Anti-Black racism (both past and present) is fundamentally rooted in white supremacist ideology and the economic profits of the colonial and neo-colonial oppressors; and

Whereas, Anti-Black racism cannot be eradicated without the elimination of social ghettoization and demonization of Africans and African descendants; and

Whereas, Many Africans and African descendants suffer from multi-oppressions structured around class, gender, disability, immigrant status and sexuality. These forms of oppression must be eliminated; and,

Whereas, African and African descendant women play, and have always played, a fundamental role in the development and maintenance of our families, peoples, communities and nations, even though historically they have faced the worst conditions, the greatest marginalization and systematic exclusion. Women and men, and children and youth of both genders are equal and must be treated so; and,

Whereas, Racism is a major health determinant. Historical and current discrimination, as well as colonial and neo-colonial policies against Africans and African descendants have resulted in Africans and African descendants having significantly lower health status, less or no access to health care and poorer quality health care;

Whereas, AIDS represents a human genocide, disproportionally victimizing African people, both on the continent and in the Diaspora and,

Whereas, Media and new technologies (including the internet) play a significant role in the maintenance of structural and cultural anti-black racism; and,

Whereas, Environmental racism refers to any government, military, industry or other institution's action, or failure to act, which has a disproportionate negative environmental impact on Africans and African descendants, on Indigenous peoples, Latino, Asian, migrant or other ethnic groups or the places where they live. Environmental racism, although not new, is a recent example of the historical double standard as to what is acceptable in certain communities, villages or cities and not in others. The mobility of corporations has made it possible for them to seek the greatest profit, the least government and environmental regulations and the best tax incentives, anywhere in the world. Natural resource extraction techniques, chemical uses and disposal of wastes unacceptable in white communities are routinely employed in African descendants communities; and,

Whereas, Africans and African descendants are victims of grave discriminatory treatment in the legal and judicial processes as well as police procedures (specifically police brutality). This includes the framing up of accusations against Africans and African descendants, the duration of prison sentences, the inhuman state of prisons and, where it exists, the death penalty which particularly affects Africans and African descendants; and,

Whereas, To ensure the future of all Africans, special attention must be given to protecting and empowering African indigenous peoples, language groups and cultures both inside and outside the African continent; and,

Restoring Africa, the Motherland

Whereas, The development of Africa has been greatly impeded by the global imbalances in power created by slavery, colonialism, and other forms of exploitation and is maintained and extended today by neo-colonial policies and practices including the pillage of the human and material resources of Africa and the draining of its financial resources by foreign debt services; and,

Whereas, Current day slavery has just taken other forms and the right to life and freedom of African people is being regularly violated with complete indifference in Western countries and by African dictators who are very often supported and protected by Western countries; and,

Whereas, The world major powers are plundering the African continent through a "debt" which has already been paid off three times over and to which the African states assign more than 50% of their national budgets; and,

Whereas, To ensure total control over the enslaved Africans and African descendants, the Western slaveholding states resorted to systematic violence, brain-washing, falsifying and negating African history and values while enhancing Western history and values in a policy of cultural imperialism; and,

Whereas, Africans and African descendants have significantly contributed to world history, their achievements need to be re-assessed within the context of the significant positive contributions made by Africa culture, Africans and African descendants; and,

Whereas, In a world where people are valued and devalued according to a given level of economic development, it is essential that the economic development of Africa be promoted as a means of fighting anti-black racism; and

Now, therefore,

Africans and African Descendants from across the world, gathered in Vienna, Austria, in unity and solidarity born of the common African root, recognition of sharing a common history—that of the African Slave Trade, Slavery, and Colonialization—and a continuing common experience of anti-Black racism, which root, history and experience bind us as a unique community; and

Respectful of the Memory of Our Ancestors and the ultimate sacrifice which they paid, and mindful that this memory must never be forgotten; and

As a Community, Committed to the elimination [of] anti-Black racism wherever it occurs in the World; and

Cognizant of the Enormity of the depredations of the Black Holocausts (Slavery and Colonialization) and the significance of these historical epochs for the world; and,

In fraternity with all peoples imbued with a sense of genuine respect for the rights of people of all races, ethnicities and creeds; and,

In abhorrence of all forms of African Slavery and the African Slave Trade (trans-Atlantic, trans-Saharan and trans-Indian Ocean) and the Colonization of Africa;

BE IT RESOLVED that this Assembly:

Black Holocausts (Slavery and Colonization)

CONDEMNS AFRICAN SLAVERY in all its manifestations (trans-Atlantic, trans-Saharan and trans-Indian Ocean) and calls on the United Nations and the governments of the World to do likewise;

DECLARES AFRICAN SLAVERY AND COLONIZATION and the atten dant unprecedented genocide and systematic violations of human rights and the rights of Africans and African descendant People, as Crimes Against Humanity;

CALLS, SPECIFICALLY, ON former European countries and American slave-holding States and all those who benefitted [sic] from the slave trade and colonization of Africa to unconditionally and separately adopt a Declaration of recognition of the Black Holocausts (Slave Trade/Slavery and Colonization) as Crimes Against Humanity;

CALLS, SPECIFICALLY, ON former European and American slave-holding States and all those who benefitted [sic] from the slave trade and colonization of Africans to unconditionally and separately adopt a Declaration which asks for forgiveness for the exactions committed during the Slave Trade/Slavery and Colonization and for their lasting effects on the Africans and African Descendants, in psychological spheres as well as on economical, social, political and cultural ones;

CALLS ON THE UNITED NATIONS AND GOVERNMENTS of the World to make it an offence, punishable by law, for anyone to deny the existence of the Black Holocausts (African Slave Trade/Slavery and Colonization);

CALLS ON FORMER EUROPEAN AND AMERICAN SLAVE-HOLDING STATES and all those who benefitted [sic] from the slave trade and colonization of Africans to acknowledge the principle of reparations for the cultural, demographic, economic, political, social and moral wrongs of the Slave Trade/Slavery and Colonization and that the Africans and African descendants victims of the Slave Trade/Slavery and Colonization reserve the right to determine the form and manner of reparations; and,

DEMAND THAT THE Governments of the World condemn the trans-Saharan and Indian Ocean slave trade which, like the trans-Atlantic slave trade, brought serious damages to Africa. Unlike the trans-Atlantic slave trade, vestiges of the trans-Saharan slave trade continues [sic] [to] this day unabated (specifically in Mauritania and Sudan); and, call on the governments of Mauritania and Sudan to recognize this problem and to eradicate it completely [sic].

CALL on the German and Italian Government[s] to ask for forgiveness for the exactions and genocide committed during the World War [II] by the Nazis and Fascist[s] against Africans and African descendants; recognizing that African and African descendant victims of Nazism have the same right to compensatory measures as Jews or Romas;

and,

CALLS ON STATES, SURVIVING CORPORATE INTERESTS, CHURCHES AND NON-GOVERNMENTAL AGENCIES involved in the trans-Atlantic slave trade, the resulting slavery and colonization to acknowledge their wrongdoings and accept the principle of restitution and that the Africans and African descendants victims of the Slave Trade/Slavery and Colonization reserve the right to determine the form and manner of reparations; and,

Eliminating Anti-Black Racism

DEMANDS THAT GOVERNMENTS AND ORGANIZATIONS recognize anti-Black racism as a form of racism which has its own specificity in the same way as anti-Semitism and to be differentiated from all other forms of racism, discrimination and intolerance; and,

CALLS ON GOVERNMENTS AND OTHERS TO condemn any political, economic or social structure that has the effect of promoting, encouraging, or facilitating anti-Black racism; and,

DEMAND THAT States eliminate racial disparities in education, housing, economic development, health and health care, [the] environment, civil and criminal justice; and,

DEMAND THAT States adopt effective mechanisms for monitoring and eliminating all forms of overt and covert racial discrimination, placing particular emphasis on institutional and structural anti-Black racism in education, housing, economic development, health and health care, environment, civil and criminal justice; and,

CALL ON States, and United Nations organizations (such as World Health Organization) to routinely and systematically collect race, gender and socio-economic class data related to education, housing, economic development, health and health care, environment, civil and criminal justice; and,

DEMAND THAT STATES stop the criminalization of blackness immediately.

REQUEST THAT a representative of the Africans and African Descendants Caucus be allowed to address the World Conference against Racism, Racial

Discrimination, Xenophobia and Related Forms of Intolerance in South Africa; and,

DEMAND THAT ALL ORGANIZATIONS (multilateral, financial, development and human rights) formulate diagnostic indicators of the impact of their policies and programs on African and African descendant communities; and,

DEMAND THAT States, and the international community, develop effective anti-discrimination laws which provide an adequate institutional framework for redress that is specific to eliminating institutional and structural anti-Black discrimination (both overt and covert); and,

URGE states to institute educational steps to combat racism including challenging racist language and eradication of words and terms with a racist content especially when used by authorities; and adopting a prohibition against racist documents particularly books for children which convey a depreciative image of Africans and African Descendants; and,

CALL on civil society groups to help develop advocacy strategies that link environmental issues (including environmental racism) to human rights; and Governments adopt and enforce legislation and policies that protect society from environmental racism; and,

CALL on the United Nations to support a world institute dedicated to research, fact finding and resource networking for Africans, African descendants and related issues. The research should serve to bridge the gap between the *past*, by presenting African history according to credible African resources, the *present*, by monitoring the overall life conditions of Africans and African descendants worldwide and the *future*, by implementing its' [sic] research in informal and formal education to change attitudes, perceptions and promote understanding; and,

REQUEST the media of the world and providers of Internet services to implement initiatives for increasing public awareness of anti-racist and tolerant behavior towards Africans and promote a positive and valorizing image of Africans; and,

URGE States and organizations to give special attention to adolescents and young people of African descent in terms of empowerment, training, mentoring and possibilities to exercise responsibilities; Attention must be given to activities promoting a healthy and balanced African identity for children and youth; Youth participation must be se- cured on national and international levels of political decision making; and,

URGE the international community to take practical steps to understand the political nature of the AIDS epidemic and to improve prevention strategies, testing material, access to medicines and care for those infected with AIDS; and,

CALLS ON AFRICANS AND AFRICAN DESCENDANTS to recognize that the struggle against anti-black racism is inevitably linked with the struggle against poverty, racism against others, imperialism, globalization and war. Africans and African descendants express solidarity with other peoples who are similarly oppressed and exploited; and,

Restoring Africa, the Motherland

CALL ON AFRICANS AND AFRICAN DESCENDANTS TO END conflicts based on ethnic divisions which is tearing the African continent apart through ethnic genocide, ethnic cleansing and ethnic culture war; the struggle against racism must go hand in hand with struggle against negative ethnicity in Africa; and

CALL ON AFRICAN NATIONS to take legal action and give priority to the equitable redistribution of stolen, possessed and occupied land on the continent; and call on the international community to support such actions; and,

CALL on African governments to adopt policies to grant all Africans and African descendants the possibility to return home and settle without limitations or discrimination; and,

DEMAND that European, American and other governments repatriate funds stolen from African countries/people and stored in European and American banks to the African countries of their origin; and,

URGE the debt-holding countries to take practical steps toward the cancellation of the "debt" of African States; and,

DEMAND THAT THE MANY ART[I]FACTS AND ANTIQUITIES of African civilization which have been stolen or taken out of the country without permission be returned or that the countries from which these antiquities were taken be compensated; and,

DEMAND THAT THE TRAFFICKING OF AFRICAN AND AFRICAN DESCENDANT women, children and youth for sex, and for forced labour and various forms of enslavement be stopped in both locations receiving victims of trafficking, and in locations of origin. International, local/national, and other media are urged to continue and increase their much-needed work of reporting on these crimes; and,

CALL ON AFRICANS AND AFRICAN DESCENDANTS to urgently free themselves from slave and colonial mentality and attitudes. The rich African cultural heritage at our disposal serve[s] as the first step in a real liberation and renaissance of Africa and its people all over the World.

Source: Excerpt from "Paper Trail: World Conference against Racism, Xenophobia, and Related Intolerance," *Souls* 4, no.3 (May 2002), pp. 69–82.

SELECT BIBLIOGRAPHY:
"The Vienna Declaration and Plan of Action: African and African Descendents Caucus", 2001) academic.udayton.edu/race/06hrights/WCAR2001/NGOFORUM/Victims.htm.
Carol Barton, "UN World Conference against Racism-Breaking the Silence," World Conference Against Racism (2001) www.wicej.addr.com/wcar_docs/index.html.
Salih Booker and William Minter, "Global Apartheid," *Peace Research Abstracts* 40, no. 2 (2003), pp. 123–261.

Linda Burnham, "The Light of History," *Souls* 4, no. 1 (January 2002), pp. 15–19.

Gernot Kohler, *Global Apartheid* (New York: Institute for World Order, 1978).

———, "The Three Meanings of Global Apartheid: Empirical, Normative, Existential," *Alternatives* 20, no. 3 (1995), pp. 403.

Leith Mullings, "Race and Globalization," *Souls* 6, no. 2 (June 2004), pp. 1–9.

Scott Sherman, "Target Ford," *Nation* 282, no. 22 (June 5, 2006), pp. 13–20.

J. Michael Turner, "The Road to Durban—and Back," *NACLA Report on the Americas* 35, no. 6 (May/ June 2002), pp. 31–35.

⚡ **20** ⚡

African Americans Respond to Terrorism and War

On September 11, 2001, terrorist attacks destroyed the World Trade Center towers in New York City. These crimes against humanity claimed the lives of nearly 3,000 people, including passengers on the planes that crashed into the towers or to the ground. Another terrorist attack took place at the Pentagon, where more than 100 people were killed. Like most Americans, African Americans were outraged by these attacks and supported military retaliation against the Al Qaeda terrorist network in Afghanistan. However, when the attacks were used by the Bush administration as justification for undermining civil liberties incarcerating Muslims and people of Middle Eastern descent based on their religion or ethnic background alone, many black Americans protested.

Representative Barbara Lee was the only member of Congress to oppose authorizing the Bush administration to use military force to invade Afghanistan. After the initiation of the "War on Terror" and the establishment of the Office of Homeland Security, the majority of African-American leaders vigorously protested the curtailment of civil liberties and the unilateral expansion of U.S. militarism in the Muslim world. As the war expanded into Iraq in 2003 a significant number of U.S. soldiers and Iraqi war veterans turned against the war, citing the failure to find weapons of mass destruction in the country and the massive cost to the U.S. taxpayer.

⚡

"BARBARA LEE'S STAND"

When Congress voted to authorize the Bush Administration to use military force in response to the September 11 terror attacks on the World Trade Center and the Pentagon, Representative Barbara Lee stood alone in opposition to what she saw as a "rush to judgment." Lee, the California Democrat who holds the Bay Area seat once occupied by antiwar activist Ron Dellums, spoke with John Nichols, The Nation's Washington correspondent, this week.

THE NATION: How did you reach the decision to oppose authorizing the use of force?

LEE: I was at the National Cathedral in Washington. I went to the memorial service on the Friday after the attacks and I prayed. I said to myself, "You've got to figure this one out." I was dealing with all the grief and sorrow and the loss of life, and it was very personal because a member of my staff had lost a cousin in the Pennsylvania crash. I was thinking about my responsibility as a member of Congress to try to insure that this never happens again. I listened to the remarks of the clergy. Many of them made profound statements. But I was struck by what one of them said: "As we act, let us not become the evil that we deplore." That was such a wise statement, and it reflected not only what I was feeling but also my understanding of the threats we continue to face. When I left the cathedral, I was fairly resolved.

THE NATION: Were you also concerned about the constitutional implications of the vote?

LEE: Absolutely. Given the three branches of government, and given that each has a role in the making of monumental decisions such as this, I thought the Congress had a responsibility in this instance especially to step back and say, "Let's not rush to judgment. Let us insist that our democracy works by insuring that the checks and balances work and that the Congress is a part of the decision-making process in terms of when we go to war and with whom. . . . I think we disenfranchised the American people when we took their representatives out of the decision-making on whether to go to war with a specific nation.

THE NATION: Were you surprised that no other members of Congress voted with you?

LEE: It never dawned on me that I would cast the only vote against this resolution. Many members asked me to change my position. They were friends, and they said, "You do not want to be out there alone." I said, "Oh, no, don't worry. There will be others." When there weren't, I said, "Oh my God." I could not believe it. It was an awesome feeling. And a lonely feeling.

THE NATION: You mentioned that other members said, "You don't want to be out there alone." Do you think other members shared your concerns but were unwilling to cast a risky vote with emotions running so high?

LEE: If you read the floor statements. you'll see that there are many members of Congress who share my concerns. I think that, when I cast that vote, I was speaking for other people in Congress and outside Congress who want a more deliberative approach.

THE NATION: At the same time, you have received precisely the sort of criticism that most politicians fear.

LEE: I've been called a traitor, a coward, a communist, all the awful stuff. It's been quite difficult for me. But I still believe that I cast the right vote. My district, I think, understands this vote. . . . I've gotten probably 20,000 e-mails. At first, there were a lot of very harsh messages. But now we are hearing more from people who are saying, "Yes, let's use some restraint. Yes, let's break the cycle of violence if we can." I think the further we get away from that tragic day, the more we will hear those voices of reason.

Iraq Veterans Against the War

Why we're against the War
Q: Why are veterans, active duty, and National Guard men and women opposed to the war in Iraq?

A: Here are 10 reasons we oppose this war:

The Iraq war is based on lies and deception.
The Bush Administration planned for an attack against Iraq before September 11th, 2001. They used the false pretense of an imminent nuclear, chemical and biological weapons threat to deceive Congress into rationalizing this unnecessary conflict. They hide our casualties of war by banning the filming of our fallen's caskets when they arrive home, and when they refuse to allow the media into Walter Reed Hospital and other Veterans Administration facilities which are overflowing with maimed and traumatized veterans.

The Iraq war violates international law.
The United States assaulted and occupied Iraq without the consent of the UN Security Council. In doing so they violated the same body of laws they accused Iraq of breaching.

Corporate profiteering is driving the war in Iraq.
From privately contracted soldiers and linguists to no-bid reconstruction contracts and multinational oil negotiations, those who benefit the most in this conflict are those who suffer the least. The United States has chosen a path that directly contradicts President Eisenhower's farewell warning regarding the military industrial complex. As long as those in power are not held accountable, they will continue. . .

Overwhelming civilian casualties are a daily occurrence in Iraq.
Despite attempts in training and technological sophistication, large-scale civilian death is both a direct and indirect result of United States aggression in Iraq. Even the most conservative estimates of Iraqi civilian deaths number over 100,000. Currently over 100 civilians die *every day* in Baghdad alone.

Soldiers have the right to refuse illegal war.
All in service to this country swear an oath to protect and defend the Constitution of the United States against all enemies, both foreign and domestic. However, they are prosecuted if they object to serve in a war they see as illegal under our Constitution. As such, our brothers and sisters are paying the price for political incompetence, forced to fight in a war instead of having been sufficiently trained to carry out the task of nation-building.

Service members are facing serious health consequences due to our Government's negligence.
Many of our troops have already been deployed to Iraq for two, three, and even four tours of duty averaging eleven months each. Combat stress, exhaustion, and bearing witness to the horrors of war contribute to Post Traumatic Stress Disorder (PTSD), a serious set of symptoms that can lead to depression, illness, violent behavior, and even suicide. Additionally, depleted uranium, Lariam, insufficient body armor and infectious diseases are just a few of the health risks which accompany an immorally planned and incompetently executed war. Finally, upon a soldier's release, the Veterans Administration is far too under-funded to fully deal with the magnitude of veterans in need.

The war in Iraq is tearing our families apart.
The use of stop-loss on active duty troops and the unnecessarily lengthy and repeat active tours by Guard and Reserve troops place enough strain on our military families, even without being forced to sacrifice their loved ones for this ongoing political experiment in the Middle East.

The Iraq war is robbing us of funding sorely needed here at home.
$5.8 billion per month is spent on a war which could have aided the victims of Hurricane Katrina, gone to impoverished schools, the construction of hospitals and health care systems, tax cut initiatives, and a host of domestic programs that have all been gutted in the wake of the war in Iraq.

The war dehumanizes Iraqis and denies them their right to self-determination.
Iraqis are subjected to humiliating and violent checkpoints, searches and home raids on a daily basis. The current Iraqi government is in place solely because of the U.S. military occupation. The Iraqi government doesn't have the popular support of the Iraqi people, nor does it have power or authority. For many Iraqis the current government is seen as a puppet regime for the U.S. occupation. It is undemocratic and in violation of Iraq's own right to self-governance.

Our military is being exhausted by repeated deployments, involuntary extensions, and activations of the Reserve and National Guard.
The majority of troops in Iraq right now are there for at least their second tour. Deployments to Iraq are becoming longer and many of our service members are facing involuntary extensions and recalls to active duty. Longstanding policies to limit the duration and frequency of deployments for our part-time National

Guard troops are now being overturned to allow for repeated, back-to-back tours in Iraq. These repeated, extended combat tours are taking a huge toll on our troops, their families, and their communities.

Sources: (1)"Barbara Lee's Stand," *The Nation* (October 8, 2001), p. 5. (2) "Iraq Veterans against the War," www.ivaw.org/about.

SELECT BIBLIOGRAPHY:

Patricia Foulkrod, *The Ground Truth*, Universal City: Universal Studios Home Entertainment, 2006. DVD Video.

Derrick Z. Jackson, "Blacks Have Good Cause to Oppose War in Iraq," *Boston Globe* (February 26, 2003), p. A19.

Yvonne Latty, *In Conflict: Iraq War Veterans Speak out on Duty, Loss, and the Fight to Stay Alive* (Sausalito: PoliPoint Press, 2006).

Yvonne Latty and with photographs by Ron Tarver, *We Were There: Voices of African American Veterans from World War II to the War in Iraq* (New York: Amistad, 2004).

Bill Maher, Ann Coulter, and Dennis Miller, "Weapons of Mass Seduction: The War in Iraq and Inside the U.S.," in *Debating Race with Michael Eric Dyson*, ed. by Michael Eric Dyson (New York: Basic Civitas, 2007).

Julianne Malveaux and Reginna A. Green, eds., *The Paradox of Loyalty: An African American Response to the War on Terrorism*, 2nd ed. (Chicago: Third World Press, 2004).

Manning Marable, "Racism in a Time of Terror," *Souls* 4, no. 1 (January 2002), pp. 1–14.

Barack Obama, "Remarks of Senator Barack Obama: Turning the Page in Iraq" (September 12, 2007) www.barackobama.com/2007/09/12/remarks_of_senator_barack_obam_23 .php.

Martha J. Simmons and Frank A. Thomas, eds., *9.11.01: African American Leaders Respond to an American Tragedy* (Valley Forge: Judson Press, 2001).

~ 21 ~

The "Personal Responsibility vs. Institutional Racism Debate" Bill Cosby vs. Michael Eric Dyson

In the early twentieth-first century, a national debate erupted between social policy researchers and educators over the escalating crisis of the "criminalization of black youth." Statistical evidence mounted across the country that African-American young people, as a group, had become stigmatized as antisocial, delinquent, and potentially violent. Such stereotypes profoundly effected the administrative treatment of black youth inside educational institutions. For example, in Oakland, California, during the 2004–2005 school year, black males comprised 28 percent of the city's public school students but accounted for 53 percent of all suspensions. Nationwide that same year, black youth were 17.1 percent of all public school students, but 32.7 percent of expulsions. As of 2000, black youth comprised only 15 percent of their national age cohort, but represented 29 percent of all youth arrested, and 44 percent of all youth in juvenile correctional facilities.

Social conservatives and some religious leaders in the black community began to argue that such social devastation was the result of irresponsible behavior by African-American young people. They criticized the bawdy language of hip-hop music and other elements of black popular culture as socially destructive and nihilistic.

Cosby Summary

It was from this perspective that comedian and philanthropist Bill Cosby addressed an NAACP-sponsored event celebrating the fiftieth anniversary of the May 19, 1954 *Brown v. Board of Education* decision, outlawing the legal racial segregation of public schools. Cosby recognized the accomplishment of that legal victory, but he was far more concerned with what he considered social deviance and violence by young blacks who comprised a post-*Brown* generation.

Cosby attributed the socioeconomic inequalities and problems that were devastating the national black community to antisocial behaviors, criminality and the absence of parental control in African-American households. He ridiculed the clothing, language and hip-hop cultural style of black young people. "Are you not paying attention, people with their hat on backwards, pants down around the crack. Isn't that a sign of something?" Inner-city blacks who claim that their cultural values are drawn from Africa, Cosby implied, were simply fooling themselves. "What part of Africa did this come from? We are not Africans. Those people are not Africans, they don't know a damned thing about Africa." Cosby made fun of the African and Islamic names many young blacks have. "With names like Shaniqua, Shaliqua, Mohammed, and all that crap and all of them are in jail. . . . What's the point of giving them strong names if there is not parenting and values backing it up."

Cosby's rant was laced with humorous asides, but his core message was profoundly conservative, and critical of African-American young people and their popular culture. It said virtually nothing about factors such as racial discrimination within educational institutions and the criminal justice system that have negatively affected black youth. Nevertheless, the national media eagerly picked up Cosby's anti–hip-hop polemic and media pundits debated the implications of Cosby's arguments. Many suggested that affirmative action was not only no longer necessary, but for criminalized black youths it was undeserved. In the preparation of this anthology, Cosby's representatives refused to extend permission to reprint the entire text of the comedian's remarks. However, due to the significance of the issues involved, the editors have presented a brief summary of Cosby's statement (above) and, to accompany it, a critical response by cultural critic and religious studies scholar Michael Eric Dyson.

Dyson Response

Cosby's overemphasis on personal responsibility, not structural features, wrongly locates the source of poor black suffering—and by implication its remedy—in the lives of the poor. When you think the problems are personal, you think the solutions are the same. If only the poor were willing to work harder, act better, get educated, stay out of jail and parent more effectively, their problems would go away. It's hard to argue against any of these things in the abstract; in principle such suggestions sound just fine. But one could do all of these things and still be in bad shape at home, work or school. For instance, Cosby completely ignores shifts in the economy that give value to some work while other work, in the words of William Julius Wilson, "disappears." In our high-tech, high-skilled economy where low-skilled work is being scaled back, phased out, exported, or severely under-compensated, all the right behavior in the world won't create better jobs with more pay. And without such support, all the goals that Cosby expresses for the black poor are not likely to become reality. If the rigidly segregated educational system continues to miserably fail poor blacks by failing to prepare their children for the world of work, then admonitions to "stay in school" may ring hollow.

In this light, the imprisonment of black people takes on political consequence. Cosby may be right that most black folk in jail are not "political prisoners," but it doesn't mean that their imprisonment has not been politicized. Given the vicious way blacks have been targeted for incarceration, Cosby's comments about poor blacks who end up in jail are dangerously naïve and empirically wrong. Cosby's critique of criminal behavior among poor blacks neglects the massive body of work that catalogs the unjust imprisonment of young blacks. This is not to suggest an apologia for black thugs; instead, it suggests that a disproportionate number of black (men) are incarcerated for nonviolent drug offenses. Moreover, Cosby seems to offer justification for the police killing a young black for a trivial offense (the theft of a Coca-Cola or pound cake), neglecting the heinous injustices of the police against blacks across the land. Further, Cosby neglects to mention that crime occurs in all classes and races, though it is not equally judged and prosecuted.

Cosby also slights the economic, social, political and other structural barriers that poor black parents are up against: welfare reform, dwindling resources, export of jobs and ongoing racial stigma. And then there are the problems of the working poor: folk who rise up early every day and often work more than forty hours a week, and yet barely, if ever, make it above the poverty level. We must acknowledge the plight of both poor black (single) mothers and poor black fathers, and the lack of social support they confront. Hence, it is incredibly difficult to spend as much time with children as poor black parents might like, especially since they will be demonized if they fail to provide for their children's basic needs. But doing so deflects critical attention and time from child—rearing duties-duties that are difficult enough for two-parent, two-income, intact middle-class families.[2] The characteristics Cosby cites are typical of all families that confront poverty the world over. They are not indigenous to the black poor; they are symptomatic of the predicament of poor people in general. And Cosby's mean-spirited characterizations of the black poor as licentious, sexually promiscuous, materialistic and wantonly irresponsible can be made of all classes in the nation. . . .

Cosby's views on education have in some respects changed for the worse. His earlier take on the prospects of schooling for the poor was more humane and balanced. In his 1976 dissertation, Cosby argued against "institutional racism" and maintained that school systems failed the poorest and most vulnerable black students. It is necessary as well to acknowledge the resegregation of American education (when in truth it was hardly desegregated to begin with). The failure of Brown v. Board to instigate sufficient change in the nation's schools suggests that the greatest burden and responsibility—should be on crumbling educational infrastructures. In suburban neighborhoods, there are $60-million schools with state-of-the-art technology, while inner city schools fight desperately for funding for their students. And anti-intellectualism, despite Cosby's claims, is hardly a black phenomenon; it is endemic to the culture. Cosby also spies the critical deficiency of the black poor in their linguistic habits, displaying his ignorance about "black English" and "Ebonics." But the intent of Ebonics, according to its advocates, is to help poor black youth speak "standard" English while retaining an appreciation for their dialects and "native tongues." All of this suggests that structural barriers, much more than personal desire, shape the educational experiences of poor blacks. In fact, Fat Albert and the Cosby Kids, Cosby's lauded '70s television cartoon series, won greater acceptance for a new cast of black identities and vernacular language styles. Cosby has made money and gained further influence from using forms of Black English he now violently detests. . .

Cosby also contends that black folk can't blame white folk for our plight. His discounting of structural forces and his exclusive focus on personal responsibility, and black self-help, ignore the persistence of the institutional racism Cosby lamented in his dissertation. To be sure, even when black folk argued for social justice, we never neglected the simultaneous pursuit of personal responsibility and self-help, since that's often the only help we had. In the end, Cosby's views may make white and black liberal fence—sitters unfairly critical of the black poor. Cosby may even convince them that personal behavior will help the poor more than social programs, thus letting white and black elites off the hook. . .

Sources: Dr. Bill Cosby speaks at the 50th anniversary commemoration of the *Brown v. Topeka Board of Education* Supreme Court Decision, May 17, 2004.
Excerpt from Michael Eric Dyson, *Is Bill Cosby Right?: Or Has the Black Middle Class Lost Its Mind?* (New York: Basic Civitas Books, 2005) pg. 6–14.

SELECT BIBLIOGRAPHY:

Damian Bruce, "Poor Excuse: Cosby and the Politics of Disgust," in *Debating Race with Michael Eric Dyson*, ed. by Michael Eric Dyson (New York: Basic Civitas, 2007).

Bill Cosby and Alvin F. Poussaint, *Come on, People on the Path from Victims to Victors* (Nashville: Thomas Nelson, 2007).

Juan Williams, *Enough: The Phony Leaders, Dead-End Movements, and Culture of Failure That Are Undermining Black America—and What We Can Do About It* (New York: Crown Publishers, 2006).

22

U.S. Senate Resolution Against Lynching, *2005*

Between 1880 and 1940, nearly five thousand Americans, most of whom were black, were lynched in the United States. For many decades, the NAACP pressured the U.S. Congress to pass federal legislation outlawing the crime of lynching. Southern white opposition repeatedly blocked these efforts in Congress. Scholars contend that lynching was a form of social control and domination for "uppity" blacks, thus asserting white supremacy throughout the South. On June 13, 2005, the 109th Congress passed Senate Resolution 39, "apologizing to the victims of lynching and the descendents of those lynchings for the failure of the Senate to enact anti-lynching legislation." After the passage of the resolution, eight white senators, all Republicans, refused to sign the document. Although the resolution was an unprecedented occasion, scholars have noted that despite the passage of the resolution black people continue to experience incidents of extreme brutality and extra legal terrorism in the United States.

109th CONGRESS
1st Session
S. RES. 39

Apologizing to the victims of lynching and the descendants of those victims for the failure of the Senate to enact anti-lynching legislation.

IN THE SENATE OF THE UNITED STATES
February 7, 2005

Ms. LANDRIEU (for herself, Mr. ALLEN, Mr. LEVIN, Mr. FRIST, Mr. REID, Mr. ALLARD, Mr. AKAKA, Mr. BROWNBACK, Mr. BAYH, Ms. COLLINS, Mr. BIDEN, Mr. ENSIGN, Mrs. BOXER, Mr. HAGEL, Mr. CORZINE, Mr. LUGAR, Mr. DAYTON, Mr. MCCAIN, Mr. DODD, Ms. SNOWE, Mr. DURBIN, Mr. SPECTER, Mr. FEINGOLD, Mr. STEVENS, Mrs. FEINSTEIN, Mr. TALENT, Mr. HARKIN, Mr. JEFFORDS, Mr. JOHNSON, Mr. KENNEDY, Mr. KOHL, Mr. LAUTENBERG, Mr. LEAHY, Mr. LIEBERMAN, Mr. NELSON of Florida, Mr. PRYOR, Mr. SCHUMER, Ms. STABENOW, Mr. SALAZAR, Mr. VITTER, Mr. OBAMA, Mrs. LINCOLN, Mr. SANTORUM, Mr. SARBANES, Mr. KERRY,

Mr. BYRD, Mr. COBURN, Mr. COLEMAN, Mr. CRAIG, Ms. MIKULSKI, Mrs. MURRAY, Ms. CANTWELL, Mr. DEMINT, Mr. DOMENICI, Mr. DORGAN, Mr. INOUYE, Mrs. CLINTON, Mr. NELSON of Nebraska, Mr. CARPER, Mr. GRAHAM, Mr. BURR, Mr. MCCONNELL, Mr. BUNNING, Mr. MARTINEZ, Mr. BURNS, Mr. DEWINE, Mrs. DOLE, Mr. ROCKEFELLER, Mr. THUNE, Mr. WYDEN, Mr. WARNER, Mr. BAUCUS, Mr. ROBERTS, Mr. CHAFEE, Mr. SESSIONS, Mr. BOND, Mr. CHAMBLISS, Mr. ISAKSON, and Mr. INHOFE) submitted the following resolution; which was referred to the Committee on the Judiciary

June 13, 2005

Committee discharged; considered and agreed to

RESOLUTION
Apologizing to the victims of lynching and the descendants of those victims for the failure of the Senate to enact anti-lynching legislation.

Whereas the crime of lynching succeeded slavery as the ultimate expression of racism in the United States following Reconstruction;

Whereas lynching was a widely acknowledged practice in the United States until the middle of the 20th century;

Whereas lynching was a crime that occurred throughout the United States, with documented incidents in all but 4 States;

Whereas at least 4,742 people, predominantly African-Americans, were reported lynched in the United States between 1882 and 1968;

Whereas 99 percent of all perpetrators of lynching escaped from punishment by State or local officials;

Whereas lynching prompted African-Americans to form the National Association for the Advancement of Colored People (NAACP) and prompted members of B'nai B'rith to found the Anti-Defamation League;

Whereas nearly 200 anti-lynching bills were introduced in Congress during the first half of the 20th century;

Whereas, between 1890 and 1952, 7 Presidents petitioned Congress to end lynching;

Whereas, between 1920 and 1940, the House of Representatives passed 3 strong anti-lynching measures;

Whereas protection against lynching was the minimum and most basic of Federal responsibilities, and the Senate considered but failed to enact anti-lynching legislation despite repeated requests by civil rights groups, Presidents, and the House of Representatives to do so;

Whereas the recent publication of 'Without Sanctuary: Lynching Photography in America' helped bring greater awareness and proper recognition of the victims of lynching;

Whereas only by coming to terms with history can the United States effectively champion human rights abroad; and

Whereas an apology offered in the spirit of true repentance moves the United States toward reconciliation and may become central to a new understanding, on which improved racial relations can be forged: Now, therefore, be it

Resolved, That the Senate—

(1) apologizes to the victims of lynching for the failure of the Senate to enact anti-lynching legislation;

(2) expresses the deepest sympathies and most solemn regrets of the Senate to the descendants of victims of lynching, the ancestors of whom were deprived of life, human dignity, and the constitutional protections accorded all citizens of the United States; and

(3) remembers the history of lynching, to ensure that these tragedies will be neither forgotten nor repeated.

SOURCE: Senate, "Apologizing to the Victims of Lynching and the Descendants of Those Victims for the Failure of the Senate to Enact Anti-Lynching Legislation" (Washington, DC: U.S. Government Printing Office, 2005).

SELECT BIBLIOGRAPHY:

"Eight U.S. Senators Decline to Cosponsor Resolution Apologizing for Failure to Enact Anti-Lynching Legislation," *Journal of Blacks in Higher Education Weekly Bulletin* (June 30, 2005).

Alfred L. Brophy, *Reparations: Pro & Con* (Oxford: Oxford University Press, 2006).

W. Fitzhugh Brundage, ed., *Under Sentence of Death: Lynching in the South* (Chapel Hill: University of North Carolina Press, 1997).

Jacqueline Denise Goldsby, *A Spectacular Secret: Lynching in American Life and Literature* (Chicago: University of Chicago Press, 2006).

Amy Goodman and Juan Gonzalez, "Senate Apologizes for Not Enacting Anti-Lynching Legislation, a Look at Journalist and Anti-Lynching Crusader Ida B. Wells," *Democracy Now* (June 14, 2005), www.democracynow.org/2005/6/14/senate_apologizes_for_not_enacting_anti.

Jacqueline Jones Royster, ed., *Southern Horrors and Other Writings: The Anti-Lynching Campaign of Ida B. Wells, 1892–1900, The Bedford Series in History and Culture* (Boston: Bedford Books, 1997).

Julius Eric Thompson, *Lynchings in Mississippi: A History, 1865–1965* (Jefferson: McFarland & Company, 2007).

⚯ 23 ⚯

Hurricane Katrina Crisis, *2005*

Hurricane Katrina hit the southern U.S. coastline bordering the Gulf of Mexico on August 29, 2005, with Mississippi, southwestern Alabama, and Louisiana suffering the most devastation. The storm resulted in tens of billions of dollars in property damage and the loss of more than 1,000 lives. When the levees were breached, New Orleans was overwhelmed by massive flooding. Local residents were forced to remain in the Superdome and Convention Center for days without adequate food, running water, or toilets. Generally agreed to be a national disgrace, the response of the U.S government was woefully inadequate. Much of the national media presented racially biased stereotypes in describing black victims of the flood. The documentary by filmmaker Spike Lee, "When the Levees Broke: A Requiem in Four Acts" provided an analysis of the aftermath and the stories of victims, those who stayed in New Orleans and those who were dispersed to other states.

"THIS IS CRIMINAL"

It's criminal. From what you're hearing, the people trapped in New Orleans are nothing but looters. We're told we should be more "neighborly." But nobody talked about being neighborly until after the people who could afford to leave . . . left.

If you ain't got no money in America, you're on your own. People were told to go to the Superdome, but they have no food, no water there. And before they could get in, people had to stand in line for 4–5 hours in the rain because everybody was being searched one by one at the entrance.

I can understand the chaos that happened after the tsunami, because they had no warning, but here there was plenty of warning. In the three days before the hurricane hit, we knew it was coming and everyone could have been evacuated.

We have Amtrak here that could have carried everybody out of town. There were enough school buses that could have evacuated 20,000 people easily, but they just let them be flooded. My son watched 40 buses go underwater—they just wouldn't move them, afraid they'd be stolen.

People who could afford to leave were so afraid someone would steal what they own that they just let it all be flooded. They could have let a family without a vehicle borrow their extra car, but instead they left it behind to be destroyed.

There are gangs of white vigilantes near here riding around in pickup trucks, all of them armed, and any young Black they see who they figure doesn't belong in their community, they shoot him. I tell them, "Stop! You're going to start a riot."

When you see all the poor people with no place to go, feeling alone and helpless and angry, I say this is a consequence of HOPE VI. New Orleans took all the HUD money it could get to tear down public housing, and families and neighbors who'd relied on each other for generations were uprooted and torn apart.

Most of the people who are going through this now had already lost touch with the only community they'd ever known. Their community was torn down and they were scattered. They'd already lost their real homes, the only place where they knew everybody, and now the places they've been staying are destroyed.

But nobody cares. They're just lawless looters . . . dangerous.

The hurricane hit at the end of the month, the time when poor people are most vulnerable. Food stamps don't buy enough but for about three weeks of the month, and by the end of the month everyone runs out. Now they have no way to get their food stamps or any money, so they just have to take what they can to survive.

Many people are getting sick and very weak. From the toxic water that people are walking through, little scratches and sores are turning into major wounds.

People whose homes and families were not destroyed went into the city right away with boats to bring the survivors out, but law enforcement told them they weren't needed. They are willing and able to rescue thousands, but they're not allowed to.

Every day countless volunteers are trying to help, but they're turned back. Almost all the rescue that's been done has been done by volunteers anyway.

My son and his family—his wife and kids, ages 1, 5 and 8—were flooded out of their home when the levee broke. They had to swim out until they found an abandoned building with two rooms above water level.

There were 21 people in those two rooms for a day and a half. A guy in a boat who just said "I'm going to help regardless" rescued them and took them to Highway I-10 and dropped them there.

They sat on the freeway for about three hours, because someone said they'd be rescued and taken to the Superdome. Finally they just started walking, had to walk six and a half miles.

When they got to the Superdome, my son wasn't allowed in—I don't know why—so his wife and kids wouldn't go in. They kept walking, and they happened to run across a guy with a tow truck that they knew, and he gave them his own personal truck.

When they got here, they had no gas, so I had to punch a hole in my gas tank to give them some gas, and now I'm trapped. I'm getting around by bicycle.

People from Placquemine Parish were rescued on a ferry and dropped off on a dock near here. All day they were sitting on the dock in the hot sun with no food, no water. Many were in a daze; they've lost everything.

They were all sitting there surrounded by armed guards. We asked the guards could we bring them water and food. My mother and all the other church ladies were cooking for them, and we have plenty of good water.

But the guards said, "No. If you don't have enough water and food for everybody, you can't give anything." Finally the people were hauled off on school buses from other parishes.

You know Robert King Wilkerson (the only one of the Angola 3 political prisoners who's been released). He's been back in New Orleans working hard, organizing, helping people. Now nobody knows where he is. His house was destroyed. Knowing him, I think he's out trying to save lives, but I'm worried.

The people who could help are being shipped out. People who want to stay, who have the skills to save lives and rebuild are being forced to go to Houston.

It's not like New Orleans was caught off guard. This could have been prevented.

There's military right here in New Orleans, but for three days they weren't even mobilized. You'd think this was a Third World country.

I'm in the Algiers neighborhood of New Orleans, the only part that isn't flooded. The water is good. Our parks and schools could easily hold 40,000 people, and they're not using any of it.

This is criminal. These people are dying for no other reason than the lack of organization.

Everything is needed, but we're still too disorganized. I'm asking people to go ahead and gather donations and relief supplies but to hold on to them for a few days until we have a way to put them to good use.

I'm challenging my party, the Green Party, to come down here and help us just as soon as things are a little more organized. The Republicans and Democrats didn't do anything to prevent this or plan for it and don't seem to care if everyone dies.

Source: Malik Rahim, "'This Is Criminal': Malik Rahim Reports from New Orleans" (September 1, 2005) www.cwsworkshop.org/katrinareader/node/268.

SELECT BIBLIOGRAPHY:

"Race an Issue in Katrina Response: Lawmakers Voice Opinions on Role of Skin Color in Rescue Efforts," CBS News (Sept. 3, 2005) www.cbsnews.com/stories/2005/09/03/katrina/main814623.shtml.

Darwin Bond Graham, "The New Orleans That Race Built: Racism, Disaster, and Urban Spatial Relationships," *Souls* 9, no. 1 (January–March 2007), pp. 4–18.

Douglas Brinkley, *The Great Deluge: Hurricane Katrina, New Orleans, and the Mississippi Gulf Coast* (New York: Morrow, 2006).

Michael Eric Dyson, *Come Hell or High Water: Hurricane Katrina and the Color of Disaster* (New York: Basic Civitas, 2006).

Kevin Michael Foster, "Are They Katrina's Kids or Ours?: The Experience of Displaced New Orleans Students in Their New Schools and Communities," *Souls* 9, no. 1 (2007), pp. 45–52.

Chester W. Hartman and Gregory D. Squires, eds., *There Is No Such Thing as a Natural Disaster: Race, Class, and Hurricane Katrina* (New York: Routledge, 2006).

Jed Horne, *Breach of Faith: Hurricane Katrina and the near Death of a Great American City* (New York: Random House, 2006).

Spike Lee, *When the Levees Broke: A Requiem in Four Acts*, New York: HBO Documentary Films, 2006. DVD Video.

Manning Marable and Kristen Clarke, eds., *Seeking Higher Ground: The Hurricane Katrina Crisis, Race, and Public Policy Reader* (New York: Palgrave Macmillan, 2008).

Betsy Reed, ed., *Unnatural Disaster: The Nation on Hurricane Katrina* (New York: Nation Books, 2006).

Lydia Sargent, *The Katrina Crisis: Race, Class, & Disaster in New Orleans*, Woods Hole: Z Video Productions, 2006. DVD Video.

David Dante Troutt, ed., *After the Storm: Black Intellectuals Explore the Meaning of Hurricane Katrina* (New York: New Press, 2006).

24

Barack Obama's Presidential Campaign, *2007–2008*

In the aftermath of the federal government's irresponsible actions connected with the 2005 Hurricane Katrina crisis, many African-Americans became more pessimistic about their ability to impact national politics. So when in early 2007, a young, first-term senator from Illinois named Barack Hussein Obama (1961–), an African American, announced his candidacy for the presidency most blacks doubted that he would be successful. Some African American critics, noting that his mother had been white, questioned his racial authenticity. Obama's political message, moreover, was a sharp departure from the protest-style of Jesse Jackson's Rainbow Coalition campaigns of the 1980s. Obama was a liberal progressive, but his style down played "race," and emphasized consensus issues that brought people together regardless of color, class, or gender. As late as December 2007, in public opinion surveys, a majority of African Americans favored New York Senator Hillary Clinton over Obama for the presidency.

But in a stunning triumph, Obama defeated Clinton and other Democratic challengers in the Iowa caucus, in January 2008, where blacks represented less than 2 percent of all voters. In the following months Obama won a series of primaries and caucuses in many states with relatively few blacks or other racialized minorities. Obama consistently won majorities among voters under age thirty, college-educated voters, and voters earning over $50,000 annually. By the South Carolina Democratic primary, the vast majority of blacks swung their allegiance behind Obama, and by the final races the candidate's African-American support exceeded 90 percent. Winning the Democratic Party's presidential nomination in August 2008, Obama subsequently ran what many media observers described as a near-flawless campaign. On November 4, 2008, Obama easily defeated his Republican opponent, Arizona senator John McCain, winning nearly 53 percent of the popular vote.

The rise of a Barack Obama was at a certain level inevitable. Demographically, the white majority population will begin to decline in several years. Latinos, Asians, African Americans, and other racialized minorities will outnumber whites by 2042, according to Census Bureau projections. But the larger question is what the Obama victory portends for the realization of racial justice, or "freedom," that remains the central motivating factor behind the African-American struggle. Is

Obama's victory a statement of symbolic representation for blacks, or will it be translated into a transformed political environment with greater opportunities and fewer inequalities for people of color?

~

KEYNOTE ADDRESS AT THE 2004 DEMOCRATIC NATIONAL CONVENTION
Excerpts are from speech as prepared for delivery.
Tonight is a particular honor for me because, let's face it, my presence on this stage is pretty unlikely. My father was a foreign student, born and raised in a small village in Kenya. He grew up herding goats, went to school in a tin-roof shack. His father, my grandfather, was a cook, a domestic servant.

But my grandfather had larger dreams for his son. Through hard work and perseverance my father got a scholarship to study in a magical place: America, which stood as a beacon of freedom and opportunity to so many who had come before. While studying here, my father met my mother. She was born in a town on the other side of the world, in Kansas. Her father worked on oil rigs and farms through most of the Depression. The day after Pearl Harbor he signed up for duty, joined Patton's army and marched across Europe. Back home, my grandmother raised their baby and went to work on a bomber assembly line. After the war, they studied on the GI Bill, bought a house through FHA, and moved west in search of opportunity.

And they, too, had big dreams for their daughter, a common dream, born of two continents. My parents shared not only an improbable love; they shared an abiding faith in the possibilities of this nation. They would give me an African name, Barack, or "blessed," believing that in a tolerant America your name is no barrier to success. They imagined me going to the best schools in the land, even though they weren't rich, because in a generous America you don't have to be rich to achieve your potential. They are both passed away now. Yet, I know that, on this night, they look down on me with pride.

I stand here today, grateful for the diversity of my heritage, aware that my parents' dreams live on in my precious daughters. I stand here knowing that my story is part of the larger American story, that I owe a debt to all of those who came before me, and that, in no other country on earth, is my story even possible. Tonight, we gather to affirm the greatness of our nation, not because of the height of our skyscrapers, or the power of our military, or the size of our economy. Our pride is based on a very simple premise, summed up in a declaration made over two hundred years ago, "We hold these truths to be self-evident, that all men are created equal. That they are endowed by their Creator with certain inalienable rights. That among these are life, liberty and the pursuit of happiness."

That is the true genius of America, a faith in the simple dreams of its people, the insistence on small miracles. That we can tuck in our children at night and know they are fed and clothed and safe from harm. That we can say what we think, write what we think, without hearing a sudden knock on the door. That we can have an idea and start our own business without paying a bribe or hiring somebody's son. That we can participate in the political process without fear of retribution, and that our votes will he counted—or at least, most of the time.

This year, in this election, we are called to reaffirm our values and commitments, to hold them against a hard reality and see how we are measuring up, to the legacy of our forbearers, and the promise of future generations. And fellow Americans— Democrats, Republicans, Independents—I say to you tonight: we have more work to do. More to do for the workers I met in Galesburg, Illinois, who are los- ing their union jobs at the Maytag plant that's moving to Mexico, and now are hav- ing to compete with their own children for jobs that pay seven bucks an hour. More to do for the father I met who was losing his job and choking back tears, wondering how he would pay $4,500 a month for the drugs his son needs without the health benefits he counted on. More to do for the young woman in East St. Louis, and thousands more like her, who has the grades, has the drive, has the will, but doesn't have the money to go to college.

Don't get me wrong. The people I meet in small towns and big cities, in diners and office parks, they don't expect government to solve all their problems. They know they have to work hard to get ahead and they want to. Go into the collar counties around Chicago, and people will tell you they don't want their tax money wasted by a welfare agency or the Pentagon. Go into any inner city neighborhood, and folks will tell you that government alone can't teach kids to learn. They know that parents have to parent, that children can't achieve unless we raise their expectations and turn off the television sets and eradicate the slander that says a black youth with a book is acting white. No, people don't expect government to solve all their problems. But they sense, deep in their bones, that with just a change in priorities, we can make sure that every child in America has a decent shot at life, and that the doors of opportunity remain open to all. They know we can do better. And they want that choice.

In this election, we offer that choice. Our party has chosen a man to lead us who embodies the best this country has to offer. That man is John Kerry. . . .

. . . John Kerry believes in America. And he knows it's not enough for just some of us to prosper. For alongside our famous individualism, there's another ingredi- ent in the American saga.

A belief that we are connected as one people. If there's a child on the south side of Chicago who can't read, that matters to me, even if it's not my child. If there's a senior citizen somewhere who can't pay for her prescription and has to choose between medicine and the rent, that makes my life poorer, even if it's not my grandmother. If there's an Arab American family being rounded up without benefit of an attorney or due process, that threatens my civil liberties. It's that fundamental belief—I am my brother's keeper, I am my sister's keeper—that makes this country work. It's what allows us to pursue our individual dreams, yet still come together as a single American family. "E pluribus unum." Out of many, one. . . .

We are one people, all of us pledging allegiance to the stars and stripes, all of us defending the United States of America.

In the end, that's what this election is about. Do we participate in a politics of cynicism or a politics of hope? John Kerry calls on us to hope. John Edwards calls on us to hope. I'm not talking about blind optimism here—the almost willful ignorance that thinks unemployment will go away if we just don't talk about it, or the health care crisis will solve itself if we just ignore it. No, I'm talking about something more substantial. It's the hope of slaves sitting around a fire singing freedom songs; the hope of immigrants setting out for distant shores; the hope of a young naval lieutenant bravely patrolling the Mekong Delta; the hope of a millworker's son who dares to defy the odds; the hope of a skinny kid with a funny name who believes that America has a place for him, too. The audacity of hope!

～

REMARKS OF SENATOR BARACK OBAMA: "A MORE PERFECT UNION"
As Prepared for Delivery
"We the people, in order to form a more perfect union."

Two hundred and twenty one years ago, in a hall that still stands across the street, a group of men gathered and, with these simple words, launched America's improbable experiment in democracy. Farmers and scholars; statesmen and patriots who had traveled across an ocean to escape tyranny and persecution finally made real their declaration of independence at a Philadelphia convention that lasted through the spring of 1787.

The document they produced was eventually signed but ultimately unfinished. It was stained by this nation's original sin of slavery, a question that divided the colonies and brought the convention to a stalemate until the founders chose to allow the slave trade to continue for at least twenty more years, and to leave any final resolution to future generations.

Of course, the answer to the slavery question was already embedded within our Constitution—a Constitution that had at its very core the ideal of equal citizenship under the law; a Constitution that promised its people liberty, and justice, and a union that could be and should be perfected over time.

And yet words on a parchment would not be enough to deliver slaves from bondage, or provide men and women of every color and creed their full rights and obligations as citizens of the United States. What would be needed were Americans in successive generations who were willing to do their part—through protests and struggle, on the streets and in the courts, through a civil war and civil disobedience and always at great risk—to narrow that gap between the promise of our ideals and the reality of their time.

This was one of the tasks we set forth at the beginning of this campaign—to continue the long march of those who came before us, a march for a more just, more equal, more free, more caring and more prosperous America. I chose to run for the presidency at this moment in history because I believe deeply that we cannot solve the challenges of our time unless we solve them together—unless we perfect our union by understanding that we may have different stories, but we hold common hopes; that we may not look the same and we may not have come from the same place, but we all want to move in the same direction—towards a better future for our children and our grandchildren.

This belief comes from my unyielding faith in the decency and generosity of the American people. But it also comes from my own American story.

I am the son of a black man from Kenya and a white woman from Kansas. I was raised with the help of a white grandfather who survived a Depression to serve in Patton's Army during World War II and a white grandmother who worked on a bomber assembly line at Fort Leavenworth while he was overseas. I've gone to some of the best schools in America and lived in one of the world's poorest nations. I am married to a black American who carries within her the blood of slaves and slaveowners—an inheritance we pass on to our two precious daughters. I have brothers, sisters, nieces, nephews, uncles and cousins, of every race and every hue, scattered across three continents, and for as long as I live, I will never forget that in no other country on Earth is my story even possible.

It's a story that hasn't made me the most conventional candidate. But it is a story that has seared into my genetic makeup the idea that this nation is more than the sum of its parts—that out of many, we are truly one.

Throughout the first year of this campaign, against all predictions to the contrary, we saw how hungry the American people were for this message of unity. Despite the temptation to view my candidacy through a purely racial lens, we won commanding victories in states with some of the whitest populations in the country.

In South Carolina, where the Confederate Flag still flies, we built a powerful coalition of African Americans and white Americans.

This is not to say that race has not been an issue in the campaign. At various stages in the campaign, some commentators have deemed me either "too black" or "not black enough." We saw racial tensions bubble to the surface during the week before the South Carolina primary. The press has scoured every exit poll for the latest evidence of racial polarization, not just in terms of white and black, but black and brown as well.

And yet, it has only been in the last couple of weeks that the discussion of race in this campaign has taken a particularly divisive turn.

On one end of the spectrum, we've heard the implication that my candidacy is somehow an exercise in affirmative action; that it's based solely on the desire of wide-eyed liberals to purchase racial reconciliation on the cheap. On the other end, we've heard my former pastor, Reverend Jeremiah Wright, use incendiary language to express views that have the potential not only to widen the racial divide, but views that denigrate both the greatness and the goodness of our nation; that rightly offend white and black alike.

I have already condemned, in unequivocal terms, the statements of Reverend Wright that have caused such controversy. For some, nagging questions remain. Did I know him to be an occasionally fierce critic of American domestic and foreign policy? Of course. Did I ever hear him make remarks that could be considered controversial while I sat in church? Yes. Did I strongly disagree with many of his political views? Absolutely—just as I'm sure many of you have heard remarks from your pastors, priests, or rabbis with which you strongly disagreed.

But the remarks that have caused this recent firestorm weren't simply controversial. They weren't simply a religious leader's effort to speak out against perceived injustice. Instead, they expressed a profoundly distorted view of this country—a view that sees white racism as endemic, and that elevates what is wrong with America above all that we know is right with America; a view that sees the conflicts in the Middle East as rooted primarily in the actions of stalwart allies like Israel, instead of emanating from the perverse and hateful ideologies of radical Islam.

As such, Reverend Wright's comments were not only wrong but divisive, divisive at a time when we need unity; racially charged at a time when we need to come together to solve a set of monumental problems—two wars, a terrorist threat, a falling economy, a chronic health care crisis and potentially devastating climate change; problems that are neither black or white or Latino or Asian, but rather problems that confront us all.

Given my background, my politics, and my professed values and ideals, there will no doubt be those for whom my statements of condemnation are not enough. Why associate myself with Reverend Wright in the first place, they may ask? Why not join another church? And I confess that if all that I knew of Reverend Wright were the snippets of those sermons that have run in an endless loop on the television and You Tube, or if Trinity United Church of Christ conformed to the caricatures being peddled by some commentators, there is no doubt that I would react in much the same way

But the truth is, that isn't all that I know of the man. The man I met more than twenty years ago is a man who helped introduce me to my Christian faith, a man who spoke to me about our obligations to love one another; to care for the sick and lift up the poor. He is a man who served his country as a U.S. Marine; who has studied and lectured at some of the finest universities and seminaries in the country, and who for over thirty years led a church that serves the community by doing God's work here on Earth—by housing the homeless, ministering to the needy, providing day care services and scholarships and prison ministries, and reaching out to those suffering from HIV/AIDS.

In my first book, *Dreams From My Father*, I described the experience of my first service at Trinity:

"People began to shout, to rise from their seats and clap and cry out, a forceful wind carrying the reverend's voice up into the rafters. . . . And in that single note—hope!—I heard something else; at the foot of that cross, inside the thousands of churches across the city, I imagined the stories of ordinary black people merging with the stories of David and Goliath, Moses and Pharaoh, the Christians in the lion's den, Ezekiel's field of dry bones. Those stories—of survival, and freedom, and hope—became our story, my story; the blood that had spilled was our blood, the tears our tears; until this black church, on this bright day, seemed once more a vessel carrying the story of a people into future generations and into a larger world. Our trials and triumphs became at once unique and universal, black and more than black; in chronicling our journey, the stories and songs gave us a means to reclaim memories that we didn't need to feel shame about . . . memories that all people might study and cherish—and with which we could start to rebuild."

That has been my experience at Trinity. Like other predominantly black churches across the country, Trinity embodies the black community in its entirety—the doctor and the welfare mom, the model student and the former gang-banger. Like other black churches, Trinity's services are full of raucous laughter and sometimes bawdy humor. They are full of dancing, clapping, screaming and shouting that may seem jarring to the untrained ear. The church contains in full the kindness and cruelty, the fierce intelligence and the shocking ignorance, the struggles and successes, the love and yes, the bitterness and bias that make up the black experience in America.

And this helps explain, perhaps, my relationship with Reverend Wright. As imperfect as he may be, he has been like family to me. He strengthened my faith, officiated my wedding, and baptized my children. Not once in my conversations with him have I heard him talk about any ethnic group in derogatory terms, or treat whites with whom he interacted with anything but courtesy and respect. He contains within him the contradictions—the good and the bad—of the community that he has served diligently for so many years.

I can no more disown him than I can disown the black community. I can no more disown him than I can my white grandmother—a woman who helped raise me, a woman who sacrificed again and again for me, a woman who loves me as much as she loves anything in this world, but a woman who once confessed her fear of black men who passed by her on the street, and who on more than one occasion has uttered racial or ethnic stereotypes that made me cringe.

These people are a part of me. And they are a part of America, this country that I love.

Some will see this as an attempt to justify or excuse comments that are simply inexcusable. I can assure you it is not. I suppose the politically safe thing would be to move on from this episode and just hope that it fades into the woodwork. We can dismiss Reverend Wright as a crank or a demagogue, just as some have dismissed Geraldine Ferraro, in the aftermath of her recent statements, as harboring some deep-seated racial bias.

But race is an issue that I believe this nation cannot afford to ignore right now. We would be making the same mistake that Reverend Wright made in his offending sermons about America—to simplify and stereotype and amplify the negative to the point that it distorts reality.

The fact is that the comments that have been made and the issues that have surfaced over the last few weeks reflect the complexities of race in this country that we've never really worked through—a part of our union that we have yet to perfect. And if we walk away now, if we simply retreat into our respective corners, we will never be able to come together and solve challenges like health care, or education, or the need to find good jobs for every American.

Understanding this reality requires a reminder of how we arrived at this point. As William Faulkner once wrote, "The past isn't dead and buried. In fact, it isn't even past." We do not need to recite here the history of racial injustice in this country. But we do need to remind ourselves that so many of the disparities that exist in the African-American community today can be directly traced to inequalities passed on from an earlier generation that suffered under the brutal legacy of slavery and Jim Crow.

Segregated schools were, and are, inferior schools; we still haven't fixed them, fifty years after *Brown v. Board of Education*, and the inferior education they provided, then and now, helps explain the pervasive achievement gap between today's black and white students.

Legalized discrimination—where blacks were prevented, often through violence, from owning property, or loans were not granted to African-American business owners, or black homeowners could not access FHA mortgages, or blacks were excluded from unions, or the police force, or fire departments—meant that black families could not amass any meaningful wealth to bequeath to future generations. That history helps explain the wealth and income gap between black and white, and the concentrated pockets of poverty that persists in so many of today's urban and rural communities.

A lack of economic opportunity among black men, and the shame and frustration that came from not being able to provide for one's family, contributed to the erosion of black families—a problem that welfare policies for many years may have worsened. And the lack of basic services in so many urban black neighborhoods— parks for kids to play in, police walking the beat, regular garbage pick-up and building code enforcement—all helped create a cycle of violence, blight and neglect that continue to haunt us.

This is the reality in which Reverend Wright and other African-Americans of his generation grew up. They came of age in the late fifties and early sixties, a time when segregation was still the law of the land and opportunity was systematically constricted. What's remarkable is not how many failed in the face of discrimination, but rather how many men and women overcame the odds; how many were able to make a way out of no way for those like me who would come after them.

But for all those who scratched and clawed their way to get a piece of the American Dream, there were many who didn't make it—those who were ultimately defeated, in one way or another, by discrimination. That legacy of defeat was passed on to future generations—those young men and increasingly young women who we see standing on street corners or languishing in our prisons, without hope or prospects for the future. Even for those blacks who did make it, questions of race, and racism, continue to define their worldview in fundamental ways. For the men and women of Reverend Wright's generation, the memories of humiliation and doubt and fear have not gone away; nor has the anger and the bitterness of those years. That anger may not get expressed in public, in front of white co-workers or white friends. But it does find voice in the barbershop or around the kitchen table. At times, that anger is exploited by politicians, to gin up votes along racial lines, or to make up for a politician's own failings.

And occasionally it finds voice in the church on Sunday morning, in the pulpit and in the pews. The fact that so many people are surprised to hear that anger in some of Reverend Wright's sermons simply reminds us of the old truism that the most segregated hour in American life occurs on Sunday morning. That anger is not always productive; indeed, all too often it distracts attention from solving real problems; it keeps us from squarely facing our own complicity in our condition, and prevents the African-American community from forging the alliances it needs to bring about real change. But the anger is real; it is powerful; and to simply wish it away, to condemn it without understanding its roots, only serves to widen the chasm of misunderstanding that exists between the races.

In fact, a similar anger exists within segments of the white community. Most working- and middle-class white Americans don't feel that they have been particularly privileged by their race. Their experience is the immigrant experience—as far as they're concerned, no one's handed them anything, they've built it from scratch. They've worked hard all their lives, many times only to see their jobs shipped overseas or their pension dumped after a lifetime of labor. They are anxious about their futures, and feel their dreams slipping away; in an era of stagnant wages and global competition, opportunity comes to be seen as a zero sum game, in which your dreams come at my expense. So when they are told to bus their children to a school across town; when they hear that an African American is getting an advantage in landing a good job or a spot in a good college because of an injustice that they themselves never committed; when they're told that their fears about crime in urban neighborhoods are somehow prejudiced, resentment builds over time.

Like the anger within the black community, these resentments aren't always expressed in polite company. But they have helped shape the political landscape for at least a generation. Anger over welfare and affirmative action helped forge the Reagan Coalition. Politicians routinely exploited fears of crime for their own electoral ends. Talk show hosts and conservative commentators built entire careers unmasking bogus claims of racism while dismissing legitimate discussions of racial injustice and inequality as mere political correctness or reverse racism.

Just as black anger often proved counterproductive, so have these white resentments distracted attention from the real culprits of the middle class squeeze—a corporate culture rife with inside dealing, questionable accounting practices, and short-term greed; a Washington dominated by lobbyists and special interests; economic policies that favor the few over the many. And yet, to wish away the resentments of white Americans, to label them as misguided or even racist, without recognizing they are grounded in legitimate concerns—this too widens the racial divide, and blocks the path to understanding.

This is where we are right now. It's a racial stalemate we've been stuck in for years. Contrary to the claims of some of my critics, black and white, I have never been so naïve as to believe that we can get beyond our racial divisions in a single election cycle, or with a single candidacy—particularly a candidacy as imperfect as my own.

But I have asserted a firm conviction—a conviction rooted in my faith in God and my faith in the American people—that working together we can move beyond some of our old racial wounds, and that in fact we have no choice if we are to continue on the path of a more perfect union.

For the African-American community, that path means embracing the burdens of our past without becoming victims of our past. It means continuing to insist on a full measure of justice in every aspect of American life. But it also means binding our particular grievances—for better health care, and better schools, and better jobs—to the larger aspirations of all Americans—the white woman struggling to break the glass ceiling, the white man whose been laid off, the immigrant trying to feed his family. And it means taking full responsibility for own lives—by demanding more from our fathers, and spending more time with our children, and reading to them, and teaching them that while they may face challenges and discrimination in their own lives, they must never succumb to despair or cynicism; they must always believe that they can write their own destiny.

Ironically, this quintessentially American—and yes, conservative—notion of self-help found frequent expression in Reverend Wright's sermons. But what my former pastor too often failed to understand is that embarking on a program of self-help also requires a belief that society can change.

The profound mistake of Reverend Wright's sermons is not that he spoke about racism in our society. It's that he spoke as if our society was static; as if no progress has been made; as if this country—a country that has made it possible for one of his own members to run for the highest office in the land and build a coalition of white and black; Latino and Asian, rich and poor, young and old—is still irrevocably bound to a tragic past. But what we know—what we have seen—is that America can change. That is the true genius of this nation. What we have already achieved gives us hope—the audacity to hope—for what we can and must achieve tomorrow.

In the white community, the path to a more perfect union means acknowledging that what ails the African-American community does not just exist in the minds of black people; that the legacy of discrimination—and current incidents of discrimination, while less overt than in the past—are real and must be addressed. Not just with words, but with deeds—by investing in our schools and our communities; by enforcing our civil rights laws and ensuring fairness in our criminal justice system; by providing this generation with ladders of opportunity that were unavailable for previous generations. It requires all Americans to realize that your dreams do not have to come at the expense of my dreams; that investing in the health, welfare, and education of black and brown and white children will ultimately help all of America prosper.

In the end, then, what is called for is nothing more, and nothing less, than what all the world's great religions demand—that we do unto others as we would have them do unto us. Let us be our brother's keeper, Scripture tells us. Let us be our sister's keeper. Let us find that common stake we all have in one another, and let our politics reflect that spirit as well.

For we have a choice in this country. We can accept a politics that breeds division, and conflict, and cynicism. We can tackle race only as spectacle—as we did in the OJ trial—or in the wake of tragedy, as we did in the aftermath of Katrina—or as fodder for the nightly news. We can play Reverend Wright's sermons on every channel, every day and talk about them from now until the election, and make the only question in this campaign whether or not the American people think that I somehow believe or sympathize with his most offensive words. We can pounce on some gaffe by a Hillary supporter as evidence that she's playing the race card, or we can speculate on whether white men will all flock to John McCain in the general election regardless of his policies.

We can do that.

But if we do, I can tell you that in the next election, we'll be talking about some other distraction. And then another one. And then another one. And nothing will change.

That is one option. Or, at this moment, in this election, we can come together and say, "Not this time." This time we want to talk about the crumbling schools that are stealing the future of black children and white children and Asian children and Hispanic children and Native American children. This time we want to reject the cynicism that tells us that these kids can't learn; that those kids who don't look like us are somebody else's problem. The children of America are not those kids, they are our kids, and we will not let them fall behind in a 21st century economy. Not this time.

This time we want to talk about how the lines in the Emergency Room are filled with whites and blacks and Hispanics who do not have health care; who don't have the power on their own to overcome the special interests in Washington, but who can take them on if we do it together.

This time we want to talk about the shuttered mills that once provided a decent life for men and women of every race, and the homes for sale that once belonged to Americans from every religion, every region, every walk of life. This time we want to talk about the fact that the real problem is not that someone who doesn't look like you might take your job; it's that the corporation you work for will ship it overseas for nothing more than a profit.

This time we want to talk about the men and women of every color and creed who serve together, and fight together, and bleed together under the same proud flag. We want to talk about how to bring them home from a war that never should've been authorized and never should've been waged, and we want to talk about how we'll show our patriotism by caring for them, and their families, and giving them the benefits they have earned.

I would not be running for President if I didn't believe with all my heart that this is what the vast majority of Americans want for this country. This union may never be perfect, but generation after generation has shown that it can always be perfected. And today, whenever I find myself feeling doubtful or cynical about this possibility, what gives me the most hope is the next generation—the young people whose attitudes and beliefs and openness to change have already made history in this election.

There is one story in particularly that I'd like to leave you with today—a story I told when I had the great honor of speaking on Dr. King's birthday at his home church, Ebenezer Baptist, in Atlanta.

There is a young, twenty-three year old white woman named Ashley Baia who organized for our campaign in Florence, South Carolina. She had been working to organize a mostly African-American community since the beginning of this campaign, and one day she was at a roundtable discussion where everyone went around telling their story and why they were there.

And Ashley said that when she was nine years old, her mother got cancer. And because she had to miss days of work, she was let go and lost her health care. They had to file for bankruptcy, and that's when Ashley decided that she had to do something to help her mom.

She knew that food was one of their most expensive costs, and so Ashley convinced her mother that what she really liked and really wanted to eat more than anything else was mustard and relish sandwiches. Because that was the cheapest way to eat.

She did this for a year until her mom got better, and she told everyone at the round-table that the reason she joined our campaign was so that she could help the millions of other children in the country who want and need to help their parents too.

Now Ashley might have made a different choice. Perhaps somebody told her along the way that the source of her mother's problems were blacks who were on welfare and too lazy to work, or Hispanics who were coming into the country illegally. But she didn't. She sought out allies in her fight against injustice.

Anyway, Ashley finishes her story and then goes around the room and asks everyone else why they're supporting the campaign. They all have different stories and reasons. Many bring up a specific issue. And finally they come to this elderly black man who's been sitting there quietly the entire time. And Ashley asks him why he's there. And he does not bring up a specific issue. He does not say health care or the economy. He does not say education or the war. He does not say that he was there because of Barack Obama. He simply says to everyone in the room, "I am here because of Ashley."

"I'm here because of Ashley." By itself, that single moment of recognition between that young white girl and that old black man is not enough. It is not enough to give health care to the sick, or jobs to the jobless, or education to our children.

But it is where we start. It is where our union grows stronger. And as so many generations have come to realize over the course of the two-hundred and twenty one years since a band of patriots signed that document in Philadelphia, that is where the perfection begins.

Source: Excerpts from (1) Barack Obama, "Keynote Address at the 2004 Democratic National Convention" (July 27, 2004) and (2) Barack Obama, "A More Perfect Union," (March 18, 2008).

SELECT BIBLIOGRAPHY:

David Mendell, *Obama: From Promise to Power* (New York: Amistad/HarperCollins, 2007).

Barack Obama, *The Audacity of Hope: Thoughts on Reclaiming the American Dream* (New York: Crown Publishers, 2006).

———, *Barack Obama in His Own Words*, ed. by Lisa Rogak (New York: Carroll & Graf, 2007).

———, *Barack Obama: Speeches 2002–2006*, ed. by Maureen Harrison and Steve Gilbert (Carlsbad: Excellent Books, 2007).

———, *Dreams from My Father: A Story of Race and Inheritance*, rev. ed. (New York: Three Rivers Press, 2006).

John K. Wilson, *Barack Obama: This Improbable Quest* (Boulder: Paradigm, 2008).

ADDITIONAL RESOURCES:

Robert D. Bullard, ed., *The Black Metropolis in the Twenty-First Century: Race, Power, and Politics of Place* (Lanham, MD: Rowman & Littlefield, 2007).

Michael Eric Dyson, *April 4, 1968: Martin Luther King, Jr.'s Death and How It Changed America* (New York: Basic Civitas Books, 2008).

Patricia Hill Collins, *From Black Power to Hip Hop: Racism, Nationalism, and Feminism, Politics, History, and Social Change* (Philadelphia: Temple University Press, 2006).

Jacqueline Jones, *Labor of Love, Labor of Sorrow: Black Women, Work, and the Family from Slavery to the Present* (New York: Vintage Books, 1995).

Manning Marable, Ian Steinberg, and Keesha Middlemass, eds., *Racializing Justice, Disenfranchising Lives: The Racism, Criminal Justice, and Law Reader*, Critical Black Studies Series (New York: Palgrave Macmillan, 2007).

Leith Mullings, "Losing Ground: Harlem, the War on Drugs, and the Prison Industrial Complex, *Souls*, 5, no. 2 (June 2003), pp. 1–21.

——, *On Our Own Terms: Race, Class, and Gender in the Lives of African American Women* (New York: Routledge, 1997).

Michael Omi and Howard Winant, *Racial Formation in the New Millennium*, Critical Social Thought (London: Routledge, 2008).

Nell Irvin Painter, *Creating Black Americans: African-American History and Its Meanings, 1619 to the Present* (New York: Oxford University Press, 2007).

James B. Stewart, ed., *African Americans and Post-Industrial Labor Markets* (New Brunswick: Transaction, 1997).

PERMISSIONS

SECTION ONE: FOUNDATIONS, 1768–1861

1. Excerpt from *Complete Writings by Phillis Wheatley*, intro. by Vincent Carretta, ed. by Vincent Carretta. Copyright 2001 by Vincent Carretta. Used by permission of Viking Penguin, a division of Penguin Group (USA) Inc.

2. Excerpt from Olaudah Equiano, *The Interesting Narrative of the Life of Olaudah Equiano, or Gustav Vasa, the African in 2 volumes* (New York, 1789 and 1791).

3. Prince Hall, "Thus Doth Ethiopia Stretch Forth Her Hand from Slavery, to Freedom and Equality." Excerpt of speech delivered at black Masonic lodge, Menotomy, Massachusetts, June 24, 1797. Originally published in William C. Nell, *The Colored Patriots of the American Revolution* (Boston: R. F. Wallcut, 1855), pp. 61–64; also in Philip S. Foner, ed., *The Voice of Black America* (New York: Simon and Schuster, 1972), pp. 13–15.

4. "The Founding of the African Methodist Episcopal Church." Excerpt from Richard Allen, *The Life, Experience and Gospel Labors of the Rt. Rev. Richard Allen* (Philadelphia: Lee & Yocum, 1888), pp. 11–17, 23–24.

5. "David Walker's Appeal, *1829–1830*." Excerpt from David Walker, *David Walker's Appeal in Four Articles; Together with a Preamble, to the Coloured Citizens of the World, but in Particular and Very Expressly, to those of the United States of America* (Boston: Revised and published by David Walker, 3rd ed., 1830).

6. "The Statement of Nat Turner, *1831*." "Autobiographical Statement of Nat Turner," published in Thomas R. Gray, ed., *The Confessions of Nat Turner, the leader of the late insurrection in Southampton, Va.* (Baltimore: 1831).

7. "Slaves Are Prohibited to Read and Write by Law, *1831*." "Act Passed by the General Assembly of the State of North Carolina at the Session of 1830–1831" (Raleigh: 1831).

8. "Mrs. Stewart's Farewell Address to Her Friends in the City of Boston, Delivered September 21, 1833," published as *Productions of Mrs. Maria W. Stewart* (Boston: William Lloyd Garrison and Knapp, 1832).

9. "A Slave Denied the Rights to Marry, *1834*." Letter from Milo Thompson (slave) to Louisa Bethley, October 15, 1834, in Dwight L. Diamond, ed., *Letters of James G. Birney, 1831–1857*, Vol. I (New York: Appleton-Century, 1938), p. 144.

10. "The Selling of Slaves, *1835*." Advertisement, "Hewlett and Bright Sale of Valuable Slaves," New Orleans, May 13, 1835. Copy at the New-York Historical Society.

11. "Solomon Northrup Describes a New Orleans Slave Auction, *1841*." Solomon Northrup, *Twelve Years a Slave* (Auburn, N.Y.: 1853), p. 78.

12. "Cinque and the *Amistad* Revolt, *1841.*" Excerpts from the *United States Appellants v. the Libellants and Claimants of the Schooner Amistad,* Supreme Court of the United States, 15 Pet. (40 U.S.) 581, 587 (1841).

13. "Let Your Motto Be Resistance!" *Henry Highland Garnet, 1843.* "An Address to the Slaves of the United States of America," 1843, reprinted in Garnet, *A Memorial Discourse by Rev. Henry Highland Garnet* (Philadelphia: Joseph M. Wilson, 1865), pp. 44–51.

14. "Slavery as It Is," *William Wells Brown, 1847.* "A Lecture Delivered before the Female Anti-Slavery Society of Salem at Lyceum Hall, November 4, 1847, by William Wells Brown, A Fugitive Slave," reported by Henry M. Parkhurst, Boston, 1847.

15. "A'n't I a Woman?" *Sojourner Truth, 1851.* (1) Excerpt from *The Anti-Slavery Bugle,* June 21, 1851; and (2) Reported in Elizabeth Cady Stanton, Susan B. Anthony, and M. J. Gage, *History of Women Suffrage,* Vol. I (Rochester, N.Y.: 1887).

16. Mary Ann Shadd Cary, excerpts from *A Plea for Emigration, or Notes of Canada West,* ed. by Richard Almonte. Toronto: The Mercury Press, 1998, pp. 43–44 and 88–89. Reprinted by permission.

17. "A Black Nationalist Manifesto," *Martin R. Delany, 1852.* Excerpt from *The Condition, Elevation, Emigration, and Destiny of the Colored People of the United States, Politically Considered* (Philadelphia: Privately Printed, 1852).

18. "What to the Slave Is the Fourth of July?" *Frederick Douglass, 1852.* From: Alice Moore Dunbar, ed., *Masterpieces of Negro Eloquence* (New York: Bookery Publishing, 1914), pp. 42–47.

19. "No Rights That a White Man Is Bound to Respect": The Dred Scott Case and Its Aftermath. From: (1) Dred Scott petitions for his freedom, July 1847, Missouri Court Records, St. Louis; (2) Roger B. Taney, excerpt from *"Obiter Dictum* on Dred Scott v. Sandford," 1857; and (3) Excerpt from Frederick Douglass, "A Most Scandalous and Devilish Perversion of the Constitution," speech denouncing the Dred Scott decision, May 1857.

20. "Whenever the Colored Man Is Elevated, It Will Be by His Own Exertions," *John S. Rock, 1858.* Speech from *The Liberator,* March 12, 1858.

21. "The Spirituals: 'Go Down, Moses' and 'Didn't My Lord Deliver Daniel.'" Traditional spirituals.

SECTION TWO: RECONSTRUCTION AND REACTION, 1861–1915

1. "What the Black Man Wants," *Frederick Douglass, 1865.* Excerpt from "What the Black Man Wants," speech delivered in 1865.

2. "Henry McNeal Turner, Black Christian Nationalist." Speech delivered on September 3, 1868, before the Georgia State Legislature.

3. "Black Urban Workers during Reconstruction." (1) Excerpt, "The National Colored Labor Convention, 1869," *American Workman,* Boston (December 25, 1869), p. 2; and (2) excerpt, article on African-American workers in Baltimore, *New York Tribune* (September 1, 1870).

4. "Labor and Capital Are in Deadly Conflict," *T. Thomas Fortune, 1886.* Speech delivered on April 20, 1886, Brooklyn Literary Union, printed in the *New York Freeman,* May 1, 1886.

5. "Edward Wilmot Blyden and the African Diaspora." Lecture delivered at the American Colonization Society, Washington, D.C., January 19, 1890.

6. "The Democratic Idea Is Humanity," *Alexander Crummell, 1888*. Excerpt from 1888 speech, "The Race Problem in America," in *Africa and America: Addresses and Discourses* (Springfield, Mass.: Wiley, 1891), pp. 39–57.

7. "A Voice from the South," *Anna Julia Cooper, 1892*. Excerpt from *A Voice from the South, By a Black Woman from the South* (Xenia, Ohio: Aldine Printing House, 1892).

8. "The National Association of Colored Women: Mary Church Terrell and Josephine St. Pierre Ruffin." From: (1) Mary Church Terrell, "The Progress of Colored Women," excerpt from a speech originally published in *The Voice of the Negro* (July 1904), pp. 292– 94; and (2) Josephine St. Pierre Ruffin, excerpt from "Letter to the Ladies of the Georgia Educational League," June 1889, published in Alice Moore Dunbar, ed., *Masterpieces of Negro Eloquence* (New York: Bookery Publishing, 1914), pp. 173–76.

9. "Ode to Ethiopia," "We Wear the Mask," and "Sympathy." In *The Collected Poetry of Paul Laurence Dunbar*, ed. Joanne Braxton, pp. 15–16, 71, 102. Copyright 1993 by the Rector and Visitors of the University of Virginia. Reprinted by permission of the University of Virginia Press.

10. "Booker T. Washington and the Politics of Accommodation." (1) Excerpt from "Atlanta Exposition Address," delivered in Atlanta, Georgia, September 18, 1895, reprinted in Washington, *Up from Slavery: An Autobiography* (New York: Doubleday, Page, 1900); (2) excerpt from "The Fruits of Industrial Training," originally printed in *The Negro in Business* (Boston: Hertel, Jenkins, 1907); and (3) "My View of Segregation Laws," *New Republic* 5, no. 57 (December 4, 1915), pp. 113–14.

11. "William Monroe Trotter and the *Boston Guardian*." Excerpt from editorial, *Boston Guardian*, December 20, 1902.

12. "Race and the Southern Worker." From: (1) "A Negro Woman Speaks," *The Independent* 54 (September 18, 1902), pp. 2221–24; (2) "The Race Question a Class Question," *The Worker* (October 2, 1904); and (3) "Negro Workers!" appeal drafted by the Committee of Defense, Brotherhood of Timber Workers, Alexandria, Louisiana, published in *Solidarity* (September 28, 1912).

13. "Ida B. Wells-Barnett, Crusader for Justice." Excerpt from speech delivered at the National Negro Conference, 1909 (*Proceedings: National Negro Conference*, 1909, pp. 174–79).

14. "William Edward Burghardt Du Bois." Excerpts from "The Conservation of Races," paper presented to the American Negro Academy, Occasional Papers, No. 2 (Washington, D.C., 1897); and (2) excerpts from chapter I, "Of Our Spiritual Strivings," and chapter II, "Of the Dawn of Freedom," from *The Souls of Black Folk* (Chicago: A.C. McClurg, 1903).

15. "The Niagara Movement, *1905*." From: "The Niagara Movement Declaration of Principles," 1905. Originally published in the *Cleveland Gazette*, July 22, 1905.

16. "Hubert Henry Harrison, Black Revolutionary Nationalist." Excerpt from speech originally delivered in about 1912, first published in Harrison, *The Negro and the Nation* (New York: 1917[?]), pp. 48–58.

SECTION THREE: FROM PLANTATION TO GHETTO, 1915–1954

1. "Black Conflict over World War I." From: (1) W. E. B. Du Bois, "Close Ranks," *Crisis* 16 (July 1918), reprinted by permission of *The Crisis*; (2) excerpt from Hubert H. Harrison, "The Descent of Du Bois," in *When Africa Awakens* (New York: Porro Press,

1920); and (3) Du Bois, "Returning Soldiers," *The Crisis* 18 (May 1919), pp. 13–14, reprinted by permission of *The Crisis*. The editors wish to thank the Crisis Publishing Co., Inc., the publisher of the magazine of the National Association for the Advancement of Colored People, for the use of the material from *The Crisis*.

2. From: "If We Must Die," *Liberator* 2 (July 1919), p. 21. Reprinted from *Selected Poems of Claude McKay* (New York: Bookman Associates, 1953), p. 36.

3. "Black Bolsheviks: Cyril V. Briggs and Claude McKay." (1) "What the African Blood Brotherhood Stands For," originally published in the *Communist Review* [London] 2 (April 1922), pp. 448–54; and (2) Claude McKay, excerpt from "Soviet Russia and the Negro," originally published in *The Crisis* 27 (December 1923), pp. 61–65, and (January 1924), pp. 114–18, reprinted by permission of *The Crisis*. The editors wish to thank the Crisis Publishing Co., Inc., the publisher of the magazine of the National Association for the Advancement of Colored People, for the use of the material from *The Crisis*.

4. "Marcus Garvey and the Universal Negro Improvement Association." (1) Excerpt from "Declaration of Rights of the Negro Peoples of the World," August 1920, originally published in Amy Jacques Garvey, ed., *Philosophy and Opinions of Marcus Garvey*, Vol. 2 (New York: Universal Publishing House, 1925), pp. 135–42; (2) "An Appeal to the Conscience of the Black Race to See Itself," in *Philosophy and Opinions of Marcus Garvey*; and (3) excerpt from "An Exposé of the Caste System among Negroes," in *Philosophy and Opinions of Marcus Garvey*, Vol. 2, pp. 55–61.

5. "Women as Leaders," from *The Negro World* (October 25, 1925).

6. "Langston Hughes and the Harlem Renaissance." From: (1) "The Negro Artist and the Racial Mountain," *The Nation* 122 (June 23, 1926), reprinted with permission. For subscription information to *The Nation*, call 1-800-333-8536. Portions of each week's *Nation* magazine can be accessed at www.thenation.com; (2) "My America," from *What the Negro Wants*, ed. by Rayford W. Logan (Chapel Hill: University of North Carolina Press, 1944), pp. 299–307. Copyright 1944 by the University of North Carolina Press, renewed 1974 by Rayford W. Logan. Used by permission of the publisher; and (3) "I, Too" and "Harlem," from *The Collected Poems by Langston Hughes*, ed. by Arnold Rampersad with David Roessel, associate editor (New York: Alfred A. Knopf, 1994). Copyright 1994 by the Estate of Langston Hughes. Reprinted by permission of Alfred A. Knopf, Inc., a division of Random House, Inc.

7. "The Negro Woman and the Ballot," from *Messenger* 9 (April 1927), p. 111.

8. "James Weldon Johnson and Harlem in the 1920s." Excerpt from "Harlem: The Culture Capital," originally written in 1925 and published in Alain Locke, ed., *The New Negro* (New York: Albert and Charles Boni, 1925), pp. 301–11.

9. "Black Workers in the Great Depression." From: "The Negro Worker: A Problem of Progressive Labor Action," *The Crisis* 37, no. 3 (March 1930), pp. 83–85. The editors wish to thank the Crisis Publishing Co., Inc., the publisher of the magazine of the National Association for the Advancement of Colored People, for the use of the material from *The Crisis*.

10. "The Scottsboro Trials, *1930s*." From: "Scottsboro Boys Appeal from Death Cells to the Toilers of the World," originally published in *The Negro Worker* 2, no. 5 (May 1932), pp. 8–9.

11. "You Cannot Kill the Working Class," *Angelo Herndon, 1933*. From: (1) Angelo Herndon's Speech to the Jury, January 17, 1933; and (2) excerpt from Angelo Herndon, *You Cannot Kill the Working Class* (New York: International Labor Defense and League

of Struggle for Negro Rights, 1937–?).

12. Excerpts reprinted by permission of Nell Irvin Painter, from *The Narrative of Hosea Hudson: His Life as a Negro Communist in the South*, edited by Nell Irvin Painter. Cambridge, Mass.: Harvard University Press, 1979.

13. "Breaking the Bars to Brotherhood," *Mary McLeod Bethune, 1935*. Excerpts from speech located in the Mary McLeod Bethune Papers, Amistad Research Center, Tulane University, New Orleans.

14. "Adam Clayton Powell, Jr., and the Fight for Black Employment in Harlem." From: "Soap Box," *Amsterdam News*, May 7, 1938; and "Platform for Job Campaign," *Amsterdam News*, May 14, 1938.

15. "Black Women Workers during the Great Depression." From: (1) Elaine Ellis, "Women of the Cotton Fields," *The Crisis* 45 (October 1938), pp. 333, 342, reprinted by permission; and (2) Naomi Ward, "I Am a Domestic," *New Masses* 35 (June 25, 1940), pp. 20–21. The editors wish to thank the Crisis Publishing Co., Inc., the publisher of the magazine of the National Association for the Advancement of Colored People, for the use of the material from *The Crisis*.

16. "Southern Negro Youth Conference, *1939*." From: "Call to Third All-Southern Negro Youth Conference," issued in March 1939.

17. "A. Philip Randolph and the Negro March on Washington Movement, *1941*." From: (1) Excerpt from "Call to the March, July 1, 1941," originally published in *The Black Worker*, May 1941; and (2) "Why Should We March?" *Survey Graphic* 31 (November 1942), pp. 488–89.

18. "Charles Hamilton Houston and the War Effort among African Americans, *1944*." From: "The Negro Soldier," reprinted with permission from the *Nation* 159 (October 21, 1944), pp. 406–07. For subscription information to the *Nation*, call 1-800-333-8536. Portions of each week's *Nation* magazine can be accessed at www.thenation.com.

19. "An End to the Neglect of the Problems of the Negro Woman!" *Claudia Jones, 1949*. From essay originally published in *Political Affairs* (1949).

20. "The Negro Artist Looks Ahead," *Paul Robeson, 1951*. Excerpt from "The Negro Artist Looks Ahead," originally published in *Masses and Mainstream* (January 1952), pp. 7–14.

21. "Thurgood Marshall: The *Brown* Decision and the Struggle for School Desegregation." Excerpt from the Edwin Rogers Embree Memorial Lectures of Thurgood Marshall at Dillard University, New Orleans, Spring 1954.

SECTION FOUR: WE SHALL OVERCOME, 1954–1975

1. From: (1) Letter from Jo Ann Robinson to W. J. Gayle, May 21, 1954, reprinted by permission of the University of Tennessee Press. From *The Montgomery Bus Boycott and the Women Who Made It: The Memoir of Jo Ann Gibson Robinson*, edited, with a foreword, by David J. Garrow (Knoxville: University of Tennessee Press, 1987). Copyright 1987 by the University of Tennessee Press; (2) "Rosa L. Parks" from *My Soul Is Rested* by Howell Raines, copyright 1977 Howell Raines. Used by permission G. P. Putnam's Sons, a division of Penguin Group (USA) Inc.; and (3) excerpts from an account by Jo Ann Robinson, from David J. Garrow, ed., *The Montgomery Bus Boycott and the Women Who Made It: The Memoir of Jo Ann Gibson Robinson*. Copyright 1987 by the University of Tennessee Press, pp. 43–47,

61–63, 112–13, 161–63.

2. "Roy Wilkins and the NAACP." Excerpt from an address delivered on February 24, 1956, NAACP Southeast Regional Convention, Charleston, South Carolina, originally published in *The Crisis* 46 (April 1956), pp. 197–201, 254–55, reprinted with permission. The editors wish to thank the Crisis Publishing Co., Inc., the publisher of the magazine of the National Association for the Advancement of Colored People, for the use of the material from *The Crisis*.

3. "The Southern Christian Leadership Conference, 1957." From: "This is SCLC," pamphlet printed as mimeograph by the SCLC in Atlanta, Georgia, in 1957.

4. "Student Nonviolent Coordinating Committee and the Sit-In Movement, 1960." From: "Statement of Purpose," drafted for the Student Nonviolent Coordinating Committee by the Rev. James Lawson, May 14, 1960, mimeographed document.

5. "Freedom Songs, 1960s." Traditional songs: "We Shall Overcome" and "Ain't Gonna Let Nobody Turn Me 'Round."

6. "We Need Group-Centered Leadership," *Ella Baker*. From: "Bigger than a Hamburger," *Southern Patriot* 18 (June 1960).

7. "Martin Luther King, Jr., and Nonviolence, 1957 and 1963." From: (1) Excerpts from "Nonviolence and Racial Justice," copyright 1957 by Martin Luther King, Jr., copyright renewed 1985 by Coretta Scott King; and (2) "I Have a Dream" speech delivered at the March on Washington, August 28, 1963, copyright 1963 by Martin Luther King, Jr., copyright renewed 1991 by Coretta Scott King. Both are reprinted by arrangement with The Heirs to the Estate of Martin Luther King, Jr., c/o Writers House, Inc., as agent for the proprietor.

8. "The Revolution Is at Hand," *John R. Lewis, 1963*. From: Speech by John Lewis, delivered at the March on Washington, August 28, 1963, courtesy of U.S. Representative John Lewis.

9. "The Salvation of American Negroes Lies in Socialism," *W. E. B. Du Bois*. Excerpt from "The Negro and Socialism," in Helen Alfred, ed., *Toward a Socialist America* (New York: Peace Publications, 1958), pp. 179–91.

10. "The Special Plight and the Role of Black Women," *Fannie Lou Hamer*. Excerpt from a speech delivered at the NAACP Legal Defense Fund Institute, New York City, May 7, 1971, pp. 609–14.

11. "SNCC Position Paper: Women in the Movement," *1964*. From: "Student Nonviolent Coordinating Committee Position Paper: Women in the Movement," text made available through the Institute of Advanced Technology in the Humanities, University of Virginia at Charlottesville, April 18, 1998.

12. "Elijah Muhammad and the Nation of Islam." Excerpt from "Program and Position" of the Nation of Islam, in Clifton E. Marsh, *From Black Muslims to Muslims: The Transition from Separatism to Islam, 1930–1980* (Metuchen, N.J.: Scarecrow Press, 1984), pp. 62–64.

13. "Malcolm X and Revolutionary Black Nationalism." From: (1) "The Ballot or the Bullet" speech delivered in Cleveland, Ohio, April 3, 1964, reprinted in *Malcolm X Speaks* (New York: Merit Publishers, 1965), pp. 23–44. Copyright 1965, 1989 by Betty Shabazz and Pathfinder Press, reprinted by permission; and (2) "Statement of the Basic Aims and Objectives of the Organization of Afro-American Unity," June 28, 1964, reprinted in George Breitman, ed., *The Last Year of Malcolm X: The Evolution of a Revolutionary* (New York: Merit Publishers, 1967), pp. 105–11. Copyright Pathfinder

Press, reprinted by permission.

14. "Black Power." From: (1) Stokely Carmichael, excerpt from "What We Want," *New York Review of Books* 7, no. 4 (September 22, 1966), pp. 5–6, 8; (2) SNCC, "Position Paper on Black Power," published in the *New York Times*, August 5, 1966; and (3) Bayard Rustin, excerpt from "'Black Power' and Coalition Politics," *Commentary* 42 (September 1966), pp. 35–40.

15. "CORE Endorses Black Power," *Floyd McKissick, 1967.* Excerpts from speech delivered at the "National Conference of Black Power," Newark, New Jersey, July 20–23, 1967. Originally published in the *New York Times*, July 30, 1967.

16. "To Atone for Our Sins and Errors in Vietnam," *Martin Luther King, Jr., 1967.* Excerpt from "Testament of Hope" speech delivered at Riverside Church, New York City, April 4, 1967, copyright 1967 by Martin Luther King, Jr., copyright renewed by the Martin Luther King, Jr. Estate. Reprinted by arrangement with The Heirs to the Estate of Martin Luther King, Jr., c/o Writers House, Inc., as agent for the proprietor.

17. "Huey P. Newton and the Black Panther Party for Self-Defense." From: (1) "The Black Panther Program: What We Want, What We Believe," October 1966; (2) "Rules of the Black Panther Party," Central Headquarters, Oakland, California; and (3) Excerpt from Huey P. Newton, "On the Defection of Eldridge Cleaver from the Black Panther Party and the Defection of the Black Panther Party from the Black Community," *Black Panther Intercommunal News Service*, April 17, 1971.

18. "The People Have to Have the Power," *Fred Hampton.* Excerpts from *"Fred Speaks": Fred Hampton 20th Commemoration* (Chicago: December 4th Committee, 1989).

19. "I Am a Revolutionary Black Woman," *Angela Y. Davis, 1970.* Excerpts from "I Am a Revolutionary Black Woman," published originally in *Muhammad Speaks* (December 1970).

20. "Our Thing Is DRUM!" *The League of Revolutionary Black Workers.* From: "General Program (Here's Where We're Coming From)," *General Policy Statement and Labor Program* (Highland Park, MI: League of Revolutionary Black Workers, 1970).

21. Attica: "The Fury of Those Who Are Oppressed," *1971.* From: "The Five Demands: To the people of America," reprinted from *A Time to Die: The Attica Prison Revolt* by Tom Wicker by permission of the University of Nebraska Press. Copyright 1975 by Tom Wicker.

22. "The National Black Political Convention, Gary, Indiana, *March 1972.*" From: "The Gary Declaration," from "The National Black Political Agenda" (Washington, D.C.: National Black Political Convention, 1972).

23. "There Is No Revolution Without the People," *Amiri Baraka, 1972.* From: (1) Excerpt from Baraka, "The Pan-African Party and the Black Nation," in Robert Chrisman and Nathan Hare, *Pan-Africanism* (Indianapolis: Bobbs-Merrill, 1974), pp. 114–26; and (2) "A Poem for Black Hearts" reprinted by permission of Sterling Lord Literistic, as agents for the author. Copyright by Amiri Baraka.

24. "My Sight Is Gone But My Vision Remains," *Henry Winston.* From: (1) "On Returning to the Struggle" published with permission from *Political Affairs* 40, no. 8 (August 1961), pp. 1–2; and (2) excerpt from "A Letter to my Brothers and Sisters" with

permission from *Political Affairs* 52, no. 2 (February 1973), pp. 13–21.

SECTION FIVE: THE FUTURE IN THE PRESENT, 1975 TO THE PRESENT

1. "Combahee River Collective Statement, *1977*." From: "Combahee River Collective: A Black Feminist Statement," copyright 1979 by Zilla R. Eisenstein. Reprinted by permission of the Monthly Review Foundation.

2. "Women in Prison: How We Are," *Assata Shakur, 1978*. Excerpt from "Women in Prison: How We Are" with permission from *Black Scholar* 9, no. 7 (April 1978), pp. 50–57.

3. "It's Our Turn," *Harold Washington, 1983*. From: "Harold Washington's Announcement of Candidacy for the Democratic Nomination for Mayor of Chicago," from Dempsey J. Travis, *Harold: The People's Mayor* (Chicago: Urban Research Press, 1989), used by permission of Ramon Price for the Washington Estate.

4. Reprinted by permission from *Sister Outsider*, by Audre Lorde. Copyright 1984, 2007 by Audre Lorde. Berkeley, Calif.: Crossing Press, www.tenspeed.com.

5. "Shaping Feminist Theory," *bell hooks, 1984*. Excerpt from "Black Women: Shaping Feminist Theory," from bell hooks, *Feminist Theory: From Margin to Center* (Boston: South End Press, 1984), pp. 1–15.

6. "The Movement against Apartheid: Jesse Jackson and Randall Robinson." From: (1) Jesse L. Jackson, "Don't Adjust to Apartheid," with permission from *Black Scholar* 16, no. 6 (November/December 1984), pp. 39–43; and (2) Clarence Lusane, "State of the U.S. Anti-Apartheid Movement: An Interview with Randall Robinson," with permission from *Black Scholar* 17, no. 6 (November/December 1985), pp. 40–42.

7. "Keep Hope Alive," *Jesse Jackson, 1988*. From: "Common Ground and Common Sense," address delivered July 20, 1988, reprinted in *Vital Speeches* 54, no. 21 (August 15, 1988), pp. 649–53.

8. "Afrocentricity," *Molefi Asante, 1991*. From: "The Afrocentric Idea in Education," *Journal of Negro Education* 60, no. 2 (Spring 1991), pp. 170–80. Copyright 1991 by Howard University.

9. "The Anita Hill–Clarence Thomas Controversy, *1991*." From: (1) "African-American Women in Defense of Ourselves"; and (2) June Jordan, "Can I Get a Witness?" Both are reprinted with permission from *Black Scholar* 22, nos. 1 and 2 (Winter/Spring 1991), pp. 56–58, 155.

10. "Race Matters," *Cornel West, 1991*. From: "Nihilism in Black America," *Dissent* (Spring 1991).

11. "Black Demogogues and Pseudo-Scholars," by Henry Louis Gates, Jr. Copyright 1992 by Henry Louis Gates, Jr. Originally published in the *New York Times*. Reprinted by permission of the author.

12. "Crime—Causes and Cures," *Jarvis Tyner, 1994*. Reprinted by the courtesy of Jarvis Tyner, Vice Chairman, Communist Party USA.

13. "Louis Farrakhan: The Million Man March, *1995*." Excerpt from Farrakhan's speech at the Million Man March, Washington, D.C., October 16, 1995.

14. "A Voice from Death Row," *Mumia Abu-Jamal*. From: Jamal News Service, 1998.

15. "Let Justice Roll Down Like Waters," *African-American Prisoners in Sing Sing, 1998*. From: (1) Statement by Sing Sing Prisoners, May 1998, pp. 36–38; (2) Michael J. Love, "The Prison-Industrial Complex: An Investment in Failure," pp. 24–25; and (3)

Willis L. Steele, Jr., "River Hudson," in Pamphlet, *Voices of the Class of 1998: Master of Professional Studies Program at Sing Sing Correctional Facility* (New York: New York Theological Seminary, 1998), pp. 34–35.

16. "Black Radical Congress, *1998*." From: (1) "BRC Principles of Unity"; (2) The "Call to Congress"; and (3) "The Freedom Agenda of the BRC." Copies in possession of the editors.

17. Letter to Governor Bush from Chairperson Mary Frances Berry, U.S. Commission on Civil Rights, March 8, 2001. Reprinted by permission of Mary Frances Berry.

18. "Protocol for Peace, Point 1: Proclamation," reprinted by permission of the estate of Stanley Tookie Williams.

19. Excerpt from "Paper Trail: World Conference against Racism, Xenophobia and Related Intolerance," *Souls* 4, no. 3 (Summer 2002), pp. 69–82. Reprinted by permission.

20. John Nichols, "Barbara Lee's Stand," *Nation*, October 8, 2001. Reprinted by permission. For subscription information, call 1-800-333-8536. Portions of each week's *Nation* magazine can be accessed at http://www.thenation.com. From "Iraq Veterans against the War," www.ivaw.org.

21. Michael Eric Dyson, *Is Bill Cosby Right? Or Has the Black Middle Class Lost its Mind?* (New York: Basic Civitas Books, 2005), pp. 6–14 (excerpts). Reprinted by permission of Civitas, a member of the Perseus Books Group.

INDEX

ABOUT THE EDITORS

One of America's most influential interpreters of the African-American experience is **Manning Marable**. Marable is currently the M. Moran Weston and Black Alumni Professor of African-American Studies, professor of public affairs, history and political science, and director of the Center for Contemporary Black History (CCBH) at Columbia University in New York City. For ten years, he was founding director of Columbia's Institute for Research in African-American Studies (1993 to 2003). A prolific writer, since 1975 Marable has produced 15 books, 13 edited volumes, and over 400 articles in academic journals, anthologies, encyclopedias, and related publications. Marable's major works include *How Capitalism Underdeveloped Black America* (1983); *Beyond Black and White* (1995); *The Great Wells of Democracy* (2002); and *Living Black History* (2006). Since 1999, he has also been founding editor of the quarterly academic publication *Souls: A Critical Journal of Black Politics, Culture and Society*.

Leith Mullings is Distinguished Professor of Anthropology at the Graduate Center, City University of New York. Her books include: *Therapy, Ideology and Social Change: Mental Healing in Urban Ghana* (1984); *Cities of the United States* (editor, 1987); *On Our Own Terms: Race, Class and Gender in the Lives of African American Women* (1997); *Stress and Resilience: The Social Context of Reproduction in Central Harlem* (2001, with Alaka Wali); *Freedom: A Photohistory of the African American Struggle* (2002, with Manning Marable); *Gender, Race, Class and Health: An Intersectional Approach* (2005, coedited with Amy Schulz). In addition, she has written numerous articles and book chapters on stratification, ethnicity, race, gender, health, globalization, participatory research, public policy, and social movements. She is currently working on an edited volume, *Rethinking Global Justice: Social Movements in the African Diaspora*, forthcoming in 2009. Mullings has served on the executive boards of the American Ethnological Society and the American Anthropological Association. Her awards include the Chair in American Civilization at the École des Hautes Études en Sciences Sociales in Paris and the Prize for Distinguished Achievement in the Critical Study of North America from the Society for the Anthropology of North America.